Essential Oils

Animal
Desk Reference

LIFE SCIENCE
PRODUCTS & PUBLISHING

FIRST EDITION

First Edition

Copyright © May 2017 • Life Science Publishing
1-800-336-6308 • www.Discoverlsp.com

ISBN 978-0-9983136-5-8

Printed in the United States of America

Contents

Section 1

Introduction...1

Chapter 1

Plants and Animals.................................5

Chapter 2

Essential Oils and Animals: an Overview...........11

Chapter 3

Application.......................................19
External Methods 19
Raindrop Technique.................................25
Internal Methods...................................27
Sample Suggested Use per Species 31

Section 2

Chapter 4

Single Essential Oils............................35
 Amazonian Ylang Ylang 38
 Angelica 38
 Anise 38
 Basil/Basil Vitality..............................39
 Bergamot/ Bergamot Vitality 39
 Biblical Sweet Myrrh..............................40
 Black Pepper/Black Pepper Vitality 40
 Black Spruce 41
 Blue Cypress 41
 Blue Tansy 41
 Calamus 41
 Canadian Fleabane.................................42
 Cardamom/Cardamom Vitality........................42

Carrot Seed/Carrot Seed Vitality 43
Cassia.................................. 43
Cedarwood 43
Celery Seed/Celery Seed Vitality 44
Cinnamon Bark/Cinnamon Bark Vitality . 44
Cistus................................. 44
Citronella 45
Citrus Hystrix/Combava 45
Clary Sage 45
Clove/Clove Vitality.................... 46
Copaiba/Copaiba Vitality
   (Balsam Copaiba)..................... 46
Coriander/Coriander Vitality 47
Cumin 47
Cypress 48
Dalmatia Bay Laurel 48
Dalmatia Juniper...................... 48
Dalmatia Sage 49
Davana 49
Dill/Dill Vitality 49
Dorado Azul 50
Douglas Fir........................... 50
Elemi 50
Eucalyptus Blue 51
Eucalyptus Citriodora 51
Eucalyptus Globulus................... 51
Eucalyptus Radiata 52
Eucalyptus Staigeriana 52
Fennel/Fennel Vitality 52
Frankincense/Frankincense Vitality 53
Frereana Frankincense................. 53
Galbanum 54
Geranium 54
German Chamomile/German
   Chamomile Vitality 55
Ginger/Ginger Vitality 55
Goldenrod 56
Grapefruit/Grapefruit Vitality 56
Helichrysum 56
Hinoki 57
Hong Kuai 57
Hyssop 57
Idaho Balsam Fir (Balsam Canada)....... 58
Idaho Blue Spruce..................... 58
Idaho Ponderosa Pine 58
Idaho Tansy 59

Ishpingo 59
Jade Lemon/Jade Lemon Vitality........ 59
Jasmine................................ 60
Juniper 60
Laurus Nobilis/Laurus Nobilis
   Vitality (Bay Laurel) 61
Lavandin............................... 61
Lavender/Lavender Vitality 61
Ledum................................. 62
Lemon/Lemon Vitality.................. 62
Lemongrass/Lemongrass Vitality........ 63
Lemon Myrtle.......................... 63
Lime/Lime Vitality 64
Mandarin 64
Manuka................................ 65
Marjoram/Marjoram Vitality 65
Mastrante.............................. 66
Melaleuca Ericifolia.................... 66
Melaleuca Quinquenervia (Niaouli) 66
Melissa 67
Micromeria 67
Mountain Savory/Mountain
   Savory Vitality 67
Myrrh.................................. 68
Myrtle 68
Neroli (Bitter Orange).................. 69
Northern Lights Black Spruce 69
Nutmeg/Nutmeg Vitality 69
Ocotea................................ 70
Orange/Orange Vitality................. 70
Oregano/Oregano Vitality 71
Palmarosa.............................. 71
Palo Santo 71
Patchouli 72
Peppermint/Peppermint Vitality 72
Petitgrain 73
Pine 73
Plectranthus Oregano 73
Ravintsara 74
Roman Chamomile..................... 74
Rose 74
Rosemary/Rosemary Vitality 75
Rosewood 76
Royal Hawaiian Sandalwood............ 76
Ruta 76
Sacred Frankincense 77

Sacred Sandalwood 77
Sage/Sage Vitality 77
Spanish Sage. 78
Spearmint/Spearmint Vitality 79
Spikenard. 79
Tangerine/Tangerine Vitality 79
Tarragon/Tarragon Vitality 80
Tea Tree. 80
Thyme/Thyme Vitality 80
Tsuga 81
Valerian. 81
Vanilla 81
Vetiver. 82
Western Red Cedar 82
White Fir 82
White Lotus 83
Wintergreen 83
Xiang Mao 84
Yarrow 84
Ylang Ylang 85
Yuzu 85

Chapter 5

Essential Oil Blends **87**

3 Wise Men 88
Abundance 88
Acceptance 88
Amoressence 88
Aroma Ease 88
Aroma Life 88
Aroma Siez. 88
Aroma Sleep 88
Australian Blue 88
Awaken. 88
Believe. 89
Bite Buster 89
Brain Power 89
Breathe Again Roll-On. 89
Build Your Dream. 89
Christmas Spirit 89
Citrus Fresh/Citrus Fresh Vitality 89
Clarity 89
Common Sense 89
Cool Azul 90
Deep Relief Roll-On 90
DiGize /DiGize Vitality 90

Divine Release 90
Dragon Time 90
Dream Catcher 90
Egyptian Gold. 90
EndoFlex/EndoFlex Vitality 90
En-R-Gee. 90
Envision 91
Evergreen Essence 91
Exodus II 91
Forgiveness 91
Freedom 91
Gathering 91
GeneYus 92
Gentle Baby 92
GLF / GLF Vitality 92
Gratitude 92
Grounding 92
Harmony. 92
Highest Potential. 92
Hope 93
Humility 93
ImmuPower. 93
Infect Away 93
Inner Child 93
Inner Harmony 93
Inspiration 93
Into the Future 93
InTouch. 94
Joy 94
JuvaCleanse/JuvaCleanse Vitality. 94
JuvaFlex /JuvaFlex Vitality. 94
Lady Sclareol. 94
Light the Fire. 94
Live with Passion 94
Live Your Passion 94
Longevity /Longevity Vitality 94
Magnify Your Purpose 95
Melrose. 95
Mendwell 95
M-Grain. 95
Mister. 95
Motivation. 95
Oola Balance 95
Oola Faith 95
Oola Family 96
Oola Field 96

Oola Finance 96
Oola Fitness 96
Oola Friends 96
Oola Fun 96
Oola Grow 96
Owie 97
PanAway 97
ParaGize 97
Peace & Calming 97
Peace & Calming II 97
Present Time 97
PuriClean 97
Purification 97
Raven 98
R.C. 98
Reconnect 98
Red Shot 98
Release 98
Relieve It 98
RepelAroma 98
RutaVaLa 98
RutaVaLa Roll-On 99
Sacred Mountain 99
SARA 99
SclarEssence/SclarEssence Vitality 99
Sensation 99
Shutran 99
Sleepylze 99
Slique Essence 99
SniffleEase 100
Stress Away 100
Stress Away Roll-On 100
Surrender 100
T-Away 100
The Gift 100
Thieves/Thieves Vitality 101
Tranquil Roll-On 101
Transformation 101
Trauma Life 101
T.R. Care 101
TummyGize 102
Valor 102
Valor II 102
White Angelica 102
White Light 102

Chapter 6

Animal Products **103**
Animal Scents Dental Pet Chews 103
Animal Scents Ointment 103
Animal Scents Shampoo 104
Infect Away 104
Mendwell 104
ParaGize 104
PuriClean 104
RepelAroma 105
T-Away 105

Equine Animal Products
Massage Oil 105
Shampoo 105
Tail & Mane Sheen 105

Chapter 7

Nutritional Support **107**
Nutritional Supplements **107**
AgilEase 107
AlkaLime 107
Allerzyme 108
BLM 108
ComforTone 108
CortiStop 108
Detoxzyme 108
Digest & Cleanse 109
EndoGize 109
Essentialzyme 109
Essentialzymes-4 109
Estro 110
FemiGen 110
ICP 110
ImmuPro 110
Inner Defense 111
JuvaSpice 111
JuvaTone 111
JuvaPower 111
K&B 112
KidScents MightyVites 112
KidScents MightyZyme 112
Life 9 113
Longevity Softgels 113

Master Formula 113
MindWise 114
Mineral Essence 114
MultiGreens 114
NingXia Nitro 115
NingXia Red 115
Ningxia Wolfberry.................. 115
OmegaGize[3] 115
ParaFree 116
PD 80/20 116
PowerGize 116
Power Meal 116
Pure Protein Complete Vanilla Spice ... 117
Rehemogen 117
SleepEssence 117
Slique Tea 117
Sulfurzyme 117
Super B 118
Super C 118
Super C Chewable 118
Super Cal 118
Thyromin 119
Yacon Syrup....................... 119

Chapter 8

Body and Environment................121
Body Care Products 121
ART Renewal Serum 121
ART Sheerlumé Brightening Cream.... 121
Cel-Lite Magic Massage Oil........... 122
ClaraDerm 122
Cool Azul Pain Relief Cream 122
Cool Azul Sports Gel 122
Dragon Time Massage Oil 122
Genesis Hand & Body Lotion 122
LavaDerm Cooling Mist 123
Lavender Hand & Body Lotion 123
Ortho Ease Massage Oil............. 123
Ortho Sport Massage Oil 123
Progessence Plus 123
Regenolone Moisturizing Cream 123
Relaxation Massage Oil 124
Rose Ointment 124
Sensation Hand & Body Lotion 124
Sensation Massage Oil 124

Thieves Dentarome Plus Toothpaste .. 124
Thieves Dentarome Ultra Toothpaste . 125
Thieves Fresh Essence Plus
    Mouthwash 125
Thieves Waterless Hand Purifier 125
V-6 Vegetable Oil Complex........... 125
Wolfberry Eye Cream 125
Environmental Care Products
Thieves Foaming Hand Soap 126
Thieves Fruit & Veggie Spray 126
Thieves Household Cleaner 126
Thieves Laundry Soap 126
Thieves Spray..................... 126

Section 3

Quick Reference Guide 128
Single EO Application Codes...........130
Blends Application Codes 133

Chapter 9

Bird (Avian) 135
Introduction.......................135
Safety Guidelines 135
Bird (Avian) Conditions...............136
Apoplexy 136
Aspergillosis 136
Avian Influenza 137
Blackhead 137
Blockage.......................... 137
Bumblefoot....................... 137
Capillaria......................... 138
Chlamydiosis...................... 138
Coccidiosis....................... 139
Coryza 139
Cramp 139
Dehydration 140
Escherichia Coli 140
Fluke or Flat Worms 140
Fowl Cholera...................... 140
French Moult...................... 141
Frostbite 141
Frounce.......................... 141
Gapeworms........................ 142
Gout............................. 142

Haemoproteus 142
Herpes.................................. 142
Impaction............................... 143
Lead Poisoning.......................... 143
Leucocytozoonosis...................... 143
Lice.................................... 143
Maggots 144
Malaria 144
Metabolic Bone Disease 144
Newcastle Disease 144
Parasites 145
Pneumonia 145
Poisoning 145
Poultry Ticks 146
Pox 146
Seizures................................ 146
Sinusitis................................ 147
Sour Crop 147
Stargazing 147
Tapeworms 148
Torticollis 148
Tuberculosis 149
Uropygial Gland Infection 149
West Nile Virus 149
Wingtip Edema 150

Chapter 10

Cats (Feline) 151
Introduction............................151
Safety Guidelines......................151
Cat (Feline) Conditions 151
Abscess................................ 154
Acne................................... 154
Allergies 154
Appetite, Poor 155
Arthritis................................ 155
Asthma 155
Behavior Modification 156
Blood Disorders (Blood Clots).......... 156
Blood Disorders (Anemia) 157
Bones, Broken.......................... 157
Cancer................................. 157
Cardiomyopathy, Hypertrophic 158
Conjunctivitis 159
Constipation 159
Dandruff................................ 159
Dental Disorders 159

Deworming 160
Diabetes 160
Diarrhea 161
Distemper 161
Ear Infection 161
Euthanasia 176
Eye Conditions 162
Fatty Liver Syndrome 162
Feline Immunodeficiency Virus 162
Feline Infectious Peritonitis 163
Feline Leukemia........................ 162
Flea Infestations....................... 163
Glaucoma.............................. 164
Hairballs 164
Heart Conditions 165
Heartworm 165
Herpesvirus 165
Hospice Care 176
Hypertension 166
Hyperthyroidism 166
Hypoglycemia 166
Inappropriate Urination / Elimination .. 167
Kidney Failure / Disease 167
Kitty Litter 153
Kitty Raindrop.......................... 153
Lacerations 168
Lameness 168
Liver Disease 168
Mast Cell Tumor 169
Mastitis 169
Neurological Conditions................ 169
Pain 170
Parasites 170
Pregnancy and Birthing 171
Pyometra 171
Respiratory Conditions 171
Seizures................................ 172
Skin Conditions 172
Squamous Cell Carcinoma, Oral........ 173
Toxoplasmosis 173
Trauma 174
Urinary Tract Conditions............... 174
Vaccination Reactions / Vaccinosis 175
Wounds................................. 175
Hospice Care and Euthanasia 176
Testimonials...........................177

Chapter 11

Dogs (Canine) **181**
Introduction. **181**
Safety Guidelines **181**
Raindrop Technique for Dogs **183**
Quick Reference Guide **184**
Mitch Seavey's Iditarod Champions **186**
Dog (Canine) Conditions **192**

   Abscess. 192
   Abuse 192
   Aggression. 193
   Allergies 194
   Anemia 194
   Anorexia 195
   Anxiety 195
   Arthritis. 196
   Barking Excessively. 197
   Boredom. 197
   Broken Bones 197
   Brucella Canis 198
   Calluses. 198
   Cancer. 199
   Chewing - Destructive. 200
   Cognitive Dysfunction. 200
   Conjunctivitis 200
   Constipation 201
   Coprophagia. 201
   Cornea. 201
   Coronavirus. 202
   Cough 202
   Courage 203
   Cruciate Ligament Injury 203
   Cystitis. 203
   Dental Disease 203
   Detoxification. 204
   Deworming 204
   Diabetes 205
   Diarrhea 205
   Ear Mites/Infections 206
   Epulis. 206
   False Pregnancy 207
   Fatty Liver. 206
   Fever 207
   Fleas. 208
   Foreign Object 208

   Gallbladder 208
   Gastric Dilatation Volvulus. 209
   Gastric Ulcers 209
   Giardia. 210
   GI Conditions 210
   Gingivitis 210
   Glaucoma. 211
   Heart Conditions 211
   Heartworm 211
   Histiocytoma. 212
   Hit by Car 212
   Horner's Syndrome. 213
   Hot Spots 213
   Hyperthermia 213
   Hypothyroidism. 214
   Incontinence. 214
   Inflammatory Bowel Disease. 214
   Kennel Cough. 215
   Kidney Disease. 215
   Lacerations 216
   Lick Granuloma 216
   Lipoma 217
   Liver Disease. 217
   Mastitis 217
   Megaesophagus 218
   Muscle Wasting 218
   Neurologic Conditions 218
   Obedience Training 219
   Pain 219
   Pancreatitis 220
   Parasites 220
   Parvo 221
   Patella 221
   Pregnancy & Delivery. 221
   Pyometra 222
   Respiratory Infections 222
   Ringworm 223
   Sarcoptic Mange 223
   Sebaceous Cysts 224
   Seborrhea Oleosa 224
   Seizures. 225
   Skin Tags. 225
   Spondylosis Deformans 225
   Steroid Alternative 226
   Submissive Urination. 226
   Thrombocytopenia. 227

Tick Bites/Disease 227
Urinary Conditions 228
Vaccinosis. 228
Vestibular Disease. 228
Viral Conditions 229
Vomiting. 229
Warts 230

Testimonials. .230

Chapter 12

Fish Conditions 245
Amoebic Gill Disease 245
Bacterial Diseases 245
Columnaris 246
Disease, General 246
Fungal Diseases 246
Furunculosis in Farmed Salmon. 246
Ichthyophthirius multifiliis. 246
Inflammation 247
Koi Herpes 247
Parasite Diseases 247
VHS. 248
Whirling Disease 248

Testimonials. .248

Chapter 13

Horses (Equine). 249
Introduction. .249
Safety Guidelines 249
Diet and Nutrition 251
Equine First Aid. 252
Quick Reference Guide 253
Raindrop Technique 256
Feelings Kit 260
Horse (Equine) Conditions. 261
Abscess. 261
Anesthesia Detoxification 261
Arthritis. 261
Autoimmune Disorders. 262
Back/Spinal Conditions. 262
Birthing and Delivery. 263
Birthing & Delivery (Mismothering) 263
Bone Conditions 265
Bruised Soles. 266
Canker. 266
Castration. 267

Choking 268
Clubfoot 268
Coffin Bone Infection 267
Cold and Influenza 268
Colic/Impaction 269
Contracted Tendons. 271
COPD/Heaves 271
Corns 272
Cough 272
Cushing's Disease 273
Cuts 274
Deworming 275
Diabetes Mellitus. 273
Diarrhea 275
Ear Fungus 276
Ear Plaque 276
Edema/Cellulitis. 276
Ehrlichia/Anaplasmosis. 277
Encephalitis. 277
EPM 278
Equine Herpes Virus 278
Equine Viral Arteritis. 279
Eye Conditions 280
Fever 281
First Aid. 252
Gastric Ulcers 281
Girth Galls 282
Greasy Heel 282
Heaves. 282
Hendra Virus 283
Hives 284
Hoof Abscess 284
Hoof Infections. 285
Hormonal Disorders. 286
Hormonal Disorders—
    Stallion and Mare Reproduction 286
Hypoadrenocorticism 286
Impaction Colic 287
Inflammation 287
Insect Bite 288
Insulin Resistance 289
Kidney Disease. 289
Laminitis. 290
Lice. 290
Liver Disease. 291
Lyme Disease 291
Mange. 292

Melanoma 292
Moon Blindness 293
Muscular Conditions 294
Navicular Syndrome 294
Nervous System Disorders 295
Onchocerciasis 296
Open Wounds 316
Pain 296
Parasites 297
Pelodera 297
Periostitis 298
Pigeon Fever 298
Potomac Fever 299
Proud Flesh 299
Puncture Wound 300
Pythiosis 300
Queensland Itch 301
Rabies 301
Raindrop Technique 257
Rain Rot 302
Respiratory Conditions 302
Rhodococcal Pneumonia 303
Ringbone 303
Ringworm 304
Rotavirus Diarrhea 304
Sarcoids 305
Scratches 306
Screw Worm 306
Sesamoiditis 306
Splints 307
Strangles 308
Swollen Sheath 308
Tendon Conditions 309
Tetanus 309
Thrush 310
Tick Bites 311
Transporting 311
Tumors 312
Tying Up 313
Vaccination Detoxification 313
Warts 313
West Nile Virus 314
White Line Disease 315
Windgalls 315
Wounds 316

Testimonials 317

Chapter 14:

Livestock and Wildlife 325
Bovidae and Cervidae 325
Bovidae and Cervidae Conditions 326
Abscess 326
Aches and Pains 326
Afterbirth Not Expelling 327
Anesthesia Detoxification or
    Tranquilization Reversal 327
Black Quarter 328
Bloat or Colic 328
Bottle Babies in Cervidea and Botinae . . 328
Botulism 328
Broken Bones 329
Broken Horns 329
Cattle Measles 330
Cold or Influenza 330
Cuts, Scrapes, and Abrasions 330
Foot Rot 331
Grass Tetany 331
Hardware Disease 331
Lactate or Lactic Acid 331
Lumpy-Skin Disease 332
Mastitis 332
Myopathy 332
Parasites 333
Prussic Acid Poisoning 333
Puncture Wound 333
Respiratory Care 333
Tetanus 334
Three-Day Stiff Sickness 334
Tick Damage 334
Worms 334

Deer-Specific Conditions 335
Anesthesia Support 335
Bovine Tuberculosis 335
Brain Abscess 336
Corn Toxicity 336
Hair Loss Syndrome 336
Lice 337
Lyme Disease 337
Mange 337
Nasal Bots 338
Parasites 338
Wounds 338

Goat and Sheep Conditions............**339**
Acetonemia................... 339
Allergic Dermatitis............ 339
Anemia 339
Anthrax..................... 340
Arthritis.................... 340
Bloat....................... 340
Bluetongue 340
Bronchitis.................. 341
Caseous Lymphadenitis 341
Chlamydiosis................ 341
Coccidiosis................. 342
Colibacillosis............... 342
Contagious Ecthyma 342
Cystitis.................... 342
Deworming................. 343
Dysentery.................. 343
Enterotoxemia 343
Eye Conditions 343
Foot-and-Mouth Diseases Virus 344
Fungal Infections........... 344
Goat Pox and Sheep Pox....... 344
Heat Stress................. 345
Hemorrhagic Septicemia 345
Hypocalcaemia 345
Indigestion 345
Johne's Disease 346
Labial Dermatitis............ 346
Lice........................ 346
Liver Fluke 347
Mange..................... 347
Mastitis 347
Melioidosis................. 348
Metritis 348
Mycoplasmosis.............. 348
Nitrate Poisoning............ 349
Pesticide Poisoning 349
Pneumonia 349
Polioencephalomalacia........ 350
Post Birth 350
Rabies 350
Rickets.................... 350
Salmonella Infection 351
Scabby Mouth 351
Tetanus 351
Ticks...................... 352
Tuberculosis 352

Urea Poisoning.............. 352
Warts 353
Worm Infestations........... 353

Alpaca and Llama Conditions.........**354**
Foot and Mouth Disease.............. 354
Heat Stress................. 354
Hypocalcemia............... 354
Hypothyroidism............. 355
Ketosis.................... 355
Sunburn 355
Urolithiasis................ 356

Poultry Conditions....................**355**
Air Sac Mite 356
Aspergillosis 357
Avian Chlamydiosis 357
Avian Encephalomyelitis....... 357
Avian Influenza 357
Avian Metapneumovirus 358
Bordetellosis 358
Botulism................... 358
Candidiasis 359
Coccidiosis................. 359
Coronaviral Enteritis......... 359
Crop Impaction and Stasis............ 359
Cryptosporidiosis 360
Duck Viral Hepatitis 360
Ectoparasites............... 360
Fatty Liver Hemorrhagic Syndrome 361
Feather Pecking and Bullying 361
Fowl Cholera............... 361
Fowlpox 361
Gangrenous Dermatitis............... 362
Giardia.................... 362
Goose Parvovirus Infection 362
Helminthiasis 362
Hemorrhagic Enteritis/
    Marble Spleen Disease.............. 363
Hexamitiasis 363
Infectious Bronchitis.......... 363
Infectious Bursal Disease 363
Infectious Coryza............ 364
Infectious Laryngotracheitis 364
Lice....................... 364
Marek's Disease 364
Mites 365
Molting 365

Mycoplasma 365
Mycotoxicoses 366
Newcastle Disease 366
Osteomyelitis 366
Quail Bronchitis 366
Riemerella Anatipestifer Infection 367
Rotaviral Infections 367
Salmonellosis 367
Scald 368
Trichomoniasis 368
Viral Infections 368
Worms 369

Swine (Pig) Conditions **369**
Abscesses 369
Anemia 369
Arthritis/Joint infection 369
Aujeszky's Disease 370
Bacterial Infections/Diseases 370
Blue Eye Disease 370
Diarrhea 370
Dipped Shoulder 371
Foot-and-Mouth Disease 371
Fractures 371
Gastric Ulcers 371
Glässer's Disease 372
Hematoma 372
Intestinal Torsion 372
Large Roundworm 372
Mange 373
Mastitis 373
Metritis 373
Navel Bleeding 373
Parasites 374
Parvovirus 374
Pneumonia 374
Porcine Influenza 374
Porcine Reproductive and
   Respiratory Syndrome 375
Respiratory Conditions 375
Ruptures 375
Swine Dysentery 375
Udder Edema 376

Livestock and Wildlife Breeding **376**
Rut 376

Exotic and Wild Animals **377**

Raccoon Conditions **378**
Conjunctivitis 378
Distemper 378
Giardia 379
Leptospirosis 379
Parasites 380
Pneumonia 380
Salmonellosis 381
Skin Infestations 381

Rogue Animals **382**
Testimonials **383**

Chapter 15

Pocket Pets **385**
Introduction **385**
Safety Guidelines **385**
Raindrop Technique **386**
Pocket Pet Conditions **387**
Adrenal Disease 387
Anesthesia Support 387
Aplastic Anemia 388
Appetite Loss 388
Barbering 389
Bloat 389
Bone Fracture 390
Breathing Issues 390
Calcium Metabolism 391
Colds 391
Conjunctivitis 392
Constipation 392
Coprophagy 393
Dental Disease 393
Diarrhea 394
Distemper 394
Ear Infection 395
Ear Masses 395
Enteritis 396
Environmental Terrain 396
Epilepsy 397
Eye Tears 397
Fever 398
Fleas and Ear Mites 398
Fungal Infections 399
Fur Chewing 399
Gastroenteritis 400

Gastrointestinal Foreign Body 400
Gastrointestinal Stasis 400
Hair Coat. 400
Heart Murmur. 401
Heat Stroke 401
Insulinomas. 402
Irritable Bowel Syndrome. 402
Joint Issues 403
Kidney Disease. 403
Kidney Disorders 404
Lead Poisoning. 404
Lumps 405
Lymphoma 405
Mammary Glands 406
Mange, Fleas and Mites. 406
Neurological Disease 407
Parasites 407
Pneumonia 408
Pododermatitis 409
Protein Digestion 409
Pyometra 410
Raindrop Technique 386
Respiratory Infection and Pasteurellosis 410
Respiratory Issues 411
Ringtail 411
Ringworm 411
Salmonellosis 412
Scurvy 412
Skin, Dry. 413
Skin Infections 413
Skin Infestations 413
Slobbers 414
Sore Hocks. 414
Stomach Ulcers 414
Tail Slip 414
Tear Glands 415

Teeth, Overgrown 416
Thiamine Deficiency. 416
Tumors, Benign 416
Tumors, Reproductive 417
Tumors, Skin and Belly Areas. 417
Tumors, Skin Swellings 418
Tumors, Surface Skin Areas 418
Tyzzer's Disease 418
Urinary Calculi 418
Viral Infections 419
Wobbly Hedgehog Syndrome 419
Wounds. 420
Wry Neck 421

Tips for Healthy Rabbits **421**
Bedding 421
Diet. 422

Testimonials. **423**

Chapter 16

Reptiles **425**
Safety Guidelines **426**
Reptile Conditions **425**
Burns 425
External Parasites 427
Injuries/Wounds 427
Internal Parasites 428
Metabolic Bone Disease 428
Shedding Problems 428
Stomatitis. 429
Upper Respiratory
    Infection/Pneumonia. 429

Testimonial. **429**

Index

Index 431

Section 1

Introduction

Ancient cultures revered animals, celebrating their unique qualities, their perceived strengths, and the observed behaviors within the food chain. The Egyptians, Mesopotamians, and Hindus all associated divine beings with animals. Native American cultures celebrated them as a rich part of their cosmology centering on the Great Spirit or the Great Mystery. They viewed seasons, weather, plants, animals, earth, water, sky and fire as part of the whole collective of humanity.

With the domestication of animals, humans took on greater responsibility—recognizing that their livelihoods depended greatly on the health and well-being of animals in their care. This tradition continued into the age of the Industrial Revolution. But over time, industrial profits and superfluous competitive breeding have compromised nature's biodiversity, effectively threatening the health of our domesticated animals by diminishing the strength of their genetic code.

With industrial food production and highly refined diets, both animals and humans alike face challenges in getting proper nutrition and healthy support. Food contains more energy and fewer enzymes, potentially causing a rise in obesity and, inversely, a decline in nutrition.

As a result, humans are faced with a choice: to enrich and supplement their diets or face a reduced quality of life. It is a curious irony that with technology and the ability to produce more *efficiently* than ever before, we have lost the *effectiveness* of one of our most powerful sources of health—the foods we ingest.

This same challenge has trickled down to the animals in our care. Animals and humans are more closely tied than the modern age would have us believe.

When we feed our animals with inferior food products, we effectively ingest those same inferior foods. When we use hormones and genetically modified foods on animals that produce food products (or become food products themselves), we potentially affect our own hormone health.

To Reap and to Sow

Many of the animals in our care are the result of generations of selective breeding. Despite their celebrated pedigrees, purebred animals increasingly lack the genetic diversity to keep them protected against disease and debilitating illness. They are more susceptible to congenital defects and early-onset ailments.

This is where plants and their highly complex organic compounds become all the more important. Plants respond to their environment each season. Every environmental influence affects their growth and chemical composition. Water, sunlight, soil nutrient profile, and even air quality all have potential to affect the resulting plant. In this way, they are responding to the environment, and they do everything in their power to survive. Where one plant may not be able to live in semi-drought conditions, another finds a way. They are the essence of life—seed, sprout, blossom, flower, ripen, mature, expire, and compost. They represent a total cycle of growth, development, adjustment, balance, and response. They evolve from crop to crop, season to season, and provide a varied chemical profile.

Why Essential Oils and Animals...

Throughout the course of history, essential oils have been the purest, most concentrated source of organic compounds. Their numerous supplemental benefits in the modern age are only just being explored. They have the potential to provide solutions where so much of modern science has failed. And, they have a history of guiding human scientific discovery in the realm of pharmaceutical development.

As more and more health practitioners, veterinary health professionals, and organic chemists explore the use of essential oils, the more likely they are to unearth even greater benefits to modern health and animal husbandry. In this day and age, perhaps the more natural the solution, the better it is in the long run. After a century of synthesizing molecules and using industrial means of extraction, we have discovered that some compounds, which seem to be cures can be, in fact, worse than the diseases they purport to treat.

We love our animals as part of our families. We respect them, often times, as part of our livelihood. We hope for a quality of life that benefits us both. With that in mind, we have compiled this information and organized it here as a way of providing valuable information from professionals and enthusiasts alike.

We hope you see the value in this volume, particularly as it provides a map of essential oils and animal use. It does not serve as the destination. Respectfully, that is for you to decide.

One thing is sure: we are all interconnected—animals, plants, and humans alike. We share the same atmosphere, the same water, and the same ground. As caretakers, we owe it to ourselves, our animals, and the earth itself to respect nature's balance. By respecting the biofeedback mechanisms of our world, we can ensure a better tomorrow for the generations of humans, plants, and animals to come.

Animal Care Professionals

Although essential oils were likely used in treating animals in previous centuries, the modern age of animal medicine is only re-discovering the potential role they play in natural health support. If pursuing an essential oil-based method of animal care, you'll want to seek advice of a professional veterinary health provider who specializes in holistic modalities. This may take some time and effort on your part, but be sure to do your research to find a certified professional who understands your reasons for pursuing essential oils and incorporating them into your animal care.

In the context of this volume, much of our information comes from our network of professionals who use essential oils in their various practices. They may be vet techs, veterinarians, specialized (to species) veterinarians, veterinary nutritional scientists, holistic aromatherapy practitioners specializing in animal care, or they may be professionals who care for animals that serve a specific function such as Award Winning Mitch Seavey of the famed Iditarod.

Additionally, we pull much of what we know from our large body of therapeutic-grade essential oil enthusiasts. Enthusiasts are clients of professionals who have incorporated essential oils in the daily care of their animals. They are not scientists but rather *enthusiastic* animal owners who have discovered the merits of various essential oils in helping their animals enjoy a better quality of life.

As the compilation team for this book, we advise that you consult a veterinarian (board certified by the AVMA) or equivalent when embarking on a new strategy of care.

Animals are as varied as people, and a professional with a case knowledge of your particular pet or animal will be able to advise you best as to proper care.

Now, that said, there are several veterinary health professionals who may help. You may encounter several competent people above and beyond those who are Doctors of Veterinary Medicine (DVM or VMD). You may interact with veterinary nurses, veterinary technicians, or veterinary assistants.

Additionally, para-veterinary workers are those professionals who assist a veterinary physician in the performance of their duties or carry out animal health procedures autonomously as part of a veterinary care system. Titles and credentials will vary with each country, state, and locality.

On the other end, a Veterinary Specialist may be consulted when an animal's condition requires specialized care above and beyond that which a regular veterinarian can offer. Many Veterinary Specialists require a referral in order to be seen. A Veterinary Specialist, as recognized by the AVMA, is "a graduate veterinarian who has successfully completed the process of board certification in an AVMA-recognized veterinary specialty organization (i.e., board or college). To become board certified, a veterinarian must have extensive post-graduate training and experience and pass a credential review and examinations set by the given specialty organization."

Essential Oils are becoming more widespread within the Holistic and CAM (Complementary Alternative Medicine) field, particularly for animals. As a caregiver who wants the best for the animal(s) in your charge, you might conduct research over the web. While there is extensive information and advice on many sites, blogs, and social media hotspots, be careful that you filter the information. Always cross-reference the postings you see and be sure the information is specifically tailored to animals and their respective species.

As you consult with professionals, always disclose any known allergies or serious health issues to your veterinary health professional before embarking on an essential oils care strategy. Some essential oils are contraindicated for use with certain health care conditions.

Plants and Animals

In the natural world, animals' diets were often in tandem with their environments and their needs. They migrated when those needs weren't met. They hunted the prey that ate certain plants most suitable for their survival. Animals and plants in the wild have a very connected biorhythm. Flora and fauna have always gone hand in hand.

Every Plant is, Itself, a Researcher

In a way, each plant that emerges from a seed spends its entire life researching its environment. It responds to stimuli in the soil, water, and air. Each stimulus produces a response. These responses manifest in the plant essences a complex series of volatile organic compounds (VOCs). Through continuous "testing," a plant discovers the best way to survive.

The biofeedback between a plant and its environment is constant and always evolving. Green leaf volatiles, a subset of VOCs, are emissions from plants. Parts of those emissions fall back to the ground due to rain, and the plant begins to read its environment as it takes up water.

Beyond the volatiles, many active plant essences are the key results of the extraction process, namely:

Terpenes	Sesquiterpenes	Ketones	Lactones
Alkanes	Alcohols	Carboxylic Acids	Coumarins
Phenols	Ethers	Esters	Furanoids
Monoterpenes	Aldehydes	Oxides	

All of these chemical constituents and their variable expression have a significant impact on human and animal tissues alike. When these plant essences are consumed by local fauna, their consequent wastes and exhalations return as feedback for the plant. Thus, the animal-to-plant feedback system comes full circle.

The Challenge of Modern Domestication

Domestication undoes many of an animal's natural instincts. As humans, we train and breed animals to behave a certain way. Consequently, they often learn to respond negatively to things they ordinarily wouldn't in the wild. Our challenge as caregivers is to use those instincts to help them.

Why Animals?

You may ask why there is a need for a desk reference for animals. The answer is simple—animals have their own unique considerations when it comes to essential oils. They have distinctive responses that depend upon their species, and they have different levels of sensitivity and toxicity than those of their human counterparts.

Even beyond species, each animal is unique and has a unique response to essential oils. Not only does each species have a set of sensitivities or allergies to certain compounds and a unique set of toxicity concerns, but also, just like humans, each animal is an individual.

Beyond those considerations, who doesn't want to help their pet or an animal in their care? Whether in times of distress or times of perfect health, essential oils are a valuable method for offering natural nurturing to the little (and not so little) friends who look to us to provide for them.

Additionally, the methods of administering essential oils to enhance the lives of animals are as varied as the animals themselves. When using essential oils in caring for animals or pets, it is paramount to consider:

- Their size
- Their hair (density of follicles changes the uptake of essential oils)
- Their sense of smell
- Their dependence upon humans
- Their unique species and sensitivities

Improving the Lives of Domestic Animals

Anyone who has witnessed the suffering of an animal knows without a doubt that it can suffer. In addition, any person who has cared for an animal—only to watch it suffer and be told nothing further could be done to help ease its suffering—knows what it feels like to try whatever it takes to relieve the situation.

Young Living Essential Oils is committed to natural sources and solutions, going to great lengths for purity, research, and study. Young Living personnel have extensive, traditional essential oil knowledge built on more than 30 years of natural research, so their mode is the inverse of the modern clinical approach. They have knowledge of how essential oils work on humans, they have expanded on that knowledge to experiment with how essences affect humans, and their nature is to use that knowledge as a safer means for trial and error when it comes to helping animals. This is in direct contrast to the modern establishment's approach of testing drastic quantities of toxic synthetics on laboratory animals.

Because of this commitment to purity, natural healing, and life enhancement, Young Living has attracted many accomplished professionals from the animal health field who want to understand what conventional wisdom cannot. They have amassed countless stories of people successfully using essential oils to help their animals experience a higher quality of life.

Quality of Life, Quality of Oils

Essential oils are extremely complex substances. In many cases, they are composed of hundreds of varying chemicals. It is this fingerprint of chemicals working in relative concentrations that enables their therapeutic effects. Not surprisingly, *how* an essential oil is extracted can have a dramatic effect on its ability to influence the tissues of humans and animals alike. The more the essence stays intact, the more superior its profile of chemical constituents. This book will cover those topics in greater detail in subsequent chapters; but for now, it is important to emphasize that therapeutic effects come from only the highest grade of essential oils.

As this book is intended to be a companion guide to the Essential Oils Desk Reference, most material can be referenced in greater detail in the most up-to-date volume. Nevertheless, we include a summarized version of some topics and product descriptions, mainly as a review and reference for those who might be sharing this information with other essential oil practitioners, for those readers who may not have had the opportunity to read the Essential Oils Desk Reference, or for those who simply need the information to put their animal focus into context.

Pets and Owners/Caregivers

Since pets cannot talk to their owners or veterinarians, they have to communicate in body language. Nothing is more dramatic than seeing an animal rise from being paralyzed with pain or coming to its owner in search of soothing effects after experiencing success with essential oils. Sometimes the effect of administering essential oils is so dramatic that owners would call it miraculous.

Yet others from the skeptical schools of thought often denounce the use of essential oils when it comes to animals, saying, "Do NOT use these powerful compounds and NEVER expose animals or pets—even to diffusion." We believe that such cynics have never actually tried essential oils on themselves, let alone on their pets or animals in their care.

On the contrary, thousands of essential oil users and practitioners who may not understand "how" or "why" essential oils work can certainly attest to the dramatic effects upon their pets. With pure essential oils, millions of pet owners can find successful relief for their pets where more conventional approaches have failed. The therapeutic potential for animals is enormous, and pet owners and pet health practitioners are just beginning to tap into this widely promising field.

We believe the controversy relating to essential oils is due to the varying types that are on the market. Consumers have access to many options of adulterated oils with varying degrees of purity. In fact, most oils on the market are so impure that they can barely be used in dilution on humans without adverse reactions, let alone pets of one tenth human mass.

Living by Smell

Many animals live by smell. If you have a pet and you've ever brought something home from the store, how often have you set that purchase on your floor and watched your pet go immediately to the item and give it a sniff? It's as though it isn't really *smelling* but is actually *seeing* with its sense of smell. It identifies what you brought home, where it has been, who has handled it, and where it was placed.

A human study by University of Oxford psychologists discovered that cognition significantly influences our human perception of smell. Researchers labeled an ambiguous Brie-like scent as either "body odor" or "aged cheddar cheese." Not surprisingly, the human test subjects rated the odor better when it was labeled "cheddar cheese." MRIs showed more activity in the olfactory region of the brain when subjects believed they smelled cheese.

Perhaps animals refrain from judging smells due to a lesser cognition than humans. Because of this reason, their brain activity may produce a different limbic system response than humans—or a more pronounced one of the same order.

When animals appear to dislike or not want an essential oil, it is often because it is simply a new smell or is unfamiliar. It might even remind the animal of something it doesn't like. If this is the case, then mix the oil with something the animal does like and see if the response is different. Diffuse the oil first for a day or two and then try applying it.

When we consider that an animal's sense of smell may be on the order of one hundred to thousands of times greater than ours (some dogs can detect odors that are one part per trillion), it is easy to understand that even a single drop of Lemon oil will take some getting used to.

Purity

Over the years, Young Living has bought and compiled an essential oil retention index and mass spectral reference library that contains over 400,000 components. Using this research reference library, Young Living developed its own standards to guarantee the highest possible therapeutic potency for its essential oils.

When it comes to humans, the fragrance of an essential oil can directly affect everything from their emotional state to their lifespan. The specific mechanics of the sense of smell are still being explored by scientists but have been described as working like a lock and key or an odor molecule fitting a specific receptor site. With animals having a far greater sense of smell, it stands to reason that those locks and keys would have exponentially greater possibility.

If the Animal Resists

As mentioned earlier, when animals appear to dislike or not want an essential oil, it is often because it is simply a new smell or is unfamiliar. It might even remind the animal of something it doesn't like. If this is the case, then mix the oil with something the animal does like and see if the response is different. Diffuse the oil first for a day or two and then try applying it.

It is easy to understand how strong the aroma of one drop of a pure oil is to a human, so it should be easy to understand how strong one drop might be to an animal. Just start slowly with diluted or even diffused oils, and eventually you will see a response.

Animal Detoxification

Overusing essential oils can happen to the best of us. Usually, it takes only one time before we learn our lesson. Keeping that in mind, always start with the approach of using the minimum. Overuse is not usually dangerous or toxic, but it may cause a detoxification that is uncomfortable and may temporarily make a therapeutic situation worse. The response doesn't usually last very long, but it always helps to understand what is happening.

If the animal feels worse and a blood analysis is done, the animal may be diagnosed with some kind of illness, when in reality, the animal was already sick. In some lab testing situations, this results in misguided labeling of the essential oils as "dangerous" or "harmful." In the extensive experience of Young Living researchers, the only times essential oils might be to blame are if they are adulterated and/or synthetic. Any synthetic or adulterated oil will cause an adverse reaction in any species.

Essential oils have been known to digest toxic substances; so when they come in contact with chemical residue on the skin, the oils start to work against them. It's important to eliminate any synthetic products, if possible, when using essential oils around animals. Use the most natural shampoos, moisturizers, and carrier oils.

Many animals, especially dogs, have been exposed to toxic chemicals, repeated vaccinations, or medications and need the detoxification. Because detoxification seems to be a characteristic of essential oils, sometimes it is better to start with lower oil amounts and allow the body to adjust, so you can see if a detoxification starts. Then you will know how to adjust the oils. Diffusing might be a better way to begin until the body has adjusted to the aroma of the essential oils.

Avoid using synthetic, petroleum-based, animal care products, as well as products containing ammonium or hydrocarbon-based chemicals. These include quaternary compounds such as quaternariums and polyquaternariums. These chemicals can be fatal if ingested, especially benzalkonium chloride, which, unfortunately, is used in many products on the market.

Other chemicals such as aluminum compounds, FD&C colors, formaldehyde, all parabens, talc, thimerosal, mercury, titanium dioxide, sodium lauryl sulfate, propylene glycol, and aluminum salts (to name a few) all pose toxic risks to animals and should be avoided.

If your aim is to detoxify a pet or animal in your care, consider removing any potentially hazardous preservatives and synthetic fragrances. These include methylene chloride, methyl isobutyl ketone, and methyl ethyl ketone. These are not only toxic, but they can also react with some compounds in natural essential oils. The result can be a severe case of dermatitis or even septicemia (blood poisoning).

Many chemicals are easily absorbed through the skin due to its permeability. One study found that 13 percent of BHT (butylated hydroxytoluene) and 49 percent of DDT (a carcinogenic pesticide) can be absorbed into the skin upon topical contact.

Once absorbed, many chemicals can become trapped in the fatty subdermal layers of skin, where they can leach into the bloodstream. They can remain trapped for several months or years until a topical substance like an essential oil starts to move them from their resting place and cause them to come out of the skin in an uncomfortable way.

Besides skin irritation, an animal could experience nausea, headaches, and other slight temporary effects during a detoxifying process. Even in small concentrations, these chemicals and synthetic compounds can be toxic and can compromise an animal's health.

When helping to detoxify an animal, the concern is which chemicals were used, how much, how long, and perhaps the level of toxicity in the animal's body.

If an animal has a reaction to this detoxifying process:

- Reduce the amount of oil used with dilution.
- Make drinking water freely available.
- Stop the use of any oil for a couple of days.
- Begin again slowly.

Consider using V-6 Vegetable Oil Complex, other organic vegetable or massage oils, or natural creams to dilute the oils. Use small amounts when administering essential oils to animals that may have been exposed to residue from soaps, moisturizers, and cleansers containing synthetic chemicals. Some of them—especially petroleum-based chemicals—can penetrate and remain in the skin and fatty tissues for days or even weeks after use.

Essential oils may work against such chemicals and toxins built up in the body from chemicals in food, water, and work environment. If the animals in your care have this kind of an experience using essential oils, it may be wise to start an internal cleansing program for the animal. In addition, try to increase the animal's water intake to flush toxins.

You may also want to try the following alternatives to a detoxification program to determine the cause of the problem:

- Dilute 1-3 drops of essential oil in ½ teaspoon of V-6 Vegetable Oil Complex, massage oil, or any pure vegetable oil. More dilution may be needed, depending on the size and type of the animal.

- Reduce the number of oils used at any time.

- Use single oils or oil blends one at a time.

- Reduce the amount of oil used.

- Reduce the frequency of application.

- Provide purified or distilled water.

- Ask your veterinary professional or holistic animal tech to monitor detoxification.

How Much Should I Use: An Overview

Animals respond to essential oils in much the same way as humans. Most animals are more sensitive to the effects of essential oils than humans and often seem to have a natural affinity to the beneficial influence of the oils. As animals have more hair follicles than humans, they may be able to absorb essential oils more effectively. Since sensitivity to essential oils may be due to the density of hair follicles on an animal, the more follicles per square inch of skin, the more enhanced the absorption of essential oils. Therefore, cats can absorb more essential oils through their skin more efficiently than a horse or a dog with a coarser hair coat. When we consider which animal species seem most sensitive to exposure to essential oils, it likely has a strong correlation with the density of hair follicles.

If the protocol for a human being weighing 160 pounds calls for 3-5 drops, then a horse at 1,600 pounds or more could use as much as 10 times that amount. A dog weighing 16 pounds would need as little as one tenth that amount. There is also a difference between topical and oral application, which always implies a smaller amount when starting and increasing the amount as needed.

If a human can use one drop of an essential oil to calm a headache, then diffusing might be the answer for birds, horses, or guinea pigs. While applying oils to the feet is considered the safest location for humans, that may not be the case with all species of animals. Some animals absorb more toxins, chemicals, etc., through their feet. Essential oils on the feet may start an uncomfortable detoxification. Working through the fur or hair may be the best way to begin. However, large animals such as horses often do well having oils applied to the hooves and along the frog or coronet band region.

In the initial cases of small dogs, cats, and exotic pets, essential oils should be diluted before being applied to test how each individual responds. Some species are more sensitive to different natural chemical compounds found in the oils. Be particularly careful when choosing oils that are high in sesquiterpenes, phenols, and eugenols (generally referred to as "hot oils") such as Oregano, Thyme, Clove, Mountain Savory, and Cinnamon Bark. Many small animals, especially cats, can be extremely sensitive to stronger oils. They should generally be diluted in a ratio of 6 drops of V-6 Vegetable Oil Complex to 1 drop of essential oil and so on like 8 to 1 or even 10 to 1, depending on the species and individual animal.

Percentages

Understanding percentages of dilution can be difficult for even the most experienced aromatherapist. Clear communication about how to dilute essential oils is critical for proper use, especially for animals. Describing dilution in multiple ways can be helpful for those of us without a mathematical strong suit. Confusion can ensue when someone is uncertain if the oil should be used at 90% "strong" or 90% "diluted." In most situations, it may be best to clearly describe the dilution of essential oils in terms of how many drops of essential oils are added to a certain quantity of carrier oil.

Essential Oils and Animals: The Future

Essential oils are no longer ignored in the annals of modern veterinary science. Instead, millions of people are applauding their benefits, and millions more are being introduced and educated to their potential each year. Large pharmaceutical giants continue to look to plants and their compounds as sources for their next patented drug. They spend millions of dollars on research to discover what plant compounds look most promising and which ones can be replicated synthetically in the lab.

As more and more health practitioners, doctors, scientists, veterinarians, therapists, and users of all ages venture into the world of this ancient knowledge, the methods of improving quality of life and wellness will take on new dimensions, and exciting discoveries will be made that will benefit humankind and animal kind alike.

A solution referred to as 90% can be thought of as 1 drop of essential oil in 9 drops of carrier oil. An 80% solution will be 2 drops of essential oil in 8 drops of carrier oil. Below is a quick reference for the percent of dilution in terms of drops of essential oil per carrier oil.

90% = 1 drop essential oil + 9 drops carrier oil
80% = 2 drops essential oil + 8 drops carrier oil
70% = 3 drops essential oil + 7 drops carrier oil
60% = 4 drops essential oil + 6 drops carrier oil
50% = 5 drops essential oil + 5 drops carrier oil
(also called 50:50=1 drop essential oil + 1 drop carrier oil)
40% = 6 drops essential oil + 4 drops carrier oil
30% = 7 drops essential oil + 3 drops carrier oil
20% = 8 drops essential oil + 2 drops carrier oil
10% = 9 drops essential oil + 1 drop carrier oil

General Guidelines

- For small animals (cats, small dogs, and exotics): Apply 3-5 drops of diluted (80-90%) oil mixture per application.

- For larger animals (large dogs, goats, and pigs): Apply 3-5 drops neat (dilute if using oils high in phenol) per application.

- For large animals (cattle, horses, and elephants): Apply 10-15 drops neat (dilute if using oils high in phenol) per application.

Essential Oils and Animals: An Overview

Prior to the industrial revolution, essential oils were one of the few methods people could use in helping to improve the lives of animals. It stands to reason that natural plant life has a way of nurturing the animals it supports. Why, then, do we encounter so many cautions regarding animals and essential oils?

Consider that quality and purity are of the utmost importance when it comes to animals. Many aspects of the human environment have been contaminated. All too often, greed and commercialism have tainted growing, extraction, distillation, and packaging of plant essences.

Yet, just because something is natural doesn't mean it can't have toxic effects. Poison ivy surely has inflammatory effects, and it is as natural as stinging nettle or poison oak. With that in mind, always remember that each animal is unique. Each animal will respond as an individual. While essential oils may help balance an animal, always remember:

Less is more • Gradual is better • Moderation is wise

Oils that are Generally Animal Kingdom Safe

Many oils are tried and true, having been used safely with most species, including Lavender, Helichrysum, Frankincense, Clary Sage, Elemi, Geranium, Roman Chamomile, Rosemary, Valerian, and many others.

Many of us have individual sensitivities to household cleaners, synthetic foods, petroleum-based silicones, and synthetic propylene glycol-based hair and skin products. Not surprisingly, each species has a different level of liver function, and so some of the essential oils with high phenol, monoterpene, and ketone content may need to be used sparingly. This is especially true with cats (feline species).

Members from around the world attended the ribbon cutting and opening of the distillery in Split, Croatia, October 6, 2015.

Clean Processes

Plant harvesting, extraction, and processing must all remain clean to give animals the best therapeutic experience. Steam distilled, expressed, and absolutes (that derive from the purest concretes and natural solvents) are the only acceptable oils for use.

Vertical Steam Distillation. Steam distillation has many subtle variables. These include the size and material of the extraction chamber, type of condenser and separator, temperature, pressure, and timing. Distillation is as much a science as it is an art. If the pressure or temperature is too high, or if the cooking chambers are constructed from reactive materials, the oil may not be therapeutic grade.

Vertical steam distillation offers the greatest potential for protecting the therapeutic benefits and quality of essential oils. In ancient distillation, low pressure (5 pounds or lower) and low temperature were extremely important for producing the most desired therapeutic benefits.

Temperature also has a distinct effect because it greatly alters pH, polarity, and constituents. Some compounds remain stable at lower temperatures but break down into something altogether different at higher pressure and temperature. For example, cypress requires a minimum of 24 hours of distillation at 265°F and 5 pounds of pressure to extract most of the therapeutically active constituents. By cutting distillation time by only 2 hours, the resulting extraction will be missing 18 to 20 constituents. Sadly, most commercial cypress oil is distilled for only 2.25

hours to reduce production costs, and this results in oil with little or no therapeutic value.

Expressed Oils. Expressed oils are pressed from the rind of fruits such as grapefruit, lemon, lime, mandarin, orange, and tangerine. These are rich in terpene alcohols and are usually too strong for many species of animals. While expressed oils are not technically "essential oils," they are still highly regarded for their potentially therapeutic properties. If one chooses to proceed with these oils, it is of utmost importance to source them only from organically grown crops, since pesticide residues can become highly concentrated in the oil.

Absolutes. Because solvent extraction involves the use of oil-soluble solvents such as hexane, di-methylene-chloride, and acetone and can be highly toxic to most species, it is important to avoid any oils that may have been adulterated with them.

Absolutes are technically not "essential oils" but are "essences." They are obtained from the grain alcohol extraction of a concrete, which is the solid, waxy residue derived from the extraction of plant materials, usually flower petals. This method of extraction is used primarily for botanicals where the fragrance and therapeutic parts of the plant can be unlocked only by using solvents. Jasmine and Neroli are extracted this way, and they should generally be used sparingly around animals.

Providing A Healthy Environment

Human diets today are highly deficient in nutrients but highly dense in calories. The same holds true for many animal foods on the market today. The food you choose can have a profound effect on your animal's health.

Exercise is important for the health of any animal. It sometimes takes as much commitment and discipline to make time for exercising a pet as it does an owner. Horses require very specialized equestrian exercises to keep their muscles, posture, and gait in perfect order.

When it comes to diet, never treat an animal to fast-food scraps. The prepared and processed foods that have negative effects on humans can have exponentially more on animals. Contaminated water and water treated with chemicals such as chlorine and fluoride might inhibit proper thyroid function and slow the metabolism, circulation system, and immune function in many animals.

Finally, air pollution, chemicals, cleaning products, pest-control products, changes in ozone, electromagnetic and radiation pollution from computers, cell phones, televisions, and electrical appliances may also influence the health of an animal in your care. Anything you can do to reduce these influences on your animal's health will boost the potential effects of an essential oil routine.

Essential Oil Chemistry

The vast majority of oils are produced for the sole purpose of scent—for the perfume industry. Because the therapeutic constituents aren't the priority, the distillation processes generally use high pressures, high temperatures, and chemical solvents to cut production costs and time. While these may smell great for human perfumes, they generally won't have the potentially positive effects on animals.

Veterinary scientists are only beginning to fully appreciate how chemically complex essential oils are. Many of them have literally hundreds of chemical components, some of which—even in small quantities—can contribute important therapeutic benefits.

The best way to preserve as many of these delicate aromatic constituents as possible is to steam distill plant material in small batches using low pressure and low heat, using the more traditional method of distillation that has been used for centuries in Europe.

Just as important is the use of nonreactive metals for the cooking chambers where the plants are distilled. Stainless steel reduces the possibility of alteration that occurs with the reactive metals such as aluminum or copper.

Finally, there should be no pesticides, herbicides, fungicides, agricultural chemicals of any kind, and no solvents or synthetic chemicals in the water used to grow or process the plant material. During distillation, pesticide residue leaches out of the plant material with the extracted essential oil, and this can have very harmful effects on animals of all sizes.

Realize that using the best grade of essential oils to help care for animals will potentially come with its own set of costs. Producing pure essential oils is very costly. It often requires several hundred or even thousands of pounds of raw plant material to produce a single pound of essential oil. For example, it takes 5,000 pounds of rose petals to produce approximately 1 pint of Rose oil. This makes the purest forms of these oils very expensive.

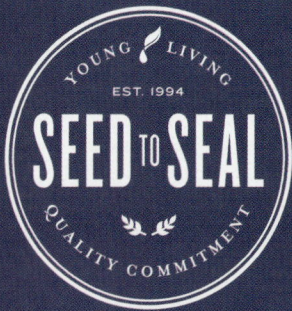

Young Living Essential Oils

is the only company dedicated to the therapeutic use and application of essential oils that is able to guarantee essential oil quality from seed to seal.

The oils that Young Living provides to consumers are extracted through steam distillation from a wide variety of plants, roots, bushes, trees, and resins and are as powerful and pure as the botanicals from which they are derived.

The life-giving energy of the essential oils that is carefully distilled from nature cannot be duplicated in a sterile laboratory. Synthetic constituents may be similar in structure but have none of the living plant energy that holds the therapeutic value of the oil that is released from the plant itself.

Young Living's Seed to Seal process guarantees a genuine, pure essential oil that has the highest therapeutic efficacy. This guarantee includes oils distilled from plants grown on Young living's own farms, sourced from experienced distillers of many generations, or purchased from distillers who have been directed and taught distilling techniques by Young Living. Consequently, their essential oils continue to be used worldwide in more clinical and university studies than any other essential oils today.

The feedback, research, and information coming from our vast population of Young Living Essential Oils users tell us that the main thing to keep in mind is to begin with the minimum amount and expand once tolerance is established. In the same common-sense way that a baby is weaned gradually from its mother's milk—or a puppy or a calf or a kitten from its mother—so too, should common sense apply with administering essential oils. Any animal flooded with multiple pure, therapeutic-grade essential oils in a single day will have aversions. If in doubt, always dilute and avoid using a heavy hand.

General Guidelines

Many of the same general guidelines that apply to humans also apply to animals. It's important to follow these rules when using essential oils, especially if you are unfamiliar with the oils and their benefits. The guidelines listed below are an overview and will be covered in greater detail in subsequent chapters. Also refer to the *Essential Oil Desk Reference* for greater detail.

Remember, no list of do's and don'ts can ever replace good, common sense. Start gradually and patiently to find what works best for each of the animals in your care.

Storage

- Always keep a bottle of a pure vegetable oil (e.g., V-6 Vegetable Oil Complex, olive oil, coconut oil, avocado oil, or any organic vegetable oil) handy when using essential oils. Vegetable oils will dilute essential oils if the essential oils cause discomfort or skin irritation.

- Keep bottles of essential oils tightly closed and store them in a cool location away from light. If stored properly, essential oils will maintain their potency for many years.

- Keep essential oils out of reach of animals. Treat the oils as you would any product for therapeutic use.

Usage

1 Essential oils rich in menthol (such as Peppermint) should not be used on the sensitive areas (e.g., belly, armpit, throat, genital area) of any animal.

2 Angelica, Bergamot, Grapefruit, Lemon, Orange, Tangerine, and other citrus oils are photosensitive and may cause a rash or dark pigmentation on skin exposed to direct sunlight or UV rays within 1-2 days after application. These should always be diluted or diffused when using with animals.

3 Keep essential oils away from the eye area and never put them directly into ears.

4 Do not touch the eye areas of any animal with essential oils on your fingers. Even in minute amounts, many essential oils will irritate eyes and mucous membranes.

5 If your animal is pregnant or nursing young, it is wise to consult a veterinary health care professional when starting any type of program. Use oils with caution and common sense. Follow the directions and dilute with V-6 Vegetable Oil Complex until you are completely familiar with the oils you are using.

6 If an animal has been diagnosed as epileptic or has a history of high blood pressure, you should consult a veterinary health care professional before using essential oils. Use extra caution with high ketone oils such as Basil, Rosemary, Sage, and Tansy. These should always be diluted or diffused when using with animals.

7 Use extra caution when using essential oils around animals with known allergies. Consult a veterinary health care professional before using. Test a small amount of diluted oil before applying neat or in Raindrop Technique.

8 The bottoms of feet might be safe locations to apply essential oils topically for humans, but they ARE NOT suitable for most animals.

9 Inhalation of essential oils can be a deep and intensive application method, particularly for respiratory congestion and illness. However, this method should not be used more than 10-15 times throughout the day without consulting a veterinary health care professional.

10 Before administering any GRAS (Generally Regarded As Safe) essential oils internally (e.g., food, water, carrier, sublingual, oral dropping), test an animal's reactions by diluting 1 drop of essential oil in 1 teaspoon of an oil-soluble liquid like olive oil, coconut oil, or rice milk. If you intend to administer more than a few drops of diluted essential oil per day, first consult a veterinary health care professional. Be aware that reactions to essential oils, both topically and orally, can be delayed as long as 2-3 days.

11 If bathing or grooming an animal, add 1-3 drops of undiluted essential oils directly to bath water. If more essential oil is desired, mix the oil first into bath salts or a species-safe bath gel base before adding to the bath water. Generally, never use more than 10 drops of essential oils in one bath. When essential oils are put directly into bath water without a dispersing agent, they can cause serious discomfort to an animal because the essential oils tend to float, undiluted, on top of the water.

Examples of Animal Exposure to Essential Oils

Fish

Fish are exposed to essential oils from plant matter decomposing in their water environment. Both the earth's oceans and freshwater contain aromatic compounds from natural plant life as well as from runoff from plant life on land.

Insects

Insects are naturally exposed to essential oils in the wild. Honeybees are currently suffering from what is considered a toxic environment with all the chemical sprays and polluted water.

Exotic Pets

Furry animals such as ferrets may use essential oils in a similar fashion as cats. For other exotic animals, use water-based diffusers. Water animals such as turtles or lizards may use the oils in the same manner as fish. Some exotic pets like citrus oils or small amounts of Citrus Fresh (1-2 drops) added to their drinking water. Use only glass, ceramic, or stainless steel water containers when using essential oils.

Birds

Birds are very sensitive to household chemicals, and bird owners know that the spray of an air freshener or the burning of a candle can be dangerous to a bird. Most household cleaners and fragrances are formulated with chemicals and other synthetic substances that are toxic to animals and humans alike, and adulterated and synthetic essential oils are no better. It has been thought that essential oils might be toxic to birds; but if they are pure, authentic, and used properly, they may benefit a wide variety of birds.

Cats

The feline species are most amenable to diffusing, especially from the water-based ultrasonic diffuser models. Cats have interesting personalities, and one cannot predict which oil any one cat may like or dislike. It is easy to tell by the cat's response to an oil if it is a good oil for that cat. The cat will either stay in or leave the room.

Some oils may be controversial, but that is usually because of low quality or adulteration. If you are uncertain, use oils that are better known and can be just as good for the need of the animal. Use applications that are well-known for their benefits. It is the same with animals as it is with humans. If one oil doesn't seem to work, then try another one and just keep experimenting until you find the right one.

Dogs

Oil application will vary depending on the size of the dog as well as the technique used. Small dogs can start with diffusing, while larger dogs can start with direct oil application. Dogs can generally use oils more freely and easily than cats and smaller-sized animals.

Cattle and Livestock

Oils may be used the same as horses for these animals. Using the oils in feed, water, and udder washes may promote health benefits when used daily.

Horses

Favorite oil applications for horses include Raindrop Technique, oral, topical applications (neat or diluted), massage, and petting. Oils may also be added to the water anytime.

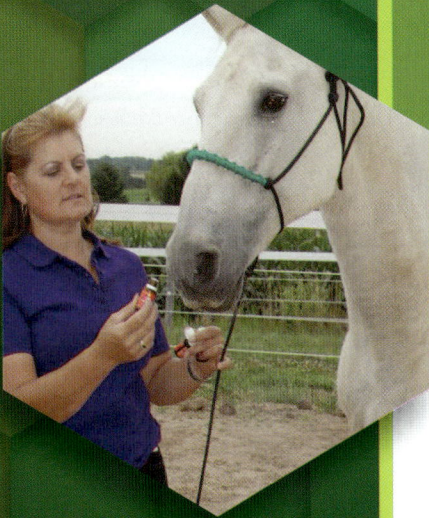

3

Application

Essential oils are used in many creative ways for nourishing, healing, and supporting the body, both human and animal. However, it does not seem to matter how essential oils are used, as long as their energy penetrates the body through topical application, ingestion and oral, or inhalation.

This chapter describes many ways of administering essential oils to animals, both external and internal. Experiment to determine what works best for your animals.

External Methods

We've established that animals are sensitive to smells. They can also be more sensitive to certain types of oils, and they may resist application due to detoxification.

One of the best properties of essential oils is that they may be easily used in the natural grooming process. They can be added to a shampoo, conditioner, or ointment. They can be brushed in dilution or petted directly into the fur with the caregiver's hands. These forms of application are easy to introduce into an animal's daily life.

Cold Compress

Another recommended topical method is a cold compress. To use this approach, apply essential oils on the location, followed by cold water packs or ice packs when treating inflamed or swollen tissues.

Frozen packages of vegetables can make excellent ice packs that conform to the shape of the area of concern. Use only freezer bags without perforations or holes and place a thin cloth or towel between the area being treated and the actual bag to prevent plastic interaction with the oils. If the cloth is too thin, the exposure to the cold may cause damage to the skin. Be sure to check the animal's skin periodically to monitor how it is reacting to the cold.

Keep the cold pack on until the swelling diminishes. For neurological problems, always use cold packs, never warm.

Caution: Eyes & Ears

Eyes and ears are sensitive areas for humans, let alone for animals who depend heavily on these heightened senses.

Essential oils may sting if applied in or around the eyes. Some oils may be painful on mucous membranes unless diluted properly. Immediate dilution is strongly recommended if skin becomes painfully irritated or if oil accidentally gets into eyes. Flushing the area with a vegetable oil should minimize discomfort almost immediately.

Misting around the eye area is the safest way to apply only Lavender oil in light concentrations. Always consult a veterinary health professional if wanting to branch out beyond this application.

As for the ears, essential oils can be helpful in the cleaning process and in keeping the outer ear tissue free of detritus, dryness, and flaking. Many conventional ear-treating pet products have essential oils as active ingredients in their ingredient lists.

The most common method is to apply 10 drops of V-6 Vegetable Oil Complex or other pure vegetable oil to a 100 percent cotton ball (cosmetic/pharmaceutical grade) and add 1-2 drops of Thieves, Purification, or Lavender (not Lavandin) essential oil or blend to the ball. Gently roll the cotton ball around your fingertips to evenly disperse the dilution. Then, with a careful grip on the ball, use it to clean just the upper visible areas inside the ear. Be sure to extract the cotton ball entirely and use a fresh one to clean the other ear.

Do Not Flush With Water! Essential oils are oil-soluble, not water-soluble. Water will only spread the oils over a larger surface, possibly worsening the problem. Use V-6 Vegetable Oil Complex, coconut oil, olive oil, or other vegetable oil to flush the essential oils. Keep eyes closed, be patient, and the sting will quickly dissipate.

Diffusing

Diffusing is its own hybrid form of administering oils. Sometimes, it is considered an internal application due to inhalation. However, many people forget that it is also a topical application. If a wounded paw is placed near a diffuser with lavender, the diffused oil begins to help ease the pain.

This is especially true when using Thieves in barns, kennels, and household rooms. The diffusing method has the ability to cleanse not only the air but also the surfaces of the room.

Because animals absorb so efficiently through their higher concentration of hair follicles, water-based diffusing near an animal is akin to topical application. This is an especially great way to apply oils to cats because:

1. They have the ability to leave the location if they are averse.
2. This provides oil exposure at lower concentrations, which may be preferable with cats' metabolic system differences.

Additionally, diffusing in conjunction with other topical applications makes a great form of layering. It enables the applied oils to be more deeply absorbed and therefore more effective.

Oils and diffusing can be specific to species. With this in mind, pay close attention to suggested oils for particular animals. Do not force animals to be in close proximity to the diffuser.

Nearly all animals will tolerate at least some degree or type of diffusing.

Water-Based Diffusing

One of the most common types of diffusing is water-based, ultrasonic diffusing. By adding drops of oil to water-based diffusers, an animal caregiver can adjust the degree of essential oil concentration that will be used to expose the animal. Concentrations can range from a toothpick dip, to a single drop, to 15 drops of essential oil in a batch of water.

Most commonly, an animal will tolerate at least a single drop of essential oil in one batch of water in a water-based diffuser. Keep in mind that dilution using a carrier oil is not necessary in these types of diffusers. Begin by adding a small amount to the diffuser and then observing the behavior of the animal for 5 minutes.

Water-Based Diffusing: Large Room

A large room is considered a closed space where an animal has more than 5 feet from any given point to move around the water-based diffuser. This is one of the better test methods for an animal. Begin by adding just 1 drop of essential oil to the water in the diffuser.

If an animal is experiencing discomfort, you can monitor behavior such as aversion, sneezing, coughing, detoxification, lethargy, increased breathing rate, panting, drooling, squinting eyes, or a change in breathing pattern.

Water-Based Diffusing: Small Room

If an animal seems to be responding positively to essential oils in a large room, you may want to try diffusing in a small room where there are fewer than 5 feet between the animal and the diffuser.

Once again, add just 1 drop to the water in the diffuser and observe the animal for 5 minutes until you've established a positive response.

Atomizing/Nebulizing Diffusing

The next step in more concentrated diffusing would be using an atomizer or nebulizer, the types that use neat essential oils. These are not water based, so the concentration will be higher. This method is usually used for larger rooms and after the animal has been observed under water-based diffusing.

This type of diffuser is often used in bars, stalls, coops, large group kennels, etc. The more sensitive an animal is, the larger the room should be, and the farther it should be kept from the diffuser.

Passive Diffusing

Passive diffusing allows the essential oil to evaporate from full concentration directly into the air. This is placing a few drops on a cotton ball or in a flat, shallow dish. It also includes when animal caregivers put oil on themselves and stand within a short distance from the animal.

Spritzing

If a diffuser is not available, an animal caregiver may still perform water-based diffusing by using a water-based spray bottle. By adding 15 drops of essential oil to a 4-oz. bottle, shaking, and then spraying, a person can easily mimic the effects of traditional diffusing.

Aural

Never put essential oils into the ear canal as they can damage delicate eardrums and nerves. Care is also needed around the eyes. Animal caregivers should always wash their hands after handling oils to prevent accidentally getting them into a pet's eyes.

Direct Topical Application

Many oils are safe to apply directly to the fur or skin of an animal. Lavender is one of the safest to apply neat, without dilution. However, the essential oil must be 100 percent pure, therapeutic-grade lavender, not a synthetic mix such as with lavandin or genetically modified lavender.

When applying most other essential oils on animals, it's a good idea to dilute the oils with V-6 or another pure vegetable oil. This is at least until you have established that the individual animal can tolerate the particular oil.

If you have established that an animal tolerates certain oils neat or diluted, you may decide to incorporate the Raindrop Technique.

If an animal suffers an injury to the patella (kneecap), applying an essential oil directly on the injury could be effective; however, it would be better to use a lighter hand and treat the entire area. Many of the pain-related oils fall into the '*hot*' class and may sensitize the skin. Always choose the method that least strains the animal's tolerance.

For optimal dilution, add 15-30 drops of essential oil to 1 oz. V-6 Vegetable Oil Complex or another pure vegetable oil.

Indirect Applications

External application to an animal may often turn into an internal application, due to natural animal licking habits. But there's more to it than just petting an animal and expecting it to lick off the oils.

Bird specialists have said that a bird's perch can be an effective way to expose them to essential oils. In the wild, they would naturally be exposed to essential oils that would be found on branches and twigs of a tree.

Cats are well-known for their self-cleaning, but they are also just as well-known for their tendency to scratch. Adding a mist to their scratching board may effectively expose them to essential oils without forcing them to be misted or undergo petting or Raindrop Technique.

Oil-Based Misting

This method follows suit with water-based misting, except that the mist happens to be vegetable oil. This may be V-6 Vegetable Oil Complex, or it could be a massage or other pure vegetable oil. This technique requires specialized bottles to handle the increased viscosity of the oil and still atomize it through the sprayer. Again, it is best to use a glass spray bottle if possible.

This method is perfect for extending the life and duration of an application. Carrier oils retain more essential oils, rather than lose so much to evaporation. Whether the result is helping to manage pain or helping to repel insects, oil based misting retains the effective compounds for a much longer timeframe.

Many animal caregivers have found that massage oils and V-6 work wonders for extending the life of insect repellant recipes. These applications also work well on helping the skin repel lice and other pests for a much longer time.

A word of caution in using oil-based misting around birds: our feathered friends need their lightweight feathers to function. Getting them too oily can weigh down the feathers so that they do not work as well as when dry. Consider using a water-based mist on birds and avoid making their specialized feathers greasy.

Peripheral Grooming and Care Products

By far, one of the best ways to administer essential oils is through the natural grooming process. Using products mentioned in this book such as Thieves Household Cleaner will help disperse the oils so that they mix evenly in water.

Using essential oils regularly as part of a daily or weekly routine may be a preventive measure to help your animal stay healthy.

Petting

One of the most natural ways to apply essential oils externally is through the common petting process. When essential oils remain on your hands when you pet an animal, you are effectively applying one of the safest dilutions. If you have any concerns about sensitizing or inflaming an area of the animal, be sure to dilute them with a pure carrier oil like V-6 or other vegetable oil.

Start by putting 10 drops of V-6 or pure carrier oil on your hands and then adding 1 or 2 drops of essential oil. Rub your hands together, spreading the oils evenly. Then pet the animal in either an all-over approach or in a specialized area.

If the animal is too small or isn't easy to pet, you may try cupping your hands and holding the animal to allow absorption.

With larger animals, you may have to try several reapplications to your hands and apply in waves and sections. Always start with proper dilution and keep a carrier oil available just in case you observe any undesirable reaction in the animal.

Tipping

It isn't advisable to put any essential oils into the ears of animals. Most species are very particular about their ears. Many are unwilling to have their ears touched and/or they resist any attention to the area. However, some individual animals love their ears massaged, petted, or lightly scratched (outer areas).

If you decide you wish to apply oils to parts of the ears for the traditionally higher absorption factor, begin by applying oils the same way you would in the petting method. Put 10 drops of carrier oil on your hands; then add 1 or 2 drops of essential oil. Rub your hands together and spread the oils evenly across the ends of your fingers. Stroke the tips of the ear or the regions around (but not in) the ear. If your animal responds well to this, consider applying the oils 2 times a day.

Vita Flex

The hooves, pads, and feet of animals are not the same as humans, even though they may seem to be similar. Consequently, the Vita Flex system doesn't have the same correspondence with most species. While many essential oil users report great results with their animals using an application to the feet, others feel the results aren't aligned with their expectations.

Also, many animals will resist application or even interaction that involves their hooves or pads. That said, of the various species, canines might respond the best to certain reflexology applications. Many essential oil enthusiasts report the correlation between points on a dog's hind paws and the body.

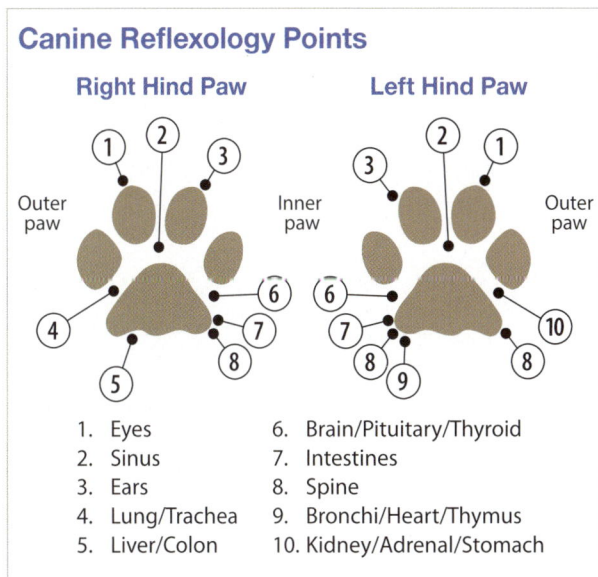

Canine Reflexology Points

Right Hind Paw   **Left Hind Paw**

Outer paw   Inner paw   Outer paw

1. Eyes
2. Sinus
3. Ears
4. Lung/Trachea
5. Liver/Colon
6. Brain/Pituitary/Thyroid
7. Intestines
8. Spine
9. Bronchi/Heart/Thymus
10. Kidney/Adrenal/Stomach

Warm Compress

Many enthusiasts report great results with compresses on animals. It's very easy to make a warm compress by placing 10 drops of V-6 Vegetable Oil Complex or other pure vegetable oil in the palms of your hands and then adding 1 or 2 drops of essential oil. Rub your hands together and apply directly to the area of concern. Then cover the location with a hot, damp towel. Cover the moist towel with a dry towel for 10-30 minutes, depending on the animal's need and/or likelihood of holding still.

As the oil penetrates the skin, the animal may experience a warming sensation. If the animal appears to be sensitive to the oil, be sure to apply a carrier or V-6 Vegetable Oil Complex.

Many animals will enjoy the warming sensation and positive outcome. If the animal is arthritic, and your compress is meant to provide relief, the animal may come to love and expect the daily routine—particularly if it reduces its pain.

Water and the Mix

Because of how animals enter water and because soaking may be necessary for an injury, it's a good idea to keep the proper dispersing agent(s) around to keep the oils from gathering into floating droplets. Essential oils may first be added to Thieves Household cleaner, Animal Scents Shampoo, or animal-friendly bath salts (such as Epsom salts) before being added to water. If soaking for an injury, go with bath salts. If soaking for grooming or cleaning, use the other two.

If the water has an agitator, that is all the better because the natural surface will be constantly moving and dispersing the essential oils. This may be true of certain aquariums, ponds with waterfalls, fountains for troughs, wading pools, and soaking ponds.

Do not, however, add oils with a dispersal agent to an aquarium or koi pond.

Water-Based Misting

Misting is a perfect form of external application, provided you have a few key tools. Because many misting or spray bottles have plastic parts that would come in contact with the essential oils, it's recommended that this method be done with specialized glass spray bottles. While some plastic components in a sprayer may be unavoidable, it is best to go as close to glass as possible.

Creating the "mist" is as easy as it sounds. Simply fill a bottle with distilled water, add the desired drops of essential oil(s), shake well, and mist the solution near the animal, near the animal's wound, or over the top of a current area of application—to layer the oils and stimulate deeper absorption. This method may also be used for applying essential oils to foods for ingestion.

This method serves as a more concentrated, less atomized form of diffusion. Some particulates may be inhaled, while others mist onto the skin or fur of an animal. The real key to even disbursement is to agitate or shake well consistently before each spray. Since essential oils and water do not mix, much like oil and vinegar in a salad dressing, shaking the solution is necessary.

Even more important, when misting an animal in this way, be sure to shield the eyes. Take a few extra seconds to maintain the protection around their eyes until the mist has fully settled. Also, it's often difficult for animals to hold still when a mist is sprayed, so keep that in mind and try to hold them steady.

Feedback from veterinary professionals indicates that most animals will respond positively to misting. Many animals will even move into the mist and like that it comes in contact with their mouth, face, and head. Unless they have a disorder that affects the blinking reflex, they will naturally keep it out of their eyes.

This works well on birds, misting the feathers and body. It also can help with large wounds where ointments would be too oily. It can work wonders on bedding, food, hay, bad-smelling areas, sensitive skin areas, and more.

Most, if not all, essential oils will work well in misting form—if not for one reason then for another. Simply use the suggested oil for the particular remedy and follow the outlined directions for combining the essential oil and distilled water. Always be aware of to which oils your animal may have individual reactions.

Try a concentration of 5 drops per ounce for smaller animals and a concentration of up to 10 drops per ounce for large animals. Consider the species and use good judgment around cats, unless the individual cat has proven to like a certain oil. If a cat seems averse to misting, try misting on your hands and then applying to the cat.

Raindrop Technique for Animals

Raindrop Technique combines soothing, relaxing, and pleasurable massage techniques with essential oils to create an effect that is greater than either alone.

The suggested use of it in subsequent chapters will have species-specific recommendations to be sure any of the oils applied neat will be tried and true from a wide array of professionals and oil enthusiasts who have met with success.

In most cases, the neat application will be followed by several drops of carrier oil within a minute or two to prevent a negative reaction. Temporary, mild warming is normal for Raindrop Technique. Typically, it is even milder than that of many capsicum creams or sports ointments in humans, but it may seem uncomfortable to some animals who do not immediately comprehend its intent.

With Raindrop Technique, prescribed oils are dispensed like drops of rain from a height of about 6 inches from the spine. Starting from the lower spine, the oils are feathered with the back of the fingers up along the vertebrae, out over the back muscles, and over the shoulders to the neck. Although the entire treatment can take 20 minutes on small animals and up to 40 minutes on larger animals (depending on the degree and intensity of the application), the oils continue to work for several days as balancing and realignment takes place.

If done properly, the technique can help to alleviate pain symptoms, ease inflammation, calm an animal, and soothe its anxiety.

The oils within a standard Raindrop Technique are usually Oregano, Thyme, Basil, Cypress, Wintergreen, Marjoram, and Peppermint. In the smaller animals, it's best to combine the oils into a single diluted solution. Because smaller animals have a difficult time staying in one spot, let alone remaining still, it's best to complete the application in one swoop.

Many animals will respond to balancing. One of the best oils to use in preparing an animal for Raindrop Technique is Valor. Start with 1-2 drops in 5 drops of V-6 or other pure carrier oil, rub evenly between palms, and begin at the lower spine of the animal. With individual animals, you may eventually work up to a neat solution if they prove to tolerate the weaker concentration.

The modified balancing technique for animals follows this general order:

1. Hold each hand over the rump/shoulder area of the animal.
2. Wait until both hands feel equal in temperature and the animal relaxes in posture.
3. Hold this for as long as it feels comfortable to you and the animal.
4. Generally, the animal will release tension and sigh deeply.

Once the animal is balanced, apply the appropriate Raindrop oils. Feather the oils with the back of the fingers from the lower spine up along the vertebrae, out over the back muscles, and over the shoulders to the base of the head.

Dripping the oils from a distance has many benefits, so modify accordingly if 6 inches seems too far for the individual animal. Each solution should be dripped along the back and spine in this same way. Be careful that the animal doesn't look up in habitual curiosity and accidentally get a drop of essential oil in its eyes or nose.

Depending on the size of the animal, use 3-6 inch strokes for evenly massaging the oils into the animal's spine and surrounding areas.

Follow with V-6 or other pure carrier oil to dilute. This will calm any of the 'hot' oils such as Oregano and Thyme and ease the response to the phenol compounds. Be particularly sensitive to how an animal responds to these oils, and always be ready to dilute for its comfort. It is better to start with a more diluted solution and draw the animal into the experience than it is to shock it into aversion.

This same technique may be used with completely different oils, especially since some animals may not tolerate the traditional Raindrop series. The important thing to remember is the technique; and while applying oils to animals has its challenges, most any of them may still benefit from the interaction with their caregivers.

While there is no right or wrong way to modifying the Raindrop Technique, it is often best to limit the application to three or four oils. Many animals simply cannot stay still long enough to receive all the oils. In general, caregivers may find that they may use the benefits of the distance drip and follow-up massage by combining the oils into specialized solutions.

Always be ready to modify your technique to accommodate the comfort of the animal. After all, the intention is to improve its quality of life and enhance its emotional and physical well-being.

Internal Methods

Animals in the wild are exposed to the complex organic compounds in essential oils in many ways. They inhale the vapors given off from natural plant respiration. They inhale the scents from flowers, broken stems and leaves, and even roots (when they dig). Also, it is important to note that animals internally *consume* many compounds in the wild that are found in 100 percent pure, therapeutic-grade essential oils.

While some people question how the higher concentrations of active organic compounds found in essential oils will affect animals internally, there is strong evidence to support the notion that many of them may tolerate certain oils quite well. That said, it is important to be mindful of the concentrated active organic compounds in essential oils in relation to physiological processes in the body.

Within the holistic world of animal health, many experts have found evidence to support the use of some oils in animal clinics, for animal first aid, and for sharing in the naturally healthier environs of an essential oils-using home. In fact, many professional caregivers, holistic veterinarians, and aromatherapy-certified veterinary technicians have marvelous anecdotal evidence of great results with oils. With so many essential oil users having such positive experiences, it's difficult to dismiss the potential benefits.

However, be conscious when you observe the animals. Watch how they respond and respect their behavior. Many will back away if they are averse. Some will sneeze. Be patient and do not force them to accept essential oils.

In the case of internal use, a caregiver may opt to administer oils in water, in feed, through a food carrier, sublingually (under the tongue), applied to the gums, orally with droppers, in gelatin or vegetable-based capsules, and rectally (retention).

When offering essential oils internally to an animal, it is critical to be sure the oils used are 100 percent pure and free of any chemicals, solvents, and adulterants.

Essential Oils in Drinking Water

When considering an internal approach to essential oils for animals, one of the best methods is to test with drinking water. While oils and water don't generally mix, the water can serve as a great dispersing medium. The concentrated oil droplets may float on top, but the general dilution will help to minimize potential reactions. The dispersed droplets in water may prove if an animal is averse to the smell and/or taste.

As you think about which oils you'd like to use with an animal in your care, start with those on the GRAS list. If you believe an oil would be palatable in your drinking water, then it may be tastier to your animals as well.

Always be sure that animals have a secondary source of drinking water in case they are averse to the water to which you've added essential oils. Remember that some animals use their water not only for drinking but also for self-cleaning and/or soaking. These animals should still have access to a secondary water source.

Water Purity

While most animals will drink from very questionable sources, it's wise to give them the purest form of water possible. After all, good health often begins with good water. Try to use purified or high quality natural spring water.

Chlorinated water is known to suppress thyroid and immune function in many animal species. If that's the case, the chlorine may interfere with the use of oils for prevention or healing. In effect, the benefits would be offset by the detriments of chemically treated water.

Safe Containers

Many containers for pet water are either wholly or partially made of plastic which can often react with essential oils and produce unhealthy compounds. If using drinking water for administering essential oils, be sure to use glass, non-reactive plastic, stainless steel, or ceramic containers. With large animals, troughs can be made of stainless steel, galvanized metal, or non-reactive plastic. If these are unavailable, try a ceramic bathtub or a large ceramic bowl or tub.

Also, be sure to mix or agitate the essential oil/water mixture. A good rule of thumb is to start with 1 drop of essential oil per quart (32 oz.) of purified or high quality, natural spring water. Glass quart bottles are excellent containers for mixing the oil into water and then pouring into the animal's drinking container.

The *Human* GRAS List

It's important not to give anything to an animal that you wouldn't likely give to yourself. However, just because human beings tolerate a particular essential oil internally does not mean that there aren't considerations for other species. Be careful how you experiment with essential oils on your animals.

The following is the human GRAS (Generally Regarded As Safe) list that shows which 100% pure, therapeutic-grade essential oils have been generally regarded as safe (GRAS) for internal consumption.

CODE: ■ Generally regarded as safe (GRAS)   ■ FDA-approved food additive   ■ Flavoring agent

Singles

Name	GRAS	FDA food additive	Flavoring agent
Anise	■	■	
Angelica	■	■	
Basil	■	■	
Bergamot	■	■	
Cajuput		■	
Cardamom		■	
Carrot Seed		■	
Cassia	■	■	
Cedarwood		■	
Celery Seed	■	■	
Cinnamon Bark	■	■	
Cinnamon Leaf	■	■	
Cistus			
Citronella	■	■	
Citrus Rinds	■	■	
Clary Sage	■	■	
Clove	■	■	
Copaiba	■	■	
Coriander	■	■	
Cumin	■	■	
Dill	■	■	
Eucalyptus Globulus	■	■	■
Elemi	■	■	■
Fennel	■	■	
Frankincense	■	■	■
Geranium	■	■	
German Chamomile	■	■	
Ginger	■	■	
Goldenrod	■		
Grapefruit	■	■	
Helichrysum	■	■	
Hyssop	■	■	
Idaho Balsam Fir		■	
Jasmine	■	■	
Juniper	■	■	
Laurus Nobilis	■	■	
Lavender	■	■	
Lavandin	■	■	
Lemon	■	■	
Lemongrass	■	■	
Lime	■	■	
Mandarin	■	■	
Marjoram	■	■	
Mountain Savory		■	
Melissa	■	■	
Myrrh	■	■	■
Myrtle	■	■	
Neroli	■	■	
Nutmeg	■	■	
Onycha (Styrax benzoin)	■	■	
Orange	■	■	
Oregano	■	■	
Palmarosa	■	■	
Patchouli	■	■	■
Pepper	■	■	
Peppermint	■	■	
Petitgrain	■	■	
Pine	■	■	■
Roman Chamomile	■	■	
Rose	■	■	
Rosemary	■	■	
Savory	■	■	
Sage	■	■	
Sandalwood	■	■	■
Spearmint	■	■	
Spruce	■	■	■
Tangerine	■	■	
Tarragon	■	■	
Tea Tree		■	
Thyme	■	■	
Tsuga	■	■	■
Valerian	■	■	■
Vetiver	■	■	
Wintergreen		■	
Yarrow		■	
Ylang Ylang	■	■	

Blends

Name	GRAS	FDA food additive	Flavoring agent
Abundance	■		
Believe		■	
Citrus Fresh	■		
Christmas Spirit	■		
DiGize	■		
EndoFlex	■		
Gratitude		■	
Joy	■		
JuvaCleanse	■		
JuvaFlex	■		
Longevity	■		
Thieves	■		
M-Grain	■		
Purification	■		
Relieve It	■		
Sacred Mountain	■		
White Angelica	■		

Essential Oils in Feed

Once you've established that an animal will tolerate oils in drinking water, you can then branch out into food. If an animal didn't necessarily love a certain oil in its drinking water, you may try adding it to food one more time, particularly if that food has flavor compatibility.

Much of an animal's food will have a fatty oil content, so adding an essential oil to it is like diluting with a carrier. A few drops could be added to soft, moist foods or to gravy on food. Experiment by mixing various essential oils with NingXia Red.

Direct Oral Administration

Some veterinary professionals will administer essential oils with this method in more extreme situations. The animal may be suffering from internal bleeding, pain, internal parasites, hives, or allergic reactions. While it is not recommended to proceed without the advice or direction of a veterinary health professional, there may be first-aid situations where essential oils can be used in this way.

Keep in mind that this kind of application may create an aversion for some animals because they have strong associations with smells, tastes, and illness. Remember that proceeding with this route may have long-term implications for more preventive use in the future. The consequent aversions may be difficult to overcome in the long term.

Buccal Cavity Application

This application uses the mucous membranes of the cheek or lip to deliver quick absorption. The animal's bottom lip may be pulled out, and drops of oil may be put in. The animal will feel the effect quickly, because capillaries in the lip will quickly carry the oil into the bloodstream. This is particularly true for dogs, horses, and livestock.

Recommendations: For a large dog, 1-3 drops are sufficient. Horses may tolerate 10-15 drops quite well.

Capsules

Many enthusiasts and professionals have found success using vegetable gelatin capsules for administering essential oils orally. Oils can be added to empty gel capsules and given to dogs by mouth. Once again, be aware of sensitivities and generally do this only under the advice of your holistic vet. These capsules are readily available at supplement supply stores as well as pharmacies and some pet supply stores.

Carriers for Ingestion

Essential oils may be mixed into agave, honey, NingXia Red, coconut oil, and vegetable oils and offered to an animal orally. Follow the directions in the *Essential Oils Desk Reference* for mixing oils into foods and for other instructions and details.

Gums

Applying directly to the gums may work very well for dogs. Try using a dilution of 1 drop of oil to 5 drops of carrier oil, mixing on your hand, and then applying a light coating of the dilution onto the gums. Be aware of sensitivities and generally do this under the advice of your holistic vet.

Recommendations: For a large dog, 1-3 drops are sufficient in dilution.

Oral Drops

This method of application is reserved most often for cats. A veterinary professional may use a drip for convalescing cats recovering from a procedure. It may be for pain or post-operative recovery. Cats often have a salivation response when given essential oils, which is quite typical. They also often salivate when traditional medicines are administered orally.

Recommendations: For a large cat, 1-2 drops will be more than enough. For a small cat, a toothpick dab up to 1 drop will be the maximum.

Sublingual Application

Sometimes, it becomes necessary to stimulate an animal recovering from a procedure, and delivering oils under the tongue is particularly effective. The mucosal membranes allow for easy absorption, and the animal responds quickly. This holds true for some emergency situations, although generally only under the supervision of a veterinary health professional.

Secondary Applications

Topical Licking

Never underestimate the functional or nervous licking that an animal will do for self-cleaning, self-healing, or due to individual habit. When an animal licks its fur or skin, it is effectively ingesting anything that has come in contact with that area. If you have "pet" your animal with essential oils on your hands, there's a good chance that the animal will lick that part of its body and ingest the oil. This can reach therapeutic levels and may be very effective, depending on the oil. Always use caution.

Rectal Instillation

This method is generally reserved for use by veterinary health professionals because it has implications according to species. It can be a very effective method of delivering the oils to an animal that may be incapacitated or may need a specialized treatment that the other methods of delivery won't facilitate.

Because of the rich blood supply and natural digestive process, much of what is instilled rectally will carry quickly to lungs and avoid passing through the liver. This can be very effective, depending on the condition of the animal and oil used.

Generally, the essential oil is diluted using V-6 Vegetable Oil Complex, and a needle-free syringe is used to introduce the resulting serum into the rectal cavity. As this can cause irritation of the anus and mucous membranes, this method should be used by professionals who are familiar with dosage and frequency.

Sample Suggested Use Per Species

Birds

Water: Because birds generally lack the same taste and smell of other animals, they respond quite readily to essential oils in their drinking water. Since birds often bathe in the same water they drink, it is important to observe and regulate how much they intake. The general rule of 1 drop of oil per quart of water applies.

Recommendations: 1 drop of Melissa per 1 quart of water. Using a glass container, shake well and pour into drinking container.

Feed: Birds have shown that they will take to essential oils in their favorite foods. Most owners will be able to identify which oils and food combinations their birds prefer. This may be multiple kinds of seed meal with Copaiba, ground fruits, citrus oils, or something as simple as warm oatmeal and Frankincense.

Due to the size of birds, it's best to start with a teaspoon of a bird's favorite food and apply a toothpick dip of essential oil. Then gradually increase the concentration up to a drop.

Recommendations: Use Citrus oils, Copaiba, Thieves, and Melissa in favorite foods.

Cats

Water: Felines tend to have aversions to essential oils more so than other species. They can be very particular about their water, and they have a right to be. Cats can be particularly sensitive to oils, and some can be toxic to them.

Be sure to experiment with minute amounts and never press the issue with cats. Also, because cats are so specific and particular, it's a good idea to try many different kinds of GRAS oils. Just be sure to provide an alternate water source when testing, and never concentrate the oil above 1 drop per quart of water.

If a cat refuses oils in drinking water, respect its aversion. You'll often have better success if you start with toothpick amounts and then bump up the concentration to 1 drop per quart.

Recommendations: Enthusiasts report success with oils such as citrus oils, Peppermint, and Melissa.

Feed: Cats may eat dry or moist foods. While most cats resist essential oils in their food, a good experiment would be to divide the meal in half and add a drop of essential oil to one half and leave the other as is. In this way, the cat will tell you if it is keen on ingesting essential oils in its food.

Recommendations: Use Copaiba, Frankincense, and citrus oils in food.

Chickens and Poultry

Water: If caring for chickens, turkeys, or other birds in a farm setting, remember that most water will not be used for bathing. Many farms use the drinking water for dispensing antibiotics. In lieu of these, some essential oils may be better suited to achieving a similar result.

Ducks and geese can contaminate their water source when it's used for both bathing and drinking. In such cases, it's best to change it frequently and add essential oils to their bathing water as well. In such cases, you may want to consider a separate source of essential oil-treated drinking water as well as a non-essential oil water source.

This works very well for flocks of chickens, turkeys, pheasants, etc. Once again, 1 drop per quart of water is the recommended dosage. Any higher concentration may cause reactions with the plastics used in automatic drinking systems.

In the case of automation, it becomes extra vital that a caregiver knows exactly how much water a flock consumes on a regular basis. That way, he or she can compare a day with regular water against a day with essential oils in the water. Should the flock not show a decrease in water consumption after essential oils are added, this would be a positive response.

Recommendations: Some of the best oils and blends to use with flocks are Purification, Thieves, and Clove.

Dogs

Water: Dogs will respond to oils more readily than cats. While the general rule of 1 drop per quart of water still applies, some dogs may tolerate a concentration up to 2 drops per quart. As usual, start small and gradually increase the concentration. Common sense applies in this case, so be sure to consult the GRAS list.

Recommendations: For dogs, try Peppermint, citrus oils, and Melissa.

Feed: This tends to be animal specific. Some dogs will eat essential oils in their food, but many may need the oils added to a carrier food. Since many dogs eat a dry kibble, it may be better to add a drop of essential oil to a chew, small side dish, or treat. If a dog eats primarily moistened foods, adding an oil to the gravy or liquid is a natural method.

Recommendations: Many enthusiasts and professionals recommend trying Frankincense, Copaiba, citrus oils, and Longevity.

Exotics

Water: The general rule of 1 drop per quart of water applies for exotic animals. Because of their size, it may be better to use a less concentrated amount such as 1 toothpick dip per quart. Once you've established that the animal tolerates this amount, feel free to work up to the 1 drop per quart.

Recommendations: 1 drop of Melissa per 1 quart of water. Using a glass container, shake well and pour into drinking water.

Ferrets

Water: *Recommendations:* 1 toothpick of Melissa or Copaiba per quart of water used as drinking and soaking water, gradually working up in concentration to the 1 drop per quart.

Feed: Many enthusiasts and professionals alike recommend NingXia Red as a ferret favorite. Due to their size, it's best to start with a teaspoon of their favorite mashed food and then apply a toothpick dip of essential oil. Then gradually increase the concentration up to a drop.

Recommendations: Use citrus oils, Copaiba, Thieves, and Melissa in favorite foods.

Horses, Cattle, and Livestock

Water: Horses and livestock respond very well to essential oils in their drinking water. The same rule of 1 drop per quart applies. Be sure to agitate the water when poured into a trough, as the oil droplets may not disperse so easily.

It's a little more difficult to avoid plastic troughs or materials when it comes to livestock. However, many of our enthusiasts and professionals alike have observed that the hard plastic troughs most commonly used for livestock are less reactive than ordinary household plastics and resist corrosion or breakdown when exposed to essential oils.

Recommendations: Horses, cattle, and other livestock seem to prefer Peppermint, Lemon, and many other oils. Start by adding 10 drops to 50-100 gallons of water and gradually increase to the 1-drop-per-quart concentration.

Feed: Horses, cattle, and farm livestock naturally ingest essential oils in their food. It takes very little effort to mix oils into oats, applesauce, NingXia Red, maple syrup, agave, molasses, and other forms of livestock feed. They even respond well to essential oils applied to hay. In fact, an air-style diffuser may prevent mold and infuse hay with beneficial amounts of essential oils.

Recommendations: Many enthusiasts and professionals recommend trying Copaiba, Frankincense, citrus oils, and Longevity.

Rabbits, Guinea Pigs, Chinchillas

Water: *Recommendations:* Add 1 drop of Melissa, Citrus Fresh, Orange, Tangerine, or other citrus oils to 1 quart of water. Using a glass container with water, shake well and pour into drinking water.

Feed: Due to the unique digestive systems of these exotics, it's important to be extra mindful when administering an essential oil orally. This method should generally be used only by a veterinary health professional or under his or her supervision or advice. These animals may be given a pureed food with essential oils in more extreme situations, and your holistic vet may recommend a regimen.

Rodents, Reptiles, and Other Exotics

Feed: Because of their diminutive size, it's best to adjust all dosages down into the toothpick method for these exotics. Really, the most common denominator in adding essential oils to foods is to find a food they really like and just introduce very small amounts to the food; or offer them a halved serving—one with oils and one without, just to determine their aversions and preferences.

Recommendations: Use citrus oils, Copaiba, Thieves, and Melissa in favorite foods.

Snakes

Water: *Recommendations:* 1 toothpick of Purification per quart of water used as drinking and soaking water, gradually working up in concentration to 1 drop per quart.

Section 2

Single Essential Oils

How to Be Sure Your Essential Oils Are Pure, Therapeutic Grade

How can you be sure that your essential oils are pure, therapeutic grade? Start by asking the following questions from your essential oil supplier:

- Are the fragrances delicate, rich, and organic? Do they "feel" natural? Do the aromas vary from batch to batch as an indication that they are painstakingly distilled in small batches rather than industrially processed on a large scale?

- Does your supplier subject each batch of essential oils through multiple chemical analyses to test for purity and therapeutic quality? Are these tests also performed by independent labs?

- Does your supplier grow and distill organically grown herbs?

- Are the distillation facilities part of the farm where the herbs are grown (so oils are freshly distilled), or do herbs wait days to be processed and lose potency?

- Does your supplier use low pressure and low temperature to produce essential oils so as to preserve all of their fragile chemical constituents? Are the distillation cookers fabricated from costly, food-grade stainless steel alloys to reduce the likelihood of the oils chemically reacting with metal?

- Does your supplier personally inspect the fields and distilleries where the herbs are grown and distilled? Do they verify that no synthetic or harmful solvents or chemicals are being used?

- How many years has your supplier been doing all of this?

How to Maximize the Shelf Life of Your Essential Oils

The highest quality essential oils are bottled in dark glass. The reason for this is two-fold. First, glass is more stable than plastic and does not "breathe" the same way plastic does. Second, the darkness of the glass protects the oil from light that may chemically alter or degrade it over time.

After using an essential oil, keep the lid tightly sealed. Bottles that are improperly sealed can result in the loss of some of the lighter, lower-molecular-weight parts of the oil. In addition, over time oxygen in the air reacts with and oxidizes the oil.

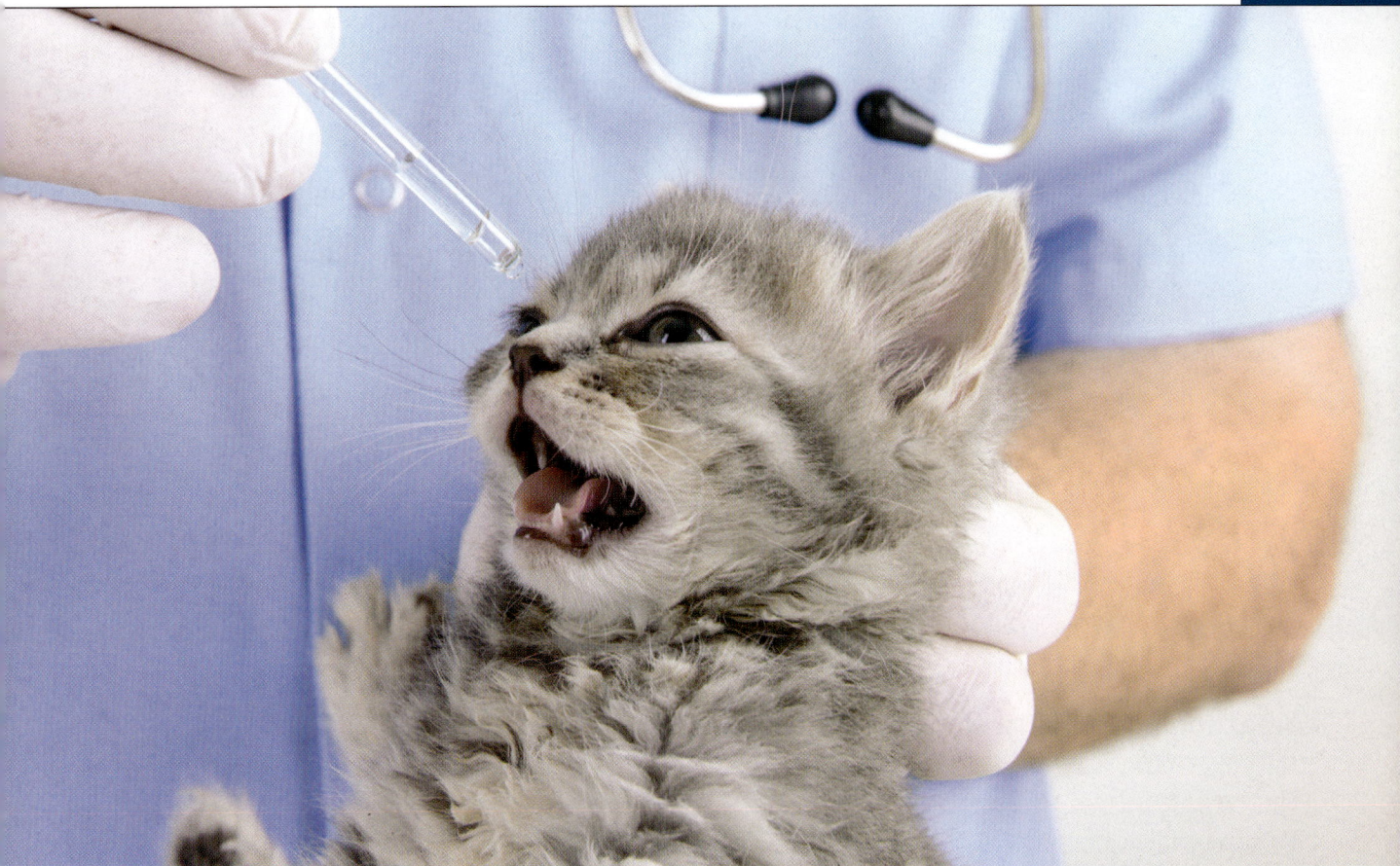

Essential oils should be stored away from light, especially sunlight—even if they are already stored in amber glass bottles. The darker the storage conditions, the longer your oil will maintain its original chemistry and quality.

Store essential oils in a cool location. Excessive heat can derange the molecular structure of the oil the same way ultraviolet light can.

Diluting Essential Oils

Most essential oils require dilution with a vegetable oil when being used either internally or externally. The amount of dilution depends on the essential oil. For example, Oregano will require four times as much dilution as that of Roman Chamomile. Vegetable oils such as V-6 Vegetable Oil Complex are specifically formulated to dilute essential oils and have a long shelf life (over two years) without going rancid. For more information on specific usage instructions for each essential oil, please see the species-specific chapters later in this book.

Guidelines

Please see the species-specific chapters for additional details on how to use the specific essential oils and blends.

Common uses: Almost all single oils can be diffused, directly inhaled, and/or applied topically.

Full-body massage: Dilute 1 drop essential oil with 15 drops of V-6 or other pure carrier oil.

Possible skin sensitivity: Test for sensitivity on small location of skin on underside of arm.

Possible sun sensitivity: Avoid direct sunlight or UV rays for up to 12 hours after applying product.

Dietary and/or culinary use: Vitality™ dietary essential oil singles and blends can be added to food for delicious, concentrated flavor or used in capsules for their supporting properties. Follow the directions on the labels.

Angelica

Anise

Amazonian Ylang Ylang
(Cananga odorata Equitoriana)

The flowering ylang ylang tree is often found in the Philippines, Indonesia, and Madagascar. Now Gary Young has also translocated trees to the Young Living Ecuador Farm, where the aromatic flowers from thousands of trees bloom every day.

Uses: While renowned for its calming effect, several studies show it brings relief for the depressed and stressed, while it increases attentiveness and alertness, causing researchers to say it is "harmonizing."

Fragrant Influence: Balances male-female energies, enhances spiritual attunement, combats anger and low self-esteem, increases focus of thoughts, filters out negative energy, restores confidence and peace

Technical Data: **Botanical Family:** Annonaceae; **Plant Origin:** Ecuador; **Extraction Method:** Steam distilled from flowers; **Key Constituents:** Benzyl Acetate (15-29%), Germacrene D (10-20%), Linalool (10-25%), Benzyl Benzoate (4-12%), p-Cresyl Methyl Ether (2-10%)

Angelica (Angelica archangelica)

Known as the "holy spirit root" or the "oil of angels" by the Europeans, angelica's healing powers were so strong that it was believed to be of divine origin. From the time of Paracelsus, it was credited with the ability to protect from the plague. The stems were chewed during the plague of 1660 to prevent infection. When burned, the seeds and roots were thought to purify the air.

Medical Properties: Anticoagulant, relaxant, antispasmodic

Uses: Throat/lung infections, indigestion, menstrual problems/PMS, symptoms of dementia

Fragrant Influence: Assists in the release of pent-up negative feelings and restores memories to the point of origin before trauma or anger was experienced

Caution: Possible sun sensitivity.

Technical Data: **Botanical Family:** Apiaceae; **Plant Origin:** Belgium, France; **Extraction Method:** Steam distilled from seed/root; **Key Constituents:** Beta-Phellandrene (60-80%), Limonene (1-4%), Alpha-Pinene (5-10%)

Anise (Pimpinella anisum)

Listed in Dioscorides' *De Materia Medica* (AD 78), Europe's first authoritative guide to medicines, which became the standard reference work for herbal treatments for over 1,700 years.

Medical Properties: Digestive stimulant, anticoagulant, anesthetic/analgesic, antioxidant, diuretic, antitumoral, anti-inflammatory

Uses: Arthritis/rheumatism, cancer

Fragrant Influence: Opens emotional blocks and recharges vital energy

Technical Data: **Botanical Family:** Apiaceae; **Plant Origin:** Turkey; **Extraction Method:** Steam distilled from the seeds (fruit); **Key Constituents:** Trans-Anethole (85-95%): Methyl Chavicol (2-4%); **ORAC:** 333,700 µTE/100g

Basil

Bergamot

Basil/Basil Vitality™
(Ocimum basilicum)

Used extensively in traditional Asian Indian medicine, basil's name is derived from "basileum," the Greek name for king. In the 16th century, the powdered leaves were inhaled to treat migraines and chest infections. The Hindu people put basil sprigs on the chests of the dead to protect them from evil spirits. Italian women wore basil to attract possible suitors. It was listed in Hildegard's Medicine, a compilation of early German medicines by highly regarded Benedictine herbalist Hildegard of Bingen (1098-1179).

Medical Properties: Powerful antispasmodic, antiviral, antibacterial, anti-inflammatory, muscle relaxant

Uses: Migraines, throat/lung infections, insect bites

Fragrant Influence: Fights mental fatigue

Cautions: Avoid use if epileptic. Do not pour oil into the ear.

Technical Data: Botanical Family: Lamiaceae; **Plant Origin:** India, Utah, France; **Extraction Method:** Steam distilled from leaves, stems, and flowers; **Key Constituents:** Methylchavicol (estragol) (70-90%), Linalol (1-20%), 1,8-Cineole (Eucalyptol) (1-7%); **ORAC:** 54,000 µTE/100g

Bergamot/ Bergamot Vitality™
(Citrus aurantium bergamia)
(also found in literature as *Citrus bergamia*)

Christopher Columbus is believed to have brought bergamot to Bergamo in Northern Italy from the Canary Islands. A mainstay in traditional Italian medicine, bergamot has been used in the Middle East for hundreds of years for skin conditions associated with an oily complexion. Bergamot is responsible for the distinctive flavor of the renowned Earl Grey Tea and was used in the first genuine eau de cologne.

Medical Properties: Calming, hormonal support, antibacterial, antidepressant

Uses: Agitation, depression, anxiety, intestinal parasites, insomnia, viral infections (herpes, cold sores)

Fragrant Influence: Relieves anxiety; mood-lifting qualities

Caution: Possible sun sensitivity.

Technical Data: Botanical Family: Rutaceae; **Plant Origin:** Italy, Morocco; **Extraction Method:** Cold pressed from the rind. Also produced by vacuum distillation. Furocoumarin-free bergamot oil is specially distilled to minimize the concentration of sun-sensitizing compounds in the oil; **Key Constituents:** Limonene (30-45%), Linalyl Acetate (22-36%), Linalol (3-15%), Gamma-Terpinene (6-10%), Beta-Pinene (5.5-9.5%)

Black Pepper

Biblical Sweet Myrrh
(Commiphora erythraea)

A close cousin to the more well-known *Commiphora myrrha,* Biblical Sweet Myrrh is also called Opoponax. Used in dozens of perfumes to impart sweet balsamic notes, this myrrh species is found in Chanel's Coco Mademoiselle and Dior's Poison. Biblical Sweet Myrrh comes from myrrh resin gathered on the island of Socotra, off the coast of Yemen, and is distilled at the Young Living farm in Salalah, Oman. Like other frankincense species, it is highly anti-inflammatory, antimicrobial, and an antioxidant.

Medical Properties: Analgesic, antioxidant, anti-inflammatory, antimicrobial, antifungal, antiviral

Fragrant Influence: Promotes spiritual awareness and is uplifting. It contains sesquiterpenes, which stimulate the limbic system of the brain (the center of memory and emotions) and the hypothalamus, pineal, and pituitary glands. The hypothalamus is the master gland of the human body, producing many vital hormones, including thyroid and growth hormone.

Technical Data: Botanical Family: Burseraceae; **Plant Origin:** Socotra Island, Yemen; **Extraction Method:** Steam distilled from resin; **Key Constituents:** Trans-Beta-Ocimene (45-65%), Cis-Alpha-Bisabolene (10-15%), Alpha-Santalene (12-20%), Trans-Alpha-Bergamotene (3-8%), Cis-Alpha-Bergamotene (1-4%)

Black Pepper/Black Pepper Vitality™
(Piper nigrum)

Used by the Egyptians in mummification, as evidenced by the discovery of black pepper in the nostrils and abdomen of Ramses II. Indian monks ate several black peppercorns a day to give them endurance during their arduous travels. In ancient times pepper was as valuable as gold or silver. When the barbarian Goth tribes of Europe vanquished Rome in 410 AD, they demanded 3,000 pounds of pepper as well as other valuables as a ransom. Traditional Chinese healers used pepper to treat cholera, malaria, and digestive problems.

Medical Properties: Analgesic, stimulates metabolism, antifungal

Fragrant Influence: Stimulating, energizing, and empowering. A 2002 study found that fragrance inhalation of pepper oil induced a 1.7-fold increase in plasma adrenaline concentration (Haze, et al.).

Technical Data: Botanical Family: Piperaceae; **Plant Origin:** Madagascar, Sri Lanka, England, India; **Extraction Method:** Steam distilled from fruit/berries; **Key Constituents:** Beta-Caryophyllene (12-29%), Limonene (10-17%), Sabinene (6-15%), Delta-3-Carene (3-15%), Alpha-Pinene (3-12%), Beta-Pinene (5-12%); **ORAC:** 79,700 µTE/100g

Black Spruce

Blue Cypress

Black Spruce *(Picea mariana)*

The Lakota Indians used black spruce to strengthen their ability to communicate with the Great Spirit. Traditionally, it was believed to possess the frequency of prosperity.

Medical Properties: Antispasmodic, antiparasitic, antiseptic, anti-inflammatory, hormone-like, cortisone-like, immune stimulant, antidiabetic

Uses: Arthritis/rheumatism, fungal infections (candida), sinus/respiratory infections, sciatica/lumbago

Fragrant Influence: Releases emotional blocks, bringing about a feeling of balance and grounding

Technical Data: **Botanical Family:** Pinaceae; **Plant Origin:** Canada; **Extraction Method:** Steam distilled from branches, needles, and twigs; **Key Constituents:** Bornyl Acetate (24-35%), Camphene (14-26%), Alpha-Pinene (12-19%), Beta-Pinene (2-10%), Delta-3-Carene (4-10%), Limonene (3-6%), Myrcene (1-5%), Santene (1-5%), Tricyclene (1-4%)

Blue Cypress *(Callitris intratropica)*

Blue cypress in ancient times was used for incense, perfume, and embalming.

Medical Properties: Anti-inflammatory, antiviral

Uses: Viral infections (herpes simplex, herpes zoster, cold sores, human papilloma virus, genital warts, etc.)

Technical Data: **Botanical Family:** Cupressaceae; **Plant Origin:** Australia; **Extraction Method:** Steam distillation from the leaves and wood of the tree; **Key Constituents:** Gamma-Eudesmol (5-12%), Guaiol (10-20%), Bulnesol (5-11%), Dihydrocolumellarin (10-25%); **ORAC:** 73,100 µTE/100g

Blue Tansy *(Tanacetum annuum)*

Moroccan Blue Tansy receives its lovely blue color from the constituent chamazulene.

Medical Properties: Anti-inflammatory, analgesic/anesthetic, antifungal, anti-itching, relaxant, hormone-like

Technical Data: **Botanical Family:** Asteraceae or Compositae (daisy); **Plant Origin:** Morocco; **Extraction Method:** Steam distilled from flowering plant; **Key Constituents:** Camphor (10-17%), Sabinene (10-17%), Beta-Pinene (5-10%), Myrcene (7-13%), Alpha-Phellandrene (5-10%), Para-Cymene (3-8%), Chamazulene (3-6%); **ORAC:** 68,800 µTE/100g

Selected Research

Zaim A, et al. Chemical Composition and Acridicid Properties of the Moroccan *Tanacetum annum* L. Essential Oils, Int J Engineering and Science 2015 May, 13-19.

Greche H, et al. Chemical Composition and Antifungal Properties of the Essential Oil of *Tanacetum annuum. J Essen Oil Res.* 2000 12(1):122-24.

Alejandro F, et al. Homoditerpenes from the essential oil of *Tanacetum annuum. Phytochem.* 1992 May 31(5):1727-30.

Alejandro F, et al. Gualianolides from *Tanacetum annuum. Phytochem.* 1990 29(11):2575-80.

Calamus *(Acorus calamus)*

Commonly known as sweet flag, this plant may have been the biblical calamus of Exodus 30:23 used in the holy anointing oil. It seems to have originated in India or Arabia but now is found in many places throughout the world. Native Americans used calamus as a medicine and a stimulant, but low doses are also believed to be calming and to induce sleep. The Penobscot people have a tradition that it saved their people from a serious illness.

Canadian Fleabane

Cardamom

Medical Properties: Antibacterial, sedative, carminative, expectorant, antispasmodic, bronchodilator, hepatoprotective

Uses: Relaxes spasms, lung infections, agitation

Fragrant Influence: Believed to induce and promote positive thoughts

Caution: Use only oil from the diploid species that does not contain β-asarone.

Technical Data: **Botanical Family:** Acoraceae; **Plant Origin:** India, Nepal, Brazil; **Extraction Method:** Steam extracted from roots; **Key Constituents:** Cis-Methyl Isoeugenol (13-21%), Syobunone (7-16%), Acorenone (5-15%), Calamuscenone (5-11%)

Canadian Fleabane (Conyza canadensis)

When bothered by rhinitis, the Zuni people inserted the crushed flowers of conyza in their nostrils for the relief of a good sneeze.

Medical Properties: Stimulates liver and pancreas, antiaging (stimulates growth hormone), antirheumatic, antispasmodic, vasodilating, reduces blood pressure, antifungal, antimicrobial

Uses: Hypertension, hepatitis, accelerated aging

Technical Data: **Botanical Family:** Compositae; **Plant Origin:** Canada; **Extraction Method:** Steam distilled from stems, leaves, and flowers (aerial parts); **Key Constituents:** Limonene (60-80%), Trans-Alpha-Bergamotene (1-10%), Trans-Beta-Ocimene (2-6%), Gamma-Curcumene (1-8%); **ORAC:** 26,700 µTE/100g

Cardamom/Cardamom Vitality™
(Elettaria cardamomum)

Called "Grains of Paradise" since the Middle Ages, it has been used medicinally by Indian healers for millennia. One of the most prized spices in ancient Greece and Rome, cardamom was cultivated by the king of Babylon around the 7th century BC.

It is mentioned in one of the oldest known medical records, the Ebers Papyrus (dating from 16th century BC), an ancient Egyptian list of 877 prescriptions and recipes.

Medical Properties: Antispasmodic (neuromuscular), expectorant, antiparasitic (worms), antioxidant, antimicrobial

Uses: Lung/sinus infection, indigestion, senility, headaches

Fragrant Influence: Uplifting, refreshing, and invigorating

Technical Data: **Botanical Family:** Zingiberaceae; **Plant Origin:** Guatemala, Sri Lanka; **Extraction Method:** Steam distilled from seeds; **Key Constituents:** Alpha-Terpinyl Acetate (45-55%), 1,8-Cineole (Eucalyptol) (16-36%), Linalol (4-7%), Linalyl Acetate (3-7%); **ORAC:** 36,500 µTE/100g

Carrot Seed

Cedarwood

Carrot Seed/Carrot Seed Vitality™
(Daucus carota)

Carrot seed oil is traditionally used for kidney and digestive disorders and to relieve liver congestion.

Medical Properties: Antiparasitic, antiseptic, purgative, diuretic, vasodilatory, antifungal

Uses: Skin conditions (eczema, oily skin, psoriasis, wrinkles), water retention, liver problems

Technical Data: **Botanical Family:** Apiaceae; **Plant Origin:** France; **Extraction Method:** Steam distilled from dried seeds; **Key Constituents:** Carotol (30-40%), Alpha-Pinene (12-16%), Trans-Beta-Caryophyllene (6-10%), Caryophyllene Oxide (3-5%)

Cassia (Cinnamomum aromaticum) (Syn. C. cassia)

Cassia is rich in biblical history and is mentioned in one of the oldest known medical records, the Ebers Papyrus (dating from 16th century BC), an ancient Egyptian list of 877 prescriptions and recipes.

Note: While its aroma is similar to cinnamon, cassia is chemically and physically quite different.

Medical Properties: Anti-inflammatory (COX-2 inhibitor), antifungal, antibacterial, antiviral, anticoagulant

Uses: Cataracts, fungal infections (ringworm, candida), atherosclerosis, anxiolytic, diabetes, arteriosclerosis

Caution: May irritate the nasal membranes if inhaled directly from diffuser or bottle

Technical Data: **Botanical Family:** Lauraceae; **Plant Origin:** China; **Extraction Method:** Steam distilled from branches, leaves, and petioles; **Key Constituents:** Trans-Cinnamaldehyde (70-88%), Trans-O, Methoxycinnamaldehyde (3-15%), Coumarine (1.5-4%), Cinnamyl Acetate (0-6%); **ORAC:** 15,170 µTE/100g

Cedarwood (Cedrus atlantica)

Throughout antiquity, cedarwood has been used in medicines. The Egyptians used it for embalming the dead. It was used as both a traditional medicine and incense in Tibet.

Medical Properties: Combats hair loss (alopecia areata), antibacterial, lymphatic stimulant

Uses: Hair loss, arteriosclerosis, ADHD, skin problems (acne, eczema)

Fragrant Influence: Stimulates the limbic region of the brain (the center of emotions), stimulates the pineal gland, which releases melatonin. Terry Friedmann, MD, found in clinical tests that this oil may treat ADD and ADHD (attention deficit disorders) in children. It is recognized for its calming, purifying properties.

Technical Data: **Botanical Family:** Pinaceae; **Plant Origin:** Morocco, USA; Cedrus atlantica is the species most closely related to the biblical Cedars of Lebanon; **Extraction Method:** Steam distilled from bark; **Key Constituents:** Alpha-Himachalene (10-20%), Beta-Himachalene (35-55%), Gamma-Himachalene (8-15%), Delta-Cadinene (2-6%); **ORAC:** 169,000 µTE/100g

Cinnamon Bark

Cistus

Celery Seed/Celery Seed Vitality™
(Apium graveolens)

Long recognized as helpful in digestion, liver cleansing, and urinary tract support. It is also said to increase milk flow in nursing mothers.

Medical Properties: Antibacterial, antioxidant, antirheumatic, digestive aid, diuretic, liver protectant

Uses: Arthritis/rheumatism, digestive problems, liver problems/hepatitis

Technical Data: **Botanical Family:** Apiaceae; **Plant Origin:** Europe; **Extraction Method:** Steam distilled from dried seeds; **Key Constituents:** Limonene (60-75%), Alpha and Beta Selinene (14-20%), Sednenolide (4-7%); **ORAC:** 30,300 µTE/100g

Cinnamon Bark/Cinnamon Bark Vitality™
(Cinnamomum zeylanicum) (Syn. C. verum)

Listed in Dioscorides' *De Materia Medica* (AD 78), Europe's first authoritative guide to medicines, which became the standard reference work for herbal treatments for over 1,700 years.

Medical Properties: Anti-inflammatory (COX-2 inhibitor), powerfully antibacterial, antiviral, antifungal, anticoagulant, circulatory stimulant, stomach protectant (ulcers), antiparasitic (worms)

Uses: Cardiovascular disease, infectious diseases, viral infections (herpes, etc.), digestive complaints, ulcers, and warts

Fragrant Influence: Thought to attract wealth

Caution: May irritate the nasal membranes if inhaled directly from diffuser or bottle.

Technical Data: **Botanical Family:** Lauraceae; **Plant Origin:** Sri Lanka, Madagascar, Ceylon; **Extraction Method:** Steam distilled from bark; **Key Constituents:** Trans-Cinnamaldehyde (50-75%), Eugenol (4-7%), Beta-Caryophyllene (3-8%), Linalol (3-9%); **ORAC:** 10,340 µTE/100g

Cistus *(Cistus ladanifer/ladaniferus)*
(also known as *Labdanum*)

Cistus is also known as "rock rose" and Rose of Sharon and has been studied for its effects on the regeneration of cells.

Medical Properties: Antiviral, antibacterial, antihemorrhagic, anti-inflammatory, supports sympathetic nervous system, immune stimulant

Uses: Hemorrhages, arthritis

Fragrant Influence: Calming to the nerves, elevates the emotions

Technical Data: **Botanical Family:** Cistaceae; **Plant Origin:** Spain; **Extraction Method:** Steam distilled from leaves and branches; **Key Constituents:** Alpha-Pinene (40-60%), Camphene (2-5%), Bornyl Acetate (3-6%), Trans-Pinocarveol (3-6%); **ORAC:** 3,860 µTE/100g

Citronella

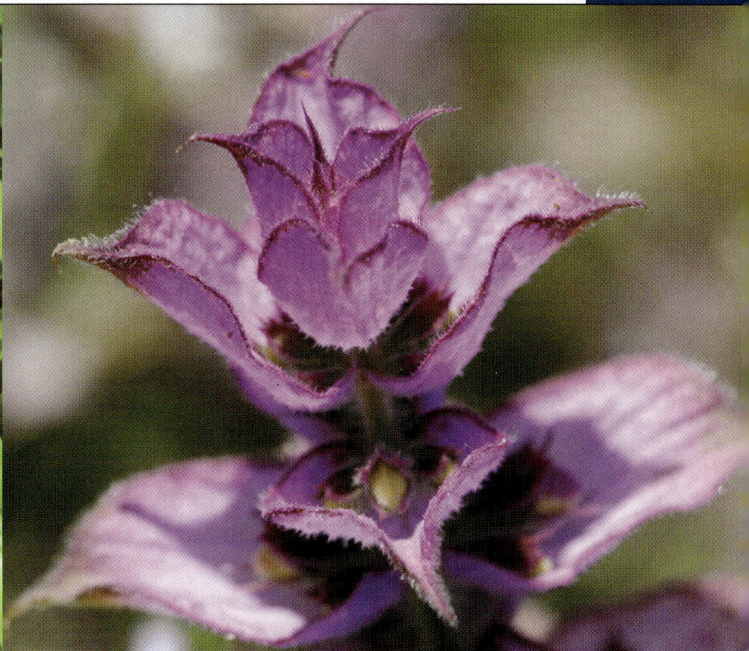

Clary Sage

Citronella (Cymbopogon nardus)

Used by various cultures to treat intestinal parasites, menstrual problems, and as a stimulant. Historically used to sanitize and deodorize surfaces. Enhanced insect repelling properties when combined with cedarwood.

Medical Properties: Powerful antioxidant, antibacterial, antifungal, insect repellent, anti-inflammatory, antispasmodic, antiparasitic (worms), relaxant

Uses: Respiratory infections, muscle/nerve pain, digestive/intestinal problems, anxiety, skin problems (acne, eczema, oily skin), skin-penetration enhancer

Fragrant Influence: Refreshing and uplifting

Technical Data: **Botanical Family:** Poaceae; **Plant Origin:** Sri Lanka; **Extraction Method:** Steam distilled from aerial parts and leaves; **Key Constituents:** Geraniol (18-30%), Limonene (5-10%), Trans-Methyl Isoeugenol (4-10%), Geranyl Acetate (5-10%), Borneol (3-8%); **ORAC:** 312,000 µTE/100g

Citrus Hystrix/Combava (Citrus hystrix)
(Also known as Kaffir lime)

Used as a flavorant and as a nausea, fainting, and headache treatment. Also used for stomachaches and dyspepsia.

Medical Properties: Anti-inflammatory, antimicrobial, antidepressant, relaxant, antitumoral, antioxidant, rich in citronellal, which possesses calmative properties

Uses: Stress, anxiety, trauma

Technical Data: **Botanical Family:** Rutaceae; **Plant Origin:** Indochina, Malaysia; **Extraction Method:** Steam distilled from leaves; **Key Constituents:** Citronnellal (65-80%), Linalol (3-6%), Citronnellol (2-5%), Isopulegol (2-4%); **ORAC:** 69,200 µTE/100g

Clary Sage (Salvia sclarea)

Clary sage seeds were historically used by soaking the seeds and using the mucilage as an eye-wash and to draw thorns or splinters from the skin. It was also used to treat skin infections, acne, digestive disorders, women's ailments, and soothe and calm the skin. Aromatically, clary sage was used to enhance the immune system, calm digestive disorders, reduce inflammation such as eczema, calm muscle spasms, and for respiratory conditions.

Medical Properties: Anticoagulant, antioxidant, antidiabetic, estrogen-like, antifungal, antispasmodic, relaxant, cholesterol-reducing, antitumoral, anesthetic

Uses: Leukemia, menstrual discomforts/PMS, hormonal imbalance, insomnia, circulatory problems, high cholesterol, insect repellant

Fragrant Influence: Enhances one's ability to dream and is very calming and stress relieving

Technical Data: **Botanical Family:** Lamiaceae; **Plant Origin:** Utah, France; **Extraction Method:** Steam distilled from flowering plant; **Key Constituents:** Linalyl Acetate (56-78%), Linalol (7-24%), Germacrene D (2-12%), Sclareol (.4-3%); **ORAC:** 221,000 µTE/100g

Clove

Copaiba

Clove/Clove Vitality™

(Syzygium aromaticum) (Syn. Eugenia caryophyllus)

The people on the island of Ternate were free from epidemics until the 16th century, when Dutch conquerors destroyed the clove trees that flourished on the islands. Many of the islanders died from the epidemics that followed.

Cloves were reputed to be part of the "Marseilles Vinegar" or "Four Thieves Vinegar" that bandits who robbed the dead and dying used to protect themselves during the 15th century plague.

Clove was listed in Hildegard's *Medicine,* a compilation of early German medicines by highly regarded Benedictine herbalist Hildegard of Bingen (1098-1179).

Healers in China and India have used clove buds since ancient times as part of their treatments.

Eugenol, clove's principal constituent, was used in the dental industry for years to numb gums.

Medical Properties: Antiaging, antitumoral, antimicrobial, antifungal, antiviral, analgesic/anesthetic, antioxidant, anticoagulant, anti-inflammatory, stomach protectant (ulcers), antiparasitic (worms), anticonvulsant, bone preserving

Uses: Antiaging, cardiovascular disease, diabetes, arthritis/rheumatism, hepatitis, intestinal parasites/infections, for numbing all types of pain, throat/sinus/lung infections, cataracts, ulcers, lice, toothache, acne

Fragrant Influence: A mental stimulant; encourages sleep, stimulates dreams, and creates a sense of protection and courage

Caution: Anticoagulant properties can be enhanced when combined with Warfarin, aspirin, etc.

Technical Data: Botanical Family: Myrtaceae; **Plant Origin:** Madagascar, Spice Islands; **Extraction Method:** Steam distilled from flower bud and stem; **Key Constituents:** Eugenol (75-87%), Eugenol Acetate (8-15%), Beta-Carophyllene (2-7%); **ORAC:** 1,078,700 µTE/100g

Copaiba/Copaiba Vitality (Balsam Copaiba)

(Copaifera officinalis, C. reticulata)

Healers and *curanderos* in the Amazon use copaiba resin for all types of pain and inflammatory disorders, both internal (stomach ulcers and cancer) and external (skin disorders and insect bites).

In Peruvian traditional medicine, three or four drops of the resin are mixed with a spoonful of honey and taken as a natural sore throat remedy. It is also employed in Peruvian and Brazilian herbal medicine systems as an anti-inflammatory and antiseptic for the urinary tract (cystitis, bladder, and kidney disorders) and in the treatment of urinary problems, stomach ulcers, syphilis, tetanus, bronchitis, and tuberculosis.

In Brazilian herbal medicine, the resin is highly regarded as a strong antiseptic and expectorant for the respiratory tract (including bronchitis and sinusitis) and as an antiseptic gargle. It is a popular home remedy in Brazil for sore throats and tonsillitis (1/2 teaspoon of resin is added to warm water).

Note: The word "Copal" is derived from the Spanish word for incense (copelli) and can refer to any number of different resinous gums or exudates

Coriander

from trees in Malaysia and South America. Copals are known as black *(Protium copal)*, white *(blanco)* *(Bursera bipinnata)*, gold *(oro) (H. courbaril)*, and Brazilian *(Copaifera langsdorfii or reticulata)*. Only the Brazilian copal or copaiba has a GRAS distinction in the U.S. and has the most published research on its anti-inflammatory effects.

Medical Properties: Anti-inflammatory (powerful), neuroprotective, antimicrobial, anxiolytic, mucolytic, antiulcer, anticancer, antiseptic, kidney stone preventative

Uses: Pain relief (strong anti-inflammatory), arthritis, rheumatism, cancer, skin disorders (psoriasis), insect bites, stomach distress, urinary disorders, sore throat, anxiety

Safety Data: Approved as a food additive in the U.S.

Technical Data: Botanical Family: Fabaceae; **Plant Origin:** Brazil; **Extraction Method:** Steam distilled (vacuum distilled) from gum resin exudate from tapped trees; **Key Constituents:** Alpha-Copaene (2-5%), Alpha-Humulene (6-10%), Beta-Caryophyllene (39-72%), Delta-Cadinene (2-3%), Delta-Elemene (2-3%), Gamma-Elemene (1-8%), Germacrene D (4-6%), Trans-Alpha-Bergamotene (3-11%)

Coriander/Coriander Vitality™
(Coriandrum sativum)

Coriander seeds were found in the ancient Egyptian tomb of Ramses II. This oil has been researched at Cairo University for its effects in lowering glucose and insulin levels and supporting pancreatic function. It has also been studied for its effects in strengthening the pancreas.

Medical Properties: Anti-inflammatory, antioxidant, sedative, analgesic, antimicrobial, antifungal, liver protectant

Uses: Diabetes, arthritis, intestinal problems, skin conditions

Fragrant Influence: Soothing and calming

Technical Data: Botanical Family: Apiaceae; **Plant Origin:** Russia; **Extraction Method:** Steam distilled from seeds (fruit); **Key Constituents:** Linalol (65-78%), Alpha-Pinene (3-7%), Camphor (4-6%), Gamma-Terpinene (2-7%), Limonene (2-5%), Geranyl Acetate (1-3.5%), Geraniol (0.5-3%); **ORAC:** 298,300 µTE/100g

Pandey A, et al. Pharmacological screening of *Coriandrum sativum* Linn. for hepatoprotective activity. *J Pharm Bioallied Sci.* 2011 Jul;3(3):435-41.

Cumin *(Cuminum cyminum)*

The Hebrews used cumin as an antiseptic for circumcision. In ancient Egypt, cumin was used for cooking and mummification.

Medical Properties: Antitumoral, anti-inflammatory, antioxidant, antiviral, antifungal, antimicrobial, digestive aid, liver protectant, immune stimulant

Cumin

Cypress

Uses: Cancer, infectious disease, digestive problems

Caution: Possible sun/skin sensitivity.

Technical Data: **Botanical Family:** Apiaceae; **Plant Origin:** Egypt; **Extraction Method:** Steam distilled from seeds; **Key Constituents:** Cuminaldehyde (16-22%), Gamma-Terpinene (16-22%), Beta-Pinene (12-18%), Para-Mentha-1,3 + 1,4-dien-7-al (25-35%), Para-Cymene (3-8%); **ORAC:** 82,400 µTE/100g

Cypress *(Cupressus sempervirens)*

The Phoenicians and Cretans used cypress for building ships and bows, while the Egyptians made sarcophagi from the wood. The Greeks used cypress to carve statues of their gods. The Greek word "sempervivens," from which the botanical name is derived, means "live forever." The tree shares its name with the island of Cypress, where it is used for worship. Cypress wood is noted for its durability, as it was used most famously for the original doors of St. Peter's Basilica at the Vatican that legends say lasted over 1,000 years.

Medical Properties: Improves circulation; is anti-infectious, antispasmodic, and an antioxidant; discourages fluid retention; improves respiration; promotes liver health

Uses: Diabetes, circulatory disorders, grounding, stabilizing

Fragrant Influence: Eases the feeling of loss and creates a sense of security and grounding. Also helps heal emotional trauma, calms, soothes anger, and helps life flow better. Can help soothe irritating coughs and minor chest discomfort.

Technical Data: **Botanical Family:** Cupressaceae; **Plant Origin:** France, Spain; **Extraction Method:** Steam distilled from branches; **Key Constituents:** Alpha-Pinene (40-65%), Beta-Pinene (0.5-3%), Delta-3-Carene (12-25%), Limonene (1.8-5%), Cedrol (0.8-7%), Myrcene (1-3.5%); **ORAC:** 24,300 µTE/100g

Dalmatia Bay Laurel *(Laurus nobilis) (Bay Laurel)*

The coastal region of Dalmatia, Croatia, is home to Dalmatia Bay Laurel. With its rich eucalyptol scent, Dalmatia Bay Laurel encourages healthy skin and enlivens massage oils when applied to the feet.

Technical Data: **Botanical Family:** Lauraceae; **Plant Origin:** Croatia; **Extraction Method:** Steam distilled from leaves and twigs; **Key Constituents:** 1,8-Cineole (Eucalyptol) (40-50%), Alpha-Terpenyl Acetate (7-14%), Alpha-Pinene (4-8%), Beta-Pinene (3-6%), Sabinene (6-11%), Linalol (2-7%); **ORAC:** 98,900 µTE/100g

Dalmatia Juniper *(Juniperus oxycedrus)*

The juniper native to the Dalmatia region of Croatia is known for its skin supporting benefits. Thriving in Croatia's rocky soil, Dalmatia Juniper was traditionally used for intestinal complaints.

Technical Data: **Botanical Family:** Cupressaceae; **Plant Origin:** Croatia; **Extraction Method:** Steam distilled from needles and branches; **Key Constituents:** Alpha-Pinene (36-56%), Limonene (10-25%), Myrcene (2-8%), Beta-Pinene (1-5%), Germacrene D (1-3.5%); Delta-Cadinene (0.8-3%); **ORAC:** 250 µTE/100g

Dill

Dalmatia Sage *(Salvia officinalis)*

Although it now grows elsewhere, sage is native to the Mediterranean area and its rich history was documented by Theophrastus and Pliny the Elder. It flourishes in the Dalmatia region of Croatia. The traditional uses of sage range from reducing fever and as a diuretic, while modern-day studies show improved cognitive function.

Technical Data: **Botanical Family:** Lamiaceae; **Plant Origin:** Croatia; **Extraction Method:** Steam distilled from leaves; **Key Constituents:** Alpha-Thujone (18-43%), Beta-Thujone (3-8.5%), 1,8-Cineole (Eucalyptol) (5.5-13%), Camphor (4.5-24.5%), Camphene (1.5-7%), Alpha-Pinene (1-6.5%), Alpha-Humulene (trace-12%); **ORAC:** 14,800 µTE/100g

Davana *(Artemisia pallens)*

Davana grows in the same areas of India as sandalwood. It has been used in India for diabetes, digestive problems (expels parasites), fighting infections, and calming anger. It has been recommended as an aphrodisiac and is often used in perfumery. It has a very rich, concentrated aroma, is usually used in only very small quantities, and is usually used as a complement in very small amounts in essential oil blends. Davana should always be diluted because it is high in ketones. The aroma tends to develop differently, depending on the individual chemistry of the person wearing the oil.

Medical Properties: Anti-infectious, antiviral, aphrodisiac, anthelmintic, calmative, analgesic, anti-inflammatory

Uses: Skin infections, headaches, emotional stress, worm infestations, sugar metabolism

Technical Data: **Botanical Family:** Asteraceae; **Extraction Method:** Steam distilled from flowers and leaves; **Key Constituents:** Davanone 1-2 (40-60%), Davana Ether 1-3 (5-10%), Ethyl Cinnamate (1-6%), Bicyclogermacrene (5-14%)

Dill/Dill Vitality™ *(Anethum graveolens)*

The dill plant is mentioned in the Papyrus of Ebers from Egypt (1550 BC). Roman gladiators rubbed their skin with dill before each match. Listed in Dioscorides' *De Materia Medica* (AD 78), Europe's first authoritative guide to medicines, which became the standard reference work for herbal treatments for over 1,700 years. It was listed in Hildegard's *Medicine,* a compilation of early German medicines by highly regarded Benedictine herbalist Hildegard of Bingen (1098-1179).

Medical Properties: Antidiabetic, antispasmodic, antifungal, antibacterial, expectorant, pancreatic stimulant, insulin/blood sugar regulator

Uses: Diabetes, digestive problems, liver deficiencies

Fragrant Influence: Calms the autonomic nervous system and, when diffused with Roman Chamomile, combats ADHD.

Technical Data: **Botanical Family:** Apiaceae; **Plant Origin:** Austria, Hungary; **Extraction Method:** Steam distilled from whole plant; **Key Constituents:** Carvone (30-45%), Limonene (15-25%), Alpha- and Beta-Phellandrene (20-35%); **ORAC:** 35,600 µTE/100g

Dorado Azul

Douglas Fir

Dorado Azul *(Dorado azul guayfolius officinalis)* *(INCI: Hyptis suaveolens)*

Until about 2006, Dorado Azul was recognized in Ecuador as only a weed. It did not even have a botanical name until D. Gary Young distilled and analyzed it for the first time and gave it its identity. It is a red liquid when distilled, and the natives use it to reverse cancer.

Medical Properties: Anti-inflammatory, antioxidant, antimicrobial, antiseptic, antihyperglycemic, gastro-protective, liver protectant, respiratory stimulant

Uses: Colds, coughs, flu, bronchitis, asthma, allergic reactions that cause constriction and compromised breathing, any compromise to the respiratory tract, hormone balancer, diabetes, vascular dilator, circulatory stimulant, arthritic and rheumatoid-type pain, reducing candida and other intestinal tract problems, digestion, hygienic action for the mouth, enhances mood

Technical Data: Botanical Family: Lamiaceae; **Plant Origin:** Ecuador; **Extraction Method:** Steam distilled from stems/leaves/flowers (aerial parts); **Key Constituents:** Alpha-Fenchol (4-12%), Beta-Pinene (7-12%), Bicyclogermacrene (4-8%), 1,8-Cineole (Eucalyptol) (23-46%), Limonene (3-7%), Sabinene (7-18%)

Douglas Fir *(Pseudotsuga menziesii)*

American Indians not only used Douglas fir for building and basketry but medicinally for ailments like headaches, stomachaches, the common cold, and rheumatism.

Medical Properties: Antitumoral, antioxidant, antifungal, pain relieving

Uses: Respiratory/sinus infections

Technical Data: Botanical Family: Pinaceae; **Plant Origin:** Idaho; **Extraction Method:** Steam distilled from wood/bark/twigs/needles; **Key Constituents:** Alpha-Pinene (25-40%), Beta-Pinene (7-15%), Limonene (6-11%), Bornyl Acetate (8-15%); **ORAC:** 69,000 µTE/100g

Elemi *(Canarium luzonicum)*

Elemi has been used in Europe for hundreds of years in salves for skin and is included in celebrated healing ointments such as baum paralytique. Used by a 17th century physician, J. J. Wecker on the battle wounds of soldiers, elemi belongs to the same botanical family as frankincense (*Boswellia carterii*) and myrrh (*Commiphora myrrha*). The Egyptians used elemi for embalming, and subsequent cultures (particularly in Europe) used it for skin care and for reducing fine lines, wrinkles, and improving skin tone.

Medical Properties: Antispasmodic, anti-inflammatory, antimicrobial, antiseptic, anticancer

Uses: Muscle/nerve pain, skin problems (scars, acne, wrinkles)

Fragrant Influence: Its spicy, incense-like fragrance is very conducive toward meditation. Can be grounding and used to clear the mind.

Technical Data: Botanical Family: Burseraceae; **Plant Origin:** Philippines; **Extraction Method:** Steam distilled from the gum/resin of the tree; **Key Constituents:** Limonene (40-72%), Alpha-Phellandrene (10-24%), Sabinene (3-8%), Elemol (1-25%)

Eucalyptus Blue

Eucalyptus Citriodora

Eucalyptus Blue *(Eucalyptus bicostata)*

Eucalyptus blue is grown and distilled on Young Living's farm in Ecuador. It is called blue gum, a tree that has been crossbred over 250 years in the wilds of the Andean Mountains in Ecuador and is a cross between Eucalyptus citriodora and Eucalyptus globulus. The native people of Ecuador have used the disinfecting leaves to cover wounds and repel insects.

Although it contains a high percentage of eucalyptol, because of its balanced chemical constituents within the eucalyptus, it is the only eucalyptus that has been found in the world today that does not cause an allergic reaction in people who have allergies to eucalyptol. Eucalyptus Blue is preferred over many of the eucalyptus species, simply because of its well-balanced chemistry and its non-allergen effect for all types of respiratory conditions. In a recent study of eight eucalyptus species, Eucalyptus bicostata had the best antiviral activity. It is a great companion to Dorado Azul.

Medical Properties: Expectorant, diaphoretic, insecticidal, oestrogenic, antifungal, antiviral, antibacterial

Uses: Supports respiratory function to promote normal breathing, relieves sore muscles, calming, invigorating

Fragrant Influence: Has a fresh, balanced, invigorating aroma

Cautions: Do not use Eucalyptus Blue as a dietary supplement. Large amounts of any eucalyptus oil may be toxic. Keep out of reach of children.

Technical Data: **Botanical Family:** Myrtaceae; **Plant Origin:** Ecuador; **Extraction Method:** Steam distilled from the leaves; **Key Constituents:** 1,8-Cineole (Eucalyptol) (40-80%), Alpha-pinene (10-30%), Aromadendrene (≤ 7%), Limonene (4-8%)

Eucalyptus Citriodora
(Eucalyptus citriodora)

Traditionally used to perfume linen closets and as an insect repellent.

Medical Properties: Analgesic, antiviral, antibacterial, antifungal, anticancer, liver protectant, expectorant, insecticidal

Uses: Fungal infections (ringworm, candida), respiratory infections, viral infections (herpes, shingles)

Technical Data: **Botanical Family:** Myrtaceae; **Plant Origin:** China; **Extraction Method:** Steam distilled from leaves; **Key Constituents:** Citronellal (75-85%), Neo-Isopulegol + Isopulegol (0-10%); **ORAC:** 83,000 µTE/100g

Eucalyptus Globulus *(Eucalyptus globulus)*

For centuries, Australian Aborigines used the disinfecting leaves to cover wounds. Shown by laboratory tests to be a powerful antimicrobial agent, *E. globulus* contains a high percentage of eucalyptol (a key ingredient in many antiseptic mouth rinses). It is often used for the respiratory system. Eucalyptus has also been investigated for its powerful insect repellent effects (Trigg, 1996). Eucalyptus trees have been planted throughout parts of North Africa to successfully block the spread of malaria.

Eucalyptus Globulus

Eucalyptus Radiata

According to Jean Valnet, MD, a solution of 2 percent eucalyptus oil sprayed on the skin will kill 70 percent of ambient staph bacteria. Some doctors still use solutions of eucalyptus oil in surgical dressings.

Medical Properties: Expectorant, mucolytic, antimicrobial, antibacterial, antifungal, antiviral, antiaging, antiulcer, antidiabetic

Uses: Respiratory/sinus infections, decongestant, rheumatism/arthritis, soothe sore muscles

Fragrant Influence: Promotes health, well-being, purification, and healing

Technical Data: Botanical Family: Myrtaceae; **Plant Origin:** China; **Extraction Method:** Steam distilled from leaves; **Key Constituents:** 1,8-Cineole (Eucalyptol) (70-90%), Alpha-Pinene (1-5%), Limonene (6-9%), Para-Cymene (1-5%); **ORAC:** 2,400 µTE/100g

Eucalyptus Radiata *(Eucalyptus radiata)*

This eucalyptus species has been treasured in folk medicine. A 2011 study conducted at Heidelberg University found that *Eucalyptus radiata* has the second highest abundance of 1,8 cineole (Eucalyptol) after *E. globulus*.

Medical Properties: Antibacterial, antiviral, expectorant, anti-inflammatory

Uses: Respiratory/sinus infections, viral infections, fights herpes simplex when combined with bergamot

Technical Data: Botanical Family: Myrtaceae; **Plant Origin:** Australia; **Extraction Method:** Steam distilled from leaves; **Key Constituents:** 1,8-Cineole (Eucalyptol) (60-75%), Alpha Terpineol (5-10%), Limonene (4-8%), Alpha Pinene (2-6%)

Eucalyptus Staigeriana
(Eucalyptus staigeriana)

This gentle eucalyptus species was valued by Australian Aborigines as a general cure-all. By 1788 it was introduced in Europe, where it was valued for treating respiratory conditions and for colic. Recent research documents staigeriana as a powerful antiparasitic as well as being highly antimicrobial.

Medical Properties: Antibacterial, diuretic, decongestant, expectorant, antiparasitic

Uses: Helps wounds, burns, and insect bites heal; suppresses coughs; relieves muscle aches

Fragrant Influences: Eucalyptus Staigeriana, also known as lemon iron bark, has a lemon-scented aroma, without the medicine-like scent of other eucalyptus oils. It can be used on people with sensitive skin.

Technical Data: Botanical Family: Myrtaceae; **Plant Origin:** Australia, Brazil; **Extraction Method:** Steam distilled from leaves; **Key Constituents:** Alpha-Phellandrene (4-7%), Limonene (4-10%), 1,8 Cineole (Eucalyptol) (15-35%), Neral (7-15%), Geranial (10-20%)

Fennel/Fennel Vitality™
(Foeniculum vulgare)

Fennel was believed to ward off evil spirits and to protect against spells cast by witches during medieval times. Sprigs were hung over doors to fend off evil phantasms. For hundreds of years, fennel seeds have been used as a digestive aid and to balance menstrual cycles. It

Frankincense

Frereana Frankincense

is mentioned in one of the oldest known medical records, the Ebers Papyrus (dating from 16th century BC), an ancient Egyptian list of 877 prescriptions and recipes. It was listed in Hildegard's *Medicine*, a compilation of early German medicines by highly regarded Benedictine herbalist Hildegard of Bingen (1098-1179).

Medical Properties: Antidiabetic, anti-inflammatory, antitumoral, estrogen-like, digestive aid, antiparasitic (worms), antiseptic, antispasmodic, analgesic, increases metabolism

Uses: Diabetes, cancer, obesity, arthritis/rheumatism, urinary tract infection, fluid retention, intestinal parasites, menstrual problems/PMS, digestive problems

Caution: Avoid using if epileptic.

Technical Data: **Botanical Family:** Apiaceae; **Plant Origin:** Hungary; **Extraction Method:** Steam distilled from the crushed seeds (fruit); **Key Constituents:** Trans-Anethole (60-80%), Fenchone (8-20%), Alpha-Pinene (1-8%), Methyl Chavicol (2-6%); **ORAC:** 238,400 µTE/100g

Frankincense/Frankincense Vitality™
(Boswellia carterii)

Also known as "olibanum," the name frankincense is derived from the Medieval French word for "real incense." Frankincense is considered the "holy anointing oil" in the Middle East and has been used in religious ceremonies for thousands of years. It was well known during the time of Christ for its anointing and healing powers and was one of

the gifts given to Christ at His birth. "Used to treat every conceivable ill known to man," frankincense was valued more than gold during ancient times, and only those with great wealth and abundance possessed it. It is mentioned in one of the oldest known medical records, Ebers Papyrus (dating from 16th century BC), an ancient Egyptian list of 877 prescriptions and recipes.

Medical Properties: Antitumoral, immuno-stimulant, antidepressant, muscle relaxing

Uses: Depression, cancer, respiratory infections, inflammation, immune-stimulating

Fragrant Influence: Increases spiritual awareness, promotes meditation, improves attitude, and uplifts spirits

Technical Data: **Botanical Family:** Burseraceae; **Plant Origin:** Somalia; **Extraction Method:** Steam distilled from gum/resin; **Key Constituents:** Alpha-Pinene (30-65%), Limonene (8-20%), Sabinene (1-8%), Myrcene (1-14%), Beta-Caryophyllene (1-5%), Alpha-Thujene (1-15%), Incensole; **ORAC:** 630 µTE/100g

Moussaieff A, et al. Incensole acetate: a novel neuroprotective agent isolated from *Boswellia carterii*. *J Cereb Blood Flow Metab.* 2008 Jul;28(7):1341-52.

Frereana Frankincense (Boswellia frereana)

This species of frankincense is native to northern Somalia, where the locals call it "Maydi" and the "King of Frankincense." Frereana incense has been a part of Eastern Orthodox and Catholic worship for hundreds of years.

Since *Boswellia carterii* also grows in Somalia, it is

Galbanum

Geranium

hard to explain why frereana has such a unique chemical composition, so different from *B. carterii* and other frankincense species. As shown by Frank and Unger, as well as E. J. Blain, frereana contains no boswellic acids. S. Hamm reports that frereana "is devoid of diterpenes of the incensole family." Now that a pure source can be guaranteed, it is hoped researchers will delve into the benefits of frereana.

There are unique constituents of frereana found in no other frankincense that have mostly been overlooked by researchers. Two frereana studies in 2010 and 2006 reported strong anti-inflammatory activity. Sadly, some trusting purchasers have received an amalgamation of cheaper frankincense resins rather than pure *Boswellia frereana*.

Political conditions in Somalia make it essential for a "feet on the ground" presence in order to secure contracts to obtain pure, high quality frereana resin. For this reason, D. Gary Young personally visited Somalia in November 2013 to contract with local clans of harvesters.

Medical Properties: Anti-inflammatory

Uses: Arthritis/rheumatism

Fragrant Influence: The aroma of frereana frankincense has a more lemony scent than carterii and is uplifting and cheering.

Technical Data: Botanical Family: Burseraceae; **Plant Origin:** Somalia; **Extraction Method:** Steam distilled from gum/resin; **Key Constituents:** Alpha-Thujene (23-45%), Alpha-Pinene (5-9%), Sabinene (1-8%), Para-Cymene (10-20%), Terpinen-4-ol (2-9%)

Galbanum *(Ferula galbaniflua)*

Mentioned in Egyptian papyri and the Old Testament (Exodus 30:34), it was esteemed for its medicinal and spiritual properties. Dioscorides, an ancient Roman historian, records that galbanum was used for its antispasmodic, diuretic, and pain-relieving properties.

Medical Properties: Antiseptic, analgesic, light antispasmodic, anti-inflammatory, circulatory stimulant, anticonvulsant

Uses: Digestive problems (diarrhea), nervous tension, rheumatism, skin conditions (scar tissue, wrinkles)

Fragrant Influence: Harmonic and balancing, amplifies spiritual awareness and meditation. When combined with Frankincense or Sandalwood, the frequency rises dramatically.

Technical Data: Botanical Family: Apiaceae; **Plant Origin:** Persia; **Extraction Method:** Steam distilled from gum/resin derived from stems and branches; **Key Constituents:** Alpha-Pinene (5-21%), Beta-Pinene (40-70%), Delta-3-Carene (2-16%), Myrcene (2.5-3.5%), Sabinene (0.3-3%); **ORAC:** 26,200 µTE/100g

Geranium *(Pelargonium graveolens)*

Geranium has been used for centuries for regenerating and healing skin conditions.

Medical Properties: Antispasmodic, antioxidant, antitumoral, anti-inflammatory, anticancer, hemostatic (stops bleeding), antibacterial, antifungal, improves blood flow, liver and pancreas stimulant,

German Chamomile

Ginger

dilates bile ducts for liver detoxification, helps cleanse oily skin; revitalizes skin cells

Uses: Hepatitis/fatty liver (Jean Valnet, MD), skin conditions (dermatitis, eczema, psoriasis, acne, vitiligo), fungal infections (ringworm), viral infections (herpes, shingles), hormone imbalances, circulatory problems (improves blood flow), menstrual problems/PMS

Fragrant Influence: Helps release negative memories and eases nervous tension; balances the emotions, lifts the spirit, and fosters peace, well-being, and hope

Technical Data: **Botanical Family:** Geraniaceae; **Plant Origin:** Egypt, India; **Extraction Method:** Steam distilled from the flowers and leaves; **Key Constituents:** Citronellol (25-36%), Geraniol (10-18%), Citronellyl Formate (5-8%), Linalol (4-8%)

German Chamomile/German Chamomile Vitality™

(Chamomilla recutita) (Syn. Matricaria recutita)

Listed in Dioscorides' *De Materia Medica* (AD 78), Europe's first authoritative guide to medicines, which became the standard reference work for herbal treatments for over 1,700 years.

Medical Properties: Powerful antioxidant, inhibits lipid peroxidation, antitumoral, anti-inflammatory, relaxant, anesthetic; promotes digestion, liver, and gallbladder health.

Uses: Hepatitis/fatty liver, arteriosclerosis, insomnia, nervous tension, arthritis, carpal tunnel syndrome, skin problems such as acne, eczema, scar tissue

Fragrant Influence: Dispels anger, stabilizes emotions, and helps release emotions linked to the past. Soothes and clears the mind.

Technical Data: **Botanical Family:** Asteraceae; **Plant Origin:** Utah, Idaho, Egypt, Hungary; **Extraction Method:** Steam distilled from flowers; **Key Constituents:** Chamazulene (2-5%), Bisabolol Oxide A (32-42%), Trans-Beta-Farnesene (18-26%), Bisbolol Oxide B (3-6%), Bisbolone Oxide A (3-6%), Cis Spiro Ether (4-8%); **ORAC:** 218,600 µTE/100g

Ginger/Ginger Vitality™ *(Zingiber officinale)*

Traditionally used to combat nausea. Women in the West African country of Senegal weave belts of ginger root to restore their mates' sexual potency.

Medical Properties: Anti-inflammatory, anticoagulant, digestive aid, anesthetic, expectorant, antifungal

Uses: Rheumatism/arthritis, digestive disorders, respiratory infections/congestion, muscular aches/pains, nausea

Fragrant Influence: Gentle, stimulating, endowing physical energy, courage

Caution: Anticoagulant properties can be enhanced when combined with Warfarin, aspirin, etc

Technical Data: **Botanical Family:** Zingiberaceae; **Plant Origin:** India, China; **Extraction Method:** Steam distilled from rhizomes/root; **Key Constituents:** Zingiberene (30-40%), Beta-Sesquiphellandrene (8-19%), 1,8-Cineole (Eucalyptol) + Beta-Phellandrene (4-10%), AR Curcumene (5-10%), Camphene (5-9%); **ORAC:** 99,300 µTE/100g

Goldenrod

Helichrysum

Goldenrod (Solidago canadensis)

The genus name, *Solidago*, comes from the Latin solide, which means "to make whole." During the Boston Tea Party, when English tea was dumped into Boston Harbor, colonists drank goldenrod tea instead, which gave it the nickname "Liberty Tea."

Medical Properties: Diuretic, anti-inflammatory, antihypertensive, liver stimulant

Uses: Hypertension, liver congestion, hepatitis/fatty liver, circulatory conditions, urinary tract/bladder conditions

Technical Data: Botanical Family: Asteraceae; **Plant Origin:** Canada; **Extraction Method:** Steam distilled from flowering tops; **Key Constituents:** Alpha-Pinene (10-24%), Germacrene D (15-37%), Myrcene (4-10%), Sabinene (5-18%), Limonene (10-20%); **ORAC:** 61,900 µTE/100g

Grapefruit/Grapefruit Vitality™

(Citrus paradisi)

Grapefruit is believed to have originated in Barbados by an accidental crossing of sweet orange (*Citrus sinensis*) and pomelo (*Citrus maxima*). When it was discovered, it was called the "forbidden fruit."

Medical Properties: Antitumoral, metabolic stimulant, antiseptic, detoxifying, diuretic, fat-dissolving, cleansing for kidneys, lymphatic and vascular system; antidepressant, rich in limonene, which has been extensively studied in over 50 clinical studies for its ability to combat tumor growth

Uses: Alzheimer's, fluid retention, depression, obesity, liver disorders, anxiety, cellulite

Fragrant Influence: Refreshing and uplifting

Caution: Possible sun sensitivity.

Technical Data: Botanical Family: Rutaceae; **Plant Origin:** South Africa and California. (Grapefruit is a hybrid between Citrus maxima and Citrus sinensis.); **Extraction Method:** Cold pressed from rind; **Key Constituents:** Limonene (88-95%), Myrcene (1-4%); **ORAC:** 22,600 µTE/100g

Helichrysum (Helichrysum italicum)

Helichrysum is also known by the names Immortelle and Everlasting. Helichrysum essential oil is renowned for its anti-inflammatory effects.

Medical Properties: Anticoagulant, anesthetic, antioxidant, antispasmodic, antiviral, liver protectant/detoxifier/stimulant, chelates chemicals and toxins, regenerates nerves

Uses: Herpes virus, arteriosclerosis, atherosclerosis, hypertension, blood clots, liver disorders, circulatory disorders, skin conditions (eczema, psoriasis scar tissue, varicose veins)

Fragrant Influence: Uplifting to the subconscious

Caution: Anticoagulant properties can be enhanced when combined with Warfarin, aspirin, etc.

Technical Data: Botanical Family: Asteraceae; **Plant Origin:** Yugoslavia, Corsica, Croatia, Spain; **Extraction Method:** Steam distilled from flower; **Key Constituents:** Neryl Acetate (3-35%), Gamma-Curcumene (10-28%), Alpha-Pinene (15-32%), Beta-Caryophyllene (2-9%), Beta-Selinene (4-8%); **ORAC:** 1,700 µTE/100g

Hong Kuai

Hyssop

Hinoki (Chamaecyparis obtusa)

Hinoki wood has been used to construct many holy temples in Japan, including Horyuji Temple and Osaka Castle, and is said to be the "tree where God stayed." Hinoki wood is resistant to decay and carries a symbolic reputation of being immortal.

Medical Properties: Contains tau-muurolene, a powerful antifungal compound; reduces agitation and hyperactivity

Uses: Antibacterial, antiviral, antidepressant, anti-inflammatory, astringent, odor eliminator, promotes hair growth, stimulates digestion, relieves pain

Fragrant Influence: Calming and centering

Technical Data: **Botanical Family:** Cupressaceae; **Plant Origin:** Southern Japan; **Extraction Method:** Steam distilled from sustainably harvested, culled wood; **Key Constituents:** Alpha-Pinene (35-60%), Gamma-Cadinene (3-8%), Delta-Cadinene (7-14%), Tau-Cadinol (7-15%), Tau-Muurolol (6-12%)

Hong Kuai (Chamaecyparis formosensis)

Hong Kuai trees grow up to 55-60 meters tall in high altitude areas of Taiwan and can live over 1,000 years. The wood of these trees is highly resistant to decay and valued for building temples. The highly scented oil was known for supporting respiratory health.

Medical Properties: Antifungal, anticancer, immune support

Uses: Fungal infections (ringworm), cancer, respiratory problems

Fragrant Influence: Calming and centering

Technical Data: **Botanical Family:** Cupressaceae; **Plant Origin:** Taiwan; **Extraction Method:** Steam distilled from sustainably harvested, culled wood; **Key Constituents:** Alpha-Pinene (4-6%), Myrtenal (3-7%), Myrtenol (11-18%), Myrtanol (13-19%), Delta-Cadinene (7-10%), Alpha-Elemol (1-4%), Tau-Muurolol (3-6%)

Hyssop (Hyssopus officinalis)

While there is some uncertainty that *Hyssopus officinalis* is the same species of plant as the hyssop referred to in the Bible, there is no question that *H. officinalis* has been used medicinally for almost a millennium for its antiseptic properties. It has also been used for opening the respiratory system.

Medical Properties: Mucolytic, decongestant, anti-inflammatory, regulates lipid metabolism, antiviral, antibacterial, and antiparasitic

Uses: Respiratory infections/congestion, parasites (expelling worms), viral infections, and circulatory disorders

Fragrant Influence: Stimulates creativity and meditation

Caution: Avoid use if epileptic.

Technical Data: **Botanical Family:** Lamiaceae; **Plant Origin:** France, Hungary, Utah; **Extraction Method:** Steam distilled from stems and leaves; **Key Constituents:** Beta-Pinene (13.5-23%), Sabinene (2-3%), Pinocamphone (5.5-17.5%), Iso-Pinochamphone (34.5-50%), Gemacrene D (2-3%), Limonene (1-4%); **ORAC:** 20,900 µTE/100g

Idaho Balsam Fir

Idaho Ponderosa Pine

Idaho Balsam Fir (Balsam Canada)
(Abies balsamea)

The balsam fir tree—a tree commonly used as a Christmas tree today—has been prized through the ages for its medicinal effects and ability to heal respiratory conditions and muscular and rheumatic pain.

Medical Properties: Anticoagulant, antibacterial, anti-inflammatory, antitumoral

Uses: Throat/lung/sinus infections, fatigue, arthritis/rheumatism, urinary tract infections, scoliosis/lumbago/sciatica

Fragrant Influence: Grounding, stimulating to the mind, and relaxing to the body

Technical Data: **Botanical Family:** Pinaceae; **Plant Origin:** Highland Flats in Naples, Idaho; **Extraction Method:** Steam distilled from leaves (needles) and branches; **Key Constituents:** Alpha-Pinene (6-9%), Beta-Pinene (14-24%), Camphene (10-15%), Limonene (1-5%); **ORAC:** 20,500 µTE/100g

Idaho Blue Spruce (Picea pungens)

Northwestern Native Americans considered the Idaho blue spruce to be a sacred tree and used it for smudging/purification rites. Spruce leaves, inner bark, gum, and twigs have been used historically by Native Americans for a variety of functions. Leaves were used as inhalants, fumigators, and revivers. The inner bark of the spruce was used for lung and throat troubles, inward troubles, in a poultice applied to wounds and for cuts and swelling, as a medicinal salt, applied to areas of inflammation, and in

an antiscorbutic drink for scurvy and colds. Spruce gum was also used for caulking canoes. Various parts of the tree were also combined and used for stomach troubles, scabs, sores, as a salve for cuts and wounds, and in a tea for scurvy and as a cough remedy.

Medical Properties: Antinociceptive (analgesic; reduces sensitivity to pain), antioxidative, antibacterial, relaxant, possibly anticancerous

Uses: Antibacterial, pain relief, insecticide, antioxidant, expectorant, induces relaxation, nAChR (nicotinic acetylcholine receptor) inhibitor, prevents oxidation of LDL, GABA agonist, antimicrobial

Fragrant Influence: Releases emotional blocks, bringing about a feeling of balance and grounding

Technical Data: **Botanical Family:** Pinaceae; **Plant Origin:** Idaho; **Extraction Method:** Steam distilled from all tree parts; **Key Constituents:** Alpha-Pinene (15-40%), Camphene (6-8%), Beta-Pinene (6-11%), Myrcene (3-7%), Limonene (18-25%), Bornyl Acetate (3-10%); **ORAC:** 575 µTE/g

Idaho Ponderosa Pine (Pinus ponderosa)

This large pine tree is native to western North America but grows throughout the temperate world. The official state tree of Montana, the ponderosa pine, gains its fragrant scent from an abundance of terpenes, including Delta-3-Carene, Beta-Pinene, Alpha-Pinene, and Limonene, listed above. A measurement by Ascending the Giants in 2011 landed a ponderosa pine in the record books as the tallest known pine (268.29 feet tall). Native Americans used the ponderosa pine to reduce coughs and fevers, while the

Idaho Tansy

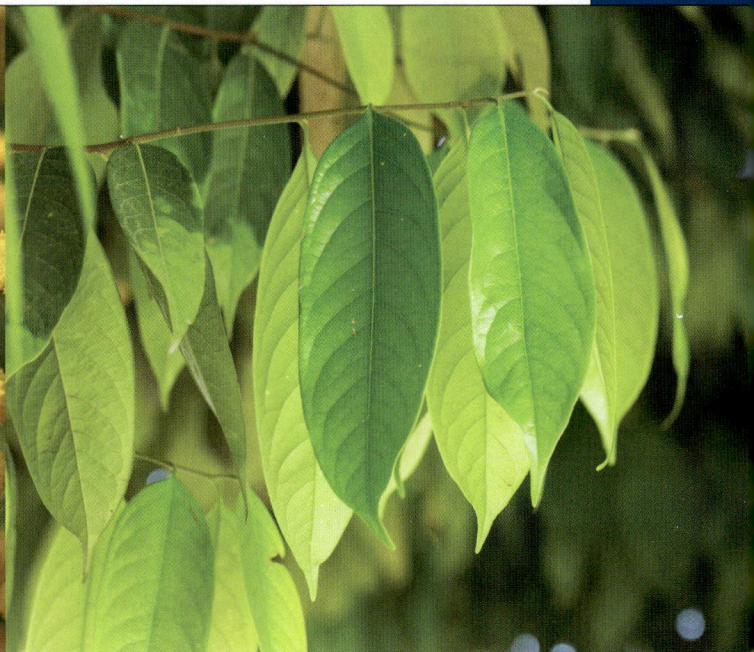

Ishpingo

pitch was used as an ointment for skin conditions. In sweat lodges, the tree boughs were used for muscular pain, and the pollen and needles were used in healing ceremonies.

Medical Properties: Antimicrobial, antifungal

Uses: Respiratory ailments, arthritis, rheumatism

Fragrant Influence: Relaxing, calming, and restorative; also emotionally uplifting

Cautions: Do not take if pregnant or planning on becoming pregnant. Not for use on children.

Technical Data: Botanical Family: Pinus; **Plant Origin:** Idaho; **Extraction Method:** Steam distilled from all tree parts; **Key Constituents:** Delta-3-Carene (35-50%), Beta-Pinene (16-30%), Alpha-Pinene (7-10%), Limonene (5-8%)

Idaho Tansy *(Tanacetum vulgare)*

This antimicrobial oil has been used extensively as an insect repellent. According to F. Joseph Montagna's herbal desk reference, it may tone the entire system (Montagna, 1990).

Medical Properties: Analgesic, antioxidant, antiviral, anticoagulant, immune stimulant, insect repellent

Uses: Arteriosclerosis, hypertension, arthritis/rheumatism

Caution: Do not use if pregnant.

Technical Data: Botanical Family: Asteraceae; **Plant Origin:** Idaho; **Extraction Method:** Steam distilled from leaves and stems; **Key Constituents:** Beta-Thujone (65-80%), Camphor (3-8%), Sabinene (1-4%), Germacrene D (3-7%)

Ishpingo *(Ocotea quixos)*

Ishpingo is a Hispanic name for Ocotea, which is distilled from the flower and fruit of a tree found in the Amazon wilderness on the ranges of the west side of the Andes Mountains. It is commonly referred to by the native people throughout Ecuador as false canilla or false cinnamon. The tree grows to a very large size, reaching up to 48 inches in diameter and over 60 feet tall, making a large canopy top. Historical usage of ocotea dates back more than 500 years, when it was used to aromatize sweets and cakes. Of 79 ocotea species' studies on PubMed, only two refer to the properties of ocotea essential oil distilled from flowers or fruit rather than the leaves and bark of the tree.

Medical Properties: Antimicrobial, antioxidant, antifungal

Technical Data: Botanical Family: Lauraceae; **Plant Origin:** Ecuador; **Extraction Method:** Steam distillation from flower/fruit; **Key Constituents:** Trans-Cinnamaldehyde (10-3%), Methyl Cinnamate (7-25%), Cinnamyl Acetate (5-18%), Alpha-Pinene (3-9%)

Jade Lemon/Jade Lemon Vitality™
(Citrus limon Eureka var. formosensis)

Taiwan and China are home to this exquisitely scented lemon variety. Unique among lemons, when fully mature it is a lovely green color, hence the name Jade Lemon. Not only is the color of this lemon unique, this essential oil has a tantalizing lemon-lime scent. Introduced at the 2014 YL convention, it has become a most beloved essential oil. Jade Lemon contains the same major constituents as Lemon essential oil but in slightly different percentages.

Jasmine

Juniper

Medical Properties: Antitumoral, antiseptic, improves microcirculation, immune stimulant (may increase white blood cells), improves memory, relaxation; rich in limonene, which has been extensively studied in over 50 clinical studies for its ability to combat tumor growth.

Uses: Used to uplift and stimulate the mind and body. Can be used in household cleaning or mixed with Citronella essential oil for a pleasant, citrus-scented insect repellant.

Technical Data: **Botanical Family:** Rutaceae; **Plant Origin:** Taiwan; **Extraction Method:** Cold pressed from rind; it takes 3,000 lemons to produce 1 kilo of oil; **Key Constituents:** Limonene (59-73%), Gamma-Terpinene (6-12%), Beta-Pinene (7-16%), Alpha-Pinene (1.5-3%), Sabinene (1.5-3%); **ORAC:** 660 µTE/100g

Jasmine *(Jasminum officinale)*

Jasmine is nicknamed the "queen of the night" and "moonlight of the grove." For centuries, women have treasured jasmine for its beautiful, seductive fragrance. It is an absolute, or essence, rather than an essential oil.

Note: One pound of jasmine oil requires about 1,000 pounds of jasmine or 3.6 million fresh, unpacked blossoms. The blossoms must be collected before sunrise, or much of the fragrance will have evaporated. The quality of the blossoms may also be compromised if they are crushed. A single pound of pure jasmine oil may cost between $1,200 and $4,500. In contrast, synthetic jasmine oils can be obtained for $3.50 per pound, but they do not possess the therapeutic qualities as the pure oil.

Medical Properties: Uplifting, antidepressant, stimulating, antibacterial, antiviral

Uses: Anxiety, depression, menstrual problems/PMS, skin problems (eczema, wrinkles, greasy), frigidity

Fragrant Influence: Uplifting, counteracts hopelessness, nervous exhaustion, anxiety, depression, indifference, and listlessness.

Technical Data: **Botanical Family:** Oleaceae; **Plant Origin:** India; **Extraction Method:** Absolute extraction from flower. Jasmine is actually an "essence" not an essential oil. The flowers must be picked at night to maximize fragrance; **Key Constituents:** Benzyl Acetate (18-28%), Benzyl Benzoate (14-21%), Linalol (3-8%), Phytol (6-12%), Isophytol (3-7%), Squalene (3-7%)

Juniper *(Juniperus osteosperma)*

Bundles of juniper berries were hung over doorways to ward off witches during medieval times. Juniper has been used for centuries as a diuretic. Until recently, French hospital wards burned sprigs of juniper and rosemary to protect from infection.

Medical Properties: Antiseptic, digestive cleanser/stimulant, purifying, detoxifying, increases circulation through the kidneys and promotes excretion of toxins, promotes nerve regeneration

Uses: Skin conditions (acne, eczema), liver problems, urinary/bladder infections, fluid retention

Laurus Nobilis

Lavandin

Fragrant Influence: Evokes feelings of health, love, and peace and may help to elevate one's spiritual awareness

Technical Data: **Botanical Family:** Cupressaceae; **Plant Origin:** Utah; **Extraction Method:** Steam distilled from stems and leaves (aerial parts); **Key Constituents:** Alpha-Pinene (20-40%), Sabinene (3-18%), Myrcene (1-6%), Camphor (10-18%), Limonene (3-8%), Bornyl Acetate (12-20%), Terpinen-4-ol (3-8%); **ORAC:** 250 µTE/100g

Laurus Nobilis/Laurus Nobilis Vitality™
(Bay Laurel) *(Laurus nobilis)*

Both the leaves and the black berries were used to alleviate indigestion and loss of appetite. During the Middle Ages, *Laurus nobilis* was used for angina, migraine, heart palpitations, and liver and spleen complaints.

Medical Properties: Antimicrobial, expectorant, mucolytic, antibacterial (staph, strep, *E. coli*), antifungal (candida), anticoagulant, anticonvulsant

Uses: Nerve regeneration, arthritis (rheumatoid), oral infections (gingivitis), respiratory infections, viral infections

Technical Data: **Botanical Family:** Lauraceae; **Plant Origin:** Croatia; **Extraction Method:** Steam distilled from leaves and twigs; **Key Constituents:** 1,8-Cineole (Eucalyptol) (40-50%), Alpha-Terpenyl Acetate (7-14%), Alpha-Pinene (4-8%), Beta-Pinene (3-6%), Sabinene (6-11%), Linalol (2-7%); **ORAC:** 98,900 µTE/100g

Lavandin *(Lavandula intermedia)*

Also known as *Lavandula* x *intermedia*, lavandin is a hybrid plant developed by crossing true lavender with spike lavender or aspic (*Lavandula latifolia*). It has been used to sterilize the animal cages in veterinary clinics and hospitals throughout Europe.

Medical Properties: Antibacterial, antifungal

Uses: Lavandin is a stronger antiseptic than lavender (*Lavandula angustifolia*). Its greater penetrating qualities make it well suited to help with respiratory, circulatory, and muscular conditions. However, its camphor content invalidates its use to soothe burns.

Fragrant Influence: Similar calming effects as lavender

Caution: Avoid using for burns; instead, use pure lavender (*Lavandula angustifolia*).

Technical Data: **Botanical Family:** Lamiaceae; **Plant Origin:** France; **Extraction Method:** Steam distilled from the flowering top; **Key Constituents:** Linalyl acetate (25-38%), Linalol (24-37%), Camphor (6-8.5%), 1,8-Cineole (Eucalyptol) (4-8%), Borneol (1.5-3.5%), Terpinen-4-ol (1.5-5%), Lavandulyl Acetate (1.5-3.5%)

Lavender/Lavender Vitality™
(Lavandula angustifolia)

The French scientist René Gattefossé was the first to discover lavender's ability to promote tissue regeneration and speed wound healing when he severely burned his arm in a laboratory explosion. Today, lavender is one of the few essential oils to still be listed in the British Pharmacopoeia.

Lavender

Ledum

Medical Properties: Antiseptic, antifungal, analgesic, antitumoral, anticonvulsant, vasodilating, relaxant, anti-inflammatory, reduces blood fat/cholesterol, combats excess sebum on skin

Uses: Respiratory infections, high blood pressure, arteriosclerosis, menstrual problems/PMS, skin conditions (perineal repair, acne, eczema, psoriasis, scarring, stretch marks), burns, hair loss, insomnia, nervous tension

Fragrant Influence: Calming, relaxing, and balancing, both physically and emotionally. Lavender has been documented to improve concentration and mental acuity.

Caution: True lavender is often adulterated with hybrid lavender (lavandin), synthetic linalol and linalyl acetate, or synthetic fragrance chemicals like ethyl vanillin.

Technical Data: **Botanical Family:** Lamiaceae; **Plant Origin:** Utah, Idaho, France; **Extraction Method:** Steam distilled from flowering top; **Key Constituents:** Linalyl Acetate (21-47%), Linalol (23-46%), Cis-Beta-Ocimene (1-8%), Trans-Beta-Ocimene (1-5%), Terpinen-4-ol (1-8%); **ORAC:** 360 µTE/100g

Ledum *(Rhododendrum groenlandicum)*

Known colloquially as "Labrador tea," ledum has been reclassified from the genus Ledum and is now classified as *Rhododendrum groenlandicum.* It is a strongly aromatic herb that has been used for centuries in folk medicine. The native people of Eastern Canada used this herb for tea, as

a general tonic, and to treat a variety of kidney-related problems. Ledum has helped protect the native people of North America against scurvy for more than 5,000 years. The Cree used it for fevers and colds.

Medical Properties: Anti-inflammatory, antitumoral, antibacterial, diuretic, liver-protectant

Uses: Liver problems/hepatitis/fatty liver, obesity, water retention

Technical Data: **Botanical Family:** Ericaceae; **Plant Origin:** North America (Canada); **Extraction Method:** Steam distilled from flowering tops; **Key Constituents:** Limonene (10-40%), Cis-Para-Mentha-1(7),8-dien-8-ol (1-12%), Trans-Para-Mentha-1(7),8-dien-8-ol (2-8%), Alpha-Selinene (4-20%), Trans-Para-Mentha-1,3,8-Triene (2-7%)

Lemon/Lemon Vitality™ *(Citrus limon)*

Lemon oil has been widely used in skin care to cleanse skin, reduce wrinkles, and combat acne. Lemon peel was used as an antiseptic, carminative, diuretic, eupeptic, a vascular stimulant and protector, and as a vitaminic (Arias, et al., 2005). It is also used as a flavorant for cleaning, cooking, and treating scurvy and a variety of other ailments.

Medical Properties: Antitumoral, antiseptic, improves microcirculation, immune stimulant (may increase white blood cells), improves memory, relaxation; rich in limonene, which has been extensively studied in over 50 clinical studies for its ability to combat tumor growth

Lemon

Lemongrass

Uses: Circulatory problems, arteriosclerosis, obesity, parasites, urinary tract infections, varicose veins, anxiety, hypertension, digestive problems, acne

Fragrant Influence: It promotes clarity of thought and purpose with a fragrance that is invigorating, enhancing, and warming.

A Mie University study found that citrus fragrances boosted immunity, induced relaxation, and reduced depression (Komori, et al., 1995).

Caution: Possible sun sensitivity.

Technical Data: Botanical Family: Rutaceae; **Plant Origin:** California, Italy; **Extraction Method:** Cold pressed from rind. It takes 3,000 lemons to produce 1 kilo of oil; **Key Constituents:** Limonene (59-73%), Gamma-Terpinene (6-12%), Beta-Pinene (7-16%), Alpha-Pinene (1.5-3%), Sabinene (1.5-3%); **ORAC:** 660 μTE/100g

Lemongrass/Lemongrass Vitality™

(Cymbopogon flexuosus)

Lemongrass is used for purification and digestion. Historically it was used for hypertension, inflammation, as a sedative, and for treatment of fevers and digestion. In a 2008 study, 91 single essential oils were tested against MRSA (Methicillin-resistant *Staphylococcus aureus*) and lemongrass. The study found that "Remarkably, lemongrass essential oil completely inhibited all MRSA growth on the plate" (Chao S, et al., 2008).

Medical Properties: Antifungal, antibacterial, antiparasitic, anti-inflammatory, regenerates connective tissues and ligaments, dilates blood vessels, improves circulation, promotes lymph flow, anticancerous. Several research articles document strong antifungal and antibacterial properties of lemongrass.

Uses: Bladder infection, respiratory/sinus infection, digestive problems, parasites, torn ligaments/muscles, fluid retention, varicose veins, salmonella, candida

Fragrant Influence: Promotes psychic awareness and purification

Technical Data: Botanical Family: Poaceae; **Plant Origin:** India, Guatemala; **Extraction Method:** Steam distilled from herb/grass; **Key Constituents:** Geranial (35-47%), Geraniol (1.5-8%), Neral (25-35%), Geranyl Acetate (1-6%); **ORAC:** 1,780 μTE/100g

Lemon Myrtle *(Backhousia citriodora)*

The aboriginal people of Australia valued lemon myrtle's flavor in cooking, calling it "bush food." It is also known as the "queen of lemon herbs." Lemon myrtle can replace lemon in milk-based foods, as it does not have lemon's curdling problems. Lemon myrtle was also widely used as a healing plant. It is the highest natural source of the constituent citral. Since citral, consisting of isomers geranial and neral, has a strong and sweet lemon scent, lemon myrtle continues to be valued in perfumery. It is used in health care and cleaning products such as soaps, shampoos, and lotions. Lemon myrtle is cultivated in Queensland and the north coast of New South Wales, Australia.

Lime

Mandarin

Medical Properties: Antiseptic, antimicrobial, antifungal, anti-inflammatory, central nervous system stimulant

Uses: Weight loss, respiratory/sinus infection, treatment of MCV (molluscum contagiosum virus) in children

Fragrant Influences: Uplifting and invigorating, lemon myrtle's fresh and sweet lemon scent encourages follow-through with goals.

Technical Data: Botanical Family: Myrtaceae; **Plant Origin:** Australia; **Extraction Method:** Steam distilled from leaves; **Key Constituents:** Geranial (45-60%), Neral (30-45%); **ORAC:** 2368 μmole TE/gram

Lime/Lime Vitality™

(Citrus latifolia or C. aurantifolia)

Primarily used in skin care and in supporting and strengthening the respiratory and immune systems.

Medical Properties: Antirheumatic, antiviral, antibacterial

Uses: Skin conditions (acne, herpes), insect bites, respiratory problems, decongests the lymphatic system, weight loss

Caution: Possible sun sensitivity.

Technical Data: Botanical Family: Rutaceae; **Plant Origin:** *C. latifolia:* Mexico, *C. aurantifolia Swingle:* Southeast Asia; **Extraction Method:** Cold expression from the rind of the unripe fruit; **Key Constituents:** Limonene (42-50%), Gamma-Terpinene (8-11%), Beta-Pinene (18-24%); **ORAC:** 26,200 μTE/100g

Mandarin *(Citrus reticulata)*

This fruit was traditionally given to Imperial Chinese officials named the Mandarins.

Medical Properties: Light antispasmodic, digestive tonic (digestoid), antifungal, and stimulates the gallbladder; rich in limonene, which has been extensively studied in over 50 clinical studies for its ability to combat tumor growth

Uses: Digestive problems, fluid retention, insomnia, anxiety, intestinal problems, skin problems (congested and oily skin, scars, acne), stretch marks (when combined with either Jasmine, Lavender, Sandalwood, and/or Frankincense)

Fragrant Influence: Appeasing, gentle, promotes happiness. A Mie University study found that citrus fragrances boosted immunity, induced relaxation, and reduced depression (Komori, et al., 1995).

Caution: Possible sun sensitivity.

Technical Data: Botanical Family: Rutaceae; **Plant Origin:** Madagascar, Italy; **Extraction Method:** Cold pressed from rind; **Key Constituents:** Limonene (65-75%), Gamma-Terpinene (16-22%), Alpha-Pinene (2-3%), Beta-Pinene (1.2-2%), Myrcene (1.5-2%); **ORAC:** 26,500 μTE/100g

Manuka

Marjoram

Manuka *(Leptospermum scoparium)*

Similar to tea tree oil but warmer, richer, and milder, manuka oil has long been used in treatment of skin, foot, and hair problems. Like tea tree oil, it is antibacterial, antiviral, and antifungal, so it can help in eliminating a wide variety of problems. Some research suggests that manuka may be more potent in fighting bacteria and fungi than tea tree oil. "Manuka" is the Maori name for the bushy tree from which the oil is produced.

Medical Properties: Antibacterial, antifungal, anti-inflammatory, anti-acne. Although research is ongoing, many believe manuka has potential in fighting antibiotic-resistant organisms, such as MRSA. A leading German aromatherapist reports that the manuka aroma is psychologically very beneficial for people who suffer from stress and anxiety. Its skin-healing properties are exceptional.

Uses: Skin infections, acne, bedsores, mild sunburn, fungal infections, itching, respiratory infections, sore throats, pain relief in muscles and joints, athletes foot and ringworm, dandruff, body odor, cold sores, dermatitis, rhinitis, tonsillitis, stress relief, sleep aid

Technical Data: **Botanical Family:** Myrtaceae; **Plant Origin:** New Zealand and Australia; **Extraction Method:** Steam distillation of chopped leaves and small stems; **Key Constituents:** Leptospermone (16-19%), Trans-Calamenene (12-16%), Flavesone (2-8%), Isoleptospermone (4-7%), Alpha-Copaene (3-6%), Cadena-3,5-diene (3-7%), Alpha-Selinene (2-5%); **ORAC:** 106,200 µTE/100g

Marjoram/Marjoram Vitality™
(Origanum majorana)

Marjoram was known as the "herb of happiness" to the Romans and "joy of the mountains" to the Greeks. It was believed to increase longevity. Listed in Dioscorides' *De Materia Medica* (AD 78), Europe's first authoritative guide to medicines, which became the standard reference work for herbal treatments for over 1,700 years. It was listed in Hildegard's *Medicine,* a compilation of early German medicines by highly regarded Benedictine herbalist Hildegard of Bingen (1098-1179).

Medical Properties: Its muscle-soothing properties help relieve body and joint discomfort. May also help soothe the digestive tract and is a general relaxant. Antibacterial, antifungal, vasodilator, lowers blood pressure, promotes intestinal peristalsis, expectorant, mucolytic.

Uses: Arthritis/rheumatism, muscle/nerve pain, headaches, circulatory disorders, respiratory infections, menstrual problems/PMS, fungal infections, ringworm, shingles, sores, spasms, and fluid retention

Fragrant Influence: Assists in calming the nerves

Technical Data: **Botanical Family:** Lamiaceae; **Plant Origin:** France, Egypt; **Extraction Method:** Steam distilled from leaves; **Key Constituents:** Terpinen-4-ol (20-33%), Gamma-Terpinene (10-17%), Linalol + Cis-4-Thujanol (4-26%), Alpha-Terpinene (6-10%), Alpha-Terpineol (2-7%), Sabinene (4-9%); **ORAC:** 130,900 µTE/100g

Mastrante

Melaleuca Quinquenervia

Mastrante *(Lippia alba)*

The plant Mastrante *(Lippia alba)* was given its botanical name by the Scottish botanist Philip Miller (1691-1771) and the British plant taxonomist N.E. Brown (1849-1934). As a result, in scientific literature it is listed as: *"Lippia alba* (Miller or Mill.) N.E. Brown."* In Brazil, it is called *"erva cidreira do campo,"* which means "lemon balm of the field." The aromatic shrub grows in southern Texas, Mexico, the Caribbean, and Central and South America.

The leaves of Mastrante are used to flavor foods, most notably molé sauces from Oaxaca, Mexico. In folk medicine it is known as a sedative, an antidepressant, and has pain-relieving properties.

Medical Properties: Antioxidant, analgesic, antibacterial, antiviral, antifungal, antispasmodic

Uses: Anti-candida agent, coughs, bronchitis, migraine headaches in women, vasorelaxant for heart disease

Fragrant Influence: This earthy aroma is grounding and calming.

Technical Data: **Botanical Family:** Verbenaceae; **Plant Origin:** Ecuador; **Extraction Method:** Steam distilled from leaves; **Key Constituents:** Carvone (35-50%), Limonene (20-30%), Germacrene D (10-17%), Alpha-Bourbonene (1-3%), Camphor (0.5-2%)

Melaleuca Alternifolia
(See Tea Tree)

Melaleuca Ericifolia *(Melaleuca ericifolia)*

The Aboriginal people of Australia used the bark of Melaleuca Ericifolia as roofing for their shelters and for blankets and paintings. Oil from the leaves was used for medicine.

Medical Properties: Powerful antibacterial, antifungal, antiviral, antiparasitic, anti-inflammatory

Uses: Herpes virus, respiratory/sinus infections

Technical Data: **Botanical Family:** Myrtaceae; **Plant Origin:** Australia; **Extraction Method:** Steam distilled from leaves and branches; **Key Constituents:** Alpha-Pinene (5-10%), 1,8-Cineole + Beta-Phellandrene (18-28%), Alpha-Terpineol (1-5%), Para-Cymene (1-6%), Linalol (34-45%), Aromadendrene (2-6%); **ORAC:** 61,100 µTE/100g

Melaleuca Quinquenervia (Niaouli)
(Melaleuca viridiflora)

A brew from the bruised leaves of *Melaleuca quinquenervia* was used by Aboriginal people in Australia for colds, headaches, and other sicknesses.

Medical Properties: Male hormone-like, anti-inflammatory, antibacterial, antiviral, and antiparasitic (amoeba and parasites in the blood), vasodilating, skin penetration enhancer (hormones)

Uses: Hypertension, urinary tract/bladder infections, respiratory/sinus infections, allergies

Technical Data: **Botanical Family:** Myrtaceae; **Plant Origin:** Australia, New Caledonia; **Extraction Method:** Steam distilled from leaves and twigs; **Key Constituents:** 1,8-Cineole (Eucalyptol) (55-75%), Alpha-Pinene (5-12%), Limonene (1-9%), Beta-Pinene (1-5%), Viridiflorol (2-6%); **ORAC:** 18,600 µTE/100g

Melissa

Mountain Savory

Melissa *(Melissa officinalis)*
(Also known as lemon balm)

Anciently, melissa was used for nervous disorders and many different ailments dealing with the heart or the emotions. It was also used to promote fertility. Melissa was the main ingredient in Carmelite water, distilled in France since 1611 by the Carmelite monks.

The University of Maryland Medical Center writes that Melissa "was used as far back as the Middle Ages to reduce stress and anxiety, promote sleep, improve appetite, and ease pain and discomfort from indigestion."

An old Arabian proverb states, "Balm makes the heart merry and joyful," which may be why Avicenna advocated the use of lemon balm in treating depression and anxiety.

Recent studies document its antiviral activities and memory and learning benefits.

Medical Properties: Anti-inflammatory, antiviral, relaxant, hypotensive, anti-oxidative, antitumoral

Uses: Viral infections (herpes, etc.), depression, anxiety, insomnia

Fragrant Influence: Brings out gentle characteristics within people. It is calming and uplifting and balances emotions. It removes emotional blocks and instills a positive outlook on life.

Technical Data: **Botanical Family:** Lamiaceae; **Plant Origin:** Utah, Idaho, France; **Extraction Method:** Steam distilled from aerial parts before flowering; **Key Constituents:** Geranial (25-35%), Neral (18-28%), Beta-Caryophyllene (12-19%); **ORAC:** 134,300 µTE/100g

Micromeria *(Micromeria fruticosa)*

Micromeria is found in Israel and in the eastern Mediterranean. It is known in folk medicine as having anti-inflammatory properties and for digestive support.

Medical Properties: Anti-inflammatory, gastroprotective

Uses: Stomach upsets

Fragrant Influence: Revitalizes and refreshes the mind

Caution: Contains high levels of pulegone. Do not use if pregnant or trying to conceive.

Technical Data: **Botanical Family:** Lamiaceae; **Plant Origin:** Israel; **Extraction Method:** Steam distilled from leaf, stem, and flower; **Key Constituents:** Pulegone (50-65%), Menthol (7-12%), Beta-Caryophyllene (3-9%), Isopulegol (3-6%), Menthone (1-5%), Neomenthol (1-5%)

Mountain Savory/Mountain Savory Vitality™ *(Satureja montana)*

Mountain savory has been used historically as a general tonic for the body.

Medical Properties: Strong antibacterial, antifungal, antiviral, antiparasitic, immune stimulant, anti-inflammatory action

Uses: Viral infections (herpes, HIV, etc.), scoliosis/lumbago/back problems

Myrrh

Myrtle

Fragrant Influence: Revitalizes and stimulates the nervous system. It is a powerful energizer and motivator.

Technical Data: Botanical Family: Lamiaceae; **Plant Origin:** France; **Extraction Method:** Steam distilled from flowering plant; **Key Constituents:** Carvacrol (22-35%), Thymol (14-24%), Gamma-Terpinene (8-15%), Carvacrol Methyl Ether (4-9%), Beta-Caryophyllene (3-7%); **ORAC:** 11,300 µTE/100g

Myrrh (Commiphora myrrha)

It is mentioned in one of the oldest known medical records, the Ebers Papyrus (dating from 16th century BC), an ancient Egyptian list of 877 prescriptions and recipes. The Arabian people used myrrh for many skin conditions such as chapped and cracked skin and wrinkles. It was listed in Hildegard's *Medicine*, a compilation of early German medicines by highly regarded Benedictine herbalist Hildegard of Bingen (1098-1179).

Medical Properties: Powerful antioxidant, antitumoral, anti-inflammatory, antibacterial, antiviral, antiparasitic, analgesic/anesthetic

Uses: Diabetes, cancer, hepatitis, fungal infections (candida, ringworm), tooth/gum infections, skin conditions (eczema, chapped, cracked, wrinkles, stretch marks)

Fragrant Influence: Promotes spiritual awareness and is uplifting. It contains sesquiterpenes, which stimulate the limbic system of the brain (the center of memory and emotions) and the hypothalamus, pineal, and

pituitary glands. The hypothalamus is the master gland of the human body, producing many vital hormones, including thyroid and growth hormone.

Technical Data: Botanical Family: Burseraceae; **Plant Origin:** Somalia; **Extraction Method:** Steam distilled from gum/resin; **Key Constituents:** Lindestrene (7-16%), Curzerene (9-32%), Furanoendesma-1,3-diene (25-50%), 2-Methoxy Furanogermacrene (1-10%), Beta-Elemene (1-9%); **ORAC:** 379,800 µTE/100g

Myrtle (Myrtus communis)

Myrtle has been researched by Dr. Daniel Pénoël for normalizing hormonal imbalances of the thyroid and ovaries, as well as balancing the hypothyroid. It has also been researched for its soothing effects on the respiratory system.

Medical Properties: Antimutagenic, liver stimulant, prostate and thyroid stimulant, sinus/lung decongestant, antispasmodic, antihyperglycemic, anti-inflammatory, antinociceptive

Uses: Thyroid problems, throat/lung/sinus infections, prostate problems, skin irritations (acne, blemishes, bruises, oily skin, psoriasis, etc.), muscle spasms

Fragrant Influence: Elevating and euphoric

Technical Data: Botanical Family: Myrtaceae; **Plant Origin:** Tunisia, Morocco; **Extraction Method:** Steam distilled from leaves; **Key Constituents:** Alpha-Pinene (15-60%), 1,8-Cineole (Eucalyptol) (15-40%), Limonene (4-18%), Myrtenyl Acetate (trace-20%); **ORAC:** 25,400 µTE/100g

Neroli

Nutmeg

Neroli (Bitter Orange) *(Citrus aurantium amara)*

Highly regarded by the ancient Egyptians for its ability to heal the mind, body, and spirit.

Medical Properties: Antiparasitic, digestive tonic, antidepressive, hypotensive (lowers blood pressure)

Uses: Hypertension, anxiety, depression, hysteria, insomnia, skin conditions (scars, stretch marks, thread veins, wrinkles)

Fragrant Influence: A natural relaxant used to treat depression and anxiety. It strengthens and stabilizes the emotions and uplifts and inspires the hopeless, encouraging confidence, courage, joy, peace, and sensuality. It brings everything into focus at the moment.

Technical Data: **Botanical Family:** Rutaceae; **Plant Origin:** Tunisia; **Extraction Method:** Steam distilled from flowers of the bitter orange tree; **Key Constituents:** Linalol (28-44%), Limonene (9-18%), Beta-Pinene (7-17%), Linalyl Acetate (3-15%), Trans-Ocimene (3-8%), Alpha-Terpineol (2-5.5%), Trans-Nerolidol (1-5%), Myrcene (1-4%)

Northern Lights Black Spruce

(Picea mariana)

The Lakota Indians used black spruce to strengthen their ability to communicate with the Great Spirit. Traditionally, it was believed to possess the frequency of prosperity.

Medical Properties: Antispasmodic, antiparasitic, antiseptic, anti-inflammatory, hormone-like, cortisone-like, immune stimulant, antidiabetic

Uses: Arthritis/rheumatism, fungal infections (candida), sinus/respiratory infections, sciatica/lumbago

Fragrant Influence: Releases emotional blocks, bringing about a feeling of balance and grounding

Technical Data: **Botanical Family:** Pinaceae; **Plant Origin:** Canada; **Extraction Method:** Steam distilled from entire tree; **Key Constituents:** Bornyl Acetate (24-35%), Camphene (14-26%), Alpha-Pinene (12-19%), Beta-Pinene (2-10%), Delta-3-Carene (4-10%), Limonene (3-6%), Myrcene (1-5%), Santene (1-5%), Tricyclene (1-4%)

Nutmeg/Nutmeg Vitality™

(Myristica fragrans)

Nutmeg was listed in Hildegard's *Medicine,* a compilation of early German medicines by highly regarded Benedictine herbalist Hildegard of Bingen (1098-1179).

Medical Properties: Anti-inflammatory, anticoagulant, antiseptic, antiparasitic, analgesic, liver protectant, stomach protectant (ulcers), circulatory stimulant, adrenal stimulant, muscle relaxing, increases production of growth hormone/melatonin

Uses: Rheumatism/arthritis, cardiovascular disease, hypertension, hepatitis, ulcers, digestive disorders, antiparasitic, nerve pain, fatigue/exhaustion, neuropathy

Technical Data: **Botanical Family:** Myristicaceae; **Plant Origin:** Tunisia, Indonesia; **Extraction Method:** Steam distilled from fruits and seeds; **Key Constituents:** Sabinene (14-29%), Beta-Pinene (13-18%), Alpha-Pinene (15-28%), Limonene (2-7%), Gamma-Terpinene (2-6%), Terpinene-4-ol (2-6%), Myristicine (5-12%); **ORAC:** 158,100 µTE/100g

Plant Name

Orange

Ocotea *(Ocotea quixos)*

Ocotea is distilled from a tree found in the Amazon wilderness, on the ranges of the west side of the Andes Mountains. It is commonly referred to by the native people throughout Ecuador as *Ishpingo* and is considered to be a false canilla or false cinnamon. The tree grows to a very large size, reaching up to 48 inches in diameter and over 60 feet tall, making a large canopy top. Historical usage of ocotea dates back more than 500 years, when it was used to aromatize sweets and cakes.

Medical Properties: Antifungal, disinfectant, anti-inflammatory

Uses: Hypertension, high blood pressure, anxiety, internal irritation, may lower insulin needs for diabetics and reduce blood sugar fluctuations, infection, digestive support

Fragrant Influence: Has a complex aroma, which may increase feelings of fullness; related to the cinnamon species but has an aroma that is different from any common cinnamon

Technical Data: **Botanical Family:** Lauraceae; **Plant Origin:** Ecuador, Central and South America; **Extraction Method:** Steam distilled from the leaves; **Key Constituents:** Beta-Caryophyllene (10-35%), Cinnamyl Acetate (1-24%), Methyl Cinnamate (4-24%), Alpha-Humulene (1-17%), Trans-Cinnamaldehyde (trace-12%)

Orange/Orange Vitality™ *(Citrus sinensis)*

Beloved for its clean, fresh scent, Orange essential oil was also shown to reduce anxiety in children awaiting dental treatment. Salivary cortisol levels were lowered as were pulse rates (Jafarzadeh, 2013).

Medical Properties: Antitumoral, relaxant, anticoagulant, circulatory stimulant. Rich in limonene, which has been extensively studied in over 50 clinical studies for its ability to combat tumor growth.

Uses: Arteriosclerosis, hypertension, cancer, insomnia, and complexion (dull and oily), fluid retention, wrinkles

Fragrant Influence: Uplifting and antidepressant. A Mie University study found that citrus fragrances boosted immunity, induced relaxation, and reduced depression (Komori, et al., 1995).

Caution: Possible sun sensitivity.

Technical Data: **Botanical Family:** Rutaceae; **Plant Origin:** USA, South Africa, Italy, China; **Extraction Method:** Cold pressed from rind; **Key Constituents:** Limonene (85-96%), Myrcene (0.5-3%); **ORAC:** 1,890 µTE/100g

Oregano

Palmarosa

Oregano/Oregano Vitality™

(Origanum vulgare) (Syn. O. majorana)

Listed in Hildegard's *Medicine,* a compilation of early German medicines by highly regarded Benedictine herbalist Hildegard of Bingen (1098-1179).

Medical Properties: Antiaging, powerful antiviral, antibacterial, antifungal, antiparasitic, anti-inflammatory, antioxidant, immune stimulant, antinociceptive, radioprotective, liver protectant

Uses: Arthritis, rheumatism, respiratory infectious diseases, infections, tuberculosis, digestive problems

Fragrant Influence: Creates a feeling of security.

Caution: High in phenols, Oregano may irritate the nasal membranes or skin if inhaled directly from diffuser or bottle or applied neat.

Technical Data: **Botanical Family:** Lamiaceae; **Plant Origin:** USA, France, Germany, Turkey; **Extraction Method:** Steam distilled from leaves; **Key Constituents:** Carvacrol (60-75%), Gamma-Terpinene (3.5-8.5%), Para-Cymene (5.5-9%), Beta-Caryophyllene (2-5%), Myrcene (1-3%), Thymol (0-5%); **ORAC:** 15,300 µTE/100g

Palmarosa *(Cymbopogon martini)*

A relative of lemongrass, palmarosa was used in temple incense by the ancient Egyptians.

Medical Properties: Antibacterial, antifungal, antiviral, supports heart and nervous system, reduces blood sugar fluctuations, stimulates new skin cell growth, regulates sebum production in skin

Uses: Fungal infections/candida, neuroprotective, cardiovascular/circulatory diseases, digestive problems, skin problems (acne, eczema)

Fragrant Influence: Creates a feeling of security. It also helps to reduce stress and tension and promotes recovery from nervous exhaustion.

Technical Data: **Botanical Family:** Poaceae; **Plant Origin:** India; **Extraction Method:** Steam distilled from leaves; **Key Constituents:** Geraniol (70-85%), Geranyl Acetate (6-10%), Linalol (3-7%); **ORAC:** 127,800 µTE/100g

Palo Santo *(Bursera graveolens)*

Palo Santo comes from the same botanical family as Frankincense, although it is found in South America. Like Frankincense, Palo Santo is known as a spiritual oil, with a deep-rooted tradition in which it was used by the Incas to purify and cleanse the air of negative energies and for good luck. It is used in South America to repel mosquitoes, for fevers, infections, and skin diseases. It is currently used by shamans of the Andes in curing ceremonies. Even its Spanish name reflects how highly this oil was regarded: *palo santo* means "holy or sacred wood."

Note: Constituents can vary depending on whether the wood is harvested from coastal or inland areas and if the trunk is red or white.

Medical Properties: Anticancerous, antiblastic, anti-inflammatory, antibacterial, antifungal, antiviral

Patchouli

Peppermint

Uses: Inflammation, regrowth of knee cartilage, joints, arthritis, rheumatism, gout, respiratory problems, reduces airborne contaminants when diffused

Technical Data: **Botanical Family:** Burseraceae; **Plant Origin:** Ecuador; **Extraction Method:** Steam distilled from the sawdust of the dead bark, wood, and branches; **Key Constituents:** Limonene (45-80%), Alpha-Terpineol (4-18%), Para-Cymene (1-6%), Carvone (0.5-6%), Beta-Bisabolene (0.5-7), Fonenol (0.5-4%)

Patchouli *(Pogostemon cablin)*

While Patchouli oil is known as an all-purpose insect repellent, it is also highly prized in the perfumery industry. Patchouli has many benefits for chapped and wrinkled skin.

Medical Properties: Relaxant, antitumoral, digestive aid that combats nausea, anti-inflammatory, antimicrobial, antifungal, insecticidal, prevents wrinkles and chapped skin, relieves itching

Uses: Hypertension, inflammatory bowel disease, skin conditions (eczema, acne), fluid retention, Listeria infection, insect repellent

Fragrant Influence: A relaxant that clarifies thoughts, allowing the discarding of jealousies, obsessions, and insecurities.

Technical Data: **Botanical Family:** Lamiaceae; **Plant Origin:** Indonesia; **Extraction Method:** Steam distilled from leaves and stems; **Key Constituents:** Patchoulol (27-35%), Bulnesene (13-21%), Alpha-Guaiene (11-16%), Beta-Patchoulene (1.8-3.5%), Beta-Caryophyllene (2-5%), Pogostol (1-2.5%), Norpatchoulenol (0.35-1%), Copaene (trace-1%); **ORAC:** 49,400 µTE/100g

Peppermint/Peppermint Vitality™
(Mentha piperita)

Peppermint is one of the oldest and most highly regarded herbs for soothing digestion. Jean Valnet, MD, studied peppermint's effect on the liver and respiratory systems. Alan Hirsch, MD, studied peppermint's ability to directly affect the brain's satiety center (the ventromedial nucleus of the hypothalamus), which triggers a sensation of fullness after meals. A highly regarded digestive stimulant.

Medical Properties: Anti-inflammatory, antitumoral, antiparasitic (worms), antibacterial, antiviral, antifungal, gallbladder/digestive stimulant, pain relieving, curbs appetite

Uses: Rheumatism/arthritis, respiratory infections (pneumonia, tuberculosis, etc.), obesity, viral infections (herpes simplex, herpes zoster, cold sores, human papilloma virus, etc.), fungal infections/candida, digestive problems, headaches, nausea, skin conditions (itchy skin, varicose veins, eczema, psoriasis, dermatitis), scoliosis/lumbago/back problems

Fragrant Influence: Purifying and stimulating to the conscious mind.

Cautions: Avoid contact with eyes, mucus membranes, sensitive skin, or fresh wounds or burns.

Technical Data: **Botanical Family:** Lamiaceae; **Plant Origin:** North America, Mediterranean area, Great Britain; **Extraction Method:** Steam distilled from leaves and stems; **Key Constituents:** Menthol (25-50%), Menthone (12-44%), Menthofuran (0.5-5%), 1.8-Cineole (Eucalyptol) (1-8%), Isomenthone (1-7%), Neomenthol (1.5-7%), Pulegone (0.5-3%), Menthyl Acetate (1-18%); **ORAC:** 37,300 µTE/100g

Petitgrain

Plectranthus Oregano

Petitgrain (Citrus aurantium amara)
(Syn. Citrus sinensis)

Petitgrain derives its name from the extraction of the oil, which at one time was from the green, unripe oranges when they were still about the size of a cherry.

Medical Properties: Antispasmodic, anti-inflammatory, relaxant, reestablishes nerve equilibrium

Uses: Insomnia, anxiety, muscle spasms, skin conditions, antitumoral

Fragrant Influence: Uplifting and refreshing to the senses; clears confusion, reduces mental fatigue and depression; stimulates the mind and improves memory.

Technical Data: Botanical Family: Rutaceae; **Plant Origin:** Paraguay, **Extraction Method:** Steam distilled from leaves and twigs; **Key Constituents:** Linalyl Acetate (40-55%), Linalol (15-30%), Alpha-Terpineol (3.5-7.5%), Geranyl Acetate (2-5%), Geraniol (2-4.5%); **ORAC:** 73,600 µTE/100g

Pine (Pinus sylvestris)

Pine was first investigated by Hippocrates, the father of Western medicine, for its benefits to the respiratory system. In 1990, Dr. Pénoël and Dr. Franchomme described pine oil's antiseptic properties in their medical textbook. Pine is also used in massage for stressed muscles and joints. It shares many of the same properties as *Eucalyptus globulus*, and the action of both oils is enhanced when blended. Native Americans stuffed mattresses with pine needles to repel lice and fleas. It was used to treat lung infections and even added to baths to revitalize those suffering from mental or emotional fatigue.

Medical Properties: Hormone-like, antidiabetic, cortisone-like, antiseptic, lymphatic stimulant

Uses: Throat/lung/sinus infections, rheumatism/arthritis, skin parasites, urinary tract infection, anticancer

Fragrant Influence: Relieves anxiety and revitalizes mind, body, and spirit. It also has an empowering, yet grounding fragrance.

Caution: Beware of pine oils adulterated with turpentine, a low-cost, but potentially hazardous, filler.

Technical Data: Botanical Family: Pinaceae (pine); **Plant Origin:** Austria, USA, Canada; **Extraction Method:** Steam distilled from needles; **Key Constituents:** Alpha-Pinene (55-70%), Beta-Pinene (3-8%), Limonene (5-10%), Delta-3-Carene (6-12%)

Plectranthus Oregano
(Plectranthus amboinicus)

The leaves of this plant have been used in traditional medicine for coughs, sore throats, and nasal congestion. Also used for infections and rheumatism, Plectranthus Oregano's flavor makes it popular for cooking, especially in soups.

Medical Properties: Antitumoral, antibacterial, antioxidant, analgesic, anti-inflammatory, antihyperlipodemic, liver protectant

Uses: Infections, cancer, arthritis, diabetes, rheumatism

Technical Data: Botanical Family: Lamiaceae; **Plant Origin:** Ecuador; **Extraction Method:** Steam distilled from leaves; **Key Constituents:** Para-Cymene (14-27%), Gamma-Terpinene (16-24%), Carvacrol (25-45%), Beta-Caryophyllene (4-11%), Alpha-Bergamotene (2-6%)

Ravintsara

Roman Chamomile

Ravintsara *(Cinnamomum camphora)*

Ravintsara is referred to by the people of Madagascar as "the oil that heals." It is antimicrobial and supporting to the nerves and respiratory system. It is also known to be clarifying, stimulating, and purifying. It also helps to clear brain fog and strengthen motivation.

Medical Properties: Antitumoral, antiviral, antibacterial

Uses: Herpes virus/viral infections (including colds, respiratory infections), throat/lung infections, hepatitis, shingles, pneumonia

Technical Data: **Botanical Family:** Lauraceae; **Plant Origin:** Madagascar; **Extraction Method:** Steam distilled from branches and leaves; **Key Constituents:** 1,8-Cineole (Eucalyptol) (50-65%), Sabinene (9-16%), Alpha-Terpineol (5-10%), Alpha-Pinene (4-6%); **ORAC:** 890 µTE/100g

Roman Chamomile
(Anthemis nobilis) (Syn. Chamaemelum nobile)

Used in Europe for skin regeneration. For centuries, mothers have used chamomile to calm crying children, combat digestive and liver ailments, and relieve toothaches.

Medical Properties: Relaxant, antispasmodic, anti-inflammatory, antiparasitic, antibacterial, anesthetic

Uses: Relieves restlessness, anxiety, ADHD, depression, insomnia, skin conditions (acne, dermatitis, eczema)

Fragrant Influence: Because it is calming and relaxing, it can combat depression, insomnia, and stress. It minimizes anxiety, irritability, and nervousness. It

may also dispel anger, stabilize the emotions, and help to release emotions that are linked to the past.

Technical Data: **Botanical Family:** Asteraceae; **Plant Origin:** Utah, France; **Extraction Method:** Steam distilled from flowering top; **Key Constituents:** Isobutyl Angelate + Isamyl Methacrylate (30-45%), Isoamyl Angelate (12-22%), Methyl Allyl Angelate (6-10%), Isobutyl n-butyrate (2-9%), 2-Methyl Butyl Angelate (3-7%); **ORAC:** 240 µTE/100g

Rose *(Rosa damascena)*

Rose has been used for the skin for thousands of years. The Arab physician, Avicenna, was responsible for first distilling rose oil, eventually authoring an entire book on the healing attributes of the rose water derived from the distillation of rose. Throughout much of ancient history, the oil was produced by enfleurage, a process of pressing the petals along with a vegetable oil to extract the essence. Today, however, almost all rose oils are solvent extracted.

Note: The Bulgarian *Rosa damascena* (high in citronellol) is very different from Moroccan *Rosa centifolia* (high in phenyl ethanol). They have different colors, aromas, and therapeutic actions.

Medical Properties: Anti-inflammatory, anti-HIV, antioxidant, anxiolytic, hepatoprotective, relaxant, reduces scarring, antiulcer, immunomodulating, cancer chemopreventive, DNA damage prevention

Uses: Hypertension, heart strengthening, anxiety, viral infections (herpes simplex), skin conditions (scarring, wrinkles, acne), ulcers

Rose

Rosemary

Fragrant Influence: Its beautiful fragrance is intoxicating and aphrodisiac-like. It helps bring balance and harmony, allowing one to overcome insecurities. The effect of rose on the heart brings good cheer with calming and a lightness of spirit.

Technical Data: Botanical Family: Rosaceae; **Plant Origin:** Bulgaria, Turkey; **Extraction Method:** Therapeutic-grade oil is steam distilled from flowers (a two-part process); **Key Constituents:** Citronellol (24-50%), Geraniol (10-22%), Nerol (5-12%), Beta-Phenylethyl Alcohol (0.5-5%); **ORAC:** 160,400 µTE/100g

Rose of Sharon (Cistus ladaniferus)

(See Cistus)

Rosemary/Rosemary Vitality™

(Rosmarinus officinalis)

Rosemary was part of the "Marseilles Vinegar" or "Four Thieves Vinegar" that bandits who robbed the dead and dying used to protect themselves during the 15th century plague. The name of the oil is derived from the Latin words for dew of the sea (ros + marinus). According to folklore history, rosemary originally had white flowers; however, they turned red after the Virgin Mary laid her cloak on the bush.

At the time of ancient Greece (about 1,000 BC), rosemary was burned as incense. Later cultures believed that it warded off devils, a practice that eventually became adopted by the sick, who then burned rosemary to protect against infection.

It was listed in Hildegard's *Medicine,* a compilation of early German medicines by highly regarded Benedictine herbalist Hildegard of Bingen (1098-1179).

Until recently, French hospitals used rosemary to disinfect the air.

Medical Properties: Liver-protecting, anti-inflammatory, antitumoral, antifungal, antibacterial, anticancer, antidepressant, hypertension moderator (high blood pressure), enhances mental clarity/concentration

Uses: Infectious disease, liver conditions/hepatitis, throat/lung infections, hair loss (alopecia areata), acne, impaired memory/Alzheimer's, weight loss

Fragrant Influence: Helps overcome mental fatigue and improves mental clarity and focus. University of Miami scientists found that inhaling rosemary boosted alertness, eased anxiety, and amplified analytic and mental ability.

Cautions: Do not use on children under 4 years of age. Do not use Rosemary for high blood pressure if already taking ACE inhibitor prescription drugs.

Technical Data: Botanical Family: Lamiaceae; **Plant Origin:** Tunisia, Morocco, Spain; **Extraction Method:** Steam distilled from leaves; **Key Constituents:** 1,8-Cineole (Eucalyptol) (38-55%), Camphor (5-15%), Alpha-Pinene (9-14%), Beta-Pinene (4-9%), Camphene (2.5-6%), Borneol (1.5-5%), Limonene (1-4%); **ORAC:** 330 µTE/100g

Rosewood

Ruta

Rosewood *(Aniba rosaeodora)*

Rosewood essential oil is antibacterial and antiviral, but it is most well-known for improving the skin. In France, it is used for natural skin rejuvenation.

Medical Properties: Antibacterial, antiviral, antiparasitic, antifungal, antimutagenic, anxiolytic, improves skin elasticity.

Uses: Fungal infections/candida, skin conditions (eczema, psoriasis)

Fragrant Influence: Empowering and emotionally stabilizing

Technical Data: Botanical Family: Lauraceae; **Plant Origin:** Brazil; **Extraction Method:** Steam distilled from wood; **Key Constituents:** Linalol (70-90%), Alpha-Terpineol (2-7%), Alpha-Copaene (trace-3%), 1,8-Cineole (Eucalyptol) (trace-3%), Geraniol (0.5-2.5%); **ORAC:** 113,200 µTE/100g

Royal Hawaiian Sandalwood™*

(Santalum paniculatum)

Used for centuries in Ayurvedic medicine for skin revitalization, yoga, and meditation. Listed in Dioscorides' *De Materia Medica* (AD 78), Europe's first authoritative guide to medicines, which became the standard reference work for herbal treatments for over 1,700 years.

Research at Brigham Young University in Provo, Utah, documented the oil's ability to inhibit several types of cancerous cells (Stevens).

Medical Properties: Antitumoral, antibacterial, antiviral, immune stimulant

Uses: Cancer, viral infections (herpes simplex, herpes zoster, cold sores, human papilloma virus, etc.), skin conditions (acne, wrinkles, scars, etc.)

Fragrant Influence: Enhances deep sleep and may help remove negative programming from the cells. It is high in sesquiterpenes that stimulate the pineal gland and the limbic region of the brain, the center of emotions. The pineal gland is responsible for releasing melatonin, a powerful immune stimulant and antitumoral agent. Can be grounding and stabilizing.

Technical Data: Botanical Family: Santalaceae; **Plant Origin:** Hawaii; **Extraction Method:** Steam distilled from wood; **Key Constituents:** Alpha-Santalol (41-55%), Beta-Santalol (16-24%); **ORAC:** 160 µTE/100g

*Royal Hawaiian Sandalwood is a trademark of Jawmin, LLC.

Ruta *(Ruta graveolens)*

Commonly known as rue. In traditional medicine it was used as a magic herb and a protection against evil. It was used to treat nervous afflictions, digestive problems, hysterics, and as an abortifacient. Formerly used to treat menstrual disorders and hysteria. Anecdotal reports suggest it has sleep-inducing properties.

Medical Properties: Anti-inflammatory, anti-diabetic, antimicrobial, hypotensive, anxiolytic, sleep promoting

Uses: Hysteria, stress, nervousness, digestion

Fragrant Influence: Calming and relaxing

Sacred Fankincense

Sacred Frankincense Resin

Caution: Possible sun sensitivity.

Technical Data: Botanical Family: Rutaceae; **Plant Origin:** Ecuador; **Extraction Method:** Steam distilled from aerial parts of the herb; **Key Constituents:** 2-Nonanone (40-53%), 2-Undecanone (35-48%), 2-Nonyl Acetate (0.5-2%), Geijerene (1-3%), 2-Decanone (1-3%)

Sacred Frankincense (Boswellia sacra)

Young Living's Sacred Frankincense oil is the first Omani Frankincense to be available to those outside of Saudi royals or the privileged of Oman. It is regarded the world over as the rarest, most sought-after aromatic in existence.

After 15 years of research, 15 trips to Oman, and numerous meetings and negotiations with Omani officials, D. Gary Young was granted the first export permit in the modern history of Oman for the release and export of the oil and permission to build a Young Living distillery in the country and to export the resulting essential oil out of Oman. Gary Young was on-site to supervise the building of Young Living's Omani distillery, and Young Living has contracted with local harvesters to secure our supply of Omani resin. This marks the first time any Westerners have been able to experience the unique spiritual properties of Sacred Frankincense essential oil.

Omani Frankincense is highly regarded as the Frankincense of the ancients and the traditional spiritual oil of biblical times. Historically, it is believed that this beautiful, white hojari resin produced the Frankincense that was taken to the Christ Child.

Science continues to document the oil's immense healing properties, which users of this oil already know.

Medical Properties: Frankincense has been tested as an anticancer agent (Ni, et al., 2012; Suhail, et al., 2011). Therapeutic-grade Frankincense oil contains boswellic acids, which are potent anti-inflammatory agents against rheumatoid arthritis and osteoporosis.

Traditional Uses: It supports skin health and treats stomach disorders, ulcers, cancer, dental and gum diseases, bad blood, infections, mental disorders, and insect bites. It is calming, meditative, relaxing, and promotes higher states of spiritual awareness and higher levels of consciousness and sensitivity.

Complement to: *Boswellia carterii*, traditional frankincense

Technical Data: Botanical Family: Burseraceae; **Plant Origin:** Oman; **Extraction Method:** Steam distilled from gum/resin; **Key Constituents:** Alpha-pinene (53-90%), Camphene (1-4%), Sabinene (1-7%), Para-cymene (0.4-4%), Limonene (2-7.5%)

Sacred Sandalwood (Santalum album)

(See Royal Hawaiian Sandalwood)

Technical Data: Botanical Family: Santalaceae; **Plant Origin:** Australia; **Extraction Method:** Steam distilled from wood; **Key Constituents:** Alpha-Santalol (41-55%), Beta-Santalol (16-24%); ORAC: 160 µTE/100g

Sage/Sage Vitality™ (Salvia officinalis)

Known as "herba sacra" or sacred herb by the ancient Romans, sage's name, *Salvia*, is derived from the word for "salvation." Sage has been used in Europe for oral infections and skin conditions. It has been recognized

Sage

Spanish Sage

for its benefits of strengthening the vital centers and supporting metabolism.

Medical Properties: Antibacterial, antifungal, antioxidant, antitumoral, anti-inflammatory, anxiolytic, hormone regulating, estrogen-like, antiviral, circulatory stimulant, gallbladder stimulant

Uses: Menstrual problems/PMS, estrogen, progesterone, and testosterone deficiencies, liver problems

Fragrant Influence: Mentally stimulating, anxiety-reducing, and helps combat despair and mental fatigue. Sage strengthens the vital centers of the body, balancing the pelvic chakra, where negative emotions from denial and abuse are stored.

Cautions: Avoid if epileptic. Avoid use on persons with high blood pressure.

Technical Data: Botanical Family: Lamiaceae; **Plant Origin:** Spain, Croatia, France; **Extraction Method:** Steam distilled from leaves; **Key Constituents:** Alpha-Thujone (18-43%), Beta-Thujone (3-8.5%), 1,8-Cineole (Eucalyptol) (5.5-13%), Camphor (4.5-24.5%), Camphene (1.5-7%), Alpha-Pinene (1-6.5%), Alpha-Humulene (trace-12%); **ORAC:** 14,800 µTE/100g

Spanish Sage (Salvia lavandulifolia)

(Also referred to as Sage Lavender)

The sage plant has been highly praised throughout history for its powers of longevity and healing. Pliny the Elder said that sage (called "salvia" by the Romans) was used as a local anesthetic for the skin and as a diuretic, in addition to other uses. It was considered a sacred herb

to the Romans and was harvested by a person wearing a white tunic, who had well-washed, bare feet.

During the Middle Ages, the plant was prized throughout Europe because of its exceptional healing effects and was used in a mixture with other herbs designed to ward off the plague.

In Spain, Spanish sage is used in cooking. It has a stronger aroma and flavor than common sage (*S. officinalis*).

Medical Properties: Antiseptic, astringent, chemopreventive, expectorant, reduces mucous, reduces fevers, purifies the blood, eliminates toxins, aids digestion, lowers blood sugar levels without affecting insulin levels, acts as a tonic to improve general health

Uses: Age-related memory loss, cuts, acne, arthritis, dandruff, colds, flu, eczema, hair loss, sweating, anxiety, headaches, asthma, laryngitis, coughs, muscular aches and pains, depression, epilepsy, soothing agent, menstrual disorders, digestive disorders. In food it is used as a spice; in manufacturing it is used as a fragrance component in soaps and cosmetics

Fragrant Influence: Camphoraceous, herbaceous, similar to rosemary

Cautions: Avoid if epileptic. Avoid use on persons with high blood pressure.

Technical Data: Botanical Family: Lamiaceae; **Plant Origin:** Central Europe and Asia Minor, esp. Spain; **Extraction Method:** Steam distilled from the leaves; **Key Constituents:** 1,8-cineole (Eucalyptol) (10-30%), Alpha-Pinene (4-11%), Limonene (2-6%), Camphor (11-36%), Linalol (0.3-4%), Alpha-Terpinyl Acetate (0.5-9%), Linalyl Acetate (0.1-5%)

Spearmint

Tangerine

Spearmint/Spearmint Vitality™
(Mentha spicata)

Spearmint is gentler than peppermint yet is beneficial for headaches and migraines, fatigue, nervous disorders, and digestive problems.

Medical Properties: Increases metabolism, antibacterial, antispasmodic, anti-inflammatory, antiseptic, mucolytic, gallbladder stimulant, digestive aid, antitumor

Uses: Obesity, intestinal/digestive disorders, nausea, hepatitis

Fragrant Influence: Opens and releases emotional blocks and brings about a feeling of balance and a lasting sense of well-being

Technical Data: Botanical Family: Lamiaceae; **Plant Origin:** Utah, China; **Extraction Method:** Steam distilled from leaves; **Key Constituents:** Carvone (45-80%), Limonene (10-30%), Cis-Dihydrocarvone (1-8%); **ORAC:** 540 µTE/100g

Spikenard *(Nardostachys jatamansi)*

Highly regarded in India as a medicinal herb. It was the one of the most precious oils in ancient times, used only by priests, kings, or high initiates. References in the New Testament describe how Mary of Bethany used spikenard oil to anoint the feet of Jesus before the Last Supper (John 12:3).

Medical Properties: Antibacterial, antifungal, anti-inflammatory, antioxidant, relaxant, immune stimulant

Uses: Insomnia, menstrual problems/PMS, heart arrhythmias, nervous tension

Fragrant Influence: Relaxing, soothing, helps nourish and regenerate the skin

Technical Data: Botanical Family: Valerianaceae; **Plant Origin:** India; **Extraction Method:** Steam distilled from roots; **Key Constituents:** Calarene (10-35%), Beta-Maaliene (4-13%), Alpha-Copaene (5-14%), Aristolene (2-9%), Seychellene (1-5%), Patchouli Alcohol (2-7%), 9-Aristolen-1-ol (1-5%); **ORAC:** 54,800 µTE/100g

Tangerine/Tangerine Vitality™
(Citrus reticulata)

Because of Tangerine essential oil's high limonene content, it is a great booster for the immune system.

Medical Properties: Antitumoral, relaxant, antispasmodic, digestive aid, and circulatory enhancer; rich in limonene, which has been extensively studied in over 50 clinical studies for its ability to combat tumor growth.

Uses: Obesity, anxiety, insomnia, irritability, lung health, learning and memory support, Alzheimer's, liver problems, digestive problems, parasites, fluid retention

Fragrant Influence: Promotes happiness, calming, helps with anxiety and nervousness. A Mie University study found that citrus fragrances boosted immunity, induced relaxation, and reduced depression (Komori, et al., 1995).

Caution: Possible sun sensitivity.

Technical Data: Botanical Family: Rutaceae; **Plant Origin:** Brazil; **Extraction Method:** Cold pressed from rind; **Key Constituents:** Limonene (90-97%), Gamma-Terpinene (0.3-3%), Myrcene (1-3%)

Tarragon

Tea Tree

Tarragon/Tarragon Vitality™
(Artemisia dracunculus)

Tarragon's botanical name is from the Greek and Latin. Artemisia is for the Greek goddess Artemis, and dracunculus is derived from the Latin for "little dragon." However intimidating the name, tarragon was recommended by the Arab healer Avicenna for bad digestion. Tarragon may have been introduced to Europe by the Crusaders returning from the Middle East.

Medical Properties: Antispasmodic, antibacterial, anti-inflammatory, antiparasitic, digestive aid, anticonvulsant, enhances insulin sensitivity

Uses: Intestinal disorders, urinary tract infection, nausea, menstrual problems/PMS

Fragrant Influence: May help alleviate deep depression

Caution: Avoid use if epileptic.

Technical Data: **Botanical Family:** Asteraceae; **Plant Origin:** Italy; **Extraction Method:** Steam distilled from leaves; **Key Constituents:** Methyl Chavicol (Estragole) (68-80%), Trans-Beta-Ocimene (6-12%), Cis-Beta-Ocimene (6-12%), Limonene (2-6%); **ORAC:** 37,900 µTE/100g

Tea Tree (Melaleuca alternifolia)

Highly regarded as an antimicrobial and antiseptic essential oil. It has high levels of terpinen-4-ol.

Medical Properties: Powerful antibacterial, antifungal, antiviral, antiparasitic, anti-inflammatory action

Uses: Fungal infections (candida, ringworm), sinus/lung infections, tooth/gum disease, water retention/hypertension, skin conditions (acne, sores)

Fragrant Influence: Promotes cleansing and purity

Technical Data: **Botanical Family:** Myrtaceae; **Plant Origin:** Australia, France; **Extraction Method:** Steam distilled from leaves; **Key Constituents:** Terpinen-4-ol (30-45%), Gamma-Terpinene (10-28%), Alpha-Terpinene (5-13%), 1,8-Cineole (Eucalyptol) (0-15%), Alpha-Terpineol (1.5-8%), Para-Cymene (0.5-12%), Limonene (0.5-4%), Aromadendrene (trace-7%), Delta-Cadinene (trace-8%), Alpha-Pinene (1-6%)

Thyme/Thyme Vitality™ (Thymus vulgaris)

Also known as Red Thyme. It is mentioned in one of the oldest known medical records, the Ebers Papyrus (dating from 16th century BC), an ancient Egyptian list of 877 prescriptions and recipes. The Egyptians used thyme for embalming. Listed in Dioscorides' *De Materia Medica* (AD 78), Europe's first authoritative guide to medicines, which became the standard reference work for herbal treatments for over 1,700 years.

Thyme was listed in Hildegard's *Medicine,* a compilation of early German medicines by highly regarded Benedictine herbalist Hildegard of Bingen (1098-1179).

Medical Properties: Antiaging, antioxidant, anti-inflammatory, antispasmodic, highly antimicrobial, antifungal, antiviral, antiparasitic. A solution of thyme's most active ingredient, thymol, is used in many over-the-counter products such as mouthwash and vapor rubs because of its purifying agents.

Thyme

Tsuga

Uses: Infectious diseases, cardiovascular disease, Alzheimer's disease, hepatitis

Fragrant Influence: It may be beneficial in helping to overcome fatigue and exhaustion after illness.

Caution: May irritate the nasal membranes or skin if

Technical Data: Botanical Family: Lamiaceae; **Plant Origin:** Mediterranean area; **Extraction Method:** Steam distilled from leaves, stems, flowers; **Key Constituents:** Thymol (37-55%), Para-cymene (14-28%), Gamma-Terpinene (4-11%), Linalol (3-6.5%), Carvacrol (0.5-5.5%), Myrcene (1-2.8%); **ORAC:** 15,960 µTE/100g

Tsuga *(Tsuga canadensis)*

Several North American Indian tribes used Tsuga for a number of complaints. To this day, it is used in modern herbalism for its antiseptic and astringent properties. Diarrhea, colitis, cystitis, and diverticulitis are treated by a tsuga tea; it can also be used as a poultice to cleanse wounds.

Medical Properties: Analgesic, antirheumatic, blood cleanser, stimulant, cell regenerating

Uses: Respiratory conditions, kidney/urinary infections, skin conditions, venereal diseases

Technical Data: Botanical Family: Pinaceae; **Plant Origin:** Canada; **Extraction Method:** Steam distilled from needles and twigs of the conifer tree commercially known as eastern hemlock; **Key Constituents:** Alpha-Pinene (18-25%), Beta-Pinene (1-3%), Camphene (13-17%), Limonene (3-5%), Bornyl Acetate (27-40%), Tricyclene (5-7%), Myrcene (2-5%); **ORAC:** 7,100 µTE/100g

Valerian *(Valeriana officinalis)*

During the last three decades, valerian has been clinically investigated for its tranquilizing properties. Researchers have pinpointed the sesquiterpenes valerenic acid and valerone as the active constituents that exert a calming effect on the central nervous system. The German Commission E has pronounced valerian to be an effective treatment for restlessness and for sleep disturbances resulting from nervous conditions.

Medical Properties: Sedative and tranquilizing to the central nervous system, antispasmodic

Uses: Insomnia, anxiety, dysmenorrhea

Fragrant Influence: Calming, relaxing, grounding, emotionally balancing

Technical Data: Botanical Family: Valerianaceae; **Plant Origin:** Belgium, Croatia; **Extraction Method:** Steam distilled from root; **Key Constituents:** Bornyl Acetate (35-43%), Camphene (22-31%), Alpha-Pinene (5-8%), Beta-Pinene (3-6%), Limonene (1-3%), Valerenal (2-8%), Myrtenyl Acetate (2-5%); **ORAC:** 6,200 µTE/100g

Vanilla *(Vanilla planifolia)*

Vanilla essential oil, created for the first time by Young Living Essential Oils, is the highest known oil in vanillin, which is similar in chemical structure to the aromatic compound eugenol, found in cloves. Recent tests conducted at independent laboratories found that the vanilla content of this vanilla oil is over 10 times higher than commercially available super-concentrated vanilla extracts. The same way that eugenol in clove oil numbs dental tissue, vanillin numbs stress and food cravings.

Vanilla

Western Red Cedar

The importance of vanillin is now being investigated by scientists who are researching the ways in which activating vanilloid-type brain receptors can enhance well-being and combat depression.

Medical Properties: Mood elevating; weakens or numbs stress and food cravings

Uses: Appetite control, depression

Fragrant Influence: Uplifts mood through vanilloid receptor action in brain

Technical Data: Botanical Family: Orchidaceae; **Plant Origin:** Brazil; **Extraction Method:** Proprietary vacuum distillation; **Key Constituents:** Vanillin (85-95%)

Vetiver *(Vetiveria zizanoides) (Syn. V. zizanioides)*

It is well known for its anti-inflammatory properties and is traditionally used for arthritic symptoms.

Medical Properties: Antiseptic, antispasmodic, relaxant, circulatory stimulant

Uses: ADHD, anxiety, rheumatism/arthritis, depression (including postpartum), insomnia, skin care (oily, aging, acne, wrinkles)

Fragrant Influence: Psychologically grounding, calming, and stabilizing. It helps us cope with stress and recover from emotional trauma.

Technical Data: Botanical Family: Poaceae; **Plant Origin:** Haiti, Ecuador; **Extraction Method:** Steam distilled from root; **Key Constituents:** Isovalencenol (1-16%), Khusimol (7-21%), Alpha-Vetivone (2-7%), Beta-Vetivone (4-14%), Beta-Vetivenene (1-8%); **ORAC:** 74,300 µTE/100g

Western Red Cedar *(Thuja plicata)*

This oil is different from Canadian Red Cedar, which is distilled from the bark of the same plant, *Thuja plicata*. This oil is not red in color, because it is derived from needles and branches.

Medical Properties: Antiseptic, antimicrobial

Uses: Throat/lung infections, urinary tract infections

Fragrant Influences: recognized for its calming, purifying properties and helping a person cope with stress and emotional traumas

Technical Data: Botanical Family: Cupressaceae; **Plant Origin:** Utah, Idaho, Canada; **Extraction Method:** Steam distilled from needles and branches; **Key Constituents:** Alpha-Thujone (60-80%), Beta-Thujone (4-7%), Alpha-Pinene (2-20%), Sabinene (2-4%)

White Fir *(Abies concolor)*

A white fir infusion of the needles was used as a bath by the Acoma and Laguna Indians to help with rheumatism. The Tewa Indians used the sap from the main stem and larger branches for cuts.

Medical Properties: Antitumoral, anticancerous, antioxidant, pain relieving

Uses: Respiratory infections, antifungal

Technical Data: Botanical Family: Pinaceae; **Plant Origin:** Idaho; **Extraction Method:** Steam distilled from wood/bark/twigs/needles; **Key Constituents:** Alpha-Pinene (8-12%), Beta-Pinene (20-30%), Camphene (7-15%), Bornyl Acetate (11-16%), Delta-Cadinene (2-7%); **ORAC:** 47,900 µTE/100g

White Lotus

Wintergreen

White Lotus *(Nymphaea lotus)*

In ancient Egypt the lotus was used widely as a religious and ceremonial icon. In 400 AD, the Christian church of Ephesus designated Mary as "The Bearer of God." The numerous churches dedicated to Mary that were built thereafter incorporated the image of the lotus, including one image of lotus leaves, flowers, and fruits surrounding a golden cross.

Medical Properties: Anticancerous, anti-inflammatory, immune supporting

Traditional Uses: White lotus was traditionally used by the Egyptians for spiritual, emotional, and physical application. Research in China found that white lotus contains anticancerous and strong immune supporting properties.

Other Uses: Inflamed eyes, jaundice, kidneys, liver spots, menstruation (promotes), palpitations, rheumatism, sciatica, sprains, sunburn, toothaches, tuberculosis, vomiting

Fragrant Influence: Stimulates a positive attitude and a general feeling of well-being

Technical Data: **Botanical Family:** Nymphaeaceae; **Plant Origin:** Egypt; **Extraction Method:** Steam distilled from the flowers; **Key Constituents:** Tetradecene (7-9%), Pentadecane (8-11%), Heptadecadiene (9-11%), Pentadecene (6-9%), Octadecene (7-10%), Ethyl-9-Hexadecenoate (9-12%), Ethyl Hexadecanoate (17-22%), Ethyl Linoleate (8-11%)

Wintergreen *(Gaultheria procumbens)*

Leaves have been chewed to increase respiratory capacity by Native Americans when running long distances and performing difficult labor. Settlers in early America had their children chew the leaves for several weeks each spring to prevent tooth decay. Wintergreen was used as a substitute for black tea during the Revolutionary War.

Medical Properties: Anticoagulant, antispasmodic, highly anti-inflammatory, vasodilator, analgesic/anesthetic, reduces blood pressure and all types of pain. Methyl salicylate, the principal constituent of wintergreen oil, has been incorporated into numerous liniments and ointments for musculoskeletal problems. The oil is also used as a flavoring agent in candies and chewing gums.

Uses: Arthritis/rheumatism, muscle/nerve pain, hypertension, arteriosclerosis, hepatitis/fatty liver

Fragrant Influence: It stimulates and increases awareness in all levels of the sensory system.

Cautions: Avoid use if epileptic. Anticoagulant properties can be enhanced when used with Warfarin or aspirin.

Technical Data: **Botanical Family:** Ericaceae; **Plant Origin:** China, North America; **Extraction Method:** Steam distilled from leaves and bark; **Key Constituent:** Methyl Salicylate (90+%); **ORAC:** 101,800 µTE/100g

Xiang Mao

Yarrow

Xiang Mao *(Cymbopogon citratus)*

This aromatic grass is sometimes called red lemongrass and has been used in folk medicine as a calming agent. It was also used to keep air in the home fresh.

Medical Properties: Chemopreventive, antimicrobial, anxiolytic, renal protective, gastroprotective, antifungal, antiparasitic, cholesterol reducer

Uses: Bladder infection, respiratory/sinus infection, digestive problems, parasites, torn ligaments/muscles, fluid retention, varicose veins, Salmonella, *Candida albicans*

Fragrant Influence: Like its close cousin, *Cymbopogon flexuosus,* this lemongrass species sharpens awareness and is a purifier

Technical Data: **Botanical Family:** Poaceae; **Plant Origin:** Taiwan; **Extraction Method:** Steam distilled from grasses; **Key Constituents:** Limonene (3-7%), Citronellal (40-50%), Citronellol (11-16%), Geraniol (15-18%), Germacrene-D (1-3%), Alpha-Elemol (1-2%)

Yarrow *(Achillea millefolium)*

The Greek Achilles, hero of the Trojan War, was said to have used the yarrow herb to help cure the injury to his Achilles tendon. Yarrow was considered sacred by the Chinese, who recognized the harmony of the Yin and Yang energies within it. It has been said that the fragrance of yarrow makes possible the meeting of heaven and earth. Yarrow was used by Germanic tribes for the treatment of battle wounds.

Medical Properties: Anti-inflammatory, hormone-like, combats scarring, supports prostate

Uses: Prostate problems, menstrual problems/PMS, varicose veins

Fragrant Influence: Balancing highs and lows, both external and internal, yarrow simultaneously inspires and grounds us. Useful during meditation and supportive to intuitive energies. Reduces confusion and ambivalence.

Technical Data: **Botanical Family:** Asteraceae; **Plant Origin:** North America, Europe, Asia; **Extraction Method:** Steam distilled from flowers, leaves, and stems; **Key Constituents:** Chamazulene (5-18%), Trans-Beta-Caryophyllene (5-13%), Germacrene D (8-25%), Sabinene (5-15%), Beta-Pinene (4-10%), 1,8-Cineole (Eucalyptol) (2-10%); **ORAC:** 55,900 µTE/100g

Ylang Ylang

Yuzu

Ylang Ylang *(Cananga odorata)*

Ylang ylang means "flower of flowers." The flowers have been used to cover the beds of newlywed couples on their wedding night. Traditionally used in hair formulas to promote thick, shiny, lustrous hair.

Flowers are picked early in the morning to maximize oil yield. The highest quality oil is drawn from the first distillation and is known as ylang ylang complete.

Medical Properties: Antispasmodic, vasodilating, antidiabetic, anti-inflammatory, antiparasitic, regulates heartbeat

Uses: Cardiac arrhythmia, cardiac problems, anxiety, hypertension, depression, hair loss, intestinal problems

Fragrant Influence: Balances male-female energies, enhances spiritual attunement, combats anger, combats low self-esteem, increases focus of thoughts, filters out negative energy, restores confidence and peace

Caution: Use sparingly if you have low blood pressure

Technical Data: **Botanical Family:** Annonaceae; **Plant Origin:** Madagascar, Ecuador; **Extraction Method:** Steam distilled from flowers; **Key Constituents:** Germacrene D (14-27%), (E,E)-Alpha-Farnesene (5-23%), Benzyl Acetate (1-15%), Geranyl Acetate (2-11%), Beta-Caryophyllene (2-19%), Benzyl Benzoate (4-8%), Linalol (2-16%), Para-Cresyl Methyl Ether (0.5-9%), Methyl Benzoate (1-5%), Benzyl Salicyclate (1-5%); **ORAC:** 130,000 µTE/100g

Yuzu *(Citrus junos)*

Thought to be a hybrid between Ichang papeda and Satsuma mandarin. Commonly used in cooking and for enhancing flavors due to the fragrant rind. There are a few reports on the use of yuzu essential oil for cosmetics and aromatherapy.

Medical Properties: Anti-inflammatory, anticancer, antidiabetic, asthma

Uses: Flavorant, inflammation, brain protection, stress

Fragrant Influence: High levels of limonene positively affect mood and heighten senses.

Caution: Possible sun sensitivity.

Technical Data: **Botanical Family:** Rutaceae; **Plant Origin:** China; **Extraction Method:** Cold-pressed from rind; **Key Constituents:** Limonene (60-85%), Beta-Phellandrene (1-5%), Gamma-Terpinene (5-15%), Linalool (0.5-3%); **ORAC:** 620 µmole TE/gram

Essential Oil Blends

This chapter describes specific blends that were formulated after years of research for both physical and emotional health. Each of these blends is formulated to maximize the synergistic effect between various oil chemistries and harmonic frequencies. When chemistry and frequency coincide, noticeable physical, spiritual, and emotional benefits can be attained.

Remember that some essential oils may be irritating to those with sensitive skin, and remember to avoid getting them in your eyes. In case you accidentally do get oil in an eye, dilute it quickly with a few drops of V-6 Vegetable Oil Complex, olive oil, or any other vegetable oil that is readily available, and call your doctor if necessary. Do not use water to rinse the eye, as water drives the oil into the tissues and creates more burning and pain.

All essential oils should be stored in a cool, dark place to preserve their fragile constituents that may dissipate over time or be damaged by harmful sunlight.

Guidelines

Please see the species-specific chapters for additional details on how to use the specific essential oils and blends.

Common uses: Almost all blends can be diffused, directly inhaled, and/or applied topically.

Full-body massage: Dilute 1 drop essential oil blend with 15 drops of V-6 or other pure carrier oil.

Possible skin sensitivity: Test for sensitivity on small location of skin on underside of arm.

Possible sun sensitivity: Avoid direct sunlight or UV rays for up to 12 hours after applying product.

Dietary and/or culinary use: Vitality™ dietary essential oils and blends can be added to food for delicious, concentrated flavor or used in capsules for their supporting properties.

3 Wise Men™

This blend of 3 Wise Men promotes feelings of reverence and spiritual awareness combined with the power of therapeutic-grade essential oils that open the subconscious. It enhances emotional equilibrium as it soothes and uplifts the heart.

Ingredients: sweet almond oil, Royal Hawaiian Sandalwood*, Juniper, Frankincense, Black Spruce, Myrrh

Abundance™

This blend exemplifies the true power of synergy. Together, all of its component oils are magnified in vibration, creating the law of attraction and the energy and frequency of prosperity and plentitude.

Ingredients: Orange, Frankincense, Patchouli, Clove, Ginger, Myrrh, Cinnamon Bark, Black Spruce

Acceptance™

Acceptance stimulates the mind, compelling us to open and accept new things, people, or relationships in life, allowing one to reach a higher potential. It also helps us to overcome procrastination and denial.

Ingredients: sweet almond oil, Coriander, Geranium, Bergamot, Frankincense, Royal Hawaiian Sandalwood, Bitter Orange (Neroli), Grapefruit, Tangerine, Spearmint, Lemon, Blue Cypress, Davana, Kaffir Lime, Ocotea, Jasmine, Matricaria (German Chamomile)

Amoressence™

A limited-edition blend available only at a Young Living Beauty School event.

Ingredients: Vetiver, Idaho Blue Spruce, Jasmine, Davana, Ocotea, Ylang Ylang, Roman Chamomile, Vanilla, Geranium

Aroma Ease™

This comforting blend has a cool, minty aroma that contains powerful essential oil constituents. Use Aroma Ease to reduce the effects of nausea and other sensations of digestive discomfort.

Ingredients: Peppermint, Spearmint, Ginger, Cardamom, Fennel

Aroma Life™

Aroma Life improves cardiovascular, lymphatic, and circulatory systems; lowers high blood pressure; and reduces stress.

Ingredients: sesame seed oil, Cypress, Marjoram, Ylang Ylang, Helichrysum

Aroma Siez™

Aroma Siez is an advanced complex of anti-inflammatory, muscle-relaxing essential oils that promote circulation and relieve headaches and tight, inflamed, aching muscles resulting from injury, fatigue, or stress.

Ingredients: Basil, Marjoram, Lavender, Peppermint, Cypress

Caution: Possible skin sensitivity.

Aroma Sleep™

AromaSleep provides a relaxing aroma to re-establish a positive energy flow to the body, helping calm your mind and feelings prior to bedtime.

Ingredients: Lavender, Geranium, Roman Chamomile, Bergamot, Tangerine, Sacred Frankincense, Valerian, Ruta

Australian Blue™

This blend includes a rare Australian aromatic called blue cypress, a part of the aboriginal pharmacopoeia for thousands of years. It is distilled from the wood of *Callitris intratropica*, the northern cypress pine, which has antiviral properties. Its aromatic influence uplifts and inspires while simultaneously grounds and stabilizes.

Ingredients: Blue Cypress, Ylang Ylang, Cedarwood, White Fir, Geranium, Grapefruit, Tangerine, Spearmint, Davana, Kaffir Lime, Lemon, Ocotea, Jasmine, Matricaria (German Chamomile), Blue Tansy, Rose

Awaken™

Five specific blends combine to awaken and enhance inner self-awareness that strengthens the desire to reach one's highest potential. It stimulates right brain creativity, amplifying the function of the pineal and pituitary glands in balancing the energy centers of the body and helps us identify our true desires and how best to pursue them.

Ingredients: Joy, Forgiveness, Present Time, Dream Catcher, Harmony

Caution: Possible sun sensitivity.

Believe™

Believe helps release the unlimited potential everyone possesses. It restores feelings of hope, making it possible to more fully experience health, happiness, and vitality.

Ingredients: Balsam Canada (Idaho Balsam Fir), Coriander, Bergamot, Frankincense, Idaho Blue Spruce, Ylang Ylang, Geranium

Caution: Possible skin sensitivity.

Bite Buster™

Bite Buster is an excellent insect repellant formulated especially for kids.

Ingredients: caprylic/capric glycerides, Idaho Tansy, Citronella, Palo Santo

Brain Power™

Brain Power promotes deep concentration and channels physical energy into mental energy. It also increases mental potential and clarity, and long-term use may retard the aging process. Many of the oils in this blend are high in sesquiterpene compounds that increase activity in the pineal, pituitary, and hypothalamus glands and thereby increase output of growth hormone and melatonin.

The oils also help dissolve petrochemicals that congest the receptor sites, clearing the "brain fog" that people experience due to exposure to synthetic petrochemicals in food, skin, hair care products, and air.

Ingredients: Royal Hawaiian Sandalwood, Cedarwood, Frankincense, Melissa, Blue Cypress, Lavender, Helichrysum

Caution: Possible skin sensitivity.

Breathe Again™ Roll-On

This supercharged version of the R.C. blend is packaged in a convenient dispenser for easy use when air pollution makes it difficult to breathe, or throat and nasal congestion strike. Contains four different eucalyptus oils and five additional essential oils, all known for their ability to relax airways, make breathing easier, and reduce coughing. In addition, these oils have anti-inflammatory characteristics.

Ingredients: caprylic/capric triglyceride, Eucalyptus Staigeriana, Eucalyptus Globulus, Laurus Nobilis (Bay Laurel), Rose Hip Seed Oil, Peppermint, Eucalyptus Radiata, Copaiba, Myrtle, Blue Cypress, Eucalyptus Blue

Build Your Dream™

A unique blend, Build Your Dream is designed to empower and give clarity to your thoughts and purpose when used aromatically.

Ingredients: Lavender, Sacred Frankincense, Melissa, Blue Cypress, Hong Kuai, Idaho Blue Spruce, Ylang Ylang, Dream Catcher, Believe, Blue Lotus

Christmas Spirit™

Christmas Spirit is a purifying blend of evergreen, citrus, and spice, reminiscent of winter holidays, and brings joy, peace, happiness, and security.

Ingredients: Orange, Cinnamon Bark, Black Spruce

Caution: Possible sun/skin sensitivity.

Citrus Fresh™/Citrus Fresh Vitality™

Citrus Fresh stimulates the right brain to amplify creativity and well-being, eradicates anxiety, and works well as an air purifier. When diffused, it adds a clean, fresh scent to any environment.

Ingredients: Orange, Tangerine, Grapefruit, Lemon, Mandarin, Spearmint

Caution: Possible sun/skin sensitivity.

Clarity™

Clarity promotes a clear mind and amplifies mental alertness and vitality. It increases energy when overly tired and brings greater focus to the spirit and mind.

Ingredients: Basil, Cardamom, Rosemary, Peppermint, Coriander, Geranium, Bergamot, Lemon, Ylang Ylang, Jasmine, Roman Chamomile, Palmarosa

Caution: Possible sun/skin sensitivity.

Common Sense™

Common Sense is a proprietary blend of pure Young Living essential oils especially formulated by D. Gary Young to increase mental acuity, improve decision-making abilities, and strengthen everyday thinking skills.

Ingredients: Frankincense, Ylang Ylang, Ocotea, Goldenrod, Ruta, Dorado Azul, Lime

Caution: Possible sun sensitivity.

Cool Azul™

Cool Azul may be applied topically after physical activities to relieve sore or stressed muscles or for a cooling, aromatic sensation.

Ingredients: Wintergreen, Peppermint, Sage, Copaiba, Oregano, Melaleuca Quinquenervia (Niaouli), Plectranthus Oregano, Lavender, Blue Cypress, Elemi, Vetiver, Caraway, Dorado Azul, Matricaria (German Chamomile)

Caution: Possible sun sensitivity.

Deep Relief Roll-On™

This convenient roll-on relieves muscle soreness and tension, soothes sore joints and ligaments, helps calm stressed nerves, and reduces inflammation. This powerful blend contains nine essential oils, most of which are known for their anti-inflammatory and pain-relieving characteristics.

This highly portable roll-on with its no-mess application is easy to carry in your pocket, purse, briefcase, etc. It also passes through airport security for "easy breathing" while flying high.

Ingredients: Peppermint, caprylic/capric triglyceride, Lemon, Balsam Canada (Idaho Balsam Fir), Clove, Copaiba, coconut oil, Wintergreen, Helichrysum, Vetiver, Dorado Azul

Caution: Possible sun sensitivity.

DiGize™/DiGize Vitality™

This blend relieves digestive problems, including indigestion, heartburn, gas, and bloating. It helps fight candida as it kills and digests parasite infestation.

Ingredients: Tarragon, Ginger, Peppermint, Juniper, Fennel, Lemongrass, Anise, Patchouli

Caution: Possible sun sensitivity.

Divine Release™

Divine Release is an elevating blend that helps release feelings of anger and promotes forgiveness to encourage the gentle characteristics within oneself for a positive outlook on life.

Ingredients: Royal Hawaiian Sandalwood, Roman Chamomile, Frankincense, Melissa, Geranium, Grapefruit, Blue Cypress, Hinoki, Helichrysum, Bergamot, Rose, Ledum, Angelica

Caution: Possible sun sensitivity.

Dragon Time™

This blend relieves PMS symptoms and menstrual discomforts, including cramping and irregular periods. It helps balance emotions, alleviating mood swings and headaches caused by hormonal imbalance.

Ingredients: Fennel, Clary Sage, Marjoram, Lavender, Yarrow, Jasmine

Caution: Possible sun sensitivity.

Dream Catcher™

This blend stimulates the emotional centers of the brain, awakening creative thoughts and enhancing dreams and visualizations, promoting greater potential for realizing your dreams and staying on your path. It also protects from negative thoughts and dreams that might cloud your vision.

Ingredients: Royal Hawaiian Sandalwood, Tangerine, Ylang Ylang, Black Pepper, Bergamot, Anise, Juniper, Geranium, Blue Cypress, Davana, Citrus Hystrix, Jasmine, Matricaria (German Chamomile), Blue Tansy, Rose, Grapefruit, Spearmint

Caution: Possible sun/skin sensitivity.

Egyptian Gold™

This is a very unique blend that combines the most valuable essences of the Middle East and Central Europe. It offers a truly enchanting aromatic effect that stimulates the central nervous system and the immune and respiratory systems.

Ingredients: Frankincense, Balsam Canada (Idaho Balsam Fir), Lavender, Myrrh, Hyssop, Northern Lights Black Spruce, Cedarwood, Vetiver, Rose, Cinnamon Bark

Caution: Possible sun sensitivity.

EndoFlex™/EndoFlex Vitality™

This blend amplifies metabolism and vitality and creates hormonal balance.

Ingredients: Spearmint, Sesame Seed Oil, Sage, Geranium, Myrtle, Matricaria (German Chamomile), Nutmeg

En-R-Gee™

This blend increases vitality, circulation, and alertness.

Ingredients: Rosemary, Juniper, Lemongrass, Nutmeg, Balsam Canada (Idaho Balsam Fir), Clove, Black Pepper

Caution: Possible skin sensitivity. Avoid contact with mucous membranes or sensitive skin.

Envision™

This blend renews focus and stimulates creative and intuitive abilities needed to achieve goals and dreams. It helps to reawaken internal drive and independence and to overcome fears and emotional blocks.

Ingredients: Black Spruce, Geranium, Orange, Lavender, Sage, Rose

Evergreen Essence™

Evergreen Essence essential oil blend has a refreshing, crisp scent that is invigorating and emotionally strengthening. With an arrangement of popular evergreen trees, the scents of pine, fir, and spruce complement one another and may assist in the release of occasional emotional blocks. Refreshing to the senses, Evergreen Essence brings a feeling of balance, peace, and security. The relaxing scent may also help clear the mind for a calming sense of meditation and reflection.

Ingredients: Idaho Blue Spruce, Ponderosa Pine, Scotch Pine, Red Fir, Western Red Cedar, White Fir, Black Pine, Pinyon Pine, Lodgepole Pine

Caution: Possible skin sensitivity.

Exodus II™

Some researchers believe that these aromatics were used by Aaron, the brother of Moses, to protect the Israelites from a plague. Modern science shows that these oils contain immune-stimulating and antimicrobial compounds. Because of the complex chemistry of essential oils, it is very difficult for viruses and bacteria to mutate and acquire resistance to them.

Ingredients: olive oil, Myrrh, Cassia, Cinnamon Bark, Calamus, Northern Lights Black Spruce, Hyssop, Vetiver, Frankincense

Caution: Possible sun/skin sensitivity. Not intended for children under 12 years of age, unless directed by a health care professional.

Forgiveness™

This blend helps to release hurt feelings and negative emotions. It also helps release negative memories, allowing one to move past emotional barriers and attain higher awareness, assisting the person to forgive and let go.

Ingredients: sesame seed oil, Melissa, Geranium, Frankincense, Royal Hawaiian Sandalwood, Coriander, Angelica, Lavender, Bergamot, Lemon, Ylang Ylang, Jasmine, Helichrysum, Roman Chamomile, Palmarosa, Rose

Caution: Possible sun/skin sensitivity.

Freedom™

This liberating blend was created to help re-establish a positive energy flow through the body to promote a sense of balance. It is part of the Freedom Collection Bundle.

Ingredients: Copaiba, Sacred Frankincense, Idaho Blue Spruce, Vetiver, Lavender, Peppermint, Palo Santo, Valerian, Ruta

Gathering™

This blend is created to help us overcome the bombardment of chaotic energy that alters our focus and takes us off our path toward higher achievements. Northern Lights Black Spruce and Vetiver have a strong effect when blended with Frankincense and Sandalwood in gathering our emotional and spiritual thoughts, helping us to achieve our potential. These oils help increase the oxygen around the pineal and pituitary glands, bringing greater harmonic frequency to receive the communication we desire.

This blend helps bring people together on a physical, emotional, and spiritual level for greater focus and clarity. It helps one stay focused, grounded, and clear in gathering motivation for self-improvement.

Ingredients: Lavender, Northern Lights Black Spruce, Geranium, Royal Hawaiian Sandalwood, Ylang Ylang, Vetiver, Cinnamon Bark, Rose

Caution: Possible skin sensitivity.

GeneYus™

Diffuse GeneYus to help young minds focus and concentrate on projects.

Ingredients: fractionated coconut oil, Sacred Frankincense, Blue Cypress, Cedarwood, Idaho Blue Spruce, Palo Santo, Melissa, Northern Lights Black Spruce, almond oil, Bergamot, Myrrh, Vetiver, Geranium, Royal Hawaiian Sandalwood, Ylang Ylang, Hyssop, Coriander, Rose

Caution: Possible sun sensitivity.

Gentle Baby™

This blend is comforting, soothing, relaxing, and beneficial for reducing stress during pregnancy. It helps reduce stretch marks and scar tissue, rejuvenates the skin, improves elasticity, and helps to reduce wrinkles.

It is particularly soothing to babies with dry, chapped skin and diaper rash. Skin issues improve when using Gentle Baby with Rose Ointment on the top of it. Gentle Baby is calming and brings a feeling of peace for tiny babies, children, and adults.

Ingredients: Coriander, Geranium, Palmarosa, Lavender, Ylang Ylang, Roman Chamomile, Bergamot (furocoumarin-free), Lemon, Jasmine, Rose

Caution: Possible sun sensitivity.

GLF™/ GLF™ Vitality™

The initials of this essential oil blend stand for **G**allbladder and **L**iver **F**lush. It is formulated with oils that help to cleanse and restore liver and gallbladder function when taken in capsules as a dietary supplement.

Ingredients: Grapefruit, Ledum, Helichrysum, Celery Seed, Hyssop, Spearmint

Caution: Possible sun sensitivity.

Gratitude™

This delightful blend is designed to elevate, soothe, and bring relief to the body while helping to foster a grateful attitude. It is also nourishing and supportive to the skin. The New Testament tells us that on one occasion, Christ healed 10 lepers (Luke 17:12-19), but only one returned to express his thanks. This blend embodies the spirit of that grateful leper.

Ingredients: Balsam Canada (Idaho Balsam Fir), Frankincense, Coriander, Myrrh, Ylang Ylang, Bergamot (furocoumarin-free), Northern Lights Black Spruce, Vetiver, Geranium

Grounding™

This blend creates a feeling of solidarity and balance. It stabilizes and grounds us so we can cope constructively with reality. When we're hurting emotionally, we resort to avoidance. When this happens, it is easy to make poor choices that lead to unhealthy relationships and unwise business decisions. We seek to escape because we do not have anchoring or awareness to know how to deal with our emotions.

Ingredients: White Fir, Black Spruce, Ylang Ylang, Pine, Cedarwood, Angelica, Juniper

Caution: Possible sun/skin sensitivity.

Harmony™

This blend promotes physical and emotional healing by creating a harmonic balance for the energy centers of the body. It brings us into harmony with all things, people, and cycles of life. It is beneficial in reducing stress, amplifying well-being, and dissipating feelings of discord. It is also uplifting and elevating to the mind, creating a positive attitude.

Ingredients: Royal Hawaiian Sandalwood, Lavender, Ylang Ylang, Frankincense, Orange, Angelica, Geranium, Hyssop, Spanish Sage, Black Spruce, Coriander, Bergamot, Lemon, Jasmine, Roman Chamomile, Palmarosa, Rose

Caution: Possible sun/skin sensitivity.

Highest Potential™

This blend elevates the mind as you gather your thoughts and mental energy to achieve your highest potential. It harmonizes several grounding, calming, inspiring, and empowering essential oils into one intoxicating blend.

Biochemist R. W. Moncrieff wrote that Ylang Ylang "soothes and inhibits anger born of frustration," which removes roadblocks and opens new vistas. The uplifting fragrance of Jasmine spurs creativity, while Lavender clears the thought processes for focused intentions.

Ingredients: Blue Cypress, Ylang Ylang, Jasmine, Cedarwood, Geranium, Lavender, Northern Lights Black Spruce, Frankincense, Royal Hawaiian Sandalwood, White Fir, Vetiver, Cinnamon Bark, Davana, Citrus Hystrix, Rose, German Chamomile, Blue Tansy, Grapefruit, Tangerine, Spearmint, Lemon, Ocotea

Caution: Possible sun/skin sensitivity.

Hope™

Hope is essential for moving forward in life. Hopelessness can cause a loss of vision, goals, and dreams. This blend helps you reconnect with a feeling of strength and grounding, restoring hope for tomorrow. It has helped many overcome suicidal depression.

Ingredients: sweet almond oil, Melissa, Juniper, Myrrh, Black Spruce

Caution: Possible skin sensitivity.

Humility™

Having humility and forgiveness helps us heal ourselves and our earth (2 Chronicles 7:14). Humility is an integral component in obtaining forgiveness and is needed for a closer relationship with God. Through the frequency and fragrance of this blend, you may arrive at a place where healing can begin.

Ingredients: caprylic/capric triglyceride, Coriander, Ylang Ylang, Bergamot (furocoumarin-free), Geranium, Melissa, Frankincense, Myrrh, Northern Lights Black Spruce, Vetiver, Bitter Orange (Neroli), Rose

Caution: Possible sun/skin sensitivity.

ImmuPower™

This blend strengthens immunity and DNA repair in the cells. It is strongly antiseptic and anti-infectious.

Ingredients: Hyssop, Mountain Savory, Cistus, Camphor (Ravintsara), Frankincense, Oregano, Clove, Cumin, Dorado Azul

Caution: Possible skin sensitivity. This blend needs to be well-diluted before using on children.

Infect Away™

Infect Away utilizes six essential oils for a gentle cleansing effect on your animal. For best results, use as the second part to a three-part system, with PuriClean being used first, then Infect Away, followed by Mendwell. It supports a healthy skin barrier.

Ingredients: caprylic/capric glycerides

Essential Oils: Myrrh, Patchouli, Dorado Azul, Palo Santo, Ecuador Plectranthus Oregano, Ocotea

Directions: Carefully apply according to the size and species of the animal. Additional dilution is recommended for smaller species.

Inner Child™

When children have been abused, they become disconnected from their inner child, or identity, which causes confusion. This fractures the personality and creates problems that tend to surface in the early- to mid-adult years, often mislabeled as a midlife crisis. This fragrance stimulates memory response and helps one reconnect with the inner self or identity. This is one of the first steps to finding emotional balance.

Ingredients: Orange, Tangerine, Ylang Ylang, Royal Hawaiian Sandalwood, Jasmine, Lemongrass, Black Spruce, Bitter Orange (Neroli)

Caution: Possible sun sensitivity.

Inner Harmony™

Inner Harmony is a calming formula that can be used to promote emotional clearing and self-renewal.

Ingredients: Geranium, Lavender, Royal Hawaiian Sandalwood, Ylang Ylang, Idaho Blue Spruce, Sacred Frankincense, Roman Chamomile, Tangerine, Orange, Northern Lights Black Spruce, Myrrh, Rose, Angelica, Vetiver, Melissa

Inspiration™

This blend is formulated to help find a calm space in our minds and bring us closer to that creative center where our higher intuition operates. These oils were traditionally used by the Native Americans to enhance spirituality, prayer, and inner awareness.

Ingredients: Cedarwood, Black Spruce, Myrtle, Coriander, Royal Hawaiian Sandalwood, Frankincense, Bergamot (furocoumarin-free), Vetiver, Ylang Ylang, Geranium

Caution: Possible sun/skin sensitivity.

Into the Future™

This blend helps one leave the past behind in order to progress with vision and excitement. So many times we find ourselves settling for mediocrity and sacrificing our own potential and success because of fear of the unknown and the future. This blend inspires determination and a pioneering spirit and creates a strong emotional feeling of being able to reach one's potential.

Ingredients: sweet almond oil, Clary Sage, Ylang Ylang, White Fir, Idaho Blue Spruce, Jasmine, Juniper, Frankincense, Orange, Cedarwood, White Lotus

Caution: Possible sun/skin sensitivity.

InTouch™

This uplifting blend can help support mood by encouraging positive energy in times of restlessness and unease and to help ground and unite the body, mind, and spirit.

Ingredients: caprylic/capric triglyceride, Vetiver, Melissa, Royal Hawaiian Sandalwood, Cedarwood, Idaho Blue Spruce

Caution: Possible sun sensitivity.

Joy™

This beautiful blend produces a magnetic energy that brings joy to the heart, mind, and soul. It inspires romance and helps overcome deep-seated grief and depression.

Ingredients: Bergamot, Ylang Ylang, Geranium, Lemon, Coriander, Tangerine, Jasmine, Roman Chamomile, Palmarosa, Rose

Caution: Possible sun/skin sensitivity.

JuvaCleanse®/ JuvaCleanse® Vitality™

The liver is the body's largest internal organ and major detoxifier. Even the toxins in the air we breathe are filtered by the liver, including chemicals from aerosol cleaners, paint, insect sprays, etc.; but eventually those filters need to be cleaned. The essential oils of Ledum, Celery Seed, and Helichrysum have long been known for their liver cleansing properties. JuvaCleanse was clinically tested in 2003 for removing mercury from body tissues.

In 2003 a study conducted by Roger Lewis, MD, at the Young Life Research Clinic in Springville, Utah, evaluated the efficacy of Helichrysum, Ledum, and Celery Seed in treating cases of advanced Hepatitis C.

In one case a 20-year-old male diagnosed with Hepatitis C had a viral count of 13,200. After taking two capsules (approx. 750 mg each) of JuvaCleanse per day for one month with no other intervention, the patient's viral count dropped more than 80 percent to 2,580.

Ingredients: Helichrysum, Ledum, Celery Seed

JuvaFlex™/JuvaFlex® Vitality™

This blend helps with liver and lymphatic detoxification. The emotions of anger and hate create toxins that are stored in the liver that can lead to sickness and disease. JuvaFlex helps break addictions to coffee, alcohol, drugs, and tobacco.

Ingredients: sesame seed oil, Fennel, Geranium, Rosemary, Roman Chamomile, Blue Tansy, Helichrysum

Lady Sclareol™

This oil, rich in phytoestrogens, is designed to be worn as an exquisite fragrance. It enhances the feminine nature by improving mood and raising estrogen levels. It may also provide relief for PMS symptoms.

Ingredients: Geranium, Coriander, Vetiver, Orange, Clary Sage, Bergamot, Ylang Ylang, Royal Hawaiian Sandalwood, Spanish Sage, Jasmine, Idaho Blue Spruce, Spearmint, Hinoki

Caution. Possible sun sensitivity.

Light the Fire™

Light the Fire is an inspiring blend with a warm, spicy aroma that can encourage feelings of power and ambition.

Ingredients: Nutmeg, Cassia, Mastrante, Ocotea, Canadian Fleabane, Lemon, Hinoki, Black Pepper, Northern Lights Black Spruce

Caution: Possible sun/skin sensitivity.

Live with Passion™

This blend revives the zest for life and improves internal energy with a combination of essential oils formulated specifically to help people attain an optimistic attitude.

Ingredients: Royal Hawaiian Sandalwood, Clary Sage, Ginger, Jasmine, Angelica, Patchouli, Cedarwood, Helichrysum, Melissa, Bitter Orange (Neroli)

Caution: Possible sun/skin sensitivity.

Live Your Passion™

Live Your Passion enhances the zest for life and improves internal energy to specifically help people go forward with motivation and excitement.

Ingredients: Orange, Royal Hawaiian Sandalwood, Nutmeg, Lime, Idaho Blue Spruce, Northern Lights Black Spruce, Ylang Ylang, Frankincense, Peppermint

Longevity™/Longevity Vitality™

This oil contains the highest antioxidant and DNA-protecting essential oils. When taken as a dietary supplement, this blend promotes longevity and prevents premature aging (see Longevity Softgels in the Nutritional Support chapter).

Ingredients: Thyme, Orange, Clove, Frankincense

Caution: Possible sun/skin sensitivity.

Magnify Your Purpose™

This blend stimulates the endocrine system for greater energy flow to the right hemisphere of the brain, activating creativity, motivation, and focus. This helps strengthen commitment to purpose, desire, and intentions until you realize your goals.

Ingredients: Royal Hawaiian Sandalwood, Sage, Coriander, Patchouli, Nutmeg, Bergamot, Cinnamon Bark, Ginger, Ylang Ylang, Geranium

Caution: Possible skin sensitivity.

Melrose™

This is a blend of four essential oils that have strong antiseptic properties to cleanse and disinfect cuts, scrapes, burns, rashes, and bruised tissue. These oils help regenerate damaged tissue and reduce inflammation. It is powerful when diffused to dispel odors, purify the air, and protect against daily radiation bombardment.

Ingredients: Rosemary, Tea Tree, Clove, Melaleuca Quinquenervia (Niaouli)

Caution: Possible skin sensitivity.

Mendwell™

Mendwell is a blend of oils that supports healthy skin repair and is specifically formulated for animals. For best results, use as the last step in a three-part system, with PuriClean and Infect Away being used first.

Ingredients: caprylic/capric glycerides

Essential Oils: Geranium, Lavender, Hyssop, Myrrh, Frankincense, Hinoki

Directions: Carefully apply according to the size and species of the animal. Additional dilution is recommended for smaller species.

M-Grain™

This blend helps relieve pain from slight headaches to severe migraine headaches. It is anti-inflammatory and antispasmodic.

Ingredients: Basil, Marjoram, Lavender, Roman Chamomile, Peppermint, Helichrysum

Caution: Possible skin sensitivity.

Mister™

This blend helps to decongest the prostate and promote greater male hormonal balance.

Ingredients: sesame seed oil, Sage, Fennel, Lavender, Myrtle, Yarrow, Peppermint

Motivation™

Motivation stimulates feelings of action and accomplishment, providing positive energy to help overcome feelings of fear and procrastination.

Ingredients: Roman Chamomile, Black Spruce, Ylang Ylang, Lavender

Oola® ** Balance™

Oola Balance is designed to align and balance your center, giving you an increase in concentration with a positive outlook. As mind and body are balanced, the ability to focus on passions, behaviors, and health are amplified for the better.

Ingredients: fractionated coconut oil, Lavender, Ylang Ylang, Frankincense, Ocotea, Idaho Blue Spruce, Royal Hawaiian Sandalwood, Balsam Canada (Idaho Balsam Fir), Sacred Frankincense, Jasmine, Northern Lights Black Spruce, Orange, Angelica, Geranium, Hyssop, Spanish Sage, Myrrh, Vetiver, Cistus, Coriander, Bergamot, Lemon, Roman Chamomile, Palmarosa, Rose

Oola® ** Faith™

This blend can awaken feelings of spirituality and humility. Inhaling the aroma may promote deeper meditation and create a greater sense of connection.

Ingredients: caprylic/capric triglyceride, Sacred Frankincense, Balsam Canada (Idaho Balsam Fir), Myrrh, Juniper, Hyssop, Cedarwood, Sage, Hinoki, Rose, Geranium, Palo Santo, Coriander, Bergamot, Lemon, Ylang Ylang, Jasmine, Roman Chamomile, Palmarosa

Caution: Possible sun sensitivity.

Oola®** Family™

This is a powerful blend that is formulated to support feelings of unconditional love, patience, and respect. It may help uplift emotions and release negative feelings to provide balance and clarity.

Ingredients: caprylic/capric triglyceride, Ylang Ylang, Lavender, Orange, Geranium, Cardamom, Tangerine, Frankincense, Cedarwood, Coriander, Pine, Royal Hawaiian Sandalwood, Lemongrass, Bergamot, Xiang Mao, Lemon, Black Spruce, Lime, Roman Chamomile, Palmarosa

Caution: Possible sun sensitivity.

Oola®** Field™

This blend encourages feelings of self-worth and strength to help you overcome barriers and reach your true, unlimited potential.

Ingredients: caprylic/capric triglyceride, Cardamom, Frankincense, Ylang Ylang, sweet almond oil, Nutmeg, Ginger, Bitter Orange (Neroli), Balsam Canada (Idaho Balsam Fir), Coriander, Black Spruce, Bergamot, Idaho Blue Spruce, Geranium

Caution: Possible sun sensitivity.

Oola®** Finance™

This Oola blend is designed to encourage positive emotions and increased feelings of abundance. Its uplifting aroma promotes a sense of clarity and alertness to help you focus on and realize financial objectives.

Ingredients: fractionated coconut oil, Frankincense, Orange, Ocotea, Balsam Canada (Idaho Balsam Fir), Royal Hawaiian Sandalwood, Basil, Geranium, Lavender, Cardamom, Coriander, Ylang Ylang, Northern Lights Black Spruce, Rosemary, Citronella (nardus), Citronella (winterianus), Bergamot (furocoumarin-free), Vetiver, Peppermint, Melissa, Myrrh, Cinnamon Bark, Lemon, Jasmine, Roman Chamomile, Palmarosa, Bitter Orange (Neroli), Rose

Caution: Possible sun sensitivity.

Oola®** Fitness™

This energizing blend is formulated to empower and promote discipline and inspiration to set and achieve fitness goals.

Ingredients: caprylic/capric triglyceride, Cypress, Copaiba, Basil, Cistus, Marjoram, Peppermint, Clary Sage, Idaho Blue Spruce, Balsam Canada (Idaho Balsam Fir), Nutmeg, Black Pepper

Oola®** Friends™

A welcoming blend, Oola Friends helps bring harmonic balance to the energy centers of the body to encourage feelings of self-worth, confidence, and awareness.

Ingredients: caprylic/capric triglyceride, Lavender, Frankincense, Blue Cypress, Orange, Royal Hawaiian Sandalwood, Palo Santo, Xiang Mao, Ylang Ylang, Mandarin, Angelica, Geranium, Hyssop, Spanish Sage, Black Spruce, Jasmine, Lemongrass, Bitter Orange (Neroli), Coriander, Bergamot, Lemon, Roman Chamomile, Palmarosa, Rose

Oola®** Fun™

This uplifting and revitalizing essential oil blend promotes euphoric emotions. The cheerful aroma boosts self-confidence and encourages the mind to enjoy life's simple pleasures.

Ingredients: caprylic/capric triglyceride, Spearmint, Cedarwood, Myrtle, Lemon, Grapefruit, Tangerine, Jasmine, Nutmeg

Caution: Possible sun sensitivity.

Oola®** Grow™

Oola Grow is designed to help you reach unlimited potential and growth in many aspects of life. Whether it's emotional, spiritual, or mental, Oola Grow gives you courage to focus on the task at hand and helps you move forward toward positive advancements and progression.

Ingredients: fractionated coconut oil, White Fir, Blue Cypress, Ylang Ylang, Roman Chamomile, almond oil, Northern Lights Black Spruce, Coriander, Geranium, Jasmine, Cedarwood, Lavender, Frankincense, Bergamot (furocoumarin-free), Clary Sage, Royal Hawaiian Sandalwood, Grapefruit, Tangerine, Spearmint, Vetiver, Lemon, Neroli, Idaho Blue Spruce, Ocotea, Juniper, Orange, Cinnamon Bark, Citrus Hystrix, Rose, White Lotus

Caution: Possible sun sensitivity.

Owie™

Apply Owie topically to improve the appearance of your child's skin and to help heal a wound.

Ingredients: caprylic/capric glycerides, Balsam Canada (Idaho Balsam Fir), Tea Tree, Helichrysum, Elemi, Cistus, Hinoki, Clove

PanAway®

This very popular blend reduces pain and inflammation, increases circulation, and accelerates healing. It relieves swelling and discomfort from arthritis, sprains, muscle spasms, cramps, bumps, and bruises.

Ingredients: Wintergreen, Helichrysum, Clove, Peppermint

Caution: Possible skin sensitivity. Not intended for children under the age of 6 without the advice of a health care professional.

ParaGize™

Created with animals in mind, ParaGize is a proprietary blend of essential oils that promotes healthy digestion and helps expel worms and parasites.

Ingredients: caprylic/capric glycerides

Essential Oils: Tarragon, Ginger, Peppermint, Juniper, Fennel, Anise, Patchouli, Lemongrass, Cumin, Spearmint, Rosemary

Directions: Carefully apply according to the size and species of the animal. Additional dilution is recommended for smaller species.

Peace & Calming®

This blend promotes relaxation and a deep sense of peace and emotional well-being, helping to dampen tensions and uplift spirits. When massaged on the bottoms of feet, it can be a wonderful prelude to a peaceful night's rest. It may calm overactive and hard-to-manage children. It also reduces depression, anxiety, stress, and insomnia. Many people use it for relief from restless leg syndrome.

Ingredients: Tangerine, Orange, Ylang Ylang, Patchouli, Blue Tansy

Caution: Possible sun/skin sensitivity.

Peace & Calming II™

Peace & Calming II has a relaxing and pleasant aroma that may contribute to calming the mind and giving a sense of overall well-being.

Ingredients: Tangerine, Orange, Ylang Ylang, Patchouli, Northern Lights Black Spruce, Matricaria (German Chamomile), Vetiver, Cistus, Bergamot, Cassia, Davana

Caution: Possible sun sensitivity.

Present Time™

This blend is an empowering fragrance that creates a feeling of being in the moment. Disease develops when we live in the past and with regret. Being in the present time is the key to progressing and moving forward.

Ingredients: sweet almond oil, Bitter Orange (Neroli), Black Spruce, Ylang Ylang

Caution: Possible sun sensitivity.

PuriClean™

PuriClean is a unique blend of eleven essential oils that is specifically formulated for animals that cleanses and refreshes the skin. For best results, use as the first step in a three-part application, with Infect Away and Mendwell being used after PuriClean.

Ingredients: caprylic/capric glycerides

Essential Oils: Citronella, Lemongrass, Rosemary, Tea Tree, Lavandin, Myrtle, Patchouli, Lavender, Mountain Savory, Palo Santo, Cistus

Directions: Carefully apply according to the size and species of the animal. Additional dilution is recommended for smaller species.

Purification®

This purifying blend cleanses and disinfects the air and neutralizes mildew, cigarette smoke, and disagreeable odors. It disinfects and cleans cuts, scrapes, and bites from spiders, bees, hornets, and wasps.

Ingredients: Citronella, Rosemary, Lemongrass, Tea Tree, Lavandin, Myrtle

Raven™

The oils of this blend fight against respiratory disease and infections such as tuberculosis, influenza, and pneumonia. It is highly antiviral and antiseptic.

Ingredients: Camphor (Ravintsara), Lemon, Wintergreen, Peppermint, Eucalyptus Radiata

Caution: For external use only. Possible sun/skin sensitivity. Not intended for children under the age of 6 without the advice of a health care professional.

R.C.™

R.C. gives relief from colds, bronchitis, sore throats, sinusitis, coughs, and respiratory congestion. It decongests sinus passages, combats lung infections, and relieves allergy symptoms.

Ingredients: Eucalyptus Globulus, Myrtle, Marjoram, Pine, Eucalyptus Radiata, Eucalyptus Citriodora, Lavender, Cypress, Black Spruce, Peppermint

Reconnect™

Apply Reconnect to help the mind to react positively and to help you reconnect to your surroundings.

Ingredients: fractionated coconut oil, Sacred Frankincense, Lavender, Blue Cypress, Cedarwood, Melissa, Idaho Blue Spruce, Palo Santo, Northern Lights Black Spruce, almond oil, Bergamot, Myrrh, Vetiver, Geranium, Royal Hawaiian Sandalwood, Ylang Ylang, Hyssop, Rose

Caution: Possible sun sensitivity.

Red Shot™

Red Shot is a limited-time-only blend that adds a delicious variation to NingXia Red.

Ingredients: Tangerine, Mandarin, Lime, Grapefruit, Cassia, Spearmint

Release™

This is a helpful blend to release anger and memory trauma from the liver in order to create emotional well-being. It helps open the subconscious mind through pineal stimulation to release deep-seated trauma. It is one of the most powerful of the emotionally supporting essential oil blends.

Ingredients: Ylang Ylang, olive oil, Lavandin, Geranium, Royal Hawaiian Sandalwood, Grapefruit, Tangerine, Spearmint, Lemon, Blue Cypress, Davana, Kaffir Lime, Ocotea, Jasmine, Matricaria (German Chamomile), Blue Tansy, Rose

Caution: Possible sun sensitivity.

Relieve It™

This blend is high in anti-inflammatory compounds that relieve deep tissue pain and muscle soreness.

Ingredients: Black Spruce, Black Pepper, Hyssop, Peppermint

Caution: Possible skin sensitivity.

RepelAroma™

A natural insect repellant for animals, RepelAroma™ is a unique combination of essential oils that helps animals enjoy the outdoors without annoyance.

Ingredients: caprylic/capric glycerides

Essential Oils: Citronella, Idaho Tansy, Palo Santo, Tea Tree

Directions: Carefully apply according to the size and species of the animal. Additional dilution is recommended for smaller species.

RutaVaLa™

RutaVaLa is a proprietary blend of *Ruta graveolens* (Ruta), Lavender, and Valerian essential oils that promotes relaxation of the body and mind, soothes stressed nerves, and induces sleep. Ruta has long been used in South America to promote the relaxation of body and mind, relieve and soothe stressed nerves, and revitalize passion.

Ingredients: Lavender, Valerian, Ruta

RutaVaLa™ Roll-On

RutaVaLa Roll-On is a proprietary blend of *Ruta graveolens* (Ruta), Lavender, and Valerian essential oils that promotes relaxation of the body and mind, soothes stressed nerves, and induces sleep. Ruta has long been used in South America to promote the relaxation of body and mind, relieve and soothe stressed nerves, and revitalize passion.

Ingredients: caprylic/capric triglyceride, Lavender, Valerian, Ruta

Sacred Mountain™

Mountain aromas instill strength, empowerment, grounding, and protection with the spiritual feeling of being in a sacred environment.

Ingredients: Black Spruce, Ylang Ylang, Balsam Canada (Idaho Balsam Fir), Cedarwood

Caution: Possible sun/skin sensitivity.

SARA™

This very specific blend enables one to relax into a mental state to facilitate the release of trauma from sexual and/or ritual abuse. SARA also helps unlock other traumatic experiences such as physical and emotional abuse.

Ingredients: sweet almond oil, Ylang Ylang, Geranium, Lavender, Orange, Cedarwood, Blue Cypress, Davana, Citrus Hystrix, Jasmine, Rose, Matricaria (German Chamomile), Blue Tansy, Grapefruit, Tangerine, Spearmint, Lemon, Ocotea, White Lotus

Caution: Possible sun/skin sensitivity.

SclarEssence™/SclarEssence Vitality™

This blend balances hormones naturally using essential oil phytoestrogens. It helps to increase estrogen levels by supporting the body's own production of hormones. It combines the soothing effects of Peppermint with the balancing power of Fennel and Clary Sage and the calming action of Spanish Sage for an extraordinary topical and aromatic blend and Vitality dietary supplement.

Ingredients: Clary Sage, Peppermint, Spanish Sage, Fennel

Caution: Possible sun sensitivity. Do not use in conjunction with any other hormone products.

Sensation™

This beautiful smell is profoundly romantic, refreshing, and arousing. It amplifies the excitement of experiencing new heights of self-expression and awareness.

Sensation is also nourishing and hydrating for the skin and is beneficial for many skin problems.

Ingredients: Coriander, Ylang Ylang, Bergamot (furocoumarin-free), Jasmine, Geranium

Shutran™

Shutran is an empowering essential oil blend that is specifically designed for men to boost feelings of masculinity and confidence.

Ingredients: Idaho Blue Spruce, Ylang Ylang, Ocotea, Hinoki, Davana, Cedarwood, Lavender, Coriander, Lemon, Northern Lights Black Spruce

Caution: Possible sun sensitivity.

SleepyIze™

SleepyIze calms and relaxes the mind and body prior to children's bedtime.

Ingredients: caprylic/capric glycerides, Lavender, Geranium, Roman Chamomile, Tangerine, Bergamot, Sacred Frankincense, Valerian, Ruta

Caution: Possible sun sensitivity.

Slique™ Essence

Slique Essence combines powerful essential oils and stevia extract to support healthy weight-management goals. It suppresses food cravings, especially when used in conjunction with Slique Tea or any of the Slique products. The oils in this blend add a flavorful and uplifting element to any day, with the added support of Spearmint to aid proper digestion. Ocotea essential oil was chosen for its irresistible cinnamon-esque aroma, which can help trigger feelings of fullness and reduce the number of unexpected cravings. Slique Essence is antibacterial, antifungal, a lipid regulator, and a glucose regulator.

Stevia is added as an all-natural sweetener that provides a pleasant, sweet taste with no added calories.

Ingredients: Grapefruit, Tangerine, Spearmint, Lemon, Ocotea, Stevia Extract

SniffleEase™

SniffleEase is a refreshing, rejuvenating blend formulated just for kids for when they have congestion.

Ingredients: caprylic/capric glycerides, Eucalyptus Blue, Palo Santo, Lavender, Dorado Azul, Ravintsara, Myrtle, Eucalyptus Globulus, Marjoram, Pine, Eucalyptus Citriodora, Cypress, Eucalyptus Radiata, Black Spruce, Peppermint

Stress Away™

This is a gentle, fragrant blend that brings a feeling of peace and tranquility to both children and adults and helps relieve daily stress and nervous tension. It helps with normal, everyday stress, improves mental response, restores equilibrium, promotes relaxation, and lowers hypertension.

Ingredients: Copaiba, Lime, Cedarwood, Vanilla, Ocotea, Lavender

Caution: Possible sun/skin sensitivity.

Stress Away™ Roll-On

This is a gentle, fragrant blend that brings a feeling of peace and tranquility to both children and adults and helps relieve daily stress and nervous tension. It helps with normal, everyday stress, improves mental response, restores equilibrium, promotes relaxation, and lowers hypertension.

Ingredients: Copaiba, Lime, Cedarwood, Vanilla, Ocotea, Lavender

Caution: Possible sun/skin sensitivity

Surrender™

This inviting oil helps one surrender aggression and a controlling attitude. Stress and tension are released quickly when we surrender willfulness.

Ingredients: Lavender, Lemon, Black Spruce, Roman Chamomile, Angelica, Mountain Savory

Caution: Possible sun/skin sensitivity.

T-Away™

T-Away™ is formulated with a powerful combination of essential oils to promote new levels of emotional freedom and joyful feelings.

Ingredients: caprylic/capric glycerides

Essential Oils: Tangerine, Lavender, Royal Hawaiian Sandalwood, German Chamomile, Frankincense, Valerian, Ylang Ylang, Black Spruce, Geranium, Davana, Orange, Angelica, Ruta (Rue), Helichrysum, Hyssop, Spanish Sage, Citrus Hystrix, Patchouli, Coriander, Blue Tansy, Bergamot (furocoumarin-free), Rose, Lemon, Jasmine, Roman Chamomile, Palmarosa

Directions: Carefully apply according to the size and species of the animal. Additional dilution is recommended for smaller species.

The Gift™

The Gift is the very "essence of Arabia," blending the oils of antiquity into a most unique and exotic fragrance. It combines seven ancient therapeutic oils to capture the spirit of Arabia.

This oil blend represents Mary's gift to Gary in honor of Shutran's noble journey through the book *The One Gift*, a historical novel depicting the wit, intrigue, sorrow, and romance of the ancient frankincense and myrrh caravans.

Out of the writings and legends of antiquity, healing mysteries unfold as we discover powerful uses for herbs and oils in healing the injuries of war, accidents, scorpion stings, and snakebites and in sacred rituals for attaining greater spiritual attunement for healing and protecting the body.

Present-day science is now documenting the properties of these oils that augment the immune system, stimulate healing, and overcome depression. Myrrh and Frankincense are being touted for their anticancer, anti-infectious, antibacterial, and antiviral abilities, as well as being a topical anesthesia and having the ability to regenerate bone and cartilage. They are the oldest known substances for their immune stimulating and healing powers to ever come out of the ancient world.

Ingredients: Balsam Canada (Idaho Balsam Fir), Sacred Frankincense, Jasmine, Northern Lights Black Spruce, Myrrh, Vetiver, Cistus

Thieves®/Thieves Vitality™

This is a most amazing blend of highly antiviral, antiseptic, antibacterial, and anti-infectious essential oils.

It was created from research based on legends about a group of 15th-century thieves who rubbed botanicals on themselves to avoid contracting the plague while they robbed the bodies of the dead and dying. When apprehended, the thieves were forced to tell what their secret was and disclosed the formula of the herbs, spices, and oils they used to protect themselves in exchange for more lenient punishment.

Studies conducted at Weber State University (Ogden, UT) during 1997 demonstrated the killing power of these amazing oils against airborne microorganisms. The analysis showed that after 10 minutes of Thieves diffusion in the air, there was an 82 percent reduction in the gram positive *Micrococcus luteus* organism bioaerosol, a 96 percent reduction in gram negative *Pseudomonas aeruginosa* organism bioaerosol, and a 44 percent reduction in *S. aureus* bioaerosol (Chao SC, et al., 1998).

Ingredients: Clove, Lemon, Cinnamon Bark, Eucalyptus Radiata, Rosemary

Caution: Possible sun/skin sensitivity.

Tranquil™ Roll-On

This proprietary blend of Lavender, Cedarwood, and Roman Chamomile essential oils, packaged in a roll-on applicator, provides convenient and portable relaxation and stress relief. All three of these oils have been well documented as being effective in reducing restlessness, decreasing anxiety, and inducing a calming feeling to mind and body. Their combined effect is uplifting as well as relaxing and can be useful in promoting sleep as well as reducing stress.

Ingredients: Lavender, Cedarwood, caprylic/capric triglyceride, Roman Chamomile, coconut oil

Caution: Possible sun sensitivity.

Transformation™

Repressed trauma and tragedy from the past may be out of sight, but they are definitely not out of mind. Memories are imprinted in our cells for better or worse. Stored negative emotions need to be replaced with joy, hope, and courage.

Transformation blend radiates with the purifying oils of Lemon and Peppermint, along with the revitalizing power of sesquiterpenes from Sandalwood and Frankincense. Idaho Blue Spruce anchors new mental programming.

Reaching into the deepest recesses of memory, Transformation empowers and upholds the changes you want to make in your belief system. Positive, uplifting beliefs are foundational for the transformation of behavior.

Ingredients: Lemon, Peppermint, Royal Hawaiian Sandalwood, Clary Sage, Sacred Frankincense, Idaho Blue Spruce, Cardamom, Ocotea, Palo Santo

Caution: Possible sun sensitivity.

Trauma Life™

The emotional trauma from accidents, death of loved ones, assault, abuse, etc., can implant its devastation deep within the hidden recesses of the mind, causing life-long problems that seem endless.

Being able to release such burdens can bring about a new "lease on life" with a return to motivation and vitality.

This blend combats stress and uproots trauma that cause insomnia, anger, restlessness, and a weakened immune response.

Ingredients: Royal Hawaiian Sandalwood, Frankincense, Valerian, Black Spruce, Davana, Lavender, Geranium, Helichrysum, Citrus Hystrix, Rose

T.R. Care™

This unique blend is designed to restore confidence and uplift emotions by reducing stress and calming the mind, body, and spirit.

Ingredients: Roman Chamomile, Tangerine, Lavender, Bergamot, Royal Hawaiian Sandalwood, Ylang Ylang, Frankincense, Valerian, Blue Cypress, Orange, Geranium, Northern Lights Black Spruce, Davana, Ruta, Jasmine, Angelica, Cedarwood, Helichrysum, Hyssop, Spanish Sage, Patchouli, Citrus Hystrix, White Fir, Blue Tansy, Vetiver, Coriander, Bergamot (furocoumarin-free), Rose, Lemon, Cinnamon Bark, Palmarosa, Matricaria (German Chamomile), Grapefruit, Spearmint, Ocotea

Caution: Possible sun sensitivity.

TummyGize™

TummyGize is a quieting, relaxing blend that can be applied to little tummies that are upset. It also supports proper digestion.

Ingredients: caprylic/capric glycerides, Spearmint, Peppermint, Tangerine, Fennel, Anise, Ginger, Cardamom

Caution: Possible sun sensitivity.

Valor®

This blend was formulated to balance energies and instill courage, confidence, and self-esteem. It helps the body self-correct its balance and alignment.

Ingredients: Black Spruce, Camphor, Geranium, Blue Tansy, Frankincense

Valor II™

This formula offers an inspiring and calming aroma that can promote empowerment and uplift the soul.

Ingredients: caprylic/capric triglyceride, Ylang Ylang, Coriander, Bergamot, Northern Lights Black Spruce, Matricaria (German Chamomile), Idaho Blue Spruce, Frankincense, Vetiver, Cistus, Cassia, Davana, Geranium

White Angelica™

Increases and strengthens the aura around the body to bring a renewed sense of strength and protection, creating a feeling of wholeness in the realm of one's own spirituality. Its frequency neutralizes negative energy and gives a feeling of security.

Ingredients: sweet almond oil, Bergamot, Myrrh, Geranium, Royal Hawaiian Sandalwood, Ylang Ylang, Coriander, Black Spruce, Melissa, Hyssop, Rose

Caution: Possible sun sensitivity.

White Light™

White Light is a balancing essential oil blend meant to elevate the mind, awaken the senses, and promote harmony with nature.

Ingredients: White Fir, White Cedar, White Spruce, White Pine

Notes

* Royal Hawaiian Sandalwood is a registered trademark of Jawmin, LLC

** Oola is a registered trademark of OolaMoola, LLC

Animal Products

Animal Scents Products

Animal Scents Dental Pet Chews

Animal Scents Dental Pet Chews are a fast and easy way to clean your pet's teeth without having to use a toothbrush. Their naturally derived ingredients help to freshen your pet's breath; your pet will love it and so will you.

Ingredients: potato starch, pea fiber, gelatin, beet pulp, tapioca syrup, glycerin, calcium carbonate, coconut oil, natural poultry flavor, safflower oil, salt, kelp powder, dill, blueberry juice, gum arabic, mixed tocopherols (preservative), green tea extract, parsley, rosemary extract

Essential Oils: Spearmint, Tarragon, Ginger, Peppermint, Juniper, Fennel, Anise, Patchouli, Lemongrass, Cumin

Directions: For 20+ lb. pets: give 2 chews per week. For 5-19 lb. pets: give ½ a chew 2 times a week. This product is intended for intermittent or supplemental feeding only. Adjust diet as needed to accommodate this chew. Consult a veterinarian for pets that are pregnant or under 5 lbs. before use.

Caution: Always offer sufficient water when giving your pet treats or food. Make sure your pet chews the treat completely, as gulping any item can be harmful. This product is not recommended for pets with a history of gulping, choking, or poor chewing capability.

Animal Scents Ointment

Animal Scents Ointment is blended with Tea Tree and Myrrh, two of nature's most powerful essential oils. It is a protective and soothing salve formulated for external use on animals. Tested in the field for many years, this ointment is typically used for minor skin irritations, cuts, and abrasions. It is designed to cover infected wounds and seal in the essential oils.

Animal Scents Ointment offers an effective yet gentle and safe approach to soothing your pets without using harmful chemicals or synthetic products.

Ingredients: mink oil, lecithin, beeswax, lanolin, sesame seed oil, wheat germ oil, rose hip seed oil

Essential Oils: Palmarosa, Carrot Seed, Geranium, Patchouli, Coriander, Idaho Balsam Fir, Myrrh, Tea Tree, Bergamot (furocoumarin-free), Ylang Ylang

Directions: Clean area and apply as needed. If using Young Living's essential oils, apply oil(s) prior to application of Animal Scents Ointment.

Animal Scents Shampoo

Animal Scents Shampoo is formulated to clean all types of animal fur and hair. It has insect-repelling and killing properties and is designed to rid hair of lice, ticks, and other insects. This all-natural shampoo contains five powerful essential oils that are blended to gently cleanse, increase luster, and enhance grooming without the harmful ingredients often found in pet care products.

Ingredients: water, decyl glucoside, coco betaine, lauryl glucoside, coco-glucoside, glycerin, glyceryl oleate, citric acid, xanthan gum, inulin, sodium levulinate, sodium anisate, sodium phytate

Essential Oils: Lavandin, Lemon, Geranium, Citronella (C. Nardus), Cintronella Java Type (C. winterianus), Northern Lights Black Spruce, Vetiver

Directions: Pour a small amount of shampoo into your palm and rub gently between your hands. Massage thoroughly into your pet's wet coat. Lather. Rinse thoroughly. Repeat if necessary.

Animal Scents Essential Oil Blends

Infect Away™

Infect Away utilizes six essential oils for a gentle cleansing effect on your animal. For best results, use as the second part to a three-part system, with PuriClean being used first, then Infect Away, followed by Mendwell. It supports a healthy skin barrier.

Ingredients: caprylic/capric glycerides

Essential Oils: Myrrh, Patchouli, Dorado Azul, Palo Santo, Ecuador Plectranthus Oregano, Ocotea

Directions: Carefully apply according to the size and species of the animal. Additional dilution is recommended for smaller species.

Mendwell™

Mendwell is a blend of oils that supports healthy skin repair and is specifically formulated for animals. For best results, use as the last step in a three-part system, with PuriClean and Infect Away being used first.

Ingredients: caprylic/capric glycerides

Essential Oils: Geranium, Lavender, Hyssop, Myrrh, Frankincense, Hinoki

Directions: Carefully apply according to the size and species of the animal. Additional dilution is recommended for smaller species.

ParaGize™

Created with animals in mind, ParaGize is a proprietary blend of essential oils that promotes healthy digestion and helps expel worms and parasites.

Ingredients: caprylic/capric glycerides

Essential Oils: Tarragon, Ginger, Peppermint, Juniper, Fennel, Anise, Patchouli, Lemongrass, Cumin, Spearmint, Rosemary

Directions: Carefully apply according to the size and species of the animal. Additional dilution is recommended for smaller species.

PuriClean™

PuriClean is a unique blend of eleven essential oils that is specifically formulated for animals that cleanses and refreshes the skin. For best results, use as the first step in a three-part application, with Infect Away and Mendwell being used after PuriClean.

Ingredients: caprylic/capric glycerides

Essential Oils: Citronella, Lemongrass, Rosemary, Tea Tree, Lavandin, Myrtle, Patchouli, Lavender, Mountain Savory, Palo Santo, Cistus

Directions: Carefully apply according to the size and species of the animal. Additional dilution is recommended for smaller species.

Gary's Equine Essentials *(Products specially formulated for equine use.)*

Massage Oil

This blend is diluted specifically for equine use to give your horse a well-deserved cool-down before, during, or after physical activity.

Ingredients: coconut oil (caprylic/capric triglyceride)

Essential Oils: Wintergreen, Peppermint, Sage, Plectranthus Oregano, Copaiba (Balsam Copaiba), Melaleuca Quinquenervia (Niaouli), Lavender, Blue Cypress, Elemi, Vetiver, Caraway, Dorado Azul, Matricaria (German Chamomile)

Directions: Apply to desired area and massage as needed. Dilute with V-6 or other pure carrier oil as needed.

Shampoo

Equine Essentials Shampoo provides safe and effective cleansing and conditioning to leave the coat smooth, lustrous, and looking its best.

Ingredients: water, decyl glucoside, alkyl polyglucoside, coco betaine, sodium methyl 2-sulfolaurate, lauryl glucoside, tetrasodium glutamate diacetate, coc-glucoside, glycerin, glyceryl oleate, citric acid, xanthan gum, inulin, sodium levulinate, disodium 2-sulfolaurate, sodium anisate, sodium phytate

Essential Oils: Clove, Lemon, Cinnamon Bark, Rosemary, Lavandin, Geranium, Citronella *(C. Nardus)*, Cintronella Java Type *(C. winterianus)*, Northern Lights Black Spruce, Vetiver

Directions: Mix a generous amount of Equine Shampoo in a bucket of warm water. Lather into a wet coat and massage. Rinse thoroughly and repeat if necessary.

Tail & Mane Sheen™

Gary's Tail & Mane Sheen smooths hair, can be used as a detangler, and brings out the hair's natural, healthy shine. Monoi oil is a fragrant oil consisting of gardenias soaked in coconut oil and is widely used among French Polynesians as a skin and hair softener.

Ingredients: coconut oil (caprylic/capric triglyceride), wheat germ oil, mink oil, monoi extract

Essential Oils: Hinoki, Northern Lights Black Spruce, Lemon, Lavender, Geranium, Royal Hawaiian Sandalwood

Directions: For best results, wash and groom before application. Spray on tail and mane and comb through to achieve a glossy appearance.

RepelAroma™

A natural insect repellant for animals, RepelAroma™ is a unique combination of essential oils that helps animals enjoy the outdoors without annoyance.

Ingredients: caprylic/capric glycerides

Essential Oils: Citronella, Idaho Tansy, Palo Santo, Tea Tree

Directions: Carefully apply according to the size and species of the animal. Additional dilution is recommended for smaller species.

T-Away™

T-Away™ is formulated with a powerful combination of essential oils to promote new levels of emotional freedom and joyful feelings.

Ingredients: caprylic/capric glycerides

Essential Oils: Tangerine, Lavender, Royal Hawaiian Sandalwood, German Chamomile, Frankincense, Valerian, Ylang Ylang, Black Spruce, Geranium, Davana, Orange, Angelica, Ruta (Rue), Helichrysum, Hyssop, Spanish Sage, Citrus Hystrix, Patchouli, Coriander, Blue Tansy, Bergamot (furocoumarin-free), Rose, Lemon, Jasmine, Roman Chamomile, Palmarosa

Directions: Carefully apply according to the size and species of the animal. Additional dilution is recommended for smaller species.

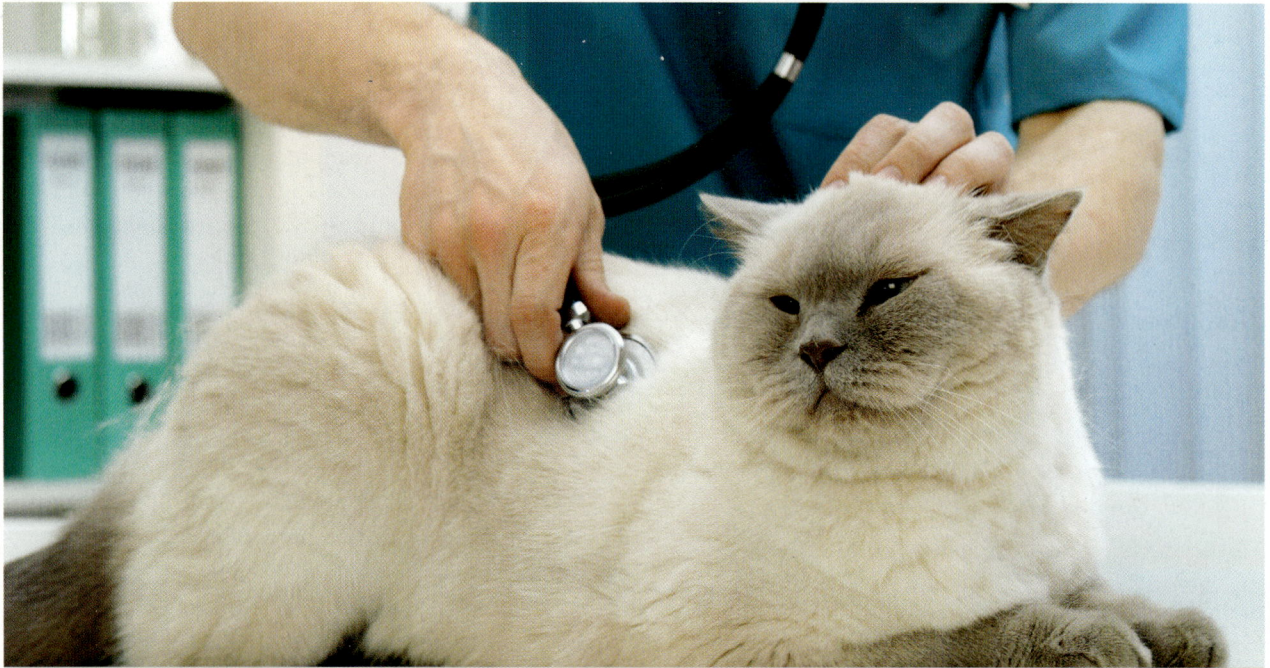

Products for First Aid for Animals

Animal Scents Ointment to seal and disinfect open wounds

Copaiba for bruising and soreness on small animals; used as a replacement for traditional Non-Steroidal Anti-Inflammatory Drugs (NSAIDs)*

Exodus II for infection and inflammation and to promote tissue regeneration

Helichrysum as a topical anesthetic and for neurologic conditions

Idaho Tansy is one of the most versatile oils for animals. It is purifying, cleansing, tissue-regenerating, anti-inflammatory, anesthetic, and is used for bruised bones, cuts, wounds, and colic. It also repels flies. Palo Santo may be used in place of Idaho Tansy.

Lavender for tissue regeneration and desensitizing the wound; effective against ringworm

Melrose for disinfecting and cleaning wounds; accelerates healing of wounds

Mountain Savory for reducing inflammation

Myrrh for infection, inflammation, and promoting tissue regeneration

Ocotea for bruising and soreness on large animals; oil of choice for diabetes

Ortho Ease to dilute essential oils and act as a pain reliever and anti-inflammatory; also has insect-repelling actions

PanAway as a pain killer if the pain originates from a broken bone rather than an open wound; make sure there is no visible, open, raw tissue.

Note: Do not apply PanAway to open wounds because it will sting and traumatize the animal. Instead, use Helichrysum and Idaho Balsam Fir to reduce bleeding and pain.

Purification is more effective than using iodine or hydrogen peroxide for washing and cleansing wounds. It also repels ticks and mites.

Roman Chamomile for tissue regeneration and desensitizing wounds

Thieves for inflammation, infection, bacteria, proud flesh (a condition where new tissue continues to rebuild itself, causing excessive granulation), and promoting tissue regeneration

Valerian can be used internally and externally for controlling pain

Vetiver can be used internally and externally for controlling pain

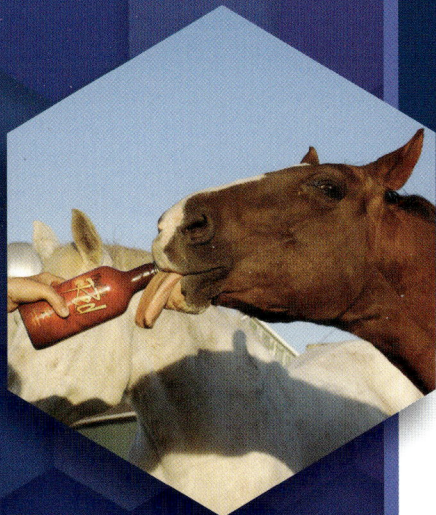

Nutritional Support

What's in it for Animals?

Similarly to humans, animals have some nutritional deficiencies as a result of a highly industrialized diet. Consequently, animal caregivers must *nourish* them, not just *feed* them. When caring for animals, we want them to be active and fit as well as pH-, vitamin-, mineral-, and enzyme-balanced. We want them to live to the higher end of their expectancy with a high quality of life.

Because nutrients have been taken out of our own food, it's no wonder their feeds are also suffering. Additionally, humans have created purebreds and domesticated animals, strategically bred to maintain ideal qualities. But this provides little genetic protection against disease. As a result, it is often desirable—if not necessary—to supplement an animal's diet with concentrated, 100 percent pure, therapeutic-grade products.

Nutritional Supplements

AgilEase™

AgilEase supports the body's response to acute inflammation in healthy animals, promotes healthy joint flexibility and mobility, and supports cartilage health.

Ingredients: frankincense resin powder, calcium fructoborate (from plant minerals), curcuminoids complex: [turmeric extract, piperine (from black pepper whole fruit extract)], collagen type II (chicken sternum extract), glucosamine sulfate, hyaluronic acid (as sodium hyaluronate), rice flour, hypromellose, silicon dioxide, potassium chloride
Essential Oils: Wintergreen, Copaiba, Clove, Northern Lights Black Spruce

AlkaLime®

This specially designed alkaline mineral powder contains an array of high-alkaline salts and other yeast- and fungus-fighting elements such as citric acid and essential oils. It may help reduce some signs of acid-based yeast and fungus dominance. Professionals and enthusiasts report success in correcting urine pH in cats and dogs. Use sparingly.

Ingredients: sodium (as sodium bicarbonate, sodium phosphate, sodium sulfate), calcium (as calcium carbonate, calcium phosphate, calcium sulfate), magnesium (as magnesium phosphate), potassium (as potassium bicarbonate, potassium chloride, potassium phosphate, potassium sulfate), lemon powder, citric acid, tartaric acid, stevia (Reb. A), silica

Essential Oils: Lemon, Lime

Caution: Consult a veterinarian if considering use for animals.

Allerzyme™

A vegetarian complex blend of enzymes, complementary botanicals, Ginger, Peppermint, and other essential oils to support proper digestion, waste elimination, and nutrient utilization. Formulated to combat allergies, gas, fermentation, fatigue, and irritable bowel syndrome, it works well for diverse animals.

Ingredients: plantain leaf, amylase, bromelain, peptidase, protease, invertase, phytase, barley grass, lipase, lactase, cellulase, alpha-galactosidase, diastase, hypromellose, water, silica

Essential Oils: Tarragon, Ginger, Peppermint, Juniper, Fennel, Lemongrass, Anise, Patchouli

BLM™ (Bones, Ligaments, and Muscles)

BLM supports normal bone and joint health. This formula combines powerful, natural ingredients enhanced with the anti-inflammatory and pain-relieving essential oils.

These ingredients support healthy cell function and encourage joint health and fluid movement.

This product is a highly effective arthritis treatment for building bones, ligaments, and muscles. The exclusive collagen and hyaluronic acid blend strengthens and rebuilds damaged joints and cartilage as it combats arthritis inflammation and bone pain.

Ingredients: sodium, manganese, Proprietary BLM Blend: [glucosamine sulfate, type II collagen (chicken sternum extract), MSM (methylsulfonylmethane)], gelatin, rice flour, magnesium stearate, silicon dioxide

Essential Oils: Idaho Balsam Fir, Wintergreen, Clove

Allergen Warning: Contains ingredients derived from shellfish.

ComforTone®

ComforTone is an effective combination of herbs and essential oils that supports the health of the digestive system by eliminating residues from the colon and enhancing its natural ability to function optimally. Because it supports normal peristalsis (the wave-like contractions that move food through the intestines), ComforTone is ideal for strengthening the system that delivers nutrients to the rest of the body.

This herbal formulation is combined with powerful essential oils that are antiparasitic, anti-inflammatory, ease intestinal cramps, help soothe the discomforts of the digestive tract, and aid in the elimination process.

Ingredients: cascara sagrada bark, psyllium seed, barberry bark, burdock root, fennel seed, garlic, echinacea root, bentonite, diatomaceous earth, ginger root, German chamomile flower extract, apple pectin, licorice root, cayenne fruit, gelatin, water, silicon dioxide

Essential Oils: Tarragon, Ginger, Tangerine, Rosemary, Anise, Peppermint, Ocotea, German Chamomile

CortiStop™

A proprietary dietary supplement designed to help the body minimize production of the stress hormone cortisol, CortiStop is used in female animals to combat the effects of Cushing's disease.

Ingredients: pregnenolone, L-a-phosphatidylserine, L-a-phosphatidylcholine, black cohosh extract, DHEA, rice flour, silica, gelatin

Essential Oils: Clary Sage, Canadian Fleabane (Conyza), Fennel, Frankincense, Peppermint

Detoxzyme®

Detoxzyme combines powerful and effective essential oils with a spectrum of fast-acting enzymes that assist in the complete digestive process, helping to detoxify and promote cleansing. The enzymes are designed to help digest starches, sugars, proteins, and fats and along with the trace minerals help the body detoxify, reducing cholesterol and triglycerides. Detoxzyme helps in opening the gallbladder duct and cleansing the liver, while promoting detoxification and parasite cleansing.

This important enzyme formula facilitates remarkable absorption of nutrients from foods and supplements. Cats and dogs benefit mostly from the antiparasitic qualities.

Ingredients: amylase, cumin seed powder, invertase, protease 4.5, glucoamylase, bromelain, phytase, lipase, cellulase, lactase, alpha-galactosidase, vegetable cellulose, rice bran, water, silica,
Essential Oils: Cumin, Anise, Fennel

Digest & Cleanse™

Digest & Cleanse is formulated to soothe the bowel, prevent gas, and stimulate the liver, gall bladder, and stomach secretions, thus aiding digestion and absorption. It is blended with clinically proven and time-tested essential oils that work synergistically. Because the essential oils are so potent, it takes only a very few drops of the oil to achieve the desired digestive and cleansing effects.

Ingredients: virgin coconut oil, fractionated coconut oil, gelatin, glycerin, aqueous coating solution (water, oleic acid, sodium alginate, medium-chain triglycerides, ethyl-cellulose, ammonium hydroxide, stearic acid)
Essential Oils: Peppermint, Caraway, Lemon, Ginger, Fennel, Anise

---

EndoGize™

When the endocrine system is not balanced, each of these body systems is unable to function properly and can put undue stress on other systems within the body. It is particularly indicated for dogs and horses with Cushing's disease, hypothyroidism, false pregnancy, pyometra, Metabolic Syndrome, urinary incontinence, prostate disease, cystic ovaries, and obesity.

Ingredients: vitamin B6 (as pyridoxine HCl), zinc (as zinc aspartate), Proprietary EndoGize Blend: [ashwaganda root, muira puama bark, L-arginine, epimedium aerial parts, tribulus terrestris fruit extract, phosphatidylcholine, soy lecithin, black pepper fruit extract, glycoamylase, acid stable protease, eurycoma longifolia root extract, amylase, cellulase], DHEA, rice flour, gelatin
Essential Oils: Ginger, Myrrh, Cassia, Clary Sage, Canadian Fleabane

---

Essentialzyme™

Essentialzyme is an advanced, multienzyme complex that promotes digestion and assists in the assimilation of nutrients. Enzyme supplementation is particularly important when the pancreas duct or common bile duct is blocked, thereby preventing enzymes from reaching the intestines.

Essentialzyme is a bilayer, Peppermint-coated caplet that combines pure essential oils, herbs, and pancreatic and plant-derived enzymes to support overall digestion. Its dual time-release technology increases its effect during digestion.

Essentialzyme helps re-establish proper enzyme balance in the digestive system and throughout the body, helps to improve intestinal flora, and may also help retard the aging process. This is a high-quality, complex enzyme formula created to help improve and aid digestion and elimination of toxic waste from the body, which in turn means more energy and vitality.

Ingredients: calcium (as di-calcium phosphate), Proprietary Delayed Release Blend (Light): [pancrealipase, pancreatin, trypsin], Proprietary Immediate Release Blend (Dark): [betaine (HCl), bromelain, thyme leaf powder, carrot powder, alfalfa sprout powder, alfalfa leaf powder, papain, cumin seed powder, Essential Oil Blend], microcrystalline cellulose, dicalcium phosphate, hydroxypropylcellulose, hydroxypropylmethylcellulose, stearic acid, silicon dioxide, croscarmellose sodium, **Coating:** sodium citrate, sodium carboxymethyl cellulose, dextrin, lecithin, dextrose, peppermint essential oil
Essential Oils: Anise, Fennel, Peppermint, Tarragon, Clove

Essentialzymes-4™

Essentialzymes-4 is a multispectral enzyme complex specially formulated to aid the digestion of dietary fats, proteins, fiber, and carbohydrates commonly found in the modern, processed diet. Essentialzymes-4 combines both animal- and plant-based enzymes into a single solution to help the body more completely break down problematic foods such as high fats and excessive starch. The dual time-release technology releases the animal- and plant-based enzymes at separate times within the digestive tract, allowing for optimal absorption of key nutrients and amino acids.

The plant-based enzymes capsule is designed to release immediately upon entering the stomach, where the pH environment is broad, acidic, and more conducive to plant-based enzyme breakdown and proper absorption.

The animal-based enzyme capsule is formulated to delay its release in the lower intestine region, where the environment is more alkaline, and the pH level is better suited for animal-based enzyme breakdown and proper absorption.

Ingredients (Yellow Capsule): protease (4.5, 6.0), amylase, cellulase, lipase, peptidase, phytase, bromelain, papain, rice flour, gelatin capsule, magnesium stearate, silicon dioxide

Essential Oils: Anise, Ginger, Rosemary, Tarragon, Fennel

Ingredients (White Capsule): bee pollen powder, pancreatin, lipase, rice flour, hypromellose capsule, magnesium stearate, silicon dioxide

Allergen Warning: Contains bee product.

Estro™

Estro is an herbal tincture containing plant-derived phytoestrogens, such as black cohosh, which are widely used in Europe as safe alternatives to synthetic estrogen. Phytoestrogens have been researched for their ability to support the body.

The essential oil of Clary Sage, containing natural sclareol, is a plant-based estrogen that is very calming and emotionally balancing. Estro combines the wonderful benefits of royal jelly, rich in amino acids, minerals, and vitamins B5 and B6, and helps to provide immune-stimulating properties and energy.

Estro is particularly indicated for dogs and horses with Cushing's disease, hypothyroidism, false pregnancy, pyometra, metabolic syndrome, urinary incontinence, prostate disease, cystic ovaries, and obesity.

Ingredients: black cohosh root, blue cohosh root, royal jelly, distilled water, ethanol

Essential Oils: Fennel, Lavender, Clary Sage

Allergen Warning: Product contains bee products.

FemiGen™

FemiGen combines whole food herbs like wild yam, damiana, and dong quai with synergistic amino acids and select hormone-balancing essential oils to supply special nutritional support to the female systems. It acts as a natural estrogen and helps balance the hormones and the reproductive system.

FemiGen is particularly indicated for dogs and horses with Cushing's disease, hypothyroidism, false pregnancy, pyometra, metabolic syndrome, urinary incontinence, prostate disease, cystic ovaries, and obesity.

Ingredients: magnesium (magnesium carbonate), damiana leaf, *Epimedium sagittatum* aerial plant, wild yam root, dong quai root, muira puama root, ginseng root,

licorice root extract, black cohosh root, L-carnitine, dimethylglycine HCI, cramp bark, squaw vine, L-phenylalanine, L-cystine, L-cysteine HCI, gelatin

Essential Oils: Fennel, Clary Sage, Sage, Ylang Ylang

ICP™

ICP is a great colon cleanser with an advanced mix of fibers that scours out residues.

A healthy digestive system is important for the proper functioning of all other systems because it absorbs nutrients that are used throughout the body. ICP provides ingredients such as psyllium, oat bran, flax, and fennel seeds to form a combination of soluble and insoluble fibers. Enhanced with a special blend of essential oils, the fibers work to decrease the buildup of wastes, dispel gas, improve nutrient absorption, and help maintain a healthy heart.

Ingredients: Proprietary ICP Blend: [psyllium seed, flax seed oil, oat bran, fennel powder, rice bran, guar gum, yucca root, cellulose], Proprietary ICP Enzyme Blend: [lipase, protease, phytase, peptidase, aloe vera leaf juice]

Essential Oils: Fennel, Anise, Tarragon, Ginger, Lemongrass, Rosemary

Caution: Using without enough liquid may cause choking. Do not use if you have difficulty swallowing.

Allergen Alert: May cause allergic reaction in animals sensitive to inhaled or ingested psyllium.

ImmuPro™

ImmuPro chewable tablets are packed with some of the most powerful immune stimulants known, including wolfberry polysaccharide and beta glucan (a polysaccharide from reishi, maitake, and *Agaricus blazei* mushrooms). Reishi, maitake, and *Agaricus blazei* organic mushrooms are the highest known sources of a rich variety of beta glucans, potent immune-stimulating polysaccharides that have been documented by numerous studies as having significant immune-boosting effects.

Reports from the field hint that these botanicals may help to boost survivor rates of cancer and stimulate both cell-mediated and humoral immunity, potentially boosting levels of macrophages, neutrophils, phagocytes, B-cells, T-cells, natural killer cells, interleukins, and interferons. ImmuPro combines complex and potent, immune-boosting minerals such as zinc, copper, and selenium. It also contains melatonin, one of the most powerful immune stimulants known. Melatonin levels steadily decrease with age, which is a factor that contributes to accelerated aging.

ImmuPro has great reports from the field regarding dogs, particularly those with cancer.

Ingredients: calcium (as c. carbonate), zinc (as z. bisglycinate), selenium (as s. glycinate chelate), copper (c. glycinate chelate), strawberry powder, wolfberry fruit polysaccharide, raspberry fruit powder, Reishi whole mushroom powder, Maitake mushroom mycelia powder, larch tree wood extract, mushroom fruit powder, melatonin, dextrose (non-GMO), hydroxylpropyl cellulose, stevia, silicon dioxide, magnesium stearate, maltodextrin (non-GMO)
Essential Oil: Orange

Inner Defense®

Inner Defense helps counter exposure to harmful germs, bacteria, poor diet, devitalized food, and polluted water and air. This proprietary essential oil blend helps boost immune systems by creating an unfriendly environment for yeast and fungus, improving digestion, supporting the respiratory system, and fighting against the invasion of destructive viruses and bacteria.

Ingredients: virgin coconut oil, fish gelatin, glycerin, water
Essential Oils: Thieves Blend: [Clove, Lemon, Eucalyptus Radiata, Rosemary, Cinnamon Bark], O3 Super Blend: [Oregano, Thyme, Lemongrass]
Allergen Warning: Product contains bee products.

JuvaPower®

JuvaPower is a high-antioxidant, whole-food vegetable powder complex that is a rich source of acid-binding foods. It is formulated with powerful, liver-supporting nutrients with intestinal cleansing benefits. JuvaPower is one of the most important and supportive supplements to take daily. It is very cleansing to the colon and to the liver. Best results from the field indicate adding to a soft, warm meal.

Ingredients: Proprietary JuvaPower Blend: [rice seed bran, spinach leaf, tomato fruit, beet root, flaxseed bran, oat bran, broccoli floret/stalk, cucumber, dill seed, barley sprout seed, ginger root and rhizome, slippery elm bark, L-taurine, psyllium seed husk, anise seed, fennel seed, aloe vera leaf extract, peppermint leaf
Essential Oils: Anise, Fennel
Allergen Alert: May cause allergic reaction in animals sensitive to inhaled or ingested psyllium.

JuvaSpice®

JuvaSpice is a healthy spice, formulated with powerful, liver-supporting nutrients and cleansing benefits. It is very similar to JuvaPower in its cleansing and supporting health benefits. Reports indicate best results by sprinkling over an animal's food and gradually increasing the amount over the course of a week.

Ingredients: Proprietary JuvaSpice Blend: [rice seed bran, spinach leaf, tomato fruit, beet root, flaxseed bran, oat bran, broccoli floret/stalk, cucumber, potassium (chloride), Redmond Real Salt*, dill seed, barley sprouted seed, cayenne pepper fruit, ginger root and rhizome, slippery elm bark, L-taurine, psyllium seed husk, anise seed, fennel seed, aloe vera leaf extract, peppermint leaf
Essential Oils: Anise, Fennel
Allergen Alert: May cause allergic reaction in animals sensitive to inhaled or ingested psyllium.

JuvaTone®

JuvaTone is a special herbal complex in tablet form designed to support the liver with an excellent source of choline, a nutrient that is vital for proper liver function and necessary for those with high-protein diets. JuvaTone also contains inositol and dl-methionine, which help with the body's process of elimination. Methionine helps recycle glutathione, a natural antioxidant crucial for normal liver function. Other ingredients include Oregon grape root, a source of the liver-supporting compound berberine, and therapeutic-grade essential oils to enhance overall effectiveness.

Fats and bile within the liver may easily become oversaturated with oil-soluble toxins, synthetic chemicals, and heavy metals. As toxins build, the liver becomes taxed and stressed, resulting in aggravating skin conditions, rashes, fatigue, headaches, muscle pain, digestive disturbances, pallor, dizziness, and mental confusion. The final products of digestion are transported through the hepatic portal vein from the colon to the liver to be cleansed. Animals in the field respond well to it, albeit when crushed and mixed into their favorite foods.

Ingredients: calcium (as dicalcium phosphate), iron (dicalcium phosphate, parsley leaf powder), copper (as copper citrate), sodium, choline (from c. bitartrate), DI-methionine, beet root, inositol, dandelion root, L-cysteine HCI, alfalfa sprout, Oregon grape root, parsley leaf powder, bee propolis, echinacea purpurea root, cellulose, silicon dioxide, magnesium stearate, cellulose film-coating

Essential Oils: Lemon, German Chamomile, Geranium, Rosemary, Myrtle, Blue Tansy

Allergen Warning: Product contains bee pollen.

K&B™

K&B is formulated to nutritionally support normal kidney and bladder health. Juniper enhances the body's efforts to maintain proper fluid balance. Parsley supports kidney and bladder function and aids overall urinary health. Uva Ursi supports both urinary and digestive system health. The 100 percent pure, therapeutic-grade essential oils added to the ingredients fortify the effectiveness of its overall use for kidney and bladder infections and other related conditions.

Ingredients: juniper berry extract, parsley leaf extract, uva-ursi leaf extract, dandelion root extract, German chamomile flower extract, royal jelly, water, ethyl alcohol

Essential Oils: Geranium, Fennel, Clove, Roman Chamomile, Sage, Juniper

Allergen Warning: Product contains bee products

KidScents® MightyVites™

KidScents MightyVites is a whole food, multinutrient that contains super fruits, plants, and vegetables that deliver the full spectrum of vitamins, minerals, antioxidants, and phytonutrients. The Ningxia wolfberry fruit is one of the highest antioxidant foods known, making it an excellent whole food with 18 amino acids; 21 trace minerals; vitamins Bl, B2, B6, C, E; polyphenols; carotenoids; magnesium; and potassium. This super-enriched, chewable vitamin is perfect for giving animals what Mother Nature intended.

Ingredients: vitamin A, vitamin C (as ascorbic acid from orange), vitamin D (as cholecalciferol), vitamin E (as d-alpha tocopheryl acid succinate), vitamin K (phytonadione), thiamine (vitamin B1 as thiamine mononitrate), riboflavin (vitamin B2), niacin (as niacinamide), vitamin B6 (as pyridoxine HCI), vitamin B6 (as pyridoxal-5-phosphate), folate (as folic

acid), vitamin B12 (methylcobalamin), biotin (vitamin H), pantothenic acid (as d-calcium pantothenate), iodine (as potassium iodide), magnesium (as magnesium oxide), zinc (from zinc yeast complex), selenium (from selenium yeast complex), copper (from copper yeast complex), chromium (from chromium yeast complex), sorbitol, fructose, natural flavors, lecithin (soy), citric acid, silica, magnesium stearate, di-calcium phosphate

MightyVites™ Wild Berry Proprietary Blend
Ingredients: grape skin powder, Ningxia wolfberry fruit, cherry juice powder, strawberry juice powder, malic acid, broccoli floret, methylsulfonylmethane, barley grass, curcumins, citrus flavonoids (from tangerine), spirulina algae, tocotrienols (from natural palm oil), olive leaf extract, boron (as boron AAC), lutein (from marigold flowers)

MightyVites™ Orange Cream Proprietary Blend
Ingredients: orange juice powder, Ningxia wolfberry fruit, malic acid, broccoli floret, methylsulfonylmethane, barley grass, curcumins, citrus flavonoids (from tangerine), spirulina algae, grape skin powder, tocotrienols (from natural palm oil), olive leaf extract, boron (as boron AAC), lutein (from marigold flowers)

KidScents® MightyZyme™

KidScents MightyZyme is an all-natural, vegetarian, chewable tablet, designed to give added enzyme nutrition to prevent any enzyme depletion. MightyZyme combines nine different digestive enzymes with several other nutrients to support healthy digestion, relieving occasional symptoms, including stomach pressure, bloating, gas, pain, and minor cramping that may occur after eating. MightyZyme chewable tablets assist with normal digestion of all foods, including proteins, carbohydrates, and fats.

Ingredients: folate (as folic acid), calcium (from calcium carbonate), Proprietary MightyZyme Blend: [lipase, alfalfa leaf powder, protease 4.5, amylase, bromelain, carrot root powder, protease 6.0, peptidase, phytase, protease 3.0, cellulase], carnauba wax, fructose, maltodextrin, apple juice concentrate, coconut oil, silica

Essential Oil: Peppermint

Life 9™

This high-potency probiotic builds and restores intestinal health. Probiotics are important because of their positive effect on the bowels. Many do not realize that the bowels are the source of health and vitality and where nutrients are absorbed into the bloodstream. They are also the command center of the immune system and eliminators of waste products. If the bowels are not working properly, optimal health is impossible and the body is vulnerable to a myriad of conditions.

For the bowels to function properly, probiotics are necessary for every intestinal physiological process and to prevent the proliferation of harmful bacteria and yeast.

Life 9 is a proprietary, high-potency combination of nine probiotic bacteria strains *(Lactobacillus acidophilus, Bifidobacterium lactis, Lactobacillus plantarum, Lactobacillus rhamnosus, Lactobacillus salivarius, Streptococcus thermophilus, Bifidobacterium breve, Bifidobacterium bifidum/biflactis, Bifidobacterium longum)* that support intestinal health and healthy immune function.

This product may be very helpful when given to animals intensively during and after illness to boost immunity and support recovery. It is especially important after animals have taken antibiotics or suffered any gastrointestinal distress.

Ingredients: *L. acidophilus, Bifidobacterium lactis, Lactobacillus plantarum, Lactobacillus rhamnosus, Lactobacillus salivarius, Streptococcus thermophilus, Bifidobacterium breve, Bifidobacterium bifidum/bif lactis, Bifidobacterium longum*, calcium carbonate, microcrystalline cellulose, Hypromellose and gellan gum delayed-release capsule, rice bran, silica

Longevity Softgels™

A daily antioxidant—a potent, proprietary blend of fat-soluble antioxidants, is as essential as a multivitamin to be taken daily. One of the most powerful antioxidant supplements available, with an ORAC score of 150,000, Longevity provides 700 times the antioxidant power of carrots. It helps prevent the damaging effects of aging, diet, and the environment using the 100 percent pure essential oils of Thyme, Orange, Frankincense, and Clove, nature's strongest antioxidant oil.

Longevity helps protect DHA levels for brain function and cardiovascular health, helps promote healthy cell regeneration, helps support the liver, helps increase immune function, and helps strengthen the nervous system.

Reports from the field indicate great use in dogs with the added benefit of discouraging insect bites.

Ingredients: virgin coconut oil, fractionated coconut oil, gelatin, water, glycerin, aqueous coating solution: [oleic acid, sodium alginate, medium-chain triglycerides, ethylcellulose, ammonium hydroxide, stearic acid], mixed tocopherols (vitamin E)
Essential Oils: Thyme, Orange, Clove, Frankincense

Master Formula

Master Formula is a full-spectrum, premium multinutrient supplement, providing vitamins, minerals, and food-based nutriment to support general health and well-being. By using a Synergistic Suspension Isolation process (SSI Technology), ingredients are delivered in three distinct delivery forms. Collectively, these ingredients provide a premium, synergistic complex to support the body.

Micronized Nutrient Capsules

Micronized Nutrient Capsules are an organic food blend of B vitamins along with chelated minerals to naturally support the body.

Ingredients: vitamin A (from beta carotene), thiamin (vitamin B1), riboflavin (vitamin B2), niacin (vitamin B3), vitamin B6 (pyridoxine), folate (vitamin B9), vitamin B12 (methylcobalamin), biotin, pantothenic acid (vitamin B5), iron (ferrous bisglycinate chelate), magnesium (magnesium glycinate chelate), zinc (zinc glycinate chelate), selenium (selenium glycinate chelate), copper (copper glycinate chelate), manganese (manganese glycinate chelate), chromium (chromium nicotinate glycinate chelate), molybdenum glycinate chelate, Proprietary Master Formula Capsule Blend: [Atlantic kelp, inositol, PABA (para amino benzoic acid), spirulina algae, barley grass, citrus bioflavonoids from lemon whole fruit powder, orange whole fruit powder, lime whole fruit powder, tangerine whole fruit powder, grapefruit whole fruit powder, Ningxia wolfberry fruit powder, olive leaf extract, boron citrate, lycopene], hypromellose, magnesium stearate (vegetable source), silicon dioxide, microcrystalline cellulose

Phyto-Caplets

Phyto-Caplets are a trace mineral complex and supporting prebiotics; a powerful fruit, vegetable, and herb extract blend along with vitamin C to help scavenge free radicals in the body.

Ingredients: vitamin C (calcium ascorbate and acerola cherry), calcium (calcium carbonate), potassium (potassium chloride), choline (choline bitartrate), Proprietary Master Formula Tablet Blend: [fructooligosaccharides, trace minerals], Spectra™ Fruit, Vegetable, and Herb Blend: [coffea arabica fruit extract, broccoli sprout seed concentrate, camellia sinensis leaf extract, onion bulb extract, apple fruit skin extract, acerola fruit extract, camu camu fruit concentrate, quercetin flower extract, tomato fruit concentrate, broccoli floret and stem concentrate, acai fruit concentrate, turmeric root concentrate, garlic clove concentrate, basil leaf concentrate, oregano leaf concentrate, cinnamon branch/stem concentrate, elderberry fruit concentrate, carrot root concentrate, mangosteen fruit concentrate, black currant fruit extract, blueberry fruit extract, sweet cherry fruit concentrate, blackberry fruit concentrate, chokeberry fruit concentrate, raspberry fruit concentrate, spinach leaf concentrate, kale leaf concentrate, bilberry fruit extract, Brussels sprout head concentrate], microcrystalline cellulose, stearic acid, croscarmellose sodium, organic maltodextrin, silicon dioxide, organic sunflower lecithin, organic palm olein, organic guar gum

Liquid Vitamin Capsule

Liquid Vitamin Capsules contain pure essential oils and fat soluble vitamins, which provide antioxidants and vitamins in a liquid delivery.

Ingredients: vitamin A (from beta carotene), vitamin D3 (cholecalciferol), vitamin E (d-alpha tocopheryl succinate), vitamin K (K2 as menaquinone-7), sunflower lecithin (non-GMO), hypromellose

Essentials Oils: Turmeric, Cardamom, Clove, Fennel, Ginger

MegaCal™

Caution: Avoid using this with animals due to its significant xylitol content.

MightyVites™ (See KidScents MightyVites)

MightyZyme™ (See KidScents MightyZyme)

MindWise™

MindWise delivers the exotic sacha inchi nut oil and a proprietary blend of pure essential oils and more to support normal brain and cardiovascular function.

Ingredients: vitamin D, Proprietary MindWise Memory Blend: [pomegranate fruit extract, rhododendron leaf extract, GPC (L-alpha glycerylphosphorylcholine), ALCAR (acetyl-L-carnitine), CoQ10 (Kaneka Q10™) (as ubiquinone), turmeric root powder, lithium orotate, sacha inchi nut oil, fractionated coconut oil, water, pomegranate juice concentrate, acai puree, glycerin, gum acacia, fruit and vegetable juice for color, natural pomegranate acai flavor, stevia, natural oil flavor, natural acai oil flavor, organic guar gum]

Essential Oils: Peppermint, Fennel, Anise, Lemon, Lime

Allergen Warning: Contains tree nuts.

Mineral Essence™

This product is a very balanced, organic, ionic mineral complex with more than 60 different minerals. Without minerals, vitamins cannot be properly assimilated or absorbed by the body. Mineral Essence has a natural electrolyte balance, helping to prevent disease and premature aging. Minerals are necessary for proper immune and metabolic functions, and essential oils enhance the bioavailability of minerals, which provides us with a superior product.

Ingredients: magnesium, chloride, trace mineral complex, honey, royal jelly

Essential Oils: Lemon, Cinnamon Bark, Peppermint

Allergen Warning: Product contains bee products.

MultiGreens™

MultiGreens is a nutritious chlorophyll formula designed to boost vitality by working with the glandular, nervous, and circulatory systems. MultiGreens is made with spirulina, alfalfa sprouts, barley grass, bee pollen, eleuthero, Pacific kelp, and 100 percent pure, therapeutic-grade essential oils. It is a natural, sustainable energy source with bioactive sea vegetables that increase vitality, nutrient-dense bee pollen, a purifying essential oil blend to increase assimilation, and an excellent source of choline, critical for energy production.

Ingredients: Proprietary MultiGreens Blend: [bee pollen, barley grass juice concentrate, spirulina, choline (as choline bitartrate), eleuthero root, alfalfa, kelp], amino acid complex: [L-arginine, L-cysteine, L-tyrosine], gelatin, silica

Essential Oils: Rosemary, Lemon, Lemongrass, Melissa

NingXia Nitro®

NingXia Nitro is an all-natural way to increase cognitive alertness, enhance mental fitness, promote energy, and support overall performance. Its benefits are derived from a wide range of powerful cognitive enhancers like wolfberry seed oil combined with therapeutic-grade essential oils. It improves physical performance, speeds up recovery, and increases overall energy reserves, while avoiding the typical caffeine crash.

Other supportive ingredients such as B vitamins, green tea extract (derived from the leaves of *Camilla sinensis* that are unfermented, a source of ECGC), choline, and Korean ginseng have been added to sharpen the mind and invigorate the senses. NingXia Nitro is a simple and convenient way for your animal to become more focused, have better mental acuity, and have enhance physical performance.

Ingredients: niacin (as niacinamide), vitamin B6 (as pyridoxine HCl), vitamin B12 (as methylcobalamin), iodine (as potassium iodide), Proprietary Nitro Energy Blend: [d-ribose, green tea leaf extract, choline (as choline bitartrate), mulberry leaf extract, Korean ginseng root extract], vanilla fruit oil, chocolate bean oil, yerba mate leaf oil, wolfberry seed oil, purified water, Nitro Fruit Juice Blend Concentrate: [sweet cherry, kiwi, blueberry, acerola, bilberry, black currant, raspberry, strawberry, cranberry], coconut nectar, natural flavors, pectin, xanthan gum
Contains 40 mg of naturally occurring caffeine.

Essential Oils: Spearmint, Peppermint, Nutmeg, Black Pepper

Allergen Warning: Contains milk and tree nut (coconut).

NingXia Red® (Juice)

Ningxia wolfberries have long been treasured in the natural health community. Their phytochemical profile is legendary: amazing polysaccharides, calcium, 18 amino acids, 21 trace minerals, beta-carotene, vitamins B1, B2, B6, and E, along with polyphenols.

It promotes free radical scavenging by providing high levels of powerful antioxidants while boosting energy. It supports brain and cognitive health as well as digestive and eye health. The nutritive power of NingXia Red fortifies the cardiovascular system and supports healthy blood pressure levels while promoting restful sleep patterns. It aids the animal's body's natural anti-inflammatory response, enhances immune function, and supports proper muscle and joint health.

This powerful antioxidant supplement drink supports immune function, liver function, and eye health.

Ingredients: sodium, Proprietary NingXia Red Blend: [whole Ningxia wolfberry puree, blueberry juice from concentrate, plum juice from concentrate, cherry juice from concentrate, aronia juice from concentrate, pomegranate juice from concentrate], water, tartaric acid, natural blueberry flavoring, pure vanilla extract, malic acid, pectin, sodium benzoate (to maintain freshness), natural stevia extract

Essential Oils: Grape, Orange, Yuzu, Lemon, Tangerine

Ningxia Wolfberry (Organic Dried)

The Ningxia wolfberry is one of earth's most powerful antioxidant fruits. It is rich in polysaccharides, with more vitamin C than oranges, more beta-carotene than carrots, and more calcium than broccoli.

Ingredients: Ningxia Organic Dried Wolfberries

OmegaGize³®

This formula blends the omega-3 fatty acids DHA and EPA with powerful CoQ10, a vitamin-like substance that powers energy in every cell while performing as an antioxidant. The fish oil complex in OmegaGize³ is derived from some of the cleanest water on the planet and is enhanced with essential oils and mixed carotenoids for stability. OmegaGize³ also contains vitamin D and vitamin E. Omega-3 essential fatty acids found in fish oil are among the best good fats for animals from all walks of life. Omega-3 fats are known to help reduce systemic inflammation and support cardiovascular, joint, eye, and brain health.

Ingredients: vitamin D (as cholecalciferol), vitamin E (as tocotrienols), Proprietary OmegaGize³ Blend: [omega-3 fatty acids (from fish oil) [eicosapentaenoic acid (EPA), docosahexaenoic acid (DHA)], Coenzyme Q10 (as ubiquinone)], gelatin, silicon dioxide, purified water, vitamin A (from mixed carotenoids)

Essential Oils: Clove, German Chamomile, Spearmint

ParaFree™

ParaFree is formulated with an advanced blend of some of the strongest essential oils studied for their cleansing abilities and antiparasitic properties. This formula also includes the added benefits of sesame seed oil and olive oil.

Ingredients: sesame seed oil, olive oil, gelatin, glycerin, deionized water

Essential Oils: Cumin, Anise (fruit oil), Fennel, Vetiver, Bay Laurel, Nutmeg, Tea Tree, Thyme, Clove, Ocotea, Dorado Azul, Tarragon, Ginger, Peppermint, Juniper, Fennel, Lemongrass, Anise, Patchouli

PD 80/20™

PD 80/20 is a dietary supplement formulated to help maximize internal health and support the endocrine system. It contains pregnenolone and DHEA, two substances produced naturally that decline with age. Pregnenolone is the key precursor for the body's production of estrogen, DHEA, and progesterone; and it also has an impact on mental acuity and memory.

DHEA is involved in maintaining the health of the cardiovascular and immune systems. As hormone levels decline with age, maintaining adequate hormone reserves becomes vital for sustaining health and preventing premature aging.

Ingredients: pregnenolone, DHEA, rice flour, gelatin

PowerGize™

PowerGize is an herbal supplement that sustains energy, boosts stamina, increases strength, and enhances physical performance.

Ingredients: ashwagandha root extract, longjack root powder, fenugreek seed extract, epimedium leaf powder, desert hyacinth root powder, tribulus fruit/leaf extract, muira puama bark powder, hypromellose, rice flour, silicon dioxide

Essential Oils: Idaho Blue Spruce, Goldenrod, Cassia

Power Meal™

A delicious, satisfying, rice-based vegetarian meal replacement that contains Ningxia wolfberries, Power Meal is rich in calcium and delivers an impressive 20 grams of protein per serving, plus a complete vitamin, mineral, and enzyme profile. It builds lean muscle mass, contains antioxidants that strengthen immunity, supports bone health, includes amino acids that enhance digestive activity, and provides the building blocks required for regeneration and energy.

Ingredients: vitamin A, vitamin C, vitamin D, vitamin E, thiamin, riboflavin, niacin, vitamin B6, folate, vitamin B12, biotin, calcium, iron, pantothenic acid, phosphorus, magnesium, zinc, selenium, copper, manganese, chromium, rice protein concentrate, rice bran and germ, Ningxia wolfberry fruit, fructose, natural flavors, apple fruit, chicory root fiber extract (FOS), medium-chain triglycerides, calcium (as tri-calcium phosphate), soy lecithin, guar gum, magnesium (from m. oxide), MSM (methylsulfonylmethane), xanthan gum, lo han kuo extract, cinnamon bark, lipase, protease 4.5, ginkgo biloba extract, protease 3.0, vitamin E (mixed tocopherols), manganese (from m. gluconate), ginger root, choline bitartrate, eleuthero root, PABA (para-aminobenzoic acid), zinc (from zinc lactate), vitamin C (as ascorbic acid), protease 6.0, phytase, vitamin A (as beta-carotene), talin, betaine HCI, peptidase, white pepper fruit, niacin (vitamin B3), selenium (from selenomethionine), clove flower bud, alpha-lipoic acid, vitamin A (from mixed carotenoids), kelp, nutmeg seed, fennel seed, copper (from copper gluconate), pantothenic acid (from calcium pantothenate) (vitamin B5), neohesperidin derivative (flavor from natural citrus), lycopene, cardamom seed, vitamin B6 (from pyridoxine HCI), thiamin HCI (vitamin B1), riboflavin (vitamin B2), lutein, chromium (from chromium aminonicotinate), zeaxanthin, astaxanthin, cholecalciferol, folic acid, biotin, vitamin B12 (from methylcobalamin)

Essential Oils: Orange, Lemon, Grapefruit, Anise, Fennel, Nutmeg

Allergen Warning: Contains ingredients derived from soy and tree nut (coconut).

Pure Protein Complete™ Vanilla Spice

Pure Protein Complete helps boost protein in animals, provides a balance of amino acids, and supports ATP production, the energy currency of the body. It is high in bioactive whey protein and low in carbohydrates, fats, and calories and is supported by a specialized enzyme blend, a low-glycemic carbohydrate matrix, and generous amounts of complementary vitamins and minerals.

Ingredients: thiamin (as thiamin hydrochloride), riboflavin, niacin, vitamin B6 (as pyridoxine hydrochloride), vitamin B12 (as methylcobalamin), biotin, pantothenic acid (as d-calcium pantothenate), calcium (as d-calcium pantothenate), zinc, Pure Protein Proprietary Blend: [rBGH-free whey protein concentrate, pea protein isolate, goat whey protein concentrate, egg albumin, organic hemp seed protein, ancient peat, apple extract], Enzyme Proprietary Complex: [alpha and beta amylase, protease, lipase, cellulase, lactase, L. acidophilus, papain, bromelain], organic evaporated cane juice crystals, natural flavors, xanthan gum, Amino Acid Blend: [L-leucine, L-isoleucine, L-valine, L-methionine, L-lysine, L-glutamine], sodium chloride, stevia rebaudiana, organic ground nutmeg, lou han guo fruit extract

Essential Oil: Orange

Allergen Warning: Contains milk- and egg-derived ingredients.

Rehemogen™

Rehemogen tincture contains herbs that were used by Native Americans to cleanse, purify, disinfect, and build the blood. It contains cascara sagrada, red clover, poke root, prickly ash bark, and burdock root, which have been historically used for their cleansing and building properties. Rehemogen is also formulated with essential oils to fortify digestion.

Reports from the field indicate great use in cats and dogs for detoxification.

Ingredients: red clover blossom, licorice root, poke root, peach bark, Oregon grape root, stillingia root, sarsaparilla root, cascara sagrada bark, prickly ash bark, burdock root, buckthorn bark, royal jelly, distilled water, ethanol

Essential Oils: Roman Chamomile, Rosemary, Thyme, Tea Tree

Allergen Warning: Product contains bee products.

SleepEssence™

Four powerful essential oils that have unique sleep-enhancing properties are combined into a vegetarian softgel for easy digestion. Lavender, Vetiver, Valerian, and Ruta essential oils mixed with the hormone melatonin help provide for a peaceful sleep.

Reports from the field suggest use for animals recuperating from procedures. Also, field reports indicate success in calming animals on nights when they or their neighborhood will be exposed to fireworks.

Ingredients: melatonin, lecithin, coconut meat oil, carrageenan, glycerin, modified cornstarch, sorbitol

Essential Oils: Lavender, Vetiver, Valerian, Mandarin, Rue

Caution: Consult a veterinarian if considering use on animals.

Slique® Tea

Slique Tea is a delicious, premium blend of wholesome and rare ingredients. It contains Ecuadorian ocotea leaf, a member of the cinnamon family traditionally used by natives for health and wellness. It acts as a powerful antioxidant. All of these ingredients are enriched with 100 percent pure, therapeutic-grade Arabian Sacred Frankincense powder, an exclusive ingredient from Young Living's distillery in Salalah, Oman.

Ingredients: jade oolong tea, inulin, ocotea leaf, Ecuadorian cacao powder, Sacred Frankincense powder, natural stevia extract

Essential Oil: Vanilla

Caution: Contains naturally occurring tea caffeine.

Sulfurzyme®

Sulfurzyme is a unique combination of MSM (methylsulfonylmethane) and Ningxia wolfberry. MSM is the protein-building compound found in breast milk, fresh fruits, and vegetables, while Ningxia wolfberry is a natural source of vitamins and antioxidants. Together, they create a new concept in balancing the immune system and supporting almost every major function of the body.

MSM has the ability to equalize water pressure inside the cells, which may provide considerable benefit for animals with arthritis, knee, joint, and tendon conditions.

Ingredients (Capsules): MSM, Ningxia wolfberry fruit powder, hypromellose, rice flour, magnesium stearate, silica

Ingredients (Powder): MSM, FOS (fructooligosaccharides), Ningxia wolfberry fruit powder, stevia leaf extract, calcium silicate

Super B™

Super B is a comprehensive source of the B vitamins essential for good health, including thiamine (vitamin B1), riboflavin (vitamin B2), niacin (vitamin B3), pyridoxine (vitamin B6), vitamin B12, biotin, folic acid, and PABA. It also includes minerals that aid in the assimilation and metabolism of B vitamins.

B vitamins are particularly important during times of stress when reserves are depleted.

When many B vitamins are combined at once in the stomach, it can cause fermentation, resulting in stomach upset. To avoid this, Super B uses a special formulation process to isolate the various vitamins so that they are released at different times.

Ingredients: thiamin (vitamin B1)(as thiamine HCI), riboflavin (vitamin B2), niacin (vitamin B3) (as nicotinic acid and niacinamide), vitamin B6 (as pyridoxine HCI), folate (vitamin B9), vitamin B12 (as methylcobalamin), biotin (vitamin B7), pantothenic acid (vitamin B5) (as d-calcium pantothenate), calcium (as dicalcium phosphate), magnesium (as m. bisglycinate chelate), zinc (as z. bisglycinate chelate), selenium (as s. glycinate complex), manganese (as m. bisglycinate chelate), PABA (para amino benzoic acid), cellulose, stearic acid, diglycerides

Essential Oil: Nutmeg

Super C™

Super C is properly balanced with rutin, biotin, bioflavonoids, and trace minerals to work synergistically, balance the electrolytes, and increase the absorption rate of vitamin C. Without bioflavonoids, vitamin C has a hard time getting inside cells, and without proper electrolyte balance and trace minerals, it will not stay there for long.

Ingredients: vitamin C (as ascorbic acid), calcium (as calcium carbonate and dicalcium phosphate), zinc (gluconate), manganese (as manganese sulfate), potassium (as potassium chloride), citrus bioflavonoids, rutin, cayenne pepper fruit, cellulose, stearic acid, magnesium stearate, vegetable food-grade coating, silica

Essential Oils: Orange, Tangerine, Grapefruit, Lemon, Lemongrass

Super C™ Chewable

Super C Chewable is the only vitamin C chewable in the world that combines citrus essential oils, citrus bioflavonoids, and whole-food, natural vitamin C in one tablet.

Super C Chewable is the most complete, biologically utilizable vitamin C supplement available that is derived from a whole-food source of acerola cherries.

Crushing 1 chewable and adding to food will get this antioxidant in your animal's body.

Ingredients: vitamin C (as ascorbic acid), acerola cherry fruit extract, camu camu whole fruit powder, rose hips fruit powder, citrus bioflavonoids (from lemon whole fruit powder, orange whole fruit powder, lime whole fruit powder, tangerine whole fruit powder, grapefruit whole fruit powder), non-GMO tapioca dextrose, sorbitol, calcium ascorbate, stevia, hydroxypropyl cellulose, stearic acid, silicon dioxide, magnesium stearate

Essential Oil: Orange

Allergen Warning: Contains milk or milk derivatives.

Super Cal™

This is a high-powered calcium, potassium, and magnesium complex that restores proper electrolyte and hormonal balance and improves muscle and bone development.

Ingredients: calcium (from calcium citrate), magnesium (from magnesium citrate), zinc (from zinc citrate), potassium (from potassium citrate), boron (as sodium borate), gelatin, stearic acid, cellulose

Essential Oils: Marjoram, Wintergreen, Lemongrass, Myrtle

Caution: Consult a veterinarian if considering use for animals.

Thyromin

A well-functioning body needs a strong thyroid. Thyromin was developed to nourish the thyroid, balance metabolism, and reduce fatigue. It contains a combination of specially selected glandular nutrients, herbs, amino acids, minerals, and therapeutic-grade essential oils and are perfectly balanced to bring about the most beneficial and nutritional support to the thyroid.

Ingredients: vitamin E (as mixed tocopherols), iodine (from kelp and potassium iodide), potassium (as potassium citrate and potassium iodide), Proprietary Thyromin Blend: [parsley leaf, thyroid powder, L-tyrosine, pituitary extract (from porcine), adrenal extract (from porcine), L-cystine, L-cysteine HCI], gelatin, magnesium carbonate, magnesium stearate

Essential Oils: Peppermint, Spearmint, Myrtle, Myrrh

Yacon Syrup

The Peruvian yacon plant resembles a yam or sweet potato but with a black skin. While deliciously sweet, Yacon Syrup contains inulin, the complex sugar that slowly breaks down into FOS (fructooligosaccharide). Inulin is not digestible so it passes through the body, with the result that it is but half the calories of other sugars. FOS is well known for its prebiotic effects and also supports microflora in the large intestine, while it promotes the absorption of calcium.

Growing in the Andes Mountains, yacon takes up valuable minerals from volcanic ash build-up, adding high mineral content to high amino acid and vitamin A content. Thus, yacon is similar to the Ningxia wolfberry in its nutrient profile.

Animals tolerate Yacon Syrup well, although it is not recommended as a supplement for them or a food source. Due to its sweetness, it may be used as a carrier for delivering internal drops of essential oils in many animals.

Ingredients: Yacon Syrup

Body and Environment

Body Care Products

ART® Renewal Serum

ART Renewal Serum is an intricate blend of exotic botanicals chosen for their unique ability to soothe and protect the most delicate areas of the face. These premium ingredients work in harmony to deeply nourish, hydrate, and help restore youthfulness to skin.

Ingredients: water, glycerin, selaginella lepidophylla extract, lactobacillus ferment, condensed herbal extracts I: speranskia tuberculata whole plant extract, eucommia ulmoides extract, glycine tomentella root extract, polygonum cuspidatum root extract, vanilla extract, niacinamide, phalaenopsis orchid flower extract, condensed herbal extracts II: torenia concolor whole plant extract, *Commiphora myrrha* resin extract, *Boswellia carterii* resin extract, spatholobus suberectus stem extract, angelica polymorpa sinensis root extract, liquidambar formosana dried fruit extract, crocus sativus flower extract, Chamomilla recutita flower extract, sodium hyaluronate, ascorbyl glucoside

Essential Oils: Sensation blend: [Coriander, Ylang Ylang, Bergamot (Furocoumarin-free), Jasmine, Geranium]

Cautions: Avoid contact with eyes. Discontinue use if irritation occurs.

ART® Sheerlumé Brightening Cream

This advanced formula combines a perfect blend of essential oils with skin-nourishing ingredients to visibly brighten and balance skin tone, unveiling a more radiant, youthful-looking glow.

Ingredients: water, glycerin, coconut alkanes, caprylic/capric tyriglyceride, glyceryl stearate SE, cetearyl alcohol, licorice root extract, sodium stearoyl lactate, centella asiatica extract, theobroma grandiflorum seed butter, physalis angulata extract, batyl alcohol, alcohol denatured, coco-caprylate/caprate, plumeria acutifolia flower extract, sodium PCA, meadowfoam seed oil, terminalia ferdinandiana fruit extract, lilium candidum leaf cell extract, sodium citrate, honeysuckle flower extract, citric acid, mallow extract, primula veris extract, alchemilla vulgaris extract, veronica officinalis extract, melissa officinalis extract, achillea millefolium extract, honeysuckle extract, sodium phytate, tocopherol

Essential Oils: Peppermint, Vetiver, Blue Cypress, Davana, Royal Hawaiian Sandalwood, Clove, Jasmine, Carrot, Spearmint, Geranium, Sacred Frankincense

Cel-Lite Magic™ Massage Oil

Cel-Lite Magic Massage Oil enhances circulation and provides nutrients that help reduce the appearance of fat and cellulite. This massage oil is formulated with pure vegetable oils, vitamin E, Grapefruit essential oil to improve skin texture, and Juniper essential oil to detoxify and cleanse.

Ingredients: caprylic/capric triglyceride, grape seed oil, wheat germ oil, sweet almond oil, olive oil

Essential Oils: Grapefruit, Cypress, Cedarwood, Juniper, Clary Sage

Allergen Warning: Contains wheat product.

ClaraDerm™

ClaraDerm spray soothes dry, chapped, or itchy skin. Its gentle blend is particularly helpful in relieving skin irritations, burning, and itching in sensitive genital areas. Its formula can also assist in controlling rashes, etc.

Ingredients: fractionated coconut oil

Essential Oils: Myrrh, Tea Tree, Lavender, Frankincense, Roman Chamomile, Helichrysum

Cool Azul® Pain Relief Cream

Young Living's Cool Azul Pain Relief Cream provides penetrating and cooling relief from your animal's minor muscle and joint aches, simple backache, arthritis, strains, bruises, and sprains. This plant-based formula combines the power of Wintergreen essential oil and Cool Azul essential oil blend, while remaining free of synthetic ingredients.

Ingredients: methyl salicylate, menthol, aloe vera leaf extract, safflower seed oil, glyceryl stearate, cetyl alcohol, stearyl alcohol, squalane, glycerin, rose hip seed oil, mango seed butter, water, alcohol, matricaria flower extract, green tea leaf extract, levulinic acid, benzyl alcohol, camphor, p-anisic acid, caraway seed oil, tocopheryl acetate

Essential Oils: Peppermint, Sage, Plectranthus Oregano, Balsam Copaiba, Melaleuca Quinquenervia (Niaouli), Lavender, Blue Cypress, Elemi, Vetiver, Dorado Azul, Matricaria (German Chamomile)

Cool Azul® Sports Gel

With 10 percent essential oils, Cool Azul Sports Gel is great to use on animals before or after physical activity.

Ingredients: aloe extract, olive oil, glycerin, menthol, arnica extract, water, camphor, sodium hyaluronate, sunflower lecithin, xanthan gum, water, matricaria extract, willow bark extract, caraway seed oil, levulinic acid, p-Anisic acid

Essential Oils: Peppermint, Wintergreen, Sage, Copaiba, Plectranthus Oregano, Melaleuca Quinquenervia (Niaouli), Lavender, Blue Cypress, Elemi, Dorado Azul, Vetiver, German Chamomile (Matricaria)

Caution: Proceed with caution when applying to sensitive skin.

Dragon Time™ Massage Oil

Dragon Time Massage Oil combines specially blended vegetable oils with pure Lavender, Ylang Ylang, and other essential oils that deliver natural phytoestrogens to balance and stabilize the body. It is especially helpful in stabilizing hormones.

Ingredients: deionized water, decyl glucoside, coco betaine, lauryl glucoside, coco-glucoside, glyceryl oleate, citric acid, glycerin, levulinic acid, p-Anisic acid, xanthan gum, inulin, sodium phytate

Essential Oils: Tangerine, Geranium, Fennel, Lavender, Sage, Marjoram, Clary Sage, Coriander, Bergamot (Furocoumarin-free), Lemon, Ylang Ylang, Jasmine, Roman Chamomile, Palmarosa, Blue Tansy

Genesis™ Hand & Body Lotion

Genesis Hand & Body Lotion is an ultra-moisturizing cream containing sweet almond oil and other natural botanicals to soothe and nourish dry, dehydrated skin.

Geranium, Jasmine, and other pure essential oils are included for their therapeutic, skin care benefits.

Ingredients: water, dimethyl sulfone (MSM), glyceryl stearate, stearic acid, glycerin, grape seed extract, sodium hyaluronate, sorbitol, rose hip seed oil, shea butter, mango seed butter, wheat germ oil, kukui seed oil, lecithin, safflower seed oil, apricot kernel oil, sweet almond oil, vitamin E (tocopheryl acetate), vitamin A (retinyl palmitate), jojoba seed oil, calendula flower extract, chamomile extract, green tea leaf extract, St. John's Wort extract, algae extract, aloe vera gel, vitamin C (ascorbic acid), gingko biloba extract

Essential Oils: Palmarosa, Coriander, Bergamot (Furocoumarin-free), Geranium, Jasmine, Lemon, Ylang Ylang, Roman Chamomile

Allergen Warning: Contains wheat product.

Lavender Hand & Body Lotion

Infused with Lavender essential oil and other plant-based ingredients, Lavender Hand & Body Lotion moisturizes and protects skin from overexposure to the elements for long-lasting hydration. This formula is certified eco-friendly and all natural.

Ingredients: water, sandalwood extract, phellodendron amurense bark extract, barley extract, cetearyl alcohol, glycerin, glyceryl stearate, sodium stearoyl lactylate, levulinic acid, p-Anisic acid, laminaria digitata, algae, xanthan gum, hydrolyzed silk, sorbic acid, astrocaryum murumuru seed butter, wolfberry seed oil, olive fruit unsaponifiables, rosemary leaf extract, vitamin E (tocopherol), sodium phytate, beeswax, aloe vera leaf extract

Essential Oils: Lavender, Lemon, Myrrh, Davana

LavaDerm Cooling Mist™

The essential oil of Lavender has been highly regarded as a burn treatment, having both antiseptic properties and an ability to reduce the formation of scar tissue.

Ingredients: water, aloe vera leaf extract, vegetable glycerin, potassium sorbate, sodium levulinate, sodium anisate, ionic trace minerals, citric acid

Essential Oils: Lavender, Northern Lights Black Spruce, Helichrysum

Ortho Ease® Massage Oil

Ortho Ease Massage Oil is a calming blend of vegetable oils and therapeutic-grade essential oils such as Wintergreen, Peppermint, Juniper, and Marjoram. This unique blend is anti-inflammatory and painkilling, ideal for strained, swollen, or torn muscles and ligaments. It also combats insect bites, dermatitis, and itching.

Ingredients: caprylic/capric triglyceride, grape seed oil, wheat germ oil, sweet almond oil, olive oil

Essential Oils: Wintergreen, Peppermint, Juniper, Eucalyptus Globulus, Lemongrass, Marjoram, Thyme, Eucalyptus Radiata, Vetiver

Allergen Warning: Contains wheat product.

Ortho Sport® Massage Oil

Ortho Sport Massage Oil is an anti-inflammatory and painkilling complex of vegetable and essential oils. Ideal for strained, swollen, or torn muscles and ligaments, it has higher phenol content than Ortho Ease and produces a greater warming sensation.

Ingredients: caprylic/capric triglyceride, grape seed oil, wheat germ oil, sweet almond oil, olive oil

Essential Oils: Wintergreen, Peppermint, Oregano, Eucalyptus Globulus, Elemi, Vetiver, Lemongrass, Thyme

Allergen Warning: Contains wheat product.

Progessence® Plus

Progessence Plus increases hormonal balance the way nature intended. It is a balancing blend designed to enhance the natural effects of progesterone. Pure USP-grade, super-micronized progesterone from wild yam is purified into a pure, therapeutic-grade essential oil-infused serum.

The first-ever, pure progesterone serum on the market, Progessence Plus has a pleasant aroma, is easily absorbed into the skin, and does not require cycling the application sites like other progesterone supplements.

Ingredients: caprylic/capric triglyceride, tocopherol, USP-grade progesterone (from wild yam extract)

Essential Oils: Copaiba, Sacred Frankincense, Cedarwood, Bergamot (Furocoumarin-free), Peppermint, Clove

Regenolone™ Moisturizing Cream

Regenolone is a natural moisturizer formulated to support proper estrogen levels in women. It contains wild yam, black and blue cohosh, Peppermint, and Wintergreen to invigorate the skin and enhance absorption.

Ingredients: water, dimethyl sulfone (MSM), fractionated coconut/palm oil, sorbitol, pregnenolone, lecithin, shea butter, wolfberry seed oil, glyceryl stearate, aloe vera leaf, sodium PCA, stearic acid, calendula flower extract, Roman chamomile flower extract, rosebud flower extract, green tea leaf extract, St. John's wort extract, ginkgo biloba leaf extract, grape seed extract, algae extract, vitamin E (tocopheryl acetate and linoleate), hydrolyzed wheat protein, locust bean gum, trace minerals, flaxseed oil, wheat germ oil, allantoin, wild yam root extract, eleuthero root extract, kelp extract, vitamin A (retinyl palmitate), black cohosh root extract, blue cohosh extract, vitamin C (ascorbic acid)

Essential Oils: Wintergreen, Peppermint, Douglas Fir, Oregano

Allergen Warning: Contains wheat products.

Relaxation™ Massage Oil

Relaxation Massage Oil promotes tranquility and eases tension to restore vitality. This formula blends specially selected vegetable oils with soothing essential oils for maximum stress relief and relaxation.

Ingredients: caprylic/capric triglyceride, grape seed oil, wheat germ oil, sweet almond oil, olive oil

Essential Oils: Tangerine, Lavender, Spearmint, Ylang Ylang, Peppermint, Coriander, Bergamot (Furocoumarin-free), Geranium

Allergen Warning: Contains wheat product.

Rose Ointment™

Rose Ointment is a deeply soothing and nourishing blend for dry skin. Rose essential oil and vitamin A improve skin texture, while Tea Tree and Rose work to rejuvenate rough, irritated skin.

Use Rose Ointment over essential oils to lock in their benefits. Though not recommended for burns initially, this ointment can be very beneficial in maintaining, protecting, and keeping the scab soft.

Ingredients: mink oil, lecithin, beeswax, lanolin, sesame seed oil, wheat germ oil, rosehip seed oil

Essential Oils: Palmarosa, Patchouli, Coriander, Myrrh, Bergamot (Furocoumarin-free), Carrot Seed, Tea Tree, Ylang Ylang, Geranium, Rose

Allergen Warning: Contains wheat product.

Sensation™ Hand & Body Lotion

Sensation Hand & Body Lotion is an ultra-moisturizing cream. Ylang Ylang encourages relaxation, Jasmine balances female energy, and Geranium nourishes and refreshes the skin. This lotion leaves the skin soft and moist while protecting it from harsh weather, chemicals, and dry air.

Ingredients: deionized water, dimethyl sulfone (MSM), glyceryl stearate, stearic acid, glycerine, grape seed extract, sodium hyaluronate, sorbitol, rose hip seed oil, shea butter, mango seed butter, wheat germ oil, kukui seed oil, safflower seed oil, apricot kernel oil, sweet almond oil, vitamin E (tocopheryl acetate), vitamin A (retinyl palmitate), jojoba seed oil, sesame seed oil, calendula extract, chamomile extract, green tea leaf extract, St. John's Wort extract, algae extract, aloe vera gel, vitamin C (ascorbic acid), gingko biloba leaf extract

Essential Oils: Ylang Ylang, Coriander, Bergamot (Furocoumarin-free), Jasmine, Geranium

Sensation™ Massage Oil

Sensation Massage Oil stimulates the senses while easing anxiety.

Ingredients: caprylic/capric triglyceride, grape seed oil, wheat germ oil, sweet almond oil, olive oil

Essential Oils: Ylang Ylang, Coriander, Bergamot (Furocoumarin-free), Jasmine, Geranium

Allergen Warning: Contains wheat product.

Thieves® Dentarome® Plus Toothpaste

Thieves Dentarome Plus Toothpaste is an advanced formula of all-natural ingredients that gently cleans and whitens teeth while harnessing the power of pure, therapeutic-grade Thieves essential oil blend for decreasing levels of damaging plaque and tartar.

Great reports from the field with canine and feline tooth brushing. Some caregivers apply with a finger brush and wipe clean with a soft, wet oral towelette.

Ingredients: water, sodium bicarbonate, vegetable glycerin, xanthan gum, ionic trace minerals, stevia leaf

Essential Oils: Peppermint, Wintergreen, Thieves blend: [Clove, Lemon, Cinnamon Bark, Eucalyptus Radiata, Rosemary]

Contains NO fluoride, sodium lauryl sulfate, sugar, synthetic chemicals, or colors.

Thieves® Dentarome® Ultra Toothpaste

Thieves Dentarome Ultra Toothpaste is a high-powered, essential oil toothpaste that provides long-lasting freshness. It emulsifies and protects essential oils from oxidation and binds essential oils to the mucus membranes in the mouth for unmatched breath-freshening and oral hygiene.

Great reports from the field with canine and feline tooth brushing. Some caregivers apply with a finger brush and wipe clean with a soft, wet oral towelette. It is also being used very successfully to pack wounds.

Ingredients: water, sodium bicarbonate, vegetable glycerin, xanthan gum, ionic trace minerals, stevia leaf
Essential Oils: Peppermint, Wintergreen, Thieves Blend: [Clove, Lemon, Cinnamon Bark, Eucalyptus Radiata, Rosemary]
Contains NO fluoride, sodium lauryl sulfate, sugar, synthetic chemicals, or colors.

Thieves® Fresh Essence Plus™ Mouthwash

Thieves Fresh Essence Plus Mouthwash blends Thieves essential oil blend and Peppermint, Spearmint, and Vetiver essential oils for an extra clean mouth and fresh breath. It contains only natural ingredients and uses a patented, time-release technology for lasting freshness.

Ingredients: water, lecithin, quillaja saponaria wood extract, potassium sorbate, stevioside, vitamin E (alpha tocopheryl), colloidal silver, citric acid
Essential Oils: Peppermint, Clove, Spearmint, Lemon, Cinnamon Bark, Vetiver, Eucalyptus Radiata, Rosemary

Thieves® Waterless Hand Purifier

This all-natural hand cleaner is designed to sanitize and refresh the hands. Thieves Waterless Hand Purifier conveniently promotes good hygiene whenever water or washing facilities are not available.

It contains Thieves blend essential oil, known for the powerful, antibacterial properties that penetrate the skin as the ethanol in this hand purifier evaporates. It also contains active skin-moisturizing ingredients to prevent dry skin.

Ingredients: alcohol (denatured with peppermint essential oil), water, aloe vera leaf powder, vegetable glycerin, hydroxylpropyl cellulose
Essential Oils: Peppermint, Thieves Blend: [Clove, Lemon, Cinnamon Bark, Eucalyptus Radiata, Rosemary]

V-6™ Vegetable Oil Complex

V-6 Vegetable Oil Complex is widely used to dilute certain essential oils and can be mixed to create custom blends, formulas, and massage oils. This oil complex nourishes the skin, is nonreactive to nearly all animals, has a long shelf life, doesn't clog pores, and will not stain fur, feathers, or fabric.

Ingredients: caprylic/capric triglyceride, sesame seed oil, grape seed oil, sweet almond oil, wheat germ oil, sunflower seed oil, olive oil
Allergen Warning: Contains wheat product.

Wolfberry Eye Cream™

Wolfberry Eye Cream is a natural, water-based moisturizer. Containing the antiaging properties of wolfberry seed oil, this cream soothes tired eyes and minimizes the appearance of bags, circles, and fine lines. Use in the evening. Repeat in the morning if desired.

Ingredients: deionized water, sorbitol, glycerin, cetearyl alcohol, glyceryl stearate, sodium stearoyl lactylate, oat kernel extract, stearic acid, caprylic/capric triglycerides, alfalfa seed extract, hydrolyzed lupine protein, levulinic acid, p-Anisic acid, sandalwood extract, phellodendron amurense bark extract, barley extract, olive fruit, wolfberry seed oil, avocado oil, kukui seed oil, rosehip seed oil, sweet almond oil, jojoba seed oil, mango seed butter, sorbic acid, witch hazel extract, allantoin, xanthan gum, shea butter, vitamin A (retinyl palmitate), sodium PCA, ascorbyl palmitate, cucumber fruit extract, hydrolyzed soy protein, hydrolyzed wheat protein, hydrolyzed wheat starch, horses chestnut seed extract, centella asiatica extract, sodium phytate, sodium hyaluronate, green tea leaf extract, ascorbic acid, sodium hydroxide, citric acid
Essential oils: Lavender, Coriander, Roman Chamomile, Frankincense, Geranium, Bergamot (Furocoumarin-free), Ylang Ylang
Allergen Warning: Contains wheat and soy products.

Environmental Care Products

Thieves® Foaming Hand Soap

Thieves Foaming Hand Soap is a natural hand-cleansing formula that contains Thieves essential oil blend, known for its powerful antibacterial properties. Thieves essential oil blend penetrates beneath the skin's surface, providing a long-lasting barrier of protection. This gentle, foaming soap also contains ingredients such as vitamin E, aloe vera, and ginkgo biloba to moisturize and soften the skin and provide a balanced pH to support the skin's natural moisture complex.

Ingredients: water, decyl glucoside, cocamidopropyl hydroxysultaine, alcohol denatured, aloe vera leaf juice, vitamin E (tocopheryl acetate), ginkgo biloba leaf extract, vitamin A (retinyl palmitate), camellia sinensis leaf extract, cetyl hydroxyethylcellulose, sodium hydroxide, citric acid

Essential Oils: Thieves: [Clove, Lemon, Cinnamon Bark, Eucalyptus Radiata, Rosemary], Orange

Caution: Avoid contact with eyes. Not for internal use.

Thieves® Fruit & Veggie Spray

Powered by five essential oils, the Thieves Fruit & Veggie Spray is formulated to quickly and naturally clean fruits and vegetables.

Ingredients: water, citric acid, decyl glucoside, glycerin, sodium citrate

Essential Oils: Lime, Thieves essential oil blend: [Clove, Lemon, Cinnamon Bark, Eucalyptus Radiata, Rosemary]

Thieves® Household Cleaner

Thieves Household Cleaner has great cleansing power and a safe, sustainable formula, which contains ingredients from renewable plant and mineral sources, vegetable-based surfactants, and great ratios of Thieves and Lemon essential oils for healthy cleaning power around animals. It's great for farms, ranches, and veterinary hospitals, a must for keeping your pet or herd's environment hygienically clean.

Dilution ratios: most cleaning applications 30 to 1; heavy degreasing 15:1; light degreasing 50 to 1; glass 50 or 100 to 1.

Ingredients: water, alkyl polyglucoside, sodium methyl 2-sulfolaurate, disodium 2-sulfolaurate, tetrasodium glutamate diacetate

Essential Oils: Thieves essential oil blend: [Clove, Lemon, Cinnamon Bark, Eucalyptus Radiata, Rosemary], Lemon

Caution: Avoid contact with eyes. Not for internal use.

Thieves® Laundry Soap

With a plant-based formula, Thieves Laundry Soap gently and naturally washes clothes without using chemicals or synthetics. Natural enzymes and powerful essential oils enhance the formula's strength and give a pleasant, light citrus scent.

Ingredients: water, decyl glucoside, sodium oleate, glycerin, caprylyl glucoside, lauryl glucoside, sodium chloride, sodium gluconate, carboxymethyl cellulose, alpha-amylase, protease, lipase

Essential Oils: Jade Lemon, Bergamot (Furocoumarin-free), Thieves essential oil blend: [Clove, Lemon, Cinnamon Bark, Eucalyptus Radiata, Rosemary]

Thieves® Spray

Thieves Spray is an all-natural, petrochemical-free antiseptic spray ideal for purifying small surfaces like doorknobs, handles, toilet seats, and any surface that needs cleansing to protect from dust, mold, and undesirable microorganisms. It also can work on larger animals to protect their ears from mites as well as misting their healing wounds.

Ingredients: alcohol denatured, water, caprylic/capric triglyceride, lecithin, polysorbate 80

Essential Oils: Thieves essential oil blend: [Clove, Lemon, Cinnamon Bark, Eucalyptus Radiata, Rosemary]

Section 3

Quick Reference Guide

Arthritis (common in older animals and purebreds)

Ortho Ease or PanAway: Massage on location or put several drops in animal feed.

Use Raindrop-like application of PanAway, Wintergreen, Pine, or Spruce and massage the location. For larger animals, use at least 2 times more oil than a normal Raindrop Technique would call for on humans.

Copaiba can be given orally as a replacement for traditional NSAID's.

For prevention: Put Power Meal or Pure Protein Complete and Sulfurzyme in feed or fodder. Small animals need 1/8 to 1/4 serving per day. Large animals need 2 to 4 servings per day.

Birthing

Gentle Baby

Bleeding

Geranium, Helichrysum, and Cistus: Shave the hair over the area being treated. For internal hemorrhage, the use of Cistus orally is recommended.

Bones (pain and spurs on all animals)

R.C., PanAway, Wintergreen, Lemongrass, and Spruce. All conifers are very powerful in the action for bones and in promoting bone health. For more effective absorption, it is helpful to shave the fur/hair away from the area being treated. AgilEase is an excellent supplement for building animal bones.

Bones (fractured or broken)

Mix PanAway with 15-25 drops of Wintergreen and Spruce. Cover the area. After 15 minutes rub in 10-15 more drops of Wintergreen and Spruce and cover with Ortho Sport Massage Oil. AgilEase can be used as a supplement to help speed bone healing.

Calming

Peace & Calming, T-Away, Trauma Life, and Lavender; domestic animals respond very quickly to the smell.

Colds and Flu

For small animals, put 1-3 drops of Exodus II, ImmuPower, DiGize, or DiGize Vitality in feed or fodder. For large animals, use 10-20 drops.

Colic

For large animals like cows, put 10-20 drops of DiGize or DiGize Vitality in feed or fodder. For small animals, use 1-3 drops.

Horse Colic Protocol: Administer 20 drops of Peppermint or Peppermint Vitality and 20 drops of DiGize or DiGize Vitality orally, as well as apply to the umbilical area of the abdomen. Repeat every 20 minutes, as needed.

Fleas and Other Parasites

Singles: Lemongrass, Tea Tree, Eucalyptus (all types), Peppermint

Blends: RepelAroma, ParaGize, DiGize; also add 1-2 drops of Lemongrass to Animal Scents Shampoo.

Oils repel fleas and other external parasites. Wash blankets with oils added to the wash during the rinse cycle. Also, place 1-2 drops of Lemongrass on the collar to help eliminate fleas.

For internal parasites, rub ParaGize and/or DiGize on the pads (bottoms) of the feet daily. Many people have reported that they have seen the parasites eliminated from the animal within days after starting this procedure.

Inflammation

Apply Ortho Ease, PanAway, Pine, Wintergreen, or Spruce on location. Put Sulfurzyme in feed. Mineral Essence may also be helpful.

Quick Reference Guide *(continued)*

Insect Repellent

Use RepelAroma. Put 10 drops each of Palo Santo, Idaho Tansy, Eucalyptus Globulus, and Peppermint in an 8-ounce spray bottle with water.

Alternate formula: Put 2 drops Pine, 2 drops Eucalyptus Globulus, and 5-10 drops Purification in a spray bottle of water. Shake vigorously and spray over area.

Ligaments/Tendons (torn or sprained)

Apply Lemongrass and Lavender (equal parts) on location and cover area. For small animals or birds, dilute essential oils with V-6 Vegetable Oil Complex (2 parts mixing oil to 1 part essential oil). Palo Santo is an excellent oil for use on smaller animals and is generally milder than Lemongrass.

Mineral Deficiencies

Mineral Essence. In one case, an animal stopped chewing on furniture once his mineral deficiency was met. Mineral deficiency is also an important aspect of anxiety in animals, so supplementing with Mineral Essence can show beneficial calming effects.

Mites (ear mites)

Apply Purification and/or Peppermint to a cotton swab and swab just the inside of the ear.

Nervous Anxiety

Valor, T-Away, Trauma Life, Roman Chamomile, Geranium, Lavender, Valerian

Pain

Helichrysum, PanAway, Relieve It, Cool Azul Pain Relief Cream, Deep Relief Roll-On, Cool Azul, Cool Azul Sports Gel, Clove, or Peppermint diluted 50/50 with V-6 Vegetable Oil Complex

Shiny Coats

Tail & Mane Sheen, Shampoo, PuriClean, Rosemary, Sandalwood, Sulfurzyme

Sinus Problems

Diffuse Raven, R.C., Pine, Myrtle, and Eucalyptus Radiata in the animal's sleeping quarters or sprinkle on the bedding. Thieves, Super C, Exodus II, and ImmuPro have been reported as being extremely beneficial for sinus and lung congestion.

Skin Cancer

Frankincense, Lavender, Clove, Myrrh; apply neat.

Ticks

To remove ticks, apply one drop of Cinnamon Bark or Peppermint on a cotton swab and apply directly to the tick. Then wait for it to release its head before removing from the animal's skin.

Trauma

T-Away, Trauma Life, Valor, Peace & Calming, Melissa, Gentle Baby, Lavender, Valerian, Roman Chamomile

Tumors or Cancers

Mix Frankincense with Ledum, Lavender, or Clove and apply on the area of tumor.

Worms and Parasites

ParaGize, ParaFree, DiGize

Wounds (open or abrasions)

PuriClean, Infect Away, Mendwell, Melrose, Helichrysum, Animal Scents Ointment

Topical Single Essential Oil Dilution Codes

Neat = Straight, undiluted
Dilution usually NOT required; suitable for all but the most sensitive skin.

50-50 = Dilute 50-50
Dilution recommended at 50-50 (1 part essential oils to 1 part V-6 Vegetable Oil Complex) for topical and internal use, especially when used on sensitive animal areas — face, neck, genital area, underarms, belly, etc.

20-80 = Dilute 20-80
Always dilute 20-80 (1 part essential oils to 4 parts V-6 Vegetable Oil Complex) before applying to the skin or taking internally.

5% = Dilute to 5% of total
Always dilute down to 5% (5 drops essential oil to 1 teaspoon V-6 Vegetable Oil Complex) before applying to the skin or taking internally.

1% = Dilute to 1% of total
Always dilute down to 1% (1 drop essential oil to 1 teaspoon V-6 Vegetable Oil Complex) before applying to the skin or taking internally.

✷ = Photosensitizing
Avoid using on skin exposed to direct sunlight or UV rays (i.e., UV lights, sunbathing animals such as dogs or cats, etc.).

Single Oil	General Human Dilution	Avian/ Reptiles/ Pocket Pets	Canine	Equine/ Livestock	Feline
Angelica ✷	Neat	Neat	Neat	Neat	Neat
Anise	Neat	20-80	Neat	Neat	50-50
Balsam Fir	Neat	Neat	Neat	Neat	Neat
Basil	50-50	5%	Neat	Neat	20-80
Bergamot ✷	Neat	Neat	Neat	Neat	Neat
Black Pepper	Neat	5%	Neat	Neat	20-80
Cassia	50-50	1%	50-50	50-50	20-80
Cedarwood	Neat	Neat	Neat	Neat	Neat
Celery Seed	Neat	Neat	Neat	Neat	Neat
Cinnamon Bark	50-50	1%	50-50	50-50	20-80
Cistus	Neat	Neat	Neat	Neat	Neat
Citronella	Neat	Neat	Neat	Neat	Neat
Clary Sage	Neat	Neat	Neat	Neat	Neat
Clove	50-50	5%	Neat	Neat	50-50
Copaiba	Neat	Neat	Neat	Neat	Neat
Coriander	Neat	Neat	Neat	Neat	Neat
Cypress	Neat	Neat	Neat	Neat	Neat
Dill	Neat	Neat	Neat	Neat	Neat
Dorado Azul	Neat	Neat	Neat	Neat	Neat
Elemi	Neat	Neat	Neat	Neat	Neat
Eucalyptus Blue	Neat	Neat	Neat	Neat	Neat
Eucalyptus Globulus	Neat	Neat	Neat	Neat	Neat
Eucalyptus Radiata	Neat	Neat	Neat	Neat	Neat
Fennel	Neat	Neat	Neat	Neat	Neat
Frankincense	Neat	Neat	Neat	Neat	Neat
Frankincense (Sacred)	Neat	Neat	Neat	Neat	Neat
Geranium	Neat	Neat	Neat	Neat	Neat
Ginger	Neat	Neat	Neat	Neat	Neat
Goldenrod	Neat	Neat	Neat	Neat	Neat
Grapefruit ✷	Neat	Neat	Neat	Neat	Neat
Helichrysum	Neat	Neat	Neat	Neat	Neat
Hyssop	Neat	Neat	Neat	Neat	Neat
Jade Lemon	Neat	Neat	Neat	Neat	Neat
Jasmine	Neat	Neat	Neat	Neat	Neat
Juniper	Neat	Neat	Neat	Neat	Neat
Laurus Nobilis	Neat	Neat	Neat	Neat	Neat

Single Oil	General Human Dilution	Avian/ Reptiles/ Pocket Pets	Canine	Equine/ Livestock	Feline
Lavender	Neat	Neat	Neat	Neat	Neat
Ledum	Neat	Neat	Neat	Neat	Neat
Lemon ✷	Neat	Neat	Neat	Neat	Neat
Lemongrass	50-50	5%	Neat	Neat	50-50
Marjoram	Neat	Neat	Neat	Neat	Neat
Melaleuca Quinquenervia	Neat	Neat	Neat	Neat	50-50
Mountain Savory	50-50	20-80	Neat	Neat	50-50
Myrrh	Neat	Neat	Neat	Neat	Neat
Myrtle	Neat	Neat	Neat	Neat	Neat
Neroli	Neat	Neat	Neat	Neat	Neat
Nutmeg	Neat	Neat	Neat	Neat	Neat
Ocotea	Neat	Neat	Neat	Neat	Neat
Orange ✷	Neat	Neat	Neat	Neat	Neat
Oregano	50-50	20-80	Neat	Neat	50-50
Palmarosa	Neat	Neat	Neat	Neat	Neat
Palo Santo	Neat	Neat	Neat	Neat	Neat
Patchouli	Neat	Neat	Neat	Neat	Neat
Peppermint	50-50	50-50	Neat	Neat	50-50
Petitgrain	Neat	Neat	Neat	Neat	Neat
Pine	Neat	Neat	Neat	Neat	Neat
Ravintsara	Neat	Neat	Neat	Neat	Neat
Rose	Neat	Neat	Neat	Neat	Neat
Rosemary	Neat	50-50	Neat	Neat	50-50
Sage	Neat	Neat	Neat	Neat	Neat
Sandalwood	Neat	Neat	Neat	Neat	Neat
Spearmint	Neat	Neat	Neat	Neat	Neat
Tangerine ✷	Neat	Neat	Neat	Neat	Neat
Tarragon	Neat	Neat	Neat	Neat	Neat
Tea Tree	Neat	Neat	Neat	Neat	50-50
Thyme	50-50	20-80	Neat	Neat	50-50
Tsuga	Neat	Neat	Neat	Neat	Neat
Valerian	Neat	Neat	Neat	Neat	Neat
Vetiver	Neat	Neat	Neat	Neat	Neat
Wintergreen	50-50	20-80	Neat	Neat	50-50
Xiang Mao	Neat	Neat	Neat	Neat	Neat
Ylang Ylang	Neat	Neat	Neat	Neat	Neat

Topical Essential Oil Blends Dilution Codes

Neat = Straight, undiluted
Dilution usually NOT required; suitable for all but the most sensitive skin.

50-50 = Dilute 50-50
Dilution recommended at 50-50 (1 part essential oils to 1 part V-6 Vegetable Oil Complex) for topical and internal use, especially when used on sensitive animal areas — face, neck, genital area, underarms, belly, etc.

20-80 = Dilute 20-80
Always dilute 20-80 (1 part essential oils to 4 parts V-6 Vegetable Oil Complex) before applying to the skin or taking internally.

5% = Dilute to 5% of total
Always dilute down to 5% (5 drops essential oil to 1 teaspoon V-6 Vegetable Oil Complex) before applying to the skin or taking internally.

1% = Dilute to 1% of total
Always dilute down to 1% (1 drop essential oil to 1 teaspoon V-6 Vegetable Oil Complex) before applying to the skin or taking internally.

☀ = Photosensitizing
Avoid using on skin exposed to direct sunlight or UV rays (i.e., UV lights, sunbathing animals such as dogs or cats, etc.).

Esential Oil Blend	General Human Dilution	Avian/ Reptiles/ Pocket Pets	Canine	Equine/ Livestock	Feline
Abundance	Neat	20-80	Neat	Neat	50-50
Acceptance	Neat	Neat	Neat	Neat	Neat
Aroma Life	Neat	Neat	Neat	Neat	Neat
Aroma Siez	Neat	20-80	Neat	Neat	50-50
Australian Blue	Neat	Neat	Neat	Neat	Neat
Awaken	Neat	Neat	Neat	Neat	Neat
Brain Power	Neat	Neat	Neat	Neat	Neat
Christmas Spirit	Neat	20-80	Neat	Neat	50-50
Citrus Fresh	Neat	Neat	Neat	Neat	Neat
Clairty	Neat	5%	Neat	Neat	20-80
Common Sense	Neat	Neat	Neat	Neat	Neat
DiGize	Neat	Neat	Neat	Neat	Neat
Dragon Time	Neat	Neat	Neat	Neat	Neat
Dream Catcher	Neat	Neat	Neat	Neat	Neat
Egyptian Gold	Neat	5%	Neat	Neat	20-80
EndoFlex	Neat	Neat	Neat	Neat	Neat
En-R-Gee	Neat	5%	Neat	Neat	20-80
Envision	Neat	Neat	Neat	Neat	Neat
Evergreen Essence	Neat	Neat	Neat	Neat	Neat
Exclte	50-50	1%	50-50	50-50	5%
Exodus II	50-50	5%	Neat	Neat	5%
Fulfill Your Destiny	Neat	20-80	Neat	Neat	20-80
Forgiveness	Neat	Neat	Neat	Neat	Neat
Gathering	Neat	Neat	Neat	Neat	Neat
Gentle Baby	Neat	Neat	Neat	Neat	Neat
GLF	Neat	Neat	Neat	Neat	Neat
Gratitude	Neat	Neat	Neat	Neat	Neat
Grounding	Neat	Neat	Neat	Neat	Neat
Harmony	Neat	Neat	Neat	Neat	Neat
Highest Potential	Neat	Neat	Neat	Neat	Neat
Hope	Neat	Neat	Neat	Neat	Neat
Humility	Neat	Neat	Neat	Neat	Neat
ImmuPower	Neat	20-80	Neat	Neat	20-80
Inner Child	Neat	Neat	Neat	Neat	Neat

Esential Oil Blend	General Human Dilution	Avian/ Reptiles/ Pocket Pets	Canine	Equine/ Livestock	Feline
Inspiration	Neat	Neat	Neat	Neat	Neat
Into The Future	Neat	Neat	Neat	Neat	Neat
Joy ☀	Neat	Neat	Neat	Neat	Neat
JuvaCleanse	Neat	Neat	Neat	Neat	Neat
JuvaFlex	Neat	Neat	Neat	Neat	Neat
Lady Sclareol	Neat	Neat	Neat	Neat	Neat
Live with Passion	Neat	Neat	Neat	Neat	Neat
Longevity	Neat	20-80	Neat	Neat	50-50
Magnify Your Purpose	Neat	Neat	Neat	Neat	Neat
Melrose	Neat	Neat	Neat	Neat	Neat
M-Grain	Neat	5%	Neat	Neat	20-80
Mister	Neat	Neat	Neat	Neat	Neat
Motivation	Neat	Neat	Neat	Neat	Neat
My Destiny	Neat	20-80	Neat	Neat	20-80
PanAway	Neat	20-80	Neat	Neat	50-50
Peace & Calming	Neat	Neat	Neat	Neat	Neat
Present Time	Neat	Neat	Neat	Neat	Neat
Purification	Neat	50-50	Neat	Neat	50-50
Raven	Neat	50-50	Neat	Neat	50-50
R.C.	Neat	Neat	Neat	Neat	Neat
Release	Neat	Neat	Neat	Neat	Neat
Relieve It	Neat	Neat	Neat	Neat	Neat
RutaVaLa ☀	Neat	Neat	Neat	Neat	Neat
RutaVaLa Roll-On ☀	Neat	Neat	Neat	Neat	Neat
Surrender	Neat	Neat	Neat	Neat	Neat
The Gift	Neat	Neat	Neat	Neat	Neat
Thieves	Neat	5%	Neat	Neat	50-50
3 Wise Men	Neat	Neat	Neat	Neat	Neat
Transformation	Neat	50-50	Neat	Neat	50-50
Trauma Life	Neat	Neat	Neat	Neat	Neat
White Angelica	Neat	Neat	Neat	Neat	Neat

Ingestion Single Essential Oil Dilution Codes

Neat = Straight, undiluted
Dilution usually NOT required; suitable for all but the most sensitive skin.

50-50 = Dilute 50-50
Dilution recommended at 50-50 (1 part essential oils to 1 part V-6 Vegetable Oil Complex) for topical and internal use, especially when used on sensitive animal areas — face, neck, genital area, underarms, belly, etc.

20-80 = Dilute 20-80
Always dilute 20-80 (1 part essential oils to 4 parts V-6 Vegetable Oil Complex) before applying to the skin or taking internally.

5% = Dilute to 5% of total
Always dilute down to 5% (5 drops essential oil to 1 teaspoon V-6 Vegetable Oil Complex) before applying to the skin or taking internally.

1% = Dilute to 1% of total
Always dilute down to 1% (1 drop essential oil to 1 teaspoon V-6 Vegetable Oil Complex) before applying to the skin or taking internally.

☀ = Photosensitizing
Avoid using on skin exposed to direct sunlight or UV rays (i.e., UV lights, sunbathing animals such as dogs or cats, etc.).

Single Oil	General Human Dilution	Avian/ Reptiles/ Pocket Pets	Canine	Equine/ Livestock	Feline
Angelica ☀	Neat	5%	50-50	50-50	5%
Anise	Neat	5%	Neat	Neat	5%
Balsam Fir	Neat	Neat	Neat	Neat	Neat
Basil	50-50	50-50	Neat	Neat	50-50
Bergamot ☀	Neat	Neat	Neat	Neat	Neat
Black Pepper	50-50	5%	50-50	50-50	5%
Cassia	20-80	1%1%	50-50	50-50	1%
Cedarwood	Neat	Neat	Neat	Neat	Neat
Celery Seed	Neat	Neat	Neat	Neat	Neat
Cinnamon Bark	20-80	1%	50-50	50-50	1%
Cistus	Neat	Neat	Neat	Neat	Neat
Citronella	Neat	Neat	Neat	Neat	Neat
Clary Sage	Neat	Neat	Neat	Neat	Neat
Clove	50-50	20-80	Neat	Neat	20-80
Copaiba	Neat	Neat	Neat	Neat	Neat
Coriander	Neat	Neat	Neat	Neat	Neat
Cypress	Neat	Neat	Neat	Neat	Neat
Dill	Neat	Neat	Neat	Neat	Neat
Dorado Azul	Neat	Neat	Neat	Neat	Neat
Elemi	Neat	Neat	Neat	Neat	Neat
Eucalyptus Blue	Neat	Neat	Neat	Neat	Neat
Eucalyptus Globulus	Neat	Neat	Neat	Neat	Neat
Eucalyptus Radiata	Neat	Neat	Neat	Neat	Neat
Fennel	Neat	Neat	Neat	Neat	Neat
Frankincense	Neat	Neat	Neat	Neat	Neat
Frankincense (Sacred)	Neat	Neat	Neat	Neat	Neat
Geranium	Neat	Neat	Neat	Neat	Neat
Ginger	Neat	Neat	Neat	Neat	Neat
Goldenrod	Neat	Neat	Neat	Neat	Neat
Grapefruit ☀	Neat	Neat	Neat	Neat	Neat
Helichrysum	Neat	Neat	Neat	Neat	Neat
Hyssop	20-80	5%	20-80	20-80	5%
Jade Lemon	Neat	Neat	Neat	Neat	Neat
Jasmine	50-50	5%	50-50	50-50	5%
Juniper	Neat	Neat	Neat	Neat	Neat
Laurus Nobilis	Neat	Neat	Neat	Neat	Neat

Single Oil	General Human Dilution	Avian/ Reptiles/ Pocket Pets	Canine	Equine/ Livestock	Feline
Lavender	Neat	Neat	Neat	Neat	Neat
Ledum	Neat	Neat	Neat	Neat	Neat
Lemon ☀	Neat	Neat	Neat	Neat	Neat
Lemongrass	50-50	20-80	50-50	50-50	20-80
Marjoram	Neat	Neat	Neat	Neat	Neat
Melaleuca Quinquenervia	Neat	Neat	Neat	Neat	Neat
Mountain Savory	50-50	5%	50-50	50-50	20-80
Myrrh	Neat	Neat	Neat	Neat	Neat
Myrtle	Neat	Neat	Neat	Neat	Neat
Neroli	20-80	5%	50-50	50-50	5%
Nutmeg	Neat	Neat	Neat	Neat	Neat
Ocotea	Neat	Neat	Neat	Neat	Neat
Orange ☀	Neat	Neat	Neat	Neat	Neat
Oregano	50-50	1%	50-50	50-50	1%
Palmarosa	Neat	Neat	Neat	Neat	Neat
Palo Santo	Neat	Neat	Neat	Neat	Neat
Patchouli	Neat	Neat	Neat	Neat	Neat
Peppermint	Neat	Neat	Neat	Neat	Neat
Petitgrain	Neat	Neat	Neat	Neat	Neat
Pine	Neat	Neat	Neat	Neat	Neat
Ravintsara	Neat	Neat	Neat	Neat	Neat
Rose	20-80	5%	50-50	50-50	5%
Rosemary	Neat	Neat	Neat	Neat	Neat
Sage	Neat	Neat	Neat	Neat	Neat
Sandalwood	Neat	Neat	Neat	Neat	Neat
Spearmint	Neat	Neat	Neat	Neat	Neat
Tangerine ☀	Neat	Neat	Neat	Neat	Neat
Tarragon	Neat	Neat	Neat	Neat	Neat
Tea Tree	Neat	Neat	Neat	Neat	Neat
Thyme	50-50	5%	50-50	50-50	5%
Tsuga	Neat	Neat	Neat	Neat	Neat
Valerian	Neat	Neat	Neat	Neat	Neat
Vetiver	Neat	Neat	Neat	Neat	Neat
Wintergreen	20-80	1%	50-50	50-50	1%
Xiang Mao	Neat	Neat	Neat	Neat	Neat
Ylang Ylang	Neat	Neat	Neat	Neat	Neat

Ingestion Essential Oil Blends Dilution Codes

Neat = Straight, undiluted
Dilution usually NOT required; suitable for all but the most sensitive skin.

50-50 = Dilute 50-50
Dilution recommended at 50-50 (1 part essential oils to 1 part V-6 Vegetable Oil Complex) for topical and internal use, especially when used on sensitive animal areas — face, neck, genital area, underarms, belly, etc.

20-80 = Dilute 20-80
Always dilute 20-80 (1 part essential oils to 4 parts V-6 Vegetable Oil Complex) before applying to the skin or taking internally.

5% = Dilute to 5% of total
Always dilute down to 5% (5 drops essential oil to 1 teaspoon V-6 Vegetable Oil Complex) before applying to the skin or taking internally.

1% = Dilute to 1% of total
Always dilute down to 1% (1 drop essential oil to 1 teaspoon V-6 Vegetable Oil Complex) before applying to the skin or taking internally.

☀ = Photosensitizing
Avoid using on skin exposed to direct sunlight or UV rays (i.e., UV lights, sunbathing animals such as dogs or cats, etc.).

Esential Oil Blend	General Human Dilution	Avian/ Reptiles/ Pocket Pets	Canine	Equine/ Livestock	Feline
Abundance	Neat	Neat	Neat	Neat	Neat
Acceptance	Neat	Neat	Neat	Neat	Neat
Aroma Life	Neat	Neat	Neat	Neat	Neat
Aroma Siez	Neat	Neat	Neat	Neat	Neat
Australian Blue	Neat	Neat	Neat	Neat	Neat
Awaken	Neat	Neat	Neat	Neat	Neat
Brain Power	Neat	Neat	Neat	Neat	Neat
Christmas Spirit	50-50	5%	Neat	Neat	5%
Citrus Fresh	Neat	Neat	Neat	Neat	Neat
Clairty	Neat	5%	Neat	Neat	5%
Common Sense	Neat	Neat	Neat	Neat	Neat
DiGize	Neat	Neat	Neat	Neat	Neat
Dragon Time	Neat	Neat	Neat	Neat	Neat
Dream Catcher	Neat	Neat	Neat	Neat	Neat
Egyptian Gold	50-50	20-80	Neat	Neat	20-80
EndoFlex	Neat	Neat	Neat	Neat	Neat
En-R-Gee	50-50	20-80	Neat	Neat	20-80
Envision	Neat	Neat	Neat	Neat	Neat
Evergreen Essence	Neat	Neat	Neat	Neat	Neat
Excite	50-50	1%	50-50	50-50	1%
Exodus II	50-50	1%	50-50	50-50	1%
Fulfill Your Destiny	Neat	Neat	Neat	Neat	Neat
Forgiveness	Neat	Neat	Neat	Neat	Neat
Gathering	Neat	Neat	Neat	Neat	Neat
Gentle Baby	Neat	Neat	Neat	Neat	Neat
GLF	Neat	Neat	Neat	Neat	Neat
Gratitude	Neat	Neat	Neat	Neat	Neat
Grounding	Neat	Neat	Neat	Neat	Neat
Harmony	Neat	Neat	Neat	Neat	Neat
Highest Potential	Neat	Neat	Neat	Neat	Neat
Hope	Neat	Neat	Neat	Neat	Neat
Humility	Neat	Neat	Neat	Neat	Neat
ImmuPower	50-50	20-80	Neat	Neat	20-80
Inner Child	Neat	Neat	Neat	Neat	Neat
Inspiration	Neat	Neat	Neat	Neat	Neat
Into The Future	Neat	Neat	Neat	Neat	Neat

Esential Oil Blend		General Human Dilution	Avian/ Reptiles/ Pocket Pets	Canine	Equine/ Livestock	Feline
Joy	☀	Neat	Neat	Neat	Neat	Neat
JuvaCleanse		Neat	Neat	Neat	Neat	Neat
JuvaFlex		Neat	Neat	Neat	Neat	Neat
Lady Sclareol		Neat	Neat	Neat	Neat	Neat
Live with Passion		Neat	Neat	Neat	Neat	Neat
Longevity		Neat	20-80	Neat	Neat	20-80
Magnify Your Purpose		Neat	Neat	Neat	Neat	Neat
Melrose		Neat	5%	Neat	Neat	5%
M-Grain		Neat	5%	Neat	Neat	5%
Mister		Neat	Neat	Neat	Neat	Neat
Motivation		Neat	Neat	Neat	Neat	Neat
My Destiny		Neat	Neat	Neat	Neat	Neat
PanAway		50-50	5%	50-50	50-50	5%
Peace & Calming		Neat	Neat	Neat	Neat	Neat
Present Time		Neat	Neat	Neat	Neat	Neat
Purification		Neat	20-80	Neat	Neat	50-50
Raven		Neat	20-80	Neat	Neat	50-50
R.C.		Neat	Neat	Neat	Neat	Neat
Release		Neat	Neat	Neat	Neat	Neat
Relieve It		Neat	Neat	Neat	Neat	Neat
RutaVaLa	☀	Neat	20-80	Neat	Neat	50-50
RutaVaLa Roll-On	☀	Neat	20-80	Neat	Neat	50-50
Surrender		Neat	Neat	Neat	Neat	Neat
The Gift		Neat	50-50	Neat	Neat	50-50
Thieves		50-50	5%	50-50	50-50	20-80
3 Wise Men		Neat	Neat	Neat	Neat	Neat
Transformation		Neat	20-80	Neat	Neat	50-50
Trauma Life		Neat	Neat	Neat	Neat	Neat
White Angelica		Neat	Neat	Neat	Neat	Neat

Each ratio is only a suggestion. Within the same species, one animal may react differently to a particular ratio than another depending on it's needs. This variation of reaction is only amplified when dealing with differing animal species. The provided ratios are given to best suite the widest audience of animals within a group. The ratios do not cover ALL possible animals and their health needs in a particular group.

Birds (Avian)

Introduction

Birds, especially parrots, are a more recent addition to the world of veterinary aromatherapy. Pet birds are extremely sensitive to household toxins, and even the spray of an air freshener or the burning of a candle can be dangerous to them.

Since many household fragrances are created with poor grade, adulterated, or synthetic essential oils, it was commonly thought that all essential oils were toxic to birds. This has been found to be **untrue**. While birds have a distinct way in which they should be exposed to essential oils, they not only benefit from but also thrive with the addition of essential oils into their lives.

Safety And Guidelines When Using Essential Oils With Birds

In terms of topical application of essential oils, birds are unique as they are generally covered in feathers. Coating feathers in essential oils can be harmful to birds. Large amounts of oil can cause some birds' feathers to clump or molt.

Birds' skin is also unique from other animals as it supports the growth of feathers. Feathers offer birds an additional measure of protection from external pathogens and the elements.

There is a tradeoff, though. With the additional protection that feathers afford, birds' skin is usually thinner and more sensitive to oils than other animals. Consideration should also be given to birds that have naturally exposed skin. Birds with naturally exposed skin generally have a much higher number of blood vessels on the exposed portion of their bodies. This allows them to do many things, including changing their exposed skin's pigment for mating purposes to thermoregulating their body temperature by rushing more blood to the exposed area to rid excess body heat. Keep this in mind whenever applying oils to those areas, as oil absorption is greatly increased there.

Because of all these factors, it has been found that the best way to safely introduce and apply oils to birds is usually by misting, spraying, or diffusing oils on or around them. Oils can still be applied topically, but diffusing or spraying is a great way to measure your bird's tolerance and acceptance of oils before direct application.

Feather Spray Recipe

A favorite technique that is being used currently with thousands of birds is the Feather Spray Recipe. This amazing spray was created by Leigh Foster and carries benefits for everything from bacterial, viral, and fungal conditions to cancer prevention and immune system support.

Place 20 drops of Lavender, 20 drops of Lemon, and 20 drops of Orange essential oils into a 4-ounce glass spray bottle. Add distilled water to fill the bottle. Shake well before each application and then mist the bird directly with the spray up to 2 times a day. Birds love this spray, including those who routinely dislike a shower from a traditional spray bottle.

Diffusing

Diffusing from a water-based diffuser is recommended for birds. Air diffusers may be used; however, they require being farther away from the bird or used in a much larger room (such as a barn or large aviary). Almost all essential oil singles and blends have been diffused around birds from water-based diffusers such as the Aria or Home Diffuser.

In general, start with 3 drops of oil added to the water of the diffuser. Monitor the bird(s) closely for the first 5-10 minutes of diffusing and gradually increase the length of time and frequency. Often, you can diffuse on an almost continual basis, bringing amazing benefits and health to your birds.

Bird (Avian) Conditions

Apoplexy

Apoplexy is marked by an uncontrollable jerking or contraction of the muscles, typically caused by hypoglycemia, vitamin B deficiency, calcium deficiency, and vitamin D3 deficiency.

Recommendations

Singles: Lavender
Blends: Stress Away Roll-On, Peace & Calming, Peace & Calming II
Nutritionals: NingXia Red

Application and Usage

Ingestion & Oral: Place the bird in a cool, dark place and administer 1 oz. of NingXia Red 2-4 times daily until levels return to normal.
Inhalation: Diffuse Stress Away Roll-On, Peace & Calming, and Peace & Calming II in bird area.

Aspergillosis

Aspergillosis, or asper, is a fungal infection. It is the most lethal type of infection that avians, particularly arctic birds, can develop and die from. Gyrfalcons, goshawks, and snowy owls, in particular, are susceptible. This can manifest in two forms. Nodular asper attacks the air sacs, lungs, and trachea. Systemic asper attacks the kidneys, liver, or other organs.

The fungus that causes asper, *Aspergillus fumigates*, is found everywhere, except in the frozen Arctic and Antarctic regions. Birds are constantly exposed to it. Elevated levels will be found in areas where there are carpets, wet or damp substances, or materials that promote the growth of fungus such as burlap, hay, or straw.

Fecal matter and dead vegetation (straw and shavings) should be kept to a minimum in any aviary enclosure. To contract the disease, the bird usually will have a depressed immune system caused by another disease, poor health, extended antibiotic use, or poor nutrition.

Recommendations

Singles: Lemon, Cedarwood, Ocotea, Copaiba, Ginger, Ravintsara
Blends: Thieves, Purification, DiGize, Exodus II
Nutritionals: NingXia Red, Life 9
Additional: Thieves Household Cleaner

Application and Usage

Ingestion & Oral: Administer orally 2-4 times daily 2 drops Cedarwood, 2 drops Ocotea, 2 drops DiGize, and 2 drops Copaiba with 1 capsule Life 9 in 1 oz. NingXia Red. Try substituting Exodus II and Ravintsara for Cedarwood and Ocotea if necessary. Once cleared, continue to administer orally NingXia Red, Ginger, Lemon, and Life 9 until the immune system is restored.

Inhalation: Diffuse Thieves, Purification, or Lemon in bird area.

Other: Wash EVERYTHING with 4 capfuls of Thieves Household Cleaner mixed into 1 gallon of water.

Avian Influenza

Avian influenza isn't typically seen in raptors; however, since the typical host is ducks and chickens, raptors can be exposed to this as well.

Recommendations

Singles: Ravintsara, Copaiba, Lemon
Blends: Raven, Exodus II, DiGize, Thieves, Purification
Nutritionals: NingXia Red, Life 9
Additional: Thieves Household Cleaner

Application and Usage

Ingestion & Oral: Administer orally 2-4 times daily 2 drops each of Ravintsara or Raven, Exodus II, DiGize, and Copaiba with 1 capsule Life 9 in 1 oz. NingXia Red. Once cleared, continue administering orally NingXia Red, Purification, and Lemon with Life 9 until immune system is restored.

Inhalation: Diffuse Thieves, Purification, and Lemon in bird area.

Other: Wash EVERYTHING with 4 capfuls of Thieves Household Cleaner mixed into 1 gallon of water.

Blackhead

Blackhead is a disease that primarily affects turkeys and chickens in commercial poultry. The cause is protozoa that can lay dormant in the ground for years. Birds that are infected excrete a watery, yellowish mute, which is a discharge that has three parts: fecal (the semisolid mass that is often colored), urate (a white, chalky material from protein metabolism), and urine (the clear water that flushes waste from the system).

The bird must be removed and the area cleaned to prevent others from developing this condition.

Recommendations

Singles: Frankincense, Copaiba, Lemon, Myrtle
Blends: ImmuPower, Purification, Egyptian Gold, Thieves

Nutritionals: Life 9, NingXia Red
Additional: Thieves Household Cleaner

Application and Usage

Ingestion & Oral: Administer orally 2-3 times daily 2-4 drops of any 1 of these oils: ImmuPower, Purification, or Egyptian Gold with 1-2 drops of each of these oils: Frankincense, Copaiba, Lemon, and Myrtle. Combine selected oils with 1 Life 9 in 1 oz. NingXia Red.

Inhalation: Diffuse Thieves or Purification in bird area.

Other: Spray the whole area, including the ground, with a strong concentrated solution of Thieves Household Cleaner and Purification every day for 10 days.

Blockage

Although not a disease, blockage may be mistaken for one. Some birds are quite greedy and will manage to swallow more than they should. These birds must be watched carefully in case they manage to swallow large, connected segments to ensure they put over the crop correctly, pass food on through, and cast appropriately. Care should be taken to not feed on top of a difficult crop of food.

Recommendations

Singles: Copaiba
Blends: DiGize, Stress Away Roll-On, Gentle Baby
Nutritionals: Life 9, NingXia Red

Application and Usage

Ingestion & Oral: Administer orally 2-3 times daily 4-6 drops each of DiGize and Copaiba with 1 capsule Life 9 in 1 oz. NingXia Red.

Inhalation: Diffuse Stress Away Roll-On or Gentle Baby in bird area.

Bumblefoot

Bumblefoot is a disease of the bottom of the feet caused by any number of bacteria. Birds have an amazing ability to heal their skin; but unfortunately, it can end up encapsulating bacteria, allowing the colony to continue producing.

In the case of bumblefoot, the bird sustained an injury, however small, to the bottom of the foot; and bacteria took hold. The skin may have continued to heal around this colony. It began as a small, hardened corn, which developed into a fevered hot spot or open sore.

Veterinarian Tips and Suggestions

Bumblefoot in ducks and chickens

Combine:

- Thyme (15 drops)
- Oregano (15 drops)
- Wintergreen (10 drops)
- Lavender (20 drops)
- Basil (20 drops)

Application:

- Add mixture to 4 oz. glass spray bottle, filling remaining volume with a carrier oil.
- Shake well and spray mixture directly onto affected animal's foot.
- As the flock's feet begin to clear, separate healed animals from animals still affected. Birds will heal at different rates, so be sure to quarantine birds that are taking longer to prevent further transmission.

Other symptoms are a bird that lies down or won't put weight onto the feet. This corn, or a spot on the foot skin, is usually an early sign of Bumblefoot. It can still be reversed relatively easily.

Untreated, bumblefoot doesn't just impact the foot and the ability to stand comfortably; it can devolve into septicemia and even kill a bird. Falcons appear to be particularly sensitive to bumblefoot, possibly from the way they strike prey.

Recommendations

Singles: Ginger, Myrrh, Copaiba, Lemon, Mountain Savory

Blends: Thieves, Exodus II, Purification

Additional: Thieves Household Cleaner

Application and Usage

Topical: Combine any 1 of these oils: Thieves, Exodus II, Ginger, or Mountain Savory with Copaiba and Myrrh. Apply and layer oils on affected feet 2 times daily.

Inhalation: Diffuse Lemon, Thieves, or Purification in bird area.

Other: Clean area with Thieves Household Cleaner weekly.

Candidiasis

Yeast infection: Symptoms include plaques in the mouth (easily mistaken for frounce, capillaria, or vitamin A deficiency), lack of appetite, vomiting, dehydration, and depression.

Recommendations

Singles: Ocotea, Copaiba, Jade Lemon, Myrtle, Lemon, Lemon Myrtle

Blends: DiGize, Purification

Nutritionals: Mineral Essence, Life 9

Application and Usage

Ingestion & Oral: Administer orally 2 times daily 2-4 drops each of Ocotea, DiGize, and Copaiba, 1 dropperful Mineral Essence, 1 capsule Life 9, and 1 drop Jade Lemon, Lemon, or Ocotea in water. Keep the bird away from ALL sugar in food and water.

Inhalation: Diffuse Purification, Lemon, Lemon Myrtle, and Myrtle in bird area.

Capillaria

Capillaria is also called small roundworms and is typically picked up from crows or small birds. These roundworms, *Capillaria amulata*, embed themselves in the lining of the esophagus, crop, or small intestine.

Recommendations

Singles: Ocotea, Copaiba

Blends: ParaGize, DiGize

Additional: Thieves Fruit & Veggie Spray

Application and Usage

Ingestion & Oral: Administer orally 3-4 drops each of ParaGize, DiGize, Ocotea, and Copaiba 2 times daily.

Other: Wash bird area with Thieves Fruit & Veggie Spray.

Chlamydiosis (Avian Chlamydia)

Chlamydiosis is also called Avian Chlamydia. It is very common in parrots and is sometimes called parrot fever. It is caused by an intracellular bacterium called *Chlamydophila psittaci*. Symptoms vary from no symptoms with latent bacteria for months to sudden death.

Some typical symptoms are inflammation of the eye (both the conjunctiva and the cornea), inflammation of the nasal membranes, and shortness of breath. Mutes may be yellowish-green or watery-grey. These bacteria can attack the air sacs, the liver, heart, spleen, or brain.

Recommendations

Singles: Copaiba, Lavender
Blends: Thieves, Melrose, Purification
Nutritionals: NingXia Red, Life 9
Additional: Thieves Household Cleaner

Application and Usage

Ingestion & Oral: Administer orally 1-2 times daily 3 drops each of Melrose, Purification, Copaiba, and Lavender with 1 capsule Life 9 in 1 teaspoon NingXia Red.

Inhalation: Diffuse Thieves, Purification, or Melrose in the bird area, placing the diffuser approximately 6 feet away from the bird.

Other: Wash bird area with Thieves Household Cleaner.

Coccidiosis

Coccidiosis is a disease of the digestive system caused by a parasitic protozoan. This protozoan appears in two forms, Isospora and Eimeria. Isospora is the form found in falconiformes and strigiformes. These develop inside the cells that line the intestinal tract. As they take over more and more cells, the cells begin leaking, preventing the bird from absorbing nutrients or liquids. This loss of blood and fluid is what causes the reddish (or red spotty) diarrhea that marks this disease. The loss of blood and fluids can be fatal.

Recommendations

Singles: Ocotea, Copaiba, Frankincense, Thyme
Blends: ParaGize, DiGize, Purification, Thieves
Nutritionals: Life 9
Additional: Thieves Household Cleaner

Application and Usage

Ingestion & Oral: Administer orally 2 times daily 3-4 drops each of ParaGize or DiGize, Ocotea, Copaiba, 2 drops each of Frankincense and Thyme, and 1 capsule Life 9 in water.

Inhalation: Diffuse Thieves or Purification in bird area.

Other: Spray the whole area, including the ground, with a strong concentrated solution of Thieves Household Cleaner and Purification every day for 10 days.

Coryza (Infectious Coryza)

Coryza is a bacterial infection that isn't typically fatal but is difficult to treat. Birds will develop swelling around their faces and discharge from their eyes and nares (nose). They also tend to develop green mutes.

Recommendations

Singles: Copaiba, Lavender
Blends: Melrose, Thieves, Purification
Nutritionals: NingXia Red
Additional: Thieves Household Cleaner

Application and Usage

Ingestion & Oral: Administer orally 1-2 times daily 2 drops each of Melrose, Purification, Copaiba, and Lavender with 1 capsule Life 9 in 1 teaspoon NingXia Red.

Inhalation: Diffuse Thieves, Purification, or Melrose in the bird area, placing diffuser approximately 6 feet away from the bird.

Other: Wash bird area with Thieves Household Cleaner.

Cramp (also called Sprattling)

Cramp affects nestling raptors that get chilled. The chick cannot regulate its body temperature and therefore is dependent on its environment (parent or incubator) for proper warmth.

When the chick gets too cold, the intestinal gut flora dies, and the chick's digestive process begins to fail. If the chick still has gut motility, then food will pass through almost undigested. If there is no gut motility, then the food sits in the chick and spoils.

Chilling causes muscle contractions and spasms in an attempt to warm the body. This inhibits the ability to process calcium. Cramp is prevented by using a brooder box, heat lamp, or heating pad.

Recommendations

Singles: Copaiba, Ginger
Blends: DiGize
Nutritionals: Life 9, NingXia Red

Application and Usage

Topical: Apply DiGize and Copaiba topically to bird's belly and feet 2-4 times daily.

Ingestion & Oral: Administer orally 2 times daily 1 capsule Life 9 in 1 tablespoon NingXia Red. If it is advanced, administer as above and add 4 drops each of DiGize and Ginger 2-3 times daily.

Dehydration

Although dehydration is not a disease, it is a common symptom and needs to be identified. One way is by pulling the skin of the upper foot away from the body, pinching it up, and noting if it remains tented or returns to the normal shape. Skin that remains pinched and tented is typical of a dehydrated animal.

You can also open the mouth to see if there is stringy, mucousy liquid across the back of the bird's mouth. If there is, then the bird is dehydrated.

Recommendations
Singles: Jade Lemon, Lemon, Ocotea
Nutritionals: Mineral Essence, NingXia Red, Life 9

Application and Usage
Ingestion & Oral: Administer 1-2 times daily 1 drop of Jade Lemon, Lemon, or Ocotea in water, 1 dropperful Mineral Essence, 1 capsule Life 9 in 1 teaspoon NingXia Red.

Escherichia Coli (E. coli)

E. coli is typically passed from infected birds through mutes and fecal matter. Typical symptoms include ruffled appearance and listlessness, although some birds display no symptoms.

Recommendations
Singles: Copaiba
Blends: Melrose, Thieves, DiGize, Purification
Nutritionals: NingXia Red, Life 9
Additional: Thieves Household Cleaner

Application and Usage
Ingestion & Oral: Administer orally 1-2 times daily 2 drops each of Melrose, Thieves, Copaiba, DiGize, and 1 capsule Life 9 in 1 teaspoon NingXia Red.
Inhalation: Diffuse Thieves, Purification, or Melrose in bird area, placing diffuser approximately 6 feet away from bird.
Other: Wash bird area with Thieves Household Cleaner.

Fluke or Flat Worms (Trematodes)

Flukes are a very common parasite, occurring in most wild raptors.

Recommendations
Singles: Patchouli, Copaiba
Blends: ParaGize, DiGize, Thieves, Purification
Nutritionals: Life 9
Additional: Thieves Household Cleaner

Application and Usage
Ingestion & Oral: Administer orally 2 times daily 3-4 drops each of ParaGize, DiGize, Patchouli, Copaiba, and 1 capsule Life 9 in water.
Inhalation: Diffuse Thieves or Purification in bird area.
Other: Spray the whole area, including the ground, with a strong concentrated solution of Thieves Household Cleaner and Purification every day for 10 days.

Fowl Cholera (Avian Cholera)

Fowl cholera is a bacterial disease uncommon in raptors, but it can occur.

There are two forms of this disease: acute and chronic. Acute fowl cholera manifests with anorexia, high fever, mucal diarrhea, mucal discharge from the mouth, and murky greenish diarrhea. The bird tends to have a ruffled appearance and generally dies quickly.

Chronic fowl cholera may just be a localized infection in the sinus cavity or joints. This is marked more by discharge from the eyes, raspy breathing, and a twisted neck (torticollis). This is typically treated with antibiotics. The bird area needs to be disinfected.

Recommendations
Singles: Copaiba
Blends: Raven, Thieves, Melrose, Purification
Nutritionals: NingXia Red, Life 9
Additional: Thieves Household Cleaner

Application and Usage
Ingestion & Oral: Administer orally 1-2 times daily 2 drops each of Melrose, Thieves, Copaiba, and Raven and 1 capsule Life 9 in 1 teaspoon NingXia Red.
Inhalation: Diffuse Thieves, Purification, Melrose, or Raven in bird area, placing the diffuser approximately 6 feet away from the bird.
Other: Wash bird area with Thieves Household Cleaner.

French Moult

In domestic avian husbandry, almost any feather abnormality is called a *French Moult*. This could be that the bird is moulting at the wrong time of year, is moulting twice in a summer, or has feathers coming in that are misshapen. It can be caused by nutrition, environment, immune system, infection, and most commonly, polyomavirus.

An improper moult in raptors, as misshapen or pinched feathers, has recently signaled the potential of West Nile Virus (WNV). This is also being seen after a bird recovers from a WNV infection.

Recommendations
Singles: Lavender, Orange, Eucalyptus Blue
Blends: Stress Away Roll-On, Gentle Baby, Sacred Mountain, Raven

Application and Usage
Topical: Make a spray in a glass spray bottle of 4 oz. pure water (not tap); 20 drops each of Gentle Baby, Lavender, and Orange; and 5 drops each of Eucalyptus Blue and Raven. Spray on bird up to 6 times daily.
Inhalation: To bring down stress, diffuse Stress Away Roll-On, Lavender, Gentle Baby, or Sacred Mountain.
Other: Combine treatment with West Nile Virus protocol found in this chapter.

Frostbite

Some birds are very hardy and tolerate cold well. Others like a Harris Hawk or Desert Falcon are sensitive to the cold. Frostbite can be very mild or extreme enough to cause tissue death and even result in the bird's death.

The usual site of damage for frostbite is the foot appearing pale and dry. Bad frostbite will eventually darken as the tissue dies and falls off. If this is suspected, immediately bring the bird into a normal living environment where it will be in a comfortable ambient temperature.

A foot can be rinsed or soaked in cool to lukewarm water or in saline to begin to warm the tissues. **Warm or hot water should never be used**.

Recommendations
Singles: Helichrysum, Cypress, Lavender, Myrrh, Sacred Frankincense
Blends: Trauma Life, Stress Away Roll-On
Nutritionals: NingXia Red, Mineral Essence
Additional: Rose Ointment

Application and Usage
Topical: Apply 2-4 times daily Helichrysum, Cypress, Lavender, and Myrrh, with Rose Ointment over the top of applied oils.
Ingestion & Oral: The bird should be kept in a warm, quiet environment; should be well hydrated with 1 oz. NingXia Red, plus 1 dropperful Mineral Essence; and should receive sufficient food.
Inhalation: Diffuse Trauma Life, Stress Away Roll-On, Sacred Frankincense, or Lavender to reduce stress.
Other: Ensure the tissue is completely healed before the bird is exposed to cold again.

Frounce (or Avian Trichomoniasis)

Frounce is a highly contagious yeast infection of the digestive tract. It is caused by a protozoan called *Trichomoniasis gallinae,* which is frequently present in the crops of pigeons. For this reason, pigeon heads and crops are generally not fed to raptors.

The typical signs of Frounce are white spots in the mouth or crop, often described as "cheesy" or "white plaques." These alone are not enough to diagnose Frounce, as plaques could be candidiasis, capillaria, or even vitamin A deficiency; but they are a hallmark of the disease. Other signs are head bowing, head flicking, difficulty breathing, or even regurgitation of food. There is a particular smell to Frounce. Green mutes may also appear.

Recommendations
Singles: Lemon, Myrtle, Ocotea, Copaiba, Jade Lemon
Blends: DiGize, Purification
Nutritionals: Mineral Essence, Life 9

Application and Usage
Ingestion & Oral: Administer 2 times daily 2-4 drops each of Ocotea, DiGize, and Copaiba; 1 drop Jade Lemon, Lemon, or Ocotea; 1 dropperful Mineral Essence; and 1 capsule Life 9 in water. Keep the bird away from ALL sugar in food and water.
Inhalation: Diffuse Purification, Lemon, or Myrtle.

Gapeworms

Gapeworms (*Syngamus trachea*) infect the tracheas of chickens, turkeys, pheasants, and guinea fowl. Symptoms are neck stretching, wheezing, and shortness of breath. Generally, death is quick, as the worms cause asphyxiation. Symptoms are coughing, wheezing, and shortness of breath.

Recommendations
Singles: Ocotea, Copaiba, Jade Lemon, Lemon, Myrtle, Ravintsara
Blends: Purification, DiGize, Raven
Nutritionals: ParaFree, Mineral Essence, Life 9

Application and Usage
Ingestion & Oral: Administer orally 2 times daily 1 capsule ParaFree; 2-4 drops Ocotea, DiGize, Raven, and Copaiba; 1 drop Jade Lemon or Lemon; 1 dropperful Mineral Essence; and 1 capsule Life 9 in water.
Inhalation: Diffuse Purification, Lemon, or Myrtle.
Other: Keep the bird away from ALL sugar in food and water.

Gout

Gout is caused by kidney problems, which leaves excess uric acid in the system that cannot be cleaned out. This is typically seen as a swelling in the foot and joints (distinguishable from bumblefoot), but internal organs sustain damage as the acid deposits on their surfaces. Nutritional deficiencies are what lead to this.

A properly hydrated bird can stave off this disease longer than a dehydrated bird. Hydration allows the bird to flush its system.

Recommendations
Singles: Copaiba, Juniper, Helichrysum, Cypress
Nutritionals: K&B

Application and Usage
Topical: Apply Copaiba and Cypress onto feet 2-3 times daily.
Ingestion & Oral: Administer orally 2-3 times daily 1 dropperful K&B and 2 drops each Copaiba, Juniper, and Helichrysum in 1 oz. pure water.

Haemoproteus

Haemoproteus is a blood infection spread by flat flies. Pigeons and doves are frequently infected with low levels, but commercial flocks are not typically seen with infection.

Recommendations
Singles: Copaiba, Helichrysum, Cypress, Lavender, Orange, Eucalyptus Blue
Blends: DiGize, Gentle Baby, Purification
Nutritionals: Rehemogen

Application and Usage
Topical: Apply Copaiba and Cypress onto feet 2-3 times daily.
Ingestion & Oral: Administer orally 2 times daily 1 dropperful Rehemogen and 2 drops each Copaiba, DiGize, and Helichrysum in 1 oz. pure water.
Other: Make a spray in a glass spray bottle of 4 oz. pure water (not tap) and 10 drops each of Gentle Baby, Lavender, Orange, Purification, and Eucalyptus Blue. Spray on bird up to 4 times daily.

Herpes (Avian Herpes)

Three closely related viruses cause avian herpes. One strain causes Pacheco's disease, another causes Marek's disease, and the rest fall into the category of "other." Birds will pass this virus through their mutes and dander.

This is noted to be particularly deadly to gyrfalcons and peregrine falcons. Goshawks are also vulnerable to developing it.

Avian herpes causes inflammations; swellings; bleeding of the liver, kidneys, and spleen; and ultimately death. Since there are several different strains, there are several different clinical signs. The progression is slow and some signs of it are tremors, seizures, swellings, and general lethargy. Fecals may be green with yellow or orange urates.

Recommendations
Singles: Copaiba, Ravintsara, Helichrysum, Eucalyptus Blue, Melissa, Lavender
Blends: Purification, DiGize, Exodus II
Nutritionals: K&B

Application and Usage
Topical: Apply Copaiba, Melissa, and Helichrysum onto feet 2-3 times daily.
Ingestion & Oral: Administer orally 1-2 times daily 1 dropper full K&B; 2 drops each Copaiba, DiGize,

Ravintsara, Helichrysum, and Exodus II; 4 drops each Eucalyptus Blue and Melissa; and 1 oz. pure water.

Other: Make a spray in a glass spray bottle of 4 oz. pure water (not tap) and 10 drops each of Melissa, Lavender, Helichrysum, Purification, and Eucalyptus Blue. Spray on bird up to 4 times daily.

Impaction

Impaction of the crop, gizzard, or stomach is fairly uncommon. Flooring materials, such as wood shavings or sand, can be ingested. They impact in the bird, begin to breed bacteria, and create a crop infection. Plenty of water will help many things either move through the system or be cast back up. Symptoms are usually that the bird acts active, yet shows no signs of interest in food.

Recommendations
Singles: Ginger, Peppermint, Copaiba
Blends: DiGize
Nutritionals: Life 9

Application and Usage
Topical: Topically apply 1 drop each of DiGize, Copaiba, and Peppermint to bird's belly and feet 2-4 times daily.
Ingestion & Oral: Administer orally 2 times daily 1 capsule Life 9 in 1 tablespoon water, with 2 drops each of DiGize and Ginger.

Lead Poisoning

Lead poisoning causes nervous system damage and digestive system problems. It can directly impact the kidneys, liver, blood, and reproductive and immune systems. Symptoms are shaking, weakness, nervous system oddities, brown diarrhea (chocolate milk-like), high blood pressure, and renal failure.

A quick way to diagnose is by drawing the blood and viewing under a black light. The compound created by the presence of lead in the system will cause the blood to fluoresce.

Recommendations
Singles: Copaiba, Helichrysum,
Blends: DiGize
Nutritionals: K&B, Rehemogen, NingXia Red

Application and Usage
Topical: Apply Copaiba, Helichrysum, or DiGize onto feet 2-3 times daily.
Ingestion & Oral: Administer orally 1-2 times daily 1 dropperful K&B, 1 dropperful Rehemogen, 1 tablespoon NingXia Red, and 2 drops each Copaiba, DiGize, and Helichrysum in 1 oz. of pure water.

Leucocytozoonosis

Leucocytozoonosis is a blood infection of both red and white blood cells that is transmitted by black flies. This is typically seen when the black fly population is high. Birds rapidly develop anemia, breathlessness, listlessness, and typically have a green mute; but death is very quick.

Recommendations
Singles: Copaiba, Helichrysum, Hyssop, Cedarwood, Ravintsara, Eucalyptus Blue, Eucalyptus Radiata, Eucalyptus Globulus, Lemon, Dorado Azul, Hinoki
Blends: DiGize, Raven, R.C., Thieves, Believe, Sacred Mountain
Nutritionals: K&B, Rehemogen, NingXia Red

Application and Usage
Topical: Apply Copaiba, Helichrysum, and Hyssop onto feet 2-3 times daily.
Ingestion & Oral: Administer orally 1-2 times daily 1 dropperful K&B, 1 dropperful Rehemogen, 1 tablespoon NingXia Red, and 2 drops each Copaiba, DiGize, and Helichrysum in 1 oz. of pure water.
Inhalation: Diffuse any of the following in the bird area: Cedarwood, Raven, Ravintsara, Eucalyptus Blue, Eucalyptus Radiata, Eucalyptus Globulus, R.C., Thieves, Lemon, Believe, Dorado Azul, Hinoki, or Sacred Mountain.

Lice

Louse, or Lice, is an external parasite, looking almost like a white worm but with legs. These parasites bite the bird and cause irritation. Lice tend to crawl around the vent area and lay eggs along the feather shafts.

Recommendations
Singles: Cedarwood, Orange, Helichrysum, Eucalyptus Blue, Lemongrass, Eucalyptus Radiata
Blends: Melrose, Purification

Application and Usage

Topical: Make a spray in a glass spray bottle of 4 oz. pure water (not tap) and 20 drops each of Cedarwood, Orange, Melrose, Helichrysum, Purification, Eucalyptus Radiata, and Eucalyptus Globulus. Spray on bird up to 4 times daily.

Inhalation: Combine the following and diffuse in the bird area: Cedarwood, Purification, Melrose, Lemongrass, and Eucalyptus Radiata.

Maggots

Eyass birds (in downy stage) are sometimes infested with maggots, typically in the head. This can be seen on very young birds as a grey dot at the top of the skull.

Recommendations

Singles: Helichrysum, Myrrh, Cedarwood, Lemongrass, Eucalyptus Radiata

Blends: Melrose, Purification

Additional: Thieves Household Cleaner

Application and Usage

Topical: Wash affected area with a dilution of Thieves Household Cleaner to remove maggots. Dry area. Using the layering technique, apply 2-3 drops each of Melrose, Helichrysum, Purification, and Myrrh 2-3 times daily on location of the infestation.

Inhalation: Combine Cedarwood, Purification, Melrose, Lemongrass, and Eucalyptus Radiata and diffuse in the bird area.

Malaria (Avian Malaria)

Malaria is protozoa transmitted primarily by mosquitoes, occurring when mosquito populations are high.

Birds are listless with puffy, almond-shaped eyes and may display difficulty with balance or eyesight. Birds are anemic, sometimes vomiting, and typically have a high temperature. The fecal of the mute may be any color, but the urate is a dull jade green color, as the protozoa attack the liver.

Recommendations

Singles: Copaiba, Helichrysum, Ravintsara, Hyssop, Eucalyptus Blue, Eucalyptus Radiata, Eucalyptus Globulus, Melissa

Blends: DiGize, Exodus II, R.C., Thieves

Nutritionals: NingXia Red

Application and Usage

Topical: Apply Copaiba, Ravintsara, Helichrysum, and Hyssop onto feet 2-3 times daily.

Ingestion & Oral: Administer orally 1-2 times daily 1 tablespoon NingXia Red and 2 drops each Copaiba, DiGize, Exodus II, Melissa, Ravintsara, and Helichrysum.

Inhalation: Diffuse any of the following in the bird area: Raven, Ravintsara, Eucalyptus Blue, Eucalyptus Radiata, Eucalyptus Globulus, R.C., or Thieves.

Metabolic Bone Disease (MBD)

Metabolic Bone Disease is a degenerative disease in which bone formation and density are inadequate. This is caused by many factors, including poor nutrition, inadequate nutrition during adolescence, and limited exposure to sunlight, leading to low vitamin D levels. Any of these issues usually results in a vitamin deficiency that can cause poor bone growth and development.

MBD is usually preventable through proper nutrition.

Recommendations

Nutritionals: Mineral Essence, NingXia Red, Life 9, MultiGreens, Sulfurzyme

Application and Usage

Ingestion & Oral: Administer listed Nutritionals as needed; amounts will vary for each bird.

Newcastle Disease

Newcastle disease is a highly contagious viral disease, transmitted through eating diseased birds or through infected water, food, equipment, or fecal matter. The disease attacks the nervous system with symptoms like twitching, shivering, convulsions, twisting of the neck, or paralysis. Sight may be impaired and the bird may have difficulty with breathing or coughing. Most telling is the greenish mute from infected birds.

There is no effective treatment other than supportive measures, but death is usually sudden. Controlling the virus is key. All equipment and premises should be disinfected, and infected animals must be destroyed.

This is very rare in North America.

Recommendations

Singles: Copaiba, Ravintsara, Helichrysum, Hyssop, Melissa

Blends: Thieves, Raven, Exodus II, DiGize

Nutritionals: NingXia Red

Additional: Thieves Household Cleaner

Application and Usage

Topical: Apply Copaiba, Ravintsara, Helichrysum, and Hyssop onto feet 2-3 times daily.

Ingestion & Oral: Administer orally 1-2 times daily 1 tablespoon NingXia Red and 2 drops each Copaiba, DiGize, Exodus II, Melissa, Ravintsara, and Helichrysum.

Inhalation: Diffuse any of the following in the bird area: Thieves, Raven, Ravintsara, or Exodus II.

Other: Wash everything with a strong solution of Thieves Household Cleaner immediately.

Parasites

External parasites generally affect only the plumage; and most particularly, they tend to damage the white areas of feathers. The parasites can cause the bird to look ruffled, or they can roughen the edges of feathers. This can make feathers less effective and moreover irritate the bird or transmit diseases. Feather lice tend to focus on the lighter portions of feathers.

Recommendations

Singles: Copaiba, Patchouli

Blends: ParaGize, DiGize, Purification

Nutritionals: ParaFree, Life 9

Application and Usage

Ingestion & Oral: Administer orally 1-2 times daily 1 drop ParaGize or 1 capsule ParaFree, 2-4 drops each of DiGize and Copaiba, and 1 capsule Life 9 in 1 teaspoon water.

Inhalation: Diffuse Purification or Patchouli.

Other: Keep the bird away from ALL sugar in food and water.

Pneumonia

Pneumonia is often found as a secondary disease to Asper; and sometimes when found separately, they can be mistaken for the other. It has many primary causes, including bacterial and viral.

Recommendations

Singles: Cedarwood, Lemon, Copaiba, Ravintsara

Blends: Thieves, Purification, Raven, DiGize, Exodus II, ImmuPower

Nutritionals: Life 9, NingXia Red

Additional: Thieves Household Cleaner

Application and Usage

Ingestion & Oral: Administer orally 2-4 times daily 2 drops each of Cedarwood, Raven or Ravintsara, Lemon or Exodus II, DiGize, and Copaiba; 1 capsule Life 9 in 1 oz. NingXia Red. When cleared, continue administering orally NingXia Red, Lemon, Raven or ImmuPower, and Life 9 until immune system is restored.

Inhalation: Diffuse Thieves, Purification, or Lemon in bird habitat.

Other: Wash EVERYTHING down with 4 capfuls of Thieves Household Cleaner in 1 gallon of water.

Poisoning

Many different types of poisons can affect birds. These poisons are often from things the bird has ingested or that inadvertently find their way into the bird's environment. This can include environmental contaminants that are found in pesticides, herbicides, industrial chemicals, and heavily processed food.

Be aware of chemicals that may be found in food packaging and avoid using feed and water containers that may have potentially dangerous components like lead, plastic, or Teflon.

Be especially careful to monitor any spills of dangerous chemicals like fertilizers or weed sprays in the bird's area, as many birds will forage in dirt for food, inadvertently eating anything that may have contaminated the ground.

Recommendations

Singles: Cedarwood, Helichrysum, Hyssop

Blends: DiGize, Purification, Stress Away Roll-On

Nutritionals: Rehemogen

Application and Usage

Topical: Apply the following to the feet using the layering technique 1-4 times daily: DiGize, Helichrysum, Hyssop, and Purification.

Ingestion & Oral: Administer orally 1-4 times daily 2 drops each Cedarwood, DiGize, and Helichrysum in 1 dropperful Rehemogen and 1 tablespoon pure spring water (never tap water).

Inhalation: Diffuse Purification, Cedarwood, or Stress Away Roll-On in bird area.

Poultry Ticks (Argasidae or soft ticks)

Poultry ticks are external parasites and are quite tiny, appearing to be just specks. They can be difficult to see without magnification. Within an hour, these tiny ticks will come crawling out, so treat in an area away from unaffected birds. These are also very difficult to get rid of once they infect an individual or a site.

Recommendations

Singles: Cedarwood, Lemongrass
Blends: Thieves, Purification
Additional: Thieves Household Cleaner

Application and Usage

Topical: Make a spray in a glass spray bottle of 4 oz. pure water (not tap) and 20 drops each of Cedarwood, Purification, and Lemongrass. Spray on bird up to 4 times daily.

Inhalation: Diffuse Thieves or Purification in the bird habitat.

Other: Wash EVERYTHING down with ¼ cup of Thieves Household Cleaner in 1 gallon of water.

Pox (also called Avian Pox)

Pox is a slow-spreading viral disease. It is easily transmitted through several vectors, including contact with infected individuals; ingestion of dander, fecal/mute matter, etc., of infected individuals; and even contact with surfaces that infected individuals have touched. It can be spread more quickly between individuals by mosquitoes.

Be very careful if an infected bird has touched a birdhouse, perch, or glove; these will need to be disinfected before another bird can touch them.

The most common form causes warty bumps to appear on the cere, legs, mouth, around the eyes, and in the upper respiratory system.

Recommendations

Singles: Copaiba, Melissa, Ravintsara
Blends: DiGize, Exodus II, ImmuPower, Raven, Purification
Nutritionals: NingXia Red
Additional: Thieves Household Cleaner

Application and Usage

Topical: Apply Copaiba, Ravintsara, Melissa, and ImmuPower onto affected area 2-3 times daily.

Ingestion & Oral: Administer orally 1-2 times daily 1 tablespoon NingXia Red and 2 drops each Copaiba, DiGize, Exodus II, Melissa, Ravintsara, and ImmuPower

Inhalation: Diffuse any of the following in the bird area: Thieves, Raven, Ravintsara, Exodus II, or Purification.

Other: Wash EVERYTHING down with 1/4 cup Thieves Household Cleaner in 1 gallon of water.

Seizures

Seizures are an affliction of the nervous system, although the initial cause may be from other sources such as metabolism. Seizures are best dealt with by placing the bird in a cool, dark place and quickly getting it to a veterinarian.

Recommendations

Singles: Cedarwood, Copaiba, Lavender
Blends: DiGize, RutaVaLa, Stress Away Roll-On

Application and Usage

Topical: Using the layering technique, apply Cedarwood, Copaiba, Lavender, RutaVaLa, and Stress Away Roll-On on feet and top of head.

Ingestion & Oral: Administer orally 1-2 drops DiGize.

Note: Get the affected bird to the veterinarian immediately.

Sinusitis

Sinusitis is a bacterial infection of the sinuses. It is most often diagnosed when the skin in front of the eye moves in and out as the bird breathes. In extreme cases, the sinus can be nearly completely blocked with swelling of the orbital sinuses. The bird will have wheezing coming from the nares in this case.

Recommendations
Singles: Copaiba, Ravintsara, Eucalyptus Blue, Eucalyptus Radiata, Eucalyptus Globulus, Myrtle, Lemon Myrtle

Blends: Thieves, Exodus II, Raven, R.C., Purification, ImmuPower, Christmas Spirit

Nutritionals: NingXia Red, Life 9

Application and Usage
Topical: Apply Copaiba, Ravintsara, Raven, or ImmuPower onto affected area and feet 2-3 times daily.

Ingestion & Oral: Administer orally 1-2 times daily 1 tablespoon NingXia Red; 1 capsule Life 9; 2 drops each Copaiba and Exodus II or Ravintsara, Raven, R.C., and Purification or ImmuPower.

Inhalation: Diffuse any of the following in the bird area: Thieves, Raven, Ravintsara, R.C., Exodus II, Purification, ImmuPower, Eucalyptus Blue, Eucalyptus Radiata, Eucalyptus Globulus, Myrtle, Lemon Myrtle, Christmas Spirit.

Sour Crop (Crop Stasis)

Sour crop is a bacterial infection of the digestive system. This is when a bird does not put over a crop into the stomach in a timely manner. The food that remains in the crop is warm and not treated with the stomach acids; so as it sits there, the bacteria grow. The bacteria may be salmonella, in which case the bacterial growth can be very difficult to manage.

Sour crop can be caused by overfeeding, dehydration, improper feeding methods, rotten food, parasitic infections, ingestion of petroleum products, crop burns, crop lacerations, and even high temperatures or bright lights. It is marked by regurgitation of the crop contents, foul-smelling breath or castings, loss of appetite, but an increase in thirst.

Birds that have not regurgitated their crop contents will need help to very carefully remove the contents and rinse the crop. It is essential to start sour crop treatment by removing all the matter that is breeding bacteria.

Often, falconers report that they had left food on the counter all day to defrost and then noticed the bird developed sour crop. Defrosting food quickly in warm water is preferred and then serving it as soon as it is defrosted. This warms the food and defrosts it quickly, so bacteria do not multiply as much. It replaces some of the water lost when the food was frozen, helping to keep the bird hydrated.

Birds that are sick, weak, or stressed are less likely to be able to handle an over-full crop and therefore are more likely to develop sour crop.

Recommendations
Singles: Copaiba, Myrtle, Ravintsara, Lemon Myrtle, Eucalyptus Blue, Eucalyptus Radiata, Eucalyptus Globulus, Ginger, Helichrysum

Blends: DiGize, Thieves, Raven, R.C., Exodus II, Purification, ImmuPower, Christmas Spirit, Peace & Calming, Stress Away Roll-On

Nutritionals: Life 9

Application and Usage
Topical: Apply 1 drop each of DiGize, Copaiba, and Lemon Myrtle to bird's belly and feet 2-4 times daily.

Ingestion & Oral: Administer orally 2 times daily 1 capsule Life 9 in 1 tablespoon water with 2 drops each of DiGize, Ginger, Copaiba, and Helichrysum.

Inhalation: Diffuse any of the following in the bird area: Thieves, Raven, Ravintsara, R.C., Exodus II, Purification, ImmuPower, Copaiba, Myrtle, Eucalyptus Blue, Eucalyptus Radiata, Eucalyptus Globulus, Lemon Myrtle, Christmas Spirit, Peace & Calming, or Stress Away Roll-On.

Stargazing (Twirling or Ataxia)

Stargazing is an affliction of the nervous system, particularly inflammation of the brain, stemming from nutritional deficiencies (primarily vitamin B1 or D3), metabolic problems, or poor management. Typically, the muscles to the sides of the neck will be contracting, causing a twitching and twisting if they contract singly. If they contract together, the muscles will pull the head directly back, pointing the beak to the sky. Stargazing effects can be reversed with sunlight and vitamin B1 (thiamine), and a whole-food diet with proper nutritionals.

However, if another disease is causing the bird to not create or process vitamins, then that must be identified. Frequently, a poor diet consisting solely of fish or organ meats will cause this. Birds fed fish must be considered for thiamine nutritionals, especially if the fish is not absolutely fresh.

Recommendations

Singles: Helichrysum, Idaho Balsam Fir, Copaiba, Cypress, Cedarwood, Jasmine, Orange, Idaho Blue Spruce, Northern Lights Black Spruce, Pine, Grapefruit, Tangerine, Lemon, Bergamot, Sacred Frankincense, Frankincense, Lemon Myrtle, Myrtle, Sacred Sandalwood, Royal Hawaiian Sandalwood

Blends: Aroma Siez, Sacred Mountain, Believe, White Angelica, Peace & Calming, Stress Away Roll-On, DiGize

Nutritionals: Life 9, NingXia Red, Mineral Essence

Application and Usage

Topical: Apply 1 drop each of Helichrysum, Idaho Balsam Fir, Aroma Siez, Copaiba, and Cypress to bird's neck and feet 2-4 times daily.

Ingestion & Oral: Administer orally 2 times daily ½ capsule Life 9, 2 drops Mineral Essence mixed in 1 oz. NingXia Red, and 1 drop each of DiGize, Copaiba, and Helichrysum.

Inhalation: Diffuse any of the following in the bird area: Cedarwood, Jasmine, Orange, Idaho Balsam Fir, Northern Lights Black Spruce, Pine, Grapefruit, Tangerine, Lemon, Bergamot, Sacred Mountain,

Sacred Frankincense, Frankincense, Lemon Myrtle, Myrtle, Sacred Sandalwood, Royal Hawaiian Sandalwood, White Angelica, Believe, Peace & Calming, or Stress Away Roll-On.

Tapeworms (see Parasites)

Tapeworms are a parasitic infestation of the digestive system. Symptoms include diarrhea, weight loss, and general malaise. If worms are seen in the mutes and they are moving, then they are more likely to be tapeworms.

Tapeworm segments tend to stand straight up when they pass through, appearing like tiny grains of rice or cucumber seeds in the mute.

Roundworms are not usually alive when they pass through the bird.

Torticollis (Wry Neck)

Torticollis is typically a symptom of another disease. It is an affliction of the nervous system, stemming from a variety of problems, including trauma to the head, heat stroke causing nerve damage, West Nile Virus, or a variety of other diseases. It shows similar symptoms to Stargazing in that the head is held in an odd position. Unlike Stargazing, the head may be twisted forward and bent up, as if looking forward, but upside-down. Other behaviors may include walking in circles instead of a straight line.

Recommendations

Singles: Copaiba, Helichrysum, Idaho Balsam Fir, Sacred Frankincense, Cypress, Cedarwood, Jasmine, Orange, Idaho Blue Spruce, Northern Lights Black Spruce, Pine, Grapefruit, Tangerine, Lemon, Bergamot, Frankincense, Sacred Sandalwood, Royal Hawaiian Sandalwood

Blends: Sacred Mountain, Believe, Trauma Life, T-Away, Gentle Baby, Peace & Calming, Stress Away Roll-On, DiGize, White Angelica

Nutritionals: Mineral Essence, NingXia Red, Life 9

Application and Usage

Topical: Apply 1 drop each of Helichrysum, Idaho Balsam Fir, Sacred Frankincense, Copaiba, Cypress, Trauma Life or T-Away, and Peace & Calming or Stress Away Roll-On to bird's head, neck, and feet 2-4 times daily.

Ingestion & Oral: Administer orally 2 times daily ½ capsule Life 9, 2 drops Mineral Essence mixed in 1 oz. NingXia Red with 1 drop each DiGize, Copaiba, and Helichrysum.

Inhalation: Diffuse any of the following in the bird area: Cedarwood, Jasmine, Orange, Idaho Balsam Fir, Idaho Blue Spruce, Northern Lights Black Spruce, Pine, Grapefruit, Tangerine, Lemon, Bergamot, Sacred Mountain, Sacred Frankincense, Frankincense, Sacred Sandalwood, Royal Hawaiian Sandalwood, White Angelica, Believe, Trauma Life, T-Away, Gentle Baby, Peace & Calming, or Stress Away Roll-On.

Tuberculosis

Avian Tuberculosis (TB) is caused by *Mycobacterium avium*, which can infect avians with suppressed immunities. The tuberculosis granulomas can infect the gastrointestinal tract, liver, or spleen. It can cause white plaques, which may be visible on x-rays. Otherwise, the organ would have to be aspirated to be detected. Other symptoms are an elevated white blood cell count and increased liver enzymes.

Avian TB can also create external lesions that appear like Avian Pox but will not respond to the same treatment. Usually, by the time external lesions are seen, the damage to the internal organs is significant, and symptoms are very apparent.

Recommendations

Singles: Copaiba, Ravintsara, Thyme, Lemon
Blends: ImmuPower, Longevity, Thieves, Exodus II, Purification, DiGize, Raven
Nutritionals: NingXia Red
Additional: Thieves Household Cleaner

Application and Usage

Topical: Using the layering technique, apply Copaiba, Ravintsara, Thyme, and ImmuPower onto feet 2-3 times daily. If feet seem irritated from the oils, apply a carrier oil over top of the essential oils.

Ingestion & Oral: Administer orally 1-2 times daily 1 tablespoon NingXia Red and 2 drops each Copaiba, DiGize, Exodus II, Longevity, Lemon, Ravintsara, and ImmuPower.

Inhalation: Diffuse any of the following in the bird area: Longevity, Lemon, Thieves, Raven, Ravintsara, Exodus II, or Purification.

Other: Wash EVERYTHING down with 1/4 cup of Thieves Household Cleaner in 1 gallon of water.

Uropygial Gland Infection

While not common, the uropygial gland, or preen gland, can sometimes become infected and is seen with a cheesy substance coming out of it. This may come from a combination of long-term illness, lack of exposure to sunlight, lack of preening, and overall poor condition.

Warm compresses, flushing or expressing it daily, and exposure to good sunlight will help clear up an infection, even within a week.

Recommendations

Singles: Helichrysum, Lavender, Ginger, Myrrh, Lemon, Ravintsara, Copaiba, Ocotea
Blends: Purification, Melrose, Thieves, Raven, Egyptian Gold, Exodus II
Nutritionals: Mineral Essence, NingXia Red
Additional: Thieves Household Cleaner

Application and Usage

Topical: Apply Helichrysum, Lavender, Purification, Ginger, Melrose, and Myrrh using the layering application technique on the affected area 2-4 times daily.

Ingestion & Oral: The bird should be kept in a warm, sunlit environment and should be well-hydrated 2 times daily with 1 oz. NingXia Red, 1 dropperful Mineral Essence, and 1 drop each of Copaiba, Ginger, and Ocotea.

Inhalation: Diffuse any of the following in the bird habitat: Lemon, Thieves, Raven, Egyptian Gold, Ravintsara, Exodus II, or Purification.

Other: Wash EVERYTHING down with 1/4 cup of Thieves Household Cleaner in 1 gallon of water.

West Nile Virus

West Nile Virus is a disease spread by mosquitoes. Some falconers are able to screen in their mews, thereby reducing the mosquito population that is able to get to their hawks.

The symptoms of this disease are loss of interest in food, weight loss, listlessness, weakness, fever, sleeping, and in highly progressed cases, tremors or seizures. Also frequently seen are squinting (one or both eyes), head tilt, staggering, shuffling, inability to focus, nasal discharge, voice change (due to the paralysis setting in the throat), and spookiness. Absolute diagnosis is through a serology panel.

Recommendations

Singles: Copaiba, Ravintsara, Helichrysum, Melissa, Lavender, Eucalyptus Blue, Lemon

Blends: Exodus II, Purification, Thieves, Raven, Egyptian Gold, DiGize

Nutritionals: NingXia Red

Additional: Thieves Household Cleaner

Application and Usage

Topical: Apply Copaiba, Exodus II, Ravintsara, and Helichrysum onto feet 2-3 times daily. Make a spray in a glass spray bottle of 4 oz. pure water (not tap) and 10 drops each of Melissa, Lavender, Helichrysum, Ravintsara, Purification, and Eucalyptus Blue. Spray on bird up to 4 times daily.

Ingestion & Oral: Administer orally 1-2 times daily 1 oz. NingXia Red and 2 drops each Copaiba, DiGize, Helichrysum, Exodus II, and Ravintsara.

Inhalation: Diffuse any of the following in the bird area: Lemon, Thieves, Raven, Egyptian Gold, Ravintsara, Exodus II, or Purification.

Other: Wash EVERYTHING down with 1/4 cup Thieves Household Cleaner in 1 gallon water.

Wingtip Edema

Wingtip Edema is also known as Dry Gangrene Syndrome. It is normally seen in young (less than 2 years old) desert climate birds such as Harris' hawks, being tethered at flight weight in cold weather (not necessarily freezing). It is believed to be a circulatory disorder.

Although exact causes are not known, there is a direct correlation with low weight, low amounts of exercise, and cold temperatures. There is also a theory that these desert birds are being overly hydrated through their food source. They are not able to properly flush that amount of water from their system under these circumstances.

Most commonly seen in the United Kingdom, the birds display a significant swelling at the wing tip. Treatment is to warm the bird gently and encourage the bird to exercise its wings, which stimulates circulation.

Recommendations

Singles: Copaiba, Cypress, Helichrysum, Lemongrass, Lavender, Orange, Ylang Ylang, Cedarwood, Jasmine, Idaho Balsam Fir, Idaho Blue Spruce, Northern Lights Black Spruce, Pine, Grapefruit, Tangerine, Lemon, Bergamot, Sacred Frankincense, Frankincense, Lemon Myrtle

Blends: Gentle Baby, Trauma Life, T-Away, Sensation, Believe, Peace & Calming, Stress Away Roll-On, White Angelica, Sacred Mountain

Nutritionals: NingXia Red, Mineral Essence

Application and Usage

Topical: Using the layering technique, apply Copaiba, Cypress, Helichrysum, and Lemongrass on affected area of wing tips and feet 2-3 times daily. Make a spray in a glass spray bottle of 4 oz. pure water (not tap) and 10 drops each of Gentle Baby, Lavender, Orange, and Ylang Ylang. Spray on bird up to 4 times daily.

Ingestion & Oral: Administer orally 1-2 times daily 1 oz. NingXia Red and 2 drops Mineral Essence.

Inhalation: Diffuse any of the following in the bird area: Trauma Life, T-Away, Cedarwood, Jasmine, Sensation, Orange, Idaho Balsam Fir, Idaho Blue Spruce, Northern Lights Black Spruce, Pine, Grapefruit, Tangerine, Lemon, Bergamot, Sacred Mountain, Sacred Frankincense, Frankincense, Lemon Myrtle, White Angelica, Believe, Peace & Calming, or Stress Away Roll-On.

Cats (Feline)

Introduction

Caring for your cats with natural products is one of the best ways to make sure they have a long and happy life. Because of felines' unique way they metabolize synthetic products and drugs, the more "green" you can make your home, the healthier your cat will be.

Healthy cats are a joy to witness—their fur is soft and shiny; they have a playful, interactive attitude; they cooperate in using the litter box faithfully—all attributes every pet owner desires.

Stress from chaotic households, tension between cats who have personality conflicts, a diet consisting primarily of dry kibble, city tap water tainted with chlorine and fluoride, and strong commercial household cleaners can cause imbalances, both mentally and physically.

Cats react in varying degrees of acceptance when offered an oil, regardless of the method used (topical, ingestion, or inhalation). Some cats readily lie beside a diffuser or near an open bottle of oil, while others will want to leave a room where oils have been applied or diffused. Because most felines have a well-developed sense of smell and taste, essential oils may cause even the most cooperative cat to shy away from oils when they are introduced. In extreme cases, cats may drool, try to run from the oils, or exhibit behavior such as hiding or trembling.

When a cat shows an abnormally strong aversion to essential oils, however, it is usually because the oils chosen are too strong or the concentration of oils being diffused is too high. Adjusting the strength of the scent is usually enough to remedy the situation. Also, by wearing essential oils on yourself, you will become a "human diffuser"; and oftentimes the cat who detests the oils on itself will accept oils on the caretaker.

Regular health checks by a qualified animal professional should be performed at least annually and preferably semiannually. Most cats, because of their strong instinct to survive, will not show signs of disease or illness until they are very sick. Symptoms such as a roughened, unkempt hair coat (when a cat stops grooming itself), drinking more water than normal, urinating or defecating outside the litter box, hiding under the bed for extended periods of time, loss of weight, and refusing to eat are all signs that your cat may be ill.

Offering your indoor cat toys, access to windows where it can observe birds or soak up the sun, and attention from you (grooming, playing with toys) can decrease boredom and stress.

Some cats enjoy a solitary life, and they live with little interaction from humans and other animals, while others crave company and feel insecure when isolated. Getting to know and honor your cat's special personality traits will help you and your cat to live in harmony.

Safety and Guidelines When Using Essential Oils for Felines

Essential oils can be used safely for cats when certain guidelines are followed. In general, essential oils must be of the highest quality—unadulterated, genuine, and pure. Many essential oil companies market their products as "organic," "natural," or even "certified pure."

Unfortunately, many of these statements may not be true, as essential oils are not regulated by federal agencies. As a result, tainted oils are often sold, unbeknownst to the consumer.

Young Living Essential Oils, with its Seed to Seal® process, assures that the oils produced and sold are of the highest standards and are safe for animals, children, and adults when used according to directions.

One of the main considerations when choosing an oil or oils for cats is the way the feline liver processes certain constituents of essential oils. Cats of all breeds have a "deficient" P450 cytochrome pathway, making it impossible for felines to break down certain metabolites of drugs, medications, and some essential oils. As a result, these metabolites can cause toxicity in the body. For example, cats cannot break down salicylate (a major component in aspirin), and this is why aspirin is contraindicated in cats. Wintergreen essential oil has naturally occurring methyl salicylate, so Wintergreen oil is generally not given to felines.

However, with careful veterinary monitoring and consultation, certain oil blends or products containing Wintergreen *may* be used safely for short periods of time. Wintergreen and products containing this oil have for the most part been omitted from this chapter, except in several cases of illness or injury, where they can be used with veterinary supervision.

Other products containing high levels of phenols should generally be avoided or used with caution. Phenols are another compound that cats have difficulty processing

in their bodies. Oils containing high levels of phenol include **Wintergreen, Basil, Clove, Oregano, Melaleuca Quinquenervia, Thyme, Mountain Savory, Tea Tree, Laurus Nobilis,** and **Cinnamon Bark.**

To avoid potentially adverse reactions when orally administering oils containing phenol, dilute 1 drop essential oil with 1 teaspoon NingXia Red to assist the cat's liver in properly metabolizing salicylate and phenol compound oils. Administer this 1-2 times daily.

Essential Oil	YLEO Phenolic Constituents
Wintergreen*	90%+ methyl salicylate
Basil	70-90% methyl chavicol
Clove	75-87% eugenol
Oregano	60-75% carvacrol
Melaleuca Quinquenervia	55-75% eucalyptol (1,8 cineole)
Thyme	37-55% thymol
Mountain Savory	22-35% carvacrol 14-24% thymol 4-9% carvacrol methyl ether
Tea Tree*	30-45% terpinen-4-ol 0-15% eucalyptol (1,8 cineole)
Laurus Nobilis	40-50% eucalyptol (1,8 cineole)
Cinnamon Bark	4-7% eugenol

*See: The Chemistry of Essential Oils, David Stewart, PhD, page 571: "Phenols are often members of other chemical families." Wintergreen contains the phenolic ester, methyl salicylate; Tea Tree contains the phenolic alcohol, terpinen-4-ol as well as eucalyptol.

General guidelines for creating a dilution

Care should also be given to creating a proper dilution with a good quality carrier oil. In general, cats need to have at least a 75 percent dilution; and up to 90 percent is often used, depending on the oil and the condition of the cat. In severely debilitated cats, a 90 percent dilution is appropriate. The same ratio is often advised for kittens and small cats.

Certain oils, such as Lavender, Copaiba, Helichrysum, and even Frankincense may be used with weaker dilutions or may even be applied neat in certain cases. Again, it is highly advisable to work with an animal care professional who is experienced with essential oil usage in cats.

Any Animal Scents product can also be administered neat as they are already diluted for use with animals.

If considering giving essential oils by mouth, please remember that cats have a huge taste aversion to certain products; so generally, essential oils are not given orally, except in extreme cases where oral administration is required. In this case, diluted oils may be syringed into the mouth. Cats will generally not drink water that has had oils added to it and may become dehydrated unless water without essential oils is available.

Diffusing essential oils can safely be done by always offering a way out for the animal if he or she expresses agitation, anxiety, tremors, or drooling. Always provide ventilation by cracking a window open or leaving the door slightly ajar. Never lock your pet in a room without a fresh air source. Some animals are more sensitive to oils and scents than others, so closely monitor while diffusing.

Kitty Raindrop

- 1 drop Oregano or Mountain Savory
- 1 drop Thyme
- 1 drop Basil
- 1 drop Cypress
- 1 drop Wintergreen
- 1 drop Marjoram
- 1 drop Peppermint

Apply each oil individually. Start by placing 1 drop of oil and 1-2 drops of V-6 or other carrier oil in your palm. Swirl the mixture with your opposite hand's fingertips and feather mixture up the feline's spine, starting from the base of the tail and ending at the base of the head. Amazingly cats often enjoy this backward stroke! If you encounter one that does not, just pet the cat "normally" from head to tail or omit the strokes all together. Gently feather stroke the oils against the grain of the hair up the spine. Depending on the severity of the condition this is used for, you can apply 1 time daily or less often, as needed.

Also apply mixture to the pads of the feline's feet, 1 oil at a time. For added effect, be sure to administer 1 teaspoon NingXia Red prior to administering the feline Raindrop Technique. For kittens, be sure to increase the dilution, mixing 1 drop essential oil with 5-8 drops of carrier oil.

Balancing the cat with Valor or Valor II (neat or diluted) can be performed prior to administering the Raindrop Technique. Place Valor or Valor II in the palms of your hands; then rub your hands together, allowing the Valor or Valor II to almost completely absorb into your palms. Place your hands over the shoulder and rump area, and the balancing procedure is completed much like that described for humans. In some situations, this step is omitted, mainly in cats who are unable to be handled easily.

Petting the Cat

This method is well tolerated by cats and seems to be far superior to dripping oils directly onto their skin. Since hair follicles may enhance absorption, spreading the essential oils over a larger area of the cat may indeed prove more effective. This method involves placing a neat or diluted oil into your hand. Circling your hands together, the essential oils are allowed to absorb in varying degrees into your skin. Once you have the amount of oil on your hands that you desire—which can vary from completely absorbed to a thin coating—you simply pet your cat. Even with oils completely absorbed into your hand, if you smell your cat after petting, you will find that it smells like essential oils. Since cats groom themselves, oral ingestion of the essential oil is also likely to occur.

Kitty Litter

Kitty litter is possibly one of the easiest methods by which to expose cats to the health benefits of essential oils. It not only replaces the toxic fragrances found in commercial kitty litter, but it also offers a way to provide preventive and continued health benefits from essential oils on a regular basis.

Start with unscented kitty litter. Staying with the same brand that you currently use is often advisable. Add 1-3 drops of your chosen essential oil to 1 cup of baking soda. Store this mixture in a glass jar and allow it to "marinade" for several hours, shaking the mixture several times. Later, you may find you can add more essential oil drops to this recipe.

Sprinkle a small amount of the baking soda mixture onto your kitty litter. Mix well. Provide a separate litter box that does not contain essential oils to make sure that your cat does not have an aversion to the essential oil that was selected. Once you are sure your cat is using the litter box with your oil selection and concentration, you can then omit the use of the plain litter box.

Nutritionals

NingXia Red is commonly given to cats without any adverse effects. When administering NingXia Red to felines, generally the best practice is to administer by diluting in water at a 1 to 1 ratio by mouth (with a child's dosing syringe if needed). Some cats will actually drink NingXia Red, but this is typically not the case. You can use a combination of essential oils with it for its anti-inflammatory effect and general support of the immune system for many conditions.

Cat (Feline) Conditions

Abscess

An abscess is a pus-filled pocket of infection that usually originates from a bite from an animal, usually another cat. The puncture wounds are often tiny and not detectable visually. However, the bacteria are often highly pathogenic and may cause a serious infection.

Swelling, heat, and pain can accompany an abscess along with drainage of pus, fever, and loss of appetite. If the abscess is located on a foot or lower leg, the cat may limp or hold the foot off the ground. This can potentially be an emergency situation, and oftentimes antibiotics are necessary and are considered the first line of treatment.

Recommendations

Singles: Myrrh, Eucalyptus Globulus, Lavender, Helichrysum, Copaiba, Hyssop, Patchouli, Bergamot, Mountain Savory, Laurus Nobilis, Ginger, Geranium, Palmarosa, Lemon

Blends: Thieves, Exodus II, Purification, PuriClean, Infect Away, T-Away, Mendwell, ImmuPower, Raven, Egyptian Gold

Nutritionals: NingXia Red, Sulfurzyme, Life 9

Additional: LavaDerm Cooling Mist, Animal Scents Ointment, ClaraDerm

Application and Usage

Topical: Use a 75-90 percent dilution in a good quality carrier oil (e.g., V-6 Vegetable Oil Complex) and apply 2 times daily.

Ingestion & Oral: Administer orally NingXia Red (½ teaspoon syringed into mouth or mixed in wet food), Sulfurzyme (1 capsule), and Life 9 (1 capsule) 1-2 times daily.

Inhalation: Diffuse any suggested oils 2 times daily.

Acne

This condition often appears as "blackheads" or black specks on the underside of the chin. In advanced cases, raised, pink pustules may be seen in addition to the black specks. It is theorized that plastic feeding or watering dishes, exposure to household chemicals, and food sensitivities, may be common culprits.

Recommendations

Singles: Copaiba, Myrrh, Lavender, Palmarosa, Ginger, Geranium, Melissa, Ocotea, Manuka, Laurus Nobilis

Blends: Thieves, Purification, Melrose, Australian Blue, Infect Away, Mendwell, PuriClean

Nutritionals: NingXia Red, Sulfurzyme

Additional: LavaDerm Cooling Mist, Animal Scents Ointment, ClaraDerm

Application and Usage

Topical: Use a 50-90 percent dilution; apply onto affected skin 2 times daily. (**Note:** Copaiba and Lavender need to be diluted 25-50 percent in adult cats.)

Ingestion & Oral: Administer orally NingXia Red (½ teaspoon, syringed into mouth or mixed in wet food) and Sulfurzyme (1 capsule) 1-2 times daily.

Allergies

There are many different causes of allergies: food sensitivity, household toxins/chemicals, environmental sensitivities (pollens, molds), parasites (external, internal), scented cat litter, digestive issues, and stress.

It is important to feed cats a diet that is preferably canned or raw (commercially prepared) food to avoid many of the carbohydrates and fillers that are included in dry cat food. Allergies can be witnessed as itchy skin/scratching, pulling out hair in chunks, sneezing clear mucus, a non-productive cough, and even diarrhea and vomiting. A thorough veterinary examination and testing is encouraged to rule out other diseases.

Recommendations

Singles: Lavender, Copaiba, Frankincense, Sacred Frankincense, Basil, Ledum, Geranium, German or Roman Chamomile, Dorado Azul, Ginger, Hinoki, Patchouli, Lemon, Ocotea, Melissa

Blends: GLF, DiGize, JuvaFlex, Harmony, Mendwell, Purification, ImmuPower, PuriClean, JuvaCleanse, ParaGize, Purification, Longevity

Nutritionals: NingXia Red, Allerzyme, Life 9, Sulfurzyme, ParaFree

Additional: LavaDerm Cooling Mist

🐱 Veterinarian Tips and Suggestions

Allergy Blend for Cats

- 10 drops Lavender
- 10 drops Roman or German Chamomile
- 10 drops Ocotea
- 10 drops Copaiba
- 10 drops Frankincense
- 10 drops Hinoki

1. Add the above oils into a bottle with 1 oz. V-6 Vegetable Oil Complex.
2. Shake well and pet a few drops onto the feline, focusing on the tummy area.

Application and Usage

Ingestion & Oral: Administer orally NingXia Red (½ teaspoon; may increase to 1 teaspoon if cat tolerates it), Allerzyme (1 capsule in moist food), and Sulfurzyme (1 capsule) 2 times daily with Life 9 (contents of ½ capsule) and ParaFree (poke capsule with a pin and squeeze 1-2 drops into food) 1 time daily.

Inhalation: Diffuse Copaiba, Lemon, and Purification.

Other: Use Kitty Raindrop 2 times weekly.

Appetite, Poor

Reluctance to eat may indicate a variety of different conditions in your cat. Pain, intestinal parasites, kidney or liver issues, viral or bacterial infections, and food sensitivities are just a few of the reasons a cat may refuse to eat.

It is imperative to get a veterinary diagnosis before trying to stimulate the appetite with essential oils or other products. In some cases, such as an intestinal blockage, it may be detrimental for the cat to ingest food.

Here are some suggestions to try before you get to your veterinarian's office:

Recommendations

Singles: Spearmint, Neroli, Orange, Roman Chamomile, German Chamomile, Lavender, Ylang Ylang, Patchouli, Ginger, Valerian, Vetiver, Copaiba, Idaho Blue Spruce, Peppermint

Blends: Peace & Calming, DiGize, Acceptance, Sacred Mountain, Stress Away Roll-On, Citrus Fresh, White Angelica, Gentle Baby

Application and Usage

Topical: Create a 25 percent dilution before applying onto the abdomen of the cat. Can apply 2 times daily.

Inhalation: Diffuse any combination of the above oils several times during the day.

Arthritis

Arthritis is more commonly found in aging cats. It can also be a complication from a previous fracture or serious injury. Therapy is aimed at decreasing inflammation as well as pain management. A good quality diet (preferably high quality canned food or a commercially prepared raw diet) is paramount in keeping the degeneration of the joints to a minimum.

Recommendations

Singles: Copaiba, Frankincense, Palo Santo, Idaho Blue Spruce, Helichrysum, Cypress, Idaho Balsam Fir, Northern Lights Black Spruce, Wintergreen

Blends: Valor II, T-Away, Evergreen Essence, Aroma Siez, Relieve It, Deep Relief Roll-On, PanAway, Relieve It

Nutritionals: NingXia Red, Sulfurzyme powder, AgilEase or BLM

Application and Usage

Topical: Mix a 75 percent oil dilution and apply to affected area 2 times daily.

Ingestion & Oral: Administer orally NingXia Red (½-1 teaspoon, mixed in moistened food or syringed into mouth), Sulfurzyme powder (¼ teaspoon), and AgilEase or BLM (1 capsule) 1-2 times daily.

Inhalation: Diffuse Stress Away Roll-On, Idaho Balsam Fir, Peace & Calming, Inner Child, and Orange.

Other: Administer Kitty Raindrop 2-3 times weekly.

Asthma

Feline asthma is usually caused by environmental allergies such as tobacco smoke, chemical sprays and air fresheners, pollens, molds, and dust. It can also be due to complications from previous viral or bacterial respiratory conditions.

Scented cat litter should always be replaced with dust-free, non-scented, natural litter.

Recommendations

Singles: Eucalyptus Radiata, Pine, Northern Lights Black Spruce, Dorado Azul, Cedarwood, Lemon Myrtle, Eucalyptus Globulus, Lavender, Myrtle, Rosemary, Eucalyptus Blue, Frankincense, Ravintsara, Idaho Blue Spruce, Lemon, Copaiba, Lemongrass

Blends: R. C., Breathe Again Roll-On, Thieves, Evergreen Essence, Purification, Raven, Clarity, En-R-Gee

Nutritionals: NingXia Red, Allerzyme

Application and Usage

Ingestion & Oral: Administer orally NingXia Red (½-1 teaspoon) and Allerzyme (1 capsule) 1 time daily.

Inhalation: Diffuse Raven, R. C., Thieves, Purification, Lemon, Cedarwood, Idaho Blue Spruce, Lemon Myrtle, and Eucalyptus Blue.

Other: Administer Kitty Raindrop (daily as needed to reduce episodes; decrease frequency to 1-2 times weekly thereafter.

Behavior Modification (Urine Spraying, Biting, Aggression, Not Using the Litter Box)

It is important to try to determine the cause of unwanted behaviors. For example, urine spraying can be either a "normal" behavior exhibited by intact males ("territory marking"), or it may occur due to stress and anxiety.

Biting and general aggression can be due to personality conflicts between other animals in the household, children who may handle the kitty roughly, pain, or anxiety caused by a chaotic environment.

Refusal to use the litter box may be due to dirty boxes, litter boxes that are in an area where the cat feels vulnerable, and most oftentimes, a signal that there is a urinary tract issue that needs veterinary attention.

Recommendations

Singles: Lavender, Orange, Copaiba, Cedarwood, Frankincense, Rose, Ylang Ylang, Hinoki, Idaho Balsam Fir, Roman Chamomile, German Chamomile, Orange, Tangerine, Neroli, Bergamot, Idaho Blue Spruce

Blends: Peace & Calming, Stress Away Roll-On, Harmony, Valor II, Joy, Inner Child, Acceptance, Grounding, Gentle Baby, T-Away, Tranquil Roll-On, Forgiveness, Trauma Life, Sacred Mountain, SARA

Nutritionals: NingXia Red, Super B

Veterinarian Tips and Suggestions

Kitty Litter Recipe

This is a great alternative to scented litter and another way for the cats to come into contact with essential oils.

- 1 cup baking soda
- 4-5 drops each Lavender, Stress Away Roll-On, Cedarwood, Gentle Baby, Purification, Sacred Mountain or Inner Child
1. Mix the oils well into the baking soda.
2. Sprinkle a tablespoon into clean litter and mix in well.
3. Re-treat with this mixture every time you remove soiled litter.

Application and Usage

Topical: Cats can be petted with 1-2 drops of oil applied on your hands. For transporting, you can add a few drops of Lavender or Peace & Calming and place in pet carrier.

Ingestion & Oral: Administer orally NingXia Red (½-1 teaspoon) and Super B (¼ tablet, crushed and mixed into moistened food) 1 time daily.

Inhalation: Diffuse oils for 30 minutes at least 3 times daily for best results.

Bladder Infections (see Urinary Tract Conditions)

Blood Disorders (Blood Clots)

In cats with heart disease (hypertrophic cardiomyopathy or valvular disorders), a life-threatening blood clot may form in the pelvic region, causing sudden, severe pain and paralysis. This is a veterinary emergency and the cat needs to receive immediate attention. The prognosis is guarded to poor, but cats who survive the condition must be monitored and treated for underlying heart disease indefinitely.

Essential oils that may help on the way to the veterinary clinic or during after care are:

Recommendations

Singles: Ylang Ylang, Lavender, Cypress, Helichrysum, Frankincense, Lemon, Valerian, Rose, Clove, Copaiba, Hyssop

Blends: Peace & Calming, Aroma Life, AromaEase, DiGize, Forgiveness, PanAway, Stress Away Roll-On

Nutritionals: NingXia Red, Rehemogen

Application and Usage

Topical: Create a dilution according to the dilution chart for felines. Place 3-4 drops on the lower abdomen and inside of hind legs as often as every 15 minutes while transporting to your veterinarian; for follow-up, apply 1 time daily. Apply a drop of Frankincense or Sacred Frankincense to the top of the head to enhance the life force and for a greater will to live.

Ingestion & Oral: Administer orally NingXia Red (1 teaspoon) and Rehemogen (½ dropperful) 2 times daily. Also try administering 1 drop each Sacred Frankincense, Copaiba, Clove, and Helichrysum in 1 teaspoon NingXia Red 1-2 times daily.

Blood Disorders (Anemia)

Anemia is a deficiency of red blood cells in the body. There are many causes for anemia, including malnutrition, kidney failure, viral infections (feline leukemia and feline immunodeficiency virus), autoimmune disease, cancer, bleeding (externally or internally), parasites, fleas, and ingestion of rat or mouse poison.

Anemic animals are often lethargic, have pale gums, and may show signs of respiratory distress. It is imperative to establish the correct diagnosis, so the appropriate treatment can be started. Oils that may help with general anemia include:

Recommendations

Singles: Frankincense, Sacred Frankincense, Cistus, Helichrysum, Copaiba, Cypress, Lemon

Blends: Aroma Life, ParaGize, GLF, DiGize, JuvaCleanse, JuvaFlex, Exodus II, ImmuPower, Longevity, Valor, Valor II

Nutritionals: NingXia Red, MultiGreens, Allerzyme, Rehemogen, Mineral Essence

Application and Usage

Topical: Create a dilution according to the dilution chart for felines. Apply 2-3 drops of diluted oils to the neck, stomach, and chest region 2-3 times daily.

Ingestion & Oral: Administer orally NingXia Red (1 teaspoon 2 times daily), Mineral Essence (1-2 drops 2 times daily), MultiGreens (1 capsule added to moistened food), Allerzyme (½ capsule 1 time daily, mixed into moistened food or NingXia Red 2-4 times daily), and Rehemogen (½ dropper 1 time daily).

Inhalation: Diffuse any combination of suggested oils.

Bones, Broken

Broken bones, or fractures, may be simple or complicated, depending on the location and severity of the injury. In addition to damaged bone, muscles, tendons, nerves, and vessels may be affected as well.

Application of essential oils should be made as close to the cast or splint as possible. Diffusing essential oils is also an effective method for delivering essential oils to the desired location.

Recommendations

Singles: Copaiba, Palo Santo, Idaho Blue Spruce, Northern Lights Black Spruce, Idaho Balsam Fir, Peppermint, Lemongrass, Cypress, Cistus, Helichrysum

Blends: PanAway, Believe, Valor, Valor II, T-Away, Grounding, Transformation, Trauma Life, Deep Relief Roll-On

Nutritionals: NingXia Red, Sulfurzyme capsules, Super C, MultiGreens, AgilEase or BLM, Mineral Essence

Application and Usage

Topical: Apply 1-2 drops of essential oils 3-4 times daily on location. Dilute appropriately.

Ingestion & Oral: Administer orally NingXia Red (½-1 teaspoon), Sulfurzyme (1 capsule, mixed into moistened food), and MultiGreens (½ capsule) 2 times daily. Also administer AgilEase or BLM (1 capsule), Super C (¼ capsule), and Mineral Essence (2-4 drops) 1 time daily.

Inhalation: Diffuse Peace & Calming, T-Away, Stress Away Roll-On, and Trauma Life.

Cancer

Cancer—whether in cats, other animals, or humans—is a multifactorial disease condition. There is never an "oil" or just one essential oil protocol that is "one size fits all."

Cancer has its own unique path it takes in each animal's body, so oftentimes the treatment protocol is tailored according to the animal's response.

Many factors need to be considered, especially diet, eliminating chemicals and other household toxins, substituting natural and chemical-free insecticides and preservatives instead of commercial products whenever possible, and keeping the animal in as stress-free of an environment as possible.

Diet: Many good quality, commercially prepared raw diets are available at higher quality pet stores. Dry kibble foods should be replaced with a raw or home-cooked diet when possible (please work with a veterinarian or veterinary nutritionist who is trained to deal with chronic illness like cancer).

Most, if not all, commercially formulated dry cat foods contain too many carbohydrates (sugar), and cancer cells thrive on sugar. In addition, dyes, preservatives, and other additives can be harmful. If a home-cooked or raw diet is not feasible, then a good quality canned diet would be the preferred option.

Chemicals in the household: Eliminate commercial cleaning products, scented cat litter, air fresheners (including sprays, plug-ins, and candles), dryer sheets, fabric softeners, perfumes, etc. These products are toxic to **all** animals and should never be used, especially with an animal suffering from any chronic illness.

Thieves Household Cleaner can safely and effectively take the place of commercial, toxin-ridden bathroom sprays, kitchen cleaning products, and can even be used to clean pet bowls and litter boxes.

Thieves Laundry Soap is a safe alternative to laundry detergents, which may have harsh scents and other chemicals.

The following is a list of potential essential oils that support the immune system and may help with your kitty's own innate healing power:

Recommendations
Singles: Frankincense, Sacred Frankincense, Copaiba, Sacred Sandalwood, Royal Hawaiian Sandalwood, Myrrh, Idaho Blue Spruce, Northern Lights Black Spruce, Idaho Balsam Fir, Tsuga, Ledum, Orange, Grapefruit, Lemon, Lavender, Hong Kuai

Blends: Valor II, Exodus II, Hope, Longevity, T-Away, Release, Harmony, Citrus Fresh, Believe, Highest Potential, Forgiveness, 3 Wise Men, Brain Power, Sacred Mountain, JuvaCleanse

Nutritionals: NingXia Red, Super C Chewable, MultiGreens, Life 9, Essentialzyme, ImmuPro, Essentialzymes-4

Application and Usage
Topical: Apply Sacred Frankincense and Copaiba with any combination of selected oils on location 2-4 times daily. You may administer the Kitty Raindrop Technique 1-2 times weekly for general immune support.

Ingestion & Oral: Administer orally 1-2 drops each of Copaiba and Sacred Frankincense 2 times daily. Also administer orally NingXia Red (Dilute the following dosages with water in a 1 to 1 mixture; use ½-1 teaspoon daily to start; increase by ½ teaspoon weekly 2 times daily during week 2; may increase to ½ oz. daily after 2 weeks), Super C Chewable (½ capsule mixed with moistened food daily), MultiGreens (½ capsule daily; increase to 2 times daily after a few days), Essentialzyme (¼ caplet 2 times daily), Life 9 (½ capsule daily), ImmuPro (1 chewable mixed in food throughout the day), and Essentialzymes-4 (½ capsule in 2 oz. NingXia Red orally 2 times daily). Administer this Feline Immune Blend 2-3 times per week.

Inhalation: Diffuse essential oils such as Stress Away Roll-On, Lavender, Cedarwood, Peace & Calming, Hope, Frankincense, or any of the oils listed in the "anxiety" section of this chapter. This can assist your kitty in maintaining a quiet, healing environment.

Cardiomyopathy, Hypertrophic

This condition occurs when the heart wall thickens (the cause is unknown), and the heart cannot effectively pump blood. Male cats are more commonly affected, and the symptoms usually don't appear until the heart's function has been compromised.

Symptoms such as decreased appetite, lethargy, increased respirations after exercise, and weight loss may be seen. Life-threatening blood clots can form in the lungs or in the arteries supplying blood to the legs. If detected early, HCM (hypertrophic cardiomyopathy) can be managed medically and with natural products.

Recommendations
Singles: Lavender, Helichrysum, Copaiba, Grapefruit, Ylang Ylang, Marjoram, Cypress, Basil, Cedarwood

Blends: Aroma Life, Stress Away Roll-On, Forgiveness, Inner Child, Tranquil Roll-On, RutaVaLa, Joy, Sensation, Believe

Nutritionals: NingXia Red, Super B, Super C Chewable

Application and Usage
Topical: 1 drop each Copaiba, Helichrysum, Cypress, Cedarwood, and Aroma Life on pads of feet and stomach area 2-4 times daily.

Ingestion & Oral: Administer orally 1 drop each of Copaiba and Helichrysum in ½ oz. NingXia Red 2 times daily, Super B (½ tablet daily), and Super C Chewable (¼ tablet daily).

Conjunctivitis (Mattery Eyes)

Conjunctivitis often accompanies upper respiratory infections in cats, especially kittens. In addition to heavy matter around the eyes, the delicate membranes (conjunctivae) can become red, swollen, and painful.

Recommendations

Singles: Frankincense, Sacred Frankincense, Lavender, Helichrysum (dilute and gently apply a small amount to the area around the eye 2 times daily). **Do NOT** apply directly into the eye.

Blends: Purification, Melrose, Australian Blue, Mendwell, PuriClean

Nutritionals: NingXia Red

Application and Usage

Topical: Administer Feline Raindrop 2 times weekly until eyes clear up.

Ingestion & Oral: Administer orally NingXia Red (½ teaspoon diluted 1:1 with water) combined with 1 drop PuriClean, Purification, and Mendwell 2 times daily.

Inhalation: Diffuse Purification, Lemon, Lavender, Cedarwood, and Manuka.

Constipation

Constipation occurs more frequently in cats on a dry kibble diet without adequate water intake. Parasites, polyps, tumors, and inflammatory bowel disease are other inciting factors. Older cats and those with decreased neurological function frequently can experience bouts of constipation. Changing the diet to a canned food with added fiber can help offset episodes of constipation.

Recommendations

Singles: Peppermint, Tarragon, Ginger, Spearmint, Copaiba

Blends: DiGize, TummyGize, ParaGize, T-Away, JuvaCleanse, JuvaFlex, Release, Transformation

Nutritionals: NingXia Red, Essentialzyme or MightyZyme, Life 9

Application and Usage

Topical: Selected oils may be stroked onto your cat's abdomen 2-3 times daily as needed.

Ingestion & Oral: Administer orally NingXia Red (½-1 teaspoon), Essentialzyme or MightyZyme (¼ tablet crushed and mixed with moistened food), and Life 9 (1 capsule) 2 times daily.

Inhalation: Diffuse Release, Lemon, and Transformation.

Crystals, Urinary (see Urinary Tract Conditions)

Dandruff (Flaky Skin, Hair Coat)

White flakes in the fur or on the skin may indicate things such as poor nutrition, external parasites, metabolic diseases, or allergies.

Also, cats who are overweight or elderly and cannot groom themselves often show signs of skin flakes. Dandruff may also be accompanied by itchiness and scratching. A good quality diet (preferably raw) will greatly improve hair coat.

Recommendations

Singles: Lavender, Lemon, Patchouli, Hinoki, Helichrysum, German Chamomile, Copaiba, Cedarwood, Rose, Roman Chamomile, Xiang Mao, Eucalyptus Globulus, Cypress, Tangerine, Rosemary.

Blends: Purification, Gentle Baby, EndoFlex, Sacred Mountain, Aroma Life, Relieve It, R.C., DiGize, Infect Away

Nutritionals: Allerzyme, Life 9, NingXia Red, MultiGreens, Mineral Essence

Additional: LavaDerm Cooling Mist, Animal Scents Ointment, ClaraDerm, Animal Scents Shampoo.

Application and Usage

Topical: Essential oils can be stroked onto the fur 1-2 times daily or may be applied Raindrop-style several times a week.

Ingestion & Oral: Administer orally Allerzyme (½ capsule mixed in moistened food), Life 9 (½ capsule mixed in moistened food), NingXia Red (½-1 teaspoon diluted), MultiGreens (½ capsule), and Mineral Essence (1-2 drops) 1 time daily.

Inhalation: Diffuse Purification, Lemon, and R.C.

Dental Disorders (Periodontal Disease, Gingivitis, Abscessed Tooth)

Cats with oral disease may quit eating (due to pain), drool, have facial swelling (abscessed tooth), or have a foul odor coming from the mouth. Veterinary care is strongly recommended, as antibiotics are often needed to control bacterial infection from spreading elsewhere in the body and to preserve the delicate structures surrounding the teeth.

A soft diet is recommended for cats with significant oral pain, as well as making sure the water is room-temperature and changed often. Raw food diets are preferred over commercially prepared canned food. Work with your veterinarian regularly, as dental issues in cats can be difficult to resolve.

Recommendations

Singles: Frankincense, Copaiba, Clove, Myrrh, Helichrysum, Melissa, Peppermint, Rosemary, Lemon, Myrtle, Eucalyptus Globulus, Blue Cypress, Lemongrass, Fennel, Ravintsara

Blends: AromaEase, Thieves, Purification, Citrus Fresh, ImmuPower, DiGize, Infect Away, Mendwell, ParaGize, PuriClean

Nutritionals: Life 9, NingXia Red, Allerzyme, MultiGreens, OmegaGize[3]

Application and Usage

Topical: Create an essential oil dilution of 10-25 percent with V-6 Vegetable Oil Complex or another good quality carrier oil. Oils can be applied near the junction of the lower jawbone and the neck, where there is a group of lymph nodes and major blood vessels. Apply oils at least 2 times daily. If there is facial swelling present, oils can be applied directly over the area.

Ingestion & Oral: Administer orally 1-2 drops of any selected oil(s) 1-2 times daily; Life 9 (½ capsule) and NingXia Red (½-1 teaspoon diluted) 1 time daily; and Allerzyme (½ capsule), MultiGreens (½ capsule), and OmegaGize[3] (puncture capsule and squeeze a few drops onto moistened food) 2 times daily.

Inhalation: Diffuse Purification and Lemon.

Deworming

It is advisable to have your cat's feces analyzed microscopically before administering deworming products. Essential oils may be used to help prevent parasite infestations; but depending on your cat's exposure to wildlife, other cats, etc., other commercial dewormers may need to be given.

Recommendations

Singles: Peppermint, Ocotea, Tarragon, Patchouli

Blends: DiGize, ParaGize, TummyGize, ImmuPower, Purification

Nutritionals: Life 9, Essentialzyme or MightyZyme, Detoxzyme, NingXia Red

Application and Usage

Topical: Mix essential oils of DiGize and ImmuPower in a 75 percent dilution. ParaGize and TummyGize may be applied using 1 drop neat over the middle of the abdomen 2 times daily.

Ingestion & Oral: Administer orally 2 drops DiGize or ParaGize 1-2 times daily, Essentialzyme or MightyZyme (¼ tablet 2 times daily), Detoxzyme (¼ contents of one capsule 2 times daily for 14 days), and Life 9 (½ capsule) and NingXia Red (½-1 teaspoon diluted) 1 time daily.

Inhalation: Diffuse Purification.

Diabetes

Diabetes in cats is mainly a preventable disease if certain guidelines are followed with diet and husbandry. Cats who are overweight or obese are many times more susceptible to developing diabetes.

Commercial dry kibble cat foods are oftentimes too high in carbohydrates and sugars, leading to metabolic issues and extra fat storage. Changing to a commercially prepared raw diet or good quality canned diet is imperative. Symptoms of diabetes can include excessive thirst, increased urination, and increased appetite with weight loss.

Working with a veterinarian (preferably holistic) is very important to know if your cat is responding to its treatment plan and to make sure blood glucose levels have normalized.

Recommendations

Singles: Ocotea, Coriander, Helichrysum, Dill, Fennel

Blends: EndoFlex, Aroma Life, Thieves

Nutritionals: NingXia Red, Essentialzyme, MultiGreens, Life 9, OmegaGize[3], Sulfurzyme, Mineral Essence

Application and Usage

Topical: Essential oils may be applied to the midsection of the abdomen or applied under the lower jawbone and the neck regions morning and night.

Ingestion & Oral: Administer orally NingXia Red (1 teaspoon diluted), Essentialzyme (½ caplet), MultiGreens (½ capsule), Life 9 (½ capsule), OmegaGize[3] (puncture capsule and squeeze 2-3 drops in moist food), and Mineral Essence (2 drops) 1 time daily; Sulfurzyme (1 capsule) 2 times daily.

Diarrhea

Diarrhea can have several causes, including bacterial and viral infections, food sensitivities, and parasites.

Recommendations

Singles: Peppermint, Tarragon, Ginger, Patchouli, Fennel

Blends: ParaGize, DiGize, TummyGize, ImmuPower, Thieves, AromaEase

Nutritionals: Life 9, Essentialzyme, Allerzyme or Detoxzyme, NingXia Red

Additional: V-6 Vegetable Oil Complex

Application and Usage

Topical: Oils can be placed over the lower abdomen 2-3 times daily. Use a 50 percent dilution made with V-6 or another good quality carrier oil.

Ingestion & Oral: Administer orally Copaiba and ParaGize (1 drop each 2 times daily) and Life 9 (½ capsule mixed into moistened food), Essentialzyme (¼ caplet), Allerzyme or Detoxzyme (½ capsule), and NingXia Red (½-1 teaspoon diluted) 1 time daily.

Inhalation: Diffuse Purification, Thieves, DiGize, Lemon, Peace & Calming, Orange, and Cedarwood.

Distemper (Feline Panleukopenia)

"Distemper" is the common name for the panleukopenia virus. It is the feline version of parvovirus. The virus causes a severe decrease in white cell production, leaving the cats vulnerable to bacterial infections as well as diarrhea, vomiting, dehydration, and oftentimes, death.

Veterinary care is crucial as most cats and kittens affected with distemper need fluid therapy and intensive nursing care. Cats that survive the virus are protected for life from another recurrence of the disease.

The panleukopenia vaccine is highly effective at preventing illness. Kittens and young cats are more susceptible to the disease, so vaccinations are highly recommended starting at 9 weeks of age.

Recommendations

Singles: Melissa, Ravintsara, Copaiba, Ocotea, Eucalyptus Blue

Blends: DiGize, ImmuPower, Thieves, Exodus II, Purification, Infect Away, ParaGize

Nutritionals: NingXia Red, ParaFree

Application and Usage

Topical: Use 75 percent oil dilution and apply 2 times daily to the neck region below the lower jawbone, on stomach area, and on pads of feet.

Raindrop therapy: Kitten recipe (90% dilution): Oregano, Thyme, Basil, Copaiba, DiGize, Exodus II, Peppermint. Apply 2-3 drops on the spine and gently feather stroke in the oils. Also, place a small drop of oil on the neck just below the lower jawbone. Raindrop in this manner can be done daily. For adult cats, use a 25 percent dilution with the oils mentioned above. Apply 4-5 drops on the spine and 1 drop on each side of the neck below the lower jawbone.

Ingestion & Oral: Administer orally NingXia Red (kittens: ⅛ teaspoon diluted daily; adult cats (½-1 teaspoon diluted daily) and syringed into mouth 2 times daily. By adding water to this mixture, kittens will maintain better hydration. Add ParaFree to diet by puncturing 1 capsule and squeezing 2-4 drops into NingXia Red.

Ear Infection

An infection in the ear(s) can result from bacteria, excess wax production, or mites. Mite infestations need to be confirmed by swabbing the ear and observing mites and/or eggs with a microscope. Chronic ear infections in cats may be caused by a dietary sensitivity. Changing the diet to a commercially prepared raw diet or home-cooked diet may help eliminate or reduce episodes of infection.

Veterinarian Tips and Suggestions

Ear Recipe for Cats

- 1 tablespoon Thieves Household Cleaner
- 5 drops Copaiba
- 5 drops Purification
- ½ teaspoon V-6 Vegetable Oil Complex
- Distilled or purified water

1. Mix oils together and pour into a 1-oz. glass bottle.
2. Saturate cotton swab with mixture; roll swab around lip of bottle to squeeze out excess.
3. Use the swab to remove visible debris from inside the ear. Do NOT insert the swab deep into the ear canal.
4. May clean ear daily with this mixture until condition is resolved.

Recommendations

Singles: Lavender, Ocotea, Copaiba, Manuka, Patchouli, Palmarosa, Laurus Nobilis, Myrrh, Hinoki, Helichrysum, Ginger, Dorado Azul, Ravintsara, Eucalyptus Globulus, Hyssop, Geranium

Blends: Purification, PuriClean, Infect Away, Mendwell, ParaGize

Nutritionals: NingXia Red

Application and Usage

Topical: Mix a 50 percent essential oil dilution for application in ears. Oils can be applied directly to the inside of the ear, but **DO NOT** apply deep into the ear canal.

Ingestion & Oral: Administer orally NingXia Red (kittens: ¼ teaspoon diluted; adult cats: ½-1 teaspoon diluted) 1 time daily.

Eye Conditions

Corneal ulcers, abrasions, and punctures may cause an eye to be weepy, cloudy, or have a white or bluish tint. These symptoms are a veterinary emergency and need to be handled by a veterinarian to determine the cause and severity of the eye condition.

Conjunctival inflammation (of the delicate membranes found just inside the eyelid) may be due to allergies, viral or bacterial infections, or injury. An eye that appears abnormally large may indicate glaucoma, which is an abnormal fluid buildup in the chambers of the eye, which can cause blindness if left untreated.

This is also a veterinary emergency, so seek veterinary care as soon as possible. Essential oils that may help until professional care can be obtained:

Recommendations

Singles: Frankincense, Myrrh, Cypress, Lavender, Copaiba, Helichrysum

Blends: PuriClean, Mendwell, Purification, Gentle Baby, Aroma Life

Nutritionals: NingXia Red, Mineral Essence

Application and Usage

Topical: Essential oils can be applied directly around the eye 2 times daily (take care not to get oils on the lid itself). Oils should be in a 10-25 percent dilution.

Ingestion & Oral: Administer orally 1 teaspoon diluted NingXia Red with 1 dropperful Mineral Essence 1 time daily.

Other: Raindrop Technique 1-2 times a week may be beneficial.

Fatty Liver Syndrome (Hepatic Lipidosis)

This is a serious condition that occurs when a cat (especially an overweight cat) suddenly stops eating due to other illnesses or injury. Extra fat is broken down quickly for energy, but a cat's liver is not designed to process large amounts of fats; and subsequently, excess fat gets stored in the liver. Liver failure, and even death, can occur if the condition is not dealt with quickly. Veterinary care is necessary; cats must be force-fed or have a stomach tube implanted if they refuse to eat. Recovery time is often lengthy.

Recommendations

Singles: Grapefruit, Helichrysum, Ledum, Peppermint, German Chamomile

Blends: JuvaFlex, JuvaCleanse, GLF, Citrus Fresh, DiGize, ParaGize, TummyGize

Nutritionals: Super B, NingXia Red, Essentialzyme, MultiGreens, K&B

Application and Usage

Topical: Essential oils should be in at least a 25 percent dilution and applied over the middle of the abdomen 2-3 times daily.

Ingestion & Oral: Administer orally ½ oz. NingXia Red (diluted), 2 drops each Helichrysum and Copaiba with either GLF or JuvaCleanse, Super B (½ tablet), Essentialzyme (¼-½ caplet), MultiGreens (½ capsule), and K&B (3 drops). Mix in moistened food and administer orally 1 time daily.

Inhalation: Diffuse Release, Peace & Calming, and Grapefruit.

Feline Leukemia (FeLV) and Feline Immunodeficiency Virus (FIV)

FeLV and FIV are viruses that are unique to cats. They can cause widespread immune suppression, leaving a cat vulnerable to other diseases and infections. Young cats are more susceptible to the viruses, but cats of any age can contract the diseases.

FeLV is transmitted through saliva and urine of infected cats, and FIV can be contracted through a bite or through fight wounds with infected felines. Both viruses can cause death, and most cats will be infected for life once the virus establishes itself in the body. Some cats are carriers only (they have the virus but do not exhibit clinical symptoms), and others show signs such as weight loss, failure to thrive, and chronic bacterial infections (respiratory, kidney, intestinal, etc.).

Recommendations

Singles: Frankincense, Sacred Frankincense, Eucalyptus Globulus, Copaiba, Melissa, Hyssop, Ravintsara, Eucalyptus Blue, Ocotea, Lemon, Raven, Egyptian Gold

Blends: Thieves, ImmuPower, Exodus II, Longevity, Citrus Fresh

Nutritionals: NingXia Red, MultiGreens, JuvaPower, Life 9, Essentialzyme

Application and Usage

Topical: Essential oils can be used in Raindrop fashion or applied around the neck, chest, and stomach area.

Ingestion & Oral: Administer orally 2 drops each Melissa, Ravintsara, Exodus II, ImmuPower, Copaiba, and K&B in ½ oz. NingXia Red with MultiGreens (½ capsule), JuvaPower (¼ teaspoon), Life 9 (½ capsule), and Essentialzyme (½ caplet) 2 times daily.

Inhalation: Diffuse any suggested oils.

Feline Infectious Peritonitis (FIP)

Feline infectious peritonitis is a viral disease caused by a mutant form of the feline coronavirus. Transmission occurs through saliva and feces, and a cat of any age can contract FIP, although it is usually seen in cats under two years of age.

Most cats who are exposed to the feline coronavirus do not progress to full-blown FIP, but those who do develop symptoms will die. Treatment is aimed at supportive care for the immune system.

Recommendations

Singles: Lemon, Melissa, Hyssop, Ravintsara, Copaiba, Dorado Azul, Mountain Savory, Thyme, Blue Cypress, Helichrysm, Ocotea, Lemongrass, Eucalyptus Blue, Basil

Blends: Thieves, Longevity, Exodus II, Hope, ImmuPower, Egyptian Gold, Raven

Nutritionals: NingXia Red, MultiGreens, Super B, MightyZyme or Essentialzyme, K&B

Application and Usage

Topical: Essential oils may be applied Raindrop style or applied to the neck, stomach, and chest areas.

Ingestion & Oral: Administer orally 2 drops of any 3 selected oils with 2 drops each of Copaiba and K&B in NingXia Red (kittens: ½ teaspoon diluted; adult cats: 1 teaspoon diluted), a pinch of MightyZyme or Essentialzyme, MultiGreens (½-1 capsule), Super B (¼ tablet) 2 times daily.

Inhalation: Diffuse any suggested oils.

Flea Infestations

Fleas, once established in a household or cat population, can be very difficult to eliminate. If there is a heavy infestation in the home and/or yard, assistance in exterminating fleas may need to be performed by a professional. Once most of the fleas are exterminated, essential oils can be used for prevention and maintenance.

ALL animals in the environment MUST be treated at the same time. Some animals are very allergic to a flea bite and will suffer from intense itching. Therefore, essential oils should be aimed also at eliminating skin allergies that can result.

Recommendations

Singles: Helichrysum, Patchouli, Citronella, Tea Tree, Palo Santo, Peppermint, Eucalyptus Radiata, Lemongrass, Spearmint, Dorado Azul, Black Pepper, Oregano

Blends: Purification, ImmuPower, RepelAroma

Nutritionals: NingXia Red, Sulfurzyme

Additional: Animal Scents Ointment (for skin irritation from flea bites), Animal Scents Shampoo (to remove fleas and flea dirt from cat), ClaraDerm (for itching)

Application and Usage

Topical: Diffusing or applying oils in Raindrop fashion or petting the feline with oils is advised. Depending on the size of your cat, a dilution of 75-90 percent or more is recommended. Also apply ParaFree on stomach area as needed.

Ingestion & Oral: Administer orally NingXia Red (½-1 teaspoon diluted daily for immune support) and Sulfurzyme powder (½ teaspoon mixed in moistened food daily).

Veterinarian Tips and Suggestions

Homemade Flea Bomb Recipe
(Use a TheraPro Premium Diffuser or equivalent.)

- 1 15-ml bottle (recycled YL bottles are perfect)
- 70 drops Peppermint
- 70 drops Oregano
- 70 drops Purification
- 70 drops Black Pepper
- 70 drops Helichrysum

1. Mix oils together and then fill a 15-ml bottle. Refill as needed.
2. Set the dials on the TheraPro Premium Diffuser to diffuse at full strength for at least 3 hours. For heavier infestations or for bigger rooms, diffuse for up to 4 hours.
3. Wash everything with a strong dilution of Thieves Household Cleaner combined with Purification, Black Pepper, and Helichrysum added to the dilution.
4. Vacuum thoroughly and wash bedding thoroughly with Thieves Laundry Soap after diffusing.
5. NOTE: This is a STRONG diffusion. Move all animals and people out of the home while diffusing; OR if the diffused air can be confined as each room is bombed, people and animals can move to a non-diffused area of the house with circulating air accordingly.

Feline Lower Urinary Tract Disease
(see Urinary Tract Conditions*)*

Giardia *(see* Diarrhea*)*

Gingivitis *(see* Dental Disorders*)*

Glaucoma

Glaucoma is a serious eye condition where watery fluid accumulates in the front chamber of the eye just behind the lens that cannot drain. Pressure builds up from the excess fluid and can cause permanent blindness if left untreated. The eye may be reddened and enlarged with a milky appearance.

Primary glaucoma is thought to be an inherited disease (Burmese and Siamese cats are more at risk). Secondary glaucoma can occur from injury, viral infections (feline leukemia, FIV, FIP), parasitic infections (toxoplasmosis), a tumor, or from severe inflammation. Seek veterinary care immediately should symptoms arise.

Recommendations
Singles: Copaiba, Helichrysum, Frankincense, Cypress, Eucalyptus Globulus, Blue Cypress, Ocotea, Sacred Frankincense, Cedarwood
Blends: M-Grain, T-Away, Trauma Life, Stress Away Roll-On, Purification, Aroma Life
Nutritionals: NingXia Red, Mineral Essence, OmegaGize³, Detoxzyme

Application and Usage
Topical: Essential oils can be applied under the eyes (use caution not to get oils directly into eyes) or can be applied to the neck and ears region directly behind and under the lower jawbone 2-3 times daily.
Ingestion & Oral: Administer orally ½ teaspoon NingXia Red diluted, 2 drops Mineral Essence, 1 drop K&B, 2 drops Copaiba, 1 drop Sacred Frankincense, 1 drop Helichrysum, a pinch of Detoxzyme, and 1 capsule OmegaGize³ dissolved 1 time daily.
Inhalation: Diffuse Purification or Transformation.

Hairballs

Hairballs are common in cats, although the condition is not considered normal. Long-haired cats and cats who groom excessively are more prone to developing hairballs. Proper digestion and intestinal motility will prevent hair from accumulating in the intestines. Changing the diet to a raw or good-quality canned food may help, as well as offering clean, purified water at all times. Frequent brushing or shaving long-haired cats may also be beneficial.

Recommendations
Singles: Peppermint, Patchouli, Ginger, Ocotea, Juniper, Tarragon
Blends: DiGize, TummyGize, ParaGize, JuvaCleanse, AromaEase
Nutritionals: Life 9, Allerzyme, NingXia Red

Application and Usage
Ingestion & Oral: Administer orally Patchouli (1 drop), DiGize (1 drop), Copaiba (2 drops), Mineral Essence (2 drops), Life 9 (½ capsule), Allerzyme (½ capsule), NingXia Red (½-1 teaspoon diluted) 2 times daily.

Heart Conditions (see also Cardiomyopathy, Hypertrophic)

Included in this category are conditions such as hypertrophic cardiomyopathy, heart murmurs, cardiac arrhythmias, and distal aortic thrombosis ("saddle thrombus"). Management of any heart condition in cats includes a good quality diet, relief from household or environmental stress, attention to other conditions such as hyperthyroidism and kidney disease.

Work with a veterinarian who can prescribe conventional pharmaceuticals, if necessary.

Recommendations
Singles: Cypress, Helichrysum, Copaiba, Marjoram, Cedarwood, Ylang Ylang, Lavender, Melissa, Rose
Blends: Stress Away Roll-On, Peace & Calming, Aroma Life, Tranquil Roll-On, RutaVaLa, Joy, Sensation
Nutritionals: NingXia Red, Super B, Super C Chewable

Application and Usage
Topical: Essential oils can be stroked on or applied directly over the chest, stomach, and neck area. Apply 4-6 times daily.
Ingestion & Oral: Administer orally Helichrysum, Copaiba, and Mineral Essence (1-2 drops each) with MindWise (1 teaspoon) and OmegaGize[3] (1 capsule) 2 times daily. Also administer orally NingXia Red (1 teaspoon diluted), Super B (¼ tablet), Super C Chewable (¼ caplet) 1 time daily.
Inhalation: Diffuse Cedarwood with any other suggested oils.

Heartworm

Feline heartworm disease is not seen as commonly as in dogs, but there is growing speculation that more cats are affected with heart worms than previously estimated. Heartworms are transmitted from infected mosquitoes carrying the heartworm larvae into a cat when the mosquito bites. Symptoms may include weight loss, anorexia, cough, and respiratory distress.

There is no medical treatment available for feline heartworm disease, and the severity of the disease depends on the cat's overall health, the number of heartworms it harbors, and the duration of infestation. Because of the typically low number of worms residing in the pulmonary arteries as well as the shorter life cycle of the worm, some cats will recover without any intervention. Others may

develop chronic respiratory issues or damage to the heart.

A good quality diet is essential to keep the immune system primed. Feeding a commercially-prepared raw diet or home cooked meal, with the guidance of a veterinary nutritionist, is paramount for full immune support.

Recommendations
Singles: Helichrysum, Copaiba, Cypress, Cedarwood, Fennel, Patchouli, Ocotea
Blends: Aroma Life, Peace & Calming, Stress Away Roll-On, ParaGize, DiGize, Purification
Nutritionals: NingXia Red, MultiGreens, Sulfurzyme, Essentialzyme, Life 9

Application and Usage
Topical: Essential oils can be applied to the chest and neck 2 times daily by using a 90 percent dilution with V-6 Vegetable Oil Complex. Apply any of the following oils individually or combined on the stomach area and the pads of the feet 2-4 times daily: DiGize, ParaGize, Helichrysum, Cedarwood, and Copaiba.
Ingestion & Oral: Administer orally DiGize, ParaGize, Helichrysum, Cedarwood, and Copaiba (1-2 drops each) with diluted NingXia Red (1 teaspoon diluted to begin with; work up gradually to 2 teaspoons), MultiGreens (½ capsule), and Life 9 (½ capsule) 1 time daily; also, Sulfurzyme (1 capsule) and Essentialzyme (¼ caplet) 2 times daily.
Inhalation: Diffuse Stress Away Roll-On, Cedarwood, Purification, and Peace & Calming.

Herpesvirus (Feline Rhinotracheitis)

Feline rhinotracheitis is a highly contagious respiratory disease in both cats and kittens. It can cause high fever, cough, nasal discharge, and may progress to the eyes, where it can attack the surface of the cornea, resulting in deep ulcers.

Many cats (especially kittens) lose their ability to smell food, so hand-feeding and syringing water into their mouths may be necessary.

Recommendations
Singles: Laurus Nobilis, Lemongrass, Copaiba, Melissa, Ravintsara, Eucalyptus Blue
Blends: ImmuPower, Exodus II, Raven, Egyptian Gold, Purification
Nutritionals: NingXia Red, MultiGreens, Life 9

Application and Usage

Topical: Essential oils can be used in Raindrop fashion or applied around the neck, stomach, feet, and chest area. Use 25 percent dilution for adult cats; 75 percent for kittens.

Ingestion & Oral: Administer orally NingXia Red diluted (kittens: ¼ -½ teaspoon; adults: ½-1 teaspoon), MultiGreens (½ capsule), Life 9 (¼ capsule) 2 times daily.

Inhalation: Diffuse Purification, ImmuPower, Egyptian Gold, and Raven.

Hypertension (High Blood Pressure) (see also Kidney Disease)

Determining the cause for high blood pressure is important for getting the condition under control. Two common reasons for high blood pressure in cats are hyperthyroidism and kidney failure.

Using essential oils and products that support both the kidneys and hormonal system may bring about redilution of the hypertension, if those are determined to be the cause.

Recommendations

Singles: Ylang Ylang, Lavender, Copaiba, Vetiver, Valerian, Cedarwood, Juniper, Myrrh, Patchouli, Angelica, Orange, Sacred Frankincense

Blends: Peace & Calming, Valor, Valor II, Stress Away Roll-On, Aroma Life, AromaEase, EndoFlex, Gentle Baby, Harmony, Trauma Life

Nutritionals: NingXia Red, Super C Chewable, Super B, OmegaGize[3], MultiGreens, Essentialzyme, Life 9, MindWise

Application and Usage

Topical: Essential oils may be applied in Raindrop fashion or gently stroked onto the neck, paws, stomach, and chest areas 2 times daily.

Ingestion & Oral: Administer orally NingXia Red diluted (½-1 teaspoon), Super C Chewable (¼-½ caplet), Super B (½ tablet), OmegaGize[3] (puncture capsule and squeeze 2-3 drops into moistened food), MultiGreens (½ capsule), and Essentialzyme (½ caplet) 1 time daily. Also administer Life 9 (¼ capsule) and MindWise (½ teaspoon) 2 times daily.

Inhalation: Diffuse Aroma Life, Peace & Calming, Cedarwood, Stress Away Roll-On, Harmony, Sacred Frankincense, Trauma Life, Angelica, and Orange.

Hyperthyroidism (Overactive Thyroid)

Hyperthyroidism is caused by a functional tumor of the thyroid gland. Excessive amounts of thyroxine (a thyroid hormone) are released into the bloodstream. This condition typically develops in older cats, and it is the most common hormonal imbalance in cats.

Symptoms such as weight loss despite a good appetite, muscle weakness, hyperactivity, and vomiting are commonly seen. Blood tests and palpation of the thyroid gland are diagnostic for the disorder.

Recommendations

Singles: Myrrh, Copaiba

Blends: EndoFlex, Peace & Calming

Nutritionals: NingXia Red, OmegaGize[3], Essentialzyme, Life 9, Sulfurzyme, Mineral Essence

Application and Usage

Topical: Essential oils can be placed on the pads of feet and neck (along the sides and front) morning and night.

Ingestion & Oral: Administer orally NingXia Red (½-1 teaspoon), OmegaGize[3] (puncture capsule and squeeze 2-3 drops into moistened food), Essentialzyme (½ caplet), and Life 9 (½ capsule) 1 time daily. Also administer orally Sulfurzyme (½ capsule) and Mineral Essence (4 drops) 2 times daily.

Inhalation: Diffuse Peace & Calming and Stress Away Roll-On.

Hyperglycemia (High Blood Glucose) (see Diabetes)

Hypoglycemia (Low Blood Sugar)

Low blood glucose levels may be seen in diabetic cats on insulin therapy and in very young kittens who are hypothermic, dehydrated, and undernourished.

Signs of hypoglycemia may be seen as weakness, incoordination, shaking or trembling, seizures, and collapse. Immediate administration of maple syrup, honey, or glucose (from a pharmacy) should be given at the first signs of low blood sugar (in diabetics). For kittens, mixing a combination of NingXia Red and maple syrup may be given orally, if the kitten is alert enough to swallow.

Recommendations

Singles: Dill

Nutritionals: Mineral Essence, NingXia Red

Veterinarian Tips and Suggestions

Recipe for Low Blood Sugar

- 2 teaspoon NingXia Red
- 1 teaspoon maple syrup
- 1 teaspoon warm water

Maple syrup or honey may be warmed (for easier mixing) by holding the container under very warm water for a short time. Combine NingXia Red, syrup, and water. Give **adult cats** 1 teaspoon of the mixture. Can be repeated in 10 minutes, if there is no change in the cat's condition. **Kittens** can be given 0.25 -0.5 ml (use oral dosing syringe) every 5 minutes, as needed. If no syringe is available, place 4-6 drops in a plastic spoon and administer orally.

Application and Usage

Topical: Rub 1 drop of Dill on the stomach area daily.

Ingestion & Oral: Administer orally NingXia Red (½ teaspoon), maple syrup (¼ teaspoon), and Mineral Essence (1 drop) 3 times daily.

Inappropriate Urination / Elimination
(Not Using the Litter Box)

There are several main reasons why cats may not use the litter box. First and most importantly, cats need clean boxes to eliminate. Cats are very fastidious in their bathroom habits, and it's especially important to clean the boxes daily at the very least and more often with multiple cats using the boxes.

A rule of thumb is to have at least one more box than the number of cats in the household. Provide litter that is free of synthetic scents and ingredients. There are a number of good litters that have natural scents from pine and cedar. A few drops of essential oils can be added to a tablespoon of baking soda and added to the litter for safe and effective odor control.

Place multiple litter boxes in different areas of the house. For elderly felines, placing a box on the main floor of your house will make it easier for them to get to the box. Also, offering a box that is wider and shallower may eliminate some litter box aversion.

Never use harsh cleaning products (such as bleach) on the boxes. Thieves Household Cleaner is a safe, effective, and pleasantly scented product to use for cleaning boxes.

Refusal to use the litter box may also indicate a urinary tract infection. A urinalysis performed by your veterinarian may reveal infection, crystals, or other abnormal components in the urine. Cats (males especially) who repeatedly enter the box but do not urinate or vocalize during their time in the box can indicate a very serious and possibly life-threatening urinary blockage. Veterinary care is needed immediately in this situation.

Recommendations
Singles: Lavender, Ylang Ylang, Cedarwood, Pine, Bergamot, Lemon, Orange, Idaho Balsam Fir

Blends: Peace & Calming, Valor, Harmony, Citrus Fresh, Evergreen Essence, Release, Purification, Trauma Life, Stress Away Roll-On, Inner Child, PuriClean, Joy, Believe

Additional: Thieves Household Cleaner (for cleaning boxes).

Application and Usage
Topical: Oils can also be petted or stroked onto the cat 2-3 times daily. Use 15 percent dilution for topical application.

Inhalation: Essential oils can be diffused in areas near the litter box. A cotton ball or two with essential oils dripped onto them can be placed near or in the litter boxes.

Kidney Failure / Disease

In older cats, kidney failure is seen frequently. Many causes have been theorized, including autoimmune disease, dietary considerations, chronic viral infections, and other medical conditions such as hypertrophic cardiomyopathy and hyperthyroidism.

The feline species was designed to obtain most of its water intake from prey. However, in modern, domestic cat diets consisting mainly of dry kibble, water content is very low. Feeding a commercially prepared raw diet or a good quality canned diet may slow down the progression of kidney deterioration or can help prevent it. Avoid commercial treats as they are laden with carbohydrates and other sugars.

Recommendations
Singles: Juniper, Ginger, Lemon, Frankincense, Myrrh, Peppermint, Helichrysum, Copaiba, Lemongrass, Sacred Frankincense

Blends: DiGize, TummyGize, Citrus Fresh, JuvaCleanse, Evergreen Essence, Aroma Life, Purification, EndoFlex

Veterinarian Tips and Suggestions

Kidney Blend

Combine the following ingredients. Split the combined mixture into equal parts and administer orally 2 times daily:

- 6 drops K&B
- 3 drops Copaiba
- 2 drops Lemon
- 2 drops Helichrysum
- 2 drops Juniper
- 1 teaspoon diluted NingXia Red
- ½ capsule Detoxzyme
- ½ capsule MultiGreens
- ½ capsule Life 9

Nutritionals: K&B, NingXia Red, Detoxzyme, Life 9, MultiGreens, Sulfurzyme

Application and Usage

Topical: Copaiba with 2-3 additional suggested essential oils can be petted/stroked onto the cat's fur, stomach area, and pads of feet. Use a 15 percent dilution, depending on the size of the cat and the severity of the kidney degeneration. Oils can be applied daily. Raindrop Technique, using the Raindrop recipe for cats, can be done 2-3 times weekly.

Ingestion & Oral: Administer orally K&B (2 drops), NingXia Red diluted (½-1 teaspoon), Life 9 (½ capsule), and Sulfurzyme (½ capsule added to moistened food) 1 time daily. Also administer MultiGreens (¼-½ capsule) and Detoxzyme (¼ capsule) 2 times daily.

Lacerations

Recommendations

Singles: Copaiba, Lavender, Cistus, Myrrh, Helichrysum

Blends: PuriClean, Infect Away, T-Away, Mendwell, Gentle Baby, Trauma Life

Additional: Animal Scents Ointment, LavaDerm Cooling Mist, Tender Tush, ClaraDerm, Rose Ointment, V-6 Vegetable Oil Complex

Application and Usage

Topical: Essential oils should be in a 10-25 percent dilution with V-6 Vegetable Oil Complex or other pure vegetable oil. Oils such as Copaiba, Lavender, and Frankincense can be applied directly to the wound. An alternative protocol involves using PuriClean to cleanse the wound and then using

Infect Away and Mendwell to help the wound heal. Tender Tush or Animal Scents Ointment may be used around the margins of the wound to keep tissues soft and pliable.

Lameness

Lameness (or limping) may be due to a bite wound abscess to the foot or leg, a sprain or fracture, or arthritis. Getting an accurate diagnosis for the lameness issue is important to know which oils to use. Oils listed below are for pain management and inflammation only. If infection is suspected, please consult your veterinarian.

Recommendations

Singles: Copaiba, Wintergreen, Basil, Cypress, Lemongrass, Idaho Blue Spruce, Idaho Balsam Fir, Palo Santo, Peppermint, Helichrysum, Marjoram

Blends: PanAway, Aroma Siez, Stress Away Roll-On, Valor II, Deep Relief Roll-On, Relieve It, Peace & Calming, Sacred Mountain

Nutritionals: NingXia Red, Sulfurzyme, AgilEase or BLM, Mineral Essence

Application and Usage

Topical: For acute inflammation and pain relief, oils may be in a 15 percent dilution and applied topically 2-3 times daily.

Ingestion & Oral: Administer orally NingXia Red (¼-1 teaspoon), Sulfurzyme (1 capsule), AgilEase or BLM (1 capsule), Mineral Essence (1-2 drops) 2 times daily.

Liver Disease (see also Fatty Liver Syndrome)

Liver disease in cats has many causes, including chemical toxicities, viral and bacterial infections, parasites, food sensitivities, autoimmune disease, cancer, to name a few. The liver receives, filters, and detoxifies the blood; so anything that is carried via the bloodstream "hits" the liver and can cause damage to the liver, bile ducts, and gallbladder.

Recommendations

Singles: Ledum, Grapefruit, Spearmint, Orange, Tangerine, Geranium, German Chamomile, Copaiba, Celery Seed, Carrot Seed, Helichrysum

Blends: JuvaFlex, JuvaCleanse, GLF, DiGize, ParaGize, TummyGize, Longevity, T-Away, Release

Nutritionals: NingXia Red, Essentialzyme, Life 9, Detoxzyme, Sulfurzyme, Super B, MultiGreens

Application and Usage

Topical: Apply Helichrysum, Copaiba, and Grapefruit on stomach area and paws daily. Administer the Raindrop Technique at least 2 times per week.

Ingestion & Oral: Administer orally Helichrysum, JuvaCleanse, and Copaiba (1-2 drops each), K&B (2 drops) NingXia Red diluted (1 teaspoon), Essentialzyme (½ caplet), Life 9 (½ capsule), Detoxzyme (½ capsule), Sulfurzyme (1 capsule), and Super B (¼ tablet) 2 times daily with MultiGreens (½ capsule) 1 time daily.

Inhalation: Diffuse Release, Lemon, Purification, and Stress Away Roll-On.

Lymphoma, Lymphosarcoma (see Cancer)

Mastitis

Mastitis is infection and inflammation of the mammary glands. Most infections occur after birthing, although mastitis is generally not common in cats. Symptoms may include hot, swollen glands; reddened and painful nipples; lethargy; and unwillingness to let kittens nurse.

Veterinary care in the form of systemic antibiotics is often needed to control infection. Kittens often need to be bottle-fed with a commercial milk replacer until the infection is under control.

Recommendations

Singles: Lavender, Copaiba, Geranium, Myrrh, Ginger, Tea Tree, Laurus Nobilis, Eucalyptus Globulus, Patchouli, Myrtle, Clove

Blends: Thieves, Purification, Stress Away Roll-On, DiGize, Melrose, Egyptian Gold, Infect Away, Mendwell, PuriClean

Nutritionals: NingXia Red diluted, Sulfurzyme, MultiGreens

Application and Usage

Topical: Essential oils should be in a 10 percent dilution created with V-6 Vegetable Oil Complex or a good quality olive or coconut oil. Apply 4-5 drops to the affected mammary glands 2 times daily. Oils can also be applied in Raindrop fashion.

Ingestion & Oral: Administer orally Ginger, Geranium, Palmarosa, Eucalyptus Globulus, Laurus Nobilis, Copaiba, and DiGize (1-2 drops each) with NingXia Red diluted (½-1 teaspoon), Sulfurzyme (½ capsule), MultiGreens (½ capsule) 2 times daily.

Inhalation: Diffuse oils for 10-15 minutes several times daily.

Mast Cell Tumor (see also Cancer)

Mast cell tumors are conglomerations of a type of white blood cell (a mast cell) that is part of the immune system. Mast cells contain histamine granules, so they function in inflammatory and allergic reactions.

Most mast cell tumors in cats are found on the head and neck but may also be discovered on the legs and trunk of the body. In some cases, tumors can spread to the intestinal tract, liver, and internal lymph nodes.

Recommendations

Singles: Lavender, Helichrysum, Frankincense, Sacred Frankincense, Myrrh, Hong Kuai, Copaiba, Sacred Sandalwood, Royal Hawaiian Sandalwood, Ocotea, Idaho Balsam Fir, Idaho Blue Spruce, Northern Lights Black Spruce, Melissa, Basil, Hyssop, Tsuga

Blends: 3 Wise Men, Stress Away Roll-On, T-Away, Mendwell, Longevity, JuvaCleanse, DiGize

Nutritionals: NingXia Red, Sulfurzyme, MultiGreens, Detoxzyme, Life 9, ImmuPro

Application and Usage

Topical: Essential oils should be in a 90 percent dilution and applied 3 times daily directly onto the mast cell tumor(s).

Ingestion & Oral: Administer orally NingXia Red diluted (1 teaspoon), Sulfurzyme (1 capsule), Multi-Greens (½ capsule), Detoxzyme (½ capsule), Life 9 (¼ capsule), and ImmuPro (½ tablet) 2 times daily.

Inhalation: Diffuse Frankincense, Sacred Frankincense, Peace & Calming, and Purification.

Mange, Mites (see Skin Conditions)

Neurological Conditions

Symptoms of nervous system issues include incoordination, tremors, head tilt, rapid eye movement, seizures, weakness, and paralysis. Viral infections, parasites, injuries to the head or spine, and tumors are the more common causes for neurologic disease. Working with your veterinarian to determine a cause for these symptoms is highly suggested, so appropriate therapies can be initiated.

Recommendations

Singles: Helichrysum, Copaiba, Cypress, Peppermint, Geranium, Juniper, Marjoram, Petitgrain

Blends: Valor, Valor II, Tranquil Roll-On, Peace & Calming, Brain Power, T-Away, ParaGize, Aroma Siez, GeneYus, Clarity

Nutritionals: Sulfurzyme, NingXia, MultiGreens, Super B

Application and Usage

Topical: Essential oils should be in a dilution and applied to the top of the head, inside ears, on the bottoms of the feet, and feathered on the spine. Starting with Valor, apply Copaiba, Cypress, and Helichrysum, finishing with Peppermint.

Ingestion & Oral: Administer orally Sulfurzyme (1 capsule), NingXia Red diluted (kittens: ¼ teaspoon; adult cats: ½-1 teaspoon), MultiGreens (½ capsule), Super B (¼ -½ tablet), and OmegaGize³ (2 capsules) 2 times daily.

Inhalation: Diffuse Clarity, Cedarwood, Transformation, and Stress Away Roll-On.

Pain

In general, cats will try to "hide" pain and illness so as not to appear vulnerable to predators. Abnormal behaviors such as hiding in closets or under beds, shaking or trembling, poor appetite, or not interacting with housemates and humans (when they did previously) may be symptoms of a feline who is in pain.

Pain raises stress hormones and suppresses the immune system, so pain management is a key factor in healing from injuries and illnesses.

Recommendations

Singles: Helichrysum, Lavender, Frankincense, Idaho Blue Spruce, Idaho Balsam Fir, Palo Santo, Copaiba, Peppermint, Northern Lights Black Spruce, Lemongrass, Cypress, Blue Cypress, Marjoram, Wintergreen

Blends: Valor, Valor II, Aroma Siez, PanAway, T-Away, Deep Relief Roll-On, Relieve It, Trauma Life

Nutritionals: NingXia Red, Sulfurzyme, AgilEase or BLM

Application and Usage

Topical: Essential oils can be applied directly over the area where the cat has pain (25 percent dilution) 2-3 times daily. Oils can also be applied in Raindrop style daily until the pain has subsided.

Ingestion & Oral: Administer orally NingXia Red diluted (1 teaspoon), Sulfurzyme (1 capsule), and AgilEase or BLM (1 capsule) 2 times daily.

Inhalation: Diffuse Stress Away Roll-On, Orange, Peace & Calming, and Lavender.

Pancreatitis (see Liver Disease)

Parasites (Internal)

A fecal analysis performed by your veterinarian will reveal if/what types of parasites your cat or kitten may have. In heavy parasitic infestations, cats may show signs of moderate to severe weight loss, poor hair coat, decreased appetite, and lethargy. Migrating roundworm larvae may cause a variety of symptoms such as cough, diarrhea, blood in the stools, and even eye problems.

Oftentimes conventional dewormers are necessary to kill the migrating larvae and adult worms. Essential oils can be used to control light populations of parasites and for prevention.

Recommendations

Singles: Ocotea, Peppermint, Fennel, Tarragon, Patchouli

Blends: DiGize, ParaGize

Nutritionals: NingXia Red, ParaFree, Detoxzyme

Application and Usage

Topical: Essential oils (15 percent dilution) can be applied directly over the middle abdomen 2 times daily for 2-4 weeks and then applied 1-2 times per week for maintenance. Periodic fecal analyses are suggested to determine if parasites are being controlled. Cats who routinely spend a lot of time outdoors, should have fecal checks performed at least 3 times yearly.

Ingestion & Oral: Administer orally NingXia Red diluted (½-1 teaspoon), ParaFree (½ capsule), and Detoxzyme (½ capsule) 2 times daily.

Pregnancy and Birthing

Essential oils can create a calmer, more accepting mother during the birth process. Oils can help kittens through the trauma of delivery as well.

Recommendations

Singles: Lavender, Sacred Frankincense, Myrrh, Roman Chamomile, Copaiba, Blue Cypress, Rose, Ylang Ylang

Blends: Peace & Calming, Gentle Baby, AromaEase, T-Away, Stress Away Roll-On, Grounding, Harmony, Valor, White Angelica, Trauma Life

Application and Usage

Topical: Frankincense, Gentle Baby, and Lavender can be placed in your hands, rubbing the palms together gently. Then stroke the newborn kitten and mother with the oils after they are dry. Fennel applied in this fashion to the mother's abdomen may stimulate milk production and letdown.

Inhalation: Essential oils should be diffused near the mother as she is preparing for parturition.

Pyometra (Uterine Infection)

Pyometra is often a medical emergency, since pus that is trapped inside the uterus can quickly cause a cat to become very toxic, and death may occur if veterinary care is not obtained in time. Pyometra is often associated with hormonal imbalances (such as a false pregnancy), or it can be caused by tissue or dead kittens remaining inside from the birthing process. Oftentimes, a foul-smelling vaginal discharge is noticed. Essential oils can be applied as an emergency measure until veterinary care is available.

Recommendations

Singles: Geranium, Copaiba, Myrrh, Palmarosa, Ginger, Rosemary, Rose, Melissa

Blends: Thieves, Exodus II, Melrose, DiGize, Purification, Egyptian Gold

Nutritionals: NingXia Red, Life 9, MultiGreens

Application and Usage

Topical: Oils can also be in a dilution of 50 percent and applied over the lower abdomen. Because of the severity of this condition, oils should be diluted to this percentage so as not to overwhelm the body as it detoxifies. A warm towel or cloth may be placed on the cat's abdomen after applying oils, for comfort and to keep body temperature from falling.

Ingestion & Oral: Administer orally NingXia Red diluted (½ teaspoon), Life 9 (½ capsule), and MultiGreens (½ capsule) 2 times daily.

Inhalation: Diffuse Purification, Thieves, and Melrose.

Respiratory Conditions (see also Allergies, Asthma, Herpesvirus, Heartworm Disease)

Coughing, sneezing, increased respiratory effort, and nasal discharge are all symptoms that may occur with various respiratory conditions. Viral and bacterial pathogens, irritation and allergies from commercial household and personal products, tobacco or wood smoke, and internal parasites can cause respiratory issues. Essential oils can be very effective in supporting and promoting a healthy respiratory tract.

Recommendations

Singles: Frankincense, Sacred Frankincense, Ravintsara, Eucalyptus Blue, Peppermint, Idaho Blue Spruce, Melissa, Rosemary, Copaiba, Myrtle, Eucalyptus Radiata, Eucalyptus Globulus, Lavender, Hinoki, Hyssop, Dorado Azul

Blends: Thieves, R.C., ImmuPower, Purification, Breathe Again Roll-On, Exodus II, Raven, Relieve It, Infect Away, PuriClean

Nutritionals: NingXia Red, Essentialzyme, Life 9, MultiGreens

Application and Usage

Topical: Essential oils should be in a 50 percent dilution or more; and 1-2 drops can be placed directly onto the cat's neck, stomach, feet, and throat area 2-3 times daily. Kitty Raindrop can be applied Raindrop style up the spine, using 4-5 drops of the blend 1 time daily.

Ingestion & Oral: Administer orally NingXia Red diluted (½-1 teaspoon), Essentialzyme (¼ caplet), Life 9 (¼ capsule), and MultiGreens (¼-½ capsule) 2 times daily.

Inhalation: Diffusing is an excellent way to deliver essential oils to the cat's respiratory tract; try diffusing Raven or R.C.

🐈 *Veterinarian Tips and Suggestions*

Feline Skin Support Spray

- 20 drops Lavender
- 10 drops Purification
- 8 drops Frankincense or Sacred Frankincense
- 8 drops Geranium
- 4 drops Myrrh
- ⅛ oz. V-6 Vegetable Oil Complex or other good quality carrier oil

1. Place the oils into a 1-oz. spray bottle.
2. Fill with purified or distilled water.
3. Shake well.
4. Spritz the fur as needed; massage into skin gently. Or spray into hands; stroke into skin as needed.

Ringworm

Ringworm is actually a fungus that affects the skin of many species of animals, including humans. Ringworm obtains its name from a characteristic round, reddened patch of scaly skin seen on humans.

In cats, lesions can include broken shafts of hair (seen mostly in patches) and flaking, roughened skin. Ringworm is commonly seen on the ears, face, legs, and feet. Fungal cultures, examination of skin flakes under a microscope, and examination with a Wood's lamp are used to definitively diagnose ringworm.

Recommendations

Singles: Geranium, German Chamomile, Tea Tree, Myrrh, Ocotea, Helichrysum, Copaiba, Hyssop, Juniper, Ginger, Blue Cypress, Lemongrass, Eucalyptus Blue, Myrtle, Hong Kuai, Dorado Azul, Palmarosa, Patchouli

Blends: DiGize, Purification, Gentle Baby, PuriClean, Infect Away, Melrose, The Gift, Egyptian Gold, Thieves

Additional: Animal Scents Ointment, LavaDerm Cooling Mist, ClaraDerm

Application and Usage

Topical: Essential oils should be in a 50-75 percent dilution before applying. Apply directly on location 2 times daily.

Inhalation: Diffuse Purification and Thieves.

Roundworms (*see* Parasites)

Sarcoma (*see* Cancer)

Seizures (*see also* Neurologic Conditions)

Seizures occur from many different causes—feline distemper virus, feline leukemia virus, toxicity to commercial flea and tick preventatives, injuries to the skull, parasites, bacterial infections, brain tumors—and more. Essential oils can be used to control a seizure until veterinary help can be obtained.

Recommendations

Singles: Lavender, Frankincense, Sacred Sandalwood, Royal Hawaiian Sandalwood, Valerian, Cedarwood, Jasmine, Hong Kuai, Ylang Ylang, Vetiver, Idaho Blue Spruce, Idaho Balsam Fir, Jasmine, Copaiba, Sacred Frankincense, Helichrysum, Geranium

Blends: Peace & Calming, Valor II, RutaVaLa, Gentle Baby, Brain Power, Believe, Lady Sclareol, Tranquil Roll-On, Stress Away Roll-On, Sacred Mountain, White Angelica

Nutritionals: NingXia Red, MindWise, OmegaGize[3], Life 9, Super B

Application and Usage

Topical: Essential oils can be applied at the back of the skull and on top of the head (use caution so as not to be bitten inadvertently). They may also be stroked onto the cat's spine and sides of the chest.

Ingestion & Oral: Administer orally NingXia Red diluted (½-1 teaspoon), MindWise (½ teaspoon), OmegaGize[3] (2 drops), Life 9 (¼ capsule), and Super B (⅛ tablet) 2 times daily.

Inhalation: Diffuse Sacred Frankincense, Peace & Calming, Stress Away Roll-On, Believe, and Sacred Mountain.

Skin Conditions (*see also* Ringworm, Fleas, Allergies)

Skin conditions in cats can have many causes—external parasites, fungal and bacterial infections, allergies, poor diet, and metabolic disorders such as diabetes and autoimmune diseases. Getting a diagnosis from your veterinarian will aid in determining what products will be most beneficial.

Recommendations

Singles: Lavender, Frankincense, Copaiba, German Chamomile, Roman Chamomile, Geranium, Myrrh, Sacred Sandalwood, Royal Hawaiian Sandalwood, Sacred Frankincense, Palmarosa, Lemon, Rose, Helichrysum, Cistus

Blends: Gentle Baby, Purification, PuriClean, Infect Away, Mendwell, Thieves, Melrose, The Gift, Sensation

Nutritionals: NingXia Red, MindWise, OmegaGize[3], Life 9, Detoxzyme

Additional: Animal Scents Shampoo, Rose Ointment, Tender Tush, ClaraDerm, Animal Scents Ointment, LavaDerm Cooling Mist, Thieves Household Cleaner (to clean litter boxes, food and water dishes, etc.)

Application and Usage

Topical: Essential oils should be in a 50 percent dilution before application to affected skin.

Ingestion & Oral: Administer orally NingXia Red diluted (½-1 teaspoon), MindWise (¼ teaspoon), OmegaGize[3] (2 drops), Life 9 (¼ capsule), and Detoxzyme (½ capsule) 2 times daily.

Inhalation: Diffuse any selected oil.

Squamous Cell Carcinoma, Oral (see also Cancer)

Squamous cell carcinoma (SCC) most commonly appear in the mouth of a cat, especially in older felines. They are usually not detectable at first; a cat may drool, have an unpleasant odor coming from the mouth, may chew its food with its head tilted, and perhaps even refuse to eat dry food. Sometimes blood-tinged saliva will be present. Unfortunately, oral SCCs are usually aggressive and require medical intervention (pain relief and antibiotic therapy), along with essential oils and other holistic modalities.

Diet should be changed to a good quality canned food or commercially prepared raw food.

Recommendations

Singles: Copaiba, Frankincense, Helichrysum, Lavender, Myrrh, Sacred Sandalwood, Royal Hawaiian Sandalwood, Idaho Blue Spruce, Rose, Sacred Frankincense, Hong Kuai, Tsuga, Idaho Balsam Fir, Northern Lights Black Spruce, Grapefruit, Palo Santo

Blends: Thieves, ImmuPower, 3 Wise Men, Transformation, Hope, Longevity, Purification

Nutritionals: NingXia Red, Life 9, ImmuPro, MultiGreens

Application and Usage

Topical: Essential oils are best placed behind and just under the lower jawbone, where there is a group of lymph nodes and blood vessels. Oils are absorbed quickly in this area. Dilute 50 percent before application and use 2-3 drops on each side. Oils can be diluted 75 percent and placed on the site of the tumor. Cats can quickly develop taste aversion to the oils, and applying them orally could be difficult for the cats.

Ingestion & Oral: Administer orally NingXia Red diluted (1-1½ teaspoons), Life 9 (¼ capsule), ImmuPro (¼ tablet), and MultiGreens (½ capsule) 2 times daily.

Inhalation: Diffuse selected oils where the cat spends most of its time.

Tapeworms (see Deworming)

Teeth (see Dental Disorders)

Thyroid (see Hyperthyroidism)

Toxoplasmosis (see also Parasites)

Toxoplasmosis is caused by a single-celled parasite called *Toxoplasma gondii.* Cats are infected by coming in contact with contaminated soil or feces (fecal-oral transmission). Clinical signs vary from mild lethargy, soft stools, and poor appetite, seizures, incoordination, eye disorders, and pneumonia.

Toxoplasmosis can affect humans, although most *T. gondii* infestations are from contaminated, undercooked meat.

Keeping a cat's immune system at its prime is the best way to prevent toxoplasmosis.

Recommendations

Singles: Hyssop, Ocotea, Fennel, Tarragon, Patchouli, Peppermint

Blends: Thieves, DiGize, ParaGize, ImmuPower

Nutritionals: NingXia Red, MultiGreens, ParaFree, Detoxzyme

Application and Usage

Topical: Apply selected oils to stomach and paw area 2 times daily. Apply Raindrop as needed.

Ingestion & Oral: Administer orally NingXia Red diluted (1 teaspoon), MultiGreens (½ capsule), ParaFree (½ capsule 2 times daily for 14 days), and Detoxzyme (¼ capsule) 2 times daily.

Inhalation: Diffuse selected oils.

Trauma (Acute)

Trauma can be any kind of physical or emotional injury, and there is almost always an emotional component to every accident or injury (fear, hopelessness, agitation, anxiety, etc.). Essential oils should be chosen for their ability to affect both the body and the spirit. Trauma can range from mild (laceration, bruising) to severe, life-threatening incidents (hit by car, animal attack, gunshot, etc.).

Recommendations

Singles: Frankincense, Sacred Frankincense, Lavender, Vetiver, Valerian, Cedarwood, Rose, Copaiba, Cistus, Helichrysum, Ylang Ylang, Jasmine, Neroli, Idaho Balsam Fir, Idaho Blue Spruce, Northern Lights Black Spruce

Blends: Valor, T-Away, Hope, Sacred Mountain, Aroma Life, PanAway, Mendwell, Release, Transformation, Harmony, Peace & Calming II, Trauma Life, Gentle Baby

Application and Usage

Topical: Essential oils should be administered as quickly as possible. If no diluting oil is available, oils can be applied "neat." For animals in shock, place Sacred Frankincense or Rose oil (1-2 drops) on top of the head for an enhanced will to live. A small drop of Sacred Frankincense may be placed on the tongue if the cat is unconscious but breathing. Oils can also be placed Raindrop style up the spine for overall support until veterinary care can be obtained.

Upper Respiratory Tract Infections
(see Respiratory Conditions)

Urinary Tract Conditions
(see also Inappropriate Urination / Elimination)

The urinary tract includes the kidneys, bladder, ureters, and urethra.

Infection, trauma, blockage (stones, mucus plugs), inflammation, and other metabolic diseases such as diabetes mellitus are all causes for disorders of the urinary tract. Male cats, because of their longer urethras, are more prone to developing life-threatening blockages when a stone or plug lodges in the narrower end of the urethra near the opening.

Cats may urinate frequently, usually in small amounts and oftentimes outside the litter box when infection or moderate to severe inflammation is present. Sometimes blood can be seen in the urine. Male cats who sit in the box for long periods of time or vocalize when trying to urinate need to be seen by a veterinarian immediately.

Switching the cat's food from dry to wet is one of the key factors in preventing urinary tract infections. Cats, in nature, obtain most of their moisture through the ingestion of live prey. They were not designed to drink large amounts of water. Also, most commercial dry cat food formulas have a high carbohydrate content, contributing to abnormal metabolic processes in the body.

A good quality canned food or commercially prepared raw diet is important to maintain proper urinary tract health. Cats should be supplied with clean, fresh, filtered or purified water daily. City tap water often contains chlorine and fluoride, which are detrimental to the body and should never be offered to animals.

Stress is an important factor in the developing of urinary tract disorders.

Recommendations

Singles: Copaiba, Frankincense, Lavender, Juniper, Geranium, Lemon, Idaho Blue Spruce, Helichrysum, Bergamot, Sacred Frankincense, Tea Tree, Eucalyptus Globulus, Lemongrass, Cedarwood

Blends: Thieves, Release, Valor II, Peace & Calming and Peace & Calming II, PanAway, T-Away, DiGize, Citrus Fresh, Purification, DiGize, ParaGize, PuriClean

Nutritionals: NingXia Red, MultiGreens, Essentialzyme, Life 9, Super C Chewable, OmegaGize[3]

Application and Usage

Topical: Essential oils should be in a 50-75 percent dilution and applied over the lower abdomen 2-3 times daily. Kitty Raindrop can be applied, adding Juniper to the mix.

Ingestion & Oral: Administer orally NingXia Red diluted (1 teaspoon), Life 9 (¼ capsule), Super C Chewable (¼ tablet), and OmegaGize³ (2 drops) 2 times daily.

Inhalation: Diffuse Purification.

Vaccination Reactions / Vaccinosis

The subjects of when to vaccinate, what to vaccinate for, and how often to vaccinate are questions that every pet guardian should discuss with careful consideration of lifestyle, risk of exposure to disease, and overall health of the animal. New research has shown that certain vaccines often protect an animal for a much longer period of time than previously thought.

However, performing titers (solutions) for diseases such as distemper, parvo, and adenovirus in dogs and distemper, rhinotracheitis, and calicivirus in cats may be a good alternative to administering annual vaccinations.

Only healthy animals should be vaccinated. This especially includes animals with autoimmune disease or any other acute or chronic medical condition. The vaccine insert sheet (which lists possible contraindications to vaccination and the components in the vaccine itself) states that only healthy cats and kittens should be vaccinated.

Unfortunately, rabies vaccinations are mandated according to state law. However, medical exemptions for rabies vaccines are allowed in certain states. In those states that allow medical exemptions, a veterinarian must submit a statement to the state veterinary board explaining why a rabies vaccine should not be administered to the animal.

Even healthy animals that are vaccinated may experience mild, moderate, or even severe reactions. The majority of symptoms are mild (lethargy, tenderness at the vaccination site; the more serious signs include stiffness, poor appetite, fever, seizures, facial swelling, edema, and collapse).

If your kitty has experienced *any* kind of reaction, please alert your veterinarian as soon as possible. Your veterinarian will want to mark your cat's medical record, so prevention of a reaction (splitting up vaccines between several appointments or administering medications to help prevent reactions) can be planned. Essential oils can be used post-vaccination to help support and balance the immune system.

Recommendations

Singles: Copaiba, Mountain Savory, Thyme, Basil, Cypress, Marjoram, Peppermint, Lavender, Frankincense, Lemon, Grapefruit, Ledum, Helichrysum, Sacred Frankincense

Blends: PanAway, T-Away, ImmuPower, JuvaFlex, Purification, Abundance, DiGize

Nutritionals: NingXia Red, MultiGreens, Super C Chewable, Super B, Detoxzyme, K&B

Application and Usage

Topical: Kitty Raindrop can be used Raindrop style on the spine 1 time daily for 2-3 days post-vaccination. Essential oils such as Copaiba, Helichrysum, Cypress, or Purification can be placed directly over the vaccine site (dilute 75 percent before administering). Apply DiGize, Copaiba, Helichrysum, or Cypress on stomach area 2 times daily.

Ingestion & Oral: Administer orally K&B (1-3 drops), Copaiba (1 drop), DiGize (1 drop), Helichrysum (1 drop), Detoxzyme (¼ capsule), NingXia Red diluted (1 teaspoon), and MultiGreens (½ capsule) 2 times daily with Super C Chewable (¼ caplet) and Super B (¼ tablet) 1 time daily.

Wounds (*see also* Trauma, Skin Conditions)

Superficial wounds (minor cuts, scrapes, abrasions) may or may not need veterinary care, depending on the severity of the injury. Wounds that have penetrated through the skin layers or puncture wounds of any kind need medical attention as soon as possible. Essential oils can be used for urgent care needs while in transit to the veterinary clinic.

Recommendations

Singles: Frankincense, Sacred Frankincense, Lavender, Copaiba, Helichrysum, Palo Santo, Rose, Cistus, Idaho Tansy, Myrrh, Tea Tree, Patchouli, Palmarosa

Blends: PuriClean, Infect Away, Mendwell, Thieves, T-Away, Gentle Baby, Melrose, Aroma Life, Purification, The Gift, Trauma Life, Stress Away, Peace & Calming

Nutritionals: NingXia Red, Life 9, MultiGreens, Sulfurzyme

Additional: Animal Scents Ointment, Rose Ointment, Tender Tush, ClaraDerm

Application and Usage

Topical: Essential oils should be in a 75 percent dilution and applied directly on the wound. Oils can also be used in Raindrop style from the base of the tail to the base of the neck.

Ingestion & Oral: Administer orally NingXia Red diluted (½-1 oz.), Life 9 (¼ capsule), MultiGreens (½ capsule), and Sulfurzyme (1 capsule) 2 times daily.

Inhalation: Oils can be diffused or stroked onto the cat as needed to keep it calm and offer pain relief. Try Gentle Baby, Stress Away Roll-On, Trauma Life, and Peace & Calming.

Essential Oils for Hospice Care and Euthanasia

There is probably no more delicate and emotional-filled topic to discuss than helping an animal companion in his or her last days retain quality of life and knowing when it's time to "let go." Many animal guardians faced with end-care and euthanasia decisions harbor feelings of anxiety, guilt, and, ultimately, grief. Working with your veterinarian or other trained animal professional will help you make informed, objective decisions about your animal.

The focus of hospice care has several components: (1) making the animal comfortable and as pain-free as possible, (2) maintaining a good human-animal bond, (3) administering subcutaneous fluids, bandage, and wound care, and (4) education as to your animal's condition and what to expect as the condition progresses.

Euthanasia performed in a loving, quiet, and accepting environment may be a much-needed option when pain and suffering are prolonged, and there is no hope for reversal of symptoms. Most animals will give clues when the end is near. Signs may include complete withdrawal from interaction with both humans and other animals in the household, extreme weakness and lethargy, inability to stand or move, vocalizing in pain even when pain meds have been administered, a glazed-over appearance to the eyes (not focusing, hazy), and refusal to eat or drink for several days.

Essential oils can play an important role in easing this period of an animal's life and are very helpful in alleviating the anxiety and guilt that the caretaker may be experiencing. Most animal guardians question whether their decision to keep on going or to let go is the "right" one, and oils can help reduce the stress surrounding this issue.

Because there are so many oils that can be used in end-of-life situations, this section will focus only on the oils for emotional and spiritual strength and enhancement.

Recommendations

Singles: Frankincense, Sacred Frankincense, Myrrh, Lavender, Cedarwood, Palo Santo, Orange, Idaho Blue Spruce, Rose, Jasmine, Sacred Sandalwood, Royal Hawaiian Sandalwood, Idaho Balsam Fir, Northern Lights Black Spruce, Sage, Cypress, Blue Cypress, Ylang Ylang

Blends: Release, Acceptance, Peace & Calming, Valor, Sacred Mountain, Faith (Inspired by Oola), Forgiveness, Hope, Gratitude, The Gift, Transformation, Inner Child, Surrender, Stress Away Roll-On, White Angelica

Application and Usage

Topical and Inhalation: Have the caretaker place a few drops of chosen oil(s) in his/her hands and rub palms together gently. Inhale oils by cupping hands over the nose. Take a few more drops of oils in the hands and stroke the top of the animal's head and neck. Offer to let the animal sniff the hands. Diffuse oils during the process of preparing the animal for the euthanasia procedure.

Note: Sacred Frankincense and Frankincense oils are described in many references as the best oils to increase spiritual awareness, as well as to provide a strong connection between the animal/person and the Creator. They are perfect oils to use in end-of-life situations, whether applied topically or inhaled.

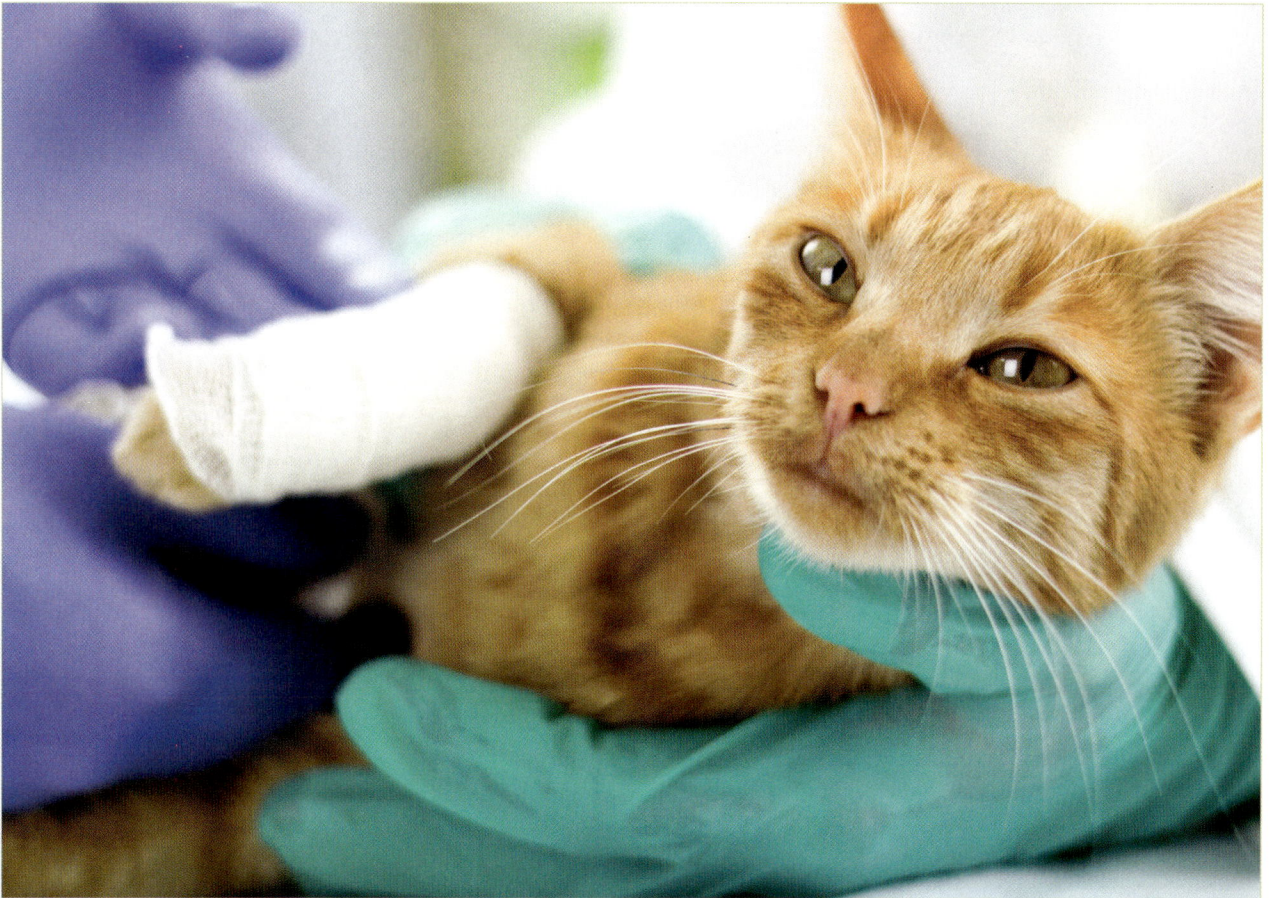

Testimonials

My grandmother's cat Oscar had mange, hair loss, was skinny, unhealthy, and just physically ill. Most of the family thought she was crazy to keep him around like he was. My grandmother asked me if I knew of anything with Young Living that would help him. That's because none of the other vet creams had worked. She started using Animal Scents Shampoo and Animal Scents Ointment. And now Oscar is fluffy and healthy!

-Heidi R.

. . . .

Marron my cat was bitten on the face during a catfight. I wiped the wound with a wet towel and a few drops of Thieves. I then applied Lavender and Tea Tree 3-4 times a day.

-Masoko H.

My friend Jessica found a stray cat and brought her into a clinic in July 2010. The veterinarian there found that the cat had ear mites, hookworms, and feline leukemia. My friend elected not to euthanize right away. After being spayed, dewormed, and treated for ear mites, the cat was in rough shape.

I approached Jessica with the idea of giving essential oils a try. We began with Melissa Hydrosol and set up a protocol of 0.1 cc to be given orally 3 times a day for 6 weeks. After the 6-week treatment protocol, you could see the improvements in the cat. Her coat was thick and luscious, her eyes were bright and clear, her gums were pink and healthy, and she had gained weight. On September 27, 2010, the feline leukemia test was taken again, and the results were negative. Jessica had the cat declawed in November and found her a new home. To this day, the cat is happy and healthy, enjoying life as she should.

-Chris S.

I found a gaping wound on my cat Tigerlily's hind end. She was licking the wound profusely and was clearly in a lot of pain. It was bleeding and oozing pus. Using a plastic syringe from the drugstore, I first irrigated Tigerlily's wound with salt water and a couple of drops of Lavender oil. I then put Melrose and Frankincense directly in the wound 2-3 times a day, followed by Animal Scents Ointment. I also put NingXia Red in Tigerlily's food 2 times a day and did two mineral soaks. It healed rapidly and by day 12, all that was left was a small scab.

-Julie B. H.

I came into a clinic with a cat that had been diagnosed with renal (kidney) failure the previous year. I had tried addressing the problem with a low-protein diet, a kidney-support supplement, and the use of fluids under the skin to help hydrate the cat and flush her kidneys. However, the cat stopped eating and drinking the previous week and would just lie around, so I had reluctantly scheduled euthanasia for her. My veterinarian recommended that I apply Geranium oil on a kidney acupuncture point on the cat 2 times a day. Two months later, I sent my vet a thank you card, telling him that the cat had started eating and drinking the next day, that I was still applying Geranium 2 times a day, and that the cat was doing great.

-John H.

I treated a cat who would urinate all over the house. For years, the owner would fold hand towels and put them in front of the litter box for the cat to urinate on and then change them out. I did an animal-human connection session with them and put together a kitty essential oil bottle for the owner to take home. During the session, I applied the first round of essential oil treatments to the cat and showed the owner how to treat at home. The cat quit urinating around the house the very next day, and to this day has not urinated outside the litter box. The cat also connects on a deeper level with her owner and other cats and dogs in the household.

-Dr. H. DVM

I volunteer at the local Humane Society, administering essential oil treatments to both dogs and cats. I typically have little to no history on the dogs and cats treated, except what the intake person can tell me. Every treatment I see instant transformation and shifting with each application of oil. On one visit, there was a cat that wasn't eating. Within minutes of getting her oil treatment, she started eating out of her bowl.

-Dr. H. DVM

I successfully treated a one-year-old cat with a mouth injury using essential oil combinations, antibiotics, wound lavage and debridement, and pain management. Healing over exposed bone occurred within four days. In my opinion, the essential oil therapy greatly enhanced the healing time. The cat made remarkable improvement in less than 24 hours. Furthermore, in just four days from the initial examination, healthy new tissue had developed over the necrotic areas and exposed bone, a process that could have taken much longer had alternative treatment not been implemented. Follow-up phone calls to the caretaker at two weeks and again at three months post-treatment resulted in reports that the cat was doing extremely well and had no complications from her ordeal.

-Dr. F. DVM

Deb, guardian of two cats named Bootie and Jeremy, started essential oil therapy on them after finding out her older cat Treetop had contracted both the feline leukemia virus and the feline immunodeficiency virus. She was diligent with administering the oils, especially after these kitties started showing symptoms suspicious of the viral infections. Bootie and Jeremy were tested in my office, and the results were negative on both cats.

-Dr. F. DVM

I examined a 15-year-old cat with a small hole on the underside of its neck that had been draining serum and occasionally pus for the past year. The cat's traditional veterinarian had sedated it and explored the wound, looking for a splinter, a weed sticker, or anything that would explain why the wound wouldn't heal. Nothing was found inside the wound. The kitty had also been on several rounds of antibiotics, which took care of the drainage, but only for a short time.

To treat the wound, I made a mixture of Thieves, Frankincense, and Patchouli diluted 75 percent in a base of extra virgin olive oil. Two drops of the mixture were applied to the lesion, and the rest of the oil mix was sent home with the owners with instructions to apply the oils 1 time daily for at least a week. Two days later, I got an email from the owners who were very happy to report that the drainage had completely stopped, and they could hardly see the hole anymore to apply the oils.

-Dr. F. DVM

Hope was a 4-month-old barn cat presented to me after it was bitten in the face by a dog. She had a fever, facial swelling, and was open-mouth breathing. I gave her one laser treatment using the Erchonia PL 5000 and one dose each of the homeopathics Ledum, Arnica, Belladonna, and Hypericum. The wound was cleaned daily with cotton balls dampened with distilled water, Lavender, Helichrysum, Myrrh, and Purification; and I applied daily Raindrop treatments for the first three days and then 2 times weekly after that. Within two days the swelling was reduced by 50 percent, and Hope began eating on her own. The wound healed completely within one month with no evidence of scarring.

-Dr. P. DVM

I have a cat that has gotten facial abscesses, 2 times (years apart). Each time, it took only 1 drop of Melrose mixed with V-6 Vegetable Oil Complex to make that abscess blow. Then I used 1 drop of Melrose with V-6 mixed with 1 drop of Lavender on day 2. Day 3 was 1 drop of Lavender mixed with V-6. Each time it worked like a charm. This cat is previously feral so not always easy to catch (she is a barn cat), so I had to use my oils wisely with her.

-Cheri L.

. . . .

Mikey, an 8-week old, domestic shorthair barn cat, was treated for feline distemper (panleukopenia), an oftentimes fatal viral disease. Panleukopenia affects the immune system by destroying protective cells lining the intestine, as well as the white cells found in the bloodstream. Mikey had a severe case; but with intensive, consistent nursing care, he made a full recovery and is now running, playing, and eating like a normal kitten.

He was given topical essential oil treatments using Oregano, Thyme, Basil, Cypress, Frankincense, Copaiba, ParaGize, and Peppermint daily. Oils were diluted by 90 percent prior to application. Two drops of the combination were applied to his neck and spine daily for one week and then every other day for the next week. He also received 0.15 ml of NingXia Red daily, given by oral syringe. For hydration, Mikey received room temperature spring water administered by oral syringe. He also was given a high-calorie, vitamin-mineral veterinary gel several times a day. Highly diluted DiGize was applied once daily on the lower abdomen for nausea and diarrhea.

-Dr. F. DVM

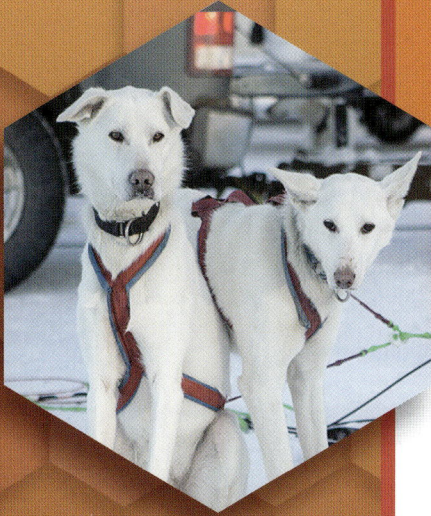

Dogs (Canine)

Introduction

Many can agree, "dogs are man's best friend." As such, we want to care for our dog(s) with the absolute best to assure long, healthy, and happy lives. Caring for your dog(s) with natural products is one of the best ways to assure this.

Have you ever considered what your personal home environment's effect may be on your best friend? The more "green" and clean you can make your home (free of toxic chemicals, cleaners, scented candles, air fresheners, furniture and carpet sprays, etc.), the healthier your dog will be.

The first line of protection your dog has is through his coat. Healthy dogs are more likely to exhibit healthy behavior. A diet consisting primarily of dry kibble, city tap water tainted with chlorine and fluoride, and toxic cleaning agents can cause imbalances, both mentally and physically.

Dogs respond in varying degrees of acceptance when offered an essential oil, regardless of the method used (topical, internal, or inhalation). Some dogs readily lie beside a diffuser or near an open bottle of oil, while others will want to leave a room where oils have been applied or diffused.

Because canines have a well-developed sense of smell and taste, essential oils may cause even the most cooperative dog to shy away from oils when they are introduced.

When a dog shows an abnormally strong aversion to essential oils, however, it is usually because the oils chosen may be too strong. Adjusting the strength of the scent is usually enough to remedy the situation. Also, by wearing essential oils on yourself, you will become a "human diffuser," and oftentimes the dog who detests the oil on itself will accept oils on the caretaker.

However, many dog owners agree that if a dog, or any animal, resists an oil, it's because it does not trust the caregiver. Please consider that as you work with your animals.

You can allow the dog to choose the essential oil itself by carefully setting out bottles. Allow the dog to go to the bottle of its choice and watch for its reactions, which may be as subtle as continually coming back to an essential oil, trying to rub the essential oil onto its shoulders or parts of its body, or as bold as picking it up and running off with it! Careful observation is a must as you perform this exercise with your dog.

Safety And Guidelines

Essential oils can be used safely in dogs if certain guidelines are followed. In general, essential oils must be of the highest quality—unadulterated, genuine, and pure. There are many essential oil companies that market their products as "organic," "natural," or even "certified pure." Unfortunately, many of these statements may not be true, since essential oils are not regulated by federal agencies. As a result, adulterated oils are often sold, unbeknown to the consumer.

Young Living Essential Oils, with its Seed to Seal process, assures that the oils produced are of the highest standards and are safe for animals, children, and adults when used according to directions.

Starting slowly should be of utmost concern when first using essential oils on your dog (unless rapid, lifesaving intervention with essential oils is required). There are 220 million olfactory receptors within a dog's nasal cavity, so a dog's sense of smell is infinitely stronger than a human's. Therefore, it is imperative to start slow so as not to overwhelm the dog. Introduce one oil at a time, using only one drop, unless the situation calls for more to produce the desired result.

Essential oils may be petted, applied neat or through a carrier oil, administered internally, misted via spray bottle, or diffused. Dilution of some essential oils may be beneficial as you determine your dog's sensitivity.

Diffusion of essential oils may be done through water diffusion. Adding 1-4 drops of a chosen essential oil to a water diffuser and diffusing in an open area is a good starting point. Allow the dog to roam freely (if possible) in the room in which the diffuser is running. This allows the dog the choice and allows the dog to be comfortable.

Never lock your pet in a room without a fresh air source. Some animals are more sensitive to oils and scents than others, so closely monitor while diffusing. Under careful supervision, diffusion can also be done in a closed room or a kennel.

Internal application may be done by adding essential oils to drinking water, inserting them directly into the mouth, putting them in a vegetable capsule, or adding them to food.

When administering essential oils through water, be sure to use a ceramic or stainless steel bowl, while offering a second water bowl without essential oils added, thus allowing the dog to have a choice.

Not all dogs will appreciate the adding of essential oils to their food. The caregivers will need to determine their own dog's needs.

Administration of essential oils via capsules is the easiest route of administration for dogs. Start by adding V-6 Vegetable Oil Complex to the capsules along with the chosen essential oils.

Two common questions are how much? and how often?

Each dog is unique in body chemistry and may react differently to each essential oil. A common-sense approach is the best answer, while noting reactions and keeping detailed notes.

Application may be once daily, once a week, or even several times daily. Determination will come through careful observation of your own dog's response. One drop may suffice in the beginning as you determine your dog's sensitivity level and individual response.

Regular health checks by a qualified animal professional should be performed at least annually and preferably semi-annually. Most dogs, because of their strong instinct to survive, will not show signs of disease or illness until they are very sick. Symptoms such as a dry, brittle coat; drinking more or less water than normal; urinating frequently or abnormal stools; abnormal weight gain or loss; refusal to eat; high temperatures; vomiting; white gums; and lethargy are all signs that your dog may be ill.

Offering your dog plenty of exercise is a must! Dogs thrive on companionship, exercise, and using their minds; whether through solving problems, training exercises, or environmental enrichment, all help to decrease boredom and stress. All dogs are pack animals and do best with structure and companionship to feel secure and ultimately exhibit healthy behavior.

Raindrop Technique for Dogs

Raindrop oils for dogs:

- Oregano
- Thyme
- Basil
- Marjoram
- Cypress
- Wintergreen
- Aroma Siez
- Peppermint
- Ortho Ease Massage Oil
- V-6 Vegetable Oil Complex (optional as needed)

Raindrop Technique has become a very common and regular treatment. It is a wonderful application for any animal. It can be a very simplified version of the application used for humans. Just use your common sense—smaller amounts of oil and much shorter time for most animals. Raindrop is used extensively on horses.

Anyone can apply the oils in the traditional Raindrop fashion and have success. The oils start working immediately upon application, and animals (and humans) will begin to feel the difference.

With dogs, the Raindrop oils are applied one at a time up the spine, dripping from approximately 6 inches above the back. For some smaller animals, the oils need to be diluted with V-6 before applying. For dogs generally under 20 pounds (9 kg), approximately 1-3 drops of each oil are applied. For dogs 20-50 pounds (9-23 kg), approximately 3-6 drops of each oil are applied. For dogs over 50 pounds (23 kg), you can generally use between 6-10 drops of each oil.

The sequence of oil application is generally Oregano, Thyme, Basil, Marjoram, Cypress, Wintergreen, Aroma Siez, Peppermint, and Ortho Ease Massage Oil. After each oil is dropped on the spine, stroke it up the back from the tail to the head. For this short version of the Raindrop Technique, the length of the strokes is not critical. Just lightly stroke or feather the oils on the animal two or three times. Just getting the oils on will stimulate circulation and overall response.

Use V-6 after applying Oregano and Thyme to avoid any discomfort or overstimulation. Use V-6 at any time when applying the oils if the pet becomes uncomfortable or agitated. Don't worry about the fur because it is a good conduit for the oils to the skin. If needed, you can apply V-6 first if you are working with an extremely sensitive animal.

Note: Applying V-6 first may dilute the oils and possibly the effectiveness of the technique. Apply V-6 and then feather the oils on top or even massage them into the skin. After all of the essential oils have been stroked in, you may work Vita Flex points at the end, which is a good way to finish.

If skin irritation occurs, just stop the application and massage in more V-6. It is amazing how fast it works, and the animal will calm right down. The irritation may come from the onset of a detoxification, which can be countered by inhaling various calming oils such as Peace & Calming, Lavender, RutaVaLa Roll-On, or even Stress Away.

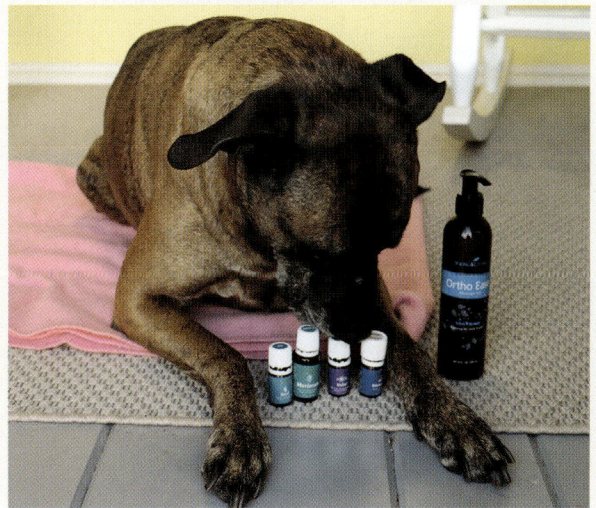

Dog (Canine) Quick Reference Guide

Bacterial

Single: Angelica, Bergamot, Black Pepper, Cedarwood, Cistus, Clove, Cinnamon Bark, Eucalyptus Blue, Eucalyptus Globulus, Eucalyptus Radiata, Geranium, Ginger, Hong Kuai, Hyssop, Laurus Nobilis, Lavender, Lemon, Lemongrass, Lemon Myrtle, Melaleuca Ericifolia, Melaleuca Quinquenervia, Mountain Savory, Myrrh, Myrtle, Nutmeg, Oregano, Palmarosa, Patchouli, Peppermint, Petitgrain, Ravintsara, Rosemary, Tea Tree, Thyme, Wintergreen, Xiang Mao

Blend: Abundance, Australian Blue, Breathe Again Roll-On, Christmas Spirit, DiGize, Egyptian Gold, En-R-Gee, Exodus II, ImmuPower, Infect Away, Longevity, M-Grain, Melrose, Mendwell, PuriClean, Purification, Raven, R.C., Relieve It, T-Away, The Gift, Thieves

Digestive

Single: Black Pepper, Cardamom, Cistus, Clove, Copaiba, Cypress, Dill, Fennel, Ginger, Grapefruit, Helichrysum, Lemon, Ocotea, Patchouli, Peppermint, Spearmint, Tarragon, Tea Tree

Blend: AromaEase, Citrus Fresh, DiGize, Egyptian Gold, En-R-Gee, EndoFlex, Gentle Baby, ImmuPower, Melrose, ParaGize, Purification, Release, Transformation

Fungal

Single: Angelica, Basil, Bergamot, Black Pepper, Blue Cypress, Cinnamon Bark, Citronella, Clove, Dorado Azul, Eucalyptus Blue, Eucalyptus Globulus, Eucalyptus Radiata, Fennel, Geranium, German Chamomile, Ginger, Goldenrod, Hong Kuai, Hyssop, Juniper, Lemongrass, Melaleuca Quinquenervia, Melissa, Mountain Savory, Myrrh, Myrtle, Ocotea, Oregano, Palmarosa, Palo Santo, Patchouli, Peppermint, Rosemary, Sage, Thyme

Blend: Abundance, AromaEase, Australian Blue, Clarity, DiGize, Egyptian Gold, En-R-Gee, Exodus II, Gathering, GLF, Gratitude, ImmuPower, Infect Away, JuvaCleanse, JuvaFlex, Longevity, M-Grain, Melrose, Mendwell, PuriClean, Purification, Raven, R.C., Relieve It, The Gift, Thieves

Liver

Single: Blue Tansy, Carrot Seed, Celery Seed, Cistus, Clove, Copaiba, Fennel, German Chamomile, Grapefruit, Helichrysum, Hyssop, Ledum, Lemongrass, Roman Chamomile, Rosemary

Blend: DiGize, GLF, ImmuPower, JuvaCleanse, JuvaFlex

Mycoplasma

Single: Basil, Blue Cypress, Blue Tansy, Clove, Copaiba, Cinnamon Bark, Cypress, Frankincense, Helichrysum, Hong Kuai, Hyssop, Melaleuca Quinquenervia, Mountain Savory, Oregano, Ravintsara, Sacred Frankincense, Thyme

Blend: DiGize, Egyptian Gold, Exodus II, Longevity, The Gift

Respiratory

Single: Basil, Blue Cypress, Cedarwood, Copaiba, Dorado Azul, Eucalyptus Blue, Eucalyptus Globulus, Eucalyptus Radiata, Frankincense, German Chamomile, Helichrysum, Hinoki, Hong Kuai, Hyssop, Idaho Balsam Fir, Idaho Blue Spruce, Lavender, Lemon Myrtle, Melaleuca Ericifolia, Melaleuca Quinquenervia, Melissa, Myrtle, Northern Lights Black Spruce, Ocotea, Oregano, Palo Santo, Peppermint, Ravintsara, Roman Chamomile, Sacred Frankincense, Sacred Mountain, Tea Tree, Wintergreen, Xiang Mao

Blend: Aroma Siez, Believe, Breathe Again Roll-On, Christmas Spirit, Clarity, Deep Relief Roll-On, Egyptian Gold, En-R-Gee, Evergreen Essence, Exodus II, Forgiveness, Gratitude, Hope, Humility, ImmuPower, Infect Away, Live with Passion, Longevity, M-Grain, Melrose, Mendwell, PanAway, ParaGize, Present Time, PuriClean, Raven, R.C., Relieve It, Stress Away, T-Away, The Gift, Thieves, Transformation, Trauma Life

Dog (Canine) Quick Reference Guide

Skin

Single: Basil, Blue Cypress, Cistus, Citronella, Clary Sage, Clove, Copaiba, Cypress, Dorado Azul, Frankincense, Geranium, German Chamomile, Helichrysum, Hinoki, Hyssop, Idaho Balsam Fir, Idaho Blue Spruce, Jasmine, Juniper, Lavender, Marjoram, Melaleuca Ericifolia, Melaleuca Quinquenervia, Melissa, Myrrh, Ocotea, Palmarosa, Palo Santo, Patchouli, Roman Chamomile, Royal Hawaiian Sandalwood, Sacred Frankincense, Sacred Sandalwood, Tea Tree, Vetiver, Ylang Ylang

Blend: Aroma Life, Australian Blue, Believe, Egyptian Gold, Gentle Baby, Harmony, Highest Potential, Infect Away, Melrose, Mendwell, ParaGize, PuriClean, Purification, Release, RutaVaLa, Sensation, T-Away, The Gift, Thieves, Valor

Viral

Single: Basil, Bergamot, Black Pepper, Blue Cypress, Breathe Again Roll-On, Cedarwood, Cistus, Citronella, Clove, Coriander, Cypress, Dorado Azul, Eucalyptus Blue, Eucalyptus Globulus, Eucalyptus Radiata, Fennel, Frankincense, Geranium, Hong Kuai, Hyssop, Juniper, Laurus Nobilis, Lemon, Lemongrass, Lemon Myrtle, Melaleuca Ericifolia, Melaleuca Quinquenervia, Melissa, Mountain Savory, Myrrh, Myrtle, Neroli, Ocotea, Oregano, Peppermint, Ravintsara, Rosemary, Sacred Frankincense, Tea Tree, Thyme, Xiang Mao

Blend: Abundance, Australian Blue, Christmas Spirit, Cinnamon Bark, Clarity, Egyptian Gold, Exodus II, Gathering, Hinoki, ImmuPower, Infect Away, Longevity, M-Grain, Melrose, Mendwell, ParaGize, PuriClean, Purification, Raven, R.C., RepelAroma, Relieve It, The Gift, Thieves

Worms

Single: Black Pepper, Blue Tansy, Clove, Fennel, Hong Kuai, Hyssop, Juniper, Lemongrass, Melaleuca Ericifolia, Melaleuca Quinquenervia, Ocotea, Patchouli, Peppermint, Spearmint, Tarragon, Tea Tree

Blend: AromaEase, Australian Blue, DiGize, Infect Away, Melrose, ParaGize, Purification

Supplement Guidelines for Dogs

Dosage amounts for canines can vary depending on many factors, including the health of your pets. When first introducing supplements to your pets, be sure to monitor their overall health to account for any reactions they may have.

Many protocols for each ailment that you'll find in this chapter will have specific guidelines on dosages when using supplements. When no specific dosage guideline is mentioned, you can refer to this section for general guidelines.

Allerzyme:	1 per 10 lbs. (12 daily max)
Digest & Cleanse:	1 per 10 lbs. (6 daily max)
Essentialzyme:	½ per 10 lbs. 1 time daily
Essentialzymes-4:	1 of each 1 time daily per 50 lbs.
Inner Defense:	1, 1 or more times daily
Life 9:	1, 1 or more times daily
Longevity Softgels:	1 per 10 lbs. (4 daily max)
MindWise:	1 oz. 1 time daily up to 50 lbs.
Mineral Essence:	1 dropperful per 10 lbs. (6 dropperfuls max)
MultiGreens:	1 per 10 lbs. (4 daily max)
NingXia Red:	1-2 oz. 2 times daily (depending upon severity)
OmegaGize³:	1 per 10 lbs. 2 times daily (12 daily max)
ParaFree:	1 per 10 lbs. (6 daily max)
Rehemogen:	1 dropperful 4 times daily per 50 lbs.
Sulfurzyme:	1 per 10 lbs. 2 times daily
Super B:	1, 1 time daily per 50 lbs.

Sled Dog Champions and Young Living Essential Oils

Mitch Seavey has run the Iditarod Trail Sled Dog Race over 20 times. One could say that mushing is in his blood. He learned to mush as a small child and helped his father prepare for the very first Iditarod Race in 1973.

Mitch ran the race himself for the first time in 1982 and then took a hiatus to raise four sons with his wife Janine. In 1995 he returned to racing and has run every Iditarod Race since, amassing a record of more than 15 top ten finishes to date, including championships in 2004, 2013, and 2017. He is the oldest musher to win at the age of 57, surpassing the record of being the oldest to win at age 53 in 2013. He is also champion of many other long distance sled dog races and travels over 5,000 miles per year by dog team.

The family tradition continues, as all four of the Seavey boys have raced sled dogs, including third son Dallas, who is also a multiple champion of the Iditarod, winning in 2012, 2014, 2015, and 2016, becoming the youngest winner.

The Seavey family owns and operates Seavey's Ididaride Sled Dog Tours in Seward, Alaska, and maintains a permanent residence and kennel in nearby Sterling.

Mitch is widely recognized as a true "dog man," with the rare ability to produce and train the best sled dogs in the world. His deep and innate understanding of his canine companions allows them to race together to their fullest potential.

A Musher's View

As a long-distance dog musher and Iditarod Race Champion, I have the pleasure of spending hours, days, and even weeks at a time on the trail with my dog team, my canine companions, enjoying the beauty of the great outdoors, traveling great distances, in awe and wonderment at their speed and power—while staring at dog rumps.

You've heard the saying "Unless you're the lead dog, the scenery never changes." It's even more true for the musher—the team member bringing up the uh, rear, so to speak.

Sled dogs are the best athletes in the world. Long and lean at 50-60 pounds, they have proportionally larger hearts than other mammals. Their oxygen uptake or VO2 max is 300 ml/kg/min, nearly double a race horse and triple the highest values recorded for a human. They can also efficiently digest 12,000 calories a day and have a unique metabolic system that allows them to convert those calories into extreme, prolonged exercise. They have a work ethic and pack mentality, which makes them able to travel great distances with their companions. I am honored to be one of those companions. They seem okay with me tagging along, too, as long as I bring lunch.

Sled dogs can run more than 120 miles a day and never seem to tire. Mile after mile, uphill and down, through howling winds, snow drifts, glaring ice, and open water—they conquer it all, with only occasional breaks to rest, eat, drink, and pee on bushes. The greatest human athletes pale in comparison.

Even with their super-canine abilities, running hard for 1,000 miles in the Iditarod Race can require support. Race drug rules are strict, so for many years I have explored natural ways to help our dogs maximize their performance.

I should confess right here that I am just a musher. Not a doctor, not a scientist, not a veterinarian. Just a musher. I have spent several decades with sled dogs, however, trying to understand what they are telling me.

You know how we humans sometimes think we hear something, but we're not sure what we heard, until we confirm it by sight? Once we lay eyes on the source, we're sure what it is. Seeing is our confirming sense. We've all said, "I'll believe it when I see it."

I've spent a lot of time around moose. I can walk right up to a herd of moose in plain sight as long as I make moose noises. They aren't sure what they are seeing, but if I grunt and thrash the brush and make moose noises, they are convinced I'm a moose. Hearing is their confirming sense. They believe it when they hear it.

A dog's confirming sense is that of smell. They experience their world largely through scent. Imagine all the stimuli presented to dogs just walking down the street. They are constantly sniffing. Sniff over here, sniff over there, stop and sniff, yank your arm nearly out of the socket to sniff the other dog. A dog park? Forget it! It's doggy Facebook. No wonder essential oils are so effective for dogs.

There are other remedies that aren't banned substances for race dogs that can be effective, but I find them difficult to use in our subzero environment, hit-or-miss on effectiveness, and too complicated. The powders, the little pills, the solutions; oops, I spilled them all in the snow. Remember, I'm just a musher.

I have heard Gary Young admonish, "Just open the bottle!" and that I can understand (let's see, lefty-loosey…). And with a sense of smell hundreds of times stronger than mine, the dogs start to benefit as soon as I complete that first step.

For many years, I have used Wintergreen essential oil on my dogs for sprains, muscle soreness and inflammation. I was introduced to essential oils by a friend and hometown holistic healer who told me to use only Young Living essential oils. I followed orders, mostly.

For the carpus (wrist) area, we use the oil under vapor-barrier film and a neoprene wrap. This creates a sweat with heat, and the oils are absorbed readily. For shoulders—triceps, biceps, tendons, and pectorals—we apply the oil twice daily under a wind-blocker fleece shoulder coat. Using these methods, we can usually heal a dog in several days at rest and even while racing.

As you may imagine, care of a large kennel of sled dogs can be expensive. Ever the "good steward," I once tried to save money with an "oil of wintergreen" that I had purchased in bulk online. It was cheap, but it did precisely nothing to help my dogs. It also had one other notable feature: wherever it was applied on the dog, it made the hair fall out! So there stood my dog after removing the wrist wraps and shoulder coat—bare shoulders, furry legs, bare wrists, and furry feet—looking like an embarrassed poodle. Even as a musher, I caught on to the fact that purity in essential oils is just as important for animals as for people.

Foot care is important for sled dogs. Each doggy foot hits the snow two million times in 1,000 miles. Times that by four feet per dog, times 16 dogs. Plus 3,000 miles in prerace training. That equals, let's see…, add the…, carry the four…, uh…, a lot. That's what it equals, a lot of dog tracks.

The most common foot problem is cracks in the skin between the toes, referred to by mushers simply as splits. Veterinarians call them "interdigital fissures," for some reason. Occasionally, the pads can also get worn or cut from many miles and abrasive snow, so mushers usually use cloth booties to protect the feet from adverse trail conditions.

There are precisely hundreds of foot remedies in the mushing world. I've used them all: Zinc Oxide Ointment, A and D Ointment, Corona Ointment, Triple Antibiotic Ointment, Bag Balm, Gold Bond, Gold Bond with Sulphur, Dr. Nelson's Pink Ointment, Dr. Schmidt's Blue Ointment, Furacin, Tuff Foot, Horseman's Dream, Musher's Secret, Ophir Gold Paw Cream, Copper Tox, Betadine, Silvadene, Povidine, bear grease, and moose drool. There, that's all of them.

For several years now the foot remedy I have used consistently is Young Living Tea Tree oil in a carrier. I put it in a small squeeze bottle and keep it in an inside pocket to keep it thawed. I apply it at least once a day during racing and hard training. The incidence of splits in my team is almost nonexistent. The oil soothes and softens the feet, and the Tea Tree is a topical and systemic antimicrobial (hah—a bit of vet talk there!). So, not only are my dogs' feet free from splits and cracks, they are free from viral, bacterial, and fungal infections. And here's the real bonus—so is the whole dog! That Tea Tree oil just sneaks right in there through the hair and follicles, and pretty soon it's doing its Tea Tree thing on the inside of the dog as well as on the outside!

So, I got a little excited there, but bear with me. Remember the part about "the scenery never changes"? Okay, there is one serious problem encountered by sled dogs running 120 miles and digesting 12,000 calories on the same day. Vets call it irritable bowel syndrome.

Whatever. I can't say here what mushers call it. It's basically a bacterial overgrowth or infection that takes advantage of inflammation in the wall of the large intestine caused by a lot of food byproduct in there while the dog is running. The result is diarrhea, straining to poop, and sometimes blood. When it's bad, several dogs may be struggling in the team at the same time. Not a happy sight, especially from behind. Imagine my excitement when I finally pieced together the fact that my Tea Tree foot ointment was combating the bad bacteria and actually helping prevent the…, um, irritable bowel syndrome. Not even Musher's Secret can do that! Lo and behold, the scenery can change.

Sled dogs are a little more closely related to their canine cousins such as wolves and coyotes than most other domestic dogs. As such, occasionally one may behave more like a wild animal than say your Golden Retriever. They try to avoid people, try not to be caught if loose, and would rather be left alone than handled. Almost without exception, however, they are perfectly content in the team with their mates. That's their comfort zone.

One such dog I had was a female named Mugsy. She was really shy, to the point of not eating when people were around and being really difficult about her feet. Once harnessed with the other dogs, she performed wonderfully and was a real asset to the team. I tried her in preliminary races; but at checkpoints, she refused to eat or sleep when bystanders or officials were present, staying on alert until we left the rest stop and returned to the wilderness. Under this added stress, try as she might, she was unable to make the Iditarod team, much less complete 1,000 miles. It seemed doubly sad to me, since her greatest happiness and peace of mind came on the trail with her comrades.

My brother also had a shy dog who was making strides in socialization—until he was scared half to death by a brown bear chasing him under the house. Bro was advised by that same hometown healer I mentioned earlier to try Geranium essential oil to calm his dog down enough to be handled. My brother claimed it worked wonders, and the pooch was eating out of his hand again. Being at least smart enough to imitate success, I tried Geranium oil on my girl Mugsy. I just put it on all four feet, on her ears, and on her nose for good measure.

I noticed right away that she actually seemed to like me messing with her feet when this stuff was involved. She even came toward me when she smelled the Geranium oil and allowed me to put it on her ears. This marked a big change in our relationship. As long as the Geranium oil was involved, my shy dog liked my attention. What a victory! So I just made a habit of putting the oil on my gloves whenever I worked with the dogs, and Mugsy was okay. She finished the Iditarod with me that winter and became one of the foundational breeding females in the kennel. Good on ya', Mugsy!

My wife, Janine, has heard me tell about Mugsy and the Geranium essential oil many times. She has this ugly little house dog which, for some inexplicable reason, everyone loves. He is talented, though, because he can snore and shed at the same time. My wife keeps a neat and clean house, so she was constantly vacuuming up dog hair, which would be okay, and I might even help, but it terrified the dog; so you know. . . . He would react to that vacuum cleaner like my brother's dog did to the bear.

I came home from a long mushing trip; and as I stumbled into the house with my arms full of gear, I could not figure out what I was seeing. The dog was flat on his back, motionless, with his legs splayed out to the sides. Yup, dead, for sure. Then I realized my wife must have killed him, for she was obviously trying to vacuum up the evidence.

"Strange behavior, Honey, and stranger still—the empty Young Living bottle on the floor. Oh, you had second thoughts and tried to revive him? Frankincense, I'll bet." Nope. Geranium.

He still sheds, but now Janine just "anointeth his head with oil" and vacuums the entire dog before the hair makes it into my soup.

A couple of years ago, just before the start of the Iditarod Race, I asked Janine and some friends at Young Living to come up with a blend for my dogs to enhance their drive and sense of invincibility. The essentials oils of Valor, Copaiba, and White Angelica were combined to make what we call the Champion Blend. I put it in a spray mister or a roll-top bottle and apply it mostly on the dogs' heads but sometimes up and down their spine. They are really attracted to it under racing conditions. I think the Champion Blend, along with Shutran and En-R-Gee, enhances the dogs' mental outlook and positive attitude when under stress. I don't know what else it does, because I'm just a musher. If my lesson from the Tea Tree foot ointment carries over, I'll bet a lot of other good stuff is happening inside the dogs, too.

After the 2014 Iditarod Race, Young Living made a short video about the team and our use of their products. Eager to show off my Champion Blend, which had been such an asset during the race that year, I pulled out a bottle and presented it to my lead dog Tanner, on camera. His reaction surprised me. Rather than press his nose into my hand with the oil and rub all over it, as he had during the race, he pulled back and shied away. No matter how

much I coaxed, his attitude was lukewarm at best. This was the same blend the whole team, and myself for that matter, had rallied around during the difficult Iditarod Race. Now, after a couple of weeks of rest, the dogs were turning up their noses at it.

Then I remembered the rest of Mugsy's story. I said I put Geranium oil on my gloves, and my shy dog loved it, right? Well, the reaction was not universal. Friendly dogs, who were usually happy to see me, pulled back a bit at the smell on my gloves. Not extreme or even negative, but definitely not the same reaction as the shy dog, Mugsy. Now, the same dogs who loved the Champion Blend when under stress were not excited about it when rested. I think we can tell something about which oils are best for dogs at a given time by their reaction to them.

Early in 2014, I became a Young Living Brand Ambassador, and our interest and involvement in essential oils redoubled. I began researching ways to incorporate more oils into our racing program. I added Lemongrass oil to the Wintergreen to help with tendon and ligament inflammation. When I considered adding Peppermint oil as well, Janine suggested that I actually look at the product catalog to see what was already available in a sports blend. Lo and behold, Ortho Sport Massage Oil contains Wintergreen, Peppermint, and Lemongrass oils, along with several others that might be useful, even though I hadn't thought of them myself. I began using Ortho Sport under therapeutic wraps, with great success.

Talon is a big, happy dog who has been on my main racing team for several years. He is a hard worker and a great eater who maintains himself well; but, since he isn't the brightest bulb in the pack, he works best in the wheel position, at the back of the team, right in front of the sled. Shortly before the 2015 Iditarod race, he got into a squabble with his mate Gnarly and got bit on the shoulder. Now, we rarely have fights between our dogs; but when it happens, it only takes a second for an injury to occur. This bite didn't look bad, only a couple of small punctures; but there seemed to be serious bruising to Talon's triceps muscle. At least he let on like there was. Since we were on the last big training trip of the season before the Iditarod Race, I decided to let Talon run with the injury and see how he did.

The risk of running with this type of injury is that discomfort can develop in another limb due to compensating. Sure enough, Talon got a sore left wrist to go with his sore right shoulder. We regularly wrapped his wrist and shoulder with Ortho Sport Massage Oil and saw improvement, but he was questionable for the big race. Then, the night before the start, tethered in temporary quarters, Talon got bit again, this time on his right front foot. Again, he had only a couple of small punctures but a badly swollen toe. Normally, that would have put him out for sure, and a replacement would have run. Come to think of it, his potential replacement was the dog that bit him! Hmm.

As we did final dog checks and harnessed the team for the start that morning, Talon was in very high spirits, romping and playing with his buddies. I could see a limp due to his latest injury but decided he didn't seem too distressed to run, and this was a good opportunity to trust this product and see the results. There was obviously no doubt in Talon's mind that he was going! Worst case, I could always send him home from a checkpoint.

I applied Ortho Sport twice daily to the triceps and wrist at rest stops and under the bootie on his toe while running. By the time we were 300 miles into the race, the shoulder and foot were causing him no discomfort, and the wrist had no swelling and was nearly pain free. I continued to wrap the wrist for another couple of days, as a precaution. This is a pretty big deal to me and Talon. These weren't major injuries but they improved—and went away altogether—while running the Iditarod Race. That's awesome, for a musher and a sled dog.

As I said, I used Ortho Sport regularly during the early part of that race. I kept two bottles in my inner pockets to keep them thawed. This product actually pours at quite low temperatures; but, in the -40°F we experienced in the 2015 Iditarod, I took no chances.

I thought it odd that I got so many comments from folks at the checkpoints about the smell of the essential oils. I suppose the Young Living logos on my gear gave them a hint.

"Boy," the checker would say, "I can sure smell those essential oils. What is that, Wintergreen?"

It surprised me because the oils are usually absorbed quickly, and the odor doesn't remain for a long time. Then I realized the backup bottle of Ortho Sport in my other pocket was leaking. A full 8 fluid ounces had been gradually introduced into my clothing over a period of a couple of days, and I had been diffusing essential oils throughout the wilderness and villages of interior Alaska. Well, as Gary Young has said, "Just open the bottle."

My own team has no trouble identifying me by the scent of essential oils. Perhaps a flight of fancy here, but I think that's important. Just like the sight of a company logo, school colors, or a national flag can have deep meaning for people, a scent can be a rallying point for dogs.

"Oh, say can you smell by the dawn's early light. . . ?"

As much as I love my Tea Tree oil foot ointment, I have now replaced it. As with my massage liniment, I had begun looking at what I could add to the Tea Tree oil to improve it as a foot ointment. I hadn't been at it all that long when, all by myself, I thought of checking the Product Guide to see what was already available. When I read the ingredient list for Animal Scents Ointment, I thought it might be the ticket. And besides, when I saw the label with those precious little animal footprints on it, I just fell in love!

Tea Tree oil is one of the ingredients, along with several other essential oils with impressive names; so I felt good about that. Because of its heavier, thicker base, the Animal Scents stays on the dogs' feet longer under booties and seems to keep them softer and the skin more hydrated. I used Animal Scents Ointment almost exclusively on my dogs' feet for the 2015 season and Iditarod Race and had the best results I've ever had for strong, healthy feet. I use it on my own hands and face regularly for dry skin and frostbite, though it's a bit "vapory" near the eyes.

Moose are my favorite wild critters. They are magnificent animals, perfectly suited to their environment. I like them as neighbors and as part of the scenery here in Alaska. I admit, also, that if it weren't for moose and caribou, my family would be hard-pressed to include red meat in our diet.

Moose have not received a passing grade in the required Neighborly Behavior class, however, nor have they completed anger management training. My petite bride has, on occasion, taken it upon herself to help with their education. She claims to have once driven a 1,200-pound moose from her garden with a 4-ounce can of mushrooms. Really? A can of mushrooms? Did she pour the stuff out on the plants to repel the moose? Did she make a noisy scarecrow from the empty can? No. Janine claims she stepped out on the deck and, with a multi-million-dollar-a-year-contract-major-league-style throw, clocked that old cow moose upside the head with a 4-ounce can of mushrooms. The cow moose staggered. She swayed. She stumbled. She asked for an aspirin and off she went, never to return again.

I don't believe her to this day. The moose I have encountered on the trail with the dog team would not be impressed by a can of mushrooms. I have fired real guns in the air, with real bullets, to scare them away; and the moose barely noticed. A 4-ounce can of mushrooms?

Late in the winter when snow is deep and browse is scarce, moose can be in a near-starvation mode. When we encounter them with a dog team, they often refuse to leave the trail. They doubtless view a team of sled dogs charging up the trail at them with the same fondness as a pack of wolves plotting to eat them. The resulting flurry of flying hoofs, fur, and fangs usually favors the moose, which outweighs an entire team of dogs by double.

Eagle, one of my race dogs, was moose-kicked in such an encounter and was injured in his lower back. We used Wintergreen oil for bruising and inflammation and saw improvement, but there was a lingering problem affecting his hind leg. I decided there may be some nerve damage involved. Please be reminded that our sufferer was consigned to the sole care of a simple musher, not a doctor or a scientist.

Now if I were wise, what would I use to help our brave Eagle? Well, I have it on good authority that the Wise Men had gold, Frankincense, and Myrrh.

"Well, Eagle, old buddy, gold is out of the question; so you can just forget about that right now. Have you seen that vet office? No, I guess you haven't, but that place is like the Taj Mahal. Where do you think they get all the money for that fancy stuff, eh, Eagle? Well, not from us."

As for Myrrh, I actually didn't know what it was unless it had something to do with those awkward-looking birds we see in the summer from the fishing boat.

So that left Frankincense, and I actually had some of that around. After about four days of massaging Frankincense essential oil into Eagle's lower back and thigh, his leg became weight bearing again. We continued with Frankincense and as we trotted him on a leash daily, the limp vanished. He began to use his leg normally and resumed training.

Two months later, and shortly after finishing the 1,000-mile Iditarod Race, Eagle was one of ten dogs I used in the 2008 centennial running of the All Alaska Sweepstakes Sled Dog Race. It was a 408-mile winner-take-all sled dog race, with the largest first-place prize in dog sledding history and the largest sports prize ever awarded in the State of Alaska.

Eagle didn't care about that. He was just overflowing with natural joy and enthusiasm as he ran that race with his buddies, often in the lead position. His run-in with Mamma Moose was but a distant memory.

It seemed pointless to tell Eagle, but we did win that race.

Eagle was a special dog to our family and especially to our son Conway. He and Eagle grew up together. Inseparable, they enjoyed countless adventures in our vast wilderness back yard. Untethered at home after a long run, hike, or bike trip, Eagle would take up his station on

the back porch and wait faithfully, for hours if necessary, for Conway to come back out and feed him, return him to his dog house, or resume the adventure.

On one such adventure, a terrible fall from a cliff on Mount Marathon in Seward, Alaska, proved disastrous for Eagle. Conway carried him down the mountain and got him to that veterinarian with the fancy offices, nice building, and fancy paintings. Eagle had a broken back and pelvis and was put down.

Okay, now stop it. It's a dog. Not your child.

Still, I wonder if I had been equipped at that time with the experience and knowledge of what these amazing pure essential oils can do for all of us, including our dogs, could Eagle have come back and walked again? Run? Even raced? I have seen amazing things with essential oils. Could Eagle's story have ended differently?

So these are a few of the experiences I've had with my sled dogs and essential oils. I'm sure there are more effective oils to use in certain situations than what this musher knows about, and I'm committed to learning as much as I can.

But like God, their Creator, essential oils don't judge me for my knowledge or lack thereof. They honor my intent.

Gary Young, founder of Young Living Essential Oils, understands that arrangement. "Just open the bottle," says he.

— Mitch Seavey
Young Living Brand Ambassador
Iditarod Trail Sled Dog Race
Grand Champion 2004, 2013, 2017

Dog (Canine) Conditions

Abscess

An abscess is a pus-filled infection pocket. It may occur on any part of the body from the mouth to the foot. Usually it follows a mild injury or stress-related issue to the tissue, which then results in a secondary infection. It always requires immediate professional veterinary attention. Abscesses often need medical intervention to open and drain the wound.

A diet free of grain, sugars, and processed preservatives may help prevent abscesses.

Always talk with your veterinarian about the cause, preventing complications, and what treatments are best for your animal.

Recommendations

Singles: Copaiba, Lavender, Ginger, Lemongrass, Clove, Oregano, Thyme, Rosemary, Ocotea, Tea Tree, Melaleuca Ericifolia, Mountain Savory, Myrrh, Black Pepper, Ravintsara, Lemon, Idaho Balsam Fir, Orange, Sacred Frankincense, Idaho Blue Spruce, Northern Lights Black Spruce

Blends: Thieves, Melrose, Exodus II, Purification, Raven, Longevity, Stress Away, Peace & Calming, DiGize

Nutritionals: Sulfurzyme, NingXia Red, Inner Defense, LavaDerm, Life 9, Detoxzyme, ParaFree, Digest & Cleanse, Mineral Essence, MultiGreens, Longevity Softgels

Additional: Thieves Household Cleaner, Animal Scents Ointment

Application and Usage

Topical: Apply any chosen single or blend combination neat, directly on the abscess. For sensitive animals, try a hot compress with Epsom salts mixed with 2 drops each of Thieves, Lavender, and Melrose. Once the abscess has opened, cleanse the area with diluted Thieves Household Cleaner and then reapply selected oils and layer with Animal Scents Ointment.

Ingestion & Oral: Administer Sulfurzyme: 1, 2 times daily per 10 lbs.; Inner Defense: 1, 1 or more times daily; Life 9: 1, 2 times daily per 50 lbs.; NingXia Red: 1-2 oz. 2 times daily (depending on severity); Mineral Essence: 1 dropperful per 10 lbs. (6 max); MultiGreens: 1 per 10 lbs. (4 max); Longevity

Softgels: 1 per 10 lbs. (4 max); 1-2 drops orally of suggested oils from Vitality line, 1-3 times daily per 10 lbs.

Inhalation: Diffuse Thieves, Melrose, Purification, Stress Away, Peace & Calming, Idaho Balsam Fir, Orange, Sacred Frankincense, Idaho Blue Spruce, Northern Lights Black Spruce, Lavender—alternate as needed.

Other: If the dog is anxious and wants to lick/clean the area or must wear an e-collar, consult the section on anxiety.

Abuse (Trauma, PTSD)

Abuse in dogs can either be deliberate or unintentional through neglect. Whatever the reason, essential oils can have helpful effects when it comes to calming or bonding with a dog that has suffered abuse.

Be especially careful and slow when introducing new oils regarding the emotional health of a canine. Watch for signs of increased anxiety or discomfort when applying oils for the first time.

Recommendations

Singles: Idaho Blue Spruce, Copaiba, Roman Chamomile, Ylang Ylang, Cypress, Cedarwood, Lavender, Frankincense, Sacred Frankincense, German Chamomile, Idaho Balsam Fir, Neroli, Vetiver, Valerian, Geranium, Orange, Northern Lights Black Spruce, Hinoki

Blends: DiGize, T- Away, Trauma Life, Valor, Valor II, Peace & Calming, Peace & Calming II, Grounding, Release, Forgiveness, Sacred Mountain, Stress Away, Acceptance, Present Time, White Angelica, Inner Child, SARA, Harmony, Hope, Tranquil Roll-On, Transformation, Joy, Gratitude, Into the Future, RutaVaLa Roll-On, Freedom, Aroma Sleep, Divine Release, Feelings Kit

Nutritionals: OmegaGize[3], PowerGize, NingXia Red, Sulfurzyme, ImmuPro, MultiGreens, Longevity Softgels, Life 9, MightyZymes

Application and Usage

Topical: Apply any of above oils to tips of ears, crown of skull, base of skull, chest area, and along spine as needed.

Ingestion & Oral: Administer orally 1-2 drops of suggested oils from the Vitality line 1-3 times daily per 10 lbs. If the dog chooses, allow it to lick oil off your hands when applying topically.

Inhalation: Diffuse chosen oils, rotating throughout the day.

Other: Start by applying Valor to forehead and feet. Apply 2 drops of Forgiveness over the heart and over the abdomen. Follow with 2 drops of Release applied over the abdomen. Apply 1 drop of T-Away or Trauma Life to the tips of the ears. Finish with applying 2 drops White Angelica onto the spine. Feather in the oils, starting at the base of the spine and moving to the top. Apply Peace & Calming, Stress Away, Lavender, or Sacred Frankincense anytime to encourage calming.

Veterinarian Tips and Suggestions

For extreme cases of abuse, try the Freedom Release Collection.

For the first 2-4 weeks of treatment, apply:

- 1 drop Valor or Valor II 2 times daily over the heart
- 1 drop Aroma Sleep 2 times daily on the back of the neck
- 1 drop Freedom on the tops of the paws 2 times daily (if the dog allows paws to be touched; if not, place along spine)
- 1 drop Inner Harmony 2 times daily over the front paws

For the next 3-8 weeks of treatment, apply:

- 1 drop Valor or Valor II on stomach and chest area
- 1 drop Transformation over the front paws 2 times daily
- 1 drop Freedom on the tops of the paws (if the dog allows paws to be touched; if not, place along the spine 2 times daily)
- 1 drop Divine Release on the crown of the head 2 times daily
- 1 drop T.R. Care on the tips of the ears 2 times daily
- 1 drop Joy over the heart 2 times daily

Aggression (Territorial, Dog-to-Dog, Possessive, Protective, Fear, Defensive, Social, Frustration-Elicited, Redirected, Pain-Elicited, Predatory, Food, Sibling Rivalry)

Aggression is the most common and most serious issue that needs to be dealt with a Professional Pet Dog Trainer or Certified Behaviorist. Care must be taken to always manage the dog and to prevent harm from being caused to any person. Management may include using dog runs, crates, proper leashes (NOT flexi-leads), proper collars, and/or muzzles.

The root cause of the aggression needs to be addressed; use essential oils in tandem with a proper behavior modification program.

Recommendations

Singles: Angelica, Cedarwood, Lavender, Frankincense, Sacred Frankincense, German Chamomile, Idaho Balsam Fir, Neroli, Vetiver, Valerian, Orange, Cypress, Northern Lights Black Spruce, Hinoki, Idaho Blue Spruce, Roman Chamomile

Blends: T- Away, Trauma Life, Valor, Valor II, Peace & Calming, Peace & Calming II, Grounding, Release, Forgiveness, Stress Away, Acceptance, Present Time, White Angelica, Inner Child, SARA, Joy, Harmony, Highest Potential, Humility, Tranquil Roll-On, Gathering, Inner Child

Nutritionals: OmegaGize[3], Life 9, Mineral Essence, MindWise, NingXia Red, Essentialzyme, Essentialzymes-4

Applications and Usage

Topical: Apply any of above oils to tips of ears, crown of skull, base of skull, sternum, top of the paws, footpads, top of inner thigh, and along spine as needed. Also apply oils to inside ear flap, NOT into ear canal.

Ingestion & Oral: Administer orally 1-2 drops of suggested oils from the Vitality line 1-3 times daily per 10 lbs. If dog chooses, allow it to lick oil off your hands when applying topically.

Inhalation: Diffuse chosen oils, rotating throughout the day.

Other: If pain related, see section on pain. If abuse related, see "Other" section under Abuse.

Veterinarian Tips and Suggestions

Aggression

- Apply Valor to head, shoulders, and chest area, adding Inner Child when applying to chest area.

- Apply Grounding to the paws.

- Apply 2 drops Forgiveness over the heart and over the abdomen.

- Follow with 2 drops Release applied over the abdomen.

- Apply 1 drop of T-Away or Trauma Life applied to the tips and flaps of the ears.

- Finish by applying 2 drops White Angelica onto the spine.

- Feather in the oils, starting at base of spine and moving to the top.

Allergies

There are two types of allergic reactions. The first is long-term, not acute in nature. The second is acute (sudden onset), which usually requires prompt veterinary intervention.

Diet changes are required to solve most allergies (even if not a specific food allergy), since they are most often caused by a dog's diet. Consider a food that's free of all grain (wheat, soy, corn, etc.), eggs, and dairy.

Environment also plays a huge factor in allergies regarding canines. Fewer than 10 percent of dogs become sensitized to the environment and manifest respiratory reactions. Look for causes such as household cleaners, carpet sprays, furniture sprays, lawn fertilizers, scented candles, plug-in fresheners, laundry detergents, and fabric softeners (dog's bedding).

Also bear in mind that canines may have adverse allergic reactions to vaccines.

Allergies may begin when the dog is 6 months to 3 years old. Itching is the most typical sign and will affect the abdomen, feet, face, and ears. This may be accompanied by excessive licking, which may lead to secondary wounds, hair loss, and scabbing. Consult a veterinary health professional.

Recommendations

Singles: Lavender, Hinoki, Copaiba, Basil, Peppermint, Lemon, Helichrysum, Roman Chamomile, Frankincense, Melissa, Ocotea

Blends: ImmuPower, Aroma Siez, Aroma Life, Harmony, DiGize, ParaGize, R.C., Breathe Again Roll-On, Purification, The Gift

Nutritionals: OmegaGize[3], Sulfurzyme, NingXia Red, Allerzyme, ImmuPro, Life 9, Detoxzyme

Additional: Thieves Household Cleaner, Animal Scents Shampoo, Thieves Laundry Soap

Application and Usage

Topical: Apply as needed any oils neat listed above, ending with Animal Scents Ointment over the top. Use Animal Scents Shampoo as needed. Raindrop Technique: The allergic dog's immune system is already compromised, so start slowly and work methodically.

Ingestion & Oral: Administer 1-2 drops of suggested oils from Vitality line 1-3 times daily per 10 lbs.; Copaiba, DiGize, Basil: 2 drops each per 10 lbs. 2 times daily; Allerzyme: 2-6 and Life 9: 1-2, 1 time daily.

Inhalation: If dealing with seasonal respiratory allergies, diffuse any of the following: Lavender, Hinoki, Copaiba, Purification, R.C., and Lemon.

Other: Often allergic dogs are anxious and need calming—refer to anxiety section if needed. Always look at diet and change if needed. Bathe dog in Animal Scents Shampoo; let shampoo sit on coat/skin for 5 minutes. Then rinse very well. Bathe dog using diluted Thieves Household Cleaner as well. Use diluted Thieves Household Cleaner to clean environment and Thieves Laundry Soap for animal bedding.

Anemia

This is a low count of red blood cells, as measured by count or hemoglobin concentration. This can be due to either a medical condition (illness or pharmaceuticals) or diet.

Anemia is classified as regenerative or nonregenerative. In regenerative cases, the bone marrow responds with increased production. In nonregenerative cases, the bone marrow doesn't respond.

Signs depend on severity and duration, but they may include pale gums, low blood pressure, increased heart rate, jaundice, lethargy, weakness, pale foot pads, respiratory stress, and loss of appetite.

Anemia is most often the result of iron and nutritional deficiencies, renal failure, viruses, autoimmune disorder, or parasitic infection. Consult a veterinary health professional to confirm diagnosis, determine a plan of treatment, and prevent complications.

Recommendations

Singles: Frankincense, Fennel, Peppermint, Helichrysum, Roman Chamomile, Ginger, Geranium, Ocotea, Copaiba, Dorado Azul, Celery Seed, Carrot Seed, Cedarwood, Lemon, Sacred Frankincense

Blends: DiGize, ParaGize, JuvaFlex, JuvaCleanse, GLF, Purification, Stress Away, Release

Nutritionals: MultiGreens, NingXia Red, Super B, Mineral Essence, Rehemogen, Essentialzymes-4, Allerzyme, Sulfurzyme, MindWise, OmegaGize[3], Digest & Cleanse, Detoxzyme

Application and Usage

Topical: Apply any of the suggested oils to stomach and chest area.

Ingestion & Oral:

Specifically use JuvaCleanse, JuvaFlex, and Roman Chamomile: 7 drops each in 00 capsule per 50 lbs. 1 time daily; 1-2 drops orally of suggested oils from Vitality line 1-3 times daily per 10 lbs.

Also administer the following orally:

Rehemogen: 1-4 dropperfuls 2-4 times daily

Mineral Essence: 3-4 dropperfuls 2 times daily

Sulfurzyme: 2 per 20 lbs. 2 times daily

Digest & Cleanse: 1-4, 1 time daily

Inhalation: Diffuse Cedarwood, Lemon, Stress Away, or Sacred Frankincense.

Other: Make sure the diet is providing the dog's needed requirements. If the condition involves heart complications, see the heart section. To aid with diet, administer the following orally: 6-20 drops each Helichrysum, Copaiba, and JuvaCleanse 2 times daily. Add 1 Life 9 and 1 Detoxzyme per 20 lbs. daily. Apply Release, JuvaFlex, and DiGize topically to stomach area 2 times daily.

Anorexia

Dogs live to eat so if there is a loss of appetite, there is often an underlying medical condition. There are many reasons, physical and psychological, that will cause dogs to eat less or stop eating.

Vaccinations may cause a dog to lose its appetite temporarily.

If your dog is interested in your food but not his or her own, this is generally more of a behavioral issue.

Keep in mind that reduced appetite is one of the first signs of any number of serious conditions. If your dog doesn't seem interested in food, immediately consult a veterinary health professional, who will help you rule out serious, underlying causes. Always check for electrolyte balance.

Treat the root condition to fully treat the anorexia.

Recommendations

Singles: Sacred Frankincense, Ginger, Peppermint, Fennel, Mountain Savory, Copaiba, Cistus, Orange, Neroli

Blends: Valor, Highest Potential, DiGize, Release, Harmony, ParaGize, Inner Child, Trauma Life, Peace & Calming, Stress Away, Purification

Nutritionals: NingXia Red, ParaFree, Detoxzyme, Mineral Essence, Life 9, Inner Defense, Digest & Cleanse, Allerzyme

Application and Usage

Topical: Apply 1-3 drops each Peppermint, Neroli, Ginger, and DiGize on the lower chest and down the abdomen.

Ingestion & Oral: Administer NingXia Red: 2 oz. 2 times daily. DiGize, Copaiba, and Ginger: 3 drops in mouth 1-2 times daily. Also administer Life 9: 1 daily or Allerzyme: 1-4 daily.

Inhalation: Diffuse or pet on the dog Inner Child, Valor, Highest Potential.

Anxiety (Separation, Fear, Phobias/Sound)

Anxiety can be due to emotional trauma, predisposition from genetics, or poor digestive health.

Separation anxiety can be very difficult to treat and will need a specific behavior modification program that can be developed by a Certified Dog Trainer or Certified Behaviorist. Dogs suffering from separation anxiety can cause harm to themselves, so special care needs to be taken to keep the dog safe.

Veterinarian Tips and Suggestions

Canine Anxiety

Recipe #1

- Combine:
- 50 drops Lavender
- 35 drops Valor/Valor II
- 30 drops Stress Away or Peace & Calming
- 15 drops Patchouli
- 15 drops Vetiver
- 20 drops Valerian

Recipe #2

- Combine:
- 10 drops Lavender
- 5 drops Sacred Sandalwood or Royal Hawaiian Sandalwood
- 10 drops Roman Chamomile or German Chamomile
- 5 drops Geranium

With both recipes, apply as needed by petting onto the dog. Specific areas include tops of paws, stomach area, or by the ears (DO NOT allow oils into the ear canal.). Also try diffusing in the dog's area.

Recommendations

Singles: Cedarwood, Lavender, Frankincense, Sacred Frankincense, German Chamomile, Idaho Balsam Fir, Neroli, Vetiver, Valerian, Orange, Hinoki, Northern Lights Black Spruce, Patchouli, Roman Chamomile, Idaho Blue Spruce, Angelica, Palo Santo, Bergamot, Ylang Ylang, Geranium, Sacred Sandalwood, Royal Hawaiian Sandalwood

Blends: Shutran, Believe, Hope, T- Away, Trauma Life, Valor, Valor II, Peace & Calming, Peace & Calming II, Grounding, Release, Forgiveness, Stress Away, Acceptance, Present Time, Harmony, White Angelica, Inner Child, SARA, Tranquil Roll-On, RutaVaLa Roll-On, Into the Future, Oola Faith, Acceptance, Joy, Feelings Kit

Nutritionals: Life 9, Essentialzymes-4, OmegaGize[3], NingXia Red, Mind Wise, Mineral Essence

Application and Usage

Topical: Apply any of above oils to tips of ears, crown of skull, base of skull, and along spine as needed. Apply 1-4 drops of Valor or Valor II at the base of the skull 2 times daily or as needed. Apply the Feelings Kit oils using the Raindrop Technique. Apply 1-2 drops Joy over the heart 2 times daily or as needed. Apply 1-4 drops Stress Away and Peace & Calming over the front paws 2 times daily or as needed. Apply White Angelica and Sacred Frankincense by placing a few drops in your hand and petting the dog.

Ingestion & Oral: If dog chooses, allow it to lick oil off your hands when applying topically. Special recommendation: Valerian 1-4 drops orally.

Inhalation: Diffuse chosen oils; you may rotate throughout the day.

Other: During thunderstorms, fireworks, or other potentially stressful times, diffuse 15 drops each of Lavender and Cedarwood or 15 drops of Peace & Calming/Peace & Calming II. Also try diffusing Stress Away, Sacred Frankincense, and Northern Lights Black Spruce. Apply Valor/Valor II or Peace & Calming/Peace & Calming II to tips of ears or pet on dog. Administer orally 1-4 drops Valerian.

Arthritis

Arthritis in dogs is a degenerative condition usually affecting mature animals and commonly caused by cruciate ligament problems. As the disease progresses, owners may find their dogs having difficulty with ordinary activity. Larger and heavier dogs are generally at greater risk. Some breeds are more predisposed than others.

Onset varies by breed and specific animal. Maintaining movement is essential—work on physical therapy to maintain joint flexibility. Also address diet needs and environment. Consult a veterinary health professional to be sure there isn't an underlying medical issue or injury.

Recommendations

Singles: Copaiba, Lemongrass, Idaho Balsam Fir, Frankincense, Helichrysum, Wintergreen, Peppermint, Northern Lights Black Spruce, Cypress, Idaho Blue Spruce, Palo Santo, Dorado Azul, Sacred Frankincense, Lavender, White Fir

Blends: PanAway, Relieve It, R.C., Cool Azul, Deep Relief Roll-On

Nutritionals: NingXia Red, Sulfurzyme, Longevity Softgels, AgilEase, BLM, OmegaGize[3], Mineral Essence, MultiGreens

Additional: Ortho Ease Massage Oil, Ortho Sport Massage Oil, Regenolone Moisturizing Cream, Cool Azul Pain Relief Cream, Cool Azul Sports Gel, V-6 Vegetable Oil Complex

Application and Usage

Topical: 1-3 drops per 5 lbs. neat on specific area using any combination of the following: PanAway, Deep Relief Roll-On, Copaiba, Lemongrass, Idaho Balsam Fir, Helichrysum, Wintergreen, Dorado Azul, Idaho Blue Spruce, Relieve It, Northern Lights

Black Spruce, White Fir, Lavender, Palo Santo, or any other suggested oil from above.

If the dog appears agitated, apply V-6 to restore comfort. Also try Regenolone Moisturizing Cream, Cool Azul Pain Relief Cream, Cool Azul Sports Cream, Ortho Sport Massage Oil, and Ortho Ease Massage Oil. Massage into painful areas daily and on areas where the dog is compensating for painful joints.

Ingestion & Oral: Vitality line: 1-2 drops orally of suggested oils 1-3 times daily per 10 lbs.; Copaiba and Helichrysum: 1-2 drops 2 times daily; Longevity Softgels: 1 daily; BLM: 2, 2 times daily; NingXia Red: 1 oz. daily; OmegaGize³: 1 per 5 lbs. daily (up to 15 daily); Sulfurzyme: 1 per 15 lbs. 2 times daily (adjust as needed); AgilEase: 1 per 5 lbs. up to 8 daily; Mineral Essence; MultiGreens.

Inhalation: This usually happens when you rub oils on their coats. To increase comfort level, use Harmony, White Angelica, Gentle Baby, Peace & Calming, Lavender, and Stress Away specifically. These will help ease agitation in your pets if they are suffering from chronic or intense pain.

Other: Maintain a healthy weight; excess weight on joints causes extra strain on compromised skeletal frame.

Veterinarian Tips and Suggestions

Boredom

Give Animal Scents Dental Chews once daily. Provide environmental enrichment in kennels by rotating a "scent of the day" utilizing various essential oils. Prepare rags with your dog's favorite oil dripped onto it and hide it along your chosen walk route BEFORE going for your walk with your dog.

Start by hiding it in easy-to-find locations and increase difficulty as your dog understands the game. Place a drop of your dog's favorite oil on toys and change out daily. During warm months, freeze a pan of water with Citrus Fresh and leave out for the dog to lick throughout the day.

Place a rag with essential oil dripped on it and hide it under a cardboard box. Have several other boxes next to it with no scented rag. Allow the dog to find the scented rag. Change out the scent each time you play the game.

Barking Excessively (see also Boredom, Anxiety, Aggression, Obedience Training)

Dogs bark excessively for many reasons. Excessive boredom is typically the prevailing reason for barking. Fear and anxiety can also be contributing factors, as well as attention-seeking behavior that is being inadvertently rewarded, being in the wrong environment, or the need for proper obedience training. Dogs will also bark a lot from excitement, especially sled dogs.

Boredom

Dogs that do not have enough physical exertion throughout the day or are lacking companionship will get bored, sometimes resulting in destructive behaviors. It is important that dogs receive plenty of exercise, companionship, structure, and environmental enrichment that challenges their minds throughout the day.

Using essential oils in tandem with proper structure, positive-based obedience training, exercise, and enrichment will benefit a dog greatly and reduce attention-seeking and destructive behaviors.

Recommendations

Singles: Peppermint, Grapefruit, Bergamot, Neroli, Basil, Ocotea, Idaho Balsam Fir, Hong Kuai, Cedarwood, Frankincense, Lemon, Orange, Tangerine, Nutmeg, Spearmint, Wintergreen, Lemongrass

Blends: Awaken, Brain Power, Citrus Fresh, Clarity, En-R-Gee, Aroma Siez, Believe, Christmas Spirit, Highest Potential, Inner Child, Inspiration, Joy, Magnify Your Purpose, Oola Fun, Purification, Stress Away, Transformation, Valor, Motivation

Nutritionals: NingXia Red, OmegaGize³

Additional: Animal Scents Dental Chews

Application and Usage

Topical: Apply chosen oils topically before exercise, obedience training, or throughout the day.

Inhalation: Diffuse oils of choice in environment.

Broken Bones

Active dogs are prone to injuries from time to time. Whether they are chasing other animals, jumping from heights, or happen to be hit by a car, bike, or person, dogs will occasionally break a bone. The following essential oil protocols are intended for first aid or recuperation after consulting a veterinary health professional.

Recommendations

Singles: Copaiba, Idaho Balsam Fir, Palo Santo, Wintergreen, Juniper, Cypress, Idaho Blue Spruce, Northern Lights Black Spruce, Helichrysum, White Fir, Sacred Frankincense, Myrrh

Blends: PanAway, Valor, Valor II, Aroma Life, T-Away, Trauma Life, Release, Cool Azul, Relieve It

Nutritionals: NingXia Red, Sulfurzyme, Longevity, AgilEase, OmegaGize³, Mineral Essence

Additional: Regenolone Moisturizing Cream, Cool Azul Pain Relief Cream

Application and Usage

Topical: Apply 3-5 drops of each single oil in layers on or by location 2-3 times daily minimum, 4-6 if able (if there is a cast, apply above and below). Also use Regenolone Moisturizing Cream, Cool Azul Pain Relief Cream, and Ortho Ease Massage Oil or Ortho Sport Massage Oil along the spine.

Ingestion & Oral: Helichrysum: 4-10 drops 2 times daily; Idaho Balsam Fir and Copaiba: 2-5 drops 2 times daily, in capsule 2-4 times daily (adjust according to dog's size); BLM or AgilEase: 2-10 daily; NingXia Red: 1-2 oz. 2 times daily; Sulfurzyme: 2 per 15 lbs. 2 times daily; Mineral Essence: 2-6 dropperfuls daily. Also apply Valerian 1-5 drops 2 times daily to help keep pet calm during healing process.

Inhalation: Often dogs need calming to let bones heal—see emotional section. Try diffusing Peace & Calming, Stress Away, Idaho Balsam Fir, Trauma Life, Inner Child, Orange.

Other: Layer Regenolone Moisturizing Cream and Cool Azul Pain Relief Cream over topically applied oils as needed.

Brucella Canis (Brucellosis)

Brucella canis poses particular risk to breeding dogs. Transmitted through ingestion of infected material or during mating, *Brucella* can also infect humans, although instances of this are rare and the infections less severe. It is the most common cause of spontaneous abortion in dogs at 45-55 days. Cases are reportable in some states. Immunization efforts have been unsuccessful. Both sexes are equally susceptible in contracting, carrying, and transmitting the organism. Dogs may also contract *Brucella* variations from infected domestic livestock, but this is rare.

Essential oil protocols may help in boosting the immune system or alleviating symptoms. Consult a veterinary health professional to confirm diagnosis, determine proper treatment, and prevent complications.

Recommendations

Singles: Tea Tree, Mountain Savory, Oregano, Ravintsara, Eucalyptus Blue, Thyme, Geranium, Ginger, Lemongrass, Eucalyptus Radiata, Rosemary, Eucalyptus Globulus, Hyssop, Laurus Nobilis, Myrrh, Copaiba

Blends: Thieves, Exodus II, ImmuPower, Melrose, Raven, Egyptian Gold, Longevity, The Gift

Nutritionals: ImmuPro, NingXia Red, MultiGreens, Life 9

Additional: Thieves Household Cleaner

Application and Usage

Topical: Administer Raindrop Technique every other day using the Raindrop oils. Apply 2-3 drops of chosen oil from suggested oils 2-3 times daily.

Ingestion & Oral: Thieves, Oregano, ImmuPower, Geranium, and Exodus II: 4 drops each (except Oregano, only 1 drop) 2-4 times daily; these oils can be administered in a capsule as well. Other oils can be used in addition or in place of ImmuPower and Exodus II; NingXia Red: 1 oz. daily; ImmuPro: 1 per 10 lbs. daily. Also try Copaiba: 1 drop per 5 lbs.

Inhalation: Diffuse Thieves, Raven, ImmuPower, or Melrose in environment—alternate oils as needed.

Other: Use Thieves Household Cleaner to disinfect and sanitize the environment.

Calluses (Pressure Sores, Hygromas)

These are thickened, wrinkled, hairless areas of skin that the body forms in response to stress, force, friction, or trauma to the skin or subcutaneous tissues. These generally affect the large and giant breeds, as well as crated, kenneled, or recumbent dogs.

The most common areas for calluses are the feet and elbows. Talk to your veterinarian for advice on prevention and treatment.

Recommendations

Singles: Geranium, Frankincense, Lavender, Copaiba, Helichrysum, Basil, Blue Cypress, Carrot Seed, Cypress, Eucalyptus Radiata, Grapefruit, Eucalyptus Globulus, Roman Chamomile, German

Chamomile, Hyssop, Laurus Nobilis, Lemon, Lemongrass, Lemon Myrtle, Marjoram, Tea Tree, Myrrh, Myrtle, Palmarosa, Palo Santo, Patchouli, Thyme, Clove, Vetiver

Blends: Melrose, Aroma Siez, Citrus Fresh, Egyptian Gold, En-R-Gee, Exodus II, Longevity, M-Grain, Purification, R.C., Raven, Relieve It, The Gift, Thieves, Transformation, Breathe Again Roll-On, Deep Relief Roll-On

Nutritionals: OmegaGize[3], NingXia Red, Sulfurzyme, Essentialzyme

Additional: Animal Scents Ointment, Animal Scents Shampoo, Rose Ointment, Thieves Household Cleaner

Application and Usage

Topical: Select two or more from suggested oils and apply liberally onto affected areas. Cover with Animal Scents Ointment or Rose Ointment. Shampoo with Animal Scents Shampoo 1 time weekly; let shampoo sit on coat for 5-10 minutes before rinsing.

Ingestion & Oral: OmegaGize[3], NingXia Red, Sulfurzyme, and Essentialzyme: 1 each 1 time daily.

Other: Be aware of environmental factors causing trauma to skin. Eliminate chemical-laden cleaning agents and clean the dog's environment with diluted Thieves Household Cleaner.

Cancer

Dogs with cancer often display symptoms such as lumps or swelling that do not go away with time. Other signs can be wounds or sores that don't heal properly as well as abnormal bleeding.

Cancer affecting internal organs, such as bladder cancer, affect dogs in other ways. For example, with bladder cancer, dogs often have blood in their urine, strain to urinate, have painful urination, and urinate often. The dog may have recurrent urinary tract infections.

Always monitor your dog's health to keep a watchful eye for unexplainable symptoms to help with early detection. Transitional cell carcinoma can also sometimes spread to the bone, in which case the dog may appear lame.

Recommendations

Singles: Copaiba, Sacred Frankincense, Idaho Blue Spruce, Grapefruit, Hong Kuai, Frankincense, Tsuga, Northern Lights Black Spruce, Palo

---

🐕 Veterinarian Tips and Suggestions

Cancer Recipe

Use veggie cap size "00" and fill with the following essential oils. Extras can be stored in the freezer. Wrap capsule in coconut oil, almond butter, or slice of sweet potato.

Morning Capsule:
- 7 drops Copaiba
- 7 drops Sacred Frankincense
- 7 drops Idaho Blue Spruce

Noon Capsule:
- 7 drops Copaiba
- 7 drops Sacred Frankincense
- 7 drops ImmuPower

Early Evening Capsule:
- 7 drops Copaiba
- 7 drops Frankincense
- 7 drops Grapefruit

Bedtime Capsule:
- 7 drops Copaiba
- 7 drops Sacred Frankincense
- 7 drops Palo Santo

Additional capsule at bedtime
- 10 drops JuvaCleanse
- 10 drops Tsuga (or Northern Lights Black Spruce)

Santo, Lavender, Helichrysum, Royal Hawaiian Sandalwood, Idaho Balsam Fir, Juniper, Orange

Blends: JuvaCleanse, Believe, ImmuPower, Citrus Fresh, Forgiveness, Release, PanAway, Relieve It

Nutritionals: Life 9, NingXia Red, ImmuPro, Mineral Essence, Essentialzyme, Detoxzyme, Sulfurzyme, MultiGreens, K&B, Digest & Cleanse, PowerGize

Application and Usage

Topical: Select Copaiba, Sacred Frankincense, Northern Lights Black Spruce, and Idaho Blue Spruce as a base and combine with 2-4 other listed oils to create a custom blend. Use 3-5 drops each and apply liberally on location 4-6 times daily. More oil per application is better. See oils listed under Anxiety to help with emotional pain and trauma when your pet is dealing with cancer. Also try Raindrop Technique up to 3 times a week.

Ingestion & Oral: NingXia Red: 2 oz. 3 times daily; Life 9: 1 time daily; ImmuPro: 2-3 times daily; Mineral Essence: 1 dropperful 3 times daily; Detoxzyme: 2 in the morning and 2 in the evening;

Sulfurzyme: 4, 2 times daily; PowerGize: 1, 2 times daily (can mix with NingXia Red); MultiGreens: 2, 2 times daily; K&B: 3-4 dropperfuls 2 times daily; Essentialzyme: 2, 2 times daily.

Other: Ensure that your dog's diet is grain-free and free of all artificial preservatives. Also be sure the dog's environment is free of toxic and household chemicals, including harmful cleaning products, toxic air fresheners, and harmful detergents in bedding wash.

Chewing - Destructive
(see also Boredom or Anxiety)

Sometimes destructive chewing can be a result of irritation in the gums. Along with the suggested protocols in Boredom and Anxiety, try administering Copaiba, Thieves, and Purification: 1-5 drops orally 2 times daily.

Cognitive Dysfunction

There are a number of conditions in which a dog loses cognitive and memory function. Most often this is the result of injury that damages specific parts of the brain. Additionally, there are some infections (encephalitis) that specifically target brain tissue.

Cognitive dysfunction may also indicate a nutritional deficiency and may be temporary. Talk to your veterinarian about suspected causes, preferred treatments, and expected outcomes.

Recommendations
Singles: Cedarwood, Frankincense, Sacred Frankincense, Dorado Azul, Lemon, Sacred Sandalwood, Royal Hawaiian Sandalwood, Peppermint, Hong Kuai, Helichrysum, Cardamom, Cypress, Idaho Balsam Fir, Jasmine, Spearmint, Vetiver, Patchouli

Blends: Brain Power, Clarity, Transformation, Three Wise Men, Citrus Fresh, Believe, DiGize, M-Grain, Purification, Infect-Away, PuriClean, T-Away, Trauma Life

Nutritionals: OmegaGize[3], MindWise, NingXia Red, ImmuPro, Longevity Softgels, Sulfurzyme, Allerzyme, Detoxzyme, NingXia Nitro

Application and Usage
Topical: Use any 2 of the suggested oils, 1-2 drops each applied on crown of head, inside tips of ears, as well as on the throat and chest area. Repeat up to 2 times daily. Other listed oils can be added to this combination, applied to chest, collar/neck, and head area.

Ingestion & Oral: Use any of the above oils, 1-4 drops orally 2-4 times daily. ImmuPro: 1 per 10 lbs. daily (2 max); OmegaGize[3]: 1 daily; NingXia Red: 1-2 oz. daily; Longevity Softgels: 1 daily per 50 lbs.; Mind-Wise: 1.5 oz. daily per 10 lbs., up to 3-4 oz. daily.

Inhalation: Diffuse any of the suggested oils in the dog's environment.

Conjunctivitis

There are several disorders of the tear ducts and lacrimal structure in dogs. They may be congenital or caused by trauma, the presence of foreign objects, or bacterial or viral infection. Determine if caused by allergies or virus—treatment will be based on the root cause. These conditions include: cherry eye (prolapsed nictitans gland), dacryocystitis (inflammation of the tear sac), absence of nasal tear duct openings, and dry eye (keratoconjunctivitis sicca).

Consult a veterinary health professional to determine cause, severity, and treatment.

Recommendations
Singles: Lavender, Copaiba, Blue Cypress, Cypress, Eucalyptus Blue, Eucalyptus Radiata, Eucalyptus Globulus, Hinoki, Hong Kuai, Hyssop, Lemon, Juniper, Laurus Nobilis, Tea Tree, Ocotea, Patchouli, Ravintsara, Petitgrain

Blends: Thieves, Exodus II, ImmuPower, Melrose, M-Grain, Infect Away, Mendwell, PuriClean, Purification, Raven, R.C., Stress Away, The Gift, Breathe Again Roll-On.

Nutritionals: NingXia Red, Inner Defense, Life 9, Longevity Softgels, Digest & Cleanse

Application and Usage
Topical: Apply 1 drop Lavender, Copaiba, and any one of the suggested oils on fingertip and spread ½ inch below lower eye lid.

Ingestion & Oral: Use the following oils for both viral and bacterial infections. Use equal parts Copaiba, suggested dosage is 2-7 drops 2 times daily, combined with any of the following 2-3 oils:

Blue Cypress, Eucalyptus Blue, Eucalyptus Globulus, Eucalyptus Radiata, Lemon, Juniper, Laurus Nobilis, Tea Tree, Ocotea, Patchouli, Ravintsara, Petitgrain, Thieves, Exodus II, ImmuPower, Melrose, M-Grain, Infect Away, Mendwell, PuriClean, Purification, Raven, R.C., The Gift

Inhalation: Diffuse any choice of oils in environment.

Constipation

In dogs, constipation is generally caused by dehydration and food choices. Be sure the dog has plenty of fresh water and has access to it at all times.

Also, several dog-friendly high-fiber fruits and vegetables may help. Consider giving the dog bite-sized pieces of the following as treats: cantaloupe, fresh green beans, spinach, pumpkin, blueberries, watermelon, asparagus, broccoli, and carrots.

If the dog is particularly uncomfortable, consider a pediatric rectal suppository. Consult a veterinary health professional to rule out more serious causes and to be sure that the condition hasn't caused secondary infection to the anal glands.

Recommendations
Singles: Peppermint, Ginger, Black Pepper, Fennel, Spearmint
Blends: DiGize, Copaiba
Nutritionals: Essentialzyme, ICP, Life 9, ComforTone, JuvaTone, Detoxzyme, Digest & Cleanse
Application and Usage
Topical: Apply 1-2 drops of listed oils and massage in circular motions on abdomen. Layer oils and apply 2-3 times daily.
Ingestion & Oral: DiGize in aloe vera gel in food works best. DiGize, Fennel, and Copaiba: give 1-2 drops each in a capsule 1-2 times daily. Essential-zyme: ½ per 10 lbs. 1 time daily; Life 9: 1 per 25 lbs. 1 time daily; ICP: ½ teaspoon per 20 lbs.; Comfor-Tone: 1, 1-2 times daily; JuvaTone: ½, 1-2 times daily

Coprophagia

When dogs eat stool, it is generally due to lack of balanced nourishment. It is most common in puppies. Most puppies will outgrow the practice, though it may require mild discouragement. Most adult dogs will abandon this behavior when their vitamins, minerals, and enzymes are brought into balance.

Be sure to consult a veterinarian to rule out medical problems that could lead to coprophagia.

Recommendations
Singles: Peppermint, Copaiba, Basil, Ocotea, Ginger, Fennel, Oregano
Blends: DiGize, ParaGize, AromaEase, TummyGize
Nutritionals: Essentialzyme, MultiGreens, NingXia Red, Mineral Essence, Life 9, Digest & Cleanse, Detoxzyme, Master Formula

Application and Usage
Topical: Apply Peppermint and DiGize liberally on abdomen.
Ingestion & Oral: Essentialzyme: ½ per 10 lbs. 2 times daily; Life 9: 1 per 25 lbs. 1 time daily; NingXia Red: 1 oz. daily; Mineral Essence: 1 dropperful per 20 lbs. 2 times daily. Continue for 1 week. If condition lessens, continue; if no change, add more Mineral Essence combined with Master Formula.

Cornea (Abrasion, Ulcers, Eye Conditions)

Corneal ulcers may occur if the eye isn't producing enough lubricating tears. Additionally, they may develop following scratches or other injuries. Corneal lacerations are generally the result of bites, self-inflicted trauma, and other accidents. In these cases, the wound may need sutures.

Signs that your dog's eyes are suffering from a serious condition are discharge with crust, tearing up, red or white eyelid linings, tear-stained fur, closed eye(s), cloudiness or change in eye color, visible third eyelid, and unequal pupil sizes.

Consult a veterinary health professional to determine cause and course of treatment. DO NOT APPLY ANY OILS DIRECTLY INTO THE EYE.

Recommendations
Singles: Lavender, Frankincense, Copaiba, Helichrysum, Cypress, Cistus, Sacred Frankincense, Cedarwood, Lemon
Nutritionals: NingXia Red, Longevity Softgels

Application and Usage
Topical: Apply 2 drops Lavender, Cypress, Helichrysum, and Copaiba on fingertip and spread ½ inch below lower eye lid. Layer in order listed or apply singly starting with Lavender.

Ingestion & Oral: NingXia Red: 1 oz. 2 times daily. Longevity Softgels: 1 per 50 lbs. daily.

Inhalation: Diffuse Cedarwood and Lemon with any other suggested oils.

Coronavirus (Canine Enteric Coronavirus, Canine Respiratory Coronavirus, Coronaviridae)

This viral family causes mild to significant gastrointestinal distress. Infection may become more pronounced as it makes the dog more susceptible to secondary canine parvovirus infection. The two infections in tandem are often fatal.

Thieves Household Cleaner will destroy the virus on contact. Dogs may be vaccinated against coronavirus. A second type has been shown to cause respiratory disease in dogs. Consult a veterinary health professional.

Recommendations

Singles: Lemongrass, Ocotea, Laurus Nobilis, Melissa, Eucalyptus Blue, Ravintsara, Oregano, Copaiba, Tea Tree

Blends: DiGize, Thieves, Exodus II, ImmuPower, Egyptian Gold, Raven, Melrose

Nutritionals: ImmuPro, NingXia Red, Inner Defense, Life 9, MultiGreens, Essentialzyme, Detoxzyme, Digest & Cleanse

Additional: Thieves Household Cleaner

Application and Usage

Topical: Raindrop Technique daily, DiGize, Copaiba, and Exodus II with any other selected oil 3-4 times daily on abdomen.

Inhalation: Diffuse Thieves, ImmuPower, Melrose, and Raven.

Ingestion & Oral: ImmuPower, Exodus II, DiGize, Melissa, Eucalyptus Blue, Raven, and Ravintsara: 1-5 drops each 2 times daily of any 4 oils combined with 5 drops Copaiba. NingXia Red: 1 oz. 2 times daily; Inner Defense: 1 per 50 lbs.; Life 9: 1 per 20 lbs.; Detoxzyme: 1-4, 2 times daily; Digest & Cleanse: 1, 1-2 times daily.

Other: Use Thieves Household Cleaner to disinfect and sanitize the environment.

Cough (Tracheobronchitis) (see also Kennel Cough)

While it's normal for a dog to cough on occasion to clear dust, irritation, or something strong they sniffed, a lingering, periodic cough may be the sign of a more serious problem. Some coughs can develop from inhaling dangerous bacteria and viruses.

If the cough doesn't clear after 15 or 20 minutes and continues regularly over the next few hours, it may be the early sign of infection. One of the most common is kennel cough. Consult a veterinary health professional to confirm the cause, seriousness, and treatment.

Recommendations

Singles: Mountain Savory, Eucalyptus Blue, Eucalyptus Radiata, Eucalyptus Globulus, Hyssop, Lemongrass, Rosemary, Copaiba, Black Pepper, Oregano, Melissa, Ravintsara

Blends: R.C., Breathe Again Roll-On, ImmuPower, Aroma Siez, Thieves, Raven, Exodus II, Purification

Nutritionals: Life 9, NingXia Red, Inner Defense

Additional: Thieves Household Cleaner

Application and Usage

Topical: Apply Raven, R.C., Copaiba, and any other suggested oils on chest, stomach, and throat area 2 times daily.

Ingestion & Oral: Place 1-5 drops of chosen oil in the dog's water bowl or administer in a capsule. Always have plain water as an option when presenting oil-infused water to canines. If the dog is hesitant to drink or shows signs of discomfort, remove the water. Repeat until the dog feels comfortable and readily drinks the oil-infused water. Administer the following. Life 9: 1 daily; NingXia Red: 1 oz. 2 times daily; Inner Defense: 1 per 50 lbs. daily. Also try combining 5 drops each of R.C., Copaiba, and Raven with 1 drop Black Pepper. Combine mixture and administer orally in a capsule.

Inhalation: Diffuse nonstop around the dog; rub a few drops in your hands and place gently over dog's muzzle.

Other: Use Thieves Household Cleaner to clean and sanitize the area.

Courage (Confidence, Trust)

Cowering, whining, hanging ears, submissive urination, and a tucked tail are some of the bigger clues that show a dog is anxious, uncomfortable, or scared.

Recommendations

Singles: Bergamot, Cedarwood, Frankincense, Sacred Sandalwood, Royal Hawaiian Sandalwood, Orange, Neroli, Cypress, Northern Lights Black Spruce, Roman Chamomile, Idaho Blue Spruce

Blends: Shutran, Acceptance, Believe, Present Time, Sacred Mountain, Surrender, Valor, Valor II, White Angelica, Oola Grow, Oola Faith, Trauma Life, Inspiration, Peace & Calming, Stress Away, Joy, Inner Child, Release

Nutritionals: Life 9, Essentialzymes-4, NingXia Red, Mineral Essence, OmegaGize^3, Master Formula

Application and Usage

Topical: Apply chosen oils to tips of ears, base of skull, pads of feet, and up the spine as needed.

Inhalation: Diffuse chosen oils, rotating frequently.

Cruciate Ligament Injury

This kind of injury raises the risk of developing arthritis in dogs. Consult a veterinary health professional to determine full or partial tear. The protocols below should be used only as a first response or in conjunction with instructions given by a veterinary health professional.

Recommendations

Singles: Blue Cypress, Cypress, Northern Lights Black Spruce, Palo Santo, Wintergreen, Idaho Balsam Fir, Idaho Blue Spruce, Copaiba, Lemongrass, Helichrysum

Blends: Relieve It, Deep Relief Roll-On, PanAway, Cool Azul, Australian Blue

Nutritionals: AgilEase, BLM, Sulfurzyme, NingXia Red, Mineral Essence

Additional: Ortho Sport Massage Oil, Ortho Ease Massage Oil, Regenolone Moisturizing Cream, Cool Azul Pain Relief Cream, Cool Azul Sports Gel

Application and Usage

Topical: Layer Copaiba, Blue Cypress, Idaho Balsam Fir, Idaho Blue Spruce, and Lemongrass with any other suggested oils 2-4 times daily. End with Regenolone Moisturizing Cream over top.

Ingestion & Oral: AgilEase and/or BLM: 2-10 daily; Sulfurzyme: 2-10, 2 times daily; NingXia Red: 2 oz. 2 times daily; Copaiba: 10 drops 2 times daily.

Other: Use the following individually or layer with chosen oils: Ortho Sport Massage Oil, Ortho Ease Massage Oil, Regenolone Moisturizing Cream, Cool Azul Pain Relief Cream, Cool Azul Sports Gel

Cystitis (Urinary Conditions)

This is inflammation of the bladder, most often due to infection. Symptoms are blood in the urine and straining to produce a small amount of urine. Consult a veterinary health professional to treat the underlying condition and prevent complications.

Recommendations

Singles: Geranium, Copaiba, Oregano, Mountain Savory, Clove, Black Pepper, Laurus Nobilis, Ocotea, Cedarwood, Lemongrass, Tea Tree, Juniper, Fennel

Blends: Thieves, Purification, ImmuPower, Citrus Fresh, Exodus II, Melrose, Inspiration, Egyptian Gold, PuriClean, ParaGize, Longevity

Nutritionals: Inner Defense, K&B, Super C Chewable, Life 9

Additional: Thieves Household Cleaner

Application and Usage

Topical: Apply Juniper, Melrose, Geranium and Copaiba liberally directly over bladder area several times daily. Administer Raindrop Technique every other day.

Ingestion & Oral: In capsules, administer 1-5 drops each combined Lemongrass, Copaiba, and Melrose with any other suggested oils 2 times daily. K&B: 1 dropperful per 20 lbs. 2-4 times daily; Inner Defense: 1 per 20 lbs. 1 time daily; Super C Chewable: 1 per 40 lbs. daily; Life 9: 1 daily.

Inhalation: Diffuse Thieves or selected oils to promote immune-boosting power.

Other: Maintain clean surfaces, bedding, and flooring with Thieves Household Cleaner.

Dental Disease

Periodontal disease is the most common clinical condition for dogs. While mostly preventable, many owners and caregivers underestimate the speed and extent to which their dog's teeth can become plaque-ridden, calculus-set, and overcome by gingivitis.

Have your dog's teeth evaluated by your veterinary health professional on a regular basis to prevent periodontal disease from progressing into periodontitis.

Recommendations

Singles: Lemon, Peppermint, Copaiba, Myrrh, Rosemary, Oregano, Basil, Mountain Savory, Laurus Nobilis, Lemongrass, Patchouli, Palmarosa, Ravintsara, Clove, Thyme, Ocotea, Tea Tree

Blends: Thieves, Infect Away, ParaGize, PuriClean, Exodus II, Melrose, Egyptian Gold, Raven, Christmas Spirit, Citrus Fresh

Nutritionals: Essentialzyme, Detoxzyme, Life 9, Inner Defense, MultiGreens, Mineral Essence

Additional: Thieves Fresh Essence Plus Mouthwash, Thieves Dentarome Plus Toothpaste, Animal Scents Dental Pet Chews

Application and Usage

Topical: Apply diluted choice of oils on a cotton swab in gum/mouth area, or mix into paste of baking soda and coconut oil. Use old toothbrush and lightly brush gums/teeth with mixture.

Ingestion & Oral: Promote good digestion with Essentialzyme or Detoxzyme: 1 per 50 lbs. daily. Add a drop of Citrus Fresh, Lemon, or Peppermint oil to 2 quarts of water for drinking. Make sure there is plain water available along with the water containing oils.

Other: Raw, fresh diets promote overall oral health. Providing the best diet possible will help keep teeth clean. Try Thieves Mouthwash directly on gums and teeth with a clean sponge or rag. Also try Thieves Dentarome Plus Toothpaste (DO Not use any of the other Young Living toothpastes as they contain Xylitol, wonderful for humans but may be harmful to dogs.). Give Dental Pet Chews as recommended on the package. Homemade dental biscuits can be made with any of the above oils (add 5-8 drops to recipe) to promote dental/digestive health.

Detoxification

Dogs are prone to sniffing and eating many things that aren't good for them, from known poisons, to household cleaners, to grapes and raisins. If your dog ingests any of these items, you'll want to consult a veterinary health professional to be sure your animal has every possible resource for recovery.

These oil protocols will help with first aid and may assist with long-term recovery. General overall toxins— not specific to poisoning— require specific veterinary consultation.

Recommendations

Singles: Lemon, Copaiba, Tea Tree, Hyssop, Grapefruit, Orange, Helichrysum

Blends: Citrus Fresh, GLF, JuvaCleanse, JuvaFlex, DiGize, Thieves, TummyGize, ParaGize, PuriClean, Purification, Melrose

Nutritionals: Detoxzyme, K&B, Rehemogen, Life 9, NingXia Red, Sulfurzyme, JuvaTone

Application and Usage

Topical: Administer Raindrop Technique daily for 3-7 days in a row and then 1-2 times weekly. Apply JuvaFlex or DiGize over the abdomen to help process toxins out of the body 2-4 times daily.

Ingestion & Oral: GLF or JuvaCleanse combined with Copaiba: 1 drop per 10 lbs. 2-4 times daily; Detoxzyme: 1 per 15 lbs. 1-2 times daily. Also try 1 dropperful K&B and 1 dropperful Rehemogen per 20 lbs. 2 times daily or 1 Sulfurzyme and 1 Life 9, 1-2 times daily.

Inhalation: Diffuse Thieves, Lemon, and Purification to promote immune-boosting support.

Other: Provide as fresh, healthy, and organic a diet as possible to promote the body naturally detoxifying.

Deworming

If an animal has a large parasite load, please work with your animal health professional. Testing will be required to determine best treatment. The listed protocols below will assist with maintaining overall GI health. Dogs are subject to several kinds of parasites, including tapeworms, roundworms, hookworms, whipworms, and heartworms.

Most puppies receive a deworming cycle by breeders, owners, and retail pet shops. However, infection with parasites may occur with little exposure to other animals and minimal exposure to an outdoor environment.

Consult a veterinary health professional to test for various types, determine proper treatment, and prevent complications from parasites.

Recommendations

Singles: Oregano, Fennel, Tarragon, Ocotea, Patchouli, Peppermint, Lemongrass

Blends: Thieves, DiGize, Purification, ParaGize, PuriClean

Nutritionals: ParaFree, Life 9, Longevity Softgels,
Inner Defense, Digest & Cleanse
Additional: Thieves Household Cleaner

Application and Usage

Topical: Administer Raindrop treatments to help
repel parasites and promote overall health. Apply
DiGize on the abdomen liberally multiple times
daily.

Ingestion & Oral: ParaFree: 1 per 30 lbs. 2 times
daily; Life 9: 1 daily; Longevity Softgels or Inner
Defense: 1 per 50 lbs. 1 time daily. Use other oils
1-10 drops in a capsule 1-2 times daily as needed,
depending on severity.

Inhalation: Diffuse Thieves or Purification to cleanse
the environment.

Other: Help kill external parasites by using Thieves
Household Cleaner sprayed in environment and
housing.

Diabetes

Diabetes is a metabolic disorder where dogs either
produce no insulin or not enough insulin and are
therefore unable to process sugars properly. Signs include
thirst, hunger, weight loss, and excessive urination.
Consult a veterinary health professional to test blood for
sugar levels.

Recommendations

Singles: Ocotea, Coriander, Geranium, Helichrysum,
Juniper, Dill, Fennel, Mastrante, Copaiba
Blends: Joy, Aroma Life, Aroma Siez, Citrus Fresh,
Thieves, Exodus II, DiGize, JuvaCleanse
Nutritionals: Essentialzyme, Sulfurzyme, NingXia
Red, MultiGreens, OmegaGize[3], Mineral Essence

Application and Usage

Topical: Maintain overall health with Raindrop
Technique. Apply 2 or more suggested oils over the
pancreatic region daily.

Ingestion & Oral: Administer 1 drop each Ocotea
and Copaiba orally per 50 lbs. Monitor blood
glucose levels and adjust as needed. DiGize: 2 drops
orally per 50 lbs. daily; Essentialzyme: 1 per 50
lbs. daily; Sulfurzyme: 2 per 50 lbs. 2 times daily;
NingXia Red: 1-2 oz. daily; Mineral Essence: 4
dropperfuls daily; MultiGreens: 1-6 daily.

Diarrhea

Diarrhea is any condition in which a dog produces an
abnormal amount of soft or liquid feces. It may be a sign
of parasites, infection, or metabolic diseases. Electrolyte
imbalance and foods high in starch like rice and potatoes
will also cause diarrhea and gut inflammation.

Consult a veterinary health professional to determine
the cause and prevent complications.

Recommendations

Singles: Oregano, Cistus, Ginger, Copaiba,
Peppermint, Helichrysum, Spearmint, Lavender
Blends: AromaEase, DiGize, Thieves, Citrus Fresh,
Purification
Nutritionals: Essentialzyme, Life 9, Essentialzymes-4,
Inner Defense, Detoxzyme, ParaFree, Digest &
Cleanse, Master Formula
Additional: Thieves Household Cleaner

Application and Usage

Topical: DiGize 1-2 drops applied on stomach and
intestine area. All other oils can be applied in the GI
region topically. Dilute if required by pet's weight.

Ingestion & Oral: Essentialzyme: 1 per 50 lbs. daily;
Life 9: 1 per 25 lbs. 2 times daily; Inner Defense: 1
per 50 lbs. daily; ParaFree: 1 per 50 lbs. daily. Also
administer 5-20 drops of Copaiba and DiGize to
food 2-3 times daily, depending on severity and size
of animal.

Inhalation: Diffuse Citrus Fresh, Thieves, or Purification to settle upset stomach and repel bad aroma.

Veterinarian Tips and Suggestions

Other suggestions for helping with canine diarrhea

- Parasitic diarrhea: ParaFree (see parasite section)
  1 per 50 lbs. daily
- Thieves, DiGize, or Copaiba: 1-20 drops each
  with carrier oil in capsule 1-2 times daily
- Bloody diarrhea: capsule with 1-5 drops each of
  Ginger, Cistus, Helichrysum, Spearmint, Copaiba
  2-3 times daily.
- Stress diarrhea: See section on anxiety. Also limit
  intake of food and water. Administer capsule of
  1-5 drops Peppermint, Copaiba, Lavender, and
  Ginger 1-2 times daily.

Other: Maintain a bland diet and fasting if needed to allow healing in the GI region. Give enough food/treats to get supplements into dog. Avoid feeding a grain-heavy diet. Wash environment with Thieves Household Cleaner to maintain sanitation.

Ear Mites/Infections

Most animals who are fighting ear mites or infections are fighting poor health. Improving the dog's overall health and function will improve ear health. Diet can also play a large factor in ear infections and irritation.

Allergies are also something to investigate, as many ear issues involve allergic components.

Ear mites overall are quite common and cause itching, scratching, and rubbing the ear against the ground or furniture. Consult a veterinary health professional to be sure any treatment you use is effective, eradicates the mites, and prevents complications.

Recommendations

Singles: Tea Tree, Copaiba, Lemongrass, Lavender, Patchouli, Manuka, Citronella, Basil, Lemongrass, Eucalyptus Globulus, Rosemary, Hong Kuai, Geranium, Frankincense

Blends: Purification, Thieves, RepelAroma, Infect Away, Mendwell, PuriClean, DiGize

Nutritionals: NingXia Red, Life 9, ParaFree, Digest & Cleanse

Additional: Thieves Household Cleaner, Animal Scents Ointment, Animal Scents Shampoo

Application and Usage

Topical: Use caution with oils around ear canals. Put 1-3 drops of selected oils on cotton ball and rub into ear making sure no oils drip down into the ear canal. Applying oils around the base and side of the ear flap is also effective in assisting treatment of ear conditions. Administer topical application at least 2 times daily. Apply 1-2 drops of any above-listed oils around the ear base and side of head. Also apply Raindrop Technique if needed. **Never apply an oil directly into the ear canal.**

Ingestion & Oral: If there is a persistent infection or mite problem, including the following will increase the animal's health. NingXia Red: 1-2 oz. daily; Life 9: 1 per 25 lbs. daily; ParaFree or Digest & Cleanse: 1 per 50 lbs. daily.

Inhalation: Diffuse Thieves and Purification to promote immune health.

Other: Use heavily diluted Thieves Household Cleaner or Animal Scents Shampoo to cleanse the discharge around the ear. Animal Scents Ointment for sore spots in the ear flap.

Epulis (Mouth, Gums)

These are tumor-like growths on a dog's gums. They appear to sprout from the gums and could grow to displace teeth as they expand. This may lead to the dog's bite being off. They are the fourth most common tumor in dogs, particularly in boxers.

There are three types: ossifying, acanthomatous, and fibromatous. Consult a veterinary health professional to confirm that they are benign, which type, and the best form of treatment. This is an issue that needs veterinary care. The options listed are also good for after surgery.

Recommendations

Singles: Frankincense, Myrrh, Copaiba, Lavender, Idaho Balsam Fir, Idaho Blue Spruce, Northern Lights Black Spruce, Helichrysum

Blends: Thieves, Longevity, Exodus II, Egyptian Gold

Nutritionals: Sulfurzyme, NingXia Red, Longevity Softgels, ImmuPro, Life 9, MultiGreens

Application and Usage

Topical: Apply 1-3 drops of listed oils or combination of oils 2 times daily on location. Watch for irritation and adjust strength of application accordingly. If surgery is necessary, use oils around surgical site and on site when the incision is healed. Use Helichrysum, Copaiba, and Myrrh directly on surgical site.

Ingestion & Oral: Sulfurzyme: 2 per 20 lbs. 2 times daily; NingXia Red: 1-2 oz. daily; Longevity Softgels: 1 per 50 lbs. 2 times daily; ImmuPro: 1, 1-4 times daily; Life 9: 1 daily; MultiGreens: 1-6 daily.

Fatty Liver (Hepatic Lipidosis, Liver Disease)

Fatty Liver is a condition in which excessive fat in the liver cells causes abnormal bile flow and reduced hepatic function. When hepatic function deteriorates sufficiently, it will affect the liver's ability to detoxify the blood and metabolize nutrients.

This can be a primary disease or a secondary effect of obesity, diabetes, cancer, pancreatitis, hyperthyroidism, inflammatory bowel disease, kidney disease, cardiomyopathy, or starvation. Consult a veterinary health professional to determine the cause, discuss a mode of treatment, and prevent complications.

Recommendations

Singles: Grapefruit, Ledum, Helichrysum, Copaiba, Celery Seed

Blends: DiGize, JuvaCleanse, JuvaFlex, GLF, Citrus Fresh

Nutritionals: Detoxzyme, Essentialzymes-4, MultiGreens, NingXia Red, OmegaGize[3], Sulfurzyme, JuvaTone, Life 9

Application and Usage

Topical: Apply any of the above-listed oils liberally over the liver and intestinal area 1-2 times daily. Applying oils to the liver acupressure points is also helpful.

Ingestion & Oral: 1-3 drops of Copaiba and GLF or JuvaCleanse per 25 lbs. 2 times daily, depending on severity. Citrus Fresh (or other citrus oils): 1-2 drops in 2 quarts drinking water (allow dog access to plain water as well); Essentialzymes-4 or Detoxzyme: 2 per 50 lbs.; MultiGreens: 1 per 50 lbs.; NingXia Red: 2-4 oz. daily; OmegaGize[3]: 1 per 50 lbs.; Sulfurzyme: 2-6 orally per 50 lbs. 2 times daily; Life 9: 1 daily; JuvaTone: 1-4 daily.

False Pregnancy (Pseudocoyesis)

This condition usually results from hormonal imbalance. The general consensus is that a decrease of progesterone and increase of prolactin serves as the primary cause. Animals will display many of the signs of pregnancy, including nesting, weight gain, enlarged mammary glands, abdominal swelling, vomiting, lethargy, and vaginal discharge.

Consult a veterinary health professional to confirm diagnosis and determine a course of treatment to prevent complications.

Recommendations

Singles: Fennel, Clary Sage, Dorado Azul, Geranium, Lavender

Blends: EndoFlex, SclarEssence, Dragon Time, Release, Progessence Plus

Nutritionals: PD 80/20, EndoGize, Thyromin, NingXia Red, Life 9, Master Formula

Application and Usage

Topical: Apply 2-8 drops of any of the listed oils to the dog's chest, neck, and stomach 2 times daily.

Ingestion & Oral: PD 80/20: 1 per 50 lbs. daily; EndoGize: 1 per 50 lbs. daily; Thyromin: 1 per 50 lbs. daily; NingXia Red: 1 oz. 2 times daily.

Fever (Fever of Unknown Origin/FUO)

Causing an abnormally high body temperature is the immune system's response to any number of health conditions. Usually, fevers are caused by infection (viral, bacterial, parasitic, fungal), metabolic diseases, endocrine diseases, tumors, or immune-mediated inflammatory diseases (immune diseases that lack an identifiable cause).

If a dog has an elevated temperature (above 102.5°F) on at least four occasions over a 14-day period without a determinable cause, it is called a fever of unknown origin. Consult a veterinary health professional to determine cause, cross-reference the fever with other symptoms, treat the underlying condition, and prevent complications or secondary infections.

Recommendations

Singles: Peppermint, Cypress, Spearmint, Copaiba, Lavender, Thyme, Melissa, Clove, Ravintsara, Rosemary, Tea Tree

Blends: Thieves, Purification, Infect Away, ImmuPower, DiGize, Transformation, Citrus Fresh, Exodus II, Raven

Nutritionals: NingXia Red, Inner Defense, Life 9, Digest & Cleanse, ParaFree

Application and Usage

Topical: Apply 2-8 drops Peppermint, Thieves, and Cypress with any other selected suggested oils on abdomen. Other oils can be added or substituted into this blend. A cool Epsom salt bath or cloths with oils added to Epsom salts can be used to regulate the dog's temperature.

Ingestion & Oral:

1. If dealing with a fever originating from infection, give capsules with 2-20 drops of any of the suggested oils.

2. If fever is of unknown origin, use Peppermint, Copaiba, and Cypress: 1-2 drops each; Inner Defense: 1 per 50 lbs. daily; Life 9: 1 daily.

3. NingXia Red 1-2 oz. up to 2 times daily (depending upon severity).

Inhalation: Diffuse Peppermint or Transformation to help regulate the internal temperature.

Other: Determining the cause of fever will assist in the treatment.

Fleas

When dogs are troubled by fleas, they scratch and bite themselves, especially in areas such as the head, neck, and around the tail. This incessant scratching and biting may cause the dog's skin to become red and inflamed. Flea allergy dermatitis is developed by those dogs allergic to flea saliva.

Fleas can be challenging to eradicate due to their total lifecycle. Fleas develop through four stages: egg, larva, pupa, and adult.

When treating for fleas, consider bedding and any surface the dog comes in contact with such as furniture, carpeting, etc. The lifecycle through the stages will span from a few weeks to several months. Consult a veterinary health professional to be sure your treatment is effective, safe, and not contraindicated.

Recommendations

Singles: Citronella, Lemongrass, Black Pepper, Tea Tree, Rosemary, Clove, Oregano, Cinnamon Bark, Peppermint

Blends: Thieves, Purification, RepelAroma, Longevity, ParaGize

Nutritionals: ParaFree, Life 9, Longevity Softgels, NingXia Red, ImmuPower

Additional: Thieves Household Cleaner, Animal Scents Shampoo

Application and Usage

Topical: Bathe animal every 5-7 days in Animal Scents Shampoo in custom mixture (add 4-6 drops RepelAroma, Thieves, or any above-listed oils to 2 oz. Animal Scents Shampoo). Make sure to let the shampoo solution sit on the dog for at least 5 minutes after soaping to kill and repel fleas. Raindrop Technique 2 times weekly is a good preventive for external parasites.

Ingestion & Oral: If the animal is debilitated and weak, use NingXia Red: 1-2 oz. daily; and ImmuPower: 1 per 50 lbs. Also try 1 Longevity Softgel each day in solidified coconut oil.

Other: Use Thieves Household Cleaner for all surfaces that can be washed. Vacuum areas and add 1-4 drops of above-listed oils to bag or canister to help eradicate fleas. Raindrop treatment 1 time a week. Dust sleeping areas with diatomaceous earth and then spray with Thieves Spray.

Foreign Object (Accidental Ingestion)

If at all suspected, this situation requires immediate veterinary consultation. Surgery is often needed. The below recommendations will assist with recovery.

Recommendations

Singles: Copaiba, Cistus, Ginger, Peppermint, Helichrysum, Frankincense, Spearmint, Myrrh

Blends: DiGize, AromaEase, Trauma Life, T-Away

Nutritionals: NingXia Red, Life 9, Detoxzyme, Digest & Cleanse, ComforTone, Essentialzyme

Additional: Animal Scents Ointment

Application and Usage

Topical: Apply 7-8 drops DiGize, Ginger, Peppermint, Spearmint, or AromaEase to abdomen in a circular fashion. Continue as needed or until surgery is performed. After surgery, apply Helichrysum, Myrrh, Copaiba, and Animal Scents Ointment around the incision.

Ingestion & Oral: Copaiba, Peppermint, DiGize, and Helichrysum: 1-4 drops in a capsule with a carrier oil every 4 hours (depending on severity; can be increased if needed). NingXia Red: 1-2 oz. per 20 lbs. every 12 hours; Detoxzyme: 1 per 50 lbs. daily; Life 9: 1 per 25 lbs. 2 times daily; Digest & Cleanse: 1-4 daily; ComforTone: 1-3 daily.

Inhalation: Diffuse Frankincense, T-Away, and/or Trauma Life to assist with healing.

Other: Apply Animal Scents Ointment on surgical site after surgery.

Gallbladder

The most common gallbladder issue in dogs is gallbladder mucocele, a condition in which the gallbladder becomes distended with excess mucus and bile. It is most common in Cocker Spaniels and Shetland Sheepdogs, usually afflicting middle-aged dogs. The dog may appear lethargic, have decreased appetite, exhibit a low-grade fever, and have jaundice.

Another gallbladder affliction in dogs is cholecystitis, an inflammation of the gallbladder and biliary tract.

Consult a veterinary health professional for a complete blood count and chemistry profile.

Recommendations

Singles: Copaiba, Helichrysum, Lemon, Celery Seed, Cypress, Spearmint, Ginger, Peppermint

Blends: GLF, DiGize, Citrus Fresh, JuvaCleanse

Nutritionals: NingXia Red, K&B, Detoxzyme, OmegaGize[3]

Application and Usage

Topical: Apply 2-8 drops of any of the listed oils in a circular motion over the abdominal region. This can be repeated up to 1 time every hour.

Ingestion & Oral: GLF and Copaiba: 2 drops per 20 lbs. up to 2 times daily. Can use Helichrysum and/or JuvaCleanse if GLF is not available. NingXia Red: 1 oz. 2 times daily; K&B: 1 dropperful per 50 lbs.; Detoxzyme: 1 per 50 lbs.; OmegaGize[3]: 2 per 50 lbs. 2 times daily.

Inhalation: Diffuse Ginger and Peppermint to help calm nausea.

Gastric Ulcers

Gastroduodenal ulcer disease refers to ulcers or sores found in the dog's stomach and/or the first section of the small intestine, known as the duodenum.

The most common causes of gastric ulcers are NSAIDS (nonsteroidal anti-inflammatory drugs) used to treat inflammation or fever.

Other causes include accidental poisoning from plant intoxication (e.g., mushrooms, castor beans, sago palm), pesticide or rodenticide toxicity, chemical poisoning (e.g., ethylene glycol, phenol), or heavy metal poisoning (e.g., zinc, iron, arsenic).

Recommendations

Singles: Copaiba, Frankincense, Peppermint, Cistus, Lavender, Roman Chamomile, Myrrh, Ginger, Helichrysum, Orange

Blends: DiGize, JuvaCleanse, AromaEase, Peace & Calming, Stress Away, Purification

Nutritionals: NingXia Red, Life 9, Essentialzyme, Sulfurzyme, OmegaGize[3], Master Formula, Mineral Essence

Application and Usage

Topical: DiGize, Copaiba, Cistus, or Peppermint on abdomen 2-4 times daily.

Ingestion & Oral: 2-10 drops Copaiba and Cistus 2 times daily in capsule; DiGize: 2-10 drops 2 times daily in a capsule; Life 9: 1 per 25 lbs.; Essentialzyme: 1 per 50 lbs.; OmegaGize[3] 2-8 daily.

Inhalation: Diffuse Peace & Calming, Stress Away, Orange, or Purification.

Gastric Dilatation Volvulus (GDV)

This occurs when the stomach rolls or twists, cutting off blood flow. It generally occurs in large and giant breed dogs, and it is an emergency condition. Consult a veterinary health professional immediately. Without surgery, this condition is nearly always fatal. The following recommendations are for post-surgical healing and will assist with recovery.

Recommendations

Singles: Sacred Frankincense, Frankincense, Ginger, Peppermint, Spearmint, Helichrysum, Cypress, Copaiba, Myrrh, Cistus, Lemon

Blends: DiGize, AromaEase, Trauma Life, T-Away, ImmuPower, Peace & Calming

Nutritionals: NingXia Red, Life 9, Sulfurzyme, Essentialzyme, Detoxzyme

Additional: Animal Scents Ointment

Application and Usage

Topical: Apply 3-10 drops DiGize, Sacred Frankincense, Ginger, Cypress, Peppermint, ImmuPower, Copaiba, Cistus, Myrrh, Spearmint, or AromaEase to abdomen in a circular fashion. Continue as needed or until surgery is performed. After surgery, apply Helichrysum and Animal Scents Ointment around the incision.

Ingestion & Oral: Sacred Frankincense, DiGize, Copaiba, and Helichrysum: 2-10 drops in a capsule every 6 hours (depending on severity; can be increased if needed); NingXia Red: 1-2 oz. per 20 lbs. every 12 hours; Essentialzyme or Detoxzyme: 1 per 50 lbs. 2 times daily; Life 9: 1 per 25 lbs. 2 times daily; Sulfurzyme: 2 per 20 lbs.

Inhalation: Diffuse Sacred Frankincense, T-Away, Peace & Calming, and/or Trauma Life to assist with healing.

Other: Be aware of oral ingestion limits; GDV dogs are allowed only small amounts in their stomach at a time after surgery. Space out supplements across the daily treatment protocol.

Giardia

This is a gastrointestinal condition caused by infection with Giardia, a single-celled microorganism. Symptoms include diarrhea, vomiting, stomach cramps, lethargy, and nausea. Consult a veterinary health professional to determine severity, cause, and course of treatment.

Recommendations

Singles: Oregano, Geranium, Tea Tree, Ginger, Patchouli, Clove, Copaiba

Blends: Thieves, DiGize, Egyptian Gold, ImmuPower, ParaGize, Exodus II, Melrose, Purification

Nutritionals: ParaFree, Inner Defense, NingXia Red, Life 9

Additional: Thieves Household Cleaner

Application and Usage

Topical: Rub 1-2 drops each of DiGize and Copaiba with any other suggested oils on abdomen 2-4 times daily.

Ingestion & Oral: Oregano: 1 drop and Thieves: 1 drop 2 times daily for 10 days in a capsule. ParaFree: 1-2 per 50 lbs. 2 times daily for 10 days; ParaFree or Inner Defense: 1 per 50 lbs. daily; NingXia Red: 1-2 oz. daily; Life 9: 1 per 20 lbs. Also administer orally DiGize, Copaiba, Oregano, and Thieves: 2-4 drops each in a capsule 1-2 times daily, depending on size of animal and severity.

Inhalation: Diffuse Thieves, Egyptian Gold, Melrose, Purification, or Exodus II for immune boosting.

Other: Disinfect environment with Thieves Household Cleaner daily.

GI Conditions *(see also* Diarrhea)

This may be any number of conditions affecting the internal organs responsible for digestion, including the stomach and intestines. Consult a veterinary health professional to determine severity, cause, and course of treatment.

Recommendations

Singles: Oregano, Cistus, Helichrysum, Ginger, Spearmint, Copaiba, Peppermint, Fennel, Ocotea, Tarragon, Patchouli, Tea Tree, Sacred Frankincense, Lemon

Blends: AromaEase, DiGize, Thieves, ParaGize, Purification

Nutritionals: Essentialzyme, Life 9, Essentialzymes-4, Detoxzyme, Inner Defense, ParaFree, ICP, ComforTone, MightyZymes, Digest & Cleanse

Application and Usage

Topical: DiGize: 2-10 drops applied on stomach and intestine area. All other oils can be applied in the GI region topically. Dilute if required by pet's weight. Also try Raindrop Technique.

Ingestion & Oral: Essentialzyme, Essentialzymes-4 (1 of each), MightyZymes, or Detoxzyme: 1 per 50 lbs. daily; Life 9: 1 per 25 lbs. 2 times daily; Inner Defense or ParaFree: 1 per 50 lbs. daily; ComforTone: 1 per 20 lbs. daily; Digest & Cleanse: 1, 1-2 times daily.

Inhalation: Diffuse Peppermint, Purification, or Lemon to settle upset stomach, and repel bad aroma.

Other: Maintain a bland diet and fasting if needed to allow healing in the GI region. Give enough food or treats to get supplements into dog.

Gingivitis

This is an inflammation of the gums and is mostly caused by starchy foods in a dog's diet and a lack of good dental hygiene. Dogs should have their teeth brushed and scaled by a professional periodically. Give natural dental chews to bathe the teeth and gums with saliva.

Consult a veterinary health professional to determine severity, cause, and course of treatment.

Recommendations

Singles: Wintergreen, Clove, Tea Tree, Manuka, Ravintsara, Lemon, Peppermint, Copaiba, Myrrh, Spearmint, Rosemary

Blends: Thieves, DiGize, Melrose, Exodus II, ImmuPower, Egyptian Gold, Longevity, AromaEase, Citrus Fresh

Nutritionals: Essentialzyme, Detoxzyme, Life 9, Inner Defense

Additional: Animal Scents Dental Pet Chews, Thieves Fresh Essence Plus Mouthwash, Thieves Dentarome Plus Toothpaste (DO NOT use any of the other Young Living toothpastes as they contain Xylitol, which is fine for humans but may be detrimental to dogs.)

Application and Usage

Topical: Apply your choice of oils on a cotton swab in gum/mouth area.

Ingestion & Oral: Promote good digestion with Essentialzyme or Detoxzyme: 2 per 50 lbs. 2 times daily. Spray gums directly with Thieves Mouthwash daily or apply 1-2 drops Thieves to affected area. Administer Life 9: 1 daily; Inner Defense: 1 daily. Add 1 drop Citrus Fresh or Thieves to 2 quarts of water for drinking. Make sure there is plain water available along with the water containing oils.

Other: Raw, fresh diets promote overall oral health. Providing the best diet possible will help keep teeth clean. Give Dental Pet Chews as recommended on package. Homemade dental biscuits can be made with any of the above oils (add 5-8 drops to recipe) to promote dental/digestive health.

Glaucoma

This is a condition in which the pressure inside the eye poses threat of damage to the nerve or interior. It generally occurs in older dogs and may lead to blindness, if not caught early enough and properly treated. Consult a veterinary health professional to determine severity, cause, and course of treatment.

Recommendations

Singles: Sacred Frankincense, Copaiba, Helichrysum, Cypress, Lemon, Lavender

Blends: Aroma Life, 3 Wise Men, Brain Power, Purification

Nutritionals: NingXia Red, Longevity Softgels, OmegaGize[3], MindWise, Detoxzyme, Mineral Essence

Application and Usage

Topical: Apply 2 drops each Cypress, Sacred Frankincense, Helichrysum, and Copaiba on fingertip and spread around the eyes, avoiding eyelids. Layer in order listed or apply singly starting with Lavender.

Ingestion & Oral: NingXia Red: 1 oz. 2 times daily; Longevity Softgels: 1 per 50 lbs. 2 times daily; OmegaGize[3]: 2 per 50 lbs.; MindWise 1-2 tablespoons 2 times daily.

Inhalation: Diffuse Purification, Cypress, and Lemon with any other suggested oils.

Heart Conditions

These are any conditions, structural or functional, that jeopardize normal functioning of the heart. Dogs generally develop heart conditions from different medical conditions than humans. These include kidney disease, adrenal tumors, and heartworm.

Consult a veterinary health professional to determine cause and course of treatment.

Recommendations

Singles: Cypress, Helichrysum, Ylang Ylang, Frankincense, Cistus, Copaiba, Clove, Marjoram, Cedarwood, Sacred Frankincense

Blends: Aroma Life, Stress Away, Joy, Sensation

Nutritionals: NingXia Red, Longevity Softgels, OmegaGize[3], CardioGize

Application and Usage

Topical: Apply 2-4 drops of suggested selected oils over the chest/heart area 2-3 times daily. Can include Raindrop Technique to stimulate immune system.

Ingestion & Oral: Cypress, Helichrysum, Frankincense, Sacred Frankincense, Cedarwood, and/or Copaiba: 2-4 drops each in a capsule 2 times daily per 50 lbs.; NingXia Red: 1-2 oz. 2 times daily; Longevity Softgels: 1 daily; OmegaGize[3]: 1 per 50 lbs. daily; CardioGize: 1-4 per 50 lbs. daily.

Inhalation: Diffuse any of the oils listed or pet dog on chest with oil on hands for natural diffusing.

Heartworm

This is a parasitic roundworm, *Dirofilaria immitis,* conveyed between animals, primarily by mosquitoes. The adult parasites live primarily in the lung arteries and cause progressive damage to the heart and lungs.

If an animal has a large parasite load, please work with your animal health professional, discuss a course of treatment, and address potential complications. Testing will be required to determine best treatment. See also heart conditions listed above.

Recommendations

Singles: Helichrysum, Cedarwood, Copaiba

Blends: Aroma Life, ParaGize, RepelAroma, Thieves, Purification

Nutritionals: ParaFree, Life 9, Longevity Softgels, NingXia Red, MindWise, CardioGize, Detoxzyme

Additional: Thieves Household Cleaner

Application and Usage

Topical: Raindrop Technique 2 times weekly to help repel parasites and promote overall health. Apply RepelAroma or Purification to repel pests daily.

Ingestion & Oral: ParaFree: 1 per 50 lbs. 2 times daily; Life 9: 1-2 daily; Longevity Softgels: 1 per 50 lbs. 2 times daily; CardioGize: 1-4 per 50 lbs. daily; MindWise: 1 oz. daily; NingXia Red: 1-2 oz. 2 times daily; Detoxzyme: 1-4, 2 times daily; OmegaGize^3: 1-4, 2 times daily; 2-4 drops each Helichrysum, Copaiba, and Cedarwood or Aroma Life.

Inhalation: Diffuse Thieves or Purification to cleanse the environment.

Other: Help kill external parasites by using Thieves Household Cleaner sprayed in environment and housing.

Histiocytoma

This is a benign, abnormal growth in the skin cells that are part of the immune system. Dog breeds that may be more at risk for this tumor include Bulldogs, American Pit Bull Terriers, American Staffordshire Terriers, Scottish Terriers, Greyhounds, Boxers, and Boston Terriers.

Consult a veterinary health professional to confirm benignity. Work with your animal medical professional to determine the best course of treatment. Depending on the location and severity, surgery may be required. The products listed assist in post-surgical recovery.

Recommendations

Singles: Copaiba, Lavender, Lemongrass, Sacred Frankincense, Helichrysum, Myrrh, Frankincense, Tangerine, Orange, Grapefruit, Elemi

Blends: Citrus Fresh, Aroma Life, Melrose, Purification, Longevity, Mendwell, Infect Away, PuriClean

Nutritionals: Longevity Softgels, Inner Defense, NingXia Red, Sulfurzyme, Life 9, OmegaGize^3

Additional: Animal Scents Ointment

Application and Usage

Topical: Apply 2-8 drops of any of the listed oils on location 1-3 times daily, depending on the dog's skin condition. Apply Copaiba, Helichrysum, and Myrrh and layer with Animal Scents Ointment on location either before or after surgery.

Ingestion & Oral: Longevity Softgels: 1 per 50 lbs.; Inner Defense: 1 per 50 lbs.; NingXia Red: 1-2 oz. daily; Life 9: 1-2 daily; OmegaGize^3: 2-4, 2 times daily. Administer orally 2-6 drops each Copaiba, Frankincense, and Sacred Frankincense combined with any other suggested oil(s).

Hit by Car

Many breeds are instinctive darters and have been selectively bred for their motivation to chase fast-moving things. If your dog is hit by a car, render first aid and then consult a veterinary health professional to determine the extent of the damage, the best treatment strategy, and long-term prevention of potential complications. Unseen internal damage is possible and must be addressed.

There are, however, things you can do immediately to calm the dog while waiting for veterinarian treatment.

Recommendations

Singles: Frankincense, Sacred Frankincense, Lavender, Roman Chamomile, Idaho Tansy, Cistus, Copaiba, Palo Santo, Helichrysum

Blends: Trauma Life, Mendwell, T-Away, Valor, Valor II, Release, Peace & Calming, Peace & Calming II, Aroma Life

Nutritionals: Sulfurzyme, Life 9

Application and Usage

Topical: Pet the dog liberally with Trauma Life, Sacred Frankincense, Frankincense, and/or Lavender while traveling to the veterinarian.

Ingestion & Oral: Lavender, Copaiba, Cistus, or Helichrysum: 2-3 drops in mouth; Frankincense or Sacred Frankincense and Cistus: 1-2 drops under the tongue. Other oils and supplements may be needed depending on injuries sustained.

Other: Put copious amounts of Lavender, Trauma Life, Copaiba, Helichrysum, Cistus, or Idaho Tansy on any wounds and wrap with cotton, clean linen, vet wrap, or ace bandage to stop bleeding while transporting to a veterinarian.

Horner's Syndrome (Bell's Palsy)

This is a condition where select facial muscles lose their ability to respond to nerve stimuli. Generally, it results from injury to the nerves or from lesions that form on the brain, upper spinal cord, or the nerves that run from the spine to the face. It may be from trauma, infection in the middle ear, cancer of the brain or chest, medication, or intervertebral disc disease in the neck area. Consult a veterinary health professional to establish the underlying cause and best treatment strategy.

Recommendations

Singles: Cypress, Copaiba, Helichrysum, Ravintsara, Melissa, Eucalyptus Blue, Juniper, Petitgrain, Frankincense

Blends: ImmuPower, Thieves, Exodus II, Raven, RutaVaLa Roll-On, PanAway, Relieve It

Nutritionals: Sulfurzyme, MultiGreens, NingXia Red, Longevity Softgels, Life 9, Mineral Essence, Inner Defense, Detoxzyme, OmegaGize[3]

Application and Usage

Topical: Apply 2-10 drops of 1-3 of above-listed oils on location, being careful to avoid eyes and nose area. Use Raindrop Technique at least 2 times weekly to stimulate nerve regeneration.

Ingestion & Oral: Sulfurzyme: 2 per 20 lbs. or ½ teaspoon every 6 hours; MultiGreens: 2 per 50 lbs.; NingXia Red: 1-2 oz. 2 times daily.

Hot Spots (Pyotraumatic Dermatitis, Wet Eczema)

A hot spot (also known as pyotraumatic or moist dermatitis) is a condition that involves an area of skin that has become inflamed and infected. The affected skin often appears as a moist, oozing, reddened area that is painful and very itchy to the dog. Hair loss may also be seen.

Hot spots (also known as summer sores or moist dermatitis) can seemingly appear spontaneously anywhere on a dog's body; the surrounding area can rapidly deteriorate too. This moist, raw skin disorder has a variety of causes; but the most consistent factor is bacteria, fungus, or adverse reactions to food (especially grains).

Recommendations

Singles: Lavender, Hyssop, Hong Kuai, Rosemary, Lemongrass, Bergamot, Black Pepper, Tea Tree, Oregano, Thyme, Ginger, Ocotea, Mountain Savory, Geranium, Patchouli, Basil, Copaiba

Blends: Melrose, Infect Away, Thieves, Purification, Longevity, PuriClean, Egyptian Gold, Exodus II, DiGize, ImmuPower

Nutritionals: Life 9, Inner Defense, Sulfurzyme, Longevity Softgels, Digest & Cleanse

Additional: Animal Scents Shampoo, Thieves Household Cleaner

Application and Usage

Topical: Apply 3-6 drops of any selected oils and Copaiba directly on hot spot 3 times daily. Continue to apply selected oils once the wound has healed and no open sores are present.

Ingestion & Oral: Longevity Softgels: 1, 2 times daily; Life 9: 1 per 50 lbs.; Inner Defense: 1 per 50 lbs. 1 time daily; Sulfurzyme: 2 per 20 lbs. or ½ teaspoon every 6 hours; Digest & Cleanse: 1, 2 times daily.

Other: Raindrop Technique 1 time weekly; bathe every 3-5 days with Animal Scents Shampoo and rinse with highly diluted Thieves Household Cleaner.

Hygromas (Pressure Sores, Decubital Ulcers, Calluses) (*see* Calluses)

Hyperthermia

This is a state of increased body temperature and may be caused by exertion or exposure to long bouts of extreme heat and humidity. It is a form of heat stroke in dogs. Dogs do not tolerate extreme heat as well as other animals because they sweat in minimal quantities and mainly through their paws.

If external temperatures exceed 102°F, panting may not be able to cool the dog sufficiently. Avoid exercising dogs in hot weather, leaving them in hot cars, keeping them leashed on asphalt or sun-exposed concrete, and confining them in warm spaces. Be sure they have plenty of shade and fresh water. Seek immediate veterinary attention if you suspect heat stroke.

Recommendations

Singles: Peppermint, Copaiba, Cypress

Blends: Transformation, DiGize, Citrus Fresh

Application and Usage

Topical: Apply 1-5 drops Peppermint, Copaiba, and Cypress on abdomen, under arms, and on ears every 30-60 minutes.

Ingestion & Oral: Administer 1-5 drops Peppermint and Copaiba under tongue every hour.

Hypothyroidism

This is a condition in which the thyroid doesn't produce enough T3 or T4 hormone. In a majority of canine cases, hypothyroidism is caused by actual destruction of the thyroid gland. The condition is most common in adult dogs 4 to 10 years old, usually affecting mid-size to large-size breeds. In dogs, it occurs equally between the sexes.

Signs of the disease are lethargy, weight gain (with no appetite change), changes in the skin and coat, excessive shedding, and trouble keeping warm.

Eliminate exposure to chlorine- and fluoride-containing tap water and household chemicals. Consult a veterinary health professional to determine hormone levels, severity of deficiency, and mode of treatment. Involve your animal medical professional in the testing and monitoring of the endocrine system. Proper testing ensures your dog's health is maintained.

Recommendations

Singles: Lemongrass, Cypress, Copaiba, Spearmint, Myrtle, Dorado Azul

Blends: EndoFlex, Clarity, En-R-Gee, ImmuPower, Egyptian Gold

Nutritionals: Thyromin, EndoGize, PowerGize, MultiGreens, Sulfurzyme, Super B, OmegaGize[3], NingXia Red, PD 80/20, MindWise, Mineral Essence

Application and Usage

Topical: Apply 1-2 drops of EndoFlex and En-R-Gee on dog's throat and chest daily. Apply ImmuPower, Cypress, and Copaiba on pads of feet and on the stomach area. Dorado Azul and Spearmint work better for females; Myrtle, better for males.

Ingestion & Oral: Copaiba: 1-4 drops daily; Thyromin: 1-2 daily per 50 lbs.; PowerGize: 1-2 daily per 50 lbs.; MultiGreens: 1-4 daily per 50 lbs.; Sulfurzyme: 2 per 20 lbs. or ½ teaspoon every 12 hours; Mineral Essence: 2-20 drops daily.

Incontinence

Urinary incontinence occurs when a housetrained dog loses control of his bladder. Severity can range from occasional small urine leaks to complete emptying of bladder.

Causes can range from hormonal imbalance, weak bladder sphincter, urinary tract infection, urinary stones, spinal injury or degeneration, prostate disorders, kidney disease such as diabetes, and congenital abnormalities such as dementia, medication, and anatomic disorders.

Recommendations

Singles: Copaiba, Helichrysum, Juniper, Lemongrass, Marjoram, Palo Santo, Sage, Tsuga

Blends: EndoFlex, Longevity, SclarEssence

Nutritionals: K&B, Life 9, NingXia Red, Longevity Softgels, FemiGen, Estro, AgilEase, EndoGize, Sulfurzyme.

Additional: Progessence Plus

Application and Usage

Topical: Apply 1-6 drops each Copaiba, Juniper, and Lemongrass directly on stomach area 2 times daily. For female dogs with hormone-related incontinence, apply 1-3 drops Progessence Plus to area on caudal ventral abdomen over the area of the bladder 1-2 times daily.

Ingestion & Oral: Copaiba and Juniper: 2-10 drops each; K&B: 6-8 drops daily; AgilEase: 1-4 daily.

Other: Frequent Raindrop Technique administered weekly may be beneficial.

Inflammatory Bowel Disease (Idiopathic IBD)

IBD results in inflammation of the intestines, which produces chronic symptoms related to the gastrointestinal tract. This condition is caused by abnormalities with the immune system, initiated by lack of good bacteria within the digestive tract. Concentrating on supporting a healthy immune system, proper digestive health, and reducing inflammation is ideal.

Occasionally IBD is caused by a bacterial infection in the intestines. Avoid feeding the animal a diet high in grains to help prevent infection spread.

Recommendations

Singles: Helichrysum, Peppermint, Ginger, Tarragon, Copaiba, Spearmint, Frankincense, Cistus, Lemon, Sacred Frankincense, Myrrh, Lavender

Blends: DiGize, AromaEase, ImmuPower, Thieves, Peace & Calming

Nutritionals: Life 9, Essentialzyme, Sulfurzyme, NingXia Red, MindWise, OmegaGize[3]

Additional: Animal Scents Dental Pet Chews

Application and Usage

Topical: Apply liberally a combination of the following oils to abdominal area 3 times daily: DiGize, ImmuPower, Copaiba, and Myrrh.

Ingestion & Oral: Administer 1-3 drops each DiGize, Copaiba, and Cistus 2 times daily; Life 9: 1 daily; Sulfurzyme: 1-4, 2 times daily; OmegaGize[3]: 1-4 daily; Essentialzyme: 1 with each feeding daily.

Inhalation: Diffuse Peppermint and Peace & Calming.

Other: Supplementing with Life 9 is imperative, followed by enzymes. Frequent Raindrop Technique, at least 1 time weekly, may be beneficial.

Kennel Cough (Canine Infectious Tracheobronchitis) (see also Cough)

Kennel cough is canine respiratory infection caused by *Bordetella bronchiseptica* or canine parainfluenza virus. These pathogens attack the respiratory tract and cause inflammation of the upper airway. The cough can sound like a hoarse honking, often causing the coughing up of mucus.

It is highly contagious among dogs in communal areas such as dog shows, kennels, veterinary offices, dog parks, and grooming shops. Always remove feces from kennel every day.

Recommendations

Singles: Eucalyptus Blue, Eucalyptus Radiata, Laurus Nobilis, Tea Tree, Myrtle, Oregano, Peppermint, Rosemary, Ravintsara, Blue Cypress, Basil, Black Pepper, Copaiba, Cedarwood, Mountain Savory, Lemongrass, Dorado Azul, Wintergreen

Blends: R.C., Thieves, Purification, Breathe Again Roll-On, ImmuPower, Melrose, Raven, Exodus II

Nutritionals: NingXia Red, Inner Defense, Life 9

Other: Raindrop Technique

Application and Usage

Topical: Apply R.C., Thieves, Lemongrass, Oregano, or Raven to the chest area 3-4 times daily. Also administer the Raindrop Technique daily until cough clears.

Ingestion & Oral: Thieves: 10 drops or Inner Defense: 1, 1-2 times daily; NingXia Red: 1-2 oz. 2 times daily; Life 9: 1 daily.

Inhalation: Diffuse R.C., Thieves, Purification, Raven, Wintergreen, and Oregano.

Kidney Disease

Chronic kidney disease (CKD) is defined as kidney disease that has been present for months to years. Chronic renal disease (CRD), chronic renal failure (CRF), and chronic renal insufficiency (CRI) refer to the same condition. CKD is not a single disease.

There are many different causes of CKD, but by the time the animal shows signs of kidney disease, the cause may no longer be apparent. Some potential causes of CRF include:

- Congenital malformation of the kidneys (birth defects)
- Chronic bacterial infection of the kidneys with or without kidney stones (pyelonephritis)
- High blood pressure (hypertension)
- Disease associated with the immune system (e.g., glomerulonephritis, systemic lupus)
- Acute kidney disease and poisoning with venom, toxic chemicals, or antifreeze that damages the kidneys can lead to CKD.

Often the cause of CKD is unknown.

Recommendations

Singles: Copaiba, Cypress, Cistus, Geranium, Grapefruit, Helichrysum, Juniper

Blends: Aroma Life, Aroma Siez, Purification, Peace & Calming

Nutritionals: K&B, NingXia Red, Life 9, Essentialzyme

Application and Usage

Topical: Apply copious amounts of Copaiba, Cypress, Helichrysum, and Juniper to stomach area 2-4 times daily.

Ingestion & Oral: Single oils: 2-5 drops each; Life 9: 1 daily; Essentialzyme: 1, 1-2 times daily; K&B: 1 dropperful per 25 lbs. 3-4 times daily; NingXia Red: 1-2 oz. 2 times daily.

Inhalation: Diffuse Purification and Peace & Calming.

Lacerations

These are wounds caused by tearing or scraping of the tissue. They may be from minor trauma, producing damage only to the skin; or they may be more severe, causing damage to muscles, nerves, blood vessels, or tendons. Most cases are caused by sharp objects in the environment: glass, fencing, or furniture edges.

If the laceration seems superficial, you most likely can treat the wound yourself. Consult a veterinary health professional if the bleeding doesn't immediately stop with gentle pressure with a clean towel. If you suspect blunt trauma, such as being hit by a car or being bitten by another animal, seek medical attention from a veterinary professional.

Recommendations

Singles: Helichrysum, Lavender, Cistus, Copaiba, Tea Tree, Myrrh, Sacred Sandalwood, Royal Hawaiian Sandalwood, Geranium, Manuka, Idaho Tansy

Blends: Melrose, PanAway, Purification, Thieves, PuriClean, Infect Away, Mendwell, Australian Blue, Trauma Life, T-Away

Nutritionals: NingXia Red, Inner Defense, Essentialzyme, Sulfurzyme, Mineral Essence, Life 9

Additional: Animal Scents Ointment, Rose Ointment, Animal Scents Shampoo, Thieves Household Cleaner

Application and Usage

Topical: Apply in order, 2-6 drops of each directly to wound: Idaho Tansy, Cistus, Helichrysum, and Copaiba with any other selected suggested oils, ending with Myrrh and layering Animal Scents Ointment over the top of the oils. Also try washing the wound gently with Animals Scents Shampoo or diluted Thieves Household Cleaner. Apply Lavender and vitamin E oil directly on wound.

Ingestion & Oral: Administer orally 2-10 drops any combination of suggested oils (except Idaho Tansy) 2 times daily to support proper healing. Also try administering Sulfurzyme: 2-8, 2 times daily; NingXia Red: 2 oz. 2 times daily; Life 9: 1 daily; Essentialzyme: 1-2 daily.

Other: Also apply or use Animal Scents Ointment, Rose Ointment, Animal Scents Shampoo, or diluted Thieves Household Cleaner. Use Elizabethan Collar to keep dog from licking wound, preventing the healing process.

Lick Granuloma (Acral Lick Dermatitis, Hot Spots, Acute Moist Dermatitis)

Hot Spots are caused by constant licking or chewing prompted by a variety of reasons: diet, allergies, fleas, mites, underlying ear or skin infections, stress, or boredom. They are most common in dogs that have skin conditions or allergies that manifest as skin irritations. Most dogs will lick areas on the wrist joint, top of the front paw, lower hind legs, or sensitive areas of the abdomen.

Lick granulomas can progress at a notoriously fast pace and may lead to a secondary bacterial infection or pyoderma. Most often they are harmless, but they may be a secondary indicator of other conditions. Consult a veterinary health professional to rule out serious, underlying causes.

Recommendations

Singles: Black Pepper, Palmarosa, Lemongrass, Manuka, Patchouli, Blue Cypress, Dorado Azul, German Chamomile, Geranium, Helichrysum, Juniper, Lavender, Marjoram, Tea Tree, Melissa, Mountain Savory, Myrrh, Nutmeg, Ocotea, Oregano, Palo Santo, Spruce, Valerian, Vetiver, Wintergreen, Ylang Ylang, Orange, Grapefruit, Idaho Balsam Fir, Sacred Frankincense

Blends: Deep Relief Roll-On, Trauma Life, Exodus II, JuvaFlex, ImmuPower, Infect Away, Mendwell, PuriClean, ParaGize, Egyptian Gold, Longevity, Melrose, PanAway, Purification, Relieve It, Thieves, Peace & Calming, Stress Away, Inner Child, Grounding

Nutritionals: Super B, Sulfurzyme, NingXia Red, Essentialzyme, Inner Defense, Life 9, Mineral Essence, OmegaGize[3]

Additional: LavaDerm Cooling Mist, Thieves Spray, Animal Scents Ointment

Applications and Usage

Topical: Apply oils liberally directly to the hot spot 2 times daily. Spray with LavaDerm Cooling Mist or Thieves Spray. Add oils such as Helichrysum to the spray as well. To discourage licking of the area, apply 1 drop of ParaGize neat to that area.

> ### Veterinarian Tips and Suggestions
>
> ## Lick Granuloma
>
> Combine Melrose: 10 drops, Patchouli 10 drops, with Animal Scents Ointment: 1 oz. and apply 1-4 times daily with the use of an Elizabethan Collar.

Ingestion & Oral: NingXia Red: 1-2 oz. 2 times daily; OmegaGize[3]: 1-4, 2 times daily; Life 9: 1 daily; Essentialzyme: 1-2 daily; Inner Defense (to support digestive health and fight inflammation or infections): 1 daily.

Inhalation: Diffuse Thieves, Purification, Peace & Calming, Stress Away, Inner Child, Orange, Grapefruit, Grounding, Idaho Balsam Fir, Trauma Life, or Sacred Frankincense.

Other: Raindrop Technique daily if needed. Also try LavaDerm Cooling Mist, Thieves Spray, or Animal Scents Ointment. Use Elizabethan Collar to keep dog from licking wound, preventing the healing process.

Lipoma

Lipomas are benign fatty tumors that are common in older and overweight dogs. They are subcutaneous masses or tumors that develop under the skin. They are soft to the touch, painless, and flexible. Most commonly, they are smaller than a centimeter, and, in some cases, may come and go within a matter of months without treatment. Mature, obese female dogs develop these on the trunk and near the tops of the legs.

Consult a veterinary health professional to confirm diagnosis and to rule out other types of tumors.

Recommendations

Singles: Copaiba, Lemon Myrtle, Rosemary, Manuka, Grapefruit, Ledum, Lemongrass, Lemon, Thyme, Myrtle

Blends: DiGize, Purification, Citrus Fresh

Nutritionals: Detoxzyme, Longevity Softgels, OmegaGize[3], JuvaTone, Life 9, Sulfurzyme, Mineral Essence

Additional: Cel-Lite Magic Massage Oil

Application and Usage

Topical: Massage the lump up to 4 times daily with Cel-Lite Magic Massage Oil. Liberally apply Lemon, Myrtle, Lemongrass, and Copaiba with any other selected oils.

Ingestion & Oral: Citrus Fresh: in water daily; Longevity Softgels: 1, 1-2 times daily; Detoxzyme: 2-4 daily; Life 9: 1 daily; Sulfurzyme: 2-4, 2 times daily; Mineral Essence: 2-6 dropperfuls 2 times daily. Lemon Myrtle and Copaiba: 10 drops each combined 1-2 times daily.

Liver Disease

The liver is a highly regenerative, multifunctional organ in dogs. It helps to remove the toxins from your dog's system. When it is not working correctly, it can overwhelm the dog's system and cause sickness. Signs include loss of appetite, vomiting, excessive urination and thirst, jaundice (skin or eyes), weight loss, and fever.

Consult a veterinary health professional if you suspect liver disease to determine the overall health of the dog, as well as treatment options and prevention of secondary complications.

Recommendations

Singles: Helichrysum, Grapefruit, Juniper, Ledum, Myrrh, Rosemary, Tangerine, Copaiba, Celery Seed, Carrot Seed

Blends: Citrus Fresh, GLF, JuvaCleanse, JuvaFlex, DiGize, Release, Peace & Calming, Joy

Nutritionals: NingXia Red, OmegaGize[3], Sulfurzyme, Rehemogen, Detoxzyme

Application and Usage

Topical: Liberally apply Ledum, Copaiba, and JuvaFlex over the liver 3-4 times daily.

Ingestion & Oral: Add Citrus Fresh to water; Copaiba, GLF, or JuvaCleanse:10 drops each in a capsule 1-4 times daily; Detoxzyme: 2-4, 2 times daily; Sulfurzyme: 2-5, 2 times daily; NingXia Red: 1 oz. 1-4 times daily; Rehemogen: 1 dropperful 1-4 times daily.

Inhalation: Diffuse Release, Peace & Calming, Joy, or Grapefruit.

Mastitis

Mastitis is a bacterial infection in one or more of the lactating glands. This is inflammation of the mammary gland(s) due to a bacterial infection. It generally occurs after a dog has given birth.

The affected glands are hot and painful. A suffering dog may exhibit fever, lethargy, and reduced appetite. Warm compresses may help reduce the inflammation, and the puppies should be encouraged not to feed from the affected glands. Consult a veterinary health professional to determine the cause of the infection and to prevent complications.

Recommendations

Singles: Copaiba, Clove, Patchouli, Manuka, Black Pepper, Lemongrass, Tea Tree, Mountain Savory, Myrrh, Oregano

Blends: Melrose, Purification, Thieves, Infect Away, Exodus II, DiGize, Egyptian Gold

Nutritionals: Inner Defense, NingXia Red, Life 9, Detoxzyme, Sulfurzyme

Additional: Animal Scents Ointment, ClaraDerm

Application and Usage

Topical: Apply 1 drop Oregano, 3 drops Melrose, and 3 drops Copaiba to affected area. Cover oils with Animal Scents Ointment and massage onto mammary area 1-4 times daily.

Ingestion & Oral: Inner Defense: 1-2 daily; Life 9: 1 daily; Detoxzyme: 1-3, 2 times daily; Sulfurzyme: 2-5, 2 times daily.

Inhalation: Diffuse Purification, Melrose, or Thieves.

Megaesophagus (Also known as ME)

Normally the esophagus has a muscle-like action of pushing food down into the stomach, much like peristalsis in the wave-like motions of the intestine.

But with megaesophagus in an animal, the esophagus does not contract. The food may not enter the stomach, causing regurgitation, which may be aspirated into the lungs or left decaying in the esophagus. Consult a veterinary health professional.

Recommendations

Singles: Helichrysum, Juniper, Laurus Nobilis, Lavender, Marjoram, Peppermint, Copaiba, Melissa, Ocotea, Basil, Idaho Balsam Fir

Blends: DiGize, ImmuPower, Clarity, Exodus II, Aroma Siez, Mendwell, EndoFlex, Into the Future, Thieves, Purification

Nutritionals: MindWise, Super C Chewable, OmegaGize[3], NingXia Red, Sulfurzyme, MightyZymes

Application and Usage

Topical: Liberally apply DiGize, ImmuPower, Copaiba, and any other suggested oils over the esophagus 2-6 times daily.

Ingestion & Oral: Sulfurzyme: 2-5, 1-2 times daily; MightyZymes: 1-4, 2 times daily; Super C Chewable: 2-6 daily; NingXia Red: 1-2 oz. 2 times daily; MindWise: 1-2 oz. daily; OmegaGize[3]: 1-2 daily; Helichrysum and Copaiba: 2-5 drops each daily.

Inhalation: Idaho Balsam Fir, Clarity, Exodus II, Into the Future, Thieves, Purification.

Muscle Wasting (Sarcopenia)

Muscle wasting is common in older dogs and consists of the loss of lean muscle mass. Some cases are caused from lack of using muscles due to arthritic pain. However, it is most common for dogs to experience this when they lack digestive enzymes, resulting in nutritional deficiency.

Recommendations

Singles: Idaho Balsam Fir, Idaho Blue Spruce, Northern Lights Black Spruce, Basil, Cypress, Lavender, Marjoram, Wintergreen, Peppermint, Copaiba

Blends: Aroma Siez, PanAway

Nutritionals: AgilEase, BLM, Essentialzyme, OmegaGize[3], Sulfurzyme, NingXia Red, Mineral Essence, PowerGize, CardioGize, MindWise

Additional: Regenolone Moisturizing Cream, Ortho Ease Massage Oil, Ortho Sport Massage Oil

Application and Usage

Topical: Apply Idaho Balsam Fir, Aroma Siez, Copaiba, and/or Marjoram over affected areas. Layer with Regenolone Moisturizing Cream, Ortho Ease Massage Oil, or Ortho Sport Massage Oil. Apply with any other suggested oils 2-4 times daily.

Ingestion & Oral: NingXia Red: 1-2 oz. 2-4 times daily; AgilEase: 2, 1-4 times daily; BLM: 1-4, 2 times daily; Sulfurzyme: 1-5, 2 times daily; Mineral Essence: 1-2 dropperfuls 2 times daily.

Neurologic Conditions

Many conditions affect the nervous system. These may be primary or secondary and may require extensive study to determine the cause. Poor gut health can contribute to poor neurologic function.

Supporting proper gut health is imperative to re-establishing proper neurologic health. Consult a veterinary health professional to confirm diagnosis and treat the causal condition.

Recommendations

Singles: Cedarwood, Cistus, Copaiba, German Chamomile, Helichrysum, Frankincense, Lavender, Rosemary, Peppermint, Lemon, Cypress, Sacred Frankincense, Valerian, Idaho Balsam Fir, Idaho Blue Spruce, Northern Lights Black Spruce, Vetiver, Petitgrain, Hong Kuai

Blends: Brain Power, Clarity, Valor, DiGize, GeneYus, T-Away, Trauma Life, 3 Wise Men, Aroma Life, Transformation, RutaVaLa Roll-On, Stress Away

Nutritionals: MindWise, NingXia Red, Sulfurzyme, OmegaGize^3, Essentialzymes-4, Life 9, PD 80/20, Mineral Essence, Detoxzyme, MultiGreens, Super B

Additional: Thieves Household Cleaner

Application and Usage

Topical: Apply desired oils inside the tips of ears and near the brainstem. Try Sacred Frankincense, Helichrysum, Cypress, and Copaiba with any other suggested oils.

Ingestion & Oral: NingXia Red: 1-2 oz. 2-3 times daily; MindWise: 1 oz. 1-2 times daily; Sulfurzyme: 2-5, 2 times daily; Life 9: 1 daily; Mineral Essence: 2-8 dropperfuls 2 times daily; OmegaGize^3: 1-4, 2 times daily; Essentialzymes-4: 1 of each 1 time daily.

Inhalation: Diffuse Lemon, Cedarwood, Rosemary, or any other suggested oils.

Other: Clean dog's environment with diluted Thieves Household Cleaner. DO NOT use toxic chemicals anywhere near affected animal.

Obedience Training

Dogs respond best to positive reinforcement and science-based training with the use of essential oils. Working with a Certified Pet Dog Trainer is highly recommended. If dealing with specific behavior issues, please refer to individual sections and consult with a Certified Dog Trainer or Certified Behaviorist.

Recommendations

Singles: Lemon, Tangerine, Orange, Peppermint, Lavender, Frankincense, Sacred Frankincense, Palmarosa, Cedarwood, Rosemary, Ocotea, Neroli

Blends: Awaken, Acceptance, Believe, Brain Power, Citrus Fresh, Clarity, Common Sense, Dream Catcher, Gathering, GeneYus, Grounding, Harmony, Hope, Highest Potential, Inspiration, Joy, Live with Passion, Live Your Passion, Magnify Your Purpose, Motivation, Oola Field, Oola Fun, Peace and Calming, Peace and Calming II, Present Time, Sacred Mountain, Stress Away, Surrender, Transformation, Tranquil Roll-On, Valor, Valor II, White Angelica, Inner Child

Nutritionals: OmegaGize^3, Life 9, Essentialzyme, NingXia Red, MindWise, Sulfurzyme, Mineral Essence

Additional: Animal Scents Dental Pet Chews

Application and Usage

Topical: Apply any suggested oils to base of skull 15 minutes before training.

Ingestion and Oral: NingXia Red: 1 oz. 1-2 times daily; Mineral Essence: 2-6 dropperfuls 2 times daily; Life 9: 1 daily.

Inhalation: Diffuse Lemon and Peppermint in training area.

Other: Expenditure of physical exercise is helpful before beginning your training regimen. Always make training a fun and rewarding experience, something your dog and you look forward to.

Pain

Pain is a general term that is a symptom of a large percentage of diseases. Pain management is often key in preventing a dog from suffering lameness or complications. Severe pain can inhibit the healing process and suppress the immune system. Consult a veterinary health professional to discover the underlying cause.

Recommendations

Singles: Copaiba, Sacred Frankincense, Frankincense, Helichrysum, Idaho Balsam Fir, Lavender, Marjoram, Myrrh, Palo Santo, Peppermint, Wintergreen, Elemi, Northern Lights Black Spruce, Idaho Blue Spruce, Cypress, Dorado Azul, Pine

Blends: Deep Relief Roll-On, M-Grain, PanAway, Release, Relieve It, Valor, Valor II, Stress Away, Aroma Siez, Cool Azul

Nutritionals: AgilEase, BLM, Sulfurzyme, Mineral Essence, NingXia Red, Life 9, Detoxzyme, MightyZyme, ParaFree

Additional: Ortho Ease Massage Oil, Ortho Sport Massage Oil, Cool Azul Pain Relief Cream, Cool Azul Sports Gel

Pain:

Recipe #1:
- 4 drops Copaiba
- 4 drops Frankincense
- 4 drops Idaho Balsam Fir
- Combine in a vegetable capsule and give internally 2-4 times daily.

Recipe #2:
- 1-5 drops Idaho Balsam Fir
- 1-5 drops Elemi
- 1-5 drops Wintergreen
- 1-5 drops Copaiba
- Combine in capsule or in food; adjust mixture according to canine size and preference. Can be given 2-4 times daily.

Application and Usage

Topical: Liberally apply any of the above oils on your dog 1-4 times daily or as needed when dog appears to be in pain. Start with Copaiba and apply any other suggested oils. Layer or cover applied oils with Ortho Sport Massage Oil, Ortho Ease Massage Oil, Cool Azul Pain Relief Cream, or Cool Azul Sports Gel. Apply Raindrop Technique 1 time daily.

Ingestion & Oral: Administer any suggested oils directly or in a vegetable capsule 1-3 times daily. NingXia Red: 1 oz. 1-4 times daily; AgilEase: 2-4, 2 times daily; Sulfurzyme: 2-5, 2 times daily; BLM: 2-5, 2 times daily.

Pancreatitis

Pancreatic enzymes are secreted after a stimulus (getting into the garbage, table scraps, or toxins). Digestive enzymes released too quickly begin painful digestion of the pancreas, requiring immediate veterinary care. Symptoms can include diarrhea, vomiting, and abdominal pain.

Recommendations

Singles: Copaiba, Geranium, Ginger, Helichrysum, Lavender, Ocotea, Peppermint, Spearmint, Cypress, Dill, Fennel, Coriander, Cinnamon Bark, Lemongrass

Blends: DiGize, GLF, JuvaCleanse, PanAway, Relieve It, Thieves, Peace & Calming, Stress Away

Nutritionals: OmegaGize[3], Detoxzyme, Digest & Cleanse, Essentialzyme, Essentialzymes-4, Life 9, Sulfurzyme, NingXia Red, Mineral Essence, MultiGreens, Slique Essence, K&B

Application and Usage

Topical: Apply various oils from above to help with pain and inflammation. Starting with Copaiba, Thieves, DiGize, and Ocotea together, apply any other suggested oils to stomach area 2-6 times daily. Administer the Raindrop Technique 3 times a week.

Ingestion & Oral: DiGize, Copaiba, or Ocotea: 2-5 drops each in a vegetable capsule or drop in mouth 1-4 times daily depending on severity; Essentialzyme: 1-4 daily; Life 9: 1 daily; Sulfurzyme: 2-4, 2 times daily; Mineral Essence: 2-8 dropperfuls 2 times daily; NingXia Red (diluted 50/50 in water): 1 oz. 2 times daily; K&B: 4-10 drops 2 times daily; OmegaGize[3]: 2-5, 2 times daily; Slique Essence: 1-2 drops daily.

Inhalation: Diffuse Thieves, Ocotea, and Lemongrass together; Peace & Calming, Stress Away, or Lavender for calming.

Parasites

A healthy digestive tract makes it more difficult for parasites to invade the digestive system. Parasites interfere with proper digestion. As nondiscriminating eaters, dogs are particularly susceptible to parasites that live in the soil. They may also be subject to parasites transmitted by insects or questionable water sources.

Consult a veterinary health professional to confirm the type and best mode of treatment.

Recommendations

Singles: Oregano, Copaiba, Patchouli, Lemongrass, Tea Tree, Mountain Savory, Ocotea, Peppermint, Spearmint, Tarragon, Thyme, Fennel, Clove

Blends: DiGize, ParaGize, Purification, PuriClean

Nutritionals: ParaFree, Detoxzyme, Life 9

Additional: Thieves Household Cleaner

Application and Usage

Topical: Liberally apply DiGize and Copaiba on abdomen 2 times daily. Apply Raindrop Technique weekly.

Ingestion & Oral: ParaFree: 1 per 50 lbs. 2 times daily or ParaGize: 10 drops 2 times daily; Detoxzyme: 1-4, 2 times daily; Life 9: 1 daily.

Inhalation: Diffuse Purification, ParaGize, or PuriClean.

Other: Wash everything with diluted Thieves Household Cleaner.

Parvo

Parvo is a virus that causes bloody diarrhea and vomiting. The virus can live in the environment for a very long time and is resistant to many environmental disinfectants. Parvo often requires veterinary care with hospitalization.

Combine essential oils with veterinary care to maximize a favorable outcome. Start essential oil treatment immediately upon onset of viral infection.

Recommendations

Singles: Copaiba, Ginger, Cistus, Ocotea, Clove, Tea Tree, Lemongrass, Ravintsara, Mountain Savory, Melissa, Oregano, Peppermint, Tarragon, Thyme, Lavender, Idaho Balsam Fir

Blends: DiGize, ImmuPower, Purification, Thieves, Melrose, Exodus II, ParaGize, Peace & Calming, Valor, Stress Away

Nutritionals: Inner Defense, Life 9, ParaFree, Detoxzyme, NingXia Red

Additional: Thieves Household Cleaner

Application and Usage

Topical: Liberally apply Copaiba, Cistus, Thieves, Exodus II, and DiGize to the abdomen every hour. Use Peace & Calming, Valor, Stress Away, Lavender, and Idaho Balsam Fir to help relax your dog and pet on 1-4 times daily. Administer Raindrop Technique daily.

Ingestion & Oral: Combine DiGize: 5 drops, Thieves: 5 drops, Oregano: 2 drops, and Melrose: 5 drops in a vegetable capsule and administer 2 times daily. Alternate previous recipe each day with either ParaGize: 10 drops or ParaFree: 1. Also, Life 9: 1 daily; Detoxzyme: 1-4, 2 times daily; NingXia Red: 1 oz. 1-2 times daily.

Inhalation: Diffuse Thieves and Purification, rotating throughout the communal area to help prevent the spread of the virus and aid in supporting the health of dogs inflicted.

Other: Clean environment thoroughly with diluted Thieves Household Cleaner and Purification.

Patella (Luxating)

Patella luxation occurs when a dog's kneecap is dislocated from its normal anatomical position. This is a condition where the kneecap floats, dislocates, or moves out of position easily. It is particularly common in small, miniature, and toy breeds. It usually presents when the dog is middle-aged.

Most dogs can live with the discomfort. In extreme cases, surgery is required. Consult a veterinary health professional to determine severity of case.

Recommendations

Singles: Basil, Copaiba, Idaho Balsam Fir, Frankincense, Helichrysum, Lemongrass, Marjoram, Palo Santo, Spruce, Wintergreen, Idaho Blue Spruce, Northern Lights Black Spruce

Blends: Aroma Siez, Deep Relief Roll-On, PanAway, Relieve It, Release

Nutritionals: AgilEase, NingXia Red, OmegaGize[3], Sulfurzyme, MultiGreens, BLM, Mineral Essence, Life 9

Additional: Cool Azul Pain Relief Cream, Cool Azul Sports Gel, Regenolone Moisturizing Cream, Ortho Ease Massage Oil, Ortho Sport Massage Oil, Animal Scents Ointment

Application and Usage

Topical: Apply Copaiba, Lemongrass, Idaho Balsam Fir, and Idaho Blue Spruce with any other suggested oils to the kneecap 1-4 times daily. Layer over top of oils with Regenolone Moisturizing Cream. Administer the Raindrop Technique as needed.

Ingestion & Oral: NingXia Red: 1 oz. 1-2 times daily; Life 9: 1 daily; MultiGreens: 1-4 daily; BLM: 1-4, 2 times daily; Sulfurzyme: 1-5, 2 times daily; AgilEase: 1-4, 1-2 times daily; Mineral Essence: 2-6 dropperfuls 2 times daily.

Pregnancy & Delivery

Pregnancy and delivery can be very vulnerable times for both the mother and the pups. In the days following birth, several complications pose a threat to pups and the mother. Be sure to consult your veterinary health professional during the pregnancy, around the time of delivery, and the days following whelping.

Recommendations

Singles: Frankincense, Lavender, Sacred Frankincense, Copaiba, Myrrh

Blends: En-R-Gee, Gentle Baby, Stress Away, Peace and Calming II, Valor, Valor II, Aroma Siez, Purification

Nutritionals: Longevity Softgels, NingXia Red, Mineral Essence, Life 9

Additional: Thieves Household Cleaner

Application and Usage

Topical: Apply various oils to promote a calm state of mind during pregnancy and delivery. Put Myrrh and Gentle Babies on puppies' umbilical cord area after mother has cleaned the pups.

Ingestion & Oral: In the days prior to birth and days after giving birth, administer orally to the mother NingXia Red: 1-2 oz. 2 times daily; Longevity Softgels: 1-2 daily; Life 9: 1 daily; Mineral Essence: 2-6 dropperfuls 2 times daily. This will help support the mother and puppies while nursing.

Inhalation: Diffuse calming oils in the birthing room during labor.

Other: Clean whelping area with diluted Thieves Household Cleaner and Purification.

Pressure Sores (Hygromas, Calluses) (*see* Calluses)

Pyometra

Pyometra is a life-threatening infection of the uterus that occurs in unspayed females due to hormonal changes in the dog's reproductive tract. If there is no pregnancy following estrus for several cycles, the uterine lining can increase until cysts form that create an environment where bacteria can grow. Serious bacterial infection can occur that can turn fatal if not treated promptly.

Signs and symptoms usually manifest one to three months after the completion of an estrus cycle in females. Seek immediate attention from a veterinary health professional as surgery may be necessary.

The following suggestions are for the recuperation period.

Recommendations

Singles: Cistus, Copaiba, Palmarosa, Patchouli, Myrrh, Bergamot, Australian Blue, Geranium, Helichrysum, Lavender, Mountain Savory, Tea Tree, Oregano, Sage, Lavender

---

Veterinarian Tips and Suggestions

Pyometra

Combine 5 drops Copaiba, 5 drops Geranium, 5 drops Melrose, and 5 drops Myrrh together in a needleless syringe. Insert into vaginal canal 1-2 times daily according to severity.

Blends: Dragon Time, Infect Away, PuriClean, ImmuPower, Exodus II, Egyptian Gold, Melrose, Mister, Purification, Thieves, Peace & Calming II

Nutritionals: Inner Defense, NingXia Red, Estro, Life 9, Longevity Softgels, Digest & Cleanse

Application and Usage

Topical: Apply Copaiba and Thieves with any other suggested oils to abdomen to combat infection and balance hormones. Administer the Raindrop Technique 2-3 times weekly.

Ingestion & Oral: NingXia Red: 1 oz. 2 times daily; Life 9: 1 daily; Inner Defense: 1 daily; Longevity Softgels: 1 daily; Digest & Cleanse: 1 daily.

Inhalation: Diffuse Thieves, Purification, and Melrose with any other suggested oil to combat infection.

Respiratory Infections

Dogs may experience many viral and bacterial respiratory infections, both primary and secondary. Consult a veterinary health professional to determine the cause and best treatment plan.

Recommendations

Singles: Basil, Blue Cypress, Cedarwood, Copaiba, Dorado Azul, Eucalyptus Blue, Eucalyptus Globulus, Eucalyptus Radiata, Frankincense, German Chamomile, Helichrysum, Hinoki, Hong Kuai, Hyssop, Idaho Balsam Fir, Idaho Blue Spruce, Lavender, Lemongrass, Lemon Myrtle, Melaleuca Ericifolia, Melaleuca Quinquenervia, Melissa, Myrtle, Northern Lights Black Spruce, Ocotea, Oregano, Palo Santo, Peppermint, Ravintsara, Roman Chamomile, Sacred Frankincense, Sacred Mountain, Tea Tree, Wintergreen, Xiang Mao

Blends: Aroma Siez, Believe, Breathe Again Roll-On, Christmas Spirit, Clarity, Deep Relief Roll-On, Egyptian Gold, En-R-Gee, Evergreen Essence,

Exodus II, Forgiveness, Gratitude, Hope, Humility, ImmuPower, Infect Away, Live with Passion, Longevity, M-Grain, Melrose, Mendwell, PanAway, ParaGize, Present Time, PuriClean, Raven, R.C., Relieve It, Stress Away, T-Away, The Gift, Thieves, Transformation, Trauma Life

Nutritionals: NingXia Red, Inner Defense, Life 9

Application and Usage

Topical: Apply Thieves, Raven, Oregano, and Lemongrass with any selected suggested oil to chest area. Administer the Raindrop Technique daily if needed.

Ingestion & Oral: Thieves or Raven: 2-10 drops 2-3 times daily; Life 9: 1 daily; Inner Defense: 1 per 50 lbs. daily; NingXia Red: 1-2 oz. daily.

Inhalation: Diffuse any selected suggested oil.

Ringworm (Dermatophytosis)

This is a fungal skin, hair, and nails infection that afflicts animals and humans alike. Most canine cases are the result of *Microsporum canis, Trichophyton mentagrophytes,* or *Microsporum gypseum.* It is more common in hot, humid areas and generally occurs in fall and winter.

Consult a veterinary health professional to be sure treatments are effective and that there are no complications such as a secondary infection.

Recommendations

Singles: Tea Tree, Oregano, Lemongrass, Patchouli, Blue Cypress, Geranium, Myrrh, Copaiba, Basil, Bergamot, Clove, Cinnamon Bark, Dorado Azul, Ocotea, Mountain Savory, Myrtle

Blends: Thieves, Purification, Melrose, ParaGize, PuriClean, DiGize, Exodus II, Longevity, Egyptian Gold

Nutritionals: Inner Defense, ParaFree

Additional: ClaraDerm, Thieves Household Cleaner, Thieves Foaming Hand Soap, Thieves Waterless Hand Purifier, Animal Scents Shampoo, Animal Scents Ointment

Application and Usage

Topical:

1. Depending on severity—bathe dog in a solution of ⅓ Animal Scents Shampoo or Thieves Household Cleaner and warm water. Let sit on coat/skin for 5-10 minutes after shampooing; then rinse.

2. Apply blend of any above-listed oils. Oils can be applied neat around the area. Rub in Thieves Hand Purifier over affected areas.

3. Apply Animal Scents Ointment over the oils or spray ClaraDerm if needed to ease sensitivity.

Ingestion & Oral: Thieves, Melrose, and Oregano: 3-6 drops each in a capsule 1-2 times daily; Inner Defense: 1 daily; ParaGize: 1 daily for 10 days; ParaFree: 1, 1-2 times daily for 10-15 days.

Other: Clean and disinfect everywhere your dog resides with a strong solution of Thieves Household Cleaner. Use gloves when handling infected areas and use Thieves Foaming Hand Soap and Thieves Waterless Hand Purifier. **Ringworm is highly contagious and easily transferable.**

Sarcoptic Mange

This is a highly contagious skin disease caused by *Sarcoptes scabiei* mite. Intense itching often causes hair loss from scratching. Treatment generally includes quarantine until eradicated. Consult a veterinary health professional for treatment options.

Recommendations

Singles: Tea Tree, Ocotea, Clove, Basil, Geranium, Palmarosa, Laurus Nobilis, Rosemary, Lemongrass, Patchouli, Copaiba, Oregano (use Oregano orally only)

Blends: Thieves, Purification, Melrose, RepelAroma, ParaGize

Nutritionals: Inner Defense, ParaFree, Longevity Softgels, Life 9, Mineral Essence, NingXia Red, Detoxzyme

Additional: ClaraDerm, Thieves Household Cleaner, Thieves Foaming Hand Soap, Thieves Waterless Hand Purifier, Animal Scents Shampoo, Animal Scents Ointment

Application and Usage

Topical:

1. Depending on severity—bathe dog in a solution of ⅓ Animal Scents Shampoo, ⅓ Thieves Household Cleaner, and warm water. Let sit on coat/skin for 5-10 minutes after shampooing; then rinse.

2. Liberally apply blend of any above oils directly on the area 2-4 times daily. Oils can be applied neat around the area.

3. Apply Animal Scents Ointment over the oils or spray ClaraDerm.

Ingestion & Oral: ParaFree: 1, 1-2 times daily for 21 days; Inner Defense or Longevity Softgels: 1-2 daily; Life 9: 1-2 daily; ParaGize: 4-8 drops daily; Mineral Essence: 4-8 dropperfuls 1-2 times daily; Detoxzyme: 1-4, 2 times daily; NingXia Red: 1-2 oz. daily.

Inhalation: Diffuse Purification with any other suggested oils.

Other: Disinfect areas with strong solution of Thieves Household Cleaner. Use gloves when touching infected areas and use Thieves Foaming Hand Soap and Thieves Waterless Hand Purifier.

Sebaceous Cysts

These generally occur when pores or hair follicles clog. While akin to acne, canine sebaceous cysts shouldn't be lanced because of the high risk of infection. If the cyst bursts, dogs may lick the infected pus. If the cyst grows aggressively, it may be the sign of a greater problem. An aggressive cyst may pose a higher infection risk if it bursts. Some sizable cysts require stitching to close.

Often these conditions are associated with hypothyroidism issues—see list of recommendations for this topic. Zinc supplementation and diet changes are often needed.

Recommendations

Singles: Tea Tree, Lemongrass, Geranium, Ocotea, Patchouli, Clove, Basil

Blends: Purification, Infect Away, PuriClean, Thieves, Melrose, ParaGize

Nutritionals: OmegaGize[3], NingXia Red, Sulfurzyme, Inner Defense, Life 9, ParaFree, Mineral Essence

Additional: Thieves Household Cleaner, Animal Scents Ointment, Animal Scents Shampoo

Application and Usage

Topical: Depending on the cysts' severity and infectious nature, apply as follows:

1. To combat infection, layer liberally any suggested oils 2-4 times daily on location. Administer Raindrop Technique every other day.
2. To combat cystic growths, use Melrose or Purification on location 2-4 times daily.

3. Depending on severity—bathe dog in a solution of ⅓ Animal Scents Shampoo, ⅓ Thieves Household Cleaner, and warm water. Let sit on coat/skin for 5-10 minutes after shampooing; then rinse and dry.
4. Apply Animal Scents Ointment on location after applying oils and shampooing.

Ingestion & Oral: Inner Defense: 1 per 50 lbs. daily; Sulfurzyme: 1 per 20 lbs. or ½ teaspoon every 6 hours; OmegaGize[3]: 2 per 50 lbs. 2 times daily; NingXia Red: 1-2 oz. daily; Life 9: 1 daily; ParaFree: 1, 1-2 times daily for 21 days; Mineral Essence: 2-6 dropperfuls 2 times daily.

Inhalation: Diffuse any selected suggested oils.

Seborrhea Oleosa (Dander/excess oil)

This is a condition in which keratin builds up on the skin rather than sloughing off naturally. The dog's skin displays flaky (seborrheic dermatitis), greasy (seborrhea oleosa), or dry (seborrhea sicca) skin scales. It may be a primary or secondary condition. The primary condition is caused by genetics.

Secondary cases are caused by allergies, parasites, hormones, medications, or hypothyroidism. Often these conditions are associated with hypothyroidism issues. See list of recommendations for this topic. Zinc and Iodine supplementation and diet changes are often needed.

Recommendations

Singles: Tea Tree, Lavender, Geranium, Copaiba, Sage, Rosemary, Ravintsara, Patchouli, Manuka, Hong Kuai, Basil, Eucalyptus Globulus, Wintergreen, Lemongrass, Laurus Nobilis

Blends: Purification, PuriClean, Thieves, Melrose, R.C., Raven, ImmuPower, ParaGize

Nutritionals: OmegaGize[3], NingXia Red, Sulfurzyme, Inner Defense, Mineral Essence, Detoxzyme, Thyromin

Additional: Thieves Household Cleaner, Animal Scents Ointment, Animal Scents Shampoo

Application and Usage

Topical: Depending on the severity, apply as follows:

1. Liberally apply selected oils 2-4 times daily on location.
2. Administer Raindrop Technique 2 times weekly.
3. To combat oily coat, bathe in a solution of ⅓ Animal Scents Shampoo, ⅓ Thieves Household

Cleaner, and warm water. Let sit on coat/skin for 5-10 minutes after shampooing; then rinse.

Ingestion & Oral: Inner Defense: 1 per 50 lbs. daily; Sulfurzyme: 3 per 20 lbs. or ½ teaspoon every 6 hours; OmegaGize^3: 2 per 50 lbs. 2 times daily; NingXia Red: 1-2 oz. daily; Life 9: 1 daily; Mineral Essence: 4-8 dropperfuls 2 times daily; Detoxzyme: 1-4, 2 times daily; Thyromin: 1-2 daily.

Seizures

Seizures are abnormal bursts of electrical activity in the brain that cause twitching or uncontrollable shaking. Episodes can last from 30 seconds to several minutes. Dogs have seizures from epilepsy, eating poison, head injury, anemia, brain infections, kidney disease, electrolyte imbalance, and liver disease. Consult a veterinary health professional to determine the cause, severity of the case, and long-term treatment options.

Recommendations

Singles: Lavender, Frankincense, Idaho Balsam Fir, Royal Hawaiian Sandalwood, Sacred Sandalwood, Valerian, Cedarwood, Roman Chamomile, Jasmine, Hong Kuai, Helichrysum, Petitgrain, Copaiba, Sacred Frankincense, Cypress, Lemon, Jasmine

Blends: Peace & Calming, Valor II, Gentle Baby, Brain Power, 3 Wise Men, Stress Away, Grounding, Harmony

Nutritionals: MindWise, Essentialzyme, MultiGreens, OmegaGize^3, NingXia Red, Mineral Essence, Life 9

Additional: Thieves Household Cleaner, Animal Scents Shampoo

Application and Usage

Topical: Apply selected oils topically starting with Copaiba, Cypress, and Sacred Frankincense with any other selected oils to behind the skull and down the sides of the head and under the ears. Apply oils daily and during seizures (being careful to not be near the mouth).

Ingestion & Oral: MindWise: 1 tablespoon per 40 lbs. 2 times daily; Essentialzyme: 1 per 50 lbs.; MultiGreens: 1 per 50 lbs. 2 times daily; OmegaGize^3: 2-4 per 40 lbs. 2 times daily; NingXia Red: 1-2 oz. daily; Mineral Essence: 3-6 dropperfuls 2 times daily; Life 9: 1 daily.

Inhalation: Use any of the above oils to diffuse as needed. Sacred Frankincense or Idaho Balsam Fir is a good place to start; you may have to try different combinations depending on your dog's individual needs.

Other: Make sure to watch external toxins affecting the pet; use nontoxic cleaners such as Thieves Household Cleaner and Animal Scents Shampoo. Remove all scented sprays and candles; replace by diffusing with oils.

Skin Tags

These are benign skin lumps that appear in cauliflower shapes with a wart-like surface. They often appear in multiples on mature dogs. They may be surgically removed, but they may reappear at any time in multiples after removal.

Consult a veterinary health professional to confirm benignity and removal.

Recommendations

Singles: Frankincense, Grapefruit, Lemon, Lemongrass, Oregano, Sacred Frankincense, Clove, Thyme, Copaiba

Blends: Thieves, Longevity, Egyptian Gold, Citrus Fresh

Nutritionals: Digest & Cleanse, Life 9, Mineral Essence, Longevity Softgels, OmegaGize^3

Additional: Animal Scents Ointment

Application and Usage

Topical: Apply 1 drop of 2-3 selected oils directly to the area. You may have to switch combinations to find the right approach. Apply Animal Scents Ointment on location after applying oils if needed to calm irritation.

Ingestion & Oral: Citrus Fresh: in water daily; Longevity Softgels: 1 per 50 lbs. 2 times daily; OmegaGize^3: 2 per 50 lbs. 2 times daily; Life 9: 1 daily; Digest & Cleanse: 1, 1-2 times daily.

Spondylosis Deformans

This is a degenerative condition found in senior dogs in which bone spurs form along degenerative discs of the spine. These cause the spine to lose flexibility and range of motion. The bone spurs may also cause some pain or nerve damage.

Because the symptoms may be similar to other diseases, consult a veterinary health professional. Once your vet has conducted tests to rule out other conditions, treatment will focus on pain, inflammation, and flexibility.

Recommendations

Singles: Copaiba, Lemongrass, Idaho Balsam Fir, Sacred Frankincense, Frankincense, Helichrysum, Wintergreen, Cypress, Northern Lights Black Spruce, Eucalyptus Globulus, Clove, Dorado Azul

Blends: R.C., PanAway, Deep Relief Roll-On, Relieve It, Peace & Calming, Stress Away

Nutritionals: NingXia Red, Sulfurzyme, Longevity Softgels, BLM, OmegaGize^3, AgilEase, Super C Chewable, Super Cal, Detoxzyme, Mineral Essence, Life 9

Additional: Ortho Sport Massage Oil, Ortho Ease Massage Oil

Application and Usage

Topical: Apply R.C., Cypress, and Copaiba with any selected suggested oils on specific area. Ortho Sport Massage Oil and Ortho Ease Massage Oil: massage into painful areas 1 time daily and in areas where the dog is compensating for painful joints 2-4 times daily. Apply Raindrop Technique 2 times weekly until improvement is noted.

Ingestion & Oral: Longevity Softgels: 1-2 daily; BLM: 2-4, 2 times daily; NingXia Red: 1-4 oz. daily; OmegaGize^3: 2-4, 2 times daily; Sulfurzyme: 2 per 15 lbs. 2 times daily; Super C Chewable: 1 per 25 lbs.; Life 9: 1 daily; Super Cal: 2-4, 2 times daily; NingXia Red: 1-2 oz. 2 times daily; Mineral Essence: 2-4 dropperfuls 2 times daily; Detoxzyme: 1-4, 2 times daily.

Inhalation: Diffuse Peace & Calming and Stress Away.

Other: Maintain a healthy weight; excess weight on joints causes extra strain on compromised skeletal frame.

Steroid Alternative (Corticosteroid Alternative)

Synthetically enhanced corticosteroid hormones block immune system response in dogs with allergies or that have been exposed to toxins. There are many side effects of pharmacological steroid-based treatments.

While many caregivers will turn to nonsteroidal anti-inflammatory drugs, these also have potential long-term side effects. By using these essential oil alternatives, caregivers can help with symptoms while reducing exposure to side effects.

Consult a veterinary health professional to determine when and how you might try replacing corticosteroid treatments with alternatives.

Recommendations

Singles: Copaiba, Wintergreen, Helichrysum, Cypress, Blue Cypress, Sacred Frankincense, Roman Chamomile, German Chamomile, Idaho Balsam Fir, Idaho Blue Spruce, Northern Lights Black Spruce, Cedarwood

Blends: RutaVaLa Roll-On, PanAway, Relieve It, Deep Relief Roll-On, Australian Blue, Stress Away, Peace & Calming

Nutritionals: Sulfurzyme, OmegaGize^3, NingXia Red, Detoxzyme, BLM, AgilEase, Allerzyme, Mineral Essence, MindWise

Application and Usage

Topical: Copaiba, Helichrysum, Cypress, and Idaho Balsam Fir applied on location 2-6 times daily.

Ingestion & Oral: Copaiba: 2-10 drops per 50 lbs. 2-4 times daily; Sulfurzyme: ¼ teaspoon per 10 lbs. 2 times daily or 1 per 10 lbs. 2 times daily; Allerzyme: 1-4 daily; OmegaGize^3: 2-5, 2 times daily; NingXia Red: 1-4 oz. daily; MindWise: ½-1 oz. 2 times daily.

Inhalation: Diffuse Stress Away and Peace & Calming

Submissive Urination

Submissive urination is an uncontrollable, instinctive reaction to the presence of another dog or human that they feel is superior to them. Dogs may have this condition for many reasons from abuse to lack of confidence. Work on confidence-building exercises in conjunction with essential oils. It may be helpful to work with a Certified Pet Dog Trainer to help with submissive urination.

Recommendations

Singles: Lavender, German Chamomile, Frankincense, Northern Lights Black Spruce, Patchouli, Copaiba, Roman Chamomile, Sacred Frankincense, Idaho Blue Spruce, Cypress, Neroli, Palo Santo, Sacred Sandalwood, Royal Hawaiian Sandalwood

Blends: Acceptance, Gathering, Grounding, Harmony, Valor, Valor II, Inner Child, Humility,

White Angelica, T-Away, Trauma Life, Shutran
Nutritionals: K&B, Mineral Essence, NingXia Red

Application and Usage
Topical: Apply Acceptance, Grounding, White Angelica, Valor, or Valor II on ears 15 minutes before guests arrive.

Inhalation: Diffuse Valor, Valor II, or Sacred Frankincense 15 minutes before company is to arrive. Diffuse Trauma Life while sleeping.

Other: Use essential oils in combination with a positive-based obedience training program that focuses on confidence building.

Thrombocytopenia

This is a condition in which platelet count diminishes and prevents proper blood clotting. This can happen to dogs of any breed or age. It may be caused by decreased production of platelets, leukemia, extreme blood loss from an injury, hemorrhage, or infection.

Because dogs with this condition may suffer from internal bleeding or ruptured organs, it is important to consult a veterinary health professional for thorough testing.

Recommendations
Singles: Sacred Frankincense, Frankincense, Copaiba, Cistus, Helichrysum

Blends: ImmuPower

Nutritionals: NingXia Red, MultiGreens, OmegaGize[3], Sulfurzyme, Mineral Essence

Application and Usage
Topical: Apply Helichrysum, Copaiba, and Cistus on major blood vessels 4 times daily. Use the Raindrop Technique 3 times weekly.

Ingestion & Oral: NingXia Red: 1-2 oz. 2 times daily; OmegaGize[3]: 2-4, 2 times daily; Sulfurzyme: 2 per 10 lbs. 2 times daily; Mineral Essence: 3-6 dropperfuls 2 times daily; Life 9: 1 daily; Essentialzyme: 1, 1-2 times daily. Copaiba, Cistus, and Helichrysum: 3-5 drops each together in a capsule 2-3 times daily.

Inhalation: Diffuse Sacred Frankincense or Frankincense with any other selected suggested oils.

🐕 Veterinarian Tips and Suggestions

Tick Spray Recipe
Combine:
- 10 drops Purification
- 10 drops RepelAroma
- 10 drops Eucalyptus (any)
- ¼ cup Thieves Household Cleaner

Directions:
1. Combine ingredients in 4 oz. glass spray bottle.
2. Fill bottle with V-6 Vegetable Complex Oil (approx. 1 oz.).
3. Shake well; spray on dog daily. Avoid eyes and other sensitive areas.
4. Store in a cool, dry place for later use.

Tick Bites/Disease

Several diseases can be transmitted to your pet from a tick bite. Some of the most common tick-borne diseases seen in the United States are Lyme disease, Rocky Mountain spotted fever, ehrlichiosis, and tick paralysis.

Recommendations
Singles: Palo Santo, Lemongrass, all Eucalyptus oils, Cedarwood, Wintergreen, Cinnamon Bark, Oregano, Hyssop, Laurus Nobilis, Mountain Savory, Ravintsara, Black Pepper, Blue Cypress, Myrrh, Hong Kuai, Hinoki, Basil, Copaiba, Thyme, Clove, Ocotea, Lavender, Tea Tree, Rosemary

Blends: Purification, RepelAroma, Thieves, Melrose, Exodus II, Egyptian Gold, PuriClean, ParaGize, Infect Away, ImmuPower, Raven, R.C., Longevity, DiGize

Nutritionals: ParaFree, Longevity Softgels, Inner Defense, Sulfurzyme, Detoxzyme, MultiGreens, Rehemogen, Mineral Essence, Life 9

Additional: Thieves Household Cleaner, V-6 Vegetable Oil Complex

Application and Usage
Topical: Liberally apply chosen oils to tick bite several times daily for 3-5 days. Administer Raindrop Technique every other day for 2 weeks.

Ingestion & Oral: ParaFree: 1 per 25 lbs. for 10 days during tick season; Longevity Softgels: 1 per 20 lbs. daily; Inner Defense: 1 per 50 lbs. daily; Life 9: 1 daily; NingXia Red: 1-2 oz. daily; Sulfurzyme:

1-4, 2 times daily; Detoxzyme: 1-4, 2 times daily; MultiGreens: 1-3, 2 times daily; Mineral Essence: 4-8 dropperfuls daily; Rehemogen: 1 dropperful 1-2 times daily.

Inhalation: Diffuse Purification or RepelAroma to repel ticks.

Urinary Conditions (see also Incontinence, Cystitis, Bladder Cancer and Submissive Urination)

Dogs are subject to a range of urinary conditions. They may suffer from kidney stones, bladder inflammation, bladder infection, cancer, trauma, stress, prostate disease, spinal cord abnormalities, congenital anomalies, or hormonal issues. Consult a veterinary health professional to determine the cause and course of treatment.

Recommendations

Singles: Geranium, Copaiba, Oregano, Juniper, Lemongrass, Tea Tree, Basil, Manuka, Ravintsara, Mountain Savory, Helichrysum

Blends: Thieves, Purification, Melrose, Exodus II, ImmuPower

Nutritionals: Inner Defense, K&B, Life 9, NingXia Red, MultiGreens

Additional: Thieves Household Cleaner

Application and Usage

Topical: Apply selected oils and Copaiba directly on bladder/stomach area several times daily. Apply Oregano to lower lumbar region. Administer Raindrop Technique 2-3 times weekly.

Ingestion & Oral: K&B: 1 dropperful per 20 lbs. 2 times daily; Inner Defense: 1 per 20 lbs. 1 time daily; Life 9: 1 daily; MultiGreens: 1-4, 2 times daily; NingXia Red: 1-2 oz. daily; Exodus II, Basil, and Copaiba: 2-5 drops each in a vegetable capsule 2 times daily.

Inhalation: Diffuse selected suggested oils.

Other: Maintain clean surfaces, bedding, and flooring with Thieves Household Cleaner.

Vaccinosis

Some dogs will experience a stronger adverse reaction to vaccines. Reactions may include pain or swelling at the injection site, allergic responses, neurologic complications, and contamination with other live agents. Additionally, the stress of a vaccine may bring out an infection that was present in the animal but dormant.

If a caregiver knows that an animal suffers adverse reactions, he or she may want to prepare the animal in advance with supplements and essential oil treatments. The animal may benefit from continuing these treatments for weeks following the vaccination.

Consult a veterinary health professional to discuss your concerns about reactions to vaccines, both in the short term and long term. Always observe a pet following its vaccination and know the emergency signs.

Recommendations

Singles: Frankincense, Copaiba, Cedarwood, Manuka, Ledum, Helichrysum, Sacred Frankincense, Melissa, Basil, Ravintsara, Cypress

Blends: GLF, JuvaCleanse, JuvaFlex, DiGize, Thieves, Exodus II, Raven, Purification

Nutritionals: Detoxzyme, JuvaTone, MultiGreens, NingXia Red, Mineral Essence, Rehemogen

Application and Usage

Topical: Administer Raindrop Technique daily. Apply Copaiba, JuvaFlex, or DiGize over the abdomen to help process toxins out of the body. Apply Sacred Frankincense, Copaiba, Cypress, or Cedarwood on the brainstem 2-4 times daily.

Inhalation: Diffuse selected suggested oils.

Other: Provide as fresh, healthy, and organic a diet as possible to promote the body naturally detoxifying.

Vestibular Disease (Idiopathic) (see also Ear Infections)

This condition affects the dog's balance systems. Causes may be the result of old age, chronic inner ear infection, trauma to the ear, drugs that have toxic effects on the ear, tumors, calcification within the ear, hypothyroidism, or unknown cause (idiopathic). Central vestibular disease is less common and can have inflammatory causes as well as from infection, bleeding in the brain, and cancer.

Symptoms include head tilt, nausea or reduced appetite, vomiting, flicking their eyes back and forth, unsteadiness, circling in one direction, or rolling on the floor.

If there is an ear infection, reference that topic. This condition, if severe, does require veterinary intervention. Assist with recovery by using the following protocols.

Recommendations

Singles: Geranium, Clove, Tea Tree, Cypress, Juniper, Copaiba, Blue Cypress, Lemon, Helichrysum, Lavender, Ginger, Sacred Frankincense, Peppermint

Blends: Brain Power, DiGize, Australian Blue, GeneYus, 3 Wise Men, Clarity, Melrose, Valor, Transformation

Nutritionals: Essentialzyme, Life 9, NingXia Red, MindWise, Mineral Essence, OmegaGize³, Longevity

Applications and Usage

Topical: Apply Raindrop Technique every other day; include oils to address specific concerns such as nausea or neurological issues. Apply Sacred Frankincense, Cypress, Helichrysum, Copaiba and/or Brain Power: 1-2 drops per 50 lbs. at base of skull 2-3 times daily. Valor on pads of feet, base of skull, and along spine: 1-2 times daily. Apply Copaiba, Ginger, DiGize, and Peppermint if animal is nauseated.

Ingestion & Oral: NingXia Red: 1-2 oz. 2 times daily; Essentialzyme: 1 daily; Life 9: 1 daily; Longevity: 1-2 daily; OmegaGize³: 1-4, 2 times daily; MindWise: 1 oz. daily.

Inhalation: Diffuse Ginger to help with nausea, Sacred Frankincense or Clarity, Lemon or Transformation to help with neurological symptoms.

Other: Watch hydration and dietary intake; make sure the pet is receiving adequate amounts.

Viral Conditions

The top viral conditions for dogs include canine parvovirus, canine coronavirus, canine distemper, canine influenza, infectious canine hepatitis, canine herpesvirus, pseudorabies, canine minute virus, canine papilloma virus, and canine rotavirus.

Consult a veterinary health professional to confirm infection, determine best course of treatment, and prevent complications.

Recommendations

Singles: Basil, Bergamot, Black Pepper, Blue Cypress, Breathe Again Roll-On, Cedarwood, Cinnamon Bark, Cistus, Citronella, Clove, Coriander, Cypress, Dorado Azul, Eucalyptus Blue, Eucalyptus Globulus, Eucalyptus Radiata, Fennel, Frankincense, Geranium, Hong Kuai, Hyssop, Juniper, Laurus Nobilis, Lemon, Lemongrass, Lemon Myrtle, Melaleuca Ericifolia, Melaleuca Quinquenervia, Melissa, Mountain Savory, Myrrh,

Myrtle, Neroli, Ocotea, Oregano, Peppermint, Ravintsara, Rosemary, Sacred Frankincense, Tea Tree, Thyme, Xiang Mao

Blends: Abundance, Australian Blue, Christmas Spirit, Clarity, Egyptian Gold, Exodus II, Gathering, Hinoki, ImmuPower, Infect Away, Longevity, M-Grain, Melrose, Mendwell, ParaGize, PuriClean, Purification, Raven, R.C., Repel Aroma, Relieve It, The Gift, Thieves

Nutritionals: Inner Defense, Longevity Softgels, OmegaGize³, ImmuPro, Life 9, Detoxzyme, Mineral Essence, NingXia Red, MultiGreens, Essentialzyme

Additional: Thieves Household Cleaner

Application and Usage

Topical: Apply any of the above oils 2-3 times daily on stomach area and feet. Administer the Raindrop Technique 3-4 times weekly.

Ingestion & Oral: Inner Defense: 1 daily; Longevity Softgels: 1-2, 2 times daily; NingXia Red: 1-2 oz. daily; MultiGreens: 1-4 daily; Detoxzyme: 1-4, 2 times daily; Essentialzyme: 1 at mealtimes; Life 9: 1 daily; Mineral Essence: 4-8 dropperfuls daily; OmegaGize³: 1-4, 2 times daily.

Inhalation: Use any of the above-listed oils; diffuse as needed.

Other: Use Thieves Household Cleaner to cleanse areas, add to laundry, spray areas, and wipe down surfaces.

Vomiting

Dogs vomit for a variety of reasons. They may have eaten too fast, they may have eaten something that didn't settle, or it may be the sign of a serious condition or medical emergency.

Acute episodes of vomiting may be due to a foreign body, acute kidney or liver failure, heat stroke, viral or bacterial infection, parasites, pancreatitis, food intolerance, ingesting toxins, or electrolyte imbalance.

Consult a veterinary health professional to determine underlying cause. Seek emergency care if the suspected cause is a medical emergency such as swallowing a foreign body, organ failure, toxin ingestion, or heat stroke.

Recommendations

Singles: Ginger, Peppermint, Lemon, Copaiba, Spearmint, Ocotea, Fennel

Blends: DiGize, ParaGize, AromaEase

Nutritionals: Life 9, Essentialzyme, Detoxzyme, ParaFree, Longevity Softgels, Inner Defense, Digest & Cleanse

Application and Usage

Topical: Layer Ginger or DiGize and Copaiba or Peppermint on the abdomen. Add in any of the above-listed oils 2-3 times daily.

Ingestion & Oral: Life 9: 1 daily; Essentialzyme: 1, 1-2 times daily; Digest & Cleanse: 1 daily.

Inhalation: Diffuse Lemon, Ginger, Peppermint, or AromaEase.

Warts (Papillomatosis)

These are benign tumors on the skin caused by papillomavirus. In dogs, these are mostly raised, limited to surface of skin, and varied in color. Some types may progress into common forms of skin cancer. Consult a veterinary health professional to biopsy and confirm benignity.

Recommendations

Singles: Clove, Thyme, Eucalyptus Blue, Melissa, Oregano, Lemongrass, Ravintsara

Blends: Thieves, Raven, Exodus II, Melrose, ImmuPower, Purification

Nutritionals: Longevity Softgels, OmegaGize^3, Life 9, NingXia Red, Detoxzyme, JuvaTone

Additional: Animal Scents Ointment

Application and Usage

Topical: Apply selected oils directly to the area: 1-2 drops of up to 2-3 oils. You may have to switch combinations to find the right approach. Apply Animal Scents Ointment on location after applying oils.

Ingestion & Oral: Longevity Softgels: 1-2, 2 times daily; OmegaGize^3: 2 per 50 lbs. daily; Life 9: 1 daily; JuvaTone: 1-2 daily; Detoxzyme: 1-4 daily; NingXia Red: 1-2 oz. daily.

Inhalation: Diffuse Thieves, Melrose, or Purification.

Testimonials

One of my sled dogs, Danke, got her paw badly squished between two panels of a chain link fence. They had to undo the panel connectors to get her out, and it looked excruciatingly painful.

After using a cold pack and pain medication, I applied alternating combinations of Copaiba, Lemongrass, and Peppermint with Lavender, Myrrh, and Peppermint for several hours. I also massaged Danke's arm, shoulder, and back with Aroma Siez. By the next morning, Danke was running and jumping around in her kennel without a limp.

-Jean W.

It was the first race of the season for Terry and me. We loaded the dogs and arrived at the race location the night before the race. When we let the dogs out of the traveling crates, one of them, Maker, had swelling in her wrist joint and crepitus, with lateral and medial motion.

We layered Oregano, Copaiba, Lemongrass, and Peppermint on the joint and then Aroma Siez on the muscles from the wrist to the shoulder and wrapped her lower leg with neoprene for several hours.

By the next morning, Maker was bouncing around like there had been no problem, and Terry determined that she was sound to race. During the race, a problem arose with a leader, and Maker subsequently finished the race in lead position.

-Jean W.

Terry's and my sled dog named Only was diagnosed with a salivary mucocele [a cyst that forms in the mouth]. We contacted Dr. Hoke to see what could be done to avoid surgery, since surgery would limit Only's ability to run.

We decided to layer Thyme, Cypress, Thieves, and Peppermint on the site and on her feet. The swelling grew worse by the end of the day, but Only didn't seem to be in pain. By morning the swelling had decreased, and we drained some of the fluid and started antibiotics. By the next day the swelling decreased even more, with lots of drainage. The following day the mucocele passed out of the wound while I was washing it. Only was running again within a couple of days and hasn't had another problem since.

-Jean W.

. . . .

My dog Shep was either kicked or run over by one of our horses in July 2004. We found him in the paddock, paralyzed from the shoulders down. A myelogram revealed he had received an insult to the spinal cord between his shoulder blades; but other than that, there were no fractures or damaged discs. Nevertheless, he had lost all feeling, even his deep pain. In other words, he was just about as bad as he could be. The vet said there was nothing that could be done for him, and his prognosis was that he would never walk again.

I told them I was not ready to give up on him, so they said they would keep him until his temperature and the swelling in his spinal cord had subsided, and his seizures had stopped (caused by the myelogram). Then he could go home. I asked if I could come to the clinic to begin my own treatment right away, and they let me. I don't think they realized at the time that I would be smelling up their clinic with oils, but it soon became a joke among the techs that Shep smelled like pizza.

You can probably guess that I used the raindrop oils on him. I rubbed them all the way down his tail and down to the tip of his toes. I also used Helichrysum for regenerating the nerves and lavender for calming him and helping with inflammation. I also treated him with photonic light therapy. I took him home after a week and made a place for him where I could bathe him every day and move him around wheelbarrow-style (he was 80 pounds).

After a week, I saw him move a toe. The vets didn't believe it—they said it was just a reflex. After another week, I could stand him up, and he could stay there for just a second before he fell. The vets still didn't believe it. Another week went by and he was scooting around on his own; and after a few more days, he was literally running. He never recovered 100 percent. He still had some right hind leg weakness that prevented him from jumping on things and scratching with that leg, and he always had to "canter" instead of trot. But he was nowhere near being that dog who would never walk again.

-Jan E.

My dog Lila was attacked by two other dogs and had numerous puncture wounds all over her body. One wound on her inner thigh turned necrotic, and she began chewing it. I tried to keep it wrapped, but it was in such a bad place that it was hard to keep a bandage on it, and it didn't help that she would inevitably chew it off anyway. The vet said it was OK for her to clean the wound of dead tissue, but I began to get concerned because she not only chewed the necrotic tissue off, but she then began to chew the healthy tissue. Soon she had a quarter-sized hole in her leg. The vet prescribed a wound gel, which did nothing.

Finally, I decided to pack the hole with Animal Scents Ointment, bandage it, and hope that it would stay on long enough to do some good. By the time I got home that night, sure enough, she had chewed the bandage off yet again, but the hole was already closing! The wound healed in what I thought was record time, and today she has no scar, only a place where the hair does not grow.

-Jan E.

. . . .

Allie, a 12-year-old boxer/bulldog mix was diagnosed with a mass on her spleen that was bleeding. Because she was still eating well and in good spirits, we chose to treat her acute condition rather than putting her down. She recovered; but 18 months later, she developed an oral growth on her lower gums. The vet thought the growth was a metastasis of the mass on Allie's spleen. However, the vet did not want to biopsy it because she was afraid she would not be able to control the bleeding. The vet advised us to put the dog down. Allie still did not act like a sick dog; so, again, we were reluctant to end her life.

About this time, Dr. Lin and Dr. Suhail had completed some of their studies with Sacred Frankincense. We were interested in trying it, so we gave Allie the Sacred Frankincense by putting 1 drop on the tumor and the rest on her food. The tumor resolved in 60 days.

-Jan E.

I had a dog that was vomiting and couldn't keep anything down. I rubbed 2 drops of DiGize on my palms and petted her coat. I rubbed her belly, too. I put 1 drop of Ginger in some distilled water and gave her a small amount. Within 15 minutes, no more vomiting. In the past, I would have to take her for a Tagamet shot.

Another dog was bitten on the back leg by another dog. I used Lavender and PanAway on the bruise. She stopped limping and was fine in 30 minutes.

I had another dog with a cut. I put Lavender and Helichrysum in the cut, and it healed beautifully.

I diffuse Peace & Calming for separation anxiety and use Geranium in water in a spray bottle and in shampoo for fleas.

-Tanya B.

. . . .

My dog Catalina tore her tendon sheath, and the vet said she would need surgery because that issue never heals itself. I decided that because Catalina was in virtually no pain, I would try to treat the issue first.

I used Copaiba, Lemongrass, Aroma Siez, and Marjoram diluted in V-6 oil, as well as BLM, OmegaGize³, and MultiGreens. The swelling in Catalina's elbow went from the size of a golf ball to the size of a pea in just six days.

-Brette I.

. . . .

My dog Kelsie received a bad bite from another dog. I packed the wound with an herbal poultice before it was stapled together. I applied Lavender and Frankincense 2-3 times a day to reduce pain and keep Kelsie from nagging at it. I also used Purification around the outside of the wound to prevent infection and Aroma Life a few times around the outside as well. It healed remarkably fast and with no infection.

-Kendra K.

. . . .

About 7 years ago, my Flat-Coated Retriever named Sydney had a large tumor the size of my fist on the top of her head. I took her to Dr. Heidi at the Animal Hospital of Oshkosh, Wisconsin. She had biopsies done and was diagnosed with a malignant melanoma.

I didn't want to do anything radical and had a friend named Asia from Wisconsin who is an Animal Communicator doing seminars at my Pet Nutrition Store. She told me I needed Young Living Frankincense

and Ledum. I had not heard of them, but we ordered them right away.

I knew nothing else and just started putting about 10 drops each a day on the top of Sydney's head. After about 12 weeks, the tumor was gone and it never came back. That is what started me using Young Living oils in my shop, and that is what built my entire Young Living business. Sydney just passed two years ago at the good age of 15.

Young Living has changed my life, and I wouldn't want to live without the products.

-Vicki R.

. . . .

I have a 15-year-old dog that became totally deaf last autumn. About two or three months ago, I started putting Helichrysum on his ears once or twice a day. About four weeks ago, I noticed that he could hear if I yelled really loudly, and each week he seems to be hearing better and better.

-Vicki R.

. . . .

My little dog Harmony tore her ACL when she slipped into a hole at the park. The vet performed extensive blood work and found that in addition to the torn ACL, Harmony's liver enzyme levels were high. The vet strongly suggested orthopedic surgery, as well as many different types of medications, including pain-reduction and anti-inflammatory meds.

I declined all the suggested remedies and instead started using Omega Blue [now OmegaGize³], Mineral Essence, GLF, NingXia Red, and Essentialzyme. I also applied PanAway, Lemongrass, Wintergreen, Marjoram, Peppermint, and Regenolone cream to Harmony's leg twice a day.

When Harmony returned for her follow-up vet visit three weeks later, the inflammation had decreased, mobility had returned, and her liver enzyme values were declining. Today her ACL has healed and her liver enzyme levels are normal.

-Thea M.

. . . .

In January we started fostering a pregnant Pit Bull. She was due to have her puppies on the 22nd. It was about the 13th when I took her outside to go potty, and she ran off chasing a squirrel. She went full speed and being so heavily pregnant, I'm sure she must have pulled something, or then her joints were all loose. A few days later, she could barely get up and slowly just got worse.

I used some oils like Valor, Copaiba, and Ortho Ease on her back and on the one leg that I thought was causing her pain. It seemed to help a little, but she really didn't want to get up at all. I had to use food to coax her, and since this was the first animal I had worked on, I was a little unsure and felt the need to take her to the vet (as advised by the rescue agency).

The next morning, I took her to the vet, but I couldn't get her out of her crate. She just wouldn't get up and yelped when I tried to pick up her up. So my husband and I had to put the whole crate into the car to get her to the vet.

Once we got there and tried to remove the crate from the car, she actually sat up, stepped out of the crate, and walked, or I should say hobbled, into the clinic. After they had seen her and determined there was nothing they could do for her, they prescribed Tramadol and sent me home. I had to tip her out of the crate to get her to walk to the car, as again, she didn't want to get up.

Once I got home, there was no way she was going to get up for me, and I struggled to drag the crate out of the car by myself and accidentally dropped her into the snow. She finally got up and hobbled inside, needing help up the step. She went straight into her crate and didn't get up or move for the next nine hours, when I finally managed to drag her outside. Then again, she went straight back in her crate.

The next day was a Sunday, and I felt very emotionally drained. I had not been able to get her up at all, except to sit up and eat and drink. I got a call from someone who uses oils on animals a lot, and she encouraged me to do a Raindrop Technique. So, then I got the idea to drag her crate to the front door and see if she would get up more easily, since she would only have to get down the step to go potty. It worked and she made the effort to get up. I helped her down the step and back up the step. Then while she was sitting in her crate (it took a lot of effort for her to lie back down, and she would whimper), I did a quick Raindrop up her spine, using the Raindrop-in-a-bottle I had already made.

About six hours later when I tried to get her to go outside again, she got up so much more easily and more willingly. She went on to go five days past her due date (which was good so she was able to fully recover) and

delivered 15 puppies! Three did not survive, but the rest are all up for adoption! I was so thankful for Young Living at that time, as modern medicine had nothing to offer! Thank you!

-Helena K.

• •

A few years back, we were driving out in the desert, allowing our 13-year-old Siberian Husky Cirque to run alongside us. Moments later, our half-ton truck ran over him with both front and back tires. Fearing the worst, we jumped out to find him yelping and bent in half. I immediately applied Valor and Frankincense to his paws and had him lick Trauma Life out of my hand. Peace & Calming was also held over his nose.

Scooping him up we drove back home, where I contemplated having a tremendous vet bill or him dying. The next day, I took Cirque to a chiropractor friend who confirmed his spine was broken in three places.

Cirque had still been eliminating fine, so I figured his internal organs were doing ok. I thought with him being so old, I would forgo the vet and just use oils and faith. This was the summer right after hearing Gary Young speak at convention about his broken back experience, so I thought if Gary could have such faith and use oils, so could I.

That night I did a Valor balance on Cirque's paws, praying the whole time that his spine would realign. I also lifted the hair back along his spine and applied Idaho Balsam Fir, Helichrysum, Frankincense, and PanAway. By morning his spine was totally strait! Over the next week, I applied the same oils along his spine; and after three weeks, he was running around again! He had a total recovery and lived two more years.

I spent a few hundred dollars on oils for him, versus the thousands that corrective surgery would have cost. This experience has grown my faith that anything is possible with prayer and oils.

-Janessa M.

• •

Motz, my miniature Australian Shepherd, developed an ear infection in his right ear. I took him to the vet, and he was put on antibiotics. Motz improved quickly, but a week after the dog was off the antibiotics, my husband noticed that he staggered to the right when he went down the step outside. We immediately took him back to the vet, who told us that Motz had ruptured his eardrum and had an abscess that was slightly larger than a large marble. He recommended surgery. This was on a Friday.

When I got home, I called my friend who regularly uses oils on animals and asked her what oils I could use on Motz. My friend recommended Rosemary, Thyme, and Oregano. She told me to alternate the oils, putting 2-3 drops in some olive oil and rubbing the oil on the pads of the dog's feet.

By Monday the abscess had shrunk, and by Thursday it was the size of a small pea. I left the vet a message that Motz was doing better and that surgery wouldn't be necessary. He called back and was truly amazed. Motz was fully recovered by the following week and lived to the ripe old age of 12.

-Maria J.

. . . .

In 2003 I got a call from a client whose dog Katie was in acute renal failure with myoglobinuria (in which the cell walls of overexerted muscles rupture, releasing toxic proteins) caused by giving her Ibuprofen. The conventional approach of intensive intravenous fluid therapy and medications wasn't working.

I applied essential oils, including Juniper and Peppermint, to detox Katie's body. After the first day of treatment, Katie's blood levels plateaued and she steadily improved with daily treatments. Despite the vet's expectation that Katie would have to be euthanized, she left the clinic after a little more than two weeks. The vet called Katie's survival a miracle.

-Sue O.

. . . .

My dog Baruto was very sick with a disease called Babesia. He was hospitalized for a week. I used Lemon, Lavender, Purification, NingXia Red, Carrot Seed, German Chamomile, and Roman Chamomile to help. I also used the Raindrop Technique with Oregano, Thyme, Clove, and Wintergreen.

Baruto could not stand up until the last day at the hospital, but he was back to his normal self a month and a half later.

-Naoko H.

Here is my first success story with my dog! I was first introduced to Young Living Essential Oils in January of 2011. I used them personally and a little on my family and started to fall in love with my oils. In May I decided to host a wellness gathering at my home with my sponsor.

I have a small Min Pin that gets very wound up and hyper when people come to my home, always barking a lot until he is comfortable with the new people in his environment.

In anticipation of having a house full of guests and my 9-month-old baby at the time sleeping, I didn't want him barking. I thought why not lather him with some lavender and see what happens. Well... many guests arrived with little barking from my dog. While everyone was gathered in my living room listening to a fabulous presentation on the benefits of essential oils, my dog Bennet was lying on the floor in front of everyone. This is very unlike his character.

It just goes to show how well the oils can work on animals when we use them! I can't go a day without them now! Thank you, Young Living!

-Megan B.

. . . .

My Border Collie mix developed a cough, so I rubbed Peppermint on his throat a few times daily, and he soon stopped coughing. My niece's dog, an Aussie/Retriever mix, developed the cough, and I used Peppermint on him to help with his cough as well. I treated them for two days before the cough fully went away.

My niece's dog is very hyper and was staying with us for three months. I diffused Lavender to calm him down at night, so he would sleep peacefully through the night and not wake up my entire household with his roaming. It worked marvelously.

-Kimberly Z.

. . . .

I convinced the local animal shelter where I volunteer to use essential oils as part of its enrichment program. I made up seven spray bottles (one for each day) containing various oils that provide emotional-balancing, immune-boosting, and disinfecting properties. Each day they sprayed the dogs and their kennels with the essential oil of the day. The dogs enjoy the scent. The distraction of being sprayed calmed them down and minimized barking. An added bonus was that the dogs, their bedding, and the shelter smelled delightful!

Many people commented on the nice smell and asked what it was. I also often climbed into a dog's kennel and petted it with essential oils, which really relaxed it. Some of the dogs liked the scents so much that they licked my hands after being petted.

-Michelle S.

. . . .

Hachi's life has been transformed by Young Living essential oils. Three years ago, we adopted Hachi from SPCA. Eight-year-old Hachi had really bad teeth, coarse fur, was underweight, and was recovering from tick fever. A couple of months later, on a fateful night, Hachi vomited 26 times in one night and was diagnosed with severe liver inflammation. The vet put him on a drip and told us that he might not survive the night and would be gone forever.

I was devastated, but in my state of panic, thankfully, I remembered a friend, Kai, once sharing with me about the miracles of essential oils. In desperation, I called Kai, who then called Jacq (her good friend, who is passionate about oils and loves dogs), who within hours turned up at my house with bags of essential oils, ready to help Hachi. Jacq was a godsend. By the grace of God, through Jacq's kind heart, loving energy, and the power of essential oils—Valor, JuvaCleanse, JuvaFlex, GLF, and Thieves—Hachi miraculously was healed! And that began Hachi's relationship with essential oils.

A few days later, Jacq came over to perform the Raindrop Technique on Hachi to boost his immune system. Usually a dog that has problems keeping still, Hachi was so relaxed and looked completely calm. Now Hachi loves getting his regular Raindrop sessions.

Under Jacq's recommendation, I started feeding Hachi NingXia Red berries, OmegaGize[3], and Sulfurzyme; and Hachi's fur improved so much. His dark brown fur turned a shade lighter and became soft and fluffy! Every time we walk him, he never fails to get complimented on how young and healthy he looks.

Recently, Hachi has also been on ParaFree, as his heartworm prevention regimen, in place of Revolution (which may harm his liver). And Hachi's excretion has changed from dark brown to light orangey color, which, according to Jacq, is a great sign that his internal system is cleaner.

Young Living's essential oils and the Young Living angel (Jacq) have played such an essential role in Hachi's well-being; I couldn't be more grateful for them!

-Claire

. . . .

I have an 11-year-old German Shepherd named Locker, who was diagnosed with two types of very aggressive cancer. She underwent extensive surgery at the University of Florida, removing all her breast tissue, spleen, uterus, ovaries, and a lymph node.

After the histopath came back, they told me that they needed to start chemo immediately, and they might be able to buy her a couple of months at best. I had already spent nearly $4,000 on her surgery and did not have the money to do another $4,000 for the chemo treatments. So I turned to the essential oils.

For the past several months, I have been giving Locker a drop of Lemon oil in the morning and a drop of Lemongrass in the evening. It has been 11 months since her surgery, and she is still out chasing rabbits and squirrels.

They just did a complete blood panel, chest X-rays, and ultrasound of her abdomen. The doctors at the university were shocked that they could not find any trace of her cancer.

-Carol B.

. . . .

I've been with Young Living for 5 years now, and I have gone all-natural ever since. I have not regretted it! I seldom fall ill, I'm energized during the day, and I sleep peacefully at night.

My 3-year-old rescued, female dog Duchess was either allergic to her new shampoo or really stressed due to our move to another place. Her chest area had red, swollen, dry, and inflamed areas; and it spread to Duchess' face. Her face around the eyes were dry, and her fur dropped off. She was insanely scratching until it bled. Her eyes were watery and discharge was coming out.

I was a worried mommy and panic set in. I consulted my vet. My vet, knowing full well I would rather go natural for my dogs, suggested I wash Duchess' eyes with saline and clean her eye area regularly.

I also consulted Jacq, a friend who introduced me to Young Living and who loves and works a lot with animals. She advised me on what Duchess should be taking.

Jacq's recipe:

NingXia Red: 2 oz. 2 times daily

Sulfurzyme: 2, 3 times daily

OmegaGize^3: 2, 2 times daily

Allerzyme: 1, 2 times daily

Essentialzymes-4: 1 of each 2 times daily

Lavender: 1 drop orally 3 times daily

Copaiba: 1 drop orally 3 times daily

Frankincense: 1 drop orally 3 times daily

Raindrop Technique: 1 time daily

On top of this, I used organic cold-pressed extra virgin coconut oil and rubbed it into her chest area. For the discharge from her eyes, besides using saline, I dabbed Frankincense around them and tried to cup her eyes, release the cupping, and repeat a few times. I did this regularly for one and a half months.

Now Duchess is off the e-collar (cone). She hasn't been scratching under her arms, chest, or face! I continue to give her Sulfurzyme, Allerzyme, Essential-zymes-4, OmegaGize^3, and NingXia Red. Now Rain-drop Technique is done once a week.

My 3-month-old pup Marquise has started on Sulfurzyme, a bit of Allerzyme, BLM, OmegaGize^3, and Essentialzymes-4.

My dogs are now super healthy, active, full of fur, and scratch-free—just pawfect! I'm so happy with the pawsitive results! Thank you so much Young Living for the wonderful products. Next on the list is ParaFree for the two dogs and the cat!

-Deanna K.

• •

My dog Montana is a Boston Terrier. The typical life span of her breed is 13 years (typically with many medical problems at the end of their life), and Montana will be 15 years old next month. She has been using oils since she was 1-year-old. She has not had any shots. She has not taken any prescriptions from the vet. She has been in to see the vet for only a few problems in her life, all of which were treated with essential oils, NingXia Red, and Young Living supplements.

When she was 2-years-old, she got salmonella poisoning, and the vet thought she was going to die. We took her home, used NingXia Red by syringe, Thieves and DiGize over her stomach, and other oils on her ears and spine to give her strength and courage. She recovered to her normal self.

In 2010 Montana developed a hole in her left eye. The vet said the eye would need to be removed, and she may not make it. I used Frankincense, Lavender, Helichrysum, Rose, Cedarwood, Valor, and a few other oils. Within a few short days, the hole started to heal. She is a happy, healthy, and vibrant dog...who loves oils.

-Crystal P.

• •

My Labrador Tamika was terminally ill with liver and kidney cancer. When I received this news, I chose to allow her to pass with dignity and booked her in for euthanasia. I used the Raindrop Technique on her daily, adding Copaiba for pain relief. She loved it so much. I also used the oils of the Egyptian Emotional Clearing Technique to help her transition. On the night before her passing, I also used Palo Santo in generous amounts.

Her passing was done in honor and grace as she walked into the vet, no lead necessary, to receive her final treatment. Her passing was pain-free, and I was able to keep her comfortable with the help of the Spirit and Young Living oils.

-Kathleen J.

• •

I have a 3-year-old English Springer. He's a wonderful boy and has the normal Springer energy level, which means he is usually in high gear. He is a hunting dog but also very gun shy. If anyone is shooting a gun in the area, he gets so upset that he shakes like a leaf and wants to climb in my lap—50 pounds of shaking canine trying to crawl inside my clothes!

The last time this happened, I was desperate! I mixed a few drops of Lavender and Peace & Calming in my hand and held my hands over his muzzle. He didn't care for it, so then I rubbed it on my neck, which was where his face was. After a few minutes, the shaking stopped; and a short while after that, he was calm enough to get off my lap. He still would not leave my side, but believe me, it was much better.

-Janice K.

• •

I have three cats and three dogs that I have been using Young Living oils on for over a year now.

I have a 5-lb. Chihuahua, who always seems to get trampled by our bigger dog or jumps off a couch or a bed wrong and hurts his legs and joints. I apply

Copaiba and within an hour after several applications on his joints, he can walk without yelping.

I use Purification on all of my dogs for fleas, ticks, and recently heartworm, as my Shih Tzu travels six months of the year with my parents. My Shih Tzu also has dry skin, so I have used Animal Scents Ointment on her as well.

My bigger dog, a Lab/Retriever cross, gets Purification and other oils to calm him down, as he is super excitable. I have a cat that has had a urinary infection and wanting to not use her litterbox, so I applied Goldenrod and it seems to have worked. My animals are part of my family, and I want to give them the healthiest choices as well.

-Georgina M.

• •

One of my pet-sitting clients had a dog with four infected incisions. The vet cultured the infection and found out it was microbacteria. I convinced the owner that essential oils could help.

We shaved off all the dog's hair, so the wounds could be kept clean; then we sprayed her with Lavender and a solution of Thieves. We used every oil I knew to kill bacteria, starting with ImmuPower. After each bottle was empty, we used a different oil. We rotated through Egyptian Gold, Thieves, Oregano, and Inner Defense. The dog was also given Sulfurzyme on her food.

It took six months to clear up, but the vets weren't sure that antibiotics could kill these bacteria. The owner stopped using the antibiotic; and as soon as she did, there was huge progress.

-Charla S.

• •

Charlie is our little dog, half Poodle and half Japanese Spaniel. He was about 1-year old when we had to cut his fur really short because it had become too long and was matted in places. Before the grooming, he was a happy, squirrely, wiggly, round-looking darling. After the fur was cut and shaved off, he was skinny and not too pretty. He somehow knew it. He lost his zest for life; he no longer ran around happily, nor was he eager to go outside for walks. He spent the days lying under the table, and if we called his name he would not come; he did not even lift his head. He just moved his eyes and looked at us sadly. He seemed depressed and would walk only to the mailbox, no farther. He would

pull to get back to hide under the table. I do believe he was embarrassed about how he looked.

I did some research on the Internet and decided to try a drop of Valor on his paw as he was lying under the table. A couple of minutes after putting the drop of Valor on his paw, he came out from under the table, started walking energetically around the room, wagging his tail, and wanting to engage with all of us! And thus, it was Valor that in two minutes returned our lovely Charlie to us with his happy, wonderful, puppy-dog ways! Thank YOU for Valor! Incidentally, it is the oil blend that I wear every day for perfume!

Discovering these oils has been such a wonderful, joyful experience. They give us the opportunity to connect with nature, just by being able to wear them! I feel as though I have returned to some place/thing from which I did not even know I was separated! It's a privilege to be part of the Young Living way of life!

-Jaana S.

• •

My dog Rookie suffers from anxiety. We had just adopted him a few weeks before a vacation and decided to take him along. He hated the car. He was a whining, fidgeting, frothing mess within minutes of leaving the house; and we had nine hours to go.

I dropped a couple of drops of Peace & Calming onto my hand and petted Rookie's back. In no time, Rookie was calm and resting. When the oil had metabolized about two hours later, he began to get agitated again; so the kids took turns putting Peace & Calming on his back every couple of hours. It ended up being the most pleasant nine-hour car ride with an antsy dog and four children ever!

-Jaynette B.

• •

My name is Lester and I "BELIEVE" in the essential oils that Young Living has. My furkid was diagnosed with cancer in 2011, and I was doing a lot of research on using alternate treatments to "heal" her.

In 2013 I came across an article about Frankincense and cancer, and I was determined to try what Western medicine has failed to do for her. This is when I was introduced to Jacq. Besides learning about Raindrop Technique for animals, we advanced to using "Enriched" Sacred Frankincense and Myrrh on Jill, our furkid. She is no longer with us, but the information she gave us is astonishing.

A combination of Sacred Frankincense and Myrrh given orally, Raindrop Technique, and other supplements from Young Living prolonged Jill's life from what the Western medicine world gave her of only 6 months to giving her 24 months.

-Lester

· ·

My 10-year-old dog Tanner began to experience digestive problems about five years ago. I tried diet changes, homeopathic supplements, Chinese herbs, acupuncture, autosanguis therapy, you name it! All to little or no avail. He would vomit regularly, had to be hospitalized once for pancreatitis, and his stomach would always make loud, uncomfortable-sounding noises. It was awful!! He was even on metoclopramide, which I was told is given to chemo patients for nausea. It didn't work with any regularity.

Finally, I went to the Young Living convention in Orlando. I will be forever grateful! By using YL oils and changing his diet, his digestive health has dramatically improved. No more rumbly tummy and he hardly ever throws up anymore. At the first sign of a stomach upset, he gets DiGize (a couple of drops neat, petted on). He also receives a drop or two daily of Copaiba and Longevity (mixed with ½ teaspoon of coconut oil in his food). I diffuse oils 24-7 (Lemongrass, Purification, and Sacred Mountain are favorites) and pet him whenever I use any oil on myself.

He's also had Essentialzyme and NingXia Red and gets a "flea spritzer" that I make from a variety of oils mixed with water and sprayed all over. I think another huge reason for his improved health is because of mine. I no longer use any OTC's because there's an oil for everything! I've also eliminated as many toxins as possible from our lives by replacing them with YL products. Energetically speaking, he's my little mirror; and now that my health is so much better (thanks to Young Living!), he has naturally benefited as well.

-Kim G.

· ·

Toby is my 14-year-old silky Terrier/Pomeranian mix. He's a picky eater, so he has bad teeth and gums. He had to have several teeth removed two-and-a-half years ago. In addition to his medications, I also applied PanAway under his paws and some Purification in case

of infection. Toby laid around for only about 24 hours, and then he was ready to play again.

I also ran some Mineral Essence with a little bit of NingXia Red and Frankincense around Toby's remaining teeth and gums every day.

Toby also has some back problems across his hips and loin area, so I do a Valor balance on him from time to time. When Toby gets an upset stomach, I put a couple drops of DiGize on my palms and rub them over his fur. Toby has slowed down with age, but he is still going.

-David V.P.

· ·

I met a 9-year-old dog named Hope at the rescue shelter where I was working. Hope's history was vague, but she had a lot of anger and hurt. She had been returned to the shelter when a family member developed an allergic reaction to her.

After meeting Jacq and Gennet with Young Living, I decided to explore using Young Living essential oils and supplements to help with Hope's healing. Hope looked malnourished and underweight, so we added Sulfurzyme, Detoxzyme, Omega Blue [now OmegaGize³], and NingXia Red to her meals. We also applied essential oils topically, diffused them near Hope's resting area, and showered her weekly with Animal Scents Shampoo.

After about six months, Hope was healing and behaving like a normal dog. She gained weight and was growing new fur. There was a happy light in her eyes that hadn't been there before.

-Jaclyn L.

· ·

I met a stray dog named Pico, who came to the shelter bloated, very underweight, and chronically infected by heartworms. He was too weak to receive traditional treatments, so I brought him home and treated him with antibiotics and essential oils. I supplemented his diet with Sulfurzyme and NingXia Red, diffused Peace & Calming into his resting area, and applied Copaiba and Lavender topically.

Pico still wasn't doing well, so I decided to stop the antibiotics and instead used an essential oil regimen to treat the heartworms. By the next day, Pico already seemed to be doing better.

-Jaclyn L.

My dog Avante received a dog bite at a dog run. The vet gave Avante three stitches and prescribed her some medications. Instead of using these medications, I decided to try to heal Avante with essential oils. I used Lavender, and the vet was surprised by how well Avante was healing when we took her back a few weeks later. Avante's fur grew back and you can't even tell that the wound had ever been there.

-Jacq O.

I had a tiny long-coat Chihuahua puppy that got stuck during birth. We had to do a caesarian on the mother, and the puppy had inhaled meconium, which created an infection that turned into pneumonia. The prognosis wasn't good, and the vet put the puppy on a mild antibiotic as a last-ditch effort.

I had the puppy breathe essential oils 6-8 times each day for about 5-10 minutes at a time, in addition to putting oils over her lungs, under the fur, and on her head and ears at night. Over the first few weeks of using the oils, the puppy continued to live and gain weight. She eventually recovered as if she had never been ill at all.

-Liz M.

My Doberman had been wetting the bed at night while she slept at the foot of our bed. I was so tired of changing sheets and keeping her water limited. Nothing seemed to work. I knew Valor helped with bedwetting, so I thought "Heck, it's worth a try!" I rubbed her belly every night with diluted Valor, and it stopped the annoying bedwetting!

-Leeann M.

When I got home one evening, my helper told me that one of my dogs, Latte, had just been stung by a hornet. Within minutes, Latte's face was dangerously swollen, and I was too worried to move her to take her to the vet.

I applied Purification, Lavender, and Idaho Balsam Fir over Latte's face and spine and added Peace & Calming and Valor on her chest. I repeated the application four times, approximately every 40 minutes. After the last application, Latte's swelling reduced considerably. By the next morning, she was fine.

-Yvonne Z.

I got a call from my daughter that something was wrong with her female Daschund. I checked on the dog and found that a young child had sat down on her very hard a couple of times, and the dog's leg and back muscles were very tight. She was in a lot of pain.

I applied a blend of Frankincense, Idaho Balsam Fir, Marjoram, Copaiba, Idaho Tansy, and Lemongrass. I also massaged the oils on both of the dog's legs and back and then gave her a Raindrop treatment. By that evening, the dog was moving around and feeding her pups.

-Calvin J.

I own a 4-year-old Maltese/Terrier cross named Tess. When Tess has her fur trimmed (which is often) or nails clipped, she goes into a snappy frenzy. I started applying Valor on her paws and Lavender rubbed into her belly pre-clip. She is a lot more settled and calm as a result.

Tess is also prone to getting ear inflammations when the bottlebrush tree is in bloom. It can take her many weeks to recover. I made a maintenance blend for her ears using V-6 as the base and adding Lavender and Helichrysum. If she shows signs of inflammation, I add Purification to the blend as well.

-Raili T.

In 2000 my dog Jones was diagnosed with a rash caused by food allergies. I tried everything to help and nothing worked. My vet thought it might be caused by flora and fauna, so Jones was prescribed Prednisone for life and a weekly bath in Hexadine shampoo.

I left the vet's office completely deflated but had a light-bulb moment and decided to try essential oils instead. That night I gave Jones a bath with Young Living Lavender Mint Shampoo and added 4 drops each of Lavender and Thieves. The next day Jones did not itch at all. His coat immediately started glowing with shine, and the bald spots he had scratched grew back hair. I continue to give him his weekly bath, and he's never been better.

-Erica C.

My dog Buddy started acting old. He walked slowly and acted like he was in a lot of pain. Nothing showed up on the vet's X-rays or blood work; but within 24 hours, Buddy couldn't walk and was referred to a neurology vet. Buddy was diagnosed with neospora caninum attacking his spinal cord, and his prognosis was 50/50.

Dr. Hoke recommended trying Raindrop Technique and NingXia Red. Within 24 hours of his first treatment, Buddy could hobble! Three months later, he was at 97 percent of his old self.

-Lori Y.

• •

I saw a dog for aggressive and reactive displays of behavior. Due to a hind leg injury when he was 16 weeks old, this dog would not let anyone beside his owner touch him. For each treatment, I would talk with the owner and intuitively connect with the dog's energy and the energy of the oils and then select the treatment lineup. The owner would apply to oils under my guidance.

We treated the dog over a span of approximately 10 months, extending the treatment time between each treatment, with the owner treating at home with some essential oils. As of four weeks ago, the dog was happy, having fun, not being reactive, and going to agility practice and running agility trials without problems.

-Dr. H., DVM

• •

I was called in by the owner of a Bouvier labeled as severely reactive and aggressive. She was pacing, biting, and lunging. The owner was unable to walk her, and she would stand on her hind legs and rear in the presence of other dogs. The dog's third trainer was also scheduled to be there for the appointment.

I came in the house and the dog was in the hall behind a tall baby gate. She was barking, lunging, drooling, crying, and pacing. I tuned into her energy and realized she wasn't aggressive at all, just misunderstood. The owner finally let the dog out after about 20 minutes, and she immediately passed me and went to my zipped-shut essential oil kit.

After her investigation, she came directly over to me and sat between my legs to be petted. The dog then helped me select the oils to treat her without any biting or getting aggressive. Both she and the owner continue to use the oils at home, experiencing transformation together. She is now much calmer, can be walked, and allows others to touch her.

-Dr. H., DVM

A male Rhodesian Ridgeback came to me for chiropractic adjustments. He would run really hard and jam his toes on the lava rock over and over again without a present awareness. The first time I saw him, he was not completely in his body and was really unaware of his limbs and paws.

I adjusted him and used some essential oils on him. The owners also purchased some oils to apply at home. He is now playing and running around with awareness and no leg or paw injuries.

-Dr. H., DVM

• •

I attended the first segment out of six in a reactive dog training class, which was created for dogs with a history of being reactive and unable to attend other training classes. There were six dogs in the class and were each placed behind an L-shaped barrier, so they could not see another dog and start reacting/barking, etc.

Class started out with dogs behind their individual barrier, and the owners were trying to keep their dog as calm and relaxed as they could. After the first 10-15 minutes of class, I walked around to each dog and applied 2-3 oils on each. Before I could even finish, the first three dogs came out from behind their barrier and were calmly sitting 10 feet in front of the barriers without barking or reacting to the other dogs!

-Dr. H., DVM

• •

I worked with a family wanting to integrate the brother's dog into the sister's pack of four dogs. Numerous attempts had been made to mix all five dogs, but there were reactive issues and biting involved. This family was also working with a local dog trainer to help with the reactive issues.

I worked with both groups individually, selecting oils to support each and doing animal-human connection sessions at the same time. They continued treatments at home, and one evening I was able to witness the brother's first return visit with his dog to his sister's house and her dogs. The change in everyone's behavior was incredible. Just a month ago, the brother took a trip and his dog stayed successfully with his sister's dogs for about five days, with very little reactivity or other issues.

-Dr. H., DVM

A 15-year-old Siberian Husky came to me for acupuncture due to neuropathy and a lackluster look to her eye. She responded very well to acupuncture; and with permission, I applied a few essential oils after her treatment. Each time I worked on her, I would apply a few oils and watch the dog's eyes brighten up and some of her vitality come back. She responded so well that the owner came in and purchased a small bottle of Frankincense and applied it at home.

The dog now receives her oils at home daily and loves them. Even the dog sitter applies her Frankincense when her owner and sled dog team are out running races.

-Dr. H., DVM

. . . .

In November 2004, I became the owner of Otis, an English Bulldog with multiple congenital defects that his breed is known to have. After Otis went through a ruptured umbilical hernia repair, two prolapsed glands of the third eyelid, corrective soft palate surgery, and a prolapsed urethra repair, at the age of eight, he developed a mass on the lower-left jaw, consistent with osteosarcoma of the mandible.

He was given 10 drops each of Frankincense, Grapefruit, and Copaiba orally twice a day; and he was started on a regimen of Chinese herbs.

After a while, chest films suggested metastatic lesions in the lungs. I changed from using Frankincense to Sacred Frankincense orally at 10 drops twice a day (along with continued use of Grapefruit) and had his upper canine tooth removed. Otis continued wonderfully and no one would ever have known that he had cancer.

-Dr. A., DVM

. . . .

I recently gave an essential oil treatment to a young German Shepherd named Gabe, owned by a close friend. The dog was extremely shy, wouldn't focus or relax, and was completely closed around people and other dogs.

The oils were introduced slowly and gently by letting Gabe sniff the oils first and then placing the opened bottle near his nose and letting him decide if he wanted to continue to sniff it or not. Gabe accepted every oil offered to him.

Toward the end of the session, he rolled onto his side and closed his eyes, while the last few oils were placed onto his body. Even more surprising, after the treatment, Gabe would take treats out of his owner's hand, when he never would before, even after going to doggie school.

-Dr. F.

. . . .

I was introduced to essential oils by a pet owner who had been using oils for years. This owner's dog, Diamond, would not allow her to apply the oils, so her owner brought her to me for help. Diamond was a mixed breed female who was about 4 years old. She had a raised, smooth, circular greyish mass on her right muzzle. The base of the mass could be palpated deeply from inside the cheek.

Per the owner's instructions, I injected the mass with 0.1 ml of Frankincense and topically applied 1 drop of Longevity on the first day. Over the coming weeks, we used Sacred Frankincense, DiGize, Clove, Orange, Frankincense, R.C., Copaiba, Lavender, Tea Tree, Melrose, Ravintsara, Eucalyptus Globulus, Cedarwood, Idaho Balsam Fir, Acceptance, ImmuPower, Tarragon, and others. Orally, Diamond received MSM, glucosamine, ParaGize, BLM, and probiotics. We also did regular Raindrop treatments. After six months, the mass seemed smaller and has remained unchanged to date.

-Kathleen P.

. . . .

I have treated over 100 animals with Frankincense and Sacred Frankincense. My go-to for therapy is a holistic protocol that includes some type of essential oils. I have several examples of how I have helped animals with these oils.

A little Miniature Pinscher diagnosed with a malignant melanoma was tumor free within three months.

A Golden Retriever with malignant adenocarcinoma of the gastrointestinal tract was clear as of the last ultrasound.

Another Golden Retriever had adenocarcinoma of the anal gland. She remained clear after radiation and Sacred Frankincense, with better results (per the doctor) than without.

A Black Lab with mast cell tumor biopsy of a grade 4 tumor (very fast growing) after two weeks on topical Frankincense at surgery was now a grade 2 and never regrew or metastasized, even though they usually do.

-Nancy B.

• •

A male Labrador/Pit Bull/Shar Pei named Jackie had been diagnosed with arthritis of the spine, hypothyroidism, and an enlarged spleen that was possibly cancerous. Jackie was living in a daycare facility and didn't have an owner to pay for the expensive surgeries his condition required, so I was called to see if I could do anything to help.

I visited Jackie for 15-30 minutes once a week for 11 weeks, using essential oils such as Fennel, Marjoram, Sage, and Geranium as a key part of his treatment.

-Denise M., D.C.

• •

One day I noticed immediately that my Standard Poodle was shaking his ears. Even though I caught the cause of it right away, a hematoma had already started in one of his ears. His ear was thick and heavy with blood. Having worked at a veterinarian clinic in the past, I knew what the veterinarian would have to do.

I decided to try Helichrysum on it for a day or two before going the surgical route. I simply put a drop of Helichrysum directly on the ear flap and followed with Cistus. I did this four times the first day and three times the second day. I noticed improvement on the second day, with the size of ear seeming smaller. By the third day, the ear was completely back to normal. I continued with application twice a day for five days total.

-Elizabeth R., CPDT-KA

• •

My Standard Poodle developed warts in all four paws. Our veterinarian attempted to surgically remove them and could not. She prescribed a medication. My dog still had many warts.

I purchased the Premium Starter Kit strictly to try Thieves on my dog, as per another veterinarian's recommendation. That night I put 8 drops of Thieves in the diffuser, and the dogs and I went to bed as usual. The diffuser ran about 4 hours that night.

The next morning when my dog walked on the concrete patio outside, I noticed bloody paw prints being left behind. About three days later, I checked my dog's paws to see how they were doing, and there were no signs of warts at all! The warts were completely gone and never came back.

-Cheryl K.

• •

I have a pack of rescue dogs that have all sorts of behavior problems. As a dog trainer, I constantly work with them on overcoming the problems. One issue was a real problem for me every year—fireworks. Every year I couldn't leave the house as my dogs were very stressed during the Fourth of July. They paced, drooled, whined, and would even try to hurt themselves if I was not with them. It began early, as my neighbors joined in the fun, sometimes even days before.

My friend was new to Young Living and suggested I try the diffuser with Peace & Calming running to see if it made a difference. It was early in the evening, but the dogs were already stressed. I put 12 drops in the diffuser in the back bedroom. The dogs were allowed to roam freely about the house. After approximately 20 minutes, the dogs found the diffuser, laid down, and slept peacefully through the entire fireworks show! That has NEVER happened. For two more years, I continued to diffuse Peace & Calming during this stressful event for them.

The fourth year, I didn't diffuse anything at all, and they all did FINE. The oil helped to teach them to relax and was no longer needed.

-Karen W., CPDT-KA

• •

My German Shepherd was playing ball with the neighbor kids and came back non-weight bearing on one of her back legs. I immediately took her to the veterinarian, and the vet said my dog had a soft tissue injury. The doctor prescribed medications, a splint, a cone to keep her from chewing off the splint, and complete crate rest for 6 weeks. She was only allowed to get up to go outside to potty. She is an active dog!

Instead, I used PanAway, Valor, and Peppermint neat, directly to the afflicted area. Within three days, she was bearing weight; and within a week, she was completely back to her normal activities!

-Teryn J., CPDT-KA

I regularly apply Frankincense to my Maltese Mix, as she regularly suffers from seizures. I apply one drop neat to the top of her skull, once per day. If I notice signs that she is about to have a seizure, I apply another drop to her head. It always stops and goes no further when I do this.

If I miss it and find her in a full seizure, I do the same but also apply a drop to my finger and swipe it inside her cheek (I don't worry about her biting me). The seizure will stop instantly, and she will go back to her normal routine right after. Before using essential oils, she would sleep the rest of the day and not eat her food.

-Sue S.

The veterinarian told me that my dog needed to get a dental cleaning. Instead, I began giving her the Animal Scents Dental Chews, and tartar is gone. Plus, her breath smells so much better! During a follow-up visit, the veterinarian said that her teeth and gums look great!

-Kay E.

As a dog trainer and even with all the proper training I was doing with my rescue dog, I could not get him to walk through the neighborhood without jumping and reacting to every sound. A dog barking behind a fence would make my dog try to dart and pull at the leash to get away. Walking was not fun, to say the least.

After getting essential oils, I started to apply Valor before our walks. One day I noticed just how much progress my dog had made when a Pit Bull jumped and barked at him behind a steel, screen door that was only feet from the sidewalk. He barely flinched as the dog scared him and kept walking with me. Before using Valor, he would have been a mess, and I would have had to turn around and go back home.

-Karen W., CPDT-KA

In a group class, one of the dogs was acting rather aggressively toward the other dogs in the class. The dog trainer applied one drop of Vetiver to the tip of the ear and to the top of the dog's paw. Within one minute, the dog calmed down and did well the remainder of the class.

Lucy was a Black Lab mix rescued from Louisiana. She was approximately 10-months-old when her owner adopted her, and she tested negative for heartworm both in Louisiana and after she arrived in Iowa. Upon her annual blood work, everyone was shocked when she tested positive for heartworms. She had been on a preventive program, but adult heartworms had developed and had already caused damage to her heart.

Knowing what traditional treatment involved, her owner didn't want to put her through the pain and potentially dangerous side effects. I created a treatment protocol for her using Young Living essential oils, and approximately 11 months later Lucy tested negative!

-Dr. F.

Fish

Like humans and other animals, fish suffer from diseases and parasites. Fish have protective features such as scales, skin, and a mucus layer that help protect them from environmental contaminates. When fish do experience health issues, it becomes very difficult to facilitate recovery through treatment intervention.

Disease prevention is the best approach when it comes to caring for fish. The most important aspects to manage include good water quality, supportive nutrition, and proper sanitation.

Essential oils are crucial in aiding with the maintenance of these three aspects. Many essential oils will help manage the presence of bacteria, fungi, and parasites that may be in the fish's environment.

Fish Conditions

Amoebic Gill Disease (AGD)

Amoebic Gill Disease (AGD) is a potentially fatal disease of some marine fish. It is caused by *Neoparamoeba perurans*, the most important amoeba in cultured fish.

Symptoms include mucus buildup on the gills of infected fish and hyperplastic lesions, causing white spots and eventual deterioration of the gill tissue.

Recommendations:
Singles: Eucalyptus Globulus, Copaiba
Blends: R.C., Purification.

Application and Usage:
Application: Put 1 drop of each oil in tank or pond per 3-4 gallons of water.

Bacterial Diseases

Bacterial diseases can cause problems when fish become injured, sick, or stressed from another source. Some of the common bacterial diseases are fin rot, mouth rot, and skin ulcers. They can be recognized by red streaks or spots and/or swelling of the abdomen or eye. Antibiotics such as penicillin, amoxicillin, or erythromycin are effective against bacterial diseases.

Recommendations:

Singles: Tea Tree, Lemon, Copaiba, Peppermint
Blends: Purification

Application and Usage:

Application: Start with 3 drops each per gallon, adding in 1 drop of Peppermint per tank. Increase in small amounts as needed.

Columnaris

This is a symptom of disease (also referred to as cotton-mouth) in fish, which results from an infection caused by the Gram-negative, aerobic, rod-shaped bacterium *Flavo-bacterium columnare*. It was previously known as *Bacillus columnaris*, *Chondrococcus columnaris*, *Cytophaga columnaris*, and *Flexibacter columnaris*.

The bacteria are found in freshwater fish, including cultured fish reared in ponds and raceways.

This disease is most prevalent in air temperatures above 53–57°F (12–14°C). It is often mistaken for a fungal infection. Columnaris is highly contagious and the outcome is often fatal.

Recommendations:

Singles: Ginger, Lemon, Tea Tree
Blends: Purification

Application and Usage:

Application: Put 1 drop of each oil in tank or pond per 3-4 gallons of water. Repeat every day.

Disease, General

A number of diseases that affect fish are listed in this section. Columnaris, listed above, and Freshwater White Spot Disease, listed below, as examples. Lemon, Peppermint, Frankincense, Tea Tree, and Purification are good general oils to consider for fish disease.

Recommendations:

Singles: Tea Tree, Lemon, Peppermint, Frankincense
Blends: Purification

Application and Usage:

Application: Drop into water starting with 1-2 drops per 3 gallons of water, adding more in small amounts when needed.

Furunculosis in Farmed Salmon

Farmed salmon can fall prey to this disease, which causes furuncles (boils) that progress to deep lesions, hemorrhages in muscles and internal organs, and death. Be cautious about eating farmed fish.

Recommendations:

Singles: Copaiba, Tea Tree, Lemon, Ginger
Blends: Purification

Application and Usage:

Application: Start first with 4 drops of 1 of the above oils per gallon of water in pond or tank, plus Copaiba in equal parts. If desired results are not achieved, add in each additional oil 1 at a time.

Fungal Diseases

Fungal spores are found in almost all fish tanks. They can quickly colonize and create problems in fish, especially if they are injured, stressed, or already suffering from disease. Poor water quality can also lead to an increase in fungal infections.

You can easily recognize fungal infections in your aquarium because they have a telltale white fluffy appearance. In worse cases, they may take on a gray or red appearance.

Recommendations:

Singles: Copaiba, Lemon, Peppermint, Tea Tree
Blends: Purification

Application and Usage:

Application: Start with 3 drops each per gallon, adding in 1 drop of Peppermint per tank. Increase in small amounts as needed.

Ichthyophthirius multifiliis (Commonly known as freshwater white spot disease, freshwater ich, or freshwater ick)

This is a common disease of freshwater fish. It is caused by the protozoan Ichthyophthirius. Ich is one of the most common and persistent diseases in fish. The protozoan is an ectoparasite. White nodules that look like white grains of salt or sugar of up to 1 mm appear on the body, fins, and gills. Each white spot is an encysted parasite.

It is easily introduced into a fish pond or home aquarium by new fish or equipment that has been moved from one fish-holding unit to another. When the organism gets into a large fish-culture facility, it is difficult to control because of its fast reproductive cycle and its unique life stages. If not controlled, there is a 100 percent mortality rate of fish.

Whitespot is very damaging to the gills and skin. In heavily infected fish, it can cause a rapid deterioration of condition, considerable distress, and death. Infected fish have small white spots on the skin and gills and produce excess mucus due to irritation.

Whitespot causes most damage when entering and leaving the tissues of the fish. This can lead to the loss of skin and ulcers. These wounds can harm the ability of a fish to control the movement of water into its body. Damage caused to the gill tissue of an infected fish can also reduce respiratory efficiency. This means it is more difficult for the fish to obtain oxygen from the water and becomes less tolerant to low levels of dissolved oxygen.

Recommendations:

Singles: Copaiba, Tea Tree, Lemon
Blends: Purification

Application and Usage:

Application: Add 3 drops Tea Tree per gallon of water in pond or tank. If advanced, apply Copaiba and Lemon directly on affected area of the fish 1 time daily.

Inflammation

Redness and inflammation can be a symptom of an underlying problem such as anchor worms, body flukes, or ammonia poisoning. The latter condition is suggested when the fish has red and inflamed gills.

Recommendations:

Singles: Copaiba, Lemon

Application and Usage:

Application: Start with adding 3-4 drops per gallon of water, adding more if needed for desired results. Repeat every other day.

Koi Herpes

This virus is found in common carp and ornamental koi carp. Fish may recover from it but remain carriers of the virus.

The epithelial cells of koi, especially skin and gills, are attacked by the virus. Koi may survive if the temperature of the water is gradually increased to 86°F (30°C). However, this is only partially successful and may increase susceptibility to other common diseases.

Diagnosis is by enzyme-linked immunosorbent assay (ELISA).

Recommendations:

Singles: Melissa, Copaiba
Blends: Purification

Application and Usage:

Application: Add 1 drop of Purification per gallon of water in pond or tank.
Topical: Apply Melissa and Copaiba directly on affected area of the fish 1 time daily.

Parasite Diseases

Parasites can reduce fish growth, plus decrease their agility and appetite. You may see discoloration or velvet rust or gold rust in affected fish. They may also rub against objects to attempt to dislodge parasites from their skin.

If you see affected fish, physically remove parasites and clean the wound with antiseptic. Washing your fish with salt water can also reduce parasite infection. Seek professional help without delay if you feel the problem may become a serious issue.

Monitor the health of your fish and water quality regularly. Maintain good water quality at an optimal level, reduce pollution, and clean and sanitize all your equipment. Separate dead or injured fish to reduce spread of fungal and bacterial infections. Bacterial and fungal diseases can be fatal if left untreated. Make sure fish are fed proper medication and a healthy diet from a reliable source.

Recommendations:

Singles: Copaiba, Lemon, Peppermint
Blends: Purification, ParaGize, or DiGize

Application and Usage:

Application: Start with 3 drops each per gallon of water, adding 1 drop of Peppermint per tank. Increase in small amounts as needed.

VHS (Viral Hemorrhagic Septicemia)

This infection can be brought into an aquarium or pond through fish with the virus. There may be hemorrhaging of skin, muscle, and internal organs, bulging eyes, open sores, and a reddish tint to eyes, gills, fins, and skin. Fish also may exhibit no external symptoms or signs of abnormal behavior.

Recommendations:

Singles: Copaiba, Cypress, Ocotea, and Cistus

Application and Usage:

Application: Start first with 4 drops per gallon of water in pond or tank of the above oils and Copaiba of equal parts. If desired results are not achieved, add in each additional oil 1 drop at a time.

Whirling Disease

Trout, salmon, and sometimes whitefish are infected with Whirling Disease caused by the microscopic parasite *Myxobolus cerebralis*. The name comes from the abnormal tail-chasing behavior of infected fish. It is a serious problem in fish hatcheries.

Recommendations:

Singles: Copaiba, Peppermint
Blends: ParaGize, DiGize

Application and Usage:

Application: Add 4 drops of each ParaGize and DiGize, 10 drops of Copaiba, and 2 drops of Peppermint into tank or pond per 4 gallons of water.

Testimonials

White spot disease, also known as ich (*ichthyophthiriasis*), is a parasite that most tropical fish enthusiasts will, at one time or another, have to deal with. Ich is responsible for more fish deaths than any other disease. This disease is mostly found in aquarium fish due to close contact with other fish and stress involved in living in an aquarium as opposed to the open water.

I had a 10-gallon tank and a 26-gallon tank that both had fish infected by ich. To rid my aquariums of ich, I did three things. First, I raised the temperature of the aquariums to 86°F. Second, I added 2-3 drops of Frankincense essential oil for each 10 gallons of water. Third, I made sure there was an air stone to increase oxygen in the water. Frankincense will also help to increase oxygen, kill the ich virus, and purify the water. I did not lose any of the fish.

–Dale B.

With little children in the house, the children will often hit the aquarium. This causes a condition known as "shock." A fish reacts to high stress and shock by becoming vulnerable to diseases and parasites. The symptoms include clamped fins, bloating, shimmies, lack of appetite, etc.

I had a 10-gallon tank that had been hit by little children too many times. I lost about 12 fish before realizing what was happening. First, I made the tank off limits to the children to limit the stress to the fish. Second, I placed 3-4 drops of Frankincense in the water and turned off the lights. Third, I provided enough food for them to eat within a 5-minute period. Frozen brine shrimp is my favorite fish food, especially for bigger fish. I did this for three days, and everything returned to normal.

–Dale B.

There comes a time when an aquarium becomes so dirty that it needs to be clean. I have found that algae grow back very fast if you don't clean the right way. I have found that if you take out all of the rock, sand, and decorative pieces; wash all in diluted Thieves Household Cleaner; wipe down the glass; and then wash and rinse the glass, rock, and decorations thoroughly, the algae don't come back for months. It also kills all the germs and parasites that might be in the tank.

I also allow the filter to run for 4-5 hours before placing fish back into the tank. The tank smells fresh and the fish seem to thrive once they are placed back into the tank.

Note: Do not use dish soap or other chemicals as these products leave a residue that can hurt the fish. I learned this the hard way and lost fish because I used a harsh chemical to clean a tank.

–Dale B.

11

Horses (Equine)

Introduction

In a healthy world, horses naturally come into contact with essential oils. This happens every day by grazing on live plants, scratching on bark, or eating herbs and grasses. Many flavorings in horse feed such as anise, fennel, peppermint, etc., come from essential oils as well. For millennia, nature has offered these oils to horses as a wonderful way to stay healthy.

These days, more and more equines are kept in unnatural surroundings due to space and time considerations. Being kept in stalls many hours of the day due to lack of pasture space in crowded cities and suburbs without turnout on grass or kept in small pens due to growing health issues involving metabolic diseases and/or Cushing's, horses welcome the benefits of essential oils to help them stay connected to the plant world and the healing it may offer.

Safety and Guidelines When Using Essential Oils for Equines

Essential oils can be used on all of the Equidae family, including horses, mules, donkeys, mini's, and zebras. Some may need more or less dilution, depending on the oil and the individual animal. Just like in humans, animals that have red or fair hair or are finer boned (Saddlebreds, Arabians) may require more dilution than average. Stay with them for 15 to 20 minutes after you've used an essential oil to make sure they are comfortable with the oils you've used. If they indicate any discomfort such as trying to frantically lick it off, rub it off, or are upset at all, dilute the oil further, using your choice of carrier oil such as V-6 Vegetable Oil Complex, coconut oil, jojoba oil, almond oil, grape seed oil, or olive oil.

Coconut oil is naturally antifungal and doesn't require refrigeration, perfect for your barn or trailer health chest. Even hand lotion (without petrochemical ingredients or perfumes) works in a pinch. Remember, water drives essential oils in deeper, so don't try to wash it off without soap; and aloe vera or a cold or ice application will enhance the feeling of the oils.

If unsure, you can use the oil on yourself on your inner elbow area and see if the oil feels "hot" on the skin. Dilute if it feels "hot" like Oregano or Mountain Savory would, itchy, or makes you feel uneasy for any reason. Once you have experienced what the oil may feel like, you'll understand your horse's reaction a bit more easily.

It's been said that to figure out how much essential oil a horse needs, just multiply what a human might need and adjust for the weight difference. That has been proven wrong many times and is understandable, when you remember a naturally kept horse doesn't have as many toxins assaulting its body as we humans do on a daily basis. This is especially true when using essential oils for emotional support and/or release.

When introducing essential oils, you may find animals not appreciating particular scents. They may not appreciate your putting the oils on them and may not be ready to work on an emotion that a particular oil may be evoking. Since animals rarely have a say on what is done to and for them, allowing them to choose an oil from an array of four or five may endear you to them more than you know.

To avoid scent overload and/or detox reaction, do not offer a large number of different oils.

Remember to offer the oils to both nostrils, as each side of the brain processes information differently. You'll often see the horse display the upturned lip or flehmen response, which facilitates transfer of inhaled scent molecules (pheromones and possibly some other substances) into the vomeronasal organ (VNO), a specialized chemosensory structure that transmits scent molecules to centers in the brain's accessory olfactory bulbs.

Horses often want to lick the oil from your hand or grab the bottle, so hold the bottle tightly. Some may even appreciate the taste of a hot oil such as Oregano or Hyssop, where most people find it uncomfortable. A horse's taste buds are a bit different than ours and can differentiate between bitter, sour, sweet, and salty. Horses will generally avoid bitter and sour things, which in nature indicate toxic plants and foods.

Another application method that works especially well for equids that aren't comfortable with being touched is to put the oil on yourself and let your body heat gently diffuse the oil while in the animal's presence. Using oils on a buddy or another horse can also be helpful when in a herd situation.

Oils can be placed in the environment such as on stable walls, near where the animals are fed, or in a secondary water source. In many "oily" barns, Peppermint is often placed in water troughs or buckets to assist digestion, avoid colic, and to cool horses during the summer heat (like Black Friesians in the South).

Always offer a clean, non-oiled water source in case a horse doesn't care for the taste. Oils such as Thieves, citrus oils, or spice oils are added to daily rations to keep the immune system healthy or to help balance other body systems such as the endocrine, eliminative, and more.

In many oily barns, essential oils make up fly sprays, helping to avoid the toxic buildup of daily chemical sprays. Enclosed barns can economically diffuse oils and work on an entire herd at once. Think of using oils such as R.C., Raven, or Purification to combat the indoor ammonia smell in the winter, while helping the respiratory and immune systems as well.

Other products such as Thieves Household Cleaner are used everywhere from washing horses, cleaning geldings (2-3 oz. in a 5-gallon bucket of water), cleaning quarantine stalls, washing trailers, cleaning feed dishes, in foot soaks, doing windows, and cleaning moldy tack. Next time the equine dentist makes a visit, offer Thieves Mouthwash instead of the chemicals dentists often use. If your horse has nasty feet, pack them with Thieves Dentarome Ultra Toothpaste, which acts as a poultice, antibacterial, antifungal, and protective agent in one.

Regular health checks with your animal health professional are always encouraged on a semi or annual basis. You may choose to let your professional know which oils you are using on your animals. High amounts of some oils such as Wintergreen taken orally can thin the blood; and some oils and blends such as Clary Sage, Fennel, Mister, SclarEssence, and Shutran may possibly influence hormonal balance.

Rosemary, Hyssop, and potentially Peppermint are to be used cautiously for epileptics.

Not all veterinarians are familiar with the pure Seed to Seal quality of essential oils, so offer to show them your *Animal Essential Oils Desk Reference* or to experiment with your oils a bit before they pass any judgment.

Some veterinarians may have seen what can go wrong with poor quality oils and may deem ALL oils unworthy of being used on animals based on their previous cases. Be polite and remember that you are the one who makes the final decisions on your animal's care, and you are the one paying the bill. If your animal's health professional isn't hearing your concerns or isn't supportive to your animal's needs, find another. One great resource is www.ahvma.org for the American Holistic Veterinary Medicine Association.

Nutrition and Diet

Diet and Feeds: Foods safe for insulin resistance or low-inflammatory feeds

Go to www.ecirhorse.com and check the feed tab to learn which foods on the market are safe and how to calculate what might be best for your horse. This site does not sell feeds; it contains only education.

If your horse needs higher energy or exercises a lot, investigate adding fats such as organic flax, chia, or coconut. Stay away from GMO fats or those whose harvest includes glyphosate chemicals on crops such as soy, corn, canola, and some flax.

Use soaked beet pulp with no added molasses. Speedi-Beet is a non-GMO beet pulp that has a much higher yield than most. Beet pulp is a great way to provide fiber to your horse's diet. Added fiber lowers insulin levels and gives your horse a feeling of being full, which cuts appetite and hence intake. Beet pulp has about the same protein level as grass hay (9-10 percent). Grass hay and beet pulp have similar fiber. Feed only soaked beet pulp, since dry can swell in the throat and cause choking.

The sugar part of sugar beets has been mostly removed as it was processed. What is left over is beet pulp that is 97 percent "sugar free," and that is very good. Wet beet pulp is only a 3 percent ethanol soluble carbohydrate (ESC) simple sugar. Studies have proven that it will not raise insulin levels and, in fact, is a good product to feed horses. Do not get beet pulp mixed up with bran mash. Bran mash is extremely high in sugar, is minerally imbalanced, and cannot be given to horses or ponies.

CoolStance, made of Copra or coconut meal, is another good choice.

Companies such as Triple Crown or Ontario Dehy have non-GMO hay cubes. Their balance cubes are made of non-GMO beet pulp, Timothy hay, and all the minerals needed to make them a complete feed. The only other necessary ingredients are vitamin E (5 human 400 IU capsules are easy to feed and much more absorbable than dry powdered vitamin E) and Redmond Rock Salt.

The key to good treats or additions to feed is to limit the higher sugar fruits. Fresh foods supply live enzymes for horses unable to be on pasture or are seasonally restricted such as during the winter:

- Apricots
- Bananas (the browner the better, as the sugars are used in the browning)
- Beets
- Blackberries
- Blueberries
- Cantaloupe rinds
- Celery
- Cherries (pits removed)
- Coconuts
- Grapes (small amounts only)
- Grapefruit
- Lettuce (Romaine or green leaf)
- Mangoes (pit removed)
- Oranges
- Peaches (pit removed)
- Pears
- Pineapples
- Plums (pit removed)
- Pumpkins (including canned)
- Pumpkin seeds
- Raisins
- Rutabagas
- Squash
- Strawberries
- Sweet Potatoes
- Tangerines
- Turnips
- Watermelon rinds

In insulin resistance or other inflammatory conditions, **avoid:**

1. Cookies loaded in corn, oats, sugar, and molasses. The cookies at the tack shop need to also be avoided.
2. Candy. Use only stevia-sweetened treats.
3. Bran mash has lots of carbohydrates. It also has a higher Glycemic Index than many grains. Wheat bran and rice bran should be avoided. Rice bran has 8 times more starch than alfalfa cubes and over 10 times more than beet pulp.
4. Grains like corn, oats, and wheat. Even a handful is a bad choice. According to Equi-analytical, oats have a starch of 44.2 and an NSC (non-structural carbohydrate) of 48.7 making it:
   - 15 times the starch and 4 times the NSC of alfalfa
   - 4 times the NSC of low carb/high protein feeds
   - 13 times the starch of fresh grass pasture
   - 22 times the starch of wet beet pulp and 9 times the NSC
5. Certain fruits and vegetables like apples, carrots, applesauce (3 times worse than apples), watermelons
6. Other items to avoid: Everything containing sugar, including peppermint candy, sugar cubes, jelly beans, yogurt, pretzels, chips, lawn clippings, frosted mini-wheats, and other cereals

Horse (Equine) First Aid

First-Aid Kit, Including Young Living Products

This list suggests a few simple options to deal with some of the most common injuries. You can add to it as you see fit and as you can afford. This is not intended to be an exhaustive list, and it includes many suggestions from veterinarians all over the world. You can keep everything in a bucket or bag that is wrapped in plastic to keep it clean and secure.

See the following list of basic tools, wound and equipment antiseptics, solutions, ointments, and creams. This is just a selected list and by no means a comprehensive list of items you may need when working with horses. As you become more familiar with your horses and typical issues you or they will encounter, you can tailor your aid kit to become more specific to your horse's needs.

Materials

Thieves Wipes

Adhesive wrapping materials

Self-sticking adhesive wrap

Clean stable wraps, quilted bandages, or rolled cotton

Polo wraps

Women's nylon panty hose

Non-stick Telfa™ bandages

Ice-pack leg wraps (use Peppermint, Spearmint, or Cool Azul Sports Gel or Cool Azul Pain Relief Cream to assist cooling)

Hoof boot

Epsom salts

Oils, Supplements, and Cleaners

Animal Scents Ointment

Thieves Waterless Hand Purifier

Thieves Household Cleaner

Thieves Spray

Thieves

Purification

Patchouli

Melrose

Tea Tree

Lavender

Idaho Tansy

Citrus oils

Helichrysum

Peace & Calming

Copaiba

Myrrh

German Chamomile

Carrot Seed

Palmarosa

DiGize

Peppermint

AromaEase

LavaDerm Cooling Mist

Tender Tush

ClaraDerm

Mineral Essence

Saline solution

Horse (Equine) Quick Reference Guide

Bruised Ankle (e.g., from hobble injury)

Apply Melrose, Mountain Savory, Ocotea, Cool Azul, Cool Azul Pain Relief Cream, Cool Azul Sports Gel, Deep Relief Roll-On, and PanAway with Animal Scents Ointment or Ortho Sport Massage Oil to reduce tenderness, bruising, and inflammation.

Cancer

Shave area near the tumor and inject Sacred Frankincense or Frankincense with a hypodermic syringe. Alternate with Clove oil every four days. Keep saturated with Sacred Frankincense or Frankincense. If the area is open, put a plug in the opening to hold the oil in the tumor cavity. Continue for six months.

Colic (The leading cause of death in horses)

Symptoms
- Pawing the ground with head down
- Trotting in circles
- Lying down and looking bloated
- No churning or rumbling in the stomach
- Being quiet

Causes
- Eating off the ground and a mineral imbalance (getting too much dirt in the gut). The accumulated dirt can cause the gut to twist, abscess, and spasm.
- Parasites
- Eating too much alfalfa and not enough feed. Alfalfa can stress the kidneys and liver in horses. In general, grass hay is best for horses of all kinds. As a rule of thumb, the more a horse works, the more alfalfa it needs and can tolerate.
- Getting too hot

Treatment Protocol

Keep the horse standing or walking. If the horse lies down, keep the animal's head tied up to prevent him from rolling.

1st hour

Internal Use
- 8 to 10 Detoxzyme
- 15 drops of DiGize Vitality
- Put into animal's feed grain or drop inside lip.

You can open the capsules and make an enzyme and oil paste to put inside the horse's lip.

Massage
- Rub 10 drops DiGize up each flank and massage out toward umbilical area.
- Rub 10 drops DiGize around the coronet band.
- Rub DiGize on auricular points of ears.

Enema
- Mix 30 drops of DiGize in 6 oz. V-6 Vegetable Oil Complex or olive oil and insert in the horse's rectum as an enema. Do not use castor oil as it dehydrates the colon.

2nd hour
- Put 10-20 drops DiGize Vitality in the mouth and on the flanks and coronet band.

4th hour
- Repeat 1st-hour protocol except for enema.

6th hour
- Repeat 1st-hour protocol, adding 5 drops of Peppermint to the 10-20 drops of DiGize Vitality.

8th hour
- Repeat 1st-hour protocol, except for enema, and add one scoop of Power Meal or Pure Protein Complete (add to water if the animal is drinking).

10th hour
- Continue administering 6-8 Detoxzyme every 2 hours until the horse's bowels are moving well.

Distemper, Whooping Cough, or Asthma

Daily Regimen
- Mix 30 drops each of R.C. and Raven in 4 oz. of V-6 Vegetable Oil Complex and insert into the rectum.
- Put 15 drops each of R.C. and Raven in the bottom lip.
- Massage oils on the chest between the front legs and auricular points of ears.
- Apply Raindrop Technique down the spine and neck hair.
- Administer 4 Longevity Softgels.

Horse (Equine) Quick Reference Guide

Fractures/Bone Chips

Shave area around affected bone. Apply mixture of:
- 5 drops Wintergreen
- 5 drops Idaho Balsam Fir
- 2 drops Oregano (or Plectranthus Oregano)
- Add 2 tablespoons Sulfurzyme to feed.
- Continue the above regimen daily for 3 months.

Case History

In 1997 a horse's back hock was fractured with two 50-cent-sized pieces splintered off. The animal was diagnosed at stage five lameness, and the vet urged to have the animal euthanized.

After Wintergreen essential oil was applied for several months, the bone regenerated and the break healed. The horse returned to the jousting arena stronger and more powerful than ever and spent several more years entertaining the crowds.

Note: Other oils that may be effective for this condition include Helichrysum, Northern Lights Black Spruce, and Idaho Balsam Fir. Sulfurzyme may be used internally.

Hide Injuries

Case History

A 4-month-old colt had the hide on one side of its body stripped off. The wound was sprayed with Melrose to disinfect and Helichrysum to control the pain. The wound was then sealed with the formula now known as Animal Scents Ointment. Within several months, the hair and skin had completely grown in, and the animal had made a full recovery.

Hoof Infections

Case History

In 2000 a show horse received some kind of severe bite on the pastern. Although the vet diagnosed a rattlesnake bite, it may have been caused by something else.

Two weeks later, the entire pastern and coronet band were inflamed (the size of a cantaloupe), and the rotting, decaying flesh revealed a large hole where the bone was visible and had separated from the hoof.

The vet suggested amputating the foot. Instead, the following protocol was initiated:
- **Day 1:** The wound was cleaned and disinfected with Thieves and Helichrysum, and the foot was bandaged. This treatment decreased pain enough to allow the mare to put weight on the foot.
- **Day 2:** The swelling had dropped by 50 percent. The wound was again cleaned with Thieves and Helichrysum and then packed with Animal Scents Ointment.
- **Days 3 to 14:** The wound was washed morning and night with Thieves, Melrose, and Helichrysum and packed with Animal Scents Ointment.
- **Result:** Today the animal walks with no discomfort. A brand new hoof has appeared with only a small scar on the wound site. Although there was minor swelling in the pastern for a while, it had faded eight months later.

Imprinting on New Foals

Recommended Essential Oils: Valor, Highest Potential, Sacred Mountain, Joy, Surrender, Acceptance

As soon as a colt is born, pick up the foal and hold it in your arms. Massage 5-6 drops of oil along the spine and place a drop on each ear. Then rub oils all over the colt's body a few drops at a time. Lay the colt in your lap and position it with its head back, stroke its neck, and pass all the way over its nose (avoid putting any oils on the nose as it is very sensitive). Repeat every day for 21 days.

Jitteriness

To calm a horse, apply a few drops of oil on your hands and put one hand on the base of the tail and the other on the withers. The animal should relax. Relaxation is the first step to healing.

Put several drops of T-Away, Trauma Life, Surrender, Peace & Calming, or Peace & Calming II in your hand and briefly hold it up to the animal's muzzle or nostrils. If the horse pulls away and returns to it several times,

Horse (Equine) Quick Reference Guide

perhaps out of curiosity or perhaps thinking that food may appear, feed him some grain as a reward and then put your hand with oil on his muzzle and gently rub it in.

As he relaxes, work your hand around the side of his jaw and up along the neckline to the ears. Then rub his ears and the top of his head and crop. As he relaxes further, you can add more oil to the palm of your hand (Peace & Calming, Peace & Calming II, or Valerian) and continue rubbing his ears, head, and crop.

Kidney Failure

- Administer 10 drops (about ½ dropper) of K&B tincture morning and night.
- Using a Raindrop application on the spine, apply 5 drops each of Cypress and Juniper daily for 10 days.

Laxative for Foals

Put 4 drops of DiGize Vitality in bottom lip daily until bowels are moving.

Open Wounds

Case History

A large thoroughbred gelding was attacked by a cougar that clawed a chunk of flesh half the size of a soccer ball out of the horse's buttocks. The horse bled terribly, blood squirting from ruptured blood vessels.

The vet said the prognosis was grim because there was too much torn, damaged, and removed tissue. Even if the horse didn't die, the wound would leave a sizeable scar and indentation.

Treatment Protocol
Day 1

To reduce the pain and stop the bleeding, a 5 cc hypodermic syringe was filled with Helichrysum and sprayed into the wound. The horse became less jittery, and the bleeding stopped. Several minutes later a larger 10 cc syringe of Purification was sprayed into the open wound. It took over 15 ml of Purification to spray down and cover the entire wound.

After several hours, the wound was sprayed with Melrose to disinfect it and was packed with Animal Scents Ointment. To keep hair out of the wound and reduce the possibility of infection, the tail was wrapped and tied up. Because there was no way to cover or close the wound, the horse was kept in the stable to prevent him from moving around. The animal was closely monitored to reduce the possibility of reinfection caused by the animal lying down, rolling around, and scratching the wound.

Days 2-7

The horse's grain was supplemented with crushed up Essentialzyme, the yellow capsule in Essentialzymes-4, and four scoops of Power Meal, which is dense in the nutrients required for healing and tissue rebuilding.

Three times a day, the open wound was irrigated with Purification and Helichrysum. The vet came regularly to monitor the horse's progress. He remarked that he had never seen muscle tissue regenerate to such a degree.

Weeks 2 to 4

Two times a day, the open wound was irrigated with Purification and Helichrysum.

Weeks 4 to 8

Once a week, the wound was irrigated with Purification and Helichrysum until it was closed.

Results

Today, no indentation or concavity is visible, only a small, circular 2-inch scar.

Puncture Wounds

Put 1 cc of Thieves in a hypodermic syringe, insert the needle deeply into the wound, and irrigate thoroughly. Repeat 1 to 2 times a day for 2 to 3 days if still infected or swollen. Continue this process for up to 10 days.

Saddle Sores and Raw Spots

(i.e., where packs rub against flesh)

Use PuriClean, Infect Away, and Mendwell as a three-part system; may also use Melrose and Animal Scents Ointment for at least 3 days.

Horse (Equine) Quick Reference Guide

Scours (diarrhea caused by bacteria)

- Put 5 drops ParaGize or DiGize Vitality in the horse's lower lip and rub 5-8 drops in the flank.
- Place ICP in water and pour it down the throat. Continue for four days.

Screw Worm

There is a round worm called a bore or screw worm that bores into the spine of a horse (especially wild horses). It will cause a huge boil-like abscess on the spine. When lanced, a larva worm will come out of that abscess. Sometimes the abscess will actually break open and ooze.

Pour Thieves into the hole to flush out the larva worm and then fill the hole with a mixture of 12 drops of Melrose and 5 drops of Mountain Savory.

Strangles (Streptococcus equi infection)

- Perform the Raindrop Technique with Thieves.
- Apply 4 drops of Thieves Vitality on the inside of the bottom lip (for a large horse, 8 drops).
- After 2 hours repeat Raindrop Technique with Oregano Vitality (or Plectranthus Oregano) and Thyme Vitality. Put 2 drops of Oregano Vitality and 2 drops of Thyme Vitality on the inside of the bottom lip (for a large horse, 4 drops each).
- Repeat the last two steps every 2 hours until the horse begins to improve. As the horse continues to improve, alternate treatments every 4 hours, every 6 hours, and then morning and night.

Swollen Sheath

Geldings and stallions occasionally suffer from swollen sheath with an abscess and infection. It can be caused by:

- Eating hay too rich in protein. Ideal levels of protein should be 12 to 15 percent, and alfalfa hay can have protein as high as 26 percent.
- Not extracting the penis and letting it clean off.

Treatment

- Put on rubber gloves.
- Clean inside the sheath and remove debris with soap and water. Use a half cap of Thieves Household Cleaner diluted in a half gallon of water.
- Clean outside the sheath by applying Myrrh oil and Rosemary with Tea Tree. The ratio is 15 drops of Myrrh, 15 drops of Rosemary, and 10 drops of Tea Tree.
- Clean and disinfect morning and night until infection and swelling subside.
- Maintenance: The sheath should be cleaned out once a month. Make sure the horse is fed adequate water and grass hay and gets sufficient exercise to increase circulation.
- Perform a Raindrop Technique with Oregano (or Plectranthus Oregano), Thyme, and Mountain savory every 3 to 6 months.

Umbilical Cords of Newborn Foals

Instead of iodine, put Myrrh oil on the umbilical cord of newborn foals. Myrrh will dry the umbilical cord and facilitate a good separation. Exodus II can also be used to treat infections in a foal's umbilical cord.

Raindrop Technique® for Horses

Although many veterinarians have developed their own variations of this technique, the simplicity of this procedure is what makes it effective.

Raindrop Technique for horses is similar to that for humans, except that there must be practical modifications because of the difference in size and shape of the patient. Trying to exactly duplicate the human version of the Raindrop Technique on animals is not advised.

Starting Point

Apply 6 drops of Valor to the tailbone (the base of the tail where it connects with the spine). Next, place one hand on the withers and the other on the tailbone and hold for 5 minutes. There is no difference energetically whether you use your right or left hand in these spots. Once the horse relaxes (i.e., drops its head and eyelids droop), the procedure can start.

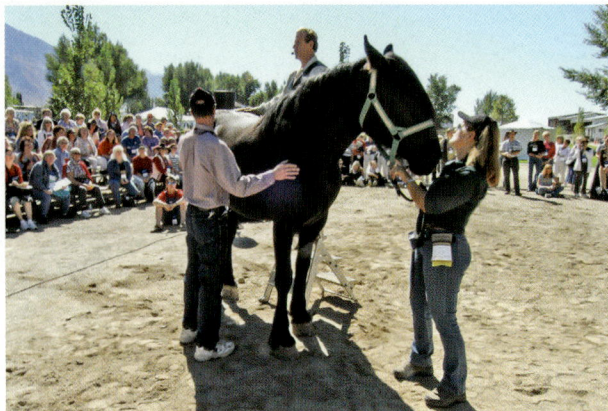

Don'ts

- Do not spend too much time stroking the horse's spine. Usually, three repetitions are sufficient.
- Avoid dripping oils on the hair of the horse's spine and stroking them in. You will be stroking against the grain of the hair, and oil will be flicked off the spine rather than rubbed in. This is not as important for animals with fine hair.
- Once you make contact with the animal on which you are applying oils, never break it.
- Do not work on the animal with multiple partners. Raindrop Technique is more effective when only one pair of hands makes continuous contact with the animal because the energy stays the same, and animals get skittish when two or more people touch them at the same time.

How to Apply Oils

- Where feasible, shave the spine area for direct application of the oil (you will use less oil).
- If shaving is not feasible, stand the hair up and part it, then drip the oil down through the hair so that the oil contacts the spine. Hold the oil 6 inches above the spine as you drop it in.
- For coarse-haired animals, stroke in the oils using small, circular motions, working from the base of the tail to the shoulders of the spine.
- For fine-haired animals, stroke in the oils using regular Raindrop Technique straight strokes.
- Spend enough time massaging to get the oils down into the skin and not sitting on top of the hair.
- When dripping the oils on the spine, use 12 drops on a draft horse, 6 drops on a saddle horse, or 3-4 drops on a miniature horse, Shetland, or Welch pony.

Additional Tips

- Carefully use your fingertips and thumb tips to perform Vita Flex along the auricular points of the ear. Be gentle. If you inflict even a little discomfort, the horse will distrust you and pull away.
- Stretching the spine is problematic in horses, so instead, place one hand over the tail, the other hand on the withers, and focus moving the energy along the spine.
- Rubbing oils around the coronet band will allow the oils to reach the bloodstream and travel through the nerves in the legs to the spine.
- Drip Marjoram and Aroma Siez into the hair of the outside muscles away from the spine and rub in with a larger circular motion massage. Idaho Tansy, Palo Santo, or Melrose—which are anti-inflammatory, anesthetic, insect-repelling, relaxing, and healing—can also be used. This is important because horses used for packing, riding, or working have extra stress placed on the spine and muscles in the back.
- Avoid having two people working on opposite sides of the horse at the same time. No two people's energy is the same, and this produces an energetic imbalance.
- Use a stool (mounting block) to reach both sides of the spine without having to break contact, potentially creating tension in the animal.
- Some people mistakenly believe that if they don't have all the oils in the Raindrop Kit, they can't do a Raindrop. You do not need to apply every oil to have an effective treatment.
- You can perform an excellent, beneficial Raindrop procedure with one oil, if that's all you have. Using just Oregano (or Plectranthus Oregano) and Thyme, Palo Santo, or even Idaho Tansy can produce excellent results. Similarly, Melrose, Tea Tree, or Mountain Savory can also be used.
- It is okay to stroke oils down off the hips and down the legs.
- It is okay to put a hot towel on the spine. In fact, it is recommended.
- Following a Raindrop Technique, you can apply a saddle blanket and then a horse blanket and leave the animal standing in the stall. Usually after about 10 minutes, it will lie down and go to sleep.

Alternate Raindrop Techniques for Horses

By Judy G.

Valor

1. Apply 5 drops to the atlas.
2. Apply 5 drops to each side of the withers and stroke into the muscles toward the base of the neck.
3. Apply 5 drops over the sacrum and pelvis.
4. Apply 2-3 drops to the bulbs of the heels or frogs on all four feet, starting with the right front foot and working in a clockwise direction.

Thyme and Oregano

1. Apply V-6 Vegetable Oil Complex or similar massage oil to the coronary bands of all four hooves before proceeding further to slow down the absorption rate of the hotter oils.
2. Apply 3 drops of Thyme first, then Oregano to the right front coronary band.
3. Do Vita Flex Technique 3 times each from the front to the inside, then from the front to the outside.
4. Continue to repeat on each of the other feet in a clockwise direction.

Cypress, Wintergreen, Basil, and Peppermint

1. In that order, use 3 drops of each and layer down the inside of each hind leg, stroking down toward the hoof 3 times in between the oils.
2. Vita Flex down the inside of the hind legs.

Thyme and Oregano

1. Suggest to drop several drops of V-6 or similar high-quality massage oil down the spine before proceeding any further to disperse the hotter oils.
2. First with Thyme, then with Oregano, drop 5 drops down the spine starting at the base of the tail and dropping from 6 inches above the horse's back.
3. Rake the oils in 3 times using a feathering motion from the base of the tail to the withers.

Cypress, Wintergreen, and Basil

1. In this order, drop 8-12 drops of each oil from 6 inches above the spine starting at the base of the tail and going up to the withers.
2. After each oil, lightly rake in the oils using a feathering motion down the spine.

Marjoram and Aroma Siez

1. Drop 5-10 drops down each side of the spine focusing on the sacrum and lumbar areas.
2. Rake in the oils with a feathering motion.

Peppermint

1. If you wish to add any extra oils, do so before Peppermint.
2. Always finish with Peppermint because it drives in the other oils. Drop the Peppermint along the spine and rake in.

Vita Flex

1. Use Vita Flex down each side of the spine from tail to withers 3 times.
2. With your fingertips, make little circles down each side of the spine 3 times.
3. Make large circles down the back muscles 3 times on each side.
4. Do the "plow" down the spine 3 times.

Other Guidelines

1. **Do not** put a heavy blanket on for several hours after doing Raindrop Technique.
2. **Do not** allow the horse to go out in direct sunlight for several hours after receiving Raindrop Technique.
3. **Do not** ride the horse until at least the following day.

Note: Although doing the hooves and legs is recommended for the greatest benefit, it is not essential. You will be giving a very therapeutic treatment by treating the poll (the area found immediately behind or right between the ears) and spine only. An easy time-saving alternative is to use Ortho Sport Massage Oil on the coronary bands and down the hind legs instead of layering on each of the oils.

The Feelings Kit Applied to Horses

Horses are just as moody as humans. Because they aren't able to express their emotions to us in words, we have to learn to read their cues. This leaves them even more vulnerable to hiding their moods inside. That said, many horses have been through some very stressful times. Show horses, rescue horses, horses that have been injured, horses that travel a lot, or horses that have passed through many owners can all benefit from essential oils.

The Feelings Collection is the perfect set of essential oils to help these wonderful beings release and move forward into the future for a more positive life.

When using the oils for support, it's always best to let the horse have the choice to smell the oils. When the horses (just like people) breathe the oils, the oils go straight into the limbic system of the brain; thus, the brain processes that oil. Sometimes they want more and sometimes they want less. Respect their wishes as you are working with them. After allowing the horses to inhale as much as they want, apply the oils topically on specific locations to further assist with balancing.

Valor (or Valor II)
1. Let the horse breathe in the oil.
2. Apply Valor to the poll, dropping down behind the ears, and following along the neck vertebrae, including sternum, shoulders, and withers.
3. Place around the bulbs of the heels and/or on the frog, as you would do in a Raindrop Session.

Harmony
1. Let the horse inhale Harmony.
2. Place a few drops of Harmony in the center of the chest, on the girth area on the left side over the approximate location of the heart. Additionally, drop along the spine from the base of the tail and ending at the poll.
3. Harmony is a wonderful blend to keep things in harmony and has great benefits when used on its own or with Valor.

Forgiveness
1. Let the horse inhale Forgiveness.
2. Apply Forgiveness on the navel and the auricular points on the inside of the ears and forehead.
3. This is a great choice on its own for horses that need help moving beyond the past.

Release
1. Let the horse inhale Release. Horses who tend to pin their ears love Release.
2. Apply Release along the right side above the liver and on the muzzle.

Present Time
1. Let the horse breathe in Present Time.
2. Apply Present Time to the chest on the approximate area over the thymus gland.
3. Rub 1-2 drops inside the upper lip, if possible. Use your intentions to direct it in. Present Time works well for horses that want to avoid the moment.

Inner Child
1. Place several drops of Inner Child in your hand and allow the horse to smell the oils; do not be surprised if it chooses to lick your hand.
2. Apply the remaining Inner Child on the forehead and heart. Allow your hand to remain there a few moments.

White Angelica
1. Put a few drops in your hand and pet the horse's whole body, starting at the forehead and finishing at the tail.

The horse will have processed a lot during this application! Give it time and space to adjust.

In addition, in the days following the use of the Feelings Collection, a horse will benefit greatly by continued use of Valor. A person may wish to continue using oils such as Trauma Life, T-Away, Joy, Highest Potential, or Into the Future to support positive emotions and a happy horse. You may choose to reapply the Feelings Kit oils daily or weekly as needed.

Horse (Equine) Conditions

Abscess

Abscess in the hoof area can be very painful and hard to diagnose. In horses, this is known as subsolar sepsis, and the most common cause is a puncture wound. The cause can be from many different problems, a stone bruise, quarter crack, gravel, out-of-balance shoeing, or injury. Most of these only pierce the subsolar soft tissue and result in a subsolar abscess.

But if the puncture penetrates synovial structures, the result can be catastrophic. Administer immediate care. Generally, the pathogens introduced by the puncture are the cause of abscess formation. If the puncture wound is in the solar area, draining the site may help prevent abscess formation. Consult your veterinary health professional.

Recommendations

Singles: Cassia, Cinnamon Bark, Laurus Nobilis, Lavender, Lemon, Lemongrass, Tea Tree, Mountain Savory, Oregano, Helichrysum, Thyme, Myrrh, Basil, Ginger, Geranium, Palmarosa, Ravintsara, Patchouli

Blends: Thieves, Purification, Exodus II, Abundance, Egyptian Gold, Longevity, PanAway, Melrose

Nutritionals: NingXia Red, Sulfurzyme

Additional: Thieves Household Cleaner, Animal Scents Ointment

Application and Usage

Topical: For 20 minutes, cover hoof/abscess with warm water, using ¼ cup Thieves Household Cleaner to 1 gallon water 2 times daily. Rub 2-3 chosen suggested oils around the coronary band or on location of the abscess 2 times daily. The goal is to reduce swelling, pain, and inflammation and to draw out toxins.

Ingestion & Oral: An internal abscess can be very tricky. The goal is to dissolve the abscess and encourage it to release. If necessary, consult your veterinarian for blood work to determine the pathology. Syringe directly into the mouth any combination of the oils listed above.

Other: Use Thieves with a hot towel and hold on area until towel is cool. Repeat 3 times daily. Once the abscess has ruptured, use Animal Scents Ointment around the area and along the drainage. Keep hole open until you are sure all of the infection is gone. Bathe affected area with Animal Scents Shampoo or diluted Thieves Household Cleaner.

Anesthesia Detoxification

Some animals have difficulty waking up fully or bouncing back after a surgery or procedure where a veterinarian used anesthesia (local or general). Horses may develop significant muscle pain and weakness in one or more muscle groups. Horses may be delayed up to two hours.

Naturopaths have long considered anesthesia to promote the formation of toxins. Symptoms range from nausea, to inflammation of the throat, to trouble standing and walking. Consult your veterinary health professional.

Recommendations

Singles: Roman Chamomile, Geranium, Grapefruit, Helichrysum, Peppermint, Juniper, Cypress, Rosemary, Tea Tree

Blends: DiGize, GLF, Longevity, JuvaCleanse

Nutritionals: NingXia Red, Rehemogen

Application and Usage

Topical: Apply 10 or more drops each of DiGize and Peppermint on stomach area.

Ingestion & Oral: Use 10-20 drops of any oil or blend listed above (DiGize is preferred). If horse is still not fully recovered, syringe into mouth 2 oz. NingXia Red and 6 dropperfuls Rehemogen.

Arthritis

This is a general term for inflammation of the joints. All joint diseases in horses will have varying degrees of inflammation. The general categories are traumatic arthritis, osteochondritis dissecans, subchondral cystic lesions, septic arthritis, and osteoarthritis. Consult your veterinary health professional to be sure of the diagnosis.

Recommendations

Singles: Copaiba, Lavender, Idaho Balsam Fir, Clove, Frankincense, Helichrysum, Lemongrass, Marjoram, Myrrh, Palo Santo, Peppermint, Pine, Idaho Blue Spruce, Vetiver, Wintergreen, Northern Lights Black Spruce, Cypress

Blends: Longevity, Aroma Siez, M-Grain, PanAway, Cool Azul, Relieve It, Deep Relief Roll-On

Nutritionals: NingXia Red, AgilEase, BLM, Sulfurzyme

Additional: V-6 Vegetable Oil Complex, Ortho Ease Massage Oil, Ortho Sport Massage Oil, Cool Azul Pain Relief Cream, Cool Azul Sports Gel

Application and Usage

Topical: Starting with Copaiba, layer any 3 chosen suggested oils on affected areas. Use any of the listed oils and/or Ortho Ease Massage Oil or Ortho Sports Massage Oil before and after exercise on joints.

Ingestion & Oral: Top dress feed 2 times daily with 2 oz. NingXia Red, 1 oz. Sulfurzyme, and 1 AgilEase or BLM.

Other: Administer Raindrop Technique weekly. If the horse has overly sensitive skin, administer 1-2 times a month, being sure to start with V-6 Vegetable Oil Complex over the back. Also, try mixing Ortho Ease Massage Oil or Ortho Sport Massage Oil with Wintergreen and rub on area. Use the following individually or layer with chosen oils: Ortho Ease Massage Oil, Ortho Sport Massage Oil, Cool Azul Pain Relief Cream, Cool Azul Sports Gel

Autoimmune Disorders

This occurs when the immune system attacks its own tissue, causing inflammation. This may be any instance in which the immune system attacks healthy cells, affecting many of the body systems. Most autoimmune disorders manifest in symptoms such as fatigue, pain, fever, inflammation, redness, heat, and swelling. Symptoms may be cyclical and vacillate between flare-up and remission. Work with your local veterinarian.

Recommendations

Singles: Frankincense, Cistus, Copaiba, Nutmeg, Ginger, Roman Chamomile, German Chamomile, Clove, Cypress, Sacred Frankincense, Helichrysum, Juniper, Laurus Nobilis, Ledum, Lemon, Lemongrass, Tea Tree, Melissa, Myrrh, Myrtle, Palo Santo, Patchouli, Ravintsara, Sacred Sandalwood, Royal Hawaiian Sandalwood, Valerian, Thyme, Palmarosa

Blends: Deep Relief Roll-On, PanAway, Cool Azul, Longevity, 3 Wise Men, Thieves, Present Time, ImmuPower, JuvaCleanse, Believe, Forgiveness, Harmony

Nutritionals: NingXia Red, Sulfurzyme, AgilEase, BLM, Mineral Essence, MindWise, Thyromin, Power Meal (for adaptogens)

Additional: V-6 Vegetable Oil Complex, Cool Azul Sports Gel, Cool Azul Pain Relief Cream

Application and Usage

Topical: Rub a few drops of chosen oils on the spine from the poll to tail, apply to stomach, femoral arteries, and coronary bands. Primary oils of choice would be Copaiba, ImmuPower, and Sacred Frankincense. Palmarosa is also known as an immune modulator.

Ingestion & Oral: Combine 5 drops each of Copaiba, ImmuPower, and Longevity with 2 oz. NingXia Red. Administer combination orally at least 2 times daily. Also try 10 drops JuvaCleanse orally for additional detox, especially heavy metal involvement. Use any of the oils listed above for additional support.

Other: Administer Raindrop Technique 1-2 times weekly. If horse has overly sensitive skin, perform Raindrop Technique just once or twice a month, being sure to start with V-6 oil over the back. Autoimmunity can have a huge emotional component to it. Use Acceptance, Believe, Forgiveness, or Harmony topically on forehead, poll, chest, and heart area. If needed for additional pain support, apply Cool Azul Sports Gel or Cool Azul Pain Relief Cream externally.

Back/Spinal Conditions

Conditions affecting the spinal column and cord may be the result of congenital disorders, inflammatory and infectious diseases, degenerative diseases, neoplasia, toxins, vascular diseases, parasites, nutritional deficiencies or excesses, injury, etc. These may include equine degenerative myeloencephalopathy, EHV-1, EPM, or equine motor neuron disease.

Most cases where back pain is present, trauma is the cause with the horse twisting or falling awkwardly. Poor fitting tack can also create back pain as can ovarian pain. The degree of pain can vary considerably and will present as any one of several symptoms. These include lameness, reluctance to perform or jump, uneven gait, rearing up, loss of muscling over the back, and changes in behavior. Pulled and/or inflamed muscle can also be a cause. Work with your vet to determine the cause and best course of action and care.

Recommendations

Singles: Copaiba, Cypress, Helichrysum, Basil, Marjoram, Wintergreen, Peppermint, Idaho Balsam Fir, Northern Lights Black Spruce, Frankincense, Sacred Frankincense, Juniper, Laurus Nobilis,

Back/Spine Conditions:

Dislocation:

Use Raindrop Technique daily, if tolerated. At the very least, use the Raindrop oils and rub them into the spine. Additionally, do the following once daily: 2 drops Valor mixed with Ortho Ease Massage Oil or Ortho Sport Massage Oil rubbed on area and around bulbs and coronary bands.

Remember to use Grounding and/or Cypress on the coronary band if you can safely work with the lower legs to draw excess energy away from the back and toward the ground, especially if horse is shod. Apply Valor or Valor II along spine, coronary band, and heel bulbs to make chiropractic adjustments hold longer. Harmony on the chakra points helps energy balance. Release essential oil blend helps with both mental and physical blocks.

Lavender, Lemongrass, Mountain Savory, Palo Santo, Palmarosa, Pine, Idaho Blue Spruce, Vetiver

Blends: Thieves, PanAway, Relieve It, Trauma Life, Valor, Valor II, Cool Azul, Deep Relief Roll On, Stress Away Roll-On

Nutritionals: NingXia Red, Sulfurzyme

Additional: V-6 Vegetable Oil Complex, Ortho Ease Massage Oil, Ortho Sport Massage Oil, Cool Azul Sports Gel, Cool Azul Pain Relief Cream, Regenolone Moisturizing Cream

Application and Usage

Topical: Starting with Copaiba, layer chosen oils on spine and either side on muscles along spine 2 times daily, finishing with Ortho Ease Massage Oil or Ortho Sport Massage Oil, Cool Azul Sports Gel, Cool Azul Pain Relief Cream, or Regenolone Moisturizing Cream. Administer the Raindrop Technique every other day. If the horse has extremely sensitive skin, do as often as can be tolerated, starting with V-6 oil. Using Release also helps both mental and physical blocks to let go. Any tree oil will be helpful in supporting the body's structure.

Ingestion & Oral: Combine 10 drops each Copaiba and Thieves with 1-2 oz. NingXia Red and 1-2 oz. Sulfurzyme. Administer combination orally at least 2 times daily.

Birthing and Delivery

Move the mare to the place where she'll deliver a few weeks prior in the evenings and make sure she is in a separate, spacious location. It should be ventilated well, disinfected, well-lit, and bedded to accommodate the delivery. This should be away from all animals that may travel, are sick, or are new to the barn.

Foaling is divided into distinct stages:

The first is often difficult to detect and occurs some hours before the foal is delivered. Signs to check for are colic-like symptoms with the mare becoming uneasy, pacing the stall, looking around at her flank, and swishing her tail. You may also see sweating and pawing at the ground. In some cases, milk may begin to squirt out. Avoid as much interference at this stage as possible. If the mare seems particularly agitated, pet her with Peace & Calming and allow her to smell Lavender.

Stage two is when the water breaks. As the muscles of the uterus contract, the foal moves into the birth canal, and the mare typically lies on her side. Stage two should last no longer than one hour and normally takes little more than 20-30 minutes. It is imperative to seek help if you suspect any difficulties or if the foal is not presenting correctly.

Recommendations

Singles: Sacred Frankincense, Frankincense, Myrrh, Lavender, Cistus, Clary Sage, Roman Chamomile, Geranium, Marjoram, Orange, Rose, Vetiver, Black Pepper, Fennel, Dill, Copaiba, Peppermint

Blends: Valor, Trauma Life, En-R-Gee, Citrus Fresh, Gentle Baby, Tranquil Roll-On, Peace & Calming, Peace & Calming II, Stress Away Roll-On

Nutritionals: NingXia Red, Mineral Essence

Additional: Relaxation Massage Oil, Ortho Ease Massage Oil, Ortho Sport Massage Oil, ClaraDerm

Application and Usage

Topical: Foal: First apply Cistus and/or Myrrh to the umbilical stump. Then apply Valor to poll, withers, and sacrum. Pet anywhere with Trauma Life and Frankincense. Also pet with any listed single or blend that the mother is particular to.

Mare: Apply Valor to poll, withers, and sacrum. Apply one of the following: Relaxation Massage Oil, Ortho Ease Massage Oil, or Ortho Sport Massage Oil and rub in gently.

Birthing and Delivery:

Mastitis:

Apply any combination of the following topically on teats and udder: Lavender, Myrrh, Geranium, Melrose, Copaiba, and ClaraDerm. For mastitis, administer the following internally: 10 drops of any combination of the following oils orally 2 times daily: Thieves, Oregano, Exodus II

Retained placenta:

This should pass within approximately 3 hours. You can encourage it to release with 30 drops each of the following oils: Copaiba, Myrrh, Thieves, Melrose, and Release via needleless syringe or turkey baster directly into the uterus.

Septicemia: Topical:

Apply 5 drops each of the following oils: Thieves or Exodus II or Mountain Savory, plus Copaiba, Peppermint, and DiGize applied to umbilical of the foal or inject 20 drops of the same oils into the vagina of the mare 2 times daily. Apply 10 drops of the same oils, plus 2 oz. NingXia Red and 10 dropperfuls Rehemogen orally 2 times daily. You may need to dilute with V-6.

Uterine Infection:

See Septicemia. Work with your veterinarian to ascertain the infection is cleared.

Ingestion & Oral: If the mare seems tired, administer Black Pepper, En-R-Gee, or Citrus Fresh in the lower lip. Give 2 oz. NingXia Red and 4-6 dropperfuls of Mineral Essence. Use Fennel or Dill to increase milk production after delivery. Copaiba and Peppermint orally can also comfort after delivery.

Inhalation: Diffuse Gentle Baby, Stress Away Roll-On, and/or Peace & Calming.

Birthing and Delivery—Mismothering

It is the mare's natural instinct to bond with the foal and allow it to suckle. In a few mares, the maternal instincts are such that the mare will not approach the foal or may even resent the foal that is attempting to nurse. Many professionals will say this cannot be reversed. This, however, is not a hard rule, and a complete reversal of

Umbilical Cords of Newborn Foals

Instead of iodine, put Myrrh oil on the umbilical cord of newborn foals. Myrrh will dry the umbilical cord and facilitate a good separation. Exodus II can also be used to treat infections in a foal's umbilical cord.

behavior from aggression to love can occur. Maiden mares are often frightened by the newborn and may even attempt to kill it. They can suddenly change and be a loving mother with intervention and assistance.

Recommendations

Singles: Lavender, Rose, Orange, Ylang Ylang

Blends: Trauma Life, Acceptance, Harmony, Valor, Transformation, Peace & Calming, Stress Away Roll-On, Gratitude, Inner Child

Nutritionals: NingXia Red

Additional: Thieves Household Cleaner

Application and Usage

Topical: Mare: Multiple times daily apply Valor or Trauma Life on poll, withers, and sacrum along with Transformation. Apply Rose over the heart and pet the mare with Acceptance and Lavender and any other suggested oils.

Foal: Pet with Harmony and put a drop in the mare's nostril. Apply Valor to poll, withers, and sacrum; Inner Child on heart, chest area, and behind the ears and down neck; and Acceptance on auricular points of the ears.

Imprinting on New Foals

Recommended Essential Oils: Valor, Highest Potential, Sacred Mountain, Joy, Surrender, Acceptance

As soon as a colt is born, pick up the foal and hold it in your arms. Massage 5-6 drops of oil along the spine and place a drop on each ear. Then rub oils all over the colt's body a few drops at a time. Lay the colt in your lap and position it with its head back, stroke its neck, and pass all the way over its nose (avoid putting any oils on the nose as it is very sensitive). Repeat every day for 21 days.

Ingestion & Oral: Put Lavender in lower lip of mare multiple times daily.

Inhalation: Diffuse Rose, Lavender, Trauma Life, Acceptance, and Harmony.

Other: Do not under any circumstance leave the mare alone with the foal. The mare should be held while the foal nurses. This process of getting the mare to accept the foal could take up to 2 weeks. If the resources are not available to protect the foal 24 hours daily, it sadly must be treated as an orphan and taken away from its mother. Try to find a nurse mare. The foal often needs to be supplemented with a milk replacer because it may not be receiving enough volume of milk from a maiden mare. Consult your veterinarian about its condition. Supplement the foal with 2-4 oz. of NingXia Red daily. Use Thieves Household Cleaner prior to delivery to clean the stall area.

Bone Conditions (Fractures)

Bone conditions are generally caused by trauma, inherited issues, congenital deformity, nutritional deficiency or excess, or improper medial lateral balance of the hooves. Osteomalacia is improper calcium/phosphorus imbalance. Excessive protein and vitamin A or D intake may inhibit proper bone development.

Other diet-related factors contributing to poor bone development may include alfalfa's calcium content, which may be imbalanced regarding other minerals in alfalfa. Consult a veterinarian nutritionist for more information,

---

▶ Veterinarian Tips and Suggestions

Bone Conditions

Apply these custom recipes topically 3 times daily for best results. They can be used separately or in conjunction with each other.

Recipe: Copaiba, Helichrysum, Cypress, Idaho Balsam Fir, Idaho Blue Spruce, Northern Lights Black Spruce, Wintergreen or PanAway, and Frankincense or Sacred Frankincense or Palo Santo

Mix equal parts of each oil, 2-5 drops each, and dilute with a small amount of V-6 Vegetable Oil Complex if necessary. If no dilution is needed, apply Regenolone Moisturizing Cream on top of applied oils. Apply 2 times daily or more as needed.

▶ Veterinarian Tips and Suggestions

Fractures/Bone Chips

Shave area around affected bone. Apply mixture of:
- 5 drops Wintergreen
- 5 drops Idaho Balsam Fir
- 2 drops Oregano (or Plectranthus Oregano)
- Add 2 tablespoons Sulfurzyme to feed.
- Continue the above regimen daily for 3 months.

Case History: In 1997 a horse's back hock was fractured with two 50-cent-sized pieces splintered off. The animal was diagnosed at stage five lameness, and the vet urged to have the animal euthanized.

After Wintergreen essential oil was applied for several months, the bone regenerated and the break healed.

---

as many feed stores know only what the feed companies tell them.

Fractures once thought of as irreparable may be treated with success. Urgent veterinary care and appropriate first aid are of paramount importance. Do not forget the importance of treating for shock. Treatment should be continued until the fracture is healed completely.

Recommendations

Singles: Copaiba, Idaho Balsam Fir, Idaho Blue Spruce, Helichrysum, Hinoki, Lemongrass, Northern Lights Black Spruce, Palo Santo, Pine, Wintergreen, Cypress

Blends: PanAway, Mendwell, Valor, Peace & Calming, Trauma Life, Believe, Aroma Siez, R.C., Cool Azul, Deep Relief Roll-On, Relieve It

Nutritionals: NingXia Red, AgilEase, MegaCal, BLM, MultiGreens, Sulfurzyme

Additional: Cool Azul Sports Gel, Cool Azul Pain Relief Cream, Regenolone Moisturizing Cream

Application and Usage

Topical: Apply any listed oil 3 times daily covering with Regenolone Moisturizing Cream over top. Also apply Valor to poll, withers, and sacrum; apply Peace & Calming to auricular points of ears; apply Trauma Life over fractured area and on poll.

Ingestion & Oral: Combine 1 AgilEase or BLM, 1 oz. of Sulfurzyme, and 3 oz. NingXia Red. Administer orally 3 times daily.

Other: For bone chips, topically use Helichrysum, R.C., Copaiba, and Wintergreen 3 times daily. Use the following individually or layer with chosen oils: Cool Azul Sports Gel, Cool Azul Pain Relief Cream, and Regenolone Moisturizing Cream.

Bruised Soles

This may be the result of uneven ground, a poorly fitted shoe, a stone injury, or dropped soles from inflammation in the foot caused by too much sugar or other toxins as the body pushes toxins farther away from its core.

Horses with flat feet or dropped soles are more susceptible to bruising and inflammation. A corn is bruising of the caudal sole at the heel buttress, which may form an abscess if untreated. Boot, pad, or shoe the horse for support and comfort.

Bruising of the sole is a common cause of lameness and the result of concussion on the sole of the foot or frog, often from riding on uneven ground. Poor shoeing and poor conformation are contributing factors. The horse may show only mild lameness; but if the trauma is severe, the horse may be extremely lame.

Recommendations

Singles: Copaiba, Cypress, Oregano, Helichrysum, Lavender, Idaho Balsam Fir, Mountain Savory, Geranium, Clove, Blue Cypress, Basil, Marjoram, Wintergreen, Idaho Blue Spruce, Northern Lights Black Spruce, Patchouli, Myrrh, German Chamomile, Roman Chamomile, Juniper, Ocotea

Blends: PanAway, Thieves, Cool Azul, Deep Relief Roll-On, Aroma Life, Melrose, Relieve It, R.C., Sacred Mountain, Australian Blue, Aroma Siez, Believe, Evergreen Essence, Purification, The Gift, Transformation, Trauma Life

Nutritionals: NingXia Red, Sulfurzyme

> ### ♘ Veterinarian Tips and Suggestions
>
> ## Bruised Ankle (e.g., from hobble injury)
>
> Apply Melrose, Mountain Savory, Ocotea, Cool Azul, Cool Azul Pain Relief Cream, Cool Azul Sports Gel, Deep Relief Roll-On, and PanAway with Animal Scents Ointment or Ortho Sport Massage Oil to reduce tenderness, bruising, and inflammation.

Additional: Thieves Household Cleaner, Thieves Dentarome Ultra Toothpaste, Cool Azul Pain Relief Cream, Cool Azul Sports Gel, Animal Scents Ointment

Application and Usage

Topical: Apply Copaiba, Oregano, Helichrysum, PanAway, and Cypress to the sole and frog of affected foot. Mix 3 gallons warm water with ¼ cup Thieves Household Cleaner and soak for 20 minutes 2 times daily. Also, apply Animal Scents Ointment or Cool Azul Pain Relief Cream on affected area after soaking and drying. Use Thieves Dentarome Ultra Toothpaste as a poultice along the frog area, especially if booting, as the frog area sweats, which can encourage pathogens if not cleaned daily.

Ingestion & Oral: Combine 2 oz. NingXia Red and 1 oz. Sulfurzyme and administered orally 2 times daily.

Cancer (*see* Tumors)

Canker

This is a chronic condition involving overproduction of the horn-producing tissues of the foot. It is a rare condition and one that is most likely to affect the hind feet. It usually starts in the heel area of the frog and appears as fronds over a milky dead cell mass. If left untreated, the condition may cause permanent lameness. Keep the hoof clean and away from mud and manure. Boot if possible, cleaning daily and poulticing with Thieves Dentarome Ultra Toothpaste.

Check mineral levels, as low minerals leave the immune system compromised. The root cause is dirty stabling, where the horse is allowed to stand in muddy conditions or on soiled bedding, coupled with poor standards, allowing bacteria to gain access.

Chronic hypertrophy of the horn-producing foot tissue is often referred to as a cancerous-type tissue in the hoof. This affects horses from all backgrounds and care conditions.

Recommendations

Singles: Oregano, Clove, Copaiba, Northern Lights Black Spruce, Cassia, Cinnamon Bark, Lemongrass, Thyme, Cypress, Idaho Blue Spruce, Palo Santo, Xiang Mao.

Blends: Thieves, Exodus II, Melrose, Longevity, DiGize

Nutritionals: NingXia Red, Longevity Softgels, MultiGreens, Sulfurzyme, Mineral Essence

Additional: Thieves Dentarome Ultra Toothpaste

Application and Usage

Topical: Apply copious amounts of chosen essential oils 3-4 times daily. Watch the horse for tenderness; you may need to dilute the oils. Use Thieves Dentarome Ultra Toothpaste as an oil carrier and poultice.

Other: Canker is difficult to treat and requires removal of all the diseased tissues. Also try Raindrop Technique on both the back and the underside of both the affected hoof and its compensatory partner.

Castration (Gelding)

Male horses that are not part of a breeding program are often gelded to avoid behavioral problems and enhance their focus and concentration. Castration is a surgical procedure performed by a veterinarian and is defined as the removal of the testicles of a male horse.

Male horses may be calm and better behaved after gelding and make better workhorses. Horse breeders use this technique to remove less desired qualities from the gene pool.

These suggestions are for post-surgery care.

Recommendations

Singles: Cistus and Helichrysum to support healing and removing sedation. After wound closes or if infected, use Idaho Balsam Fir, Lavender, Myrrh, Patchouli, Tea Tree, Copaiba, Laurus Nobilis, or Palmarosa.

Blends: Purification, Trauma Life, T-Away, PuriClean, PanAway, Cool Azul, Melrose, Mendwell, Infect Away, DiGize, Forgiveness, Into the Future, Acceptance

Nutritionals: NingXia Red, Sulfurzyme, Mineral Essence

Additional: ClaraDerm, Thieves Spray, Thieves Household Cleaner

Application and Usage

Topical: Before surgery, spray area with Thieves Spray. After surgery, while still sedated, apply Cistus, Copaiba, and Myrrh to surgical site. Also spritz a mixture of Copaiba with chosen oils on incision multiple times daily.

Ingestion & Oral: Combine 2 oz. NingXia Red, 1 oz. Sulfurzyme, and 5 drops DiGize and administer orally 2 times daily.

Other: 1 week to 1 day prior to gelding, administer Equine Raindrop Technique. Also apply Equine Raindrop Technique up to 1 week after procedure. Support the emotional change with Trauma Life, T-Away, Forgiveness, Into the Future, Acceptance. Gently clean affected area with diluted Thieves Household Cleaner after wound closes.

Coffin Bone Infection

The equine hoof is a unique appendage composed of various soft and hard connective tissue, including bone, soft tissue, a vascular network, and keratinized tissue. If any of these areas of the hoof become infected, it can jeopardize all other tissues and functionality of the hoof.

Typical causes of infection include environmental wounds (puncture), hoof cap defects (cracks, flares, contracted heels), digital instability (laminitis), and systematic issues (bacterial infections via environment or blood borne). Deep infections of structures like the Coffin Bone require intense care. Consult your veterinarian when dealing with a deep hoof infection.

Recommendations

Singles: Clove, Oregano, Idaho Blue Spruce, Idaho Balsam Fir, Cypress, Copaiba, Helichrysum, Hyssop, Lemon, Lemongrass, Cinnamon Bark, Wintergreen, Thyme, Rosemary, Melaleuca Quinquenervia, Black Pepper, Geranium, Ginger, Mountain Savory, Tea Tree

Blends: Melrose, Thieves, Raven, DiGize, Exodus II, Egyptian Gold, M-Grain

Nutritionals: NingXia Red, Sulfurzyme, AgilEase, BLM, Mineral Essence

Additional: Animal Scents Ointment

Application and Usage

Topical: Apply 6 drops each of Thieves, Clove, and Oregano with any listed oil of choice 3 times daily. Cover with Animal Scents Ointment.

Ingestion & Oral: Administer 10 drops Melrose on inside of lower lip. Also try either 4 drops DiGize, 10 drops Raven, and 10 drops Thieves combined; or 10 drops Copaiba, 5 drops Hyssop, and 10 drops Lemon combined.

Other: Continue applying suggested oils after infection is resolved to regenerate lost or damaged tissue.

Choking

Foreign objects and food can get lodged in the esophagus and cause an obstruction. Since horses cannot vomit, this must eventually pass into the stomach. This can happen with dry beet pulp, larger treats such as whole fruits and vegetables, poor dental conditions, or very fine hay. General anesthesia can also cause choking.

You can see nasal discharge of saliva, food, difficulty in swallowing, coughing, or excessive saliva production. You'll often see horses that will be anxious and will try to stretch out and/or arch the neck. Because some horses will still try to eat or drink, withhold food and water and use the oils to encourage passage of the obstruction. Call your vet while working, so you can ascertain if the blockage has truly passed and that no lung involvement has occurred.

Recommendations
Singles: Copaiba, Marjoram, Peppermint, Lavender, Vetiver, Ginger, Tarragon, Spearmint, Fennel
Blends: DiGize, AromaEase, Peace & Calming, Peace & Calming II, Stress Away Roll-On, Tranquil Roll-On, RutaVaLa, PanAway, Release, Aroma Siez, Cool Azul, R.C., Raven, Thieves, Exodus II, Mountain Savory
Nutritionals: NingXia Red
Additional: Relaxation Massage Oil, Ortho Sport Massage Oil

Application and Usage
Topical: Apply to the throat area any suggested oils 3 times daily. Apply Relaxation Massage Oil or Ortho Sport Massage Oil after applying oils.
Ingestion & Oral: Combine 10 drops each of DiGize, Copaiba, and Peppermint 2 times daily. Administer NingXia Red after choking episode is resolved; R.C. and Raven, if lung involvement is suggested; plus Thieves, Exodus II, and Mountain Savory in the food or via diffusion in a small area, such as a stall.

Clubfoot

A clubfoot refers to an abnormally upright hoof with long, contracted heels and a prominent or bulging coronary band. This is an equine condition of the flexor tendons. It can be the result of congenital formation or genetic defect, but the most common cause is chronic pain. The horse changes gait to accommodate pain, and then the tendons contract and shorten. Pain treatment of the muscles will encourage relaxation. This will also help to lengthen the gait and keep the horse from favoring the foot.

Recommendations
Singles: Copaiba, Helichrysum, Cypress, Lemongrass, Lavender, Idaho Balsam Fir, Marjoram, Palo Santo, Basil, Idaho Blue Spruce, Northern Lights Black Spruce, Wintergreen
Blends: Valor, Deep Relief Roll-On, PanAway, Cool Azul, Relieve It, Release, Aroma Siez
Nutritionals: NingXia Red, Sulfurzyme, AgilEase, BLM
Additional: Cool Azul Sports Gel, Cool Azul Pain Relief Cream, Ortho Sport Massage Oil, Relaxation Massage Oil, Regenolone Moisturizing Cream.

Application and Usage
Topical: Apply Copaiba, Marjoram, Helichrysum, and Cypress to heel bulbs, coronary band, and digital cushion 3 times daily. Apply Valor to poll, withers, and sacrum.
Other: If it is a foal, this condition can usually be corrected by an experienced blacksmith, who may choose spring shoes or extended toe to encourage the heels to spread. Use the following individually or layer with chosen oils: Cool Azul Sports Gel, Cool Azul Pain Relief Cream, Ortho Sport Massage Oil, Relaxation Massage Oil, or Regenolone Moisturizing Cream.

Cold and Influenza

The rhinovirus is similar to the cold virus that infects humans and is usually acute with mild, respiratory symptoms. It is most common in young horses, and many of the country's competitions and boarding barns require vaccination prior to entry. This, however, does not always ensure the horse doesn't get the disease.

If afflicted, rest and nutritional support will assist recovery. Diffuse in the area where the horse is kept to prevent transference to other animals. Often, if no quarantine area is available, use shower curtains or tarps on the outside of a stall to create a diffusion stall or use an equine nebulizer.

There are many variations of equine colds. Colds may or may not be accompanied by fever, mucous, cough, chest congestion, head congestion, and body aches. Spread of this virus is by infected nasal discharge, feces, or urine, following an incubation period of up to eight days.

The first symptom is usually fever with inflammation at the back of the mouth and lymph node enlargement. This is followed by a nasal discharge and a cough, which may be present for up to three weeks.

Adenovirus is very common, especially in younger horses after weaning, leading to symptoms of an upper respiratory tract infection that ranges from moderate in adults to severe in foals. In some foals, the infection can lead to severe pneumonia, which can prove fatal. Diarrhea is also a common symptom.

Recommendations

Singles: Lemon, Oregano, Ravintsara, Tea Tree, Rosemary, Thyme, Idaho Balsam Fir, Peppermint, Eucalyptus Blue, Cypress, Eucalyptus Globulus, Hyssop, Laurus Nobilis, Lavender, Basil, Melissa, Mountain Savory, Myrtle, Peppermint, Pine, Spearmint, German Chamomile, Clove, Dorado Azul, Ocotea, Idaho Blue Spruce, Lemongrass, Cedarwood, Copaiba

Blends: R.C., Raven, Egyptian Gold, Exodus II, Thieves, Longevity, Purification, Breathe Again Roll-On, Melrose

Nutritionals: Inner Defense, NingXia Red, Organic Dried Wolfberries, ImmuPro, Inner Defense, Life 9

Additional: V-6 Vegetable Oil Complex, Ortho Sport Massage Oil, Ortho Ease Massage Oil

Application and Usage

Topical: Apply Thieves, Lemongrass, Raven (or Ravintsara) and Oregano on chest and throat; then over top apply V-6. **For fever:** Apply Peppermint to poll, back of ears, and coronary bands over heart. **For sore and achy:** Use Ortho Sport Massage Oil or Ortho Ease Massage Oil. Also apply Peppermint over stomach. Apply Equine Raindrop Technique daily or every other day.

Ingestion & Oral: Use 15 drops each of 3 of the following oils of your choice: Thieves, Lemongrass, Raven, Copaiba, Exodus II, and Egyptian Gold; or give 5 Inner Defense and/or 5 Life 9 in grain 2 times daily.

Inhalation: Cough: Apply R.C. and Raven and rub around nose and on chest.

Colic/Impaction

Veterinary help should be sought as soon as symptoms are noted.

Colic is a very general term given to abdominal pain; it is not a disease or specific diagnosis. Not all colic symptoms originate from the digestive system. Ovarian pain can cause colic-like symptoms as can cystitis. Digestive-type colic can be broadly divided into several different types.

Spasmodic Colic: The most common form is caused by the muscles within the walls of the intestines going into a state of hypermotility or spasm. The most common cause is damage to the walls of the intestine from migrating parasitic larvae. Less frequently encountered triggers include behavioral problems (excitement, stress- or fear-induced colic), inappropriate physical activity or environmental factors (such as chilling), and dietary problems like feeding or drinking straight after strenuous exercise.

Symptoms may include sweating, elevation of pulse rate up to 70 beats a minute (bpm), lying down and rolling, turning around and looking at the flank, kicking at the abdomen, and in more severe cases, becoming cast (lying against a fence or wall on its back, relieving pain). Very little manure may be passed. Gut sounds are noisy and gassy but may also be silent. Symptoms come and go quickly and can be quite intense one minute and gone the next.

Impaction or constipation colic: This is likely to occur at the relatively narrow part of the large intestine. Older horses are more prone to this type, as their teeth may be poor, and they cannot break up their feed sufficiently. The underlying cause is usually dietary. Ingestion of large quantities of poor grass, straw bedding, or other indigestible feed are frequent causes. Impaction can also be due to accumulations of ingested sand, which forms masses in the gut known as sand enteroliths.

Symptoms are less dramatic than with spasmodic colic, as pain is less pronounced and gradual in onset. It may persist for several days. Affected horses often look "off" in demeanor and will lie down and/or will move with obvious discomfort. Some will roll and look at their flanks. Gut sounds are minimal or absent, and appetite is poor. Pulse is moderately elevated between 40-50 bpm. Manure is passed but in small amounts and is dry or hard in appearance.

Flatulent or gas colic: Milder forms of this colic arise from fermentation of food within the bowel leading to gas buildup within the stomach or intestines. Causes include eating unsuitable foods such as grass cuttings; horse feed with wheat, rice, and potatoes; or sudden change in concentrate diet.

Symptoms of pain are continuous. The pulse can rise to 80-100 bpm, and the mucous membranes will appear dark as the horse becomes toxic.

Colic/Impactions

This can be an emergency situation, where the horse can be in immense pain and unable to pass anything in the gut (impaction colic). Or, it can be an uneasy feeling the horse has due to gas or other abdominal pain. Call your veterinarian while you are working with the oils; you can always cancel if this passes quickly. There are many areas of the digestive tract where food can become trapped such as near the liver and can cause impaction and potential torsion, if it becomes twisted.

Do not let the horse lie down and/or roll, as this can add to the potential for twisting. Keep the horse walking to encourage movement, and a trailer ride often encourages a horse to defecate and relieve the problem, if no twist has occurred. Watch the vital signs and if they are out of normal range, alert your veterinarian and let your local surgery center know if the horse is a candidate for surgery.

During this time, use the following oils for emotional support: Peace & Calming, Peace & Calming II, Stress Away Roll-On, RutaVaLa, Tranquil Roll-On.

To clear anesthesia after surgery, use a drenching tube to insert 1 gallon castor oil with 15ml DiGize down the throat. AromaEase, Helichrysum, Longevity, JuvaCleanse, and Rehemogen may be used.

After recovery, use Sulfurzyme and Power Meal to encourage healing. Use Cel-Lite Magic Massage Oil with Cypress, Copaiba, Tangerine, and Helichrysum to move lymphatics and encourage belly inflammation to disperse. Also do gentle belly lifts with 2 people, using a beach towel under the belly and lifting for a few minutes at a time for a total of 15-20 minutes a session.

Colic is the number one cause of death in horses. Always call your veterinarian to assist in diagnosing the colic.

Symptoms
- Pawing the ground with head down
- Trotting in circles
- Lying down and looking bloated
- No churning or rumbling in the stomach
- Being quiet

Causes
- Eating off the ground and a mineral imbalance (getting too much dirt in the gut). The accumulated dirt can cause the gut to twist, abscess, and spasm.
- Parasites
- Eating too much alfalfa and not enough feed. Alfalfa can stress the kidneys and liver in horses. In general, grass hay is best for horses of all kinds. As a rule of thumb, the more a horse works, the more alfalfa it needs and can tolerate.
- Getting too hot

Treatment Protocol
Keep the horse standing or walking. If the horse lies down, keep the animal's head tied up to prevent him from rolling.

1st hour
Internal Use
- 8 to 10 Detoxzyme capsules
- 15 drops of DiGize
- Put into animal's feed grain or drop inside lip. You can open the capsules and make an enzyme and oil paste to put inside the horse's lip.

Massage
- Rub 10 drops DiGize up each flank and massage out toward umbilical area.
- Rub 10 drops DiGize around the coronet band.
- Rub DiGize on auricular points of ears.

Enema
- Mix 30 drops of DiGize in 6 oz. V-6 Vegetable Oil Complex or olive oil and insert in the horse's rectum as an enema. Do not use castor oil as it dehydrates the colon.

2nd hour
- Put 10-20 drops DiGize in the mouth and on the flanks and coronet band.

4th hour
- Repeat 1st-hour protocol except for enema.

6th hour
- Repeat 1st-hour protocol, adding 5 drops of Peppermint to the 10-20 drops of DiGize.

8th hour
- Repeat 1st-hour protocol, except for enema, and add one scoop of Power Meal or Pure Protein Complete (add to water if the animal is drinking).

10th hour
- Continue administering 6-8 Detoxzyme capsules every 2 hours until the horse's bowels are moving well.

Laxative for Foals
- Put 4 drops DiGize in bottom lip daily until bowels are moving.

Thromboembolic colic: This type of colic arises due to partial or complete obstruction of the blood supply to part of the bowel. The underlying cause is thromboemboli produced by verminous arteritis and is a consequence of poor worm control.

Signs vary with degrees of blockage ranging from mild spasmodic colic to complete death of part of the intestine with rupture, resulting in death of the horse.

Twisted intestine or displacement colic: The small intestine is suspended in the abdominal cavity by the mesentery and is free floating in the gut. This mobility can predispose the small intestine to become twisted. A twisted intestine requires immediate surgery to reposition the intestine and sometimes remove any portion of the intestine that is damaged due to restricted blood flow. In addition, both the small and large intestine can become displaced in the abdominal cavity, causing both pain and restricted blood flow. Displacement colic can be caused by gas buildup in the gut that makes the intestines buoyant and subject to movement within the gut. Displacement colic needs immediate surgical treatment.

Strangulating lipomas (also known as pedunculated lipomas) are every bit as dangerous as they sound. Diagnosis of a strangulating lipoma can be difficult, especially if some material is able to pass the constriction, and discomfort alternately eases and returns. Colic caused by a strangulating lipoma is always surgical.

Apply oils both topically and internally every 15-20 minutes while walking. Also, use a turkey baster to do a rectal implant of the oils as well if needed.

Recommendations

Singles: Copaiba, Peppermint, Tarragon, Sacred Frankincense

Blends: DiGize, ParaGize, Trauma Life, PanAway, AromaEase, Release, Relieve It, Cool Azul

Nutritionals: NingXia Red, Detoxzyme

Application and Usage

Topical: Apply 20 drops each of Copaiba, DiGize, and Peppermint to navel and abdominal area every 10-15 minutes until veterinarian arrives, and be careful not to be kicked. Massage auricular points in ears with Trauma Life or Sacred Frankincense.

Ingestion & Oral: Combine 30 drops each of Copaiba, DiGize, and Peppermint and administer orally every 20 minutes until veterinarian arrives or symptoms abate. Along with or independently of orally administered oils, add 1-2 oz. NingXia Red and 1-2 oz. Detoxzyme (open 20 capsules and mix contents in warm water to activate).

Contracted Tendons

This condition often occurs in newborn foals, and most recover with little treatment. Foals with contracted tendons appear to be up on their toes and upright in the leg, with the fetlock appearing above the foot. In the most severe case, the knee appears flexed with knuckling over at the fetlock joint. This can occur when foals are not allowed out of the stall and are on bedding that is too deep.

In newborn foals, the condition will often resolve in a few days. In older animals, deformity occurs due to uneven muscle and tendon development in relation to the growth of bone in the affected limb. Encourage movement and use the essential oils to relax and negate potential pain.

Recommendations

Singles: Copaiba, Idaho Blue Spruce, Idaho Balsam Fir, Northern Lights Black Spruce, Sacred Frankincense, Wintergreen, Basil, Lavender, Helichrysum, Lemongrass, Marjoram, Cypress

Blends: Mendwell, PanAway, Deep Relief Roll-On, Cool Azul, Release, Relieve It

Nutritionals: NingXia Red, Sulfurzyme, AgilEase, BLM

Additional: Relaxation Massage Oil, Ortho Ease Massage Oil, Ortho Sport Massage Oil, Cool Azul Sports Gel, Cool Azul Pain Relief Cream, Animal Scents Ointment

Application and Usage

Topical: Apply from back of knee along tendons to hoof 3 times daily.

Other: Use 2 oz. of one of the following: Relaxation Massage Oil, Ortho Ease Massage Oil, Ortho Sport Massage Oil, Cool Azul Sports Gel, Cool Azul Pain Relief Cream, or Animal Scents Ointment. Add 20-30 drops each of at least 4 chosen oils to whichever carrier is chosen from selected list and apply as needed.

COPD/Heaves (see also Cough)

Chronic Obstructive Pulmonary Disease (COPD) is a chronic inflammatory lung disease that causes obstructed air flow both in and out. It generally occurs during the summer months and has become the most common cause of chronic coughing in horses. Conditions are similar to asthma in humans.

The primary problem is allergy based, with susceptible horses developing hypersensitivity reaction to the inhalation of specific allergens. This is often caused by inhaling molds or fungus from bedding and/or bad hay, such as in old, damp bedding or in round bales that have gotten wet or from pollens such as grapeseed or linseed and those from trees or the grasses.

The conditions can sometimes occur in horses that have had viral or bacterial infections. This is likely to happen if the horse is returned to work too quickly, when the respiratory tract has not had time to recover and is sensitive to potential allergens and pollutants.

Symptoms may present as mild, moderate, or severe.

Affected horses should be kept outside as much as possible. Groom and clean stalls while the horse is outside. For bedding consider shredded paper or shavings. Clean the stall daily to prevent ammonia buildup, which can irritate the respiratory tract.

Dampen down or soak any hay in field cases and consider feeding vacuum packed hay, cubed hay, or pelleted hay in more severe cases. Short crop forage chaffs such as alfalfa and oat straw mixes make good hay substitutes.

Try to keep the stable as dust free as possible. Remember that allergens can travel considerable distances and that affected horses should be stabled as far away as practical from any straw or hay storage.

Recommendations

Singles: Dorado Azul, Cedarwood, Eucalyptus Globulus, Clove, Copaiba, Cypress, Helichrysum, Goldenrod, Hinoki, Hyssop, Idaho Blue Spruce, Lemongrass, Lavender, Tea Tree, Ocotea, Myrtle, Palo Santo, Ravintsara, Rosemary, Wintergreen, Hong Kuai

Blends: Raven, R.C., Breathe Again Roll-On, PanAway, Relieve It, Purification, Thieves, Exodus II, En-R-gee, The Gift, Transformation, Trauma Life

Nutritionals: NingXia Red, Sulfurzyme, Mineral Essence

Application and Usage

Topical: Layer any combination of 4-5 selected oils on throat and chest area 3-4 times daily. Administer Raindrop Technique 2 or more times a week.

Ingestion & Oral: Combine 10 drops each of Copaiba, Raven, Cedarwood, R.C., Lemongrass, and Exodus II with 1-2 oz. NingXia Red, 4-6 dropperfuls Mineral Essence, and 1-2 oz. Sulfurzyme. Administer combination orally at least 2 times daily.

Inhalation: Diffuse chosen oils with equal parts Copaiba, R.C., and Cedarwood (preferably with equine nebulizer for 20 minutes 2 times daily) in an enclosed barn or directly into the stall.

Corns (Bruised Heel)

Corns occur predominantly on the front feet. They generally arise from improper shoeing, which results in pressure on the sole. Corns occur at the inner angle of the foot formed by the wall and the bar and involve the sensitive and insensitive tissues of the sole, causing bruising. This leads to a hematoma. This may, but not always, result in the horse becoming lame.

Recommendations

Singles: Copaiba, Oregano, Wintergreen, Cypress, Lemongrass

Blends: PanAway, Relieve It, Aroma Siez, Melrose

Nutritionals: NingXia Red, Sulfurzyme, Mineral Essence.

Application and Usage

Topical: Apply copious amounts of Copaiba with 2-3 suggested oils on location multiple times daily.

Ingestion & Oral: Combine 1-2 oz. NingXia Red, 4-6 dropperfuls Mineral Essence, and 1-2 oz. Sulfurzyme. Administer combination orally at least 2 times daily.

Cough

Sound and intensity of a cough does not necessarily tell you how significant it is. Most are simply natural attempts to clear a transitory irritant from the respiratory tract; others signal more serious or chronic conditions that can jeopardize long-term health. Ignoring a seemingly minor cough can allow it to turn into a major problem. A horse coughs to remove material, mucus, or irritants from its airway, which includes throat, upper airway, and lungs.

You'll often hear them cough as a response to a dusty environment, cold weather, allergies, or during warm-up. Other more serious issues cause coughing such as viruses, inflammatory airway disease, infections, or very rarely, lungworms.

Recommendations

Singles: Eucalyptus Radiata, Cedarwood, Copaiba, Cypress, Dorado Azul, Eucalyptus Blue, Eucalyptus Globulus, Hyssop, Laurus Nobilis, Lavender,

♞ *Veterinarian Tips and Suggestions*

Distemper, Whooping Cough, or Asthma

Daily Regimen

- Mix 30 drops each of R.C. and Raven in 4 oz. of V-6 Vegetable Oil Complex and insert into the rectum.
- Put 15 drops each of R.C. and Raven in the bottom lip.
- Massage oils on the chest between the front legs and auricular points of ears.
- Apply Raindrop Technique down the spine and neck hair.
- Administer 4 Longevity Softgels.

Lemon, Lemongrass, Marjoram, Melissa, Myrtle, Oregano, Peppermint, Pine, Rosemary, Idaho Blue Spruce, Northern Lights Black Spruce, Tea Tree, Melaleuca Quinquenervia, Mastrante, Ravintsara, Hinoki, Xiang Mao, Mountain Savory, Ocotea

Blends: R.C., Raven, Thieves (especially good for mold), Aroma Siez, Egyptian Gold, Exodus II, Longevity, Melrose, Breathe Again Roll-On

Nutritionals: NingXia Red, Sulfurzyme, Life 9

Additional: Thieves Household Cleaner

Application and Usage

Topical: Rub any 3-4 suggested oils on the lung, large intestine, neck, throat, and chest area to encourage inhalation as they graze. Also perform Equine Raindrop Technique daily, if possible, but a minimum of 2-3 times a week.

Ingestion & Oral: Combine 15 drops Copaiba with one of the following oils: Raven, Hinoki, Lemongrass, Rosemary, or R.C. Administer combination 3 times daily.

Inhalation: Use oils and blends suggested above in an equine nebulizer or diffuser stall. If multiple horses are affected, run multiple diffusers in an enclosed barn. Hold diffuser containing suggested oil(s) to nostrils for 5-10 minutes. Also utilize an equine nebulizer if possible.

Other: Use Thieves Household Cleaner when cleaning the horse's area to prevent other noxious cleaners from irritating the lungs.

Cushing's Disease (Hypertrichosis) PPID

Cushing's disease, also called hyperadrenocorticism, is the most common endocrine disease in horses. The signs are due primarily to chronic excess of the hormone cortisol. Increased cortisol levels may result from one of several mechanisms such as destruction of a portion of the pituitary gland and overproduction of certain other hormones.

Unlike Cushing's disease in dogs or people, the cause is not usually related to a pituitary tumor. However, pituitary tumors do occur, particularly later in the disease.

The disorder is more often seen in older horses (although it is being diagnosed earlier of late, horses have been diagnosed as early as age 8) of any breed. Mares and geldings are most often affected.

The most striking sign is development of an abnormally long or heavy hair coat (called hypertrichosis), which can grow up to 4 to 5 inches (10 to 12 centimeters) long and is thick, wavy, and often matted. Other signs include excessive thirst and urination, increased appetite and weight, an enlarged abdomen, and bulging eyes.

♞ *Veterinarian Tips and Suggestions*

Cushing's and Diabetes Mellitus

Diabetes mellitus (often called simply Diabetes) is a chronic disorder of carbohydrate metabolism caused by either a deficiency of insulin or a resistance to insulin. Diabetes caused by a deficiency of insulin (also called primary Diabetes mellitus) is rare in horses; however, resistance to insulin (also called secondary Diabetes mellitus) is more common and tends to develop in horses with Cushing's.

A diagnosis of Diabetes mellitus is based on finding high levels of sugar in the blood and urine after a period of fasting. Treatment with insulin cannot reverse the insulin resistance seen in secondary Diabetes mellitus. Access to grass pasture must be restricted as grass can contain up to 25 percent sugar. The longer the sun is on the grass during the day, the closest to freezing it gets, or the longer the drought, the higher the sugar content of the grass.

Choose low-sugar hays (test to ascertain levels or soak for ½ hour prior to feeding), complete feeds, European beet pulp, coconut meal, etc. Do not feed iron supplements as they worsen insulin resistance.

Horses with Cushing's disease tend to have a weakened immune system and may be prone to infections (such as dental disease or respiratory infections) or parasites. A diagnosis is based on a history and signs, a physical examination, and appropriate blood tests. Potential hoof issues can occur (laminitis/founder). Advanced disease may require pharmaceutical support with either Pergolide or Prascend; oils can be used alongside to support the body.

A horse diagnosed with Cushing's disease should not be given any sugar whatsoever as it is unable to regulate its insulin levels. See dietary restriction guidelines at the beginning of this chapter.

Recommendations

Singles: Nutmeg, Clove, Rosemary, Cedarwood, Frankincense, Sandalwood, Ocotea, Ginger, Lemon, Peppermint, Cinnamon Bark, Copaiba, Coriander, Helichrysum, Ledum, Lavender, Dill, Vetiver, Idaho Balsam Fir (to lower cortisol)

Blends: Exodus II, GLF, ImmuPower, JuvaCleanse, Thieves, Believe, Stress Away Roll-On, Peace & Calming, Grounding, 3 Wise Men, Hope, EndoFlex, DiGize

Nutritionals: NingXia Red, EndoGize, Sulfurzyme, Organic Dried Wolfberries, Life 9, ParaFree, Mineral Essence

Application and Usage

Ingestion & Oral: If high blood sugar causes nausea, use DiGize and Ocotea to calm and encourage eating.

Cuts (lacerations and wounds)

Life happens in the horse world; and they often experience cuts, bruises, and wounds from fighting, scratching, and contacting brush, building materials, nails, fencing, etc. Check daily for any skin irritants or breaks and clean and treat promptly to discourage infection.

Initial treatment depends on the cause and nature of the wound. Regardless of the type of wound, start treatment by cleaning it with diluted Thieves Household Cleaner. You may first need to use a hose and water to gently remove debris.

Recommendations

Singles: Copaiba, Lavender, Frankincense, Myrrh, Lemon, Helichrysum, Cypress, Cistus, Idaho Tansy, Blue Cypress, Tea Tree, Geranium, German Chamomile, Roman Chamomile, Palmarosa, Patchouli

Blends: Thieves, Purification, PuriClean, Mendwell, Infect Away, Melrose, DiGize

---

Veterinarian Tips and Suggestions

Cuts

When you discover the wound:

Dilute Thieves Household Cleaner for initial cleaning. The wound should be unwrapped, clean, and relatively dry before oils are applied. You may also apply Thieves Spray during the cleaning process.

Stop Bleeding

Cistus, Helichrysum, Geranium, Idaho Tansy, Mineral Essence (note that Mineral Essence stings). Helichrysum is a blood adaptogen; it stems bleeding and dissolves blood clots, depending on what the body requires.

Promote Healing

Helichrysum, Patchouli, Melrose, Lavender, Copaiba, Myrrh, Sacred Frankincense, Frankincense, Roman Chamomile, Tranquil Roll-On, Geranium, German Chamomile

Clean Wound

Thieves Household Cleaner, Animal Scents Shampoo, KidScents Shampoo, Purification

Relieve Pain

PanAway, Idaho Balsam Fir, Deep Relief Roll-On, Cool Azul, Helichrysum, Valerian/Vetiver blend (equal parts)

Reduce Itching

Blue Tansy, Peppermint, Purification, Lavender, Thieves Dentarome Ultra Toothpaste as a poultice

Heal Proud Flesh

Helichrysum, Frankincense, Sacred Frankincense, Myrrh, Patchouli, Lavender, Blue Cypress; potential base for the oils: Rose Ointment, Tender Tush, Animal Scents Ointment

---

Nutritionals: Life 9, NingXia Red, Sulfurzyme, MultiGreens, Mineral Essence

Additional: Thieves Household Cleaner, Thieves Spray, Wolfberry Eye Cream, Rose Ointment, ClaraDerm, LavaDerm Cooling Mist, Animal Scents Ointment

Application and Usage

Topical: Use Copaiba, Cistus, or Helichrysum with chosen oils and apply liberally. Administer Equine Raindrop Technique once a week.

Ingestion & Oral: Combine 15 drops each of Copaiba, DiGize, and Thieves. Administer orally at least once daily.

Other: Use diluted Thieves Household Cleaner or Thieves Spray to gently clean affected area. Use the following individually or layer with chosen oils: Wolfberry Eye Cream, Rose Ointment, ClaraDerm, LavaDerm Cooling Mist, Animal Scents Ointment

Deworming

Stool samples should be tested every 3-4 months for parasites. Ideally, use essential oils the night before the full moon and for the next ten days.

Many types of worms such as large and small strongyles, roundworms, pinworms, stomach bots, and tapeworms have become resistant to many of the current pharmaceutical wormers. This can lead to stomach issues, colic, intestinal impactions, nutrient deficiencies, and overall systemic inflammation.

Using essential oils can help combat these parasites and can be used in combination with your current worming protocol. Older horses with compromised digestion may require worming more often. Always follow up with a fecal sample to ensure your choices have cleared the worms. Make sure the last worming of the year occurs after a hard frost in cold climates.

Recommendations

Singles: Fennel, Tarragon, Clove, Ocotea, Copaiba, Peppermint, Patchouli, Oregano, Hyssop, Lemon, Lemongrass, Thyme, Mountain Savory

Blends: DiGize, AromaEase, Longevity, Exodus II

Nutritionals: NingXia Red, ParaFree, Life 9, Inner Defense, Mineral Essence

Application and Usage

Ingestion & Oral: Combine 15-20 drops each of Copaiba, DiGize, and Peppermint. Administer orally at least 1 time daily. Other powerful combinations include 10 drops each of AromaEase, Fennel, and Tarragon or 10 drops Tarragon, DiGize, Ocotea, and Thyme.

Other: Worming protocols: Use 20 drops DiGize daily for 1 week starting on the full moon and quarterly through the year. Take a stool sample to the vet for verification that worms are no longer present. If worms are resistant, to the 20 drops DiGize add 20 drops Thieves, use 6-10 drops Oregano and 6 drops Patchouli for 1 week.

Diarrhea

There are many reasons why a horse may develop diarrhea, resulting in severe acute, less acute, or chronic problems. Minor cases of diarrhea in adult horses will often start to clear up within days, particularly where dietary changes are the underlying cause. In these situations, feeding hay and water are often sufficient.

Severe acute diarrhea, many cases lasting longer than 24 hours or so, and diarrhea in foals need a veterinary diagnosis. Whether chronic or acute, it can occur from infection, irritation, or inflammation. Due to potential large fluid loss, the condition can become life threatening to a horse. Some minor causes include grain overload, large salt intake, antibiotics, GMO grains, irritable bowel, and food allergies. More serious issues include peritonitis, renal failure, toxicosis, mycotoxicoses, horse tail poisoning, hyperlipidosis, thromboembolic colon disease.

Work with your veterinarian to determine causation and treatment path. Choose non-GMO feed to ease irritation and use less grain to lower sugars, which cause inflammation.

Foal Diarrhea: All Diarrhea Is Not the Same!

Rotavirus is not the only cause of foal diarrhea, although a Central Kentucky study in the late 1980s revealed that more than 90 percent of outbreaks were caused by the virus. Other causative agents of scours include the bacteria *Salmonella*, *Clostridium difficile*, *Clostridium perfringens*, *Rhodococcus equi*, and Gram negative bacteria causing septicemia (*E. coli*, *Actinobacillus*, etc.).

Parasites that can cause diarrhea include *Strongyloides westeri*, *Cryptosporidium* (usually in immunocompromised foals), and Giardia.

Non-infectious causes of scours include foal heat diarrhea; lactose intolerance; ingestion of sand, dirt, or

---

🐎 *Veterinarian Tips and Suggestions*

Diarrhea/Scours

- Put 15 drops ParaGize or DiGize Vitality plus Copaiba in the horse's lower lip and rub 5-8 drops on the stomach area.
- Place 1 teaspoon ICP in 1 quart water and syringe it down the throat. Continue for four days or until condition corrects itself.

foreign material; overfeeding; and antibiotic treatment.
Owners must remember that in some cases, the actual cause of the diarrhea cannot be determined, despite an arsenal of diagnostic tests available.

Recommendations

Singles: Copaiba, Ginger, Clove, Mountain Savory, Ocotea, Oregano, Patchouli, Peppermint, Lemongrass, Tea Tree, Tarragon, Thyme, Roman Chamomile, German Chamomile, Valerian, Lemon, Rosemary

Blends: DiGize, AromaEase, Thieves, Exodus II, Purification, Melrose, Infect Away, Peace & Calming

Nutritionals: Life 9, ParaFree, MultiGreens, Inner Defense, Power Meal, Detoxzyme, Digest & Cleanse, Mineral Essence, Essentialzyme

Additional: Thieves Household Cleaner

Application and Usage

Ingestion & Oral: Combine 15 drops each of Copaiba and DiGize, plus 5-10 drops of any suggested oils based on diagnosis. Administer combination orally at least 1 time daily.

Inhalation: Diffuse Thieves, Purification, and/or Peace & Calming if the horse is agitated.

Other: Rosemary is thought to be a possible oil for septic shock, as it suppresses endotoxin-induced activation of immune response. Also, try Thieves Household Cleaner to clean and detoxify horse's area.

Ear Fungus

Equine ear papillomas are viral-induced skin tumors, likely transmitted by blackflies. They are a type of wart and generally a cosmetic problem.

Recommendations

Singles: Copaiba, Blue Cypress, Basil, Clove, Dorado Azul, Geranium, Hong Kuai, Juniper, Lemongrass, Lemon Myrtle, Tea Tree, Mountain Savory, Myrrh, Patchouli, Ravintsara, Helichrysum, Manuka

Blends: Melrose, Purification, Thieves, Exodus II, Longevity, DiGize

Application and Usage

Topical: Apply on location any of the above-listed oils added to Copaiba, Melrose, and Purification. Ensure oils do not enter ear canal.

Ingestion & Oral: Administer orally 10 drops each Melrose, DiGize, and Copaiba 2 times daily.

Ear Plaque (see also Warts)

Use ClaraDerm spray topically and Tender Tush or Animal Scents Ointment with Helichrysum or Patchouli. Ensure the oils do NOT go deeper in the ear canal and are absorbed by the external ear itself.

Recommendations

Singles: Clove, Thyme, Lemongrass, Laurus Nobilis, Melissa, Tea Tree, Eucalyptus Globulus, Blue Cypress, Helichrysum, Ocotea, Basil, Hong Kuai, Patchouli

Blends: Thieves, Purification, Melrose, PuriClean, Infect Away, Exodus II, Egyptian Gold, The Gift

Nutritionals: Life 9, Mineral Essence, Sulfurzyme

Additional: Animal Scents Ointment, ClaraDerm

Application and Usage

Topical: Place any of the suggested oils on your fingertips and massage directly onto the affected area 2 times daily. Ensure oils do not roll into ear canal. Administer Equine Raindrop Technique 1 time a week.

Other: Apply Animal Scents Ointment or ClaraDerm directly on location.

Edema/Cellulitis (Peripheral)

Cellulitis is a term applied to an infection, normally bacterial, that spreads along the tissues underlying the surface of the skin. Affected areas are swollen or puffy and painful to touch. Edema is swelling in the tissues. It can be peripheral, in which one or more of the horse's legs becomes swollen with a puffy appearance. This is referred to as stocking up, where a horse isn't moving as much as it normally would, such as in a long trailer ride or overnight in a stall. This is relieved by normal movement once the horse moves out or exercises lightly.

> ### Veterinarian Tips and Suggestions
>
> ## Edema
>
> For hot inflammation, use Copaiba and Laurus Nobilis with Peppermint to encourage cooling, or Spearmint for geriatrics, along with Cool Azul Sports Gel. When massaging, use upward strokes towards the body core, and encourage walking if not lame to move lymphatics.

If the swelling is hot, the horse is lame, or the edema is pitting (an impression is left by light finger pressure), investigate the cause, for it may be a more serious condition. Examples may be infection; kidney, heart, or liver disease; a bite; allergies; toxins; or trauma. Call your veterinarian if it doesn't resolve quickly.

Recommendations

Singles: Lavender, Idaho Balsam Fir, Idaho Blue Spruce, Northern Lights Black Spruce, Helichrysum, Cypress, Tangerine, Palmarosa, Frankincense, Sacred Frankincense, Geranium, German Chamomile, Laurus Nobilis, Grapefruit, Tangerine, Lemongrass, Copaiba, Myrrh

Blends: Joy, Trauma Life, Aroma Life, GLF, JuvaCleanse, JuvaFlex, Purification, Thieves, Exodus II, Melrose, Citrus Fresh

Nutritionals: NingXia Red, Sulfurzyme, Life 9, K&B, Mineral Essence

Additional: Cool Azul Sports Gel, Cel-Lite Magic Massage Oil

Application and Usage

Topical: Apply Laurus Nobilis, Cypress, Copaiba, Palmarosa, and Purification to swollen areas 2-3 times daily with a thin layer of Cel-Lite Magic Massage oil over top. Use 1 drop Joy over the heart. Use Trauma Life to auricular points of the ears.

Ingestion & Oral: Combine 1-2 oz. NingXia Red, 4-6 dropperfuls Mineral Essence, and 1-2 oz. Sulfurzyme. Administer combination orally at least 2 times daily. Give Copaiba and Citrus Fresh in food, on a hay cube, or in a second bucket of water. Always leave one bucket of water with no oils to encourage normal hydration levels. Copaiba with its high beta-caryophyllene is second to none in moving inflammation. You can use it both topically and orally. It has little taste and is easy to place on the oral mucosa for internal "itis" or inflammatory conditions.

Other: Administer Equine Raindrop Technique 3-4 times a week.

Ehrlichia/Anaplasmosis

Anaplasma phagocytophilum is the new name for the agent formerly called *Ehrlichia equi* and is caused by ticks, specifically deer ticks. Symptoms can include anemia, fever, icterus (yellow mucus membranes), depression, lack of muscle coordination, loss of interest in eating, and stiff, swollen legs.

Horses of all ages can be affected, and the symptoms may appear suddenly. The disease is related to Lyme disease and Rocky Mountain Spotted Fever.

If any of these conditions present in a horse, consult your veterinarian immediately.

Recommendations

Singles: Copaiba, Peppermint, Clove, Thyme, Lemongrass, Cypress, Oregano, Tea Tree, Helichrysum, Ravintsara

Blends: DiGize, Purification, Thieves, Melrose, Exodus II, Raven

Nutritionals: Ningxia Red, Life 9, Inner Defense, Mineral Essence, MultiGreens

Application and Usage

Ingestion & Oral: Use DiGize and Copaiba with Raven or Ravintsara, 10 drops of each 3 times daily. Administer 1 oz. NingXia Red with chosen supplements 3 times daily.

Inhalation: Diffuse Thieves with Lemongrass in an enclosed barn.

Other: Equine Raindrop Technique daily.

Encephalitis

Encephalitis is defined as an acute inflammation of the brain tissues, often with secondary meningeal involvement. Although some bacterial, fungal, and autoimmune disorders can cause encephalitis, most cases are secondary to viruses. The three known strains are Western Equine Encephalitis (WEE), Eastern Equine Encephalitis (EEE), and Viral Equine Encephalitis (VEE). All are arboviruses caused by mosquitoes, ticks, etc.

Western Equine Encephalitis is a summertime infection found in more rural areas in the Western United States. Eastern Equine Encephalitis tends to occur around freshwater swampy areas that support mosquito populations. It is part of the herpes strain that affects nerves.

Work with your veterinarian as these horses may become hard to handle very quickly due to the virus's effects on the brain. IV Fluid therapy may be required as well.

Recommendations

Singles: Peppermint, Mountain Savory, Lemon, Jasmine, Laurus Nobilis (all anticonvulsants), Melissa, Manuka, Rosemary, Tea Tree, Melaleuca Quinquenervia, Copaiba, Lemongrass, Clove, Basil, Ocotea, Juniper, Geranium, Cassia, Nutmeg, German

Chamomile, Ravintsara, Oregano, Citronella, Thyme, Helichrysum, Cedarwood (to oxygenate)

Blends: Thieves, Exodus II, ImmuPower, Brain Power, Valor, Melrose, Egyptian Gold, The Gift, Grounding, Raven, Purification

Nutritionals: NingXia Red, ImmuPro, Rehemogen, MultiGreens, MindWise, OmegaGize[3], Life 9, Mineral Essence

Additional: Regenolone Moisturizing Cream, Cool Azul Sports Gel, Cool Azul Pain Relief Cream

Application and Usage

Topical: Apply Raindrop daily (if horse will tolerate), with Helichrysum, Melissa, and Copaiba applied to the poll and brain stem area. Nutmeg, Juniper, and Helichrysum are supportive to nerve tissues, as is Regenolone Moisturizing Cream. Apply other suggested oils near the jugular vein or try applying on coronary bands.

Ingestion & Oral: Feed essential oils on hay cubes if able to eat, soaked preferred. Offer Peppermint in a second water bucket to encourage temperature reduction and apply Cool Azul Sports Gel, Cool Azul Pain Relief Cream, or Copaiba to reduce inflammation. Also try 10 drops each Melissa, Peppermint, Copaiba, Raven or Ravintsara, Exodus II and Helichrysum 4 times a day in 1 oz. NingXia Red with 4 dropperfuls each Mineral Essence and Rehemogen.

Inhalation: Nebulizer (if horse is still calm), large diffuser in stall to accommodate potential recumbent horse, which may thrash about.

Other: Use your favorite oil such as Purification with additional Citronella to avoid mosquito bites, which can carry these viruses to other horses and people.

EPM (Equine Protozoal Myeloencephalitis)

A disease found in the Americas caused by a protozoan, *Sarcocystis neurona* or sporadic cases of Equine Protozoal Myeloencephalitis are associated with *Neospora hughesi*. Opossums are known carriers, and other implicated carriers are domestic cats, striped skunks, raccoons, sea otters, Pacific harbor seals, and armadillos. Work with your veterinarian and discuss your complimentary essential oil protocol.

Use the same protocols as Encephalitis with the addition of ParaFree internally.

Equine Herpes Virus (*see also* Viral Conditions)

There are five different subtypes of Equine Herpes Viruses found in horses, but Equine Herpes Virus-1 (EHV-1) and EHV-4 are the forms that result in serious clinical disease.

EHV-1 was previously known as the equine abortion virus and is most known for causing reproductive disease. This subtype is also responsible for respiratory problems (primarily rhinopneumonitis—inflammation of the upper airways and lungs) and neurological diseases. EHV-4 is also known as equine rhinopneumonitis virus and is most common among foals and yearlings. It can also cause abortion and neurological disease. Infections are common within horses up to a year old and in horses starting training.

The majority of horses will encounter this highly contagious virus during their lifetime, with infection occurring by inhalation of infected particles spread around by nose-to-nose contact or through nasal droplets in the air. Indirect infection can be through contaminated buckets, blankets, or clothing. In a proportion of horses, the virus can lie dormant and become reactivated if the immune system is stressed. The virus can enter the white blood cells and stay lodged there for some time, affecting the horse's performance and ability to fight off other infections. Call your veterinarian and limit access to barn to only necessary people.

Recommendations

Singles: Ravintsara, Lemongrass, Cypress, Tea Tree, Melaleuca Quinquenervia, Melissa, Mountain Savory, Peppermint and/or Spearmint (especially to reduce fever), Eucalyptus Globulus, Cassia, Thyme, Copaiba, Ocotea, Dorado Azul, Oregano, Clove, German Chamomile, Eucalyptus Blue, Eucalyptus Radiata

Blends: DiGize, Thieves, R.C., Raven, ImmuPower, Exodus II, Egyptian Gold, Melrose, The Gift, Valor, Valor II

Nutritionals: NingXia Red, MultiGreens, Sulfurzyme, Super C Chewable, ImmuPro, Inner Defense, Mineral Essence, Detoxzyme, Power Meal

Application and Usage

Topical: Place on the lung points, on the inside of the front legs, and on the withers area of the spine. Use Valor or Valor II and Cypress; apply to bottom of feet and frogs daily.

Equine Herpes Virus

Prevention is the best method.

Use a strong dilution of Thieves Household Cleaner on all tack, supplies, etc., that come into contact with an infected horse. Use Thieves Household Cleaner in a footbath to discourage tracking infection to other areas. Also use Thieves Spray and/or Hand Purifier. If in a barn with others, diffuse Thieves, Raven, Purification with Eucalyptus Blue, throughout the quarantine period continuously to prevent sharing with other horses.

Prevention using the following Young Living Essential Oils:

- Raven, Lemongrass, Thieves, and Ginger or Peppermint – Orally 12 drops each oil 2 times daily.
- Raindrop Technique – once every day or every other day for 2 weeks.
- Thieves or Purification – Diffuse in barn.
- Thieves Household Cleaner – Spray down whole barn and use to wash everything, including clothing and tack.
- Thieves or Purification – 12 drops oil in 4 oz. water in spray bottle – spray down trucks, everything, etc.

Treatment if diagnosed using the following Young Living Essential Oils:

- Ravintsara, Exodus II, Lemongrass, Copaiba, DiGize – Orally 12 drops each oil every 3 hours.
- ImmuPower – For immune compromised horses – Orally 6 drops 2 times daily.
- Valor or Cypress   Topically on bottoms of feet and frogs daily.
- Raindrop Technique – 2 times daily for 2 weeks.
- If budget allows, Melissa oil – 10 drops 2 times daily orally or Melissa hydrosol – 4-5 oz. in grain.
- Thieves or Purification – Diffuse in barn.
- Thieves Household Cleaner – Spray down whole barn and use to wash everything, including clothing and tack.
- Thieves or Purification – 12 drops oil and 4 oz. water in spray bottle – spray down trucks, everything, etc.

Ingestion & Oral: Combine 10-12 drops each of Ravintsara, Exodus II, Lemongrass, Copaiba, ImmuPower, and DiGize. Administer orally every 3 hours. Add Thieves, Clove, and Peppermint (with any other suggested oil(s)) on food, a hay cube, or in a second water bucket, while always leaving one plain water bucket available. If budget allows, administer orally 10 drops Melissa 2 times daily or 4-5 oz. Melissa hydrosol in grain. Give affected animal 4-6 oz. NingXia Red daily combined with any other suggested supplements.

Inhalation: Use of an Equine nebulizer or direct diffusion into a stall is best. Diffuse Eucalyptus Blue, Thieves, Exodus II, Raven, Dorado Azul

Other: No sweet treats or sweet feeds of any kind, as the sugars accelerate the virus. Administer Raindrop Technique 2 times a day for 2 weeks with Raven, Copaiba, Lemongrass, Eucalyptus Globulus, and/or Melissa.

Equine Viral Arteritis (EVA)

Equine Viral Arteritis (EVA) is an acute, contagious, viral disease, typically exhibiting fever, depression, anorexia, leukopenia, dependent edema (especially of the lower hind extremities, scrotum, and prepuce in a stallion), conjunctivitis, supra or periorbital edema, nasal discharge, respiratory distress, skin rash, temporary infertility in affected stallions, abortion, and infrequently, illness and death in young foals.

Contagion can occur by respiratory, venereal, and congenital routes or by sharing horse-handling equipment. The virus spreads through the respiratory routes during the acute phase of infection. It spreads quickly among horses kept in close quarters (at racetracks, competitions, sale barns, veterinary facilities, shelters, and breeding farms).

EVA can also be transmitted venereally by the acutely infected mare and by the acutely or chronically infected stallion. Mares can be readily infected by the venereal route after breeding to a carrier stallion, either by live cover or artificial insemination with fresh-cooled or cryopreserved semen. There is evidence that EVA can spread through embryo transfer. Infection can also be spread through indirect contact with virus-contaminated fomites (breeding, shed equipment, shanks, or twitches) or on the hands or apparel of staff and handlers.

Recommendations

Singles: Tea Tree, Melaleuca Quinquenervia, Melissa, Mountain Savory, Eucalyptus Globulus, Cassia, Ravintsara, Basil, Ocotea, Thyme, Copaiba, Dorado Azul, Palmarosa, Oregano, Lemongrass, Clove, Myrrh, Eucalyptus Blue, Oregano, German Chamomile, Cypress, Peppermint and/or Spearmint (to reduce fever)

Blends: Thieves, Raven, ImmuPower, Exodus II, Egyptian Gold

Nutritionals: NingXia Red, MultiGreens, Sulfurzyme, Super C Chewable, Mineral Essence, ImmuPro, Inner Defense

Additional: Thieves Household Cleaner, Thieves Spray, Thieves Waterless Hand Purifier, Ortho Sport Massage Oil, Ortho Ease Massage Oil

Application and Usage

Topical: Put any 3-4 of the suggested oils liberally with Cypress and Copaiba on the chest and rub on the inside of the front legs. If the area heats up, put Ortho Sport Massage Oil and Ortho Ease Massage Oil over the top. Also apply Equine Raindrop Technique daily.

Ingestion & Oral: Combine 10 drops each of Copaiba, ImmuPower, Ravintsara, Eucalyptus Blue, and Exodus II with any other chosen suggested oil(s) and administer orally or apply on food or a hay cube. In a second water bucket, add Lemon, while always leaving one plain water bucket available. Administer 2 oz. NingXia Red daily combined with other chosen suggested supplements.

Inhalation: Put any combination of the suggested oils into an equine nebulizer, or direct diffusion into a stall 2 times daily is best: Eucalyptus Blue, Thieves, Exodus II, Raven, Dorado Azul, Ravintsara, or Cypress.

Other: Use diluted Thieves Household Cleaner with Myrrh and Eucalyptus Blue to clean breeding equipment and to wash stallions. Use Thieves Household Cleaner on all tack, supplies, etc., that come into contact with an infected horse. Use Thieves Household Cleaner in a footbath to discourage tracking infection to other areas. Use Thieves Spray and/or Thieves Waterless Hand Purifier on your person to prevent transfer. If in a barn with others, diffuse Thieves, Raven, and Eucalyptus Blue throughout the quarantine period every few hours to prevent sharing with other horses.

Eye Conditions

The eyes enable the horse to see and coordinate its movement accurately and to be spatially aware of the surrounding environment. Clearly, the eye must function well for the horse to perform at its best. Other than the eyeball itself, a number of vital surrounding structures are equally important.

Injuries, although fairly common, need to be treated with the utmost respect. Injuries are a frequent result of damage by protruding nails or collision with fences or trees, especially in poor light or when the animal has been frightened. Veterinary assistance should always be sought. Cuts may need suturing to avoid distortion to the lids. Eye conditions such as any damage, corneal ulcers, film or spots, tears, discharge, or vision concerns should be evaluated as soon as possible by your veterinarian to determine potential damage to the eye itself. Infections can set in overnight, and vision problems such as blindness may result. Keep the eye covered (fly mask) to decrease light and pain.

Never apply undiluted oils directly in the eye. If oils accidentally enter the eye, flush with V-6 Vegetable Oil Complex or pure vegetable oil and follow with saline solution until irritation stops.

Recommendations

Singles: Helichrysum, Cypress, Copaiba, Lavender, Frankincense, Sacred Frankincense

Blends: Melrose, Valor, Trauma Life (for emotional support if agitated), Grounding, Peace & Calming, Peace & Calming II, RutaVaLa, Aroma Life

Nutritionals: NingXia Red has zeaxanthin and lutein to nutritionally fortify eye function and vision. Also try Sulfurzyme and Super C Chewable.

Veterinarian Tips and Suggestions

Eye Spray Recipe

Add 1 of the following oils to water in your HydroGize water bottle; charge for 3 minutes. Then put in a glass spray bottle immediately and gently mist over eye areas.

- 10 drops Lavender
- 10 drops Copaiba
- 8 drops Frankincense
- 10 drops Helichrysum
- 10 drops Cypress

Application and Usage

Topical: Apply Helichrysum, Cypress, and Copaiba as close to the eye as possible many times daily. Apply suggested oils around the outside of the eye socket and moving outwardly toward the orbit bone. Apply Lavender, Trauma Life, and Valor to withers, poll, forehead, and sacrum.

Ingestion & Oral: Administer 15 drops Melrose, Cypress, Copaiba, and 2 oz. NingXia Red 2 times a day

Other: Combine 4 oz. distilled water with 15 drops Lavender and 5 drops Helichrysum and mist gently around eye area.

Fever

Fever is a common symptom of illness and defined as a rise in body temperature in response to infection. However, a rise in body temperature can also occur where there is pain such as in colic and in many other situations such as cases of heatstroke, for example.

Recommendations

Singles: Peppermint, Copaiba, Eucalyptus Blue, Spearmint, Eucalyptus Globulus, Lavender, Tea Tree, Melaleuca Quinquenervia, Mountain Savory, Melissa, Oregano, Palo Santo, Thyme, Idaho Balsam Fir, Idaho Blue Spruce, Northern Lights Black Spruce

Blends: Thieves, Purification, R.C., Exodus II, Longevity, ImmuPower, Melrose, DiGize, Aroma Ease, Deep Relief Roll-On, PanAway, Cool Azul, Relieve It

Nutritionals: Super C Chewable, MultiGreens, Inner Defense, Digest & Cleanse, ImmuPro, NingXia Red

Additional: Thieves Household Cleaner, Cool Azul Sports Gel, Cool Azul Pain Relief Cream

Application and Usage

Topical: Combine Peppermint and Eucalyptus Blue in a spray bottle containing water and mist/spray over entire body (avoiding the eyes). Or add 10-12 drops to pail of water and sponge over body. Massage chosen oil on auricular points of ears. For any painful areas, apply Deep Relief Roll-On, PanAway, Cool Azul, Cool Azul Pain Relief Cream Cool Azul Sports Gel, Idaho Balsam Fir, Copaiba, Relieve It, Idaho Blue Spruce, or Northern Lights Black Spruce.

Ingestion & Oral: Administer orally 15 drops each Peppermint, DiGize, Copaiba, and Thieves. For additional support, administer 2-4 oz. NingXia Red daily.

Inhalation: Diffuse Eucalyptus Blue, Purification, Melrose, and R.C.

Other: Use the following individually or layer with chosen oils: Cool Azul Sports Gel or Cool Azul Pain Relief Cream. Also try Raindrop Technique 2-3 times per week. Use Thieves Household Cleaner to sanitize stalls, etc.

Founder (*see* Laminitis)

Gastric Ulcers (Equine Gastric Ulcer Syndrome/ EGUS)

This condition reflects changes in feed and the degree of stress that we place on the horse. Gastric ulceration is most likely to occur in horses undergoing training, which induces high stress levels. Removal of the stress factor inevitably leads to recovery.

Most horses with the condition do not have noticeable symptoms. Watch for loss of general condition, weight loss, anemia, low blood protein levels, and signs of mild colic and sweating after feeding. Newly weaned or stressed foals may develop ulcers. Symptoms may include frequent casting (lying against a fence or wall on its back, relieving pain from stomach acid contacting the ulcers).

Recommendations

Singles: Cistus, Copaiba, Lavender, Helichrysum, Patchouli, Peppermint, Ginger, Tea Tree, Fennel, Nutmeg, Wintergreen

Blends: DiGize, Australian Blue, Aroma Ease, Longevity, Tranquil Roll-On, Peace & Calming, Stress Away Roll-On, Inner Child, Grounding, Thieves

Nutritionals: Life 9, MultiGreens, NingXia Red, Super C Chewable, Mineral Essence

Application and Usage

Ingestion & Oral: Administer orally 20 drops each DiGize and Copaiba 2 times daily until ulcers are gone.

Other: Preventive care: Administer orally 5 drops each Copaiba and DiGize 1 time daily.

Gelding (*see* Castration)

Girth Galls (Saddle Sores)

Girth galls are open sores caused by friction between the girth or cinch and skin and are typically found where the girth meets the soft and wrinkled skin, behind the elbow. Horses are prone to injuries to the skin, tissues, and bone near the shoulder area where a poor-fitting saddle was continuously placed.

You may see hair loss, swelling, warmth, pain, infection, or just mild inflammation. These lesions, called "galls," may develop into abscesses or boils. Address the improper saddle fit and use oils to help heal these areas.

Recommendations

Singles: Lavender, Myrrh, Idaho Balsam Fir, Copaiba, Geranium, Patchouli, Sacred Sandalwood, Royal Hawaiian Sandalwood, Helichrysum, Sacred Frankincense, Tea Tree, Palmarosa, Northern Lights Black Spruce, Roman Chamomile, Rose, Blue Cypress, Cistus, Hyssop, Juniper, Ocotea, Palo Santo

Blends: Melrose, Purification, 3 Wise Men, Believe, Gentle Baby, Tranquil Roll-On, Humility, Aroma Siez, Australian Blue, Egyptian Gold, M-Grain, Mendwell, Infect Away, PuriClean, The Gift

Nutritionals: Sulfurzyme, MultiGreens, NingXia Red, Life 9, Mineral Essence

Additional: Animal Scents Ointment, Rose Ointment, Tender Tush, LavaDerm Cooling Mist, ClaraDerm, Thieves Dentarome Ultra Toothpaste

Application and Usage

Topical: Apply PuriClean, Infect Away, Mendwell, and Melrose or other chosen oils directly on top of galls and apply Animal Scents Ointment over the top 2 or more times daily.

Other: This condition is often caused by ill-fitting tack. Try to use sheepskin girths or covers. Treat galls as a cut or wound. You can poultice boils with Thieves Dentarome Ultra Toothpaste. Apply any of the following oils first and cover with Thieves Dentarome Ultra Toothpaste: Melrose, Lavender, and/or Helichrysum. Also try: Animal Scents Ointment, Rose Ointment, Tender Tush, LavaDerm Cooling Mist, ClaraDerm.

Greasy Heel (Mud Fever/Scratches)

Greasy heel is an inflammatory skin condition caused by a wet, muddy environment and the bacteria it often contains. This affects the lower legs and more often those that are white in color.

Mineral imbalances and sweet feed make horses more susceptible to this condition. Have a hair mineral analysis done to determine what the horse may need, as improper mineral levels such as low zinc can leave a horse susceptible to skin issues.

Recommendations

Singles: Lavender, Geranium, Patchouli, Tea Tree, Ravintsara, Palmarosa, Helichrysum, Lemongrass, Ginger, Hyssop

Blends: Exodus II, Thieves, ImmuPower, Raven, Melrose, Egyptian Gold, The Gift, Infect Away, PuriClean, RepelAroma

Nutritionals: Mineral Essence, NingXia Red, MultiGreens, Sulfurzyme, Super C Chewable, MindWise, Life 9

Additional: Thieves Household Cleaner, Thieves Dentarome Ultra Toothpaste

Application and Usage

Topical: Spray Thieves Household Cleaner concentrate directly on affected areas on the legs and let dry. Then wash legs 1-2 hours after, dry well, apply chosen oils, and layer Thieves Dentarome Ultra Toothpaste over top of oils. Use this application 1 time daily. Also administer Equine Raindrop Technique 2 times a week.

Heaves

This usually presents as a long, labored exhale. Cough may be present and may be productive; this is most commonly seen around feeding or exercise time. There may be wheezing, tracheal rattle, and crackles; and the abdominal muscles produce a noticeable "heave" line.

The condition is mostly caused by common environmental allergens such as dusts in hay. Moving horses to pasture with fresh grass may help. Consult a veterinary health professional to rule out serious, underlying causes, prevent serious complications, and avoid contraindications.

Recommendations

Singles: Copaiba, Peppermint, Dorado Azul, Eucalyptus Blue, Eucalyptus Globulus, Hyssop, Lavender, Lemon, Lemongrass, Marjoram, Basil,

Veterinarian Tips and Suggestions

Heaves

Look for complete feeds such as Ontario Dehy's Balance Cubes, which offer a minerally balanced complete feed. These can be fed either wet or dry, and you can easily add oils and NingXia Red to this.

An equine nebulizer can offer quicker relief, delivering the oils directly to the respiratory tissues. Include Thieves if the horse has previously been exposed to mold or eaten from round bales. Do NOT use round-baled hay and switch to a complete feed to avoid introducing more inhaled allergies. Make sure there is no mold or mildew in this horse's environment.

Myrtle, Pine, Rosemary, Northern Lights Black Spruce, Hinoki, Oregano, Peppermint, Cedarwood, Laurus Nobilis, Idaho Blue Spruce, Ocotea, Helichrysum, Ravintsara

Blends: R.C., Raven, Thieves, Breathe Again Roll-On, Aroma Siez, Melrose, Exodus II, ImmuPower, Egyptian Gold, M-Grain, JuvaCleanse (for toxin involvement reduction)

Nutritionals: NingXia Red, MultiGreens, Sulfurzyme, Mineral Essence, Super C Chewable, Organic Dried Wolfberries

Additional: Thieves Household Cleaner

Application and Usage

Topical: Use any 3 or 4 of the above oils combined with Copaiba and apply to throat, chest, and inside front legs 2 times daily. Administer Raindrop Technique 2 times weekly.

Inhalation: For the following oils, use the equine nebulizer 20 minutes 2 times daily: Copaiba with Cedarwood, Raven, Peppermint, Thieves, and Melrose. Diffuse any combination of suggested oils in an enclosed barn or stall.

Other: Whenever cleaning the barn or stall, use Thieves Household Cleaner.

Hendra Virus (see Viral Conditions)

Hendra Virus is a virus first isolated and identified in 1994, with fruit bats being determined as the natural carrier. This disease poses a Level 4 biosafety hazard to humans as the virus is zoonotic. The virus tends to attack vascular tissues throughout the body, becoming more widespread as infection progresses.

As of July 2016, 53 disease incidents involving over 70 horses were reported. These were all confined to the northeastern coast of Australia.

Diagnosis can be confirmed only by laboratory analysis. If Hendra virus is suspected, consult a veterinary health professional, prepare the animal for quarantine, and protect human handlers from crossover infection.

True Quarantine Situation

As this virus is transferable to humans, veterinarians suggest euthanizing confirmed cases to limit risk of human exposure. Concur with veterinarian professionals if Hendra Virus is diagnosed.

Be sure to use proper preventative measures when interacting with affected animals to limit your chances of contracting the virus. These steps include supplementing your own diet with Life 9, Inner Defense, and Longevity. Also diffuse Thieves, Raven, Ravintsara, Eucalyptus Blue, and Melrose in your own home to help limit the possibility of contracting the virus. Use items mentioned for precautionary effect for the rest of the herd and facility.

Recommendations

Singles: Copaiba, Ravintsara, Eucalyptus Globulus, Dorado Azul, Oregano, Clove, Tea Tree, Thyme, Peppermint, Mountain Savory, Lemongrass, Basil, Melissa, Ocotea, Helichrysum, Cedarwood

Blends: Thieves, Exodus II, ImmuPower, Egyptian Gold, The Gift, Melrose, Raven, R.C.

Nutritionals: Inner Defense, NingXia Red, Mineral Essence, Longevity Softgels, MultiGreens, Life 9, Digest & Cleanse

Additional: Thieves Household Cleaner, TheraPro Premium Diffuser or AromaLux Atomizing Diffuser

Application and Usage

Topical: Apply Raindrop Technique oils on spine of all affected horses daily (both symptom-showing horses and horses in proximity to affected horses). Apply

Copaiba with 2-4 suggested oils on throat, chest, and stomach 2-4 times daily.

Ingestion & Oral: Administer 10 drops each of Helichrysum, Melissa, Ravintsara, Eucalyptus Globulus, and Exodus II 4 times daily orally for affected animals. On an exposed horse, administer orally 5 drops of each oil 2 times daily.

Inhalation: An equine nebulizer will work the best when diffusing; use multiple times daily. Use 5 drops each Raven, Eucalyptus Globulus, Copaiba, Cedarwood, and Melissa in a nebulizer. Use the nebulizer on horses for 20 minutes 2 times daily. Sterilize between uses due to biosecurity hazards from respiratory secretions. If enclosed barn, heavily diffuse suggested oils to support the respiratory system of the barn occupants, preferably with a non-water-based diffuser such as the TheraPro Premium Diffuser or AromaLux Atomizing Diffuser. Diffusing for all barn occupants will help minimize transfer risk from affected animals to exposed animals.

Other: Clean, disinfect, and sanitize everything with a strong concentration of Thieves Household Cleaner with Cinnamon Bark oil added.

Hives (Urticaria)

Urticaria are little plaque-like eruptions that form out of edema in the dermis, and they occur in all domestic animals. Horses are most commonly affected. They may be exogenous or endogenous and may be caused by exposure to toxins, bites, medications, or chemicals. All allergens in the environment should be considered as potential causes. The wheals or plaques appear within a few minutes or hours of exposure to the causative agent. Consult a veterinary health professional to rule out serious, underlying causes.

Recommendations

Singles: Copaiba, Melissa, Basil, Lavender, Peppermint, Roman Chamomile, Myrrh, Hinoki, Geranium, German Chamomile, Dorado Azul, Oregano

Blends: Purification, Tranquil Roll-On, Hope, DiGize, AromaEase, Cool Azul, Valor

Nutritionals: Sulfurzyme, NingXia Red, Mineral Essence, Rehemogen, K&B, Longevity Softgels, Digest & Cleanse, ICP, ParaFree for GI issues, Allerzyme

Additional: ClaraDerm, LavaDerm Cooling Mist, Tender Tush

Application and Usage

Topical: Apply liberally Copaiba, Basil, Lavender, and DiGize on the stomach area, throat, jugular, and inside leg areas 2 times daily. Perform Raindrop Technique adding Copaiba between applying Valor and Oregano.

Ingestion & Oral: Administer orally 10 drops each Copaiba, Melissa, and DiGize 2 times daily until hives recede.

Inhalation: Diffuse Hinoki and Purification.

Other: Also try applying ClaraDerm, LavaDerm Cooling Mist, and/or Tender Tush topically to the affected area.

Hoof Abscess

This abscess is an infection in the hoof. Owners frequently discover their horse to be lame in 3 legs, which seems to have happened overnight.

This is one of the most common causes of lameness in horses, initiated by either a puncture wound to the sole, as consequence of a crack in the white line, or from a severe bruise to the heel. Most horses with this condition will be lame; yet in the early stages, this may not be apparent.

Veterinarian Tips and Suggestions

Hoof Abscess

Place oils in the area around the suspected abscess or hotter part of the hoof as well as on any potential entry points. Then coat with Peppermint to drive the oils in deeper and help cool the hoof.

Next, soak the hoof in warm water with Thieves Household Cleaner or Thieves Mouthwash added to soften the hoof and encourage the infection to migrate out. After 15-20 minutes, remove the hoof, dry, and use selected oils on the bulb and alongside the frog area. Also, use Thieves Dentarome Ultra Toothpaste or poultice with Thieves, etc., to draw out the infection.

Let dry in place and pad the bottom of the hoof with foam board (cutting out an area where the abscess might be for less pressure). Secure with vet wrap to give the horse a less painful surface to walk, so you can encourage movement if possible. Do not force movement. Aim to draw out infection as opposed to digging to find it, if possible.

Once infection gains hold, the foot will become extremely painful, as the hoof cannot expand as the pus builds up. By this stage, the horse is likely to be lame and not able to put the foot onto the ground for long. There will be heat in the foot, an increase in the digital pulse, and sometimes sufficient pain to cause the horse to sweat. Normally, the pus will travel the path of least resistance and will underrun the sole and travel up between the laminae to burst through at the coronary band.

Sole abscesses need to be drained to eliminate the infection and to relieve the pain. The pus normally appears as thin, grey-colored fluid.

Puncture wounds entering the region of the frog are much more serious, as infection may gain access to the navicular bursa or pedal bone. These cases sometimes need surgical intervention.

Veterinarian Tips and Suggestions

Hoof Infections

Case History

In 2000 a show horse received some kind of severe bite on the pastern. Although the vet diagnosed a rattlesnake bite, it may have been caused by something else.

Two weeks later, the entire pastern and coronet band were inflamed (the size of a cantaloupe), and the rotting, decaying flesh revealed a large hole where the bone was visible and had separated from the hoof.

The vet suggested amputating the foot. Instead, the following protocol was initiated:

Day 1: The wound was cleaned and disinfected with Thieves and Helichrysum, and the foot was bandaged. This treatment decreased pain enough to allow the mare to put weight on the foot.

Day 2: The swelling had dropped by 50 percent. The wound was again cleaned with Thieves and Helichrysum and then packed with Animal Scents Ointment.

Days 3 to 14: The wound was washed morning and night with Thieves, Melrose, and Helichrysum and packed with Animal Scents Ointment.

Result: Today the animal walks with no discomfort. A brand new hoof has appeared with only a small scar on the wound site. Although there was minor swelling in the pastern for a while, it had faded eight months later.

Recommendations

Singles: Peppermint, Copaiba, Clove, Cinnamon Bark, Cassia, Lemon, Lavender, Lemongrass, Tea Tree, Melaleuca Quinquenervia, Mountain Savory, Oregano, Thyme, Wintergreen, German Chamomile, Ginger, Palmarosa, Patchouli, Rosemary, Helichrysum, Wintergreen, Xiang Mao, Eucalyptus Globulus, Eucalyptus Radiata, Eucalyptus Blue, Bergamot, Black Pepper, Geranium, Ravintsara, Blue Cypress

Blends: Thieves, Purification, Exodus II, Abundance, Egyptian Gold, Longevity, PanAway, Deep Relief Roll-On, Raven, Relieve It, M-Grain, Melrose, Breathe Again Roll-On, ImmuPower, En-R-gee, The Gift, Christmas Spirit, DiGize

Nutritionals: NingXia Red, Longevity, Mineral Essence, Sulfurzyme

Additional: Thieves Household Cleaner, Thieves Dentarome Ultra Toothpaste, Thieves Mouthwash, Ortho Sport Massage Oil, Ortho Ease Massage Oil

Application and Usage

Topical: Soak the foot in Thieves Household Cleaner with 10 drops of any suggested blend and Epsom salt added to very warm water 2-3 times daily until pus starts draining. Once the pus is draining, you will no longer need to soak the foot. Dry foot and apply Thieves, plus other chosen oils, to abscess area and cover with Thieves Dentarome Ultra Toothpaste. Add padding such as cotton and cover foot to keep clean between soakings and cleanings. Continue to apply the chosen oils topically 2-4 times daily until the horse is 100 percent sound. Administer Raindrop Technique for both immune and balance support. If joint involvement is suspected from puncture wound entry, also apply Raindrop oils plus Thieves or Exodus II to the joint.

Ingestion & Oral: To prevent stress-induced colic, supplement orally 15 drops each Ginger and Copaiba. Also try using 10 drops of any combination of suggested oils (except Oregano) with 1-2 oz. NingXia Red orally 2 times daily until the abscess is healed.

Inhalation: Use calming, supportive oils for emotional balance such as Tranquil Roll-On, Stress Away Roll-On, Peace & Calming, Lavender, etc., if horse appears stressed.

Other: Check for imbalanced minerals, especially copper, zinc, and selenium. Also use Ortho Sport

Massage Oil or Ortho Ease Massage Oil (for compensatory leg as well), Thieves Household Cleaner, or Thieves Mouthwash to soak lame foot. After soaking, use Thieves Dentarome Ultra Toothpaste combined with suggested oils as a poultice.

Hormonal Disorders

Hormones can be a wide topic for discussion due to the many systems and pathways they affect. Horses generally fall into two different categories: 1. hormone overproduction due to a growth or calcification or 2. endocrine tissue destruction resulting in hormone deficiencies.

Another potential that is becoming more evident is potential xenoestrogen involvement, with more crops being grown systemically with glyphosate. This is an insecticide that can't be washed off, that may affect the gut bacteria, and that also includes petrochemicals that are used as surfactants during application.

Lower sugar and starch intake to reduce stress on adrenals. To get a complete picture of any hormonal issues with an equine, a blood panel may be necessary to identify the distinct areas of imbalance. You can then select the appropriate oils to administer from the suggested oils below. Discuss potential treatments with your veterinarian, if necessary.

Recommendations

Singles: Clary Sage, Sage, Nutmeg, Fennel, Idaho Balsam Fir (to lower cortisol), Myrtle, Ylang Ylang, Northern Lights Black Spruce, Idaho Blue Spruce, Patchouli, Helichrysum, Peppermint, Ginger, Ledum, Myrrh, Juniper

Blends: EndoFlex, Mister, Dragon Time, Sensation, Lady Sclareol, SclarEssence, Shutran, RutaVaLa, JuvaCleanse, GLF, DiGize, AromaEase, Progessence Plus

Nutritionals: Thyromin, EndoGize, NingXia Red, PD 80/20, Estro, FemiGen, Sulfurzyme, Mineral Essence

Application and Usage

Topical: Apply appropriate suggested oils on flanks, poll, inside front legs, inside upper portion of hind legs, and stomach area.

Ingestion & Oral: Selection of oils and dosage is dependent on blood panel results.

Inhalation: Diffuse suggested oils to calm and lower stress levels.

Hormonal Disorders—Stallion and Mare Reproduction

The control of the reproductive organs and reproductive behavior in stallions and mares is under the influence of the nervous system and hormones. Some mares will show abnormal cycles, meaning the pattern deviates from the normal, regular cycle in some way. This can occur for several reasons, leading to infertility, which can be a major problem.

Recommendations

Singles: Clary Sage, Goldenrod, Ylang Ylang, Copaiba, Fennel, Idaho Blue Spruce, Northern Lights Black Spruce

Blends: Mister, SclarEssence, Lady Sclareol, EndoFlex, Progessence Plus, Shutran

Nutritionals: NingXia Red, Sulfurzyme, Estro

Application and Usage

Ingestion & Oral: Combine 1-2 oz. NingXia Red, 4-6 dropperfuls Mineral Essence, and 1-2 oz. Sulfurzyme. Administer combination orally 2-4 times daily with the following oils:
- **Stallion:** 10 drops each Copaiba, Goldenrod, and Ylang Ylang with Shutran or Mister 2 times daily
- **Mare:** 10 drops each Clary Sage, Progessence Plus, and Copaiba 2 times daily

Inhalation: Diffuse Peace & Calming, Lavender, or Stress Away Roll-On.

Hypoadrenocorticism (Addison's Disease)

This is a deficiency of adrenal gland hormones in horses, and its cause is generally unknown. Usually, it is the result of an autoimmune condition, wherein the body destroys the hormone-production tissue in the adrenal gland.

Signs include bouts of vomiting, diarrhea, dehydration, reduced appetite, lethargy, weight loss, and a gradual loss of muscle tissue and coordination. A key diagnostic sign will be very low levels of sodium and very high levels of potassium in the blood.

Consult a veterinary health professional to rule out serious, underlying causes, prevent serious complications, and avoid contraindications.

Recommendations

Singles: Nutmeg, Fennel, Frankincense, Sacred Frankincense, Ocotea, Ginger, Peppermint, Cinnamon Bark, Copaiba, Coriander, Helichrysum, Lemongrass, Lavender, Roman Chamomile, German

Chamomile, Dill, Vetiver, Idaho Balsam Fir (to lower cortisol)

Blends: Exodus II, ImmuPower, Thieves, Believe, Stress Away Roll-On, Peace & Calming, Grounding, Hope, Tranquil Roll-On, AromaEase, EndoFlex, DiGize, En-R-Gee

Nutritionals: NingXia Red, EndoGize, Sulfurzyme, PD 80/20, Organic Dried Wolfberries, Longevity, Power Meal, Life 9, Mineral Essence, Thyromin

Application and Usage

Topical: Apply 5 drops each Nutmeg, Copaiba, Lemongrass, and EndoFlex on adrenal area 1-2 times daily. Apply Lavender, Idaho Balsam Fir, and/or Peace & Calming on the poll area 1-2 times daily. Administer Raindrop Technique with ImmuPower, Copaiba, and EndoFlex 2-3 times per week if autoimmune source is suggested.

Ingestion & Oral: Administer orally 5-10 drops each DiGize, ImmuPower, Copaiba, and Ginger 1-2 times daily. Also administer 1-2 oz. NingXia Red 4 times daily if needed.

Inhalation: Diffuse Idaho Balsam Fir, Peace & Calming, Lavender, or Stress Away Roll-On.

Other: Determine and support mineral balance required by the individual horse, not relying on off-the-shelf complete mineral balances. Choose non-starchy, low-sugar feeds that are appropriate for individual requirements to not stress the adrenals even more. If high blood sugar causes nausea, use DiGize and Ocotea to calm and encourage eating.

Impaction Colic (see also Colic and Impaction)

Call your veterinarian and/or local surgery center, if that is an option for the horse. This is a medical emergency. The horse's blood supply to a part of the digestive tract may be compromised or nonexistent. See Colic Heading for oils to use while waiting for the vet. Do not let the animal lie down or roll, if possible.

Recommendations

Singles: Copaiba, Cedarwood (for oxygenation), Peppermint, Patchouli, Cypress, Fennel, Lavender, Roman Chamomile, Idaho Balsam Fir, Sacred Frankincense

Blends: DiGize, AromaEase, Release, Aroma Siez, Deep Relief Roll-On, PanAway, Tranquil Roll-On, Peace & Calming, Gentle Baby, Stress Away Roll-On, RutaVaLa, Trauma Life

Nutritionals: NingXia Red, Sulfurzyme, Mineral Essence, Detoxzyme (empty capsules into warm water with NingXia Red and orally syringe)

Application and Usage

Topical: Apply 30 drops each of Copaiba, DiGize, and Peppermint to navel and abdominal area every 10-15 minutes until veterinarian arrives, and be careful not to be kicked. Massage auricular points in ears with Trauma Life or Sacred Frankincense.

Ingestion & Oral: Administer 30 drops each of Copaiba, DiGize, and Peppermint every 20 minutes until veterinarian arrives or symptoms abate.

Inhalation: Diffuse Peace & Calming, Lavender, Stress Away Roll-On, and Idaho Balsam Fir.

Other: Apply or diffuse calming oils such as Tranquil Roll-On, Peace & Calming, Lavender, Roman Chamomile, Gentle Baby, Stress Away Roll-On, or RutaVaLa.

Inflammation (see Cuts)

Determine the area of the body and/or causation to determine the oils and supplements to choose. Copaiba and Peppermint (dilute if any open skin) are generally the two main oils with which to start treatment.

Recommendations

Singles: Copaiba, Idaho Balsam Fir, Oregano, Peppermint

Blends: Relieve It, PanAway

Nutritionals: Sulfurzyme, NingXia Red

Additional: Regenolone Moisturizing Cream, Cool Azul Pain Relief Cream, Cool Azul Sports Gel, Ortho Sport Massage Oil, Ortho Ease Massage Oil

Application and Usage

Topical: Apply suggested oils multiple times daily followed by a cold, wet compress.

Ingestion & Oral: Administer orally 10 drops Copaiba 2-3 times daily.

Inhalation: Diffuse Peace & Calming, Lavender, Stress Away Roll-On, or Idaho Balsam Fir.

Other: Use the following individually or layer with chosen oils: Regenolone Moisturizing Cream, Cool Azul Pain Relief Cream, Cool Azul Sports Gel, Ortho Sport Massage Oil, or Ortho Ease Massage Oil.

Insect Bite

Horses are subject to a wide variety of insect pests that may spread disease, including viruses, bacteria, and parasites. Biting flies feed on their blood, and they include mosquitoes, black flies (1,000+ species), sand flies, buffalo flies, eye gnats, face flies, biting midges (gnats/no-see-ums), horse flies, stable flies, horn flies, deer flies, and ticks. The bites may be painful and cause allergic reactions. Most often, they don't pose a serious threat; but when they do, it poses a great threat to the horse's long-term health.

There are also non-biting flies that feed on bodily secretions. While these may not draw blood, they are still capable of transmitting disease. The best prevention is to keep infestations from occurring on the property. When possible, treat the grounds, stables, pasture areas, water sources, and the actual horse with bug-repelling essential oils.

If you suspect the horse has received a bite from an infection-transmitting insect, consult a veterinary health professional to test for disease and to prevent serious complications.

Horses with insect bite allergies may have any combination of hives, itchiness, hair loss, and dermatitis. Treatment must first involve avoidance and repelling insects. These insects prefer to feed at dusk and dawn. Horses can be turned out to avoid those times of the day when these insects are most likely to be active. Box fans on stalls help to keep Culicoides off horses because the insects are very small and avoid strong air currents.

Omega[3] supplementation helps the skin to recover and cope with continued exposure. Spirulina, added to feed, may lower the allergenic response.

Insect bites also include ticks and mosquitoes that can transmit diseases such as Lyme, Equine Infectious Anemia, Eastern Equine Encephalitis, Western Equine Encephalitis, Venezuelan Equine Encephalitis, and more. Check individual diseases for more information and to prevent infestations from occurring by treating stalls, grounds, ponds, water sources, animals, and yourself with essential oils. Remove any areas that hold standing water and support mosquito proliferation.

If you think that your horse is having an anaphylactic reaction to any bites, seek emergency veterinary assistance immediately. A veterinarian can give intravenous injections of epinephrine to counteract the reaction. While you are waiting, give the horse 20 to 30 drops of Copaiba on the oral mucosa along with Purification.

Recommendations

Singles: Copaiba, Peppermint, Lavender, Lemongrass, Geranium, Hyssop, Patchouli, Citronella, Palo Santo, Idaho Tansy, Eucalyptus Globulus, Ocotea, Thyme, Tea Tree, Rosemary, Hinoki, Melissa

Blends: Purification, DiGize, Melrose, Infect Away, RepelAroma, PuriClean, Longevity

Nutritionals: MultiGreens, NingXia Red, Mineral Essence, Detoxzyme, Sulfurzyme

Additional: Ortho Ease Massage Oil, Ortho Sport Massage Oil, V-6 Vegetable Oil Complex, Animal Scents Ointment, Rose Ointment

Application and Usage

Topical: Apply chosen oils on location. For allergic responses use Hinoki, Copaiba, and Melissa. Administer Raindrop Technique weekly, more often for areas with large numbers of insects.

Ingestion & Oral: Administer orally 10 drops each Longevity, Copaiba, and DiGize 1 time daily for horse in insect-dense areas. Sweet-feed fed horses seem to attract more bugs and exhibit more subsequent inflammation and reactions to bites. When Spirulina is added to the diet, it can reduce inflammatory responses to insect bites.

Inhalation: Diffuse Purification, Thieves, and Melrose.

Other: Use Animal Scents Ointment or Rose Ointment with Melrose or Purification added to lightly coat the inside of ears to discourage bites. In a thicker coat, place on open sores from fly bites. Also apply Ortho Ease Massage Oil, Ortho Sport Massage Oil, and V-6 Vegetable Oil Complex as a carrier base (it's sprayable) when applying suggested oils.

Veterinarian Tips and Suggestions

Insect Bites

Spider Bites
Apply one or all the following oils directly on bite location: Purification, Basil, Melrose, Copaiba

Bee Stings
Remove the stinger without puncturing the venom sac. Then apply Basil, Copaiba, Purification, Peppermint, PanAway, Deep Relief Roll-On, Cool Azul, Wintergreen

Tick Bites
Apply one or all the following oils directly on bite location: Longevity, Purification, Copaiba, Peppermint

Insulin Resistance

Animals with this condition are typically obese, with greater fat stores in the neck and tailhead areas. Laminitis is common. The most common sign is hyperinsulinemia, with normal blood glucose concentrations, as well as hypertriglyceridemia, increased serum leptin, and arterial hypertension. Consult a veterinary health professional to rule out serious, underlying causes; prevent serious complications; and avoid contraindications.

Sudden feed restriction should be avoided because it may lead to hyperlipidemia and further exacerbate insulin resistance. Increasing the amount and level of exercise will increase the rate of weight loss.

Particular care should be exercised if turning horses out on pasture during times of high-soluble carbohydrate content, spring and autumn, or when grass raises its sugar levels from stress due to freezing, drought, etc.

Cinnamon spice has been suggested to help, but it has no effect on balancing the insulin level, which is the main concern. However, Cinnamon Bark and Ocotea essential oils have been found to be very effective in balancing insulin.

Recommendations

Singles: Ocotea, Dill, Fennel, Coriander, Copaiba, Mastrante, Ledum, Cinnamon Bark, Idaho Balsam Fir, Nutmeg, Lavender (to calm adrenals)

Blends: DiGize, JuvaCleanse, Thieves, Exodus II, GLF, EndoFlex, Light Your Fire, Excite, Believe, Stress Away Roll-On, Peace & Calming

Nutritionals: EndoGize, NingXia Red, Sulfurzyme, Mineral Essence, MultiGreens, Essentialzymes-4, MightyZymes

Application and Usage

Topical: Apply Thieves, Copaiba, and EndoFlex on stomach area, throat, and adrenal pancreas area 2 times daily.

Ingestion & Oral: No sweet feed, sweet treats, or pelleted food that uses gluten as a binder for the animal. Administer 5-10 drops each Ocotea and Copaiba 2 times daily. Combine 1-2 oz. NingXia Red, 4-6 dropperfuls Mineral Essence, 1-2 oz. Sulfurzyme, and 1-2 MultiGreens. Administer combination orally at least 2 times daily.

Inhalation: Diffuse any suggested oil(s), particularly Thieves, for best results.

Other: Because stress levels influence cortisol and blood sugar balance, reduce stress with Idaho Balsam Fir, Believe, Stress Away Roll-On, Lavender, or Peace & Calming. High iron levels can bring on insulin resistance, and horses are rarely deficient in iron. Do not supplement with additional iron.

Kidney Disease

Equine kidneys process 10 gallons of blood on a continual basis, and only a small percentage of horses ever develop kidney conditions. However, when they do, the condition will generally go undetected until the later stages. A horse's kidneys may suffer injury from dehydration, heat stroke, certain plant and food poisons, colic, blood loss, bacterial infection, shock, or kidney stones.

Consult a veterinary health professional to rule out serious, underlying causes, prevent serious complications, and avoid contraindications.

Recommendations

Singles: Copaiba, Lemongrass, Clove, Helichrysum, Juniper, Geranium, Grapefruit, Lemon, German Chamomile, Cypress, Blue Cypress

Blends: EndoFlex, En-R-Gee, Valor, Valor II (the kidney, in Chinese medicine, houses emotion and will, both of which are supported by Valor).

Nutritionals: K&B Tincture, Detoxzyme, Organic Dried Wolfberries, NingXia Red, Inner Defense, Sulfurzyme, Rehemogen, JuvaTone, Essentialzymes-4, MindWise

Application and Usage

Topical: Administer Raindrop Technique for immune and spinal support 2-3 times per week. Also apply Cypress, Juniper, Copaiba, and Lemongrass on jugular, kidney, and femoral artery area 2-4 times daily.

Ingestion & Oral: Administer orally 20 drops each of Copaiba and Juniper or Lemongrass and 10 drops Helichrysum with 2 oz. NingXia Red and 6 dropperfuls K&B tincture at least 2-4 times daily.

Inhalation: Thieves, Purification

Lacerations (see Cuts)

Laminitis

Whenever you encounter laminitis (founder), remember these treatment steps:

1. Cool the foot without soaking.
   - R.C., Wintergreen, Peppermint
2. Stem inflammation; adjust diet to stop damage.
   - Cypress, Copaiba, Idaho Balsam Fir
3. Relieve pain.
   - Copaiba, Idaho Balsam Fir, PanAway
4. Stop the source from recurring.
   - Change feeding program and add DiGize and Copaiba orally.
5. Rebuild the hoof.
   - Copaiba, Cypress, Idaho Blue Spruce, Northern Lights Black Spruce, Lemongrass, PanAway

Laminitis (Founder)

Laminitis is a term specifically meaning inflammation of the laminae and its consequences. It can affect all four feet, although it is most common in the front. Laminae are vital structures that interlock the hoof and pedal bone. They provide an intricate suspension system that cushions the foot and leg from concussion, which occurs when the foot hits the ground. If the attachment of the pedal bone to the hoof begins to weaken and break down, the pedal bone can begin to rotate and tip downward, placing pressure on the sole of the foot and causing pain. If the rotation continues, the pedal bone will eventually protrude through the sole of the foot between the front of the frog and the toe. The rotation of the pedal bone is called foundering.

Recommendations

Singles: Cypress, Copaiba, Peppermint, Wintergreen, Clove, Helichrysum, Lavender, Lemongrass, Marjoram, Basil, Palo Santo, Pine, Idaho Blue Spruce, Northern Lights Black Spruce, Idaho Balsam Fir, Ocotea (if feed overload)

Blends: Aroma Life, Aroma Siez, Believe, DiGize, Cool Azul, Longevity, M-Grain, PanAway, Relieve It, Thieves, Peace & Calming, Stress Away Roll-On

Nutritionals: NingXia Red, Life 9, MultiGreens, Super B, Detoxzyme, Essentialzyme, Essentialzymes-4, Digest & Cleanse, Sulfurzyme

Additional: Cool Azul Sports Gel, Cool Azul Pain Relief Cream, Ortho Sport Massage Oil, Regenolone Moisturizing Cream

Application and Usage

Topical: Rub into the bulbs of the heels and inside of legs 3 times daily using 3-5 suggested oils of your choosing, layering one over the other. Apply Cool Azul Sports Gel, Cool Azul Pain Relief Cream, or Regenolone Moisturizing Cream over the top of the oils. Also try using Peppermint, Cypress, Wintergreen, and Copaiba on coronary band and bulb. Fifteen minutes later, after oils have soaked in a bit, cold hose (let the cold water run down the horse's leg), or apply cold compresses for 10-15 minutes to help oils penetrate affected area. Do NOT soak the hoof, as moisture can soften the hoof wall connection, which is already questionably damaged. Administer Raindrop Technique (adding Idaho Balsam Fir is optional) every 3 days until acute symptoms abate; then 1 time a week for 6 months until completely clear.

Ingestion & Oral: Administer orally 5-10 drops each Copaiba and DiGize with 2 oz. NingXia Red and 1 oz. Sulfurzyme at least 2 times daily.

Inhalation: Diffuse Lavender, Idaho Balsam Fir, Peace & Calming, and Stress Away Roll-On.

Other: Apply Cool Azul Sports Gel and/or Cool Azul Pain Relief Cream and Ortho Sport Massage Oil as needed (especially to compensatory limb).

Lice

Horses are prone to lice on the head, neck, mane, and base of the tail. Telltale signs are biting and rubbing infested areas. The horse may also scratch the area until it is bald and/or scratch off the top layer of skin.

Two types of lice common to horses are *Haematopinus asini* (blood-sucking) and *Damalinia equi* (biting). Usually the Haematopinus will gather at the roots of the forelock and mane, on the hairs just above the hoof, and on the area around the base of the tail. The Damalinia will manifest on the sides of the neck, flank, and base of the tail, having two tissue layers or laminae: sensitive and insensitive. The eggs (nits) will take 3-4 weeks to mature.

Several weeks of application and rotation may be required to eradicate all nits, nymphs, and adult lice. Infestations usually occur in winter or early spring, and they spread quickly and easily through a herd with direct contact of brushes, saddles, blankets, and shared stables. Consult your veterinarian to prevent any complications.

Recommendations

Singles: Orange, Citronella, Eucalyptus Globulus, Lemongrass, Ocotea, Peppermint, Thyme, Palo Santo (use one or two of the aforementioned), Tea Tree, Melaleuca Quinquenervia, Geranium, Hyssop, Patchouli

Blends: Thieves, Longevity, DiGize, Melrose, Exodus II, Egyptian Gold, RepelAroma, PuriClean, ParaGize, Infect Away, AromaEase, Purification

Nutritionals: ParaFree, Digest & Cleanse, Mineral Essence, NingXia Red, Inner Defense, MultiGreens

Additional: Animal Scents Ointment, Tender Tush, Ortho Sport Massage Oil

Application and Usage

Topical: Apply liberally Animal Scents Ointment, Tender Tush, or Ortho Sport Massage Oil mixed with any suggested oils. Administer Raindrop Technique 1 time daily until symptoms are clear.

Inhalation: Diffuse any suggested oil, particularly Melrose and Purification for best results.

Liver Disease

In most species, the liver is a very regenerative organ. In horses, this is particularly true, unless the liver is attacked by pathogens, suffers undue stress as a secondary condition, or suffers direct injury.

Early liver fibrosis can be reversed if diagnosed and treated early. Signs of insufficiency may not manifest until 60-80 percent of the liver is nonfunctional. Jaundice, weight loss, abdominal pain, colic, and unusual behavior may help to distinguish the issue from other conditions.

Liver disease can also cause photosensitization. Usually veterinarians can detect liver disease (before the liver fails) with routine blood work. Consult your veterinarian to prevent, diagnose, and treat liver disease.

Recommendations

Singles: Ledum, Lemon, Celery Seed, Helichrysum, Clove, German Chamomile, Goldenrod, Rosemary, Spearmint, Tangerine, Carrot Seed, Cardamom, Copaiba, Thyme, Grapefruit, Juniper

Blends: GLF, JuvaCleanse, JuvaFlex, Release, DiGize, ParaGize, Thieves

Nutritionals: JuvaPower, JuvaSpice, Detoxzyme, NingXia Red, JuvaTone, K&B, Life 9, MultiGreens, Inner Defense, Sulfurzyme, Mineral Essence

Additional: Thieves Household Cleaner, Thieves Spray

Application and Usage

Topical: Apply Copaiba, JuvaFlex, and Rosemary to stomach and liver area.

Ingestion & Oral: Administer orally 10 drops each Copaiba, JuvaCleanse, and DiGize with 6 dropperfuls K&B, 2 oz. NingXia Red, 2 dropperfuls Mineral Essence, and 1 oz. Sulfurzyme 2 times daily. Add Lemon or Grapefruit to water bucket. Use MultiGreens and Inner Defense if infectious causation. Use Sulfurzyme, Mineral Essence, and JuvaPower to aid in recovery.

Inhalation: Diffuse Lemon, Celery Seed, Juniper, Rosemary, Tangerine, Thieves, and Grapefruit.

Other: Choose lower protein foods and non-GMO and low-sugar feeds to keep inflammation at bay. Milk thistle and N-acetyl cysteine are great for liver support. Fresh vegetables, such as celery and cucumbers, make great low-sugar treats with live enzymes. Also try using Thieves Household Cleaner and Thieves Spray when cleaning. Do not use toxic cleaning agents, which will further stress the liver.

Lyme Disease (see also Insect Bite)

Three known tick species are capable of transmitting *Borrelia burgdorferi* (bacteria), but most infections are caused by the deer tick *Ixodes pacificus* and *Ixodes scapularis*. If Lyme is common in your region, be sure to consult your veterinary health professional to confirm infection, establish degree of infection, prevent serious complications, and avoid contraindications.

Recommendations

Singles: Copaiba, Peppermint, Mountain Savory, Lemon, Melissa, Tea Tree, Melaleuca Quinquenervia, Lemongrass, Clove, Cassia, German Chamomile, Oregano, Helichrysum, Bergamot, Black Pepper, Cinnamon Bark, Hyssop, Geranium, Hong Kuai, Laurus Nobilis, Mountain Savory, Thyme, Rosemary, Xiang Mao, Patchouli, Palmarosa, Basil, Ocotea, Ravintsara, Mastrante, Dorado Azul

Blends: Thieves, Exodus II, ImmuPower, Brain Power, Longevity, Melrose, Christmas Spirit, Infect Away, M-Grain, ParaGize, PuriClean, The Gift, Egyptian Gold, PanAway, Relieve It, DiGize

Nutritionals: NingXia Red, ImmuPro, Rehemogen, MultiGreens

Additional: Ortho Sport Massage Oil, Deep Relief Roll-On

Application and Usage

Topical: Apply any of up to 5 suggested oils to poll, spine, jugular, and inside of each leg 2 times daily. Apply Raindrop Technique every day with ImmuPower and Copaiba added if ticks or tick bites are found.

Ingestion & Oral: Combine 10 drops each DiGize, Exodus II, ImmuPower, Ocotea, and Copaiba with 6 dropperfuls Rehemogen, 2 MultiGreens, and 2 oz. NingXia Red. Administer combination orally 2-4 times daily as needed. If able to eat, administer a hay cube marinade soaked with preferred oils. Provide Peppermint and Lemon in a second water bucket to encourage temperature reduction if required or Copaiba to reduce inflammation.

Inhalation: Diffuse Thieves, Melrose, ImmuPower, Christmas Spirit, Longevity, or any potent antibacterial single oil.

Other: Use your favorite oils such as Purification to avoid tick bites. Apply Ortho Sport Massage Oil, Deep Relief Roll-On, PanAway, and Relieve It for pain and stiffness.

Mange (Mites, Chiggers)

Mange in horses comes in four varieties: sarcoptic, psoroptic, chorioptic, and demodectic.

Sarcoptic mange is the most severe in horses and is luckily quite rare.

Psoroptic mange (mane mange) has been eradicated from horses in the United States.

Chorioptic mange (leg mange) still occurs in some horses and generally infects heavy breeds (particularly Belgian, Shire, Clydesdale, and Friesian breeds). It generally responds well to treatment.

Demodectic mange in horses is extremely rare and difficult to treat. Consult a veterinary health professional to prevent serious complications and avoid contraindications.

Recommendations

Singles: Hyssop, Patchouli, Clove, Oregano, Idaho Tansy, Thyme, Peppermint, Basil, Black Pepper, Blue Cypress, Cedarwood, Dorado Azul, Goldenrod, Hinoki, Hong Kuai, Lemongrass, Tea Tree, Lemon, Mountain Savory, Ocotea, Helichrysum, Xiang

Mao, Citronella, Palo Santo, Eucalyptus Globulus, Copaiba

Blends: Thieves, Purification, Melrose, Longevity, Exodus II, Infect Away, Mendwell, ParaGize, PuriClean, RepelAroma, Egyptian Gold, DiGize, Raven, The Gift, ImmuPower

Nutritionals: MindWise, Sulfurzyme, NingXia Red, Mineral Essence

Additional: Thieves Household Cleaner, Animal Scents Shampoo, Animal Scents Ointment, Ortho Sport Massage Oil

Application and Usage

Topical: Start by bathing with Animal Scents Shampoo or Thieves Household Cleaner. Use 3-4 of any suggested oils and apply on location liberally 2-3 times daily. Cover applied oils with Animal Scents Ointment or Ortho Sport Massage Oil. Repeat 2 times daily. Administer Raindrop Technique 4-7 times a week.

Ingestion & Oral: Administer orally 10 drops each of DiGize, Thieves, Copaiba, and Melrose with 1-2 oz. NingXia Red, 4-6 dropperfuls Mineral Essence, and 1-2 oz. Sulfurzyme at least 2 times daily.

Inhalation: Diffuse in barn Thieves, Purification, Melrose, Tea Tree, or Lemon.

Other: Bathe with Thieves Household Cleaner and/or Animal Scents Shampoo. Also use Ortho Sport Massage Oil or Animal Scents Ointment.

Melanoma

Every owner of a grey horse lives in fear of melanoma, that characteristic black or brown nodule so often appearing on the skin around and under the tail. Rightly so, for estimates suggest that more than 80 percent of grey horses over the age of 15 will develop at least one melanoma tumor during its lifetime. The "why" hasn't been determined.

We know that melanoma is tumor of the melanocytes, the cells that produce skin pigment. We know that in aging grey horses, there appears to be a disturbance in the metabolism of melanin, which stimulates local overproduction of dermal pigment. Grey-horse melanomas don't appear to be linked to an overdose of sun.

Recommendations

Singles: Royal Hawaiian Sandalwood, Sacred Sandalwood, Myrrh, Hyssop, Tarragon, Orange,

Clove, Copaiba, Tsuga, Idaho Blue Spruce, Northern Lights Black Spruce, Idaho Balsam Fir, Lavender, Frankincense, Sacred Frankincense, Blue Cypress

Blends: ImmuPower, Longevity, 3 Wise Men, Egyptian Gold, Exodus II, The Gift

Nutritionals: Organic Dried Wolfberries, Super C Chewables, NingXia Red, MindWise, OmegaGize^3, Essentialzyme, Super B, Mineral Essence, Life 9, Sulfurzyme, ImmuPro

Additional: Tender Tush, Animal Scents Ointment, ClaraDerm, Ortho Ease Massage Oil, Ortho Sport Massage Oil, Thieves Dentarome Ultra Toothpaste

Application and Usage

Topical: Use 3-4 selected oils, combined with Copaiba, Frankincense, and Royal Hawaiian Sandalwood or Sacred Sandalwood. Apply topically on location 4 times daily. Apply Raindrop Technique, including Royal Hawaiian Sandalwood or Sacred Sandalwood 3 times weekly. Use Thieves Dentarome Ultra Toothpaste as a poultice.

Ingestion & Oral: Use Orange, Lemon, and other citrus oils internally, either in a second water bucket or in the food. Apply 20 drops each of Longevity, Frankincense, DiGize, and Copaiba with 1-2 oz. NingXia Red, 4-6 dropperfuls Mineral Essence, and 1-2 oz. Sulfurzyme. Administer combination orally at least 2 times daily. Avoid inflammation from sugars and grains (non-GMO feeds) and avoid using topical products containing xenoestrogens such as propylene glycol in common horse hair care products.

Inhalation: Diffuse any suggested oils. Most recommended is Frankincense.

Other: Use Tender Tush, Animal Scents Ointment, ClaraDerm, Ortho Ease Massage Oil, or Ortho Sport Massage Oil for essential oil dilution and application.

Moon Blindness (Equine Recurrent Uveitis/ERU, Periodic Ophthalmia)

This is one of the most common eye conditions for horses. It usually occurs after an initial incidence of acute uveitis. The symptoms flare and subside in cycles. However, during the periods of time when the seemingly active inflammation subsides, there is still some mild irritation. If left untreated, this syndrome may cause permanent blindness.

There are several causes, including bacteria, viruses, protozoa, parasites, and noninfectious conditions (including trauma). Treatment should reduce inflammation, minimize discomfort, and preserve vision. Consult a veterinary health professional to rule out serious, underlying causes, prevent serious complications, and avoid contraindications.

Recommendations

Singles: Copaiba, Frankincense, Blue Cypress, Cypress, Helichrysum, Palo Santo, Cistus, Clove, Roman Chamomile, German Chamomile, Hyssop, Juniper, Lavender, Lemongrass, Lemon Myrtle, Ravintsara, Sacred Frankincense, Oregano, Mountain Savory, Basil, Ocotea, Melissa, Orange

Blends: Thieves, Exodus II, Melrose, ImmuPower, The Gift, Mendwell, Infect Away, PuriClean, Egyptian Gold, Raven, Longevity, M-Grain, Aroma Life, Australian Blue, DiGize, EndoFlex, Purification, Sacred Mountain

Nutritionals: NingXia Red, Organic Dried Wolfberries, Sulfurzyme, Mineral Essence, Life 9, ImmuPro, MultiGreens

Additional: Rose Ointment

Application and Usage

Topical: Apply Frankincense or Sacred Frankincense with 5 drops each Copaiba, Cypress, and Cistus. Place around the orbit of the eye so as to not drip in the eye. Layer on top of the oils with Rose Ointment. Repeat 2-4 times daily. If autoimmune is present, apply Copaiba and EndoFlex to thyroid, kidney, and adrenal area 2 times daily. Administer Raindrop Technique 3 times per week.

Ingestion & Oral: Administer orally 10 drops each ImmuPower, Copaiba, and Exodus II with 2 oz. NingXia Red, 1 oz. Sulfurzyme, 4-6 dropperfuls Mineral Essence, and 4 MultiGreens 2 times daily. If autoimmune, administer orally 5 drops EndoFlex 2 times daily. If leptospirosis is the cause, use oils such as Thieves, Exodus II, and Oregano in feeds.

Inhalation: Diffuse Purification, Thieves, Orange, Sacred Mountain, Stress Away Roll-On, Peace & Calming, Gentle Baby.

Other: Apply Rose Ointment as needed.

Muscular Conditions

Muscle is a very specialized tissue that allows the body to move as a whole and allows parts of the body to move with respect to each other. The muscle cells or fibers are grouped in bundles. They have a good blood supply to provide the oxygen and nutrients they need to function efficiently and to also remove the waste products of muscle metabolism.

There are several types of muscle, but it is striated or skeletal muscle that composes the muscles concerned with movement and that is attached to bones by tendons. Muscles can also be attached to ligaments, cartilage, fascia, and skin. If problems are chronic, look for imbalanced mineral levels on food intake and check for imbalanced hooves.

Recommendations

Singles: Copaiba, Lavender, Basil, Marjoram, Cedarwood, Peppermint, Helichrysum, Lemongrass, Lemon, Orange, Tangerine, Lime, Grapefruit, Rosemary, Wintergreen, Elemi, Clove, Idaho Blue Spruce, Northern Lights Black Spruce, Idaho Balsam Fir, Cypress, Eucalyptus Globulus, Juniper, Blue Cypress, Dorado Azul, Mountain Savory

Blends: Mendwell, Trauma Life, Aroma Siez, Deep Relief Roll-On, PanAway, Relieve It, Release, M-Grain, Longevity, Cool Azul, Australian Blue, En-R-Gee, Transformation, RutaVaLa, RC, Valor, Valor II, Peace & Calming, Purification, Stress Away Roll-On

Nutritionals: NingXia Red, Sulfurzyme, PowerGize, Super C Chewable, Mineral Essence, AgilEase, BLM, OmegaGize[3], MindWise, MultiGreens, Life 9, Power Meal

Additional: Cool Azul Sports Gel, Cool Azul Pain Relief Cream, Regenolone Moisturizing Cream, Cel-Lite Magic Massage Oil, Relaxation Massage Oil, Ortho Sport Massage Oil, Ortho Ease Massage Oil

Application and Usage

Topical: Apply any combination of suggested oils and layer over top with Regenolone Moisturizing Cream, Ortho Sport Massage Oil, Ortho Ease Massage Oil, generously applying on location 2-4 times daily. Apply Raindrop Technique as needed.

Ingestion & Oral: Administer orally 1-2 oz. NingXia Red, 4-6 dropperfuls Mineral Essence, 1-2 oz. Sulfurzyme, and 1-2 Life 9 at least 2 times daily.

Inhalation: Diffuse Peace & Calming, Purification, Cedarwood, Stress Away Roll-On, and any citrus oils.

Other: Use Cool Azul Sports Gel or Cool Azul Pain Relief Cream. Also try Regenolone Moisturizing Cream, Cel-Lite Magic Massage Oil, and Relaxation Massage Oil. If the area involved is large, use Ortho Sport Massage Oil or Ortho Ease Massage Oil instead of Cool Azul Sports Gel or Cool Azul Pain Relief Cream.

Navicular Syndrome

Navicular disease is responsible for a large percentage of chronic forelimb lameness in horses. Several factors are involved, which makes pinpointing an exact cause difficult. It begins as pressure to the area and gradually progresses to reduced blood supply to the navicular bone, ligament, joint, bursa, and tendon. It generally afflicts mature horses.

The long-term prognosis is poor, but treatment may extend the life of the horse. Treatment will focus on trimming, proper shoeing, rest, and pain management.

Consult a veterinary health professional to rule out serious underlying causes, prevent serious complications, and avoid contraindications. Feed low-starch and low-carb food, with NO sweet feed at all.

Recommendations

Singles: Clove, Copaiba, Helichrysum, Lavender, Lemongrass, Marjoram, Idaho Balsam Fir, Cypress, Blue Cypress, Lemon, Orange, Tangerine, Lime, Grapefruit, Idaho Blue Spruce, Northern Lights Black Spruce, Wintergreen, Basil, Vetiver, Tsuga, Palo Santo, Black Pepper, Cedarwood

Blends: Aroma Life, Cool Azul, Deep Relief Roll-On, Believe, Aroma Siez, Longevity, M-Grain, Thieves, Relieve It, PanAway, Valor, Valor II, Sacred Mountain, Trauma Life, Peace & Calming, Stress Away Roll-On

Nutritionals: NingXia Red, Sulfurzyme, PowerGize, Mineral Essence, AgilEase, BLM, Life 9

Additional: Cool Azul Gel, Cool Azul Pain Relief Cream, Ortho Sport Massage Oil, Ortho Ease Massage Oil, Cel-Lite Magic Massage Oil, Regenolone Moisturizing Cream

Application and Usage

Topical: Apply any combination of at least 5 suggested oils 2-4 times daily on location or on entire leg if needed. Also apply oils on all four legs down into heel bulbs 2 times daily for additional support.

Apply Regenolone Moisturizing Cream, Cool Azul Pain Relief Cream, Ortho Sport Massage Oil, or Ortho Ease Massage Oil over the top of applied oils. Apply Valor or Valor II on poll and drip along spine 1 time daily for proper structural communication and emotional support. Administer the Raindrop Technique with Copaiba and Cool Azul.

Ingestion & Oral: Administer orally 1-2 oz. NingXia Red, 4-6 dropperfuls Mineral Essence, 1-2 oz. Sulfurzyme, and 1-2 Life 9 at least 2 times daily.

Inhalation: Diffuse Peace & Calming, Stress Away Roll-On, Lavender, Sacred Mountain, Cedarwood, or any citrus oils.

Other: Use the following individually or layer with chosen oils: Cool Azul Gel, Cool Azul Pain Relief Cream, Ortho Sport Massage Oil, Ortho Ease Massage Oil, or Cel-Lite Magic Massage Oil.

Nervous System Disorders

These may be caused by infection, injury, inflammation, heavy metals, poisoning, nutritional deficiencies, cancer, degenerative diseases, and metabolic disorders. Some injuries to the nervous system may take 24 to 48 hours to manifest.

Spinal injuries may range from mild to severe, and the results range from appearing "drunk," to limb weakness, to loss of bladder control, to paralysis.

Some metabolic disorders that may show neurological signs include low blood sugar, kidney failure, and liver disease. Consult your veterinarian for diagnosis and treatment options. Feed low-starch and low-carb food, with NO sweet feed at all. Check for mineral imbalances as well.

Recommendations

Singles: Copaiba, Helichrysum, Juniper, Frankincense, Sacred Frankincense, Elemi, Nutmeg, Wintergreen, Roman Chamomile, German Chamomile, Rosemary, Valerian, Cypress, Blue Cypress, Basil, Dorado Azul, Geranium

Blends: Cool Azul, PanAway, Deep Relief Roll-On, JuvaCleanse, Tranquil Roll-On, Relieve It, Peace & Calming, Peace & Calming II, Aroma Life, Clarity, Brain Power, Transformation

Nutritionals: OmegaGize[3], MindWise, Mineral Essence, NingXia Red, Sulfurzyme, Life 9, Super B, NingXia Nitro, PD 80/20

Veterinarian Tips and Suggestions

Nervous System Disorders

Progessence Plus:

Progesterone and its precursor compound pregnenolone are synthesized in the central nervous system by glial cells and appear to play roles in neurotransmission, helping signals get from one nerve to another. The central nervous system includes the brain, optic nerves, and spinal cord. Progesterone is synthesized by Schwann cells in the peripheral nervous system, the network that connects the nerves of the central system to the rest of the body, where it promotes myelin formation during nerve regeneration.

PD 80/20 is a supplement that contains pregnenolone, which protects cerebral function and protects against neuronal damage during injury. It is also a memory enhancer and cellular repairer—particularly of brain and nerve tissues.

Application and Usage

Topical: Apply Valor or Valor II on poll and drip along spine 1 time daily for proper structural communication and emotional support. Apply 2-3 suggested oils combined with Copaiba, Helichrysum, and Cypress and apply to affected area and on poll 2-4 times daily. Administer the Raindrop Technique 3-4 times per week; use only cool towels (heat aggravates nerve tissue).

Ingestion & Oral: Administer orally 1-2 oz. NingXia Red, 4-6 dropperfuls Mineral Essence, 1-2 oz. Sulfurzyme, and 1-2 Life 9 at least 2 times daily. For additional support, add 1 PD 80/20 with 4 OmegaGize[3] to oral regimen.

Inhalation: Diffuse Peace & Calming, Juniper, Sacred Frankincense, Cedarwood, Lavender, Stress Away Roll-On, and any citrus oil.

Additional: Progessence Plus, Ortho Ease Massage Oil, Ortho Sport Massage Oil, Cool Azul Pain Relief Cream, Cool Azul Sports Gel, and Cel-Lite Magic Massage Oil

Other: Layer the following products individually or with suggested oils: Progessence Plus, Ortho Ease Massage Oil, Ortho Sport Massage Oil, Cool Azul Pain Relief Cream, Cool Azul Sports Gel, and Cel-Lite Magic Massage Oil.

Onchocerciasis (Neck Threadworm, Ventral Midline Dermatitis)

This is an equine disease caused by the parasitic worm *Onchocerca cervicalis*. The horse contracts the worms after being bitten by a midge or gnat carrying the larvae. The best prevention is by repelling biting insects. Consult a veterinary health professional to treat acute cases and to prevent serious complications.

Recommendations

Singles: Tarragon, Tea Tree, Black Pepper, Peppermint, Patchouli, Oregano, Lemongrass, Ocotea, Thyme, Idaho Balsam Fir, Copaiba

Blends: DiGize, AromaEase, Longevity, Thieves, ParaGize, Purification, Deep Relief Roll-On, PanAway, Believe, Cool Azul

Nutritionals: ParaFree, Inner Defense, Life 9, NingXia Red, Sulfurzyme, Mineral Essence, OmegaGize³, MindWise

Additional: Ortho Ease Massage Oil, Ortho Sport Massage Oil, Cool Azul Sports Gel

Application and Usage

Topical: Liberally apply Purification and DiGize with 2-3 additional oils, 3-4 times daily on location. If the horse is sore, apply Cool Azul Sports Gel. Add Peppermint and/or Thyme to Ortho Sport Massage Oil or Ortho Ease Massage Oil to help the horse cope with the intense itching that often occurs with this infection. Use Equine Raindrop Technique 3-4 times per week. Also include neck area when administering the Raindrop Technique and add DiGize. **For Pain:** Deep Relief Roll-On, PanAway, Idaho Balsam Fir, Believe, Cool Azul, Copaiba.

Ingestion & Oral: Administer orally 15 drops each DiGize, ParaGize, Black Pepper, and Peppermint 2-3 times daily. Or administer the following supplements combined 2 times daily: 4 ParaFree, 1-2 oz. NingXia Red, 4-6 dropperfuls Mineral Essence, and 1-2 oz. Sulfurzyme.

Inhalation: Diffuse DiGize, Tarragon, Thieves, or Purification with Peppermint.

Other: Layer with oils or apply individually Ortho Ease Massage Oil, Ortho Sport Massage Oil, or Cool Azul Sports Gel. Administer OmegaGize³ and MindWise orally to provide Omega 3's for skin repair.

Veterinarian Tips and Suggestions

Pain

Recipe 1: General Pain
- Copaiba with any chosen oil intensifies it. Also, try Wintergreen with any Spruce and Cypress on joints.

Recipe 2: Wounds
- Copaiba, Helichrysum, Lavender, and/or Trauma Life

Recipe 3: Aches
- PanAway, Copaiba, and Trauma Life

Recipe 4: Dental Pain
- Copaiba, Myrrh, and Clove or Thieves

Pain

Pain in horses can be difficult to recognize, unless a caregiver is familiar with the specifics of how horses respond to the presence of pain or discomfort. Most veterinary pain assessments are based on published species-specific behaviors.

Even with these guidelines, it's difficult to assess levels of pain and severity. It is more challenging to recognize and diagnose animals in chronic pain than those with acute and traumatic pain. Consult a veterinary health professional to rule out serious underlying causes.

Recommendations

Singles: Copaiba, Clove, Helichrysum, Lavender, Lemongrass, Marjoram, Palo Santo, Peppermint, Pine, Idaho Blue Spruce, Northern Lights Black Spruce, Idaho Balsam Fir, Wintergreen, Elemi, Cypress, Oregano, Frankincense, Sacred Frankincense, Dorado Azul, Orange

Blends: Cool Azul, PanAway, Deep Relief Roll-On, Tranquil Roll-On, Aroma Life, Aroma Siez, JuvaCleanse, Longevity, M-Grain, Thieves, Relieve It, Release, DiGize, Sacred Mountain, Evergreen Essence, En-R-Gee, Believe, Transformation, Trauma Life, Stress Away Roll-On, Harmony, Gentle Baby

Nutritionals: OmegaGize³, MindWise, AgilEase, PowerGize, Mineral Essence, Super C Chewable, Organic Dried Wolfberries, NingXia Red, Sulfurzyme, Life 9

Additional: Ortho Sport Massage Oil, Ortho Ease Massage Oil, Relaxation Massage Oil, Regenolone Moisturizing Cream, Cool Azul Sports Gel, Cool Azul Pain Relief Cream

Application and Usage

Topical: Apply selected oils neat (undiluted) to area of pain multiple times daily. Rest and ice affected area. Also administer the Raindrop Technique daily to every other day as needed to mitigate pain.

Ingestion & Oral: Reduce sugars and starches to reduce inflammation.

Administer the following oils orally: Copaiba, Idaho Balsam Fir, Wintergreen, PanAway, DiGize. Administer orally any listed oil up to 40 drops total 2 times daily. Also administer orally 1-2 oz. NingXia Red, 4-6 dropperfuls Mineral Essence, 1-2 oz. Sulfurzyme, 1 AgilEase or BLM as needed.

Inhalation: Diffuse Stress Away Roll-On, Peace & Calming, Lavender, Frankincense, Sacred Mountain, Trauma Life, Harmony, Orange, and Gentle Baby.

Other: Also try Ortho Sport Massage Oil, Ortho Ease Massage Oil, Relaxation Massage Oil, Regenolone Moisturizing Cream, Cool Azul Sports Gel, and Cool Azul Pain Relief Cream. Support both the painful area and any compensatory limbs to cope with any overuse symptoms.

Papilloma Virus (see Ear Fungus or Sarcoids/Warts)

Parasites (see also Deworming)

Regular deworming is an important part of health care. All horses will have worms, which potentially can cause serious damage to the bowel, leading to digestive problems (such as colic) or damage to the associated blood vessels, leading to problems with circulation.

Other symptoms associated with heavy worm burdens include loss of condition or weight, poor appetite, diarrhea anaemia, and filling of the legs. Several types of worms affect horses: small strongyles, large strongyles, pinworms, tapeworms, ascarid worms, and bots.

Modern conventional wormers are very effective, and their value should not be underestimated. Stool samples should be tested every 3-4 months to check the parasite burden of the horse. Use the following protocol and once a year use a conventional wormer to be sure to get worms that may not have been in the stool sample but may have been in the lungs.

Recommendations

Singles: Internal parasites: Peppermint, Tarragon, Fennel, Tea Tree, Patchouli, Copaiba, Orange, Lemongrass

Blends: Internal parasites: DiGize, Thieves, JuvaCleanse, AromaEase, ImmuPower, Purification, Melrose

Nutritionals: ICP, ParaFree, Life 9

Additional: Thieves Household Cleaner

Application and Usage

Topical: Skin parasites: Wash with Thieves Household Cleaner diluted with water and 20 drops each DiGize, Copaiba, Melrose, Purification, and Orange or Lemongrass. Administer Raindrop Technique every other day until symptoms subside.

Ingestion & Oral: Internal parasites: Administer 20 drops each of 3 chosen oils. Try also 1 oz. ICP and 3 Life 9 2 times daily. Also try 4 ParaFree 2 times daily.

Inhalation: Diffuse Purification or DiGize.

Pelodera (Dermatitis)

This relatively rare, but year-round, skin condition is due to larval invasion by the nematode *Pelodera strongyloides*. Usually, these infect the horse through contact with damp bedding or muddy conditions. The larvae typically invade wounded skin, rather than healthy skin, and remain relatively confined to the area of exposure. Consult your veterinary health professional to confirm diagnosis and to prevent secondary infection or complications.

Recommendations

Singles: Tarragon, Clove, Eucalyptus Globulus, Hyssop, Lemongrass, Tea Tree, Melaleuca Quinquenervia, Mountain Savory, Ocotea, Peppermint, Thyme, Palmarosa, Idaho Tansy

Blends: Thieves, DiGize, AromaEase, Melrose, Purification, PuriClean

Nutritionals: NingXia Red, Mineral Essence, Sulfurzyme

Additional: Cool Azul Sports Gel, Thieves Dentarome Ultra Toothpaste, Animal Scents Shampoo, Thieves Household Cleaner, Thieves Spray

Application and Usage

Topical: Apply your chosen suggested oils 3 times daily directly on location. Administer Raindrop Technique every other day. Bathe horse with Animal Scents Shampoo and then rinse with 1 capful Thieves

Household Cleaner in 1 gallon water with several drops of chosen oil added. Also spot cover trouble areas with Thieves Dentarome Ultra Toothpaste.

Ingestion & Oral: Top dress feed 2 times daily with 2 oz. NingXia Red, 1 oz. Sulfurzyme, and 20 drops DiGize.

Inhalation: Diffuse Purification or DiGize.

Other: As a carrier use Cool Azul Sports Gel or Thieves Dentarome Ultra Toothpaste. Wash with and apply as needed Animal Scents Shampoo, Thieves Household Cleaner, and Thieves Spray.

Periostitis (Bucked Shins)

This is the result of high-strain, repetitive motion that takes place during aggressive training. Too much stress on the cannon bone causes greater compression on the front than on the back surface, and this results in small tears on the periosteum.

The best treatment is prevention for this condition, with trainers regulating the frequency and intensity of sessions to protect the horse from overwork at a young age. Pain and inflammation management is also key. Consult your veterinary health professional.

Recommendations

Singles: Idaho Balsam Fir, Lemongrass, Palo Santo, Pine, Wintergreen, Clove, Copaiba, Peppermint, Helichrysum, Cypress, Basil, Northern Lights Black Spruce, Idaho Blue Spruce, Dorado Azul, Myrrh, Lavender

Blends: Deep Relief Roll-On, PanAway, Cool Azul, Relieve It, Believe, Evergreen Essence, Aroma Siez, Trauma Life, Mendwell, Transformation, M-Grain, Release, Stress Away Roll-On, DiGize

Nutritionals: AgilEase, BLM, NingXia Red, Mineral Essence, Sulfurzyme, OmegaGize[3], MindWise

Additional: Ortho Sport Massage Oil, Ortho Ease Massage Oil, Relaxation Massage Oil, Regenolone Moisturizing Cream, Cool Azul Sports Gel, Cool Azul Pain Relief Cream

Application and Usage

Topical: Layer 3-5 drops of chosen oils, beginning with Copaiba, over front of cannon bones and finishing with Peppermint. Finish with recommended carrier oils, ointments, or massage oils over top of applied oils. Repeat 3 times daily.

Ingestion & Oral: Combine 2 oz. NingXia Red and 2

oz. Sulfurzyme with 20 drops each Copaiba, DiGize, and Wintergreen. Administer combination orally 2 times daily.

Other: Also try Ortho Sport Massage Oil, Ortho Ease Massage Oil, Relaxation Massage Oil, Regenolone Moisturizing Cream, Cool Azul Sports Gel, and Cool Azul Pain Relief Cream. Support both the painful area and any compensatory limbs to cope with any overuse symptoms.

Pigeon Fever (False Strangles, Pigeon Breast, Dryland Distemper)

This is a form of lymphangitis, following infection with *Corynebacterium pseudotuberculosis* bacteria. Symptoms include pus-filled sores in the chest, contagious acne, painful inflammation, small lumps or swellings, slow-healing sores, and infected mammary glands.

Your veterinary health professional may take samples from the sores to confirm infection. Treatment will focus on pain relief, rest using hot packs, poultices, or hydrotherapy.

Recommendations

Singles: Cassia, Cinnamon Bark, Laurus Nobilis, Copaiba, Lemongrass, Tea Tree, Melaleuca Quinquenervia, Mountain Savory, Oregano, Helichrysum, Thyme, Cypress, Rosemary, Tangerine, Peppermint

Blends: Thieves, Exodus II, Christmas Spirit, Purification, The Gift, Egyptian Gold, DiGize, En-R-Gee, ImmuPower, Melrose, M-Grain, Relieve It, Raven, R.C.

Nutritionals: Inner Defense, MultiGreens, NingXia Red, Mineral Essence, Super C Chewable, Longevity Softgels, Life 9, Sulfurzyme, MindWise

Additional: Thieves Dentarome Ultra Toothpaste, Cel-Lite Magic Massage Oil, Animal Scents Ointment, Tender Tush, Rose Ointment

Application and Usage

Topical: Combine Copaiba and Laurus Nobilis with any other oil and administer topically multiple times daily. Administer Raindrop Technique every day or every other day.

Ingestion & Oral: Combine 1-2 oz. NingXia Red, 4-6 dropperfuls Mineral Essence, and 1-2 oz. Sulfurzyme. Administer combination orally at least 2 times daily. Feed horse hay cubes soaked in suggested oils of choice or administer 30 drops each of Copaiba, Exodus II, Mountain Savory, and Rosemary orally combined with NingXia Red. Remove inflammatory grains and sugars from diet. Flavor second water bucket with Peppermint or citrus oil of choice.

Other: Apply oils of choice and then apply over top poultice with Thieves Dentarome Ultra Toothpaste or Cel-Lite Magic Massage Oil to draw out infection. As situation improves, apply Animal Scents Ointment, Tender Tush, or Rose Ointment intermittently and then encourage the area to dry.

Potomac Fever (see also Colic, Laminitis)

An acute enterocolitis syndrome that results in mild colic, fever, and diarrhea caused by *Neorickettsia risticii*. It may occur in spring, summer, and early fall. This may cause laminitis, a severe complication in 20-30 percent of cases.

Consult a veterinary health professional to prevent serious complications and avoid contraindications. Work with your veterinarian; horses may need IV therapy for fluids due to severe dehydration from diarrhea.

Recommendations

Singles: Clove, Oregano, Copaiba, Ocotea, Mountain Savory, Tea Tree, Melaleuca Quinquenervia, Thyme, Cassia, German Chamomile, Palmarosa, Peppermint, Rosemary, Cinnamon Bark, Eucalyptus Blue, Eucalyptus Globulus, Black Pepper, Helichrysum, Lemongrass, Cypress

Blends: Thieves, Exodus II, ImmuPower, Longevity, Melrose, AromaEase, Cool Azul, Egyptian Gold, Light the Fire, DiGize, The Gift, Purification, Raven, R.C.

Nutritionals: NingXia Red, Mineral Essence, Sulfurzyme, Life 9, Digest & Cleanse, Super C Chewable, AgilEase, BLM

Additional: Thieves Household Cleaner

Application and Usage

Topical: Apply 5-6 of any suggested oils topically along spine and on the front and back of entire leg. Administer Raindrop Technique daily as needed.

Ingestion & Oral: Administer orally 10-15 drops each of any 4-5 suggested oils starting with Copaiba and ending with Peppermint. Also administer orally 1-2 oz. NingXia Red, 4-6 dropperfuls Mineral Essence, 1-2 oz. Sulfurzyme, and 1-2 Life 9 at least 2 times daily. Additional supplements that can be added to

the above combination include Digest & Cleanse, Super C Chewables, and AgilEase or BLM.

Inhalation: Diffuse any of the suggested oils, specifically Thieves, Melrose, and Purification for best results.

Other: Use undiluted Thieves Household Cleaner for topical cleaning, stalls, footbaths, tack, etc.

Proud Flesh (see also Cuts)

Proud flesh occurs as a wound heals, when a pink granulated tissue begins to form and overflow the wound. This will eventually keep the wound from healing. It occurs on the lower legs and usually occurs around joint areas. Pressure wraps may help in addition to the oils below.

Recommendations

Singles: Helichrysum, Frankincense, Sacred Frankincense, Myrrh, Patchouli, Lavender, Geranium, Sacred Sandalwood, Royal Hawaiian Sandalwood, Copaiba, Palmarosa, Cypress, Eucalyptus Globulus, Hyssop, Lemongrass, Laurus Nobilis, Ginger, Cedarwood, Cistus, Blue Cypress

Blends: Aroma Life, 3 Wise Men, Australian Blue, Infect Away, Mendwell, PuriClean, Gentle Baby, Melrose, Believe, DiGize, Dream Catcher, Egyptian Gold, EndoFlex, En-R-Gee, Exodus II, Gratitude, ImmuPower, JuvaFlex, M-Grain, Purification, Release, The Gift, Valor, Valor II, Thieves

Nutritionals: NingXia Red, Sulfurzyme, MultiGreens, Life 9, Mineral Essence, OmegaGize^3, MindWise

Additional: Ortho Ease Massage Oil, Ortho Sport Massage Oil, Animal Scents Ointment, Rose Ointment, Tender Tush, ClaraDerm, Cel-Lite Magic Massage Oil, Regenolone Moisturizing Cream, Cool Azul Pain Relief Cream, Thieves Dentarome Ultra Toothpaste, Thieves Household Cleaner, Animal Scents Shampoo

Application and Usage

Topical: Starting with Copaiba, apply any chosen oils liberally 2-3 times daily. Wash area with Thieves Household Cleaner and Animal Scents Ointment.

Ingestion & Oral: Administer orally 1-2 oz. NingXia Red, 4-6 dropperfuls Mineral Essence, 1-2 oz. Sulfurzyme, and 1-2 Life 9 at least 2 times daily.

Inhalation: Diffuse any suggested oils, primarily Thieves, Lavender, Purification, or any citrus oil.

Other: Apply any of the following on location or

layer with accompanying suggested oil: Ortho Ease Massage Oil, Ortho Sport Massage Oil, Animal Scents Ointment, Rose Ointment, Tender Tush, ClaraDerm, Cel-Lite Magic Massage Oil, Regenolone Moisturizing Cream, Cool Azul Pain Relief Cream, Thieves Dentarome Ultra Toothpaste, Thieves Household Cleaner, Animal Scents Shampoo.

Puncture Wound

Wounds to the bottom of the foot most often occur when the horse steps on a sharp object(s) such as a nail. Puncture wounds have been classified according to the depth of penetration (superficial and deep) and location on the foot.

Recommendations

Singles: Hyssop, Wintergreen, Copaiba, Angelica, Basil, Bergamot, Black Pepper, Blue Cypress, Cistus, Clove, Cypress, Dorado Azul, Elemi, Eucalyptus Globulus, Eucalyptus Blue, Eucalyptus Radiata, Frankincense, German Chamomile, Helichrysum, Hinoki, Hong Kuai, Idaho Balsam Fir, Juniper, Laurus Nobilis, Lavender, Lemon, Lemongrass, Marjoram, Tea Tree, Manuka, Melissa, Mountain Savory, Myrrh, Myrtle, Ocotea, Palmarosa, Patchouli, Palo Santo, Ravintsara, Rosemary, Sacred Frankincense, Thyme, Xiang Mao

Blends: Valor, Trauma Life, Melrose, Raven, En-R-Gee, White Angelica, AromaEase, Aroma Siez, Australian Blue, Believe, Citrus Fresh, Clarity, DiGize, Egyptian Gold, Evergreen Essence, Exodus II, Gathering, Gentle Baby, Gratitude, Grounding, Harmony, Highest Potential, ImmuPower, Longevity, Melrose, M-Grain, Purification, Raven, R.C., Believe It, The Gift, Thieves, Infect Away, Mendwell, ParaGize, PuriClean, RepelAroma, T-Away

Nutritionals: NingXia Red, Life 9, Sulfurzyme, Inner Defense, Mineral Essence.

Additional: Thieves Household Cleaner, Animal Scents Ointment, Rose Ointment, Tender Tush, Thieves Dentarome Ultra Toothpaste

Application and Usage

Topical: Rub 2-3 drops Trauma Life on inner part of ears and on the chest. Valor or Valor II apply to the heel bulbs and all 4 hooves. Also apply Valor or Valor II to poll, withers, and sacrum. Draw hand with Valor or Valor II from withers downward toward chest area. Put White Angelica on forehead every morning. Use Thieves Household Cleaner to clean affected area by using 2 cups water to 1 capful Thieves Household Cleaner. Dry area thoroughly. Before dressing, apply 4-5 drops of any combination of suggested oils directly into wound. Layer over top of applied oils with Animal Scents Ointment or any other suggested product. Administer Raindrop Technique 2 times per week.

Inhalation: Diffuse any suggested oil but especially Lemon, Thieves, and Purification.

Ingestion & Oral: Administer orally 1-2 oz. NingXia Red, 4-6 dropperfuls Mineral Essence, 1-2 oz. Sulfurzyme, 1-2 Life 9, 20 drops each Copaiba and Thieves, and any other 2-3 suggested oils 2 times daily. Also supplement with Inner Defense.

Other: Layer applied oils with Animal Scents Ointment, Rose Ointment, Tender Tush, and Thieves Dentarome Ultra Toothpaste. When using En-R-Gee, rub up inside of front legs where they attach to the body and use 2-3 drops over the adrenal glands on back.

Pythiosis

While technically not a fungus, pythiosis is caused by a fungus-like organism (*Pythium insidiosum*). Pythiosis begins as a disease of the skin and tissues immediately beneath. Wounds associated with pythiosis often resemble proud flesh and are extremely pruritic (marked by itching). Without proper treatment, pythiosis will progress into the tendons, joints, and bones, frequently proving fatal for horses. In pythiosis, the necrotic cores are distinct from the surrounding tissue, and a seropurulent discharge from the sinuses is prominent.

> *Veterinarian Tips and Suggestions*
>
> ## Pythiosis
>
> This protocol has been used by many in the flooded areas of Texas, etc., with successful results.
>
> Add 30 ml Australian Blue and 15 ml Dill to an 8-oz. bottle of V-6 Vegetable Oil Complex; then use at a rate of 5 ml daily on feed. Do not use sweet feed or high sugar/ starch feed as they are both proinflammatory. Perform Raindrop Technique daily for 3 days in a row, then weekly until veterinarian says the condition is resolved.

Recommendations

Singles: Mountain Savory, Tea Tree, Manuka, Lemongrass, Blue Cypress, Thyme, Oregano, Palmarosa, Basil, Black Pepper, Cinnamon Bark, Cassia, Clove, Patchouli, Helichrysum, Hinoki, Copaiba

Blends: Thieves, Exodus II, Melrose, Longevity, DiGize

Nutritionals: NingXia Red, Life 9, Mineral Essence, MultiGreens, Sulfurzyme, Inner Defense, MindWise, OmegaGize[3], Super C Chewable

Additional: Thieves Spray, Thieves Dentarome Ultra Toothpaste, Ortho Sport Massage Oil, Ortho Ease Massage Oil, Cool Azul Sports Gel, Cool Azul Pain Relief Cream

Application and Usage

Topical: Apply generously on location any 4-5 suggested oils 2-3 times daily.

Ingestion & Oral: Combine 20 drops each of Copaiba, Palmarosa, DiGize, and Exodus II with 1-2 oz. NingXia Red, 4-6 dropperfuls Mineral Essence, 1-2 oz. Sulfurzyme, and 1-2 Life 9. Administer combination orally at least 2 times daily.

Inhalation: Diffuse equal parts in high concentration Hinoki, Copaiba, Purification, and Lavender in an enclosed area.

Other: Use Thieves Household Cleaner for additional topical application, cleaning stalls, and the area where the horse will be turned out. Use Thieves Spray and Thieves Dentarome Ultra Toothpaste for poulticing, along with Thyme and Peppermint added to quiet the itching. Use Ortho Sport Massage Oil, Ortho Ease Massage Oil, Cool Azul Sports Gel, or Cool Azul Pain Relief Cream to layer over applied oils.

Queensland Itch

This is a condition resulting from the bites of the Culicoides midge. Some horses have a hypersensitivity to the bites and respond with an allergic reaction to the protein molecules present in the saliva of the gnat. Consult a veterinary health professional to prevent secondary infection and complications.

The biting midges, "no-see-ums," or punkies belong to the family Ceratopogonidae. The most common biting midges are Culicoides spp. They are associated with aquatic or semiaquatic habitats; for example, mud or moist soil around streams, ponds, and marshes. Biting midges are tiny gnats (1–3 mm long) and, like black flies, inflict painful bites and suck the blood of their hosts, both people and livestock.

Recommendations

Singles: Copaiba, Tea Tree, Rosemary, Citronella, Lemongrass, Myrtle, Eucalyptus Globulus, Orange, Hinoki, Melissa, Basil, Ocotea, Idaho Tansy, Roman Chamomile, German Chamomile

Blends: Melrose, Purification, Infect Away, ParaGize, PuriClean, RepelAroma

Nutritionals: NingXia Red, Sulfurzyme, Mineral Essence, Life 9

Additional: Thieves Household Cleaner

Application and Usage

Topical: Apply chosen oils liberally to affected areas; then cover with Animal Scents Ointment 2-3 times daily.

Ingestion & Oral: Administer orally 10-20 drops each Copaiba, Purification, and Hinoki with 1-2 oz. NingXia Red, 4-6 dropperfuls Mineral Essence, 1-2 oz. Sulfurzyme, and 1-2 Life 9 at least 2 times daily.

Inhalation: Diffuse Copaiba, Purification, and Hinoki.

Other: Wash area with Thieves Household Cleaner.

Rabies

This is an emergency situation. If exposed to rabies, immediately notify your veterinarian and use the suggestions below to boost the immune system while awaiting diagnosis. Be extremely careful to avoid any bites and cover all of your open cuts and/or wounds. Rabies is a viral disease that causes inflammation of the brain and can be transmitted from animals to humans. Rabies develops usually after 20-60 days of a bite, but not less than 10 days. Horses become strange in behavior, followed by frothing and salivation. The horse will not eat or drink and will slowly become paralyzed. Death is possible within 10 days of onset of disease.

Recommendations

Singles: Copaiba, Hyssop, Black Pepper, Helichrysum, Thyme

Blends: Thieves, Purification, DiGize, ParaGize, Longevity

Nutritionals: Rehemogen, ParaFree, Life 9, JuvaPower, NingXia Red, Detoxzyme

Additional: Thieves Household Cleaner

Application and Usage

Topical: Wash any affected area on the horse with a strong solution of Thieves Household Cleaner. Dry area and apply Copaiba, Hyssop, Purification, Black Pepper, Helichrysum, and Longevity liberally on bite or affected area 2 times or more daily.

Ingestion & Oral: Administer orally 20 drops each of Copaiba, Helichrysum, Longevity, and Thyme with 3-4 ParaFree, 1 Life 9, 1 scoop JuvaPower, 1 oz. NingXia Red, and 3 Detoxzyme at least 4 times daily.

Inhalation: Diffuse Thieves, Purification, or DiGize in enclosed barn.

Other: Spray the whole area, including the ground in the barn, with ½ cup Thieves Household Cleaner in 1 gallon of water.

Rain Rot (Rain Scald, Mud Fever, Pastern Dermatitis)

This is caused by the same bacteria, *Dermatophilus congolensis*, that causes Mud Fever in horses. There are two types: the winter form and the summer form. The winter form is usually more severe, due to the length of the coat. Transmission occurs through contact with other animals, ticks, and biting flies.

Though it usually heals on its own, rain rot should generally be treated immediately to prevent it from spreading. Consult a veterinary health professional to confirm diagnosis and prevent complications.

Recommendations

Singles: Helichrysum, Lavender, Lemongrass, Tea Tree, Melaleuca Quinquenervia, Palmarosa, Dorado Azul, Ravintsara, Clove, Copaiba

Blends: Melrose, Thieves, Purification, Raven, Egyptian Gold, Exodus II, Infect Away, Mendwell, PuriClean, DiGize

Nutritionals: Sulfurzyme, OmegaGize³, NingXia Red, Mineral Essence, Life 9, MultiGreens

Additional: Animal Scents Shampoo, Animal Scents Ointment, Thieves Household Cleaner, ClaraDerm, Tender Tush, Rose Ointment, Thieves Dentarome Ultra Toothpaste

Application and Usage

Topical: Apply Lavender, Copaiba, and Purification with any suggested oils on location 2-4 times daily. Use ClaraDerm, Animal Scents Ointment, Tender Tush, Rose Ointment to layer; then use Thieves Dentarome Ultra Toothpaste to poultice the area and create a barrier while drying out the tissues. Administer Raindrop Technique two times weekly, taking care to not get hot oils in open sores.

Ingestion & Oral: Administer 20 drops each DiGize, Melrose, and Copaiba in NingXia Red.

Inhalation: Diffuse Lavender, Melrose, or Purification in enclosed area.

Other: Check mineral levels; improper copper, zinc, and selenium make it easier to have rain rot appear. In early or less severe cases, simply remove the scabs by bathing the animals with Animal Scents Shampoo, Thieves Household Cleaner, or Animal Scents Ointment to soften the scabs. Unlike most skin conditions, rain rot is not itchy, but it can be painful to the touch.

Respiratory Conditions (Bronchitis, Pneumonia, Bronchopneumonia)

Bronchitis is inflammation of the bronchi, the larger air passages that carry air to the lungs. Often this problem will lead to pneumonia, a serious respiratory condition involving inflammation of the lungs. If both the bronchi and lungs are affected, the condition is referred to as bronchopneumonia.

Bacteria, mainly Streptococci, occasionally Bordetella or Pasteurella, are often involved, although viruses, migrating parasites, and foreign material accidentally entering the lungs can also be responsible.

Remember that bacterial respiratory infections are contagious and acquired by inhalation through contact with horses carrying these bacteria or from infected nasal discharges.

Where foals are affected, the infection can enter by the navel at birth, with bacteria gaining access to the lungs via circulation. In such cases, abscesses may form in the lungs, causing significant damage and taking months to resolve. In general, foals are more often affected than adult horses, particularly where management is poor and where ventilation is inadequate. Stress has also been implicated.

Symptoms include difficulty in breathing, rapid respiration, fever, lack of appetite, and depression. A cough or nasal discharge is also sometimes present. Always seek veterinary help as pneumonia and related conditions are nearly always serious.

Recommendations

Singles: Idaho Blue Spruce, Hyssop, Oregano, Dorado Azul, Copaiba, Northern Lights Black Spruce, Cedarwood, Ravintsara, Eucalyptus Globulus, Eucalyptus Radiata, Eucalyptus Blue, Goldenrod, Lemongrass, Mountain Savory, Tea Tree, Black Pepper, Helichrysum, Wintergreen, Peppermint

Blends: Raven, Thieves, R.C., Exodus II, Egyptian Gold, Melrose, Purification

Nutritionals: NingXia Red, Life 9, Sulfurzyme, Mineral Essence, Inner Defense, Rehemogen

Application and Usage

Topical: Apply Oregano, Copaiba, Cedarwood, Dorado Azul, Idaho Blue Spruce, and Peppermint liberally on throat and chest area 2 times daily. Apply the Raindrop Technique every day for 5 days, then every 3 days until completely resolved.

Ingestion & Oral: Administer orally 20 drops each of any suggested oil with 4 Inner Defense, 10 dropperfuls Rehemogen, 1-2 oz. NingXia Red, 4-6 dropperfuls Mineral Essence, 1-2 oz. Sulfurzyme, and 1-2 Life 9 at least 2 times daily.

Inhalation: Diffuse Copaiba, Ravintsara, Idaho Blue Spruce, and any other suggested oil, except Oregano, in an enclosed area. Also try holding equine nebulizer to nostrils for 20 minutes 2 times daily using 3-5 drops of each oil.

Rhodococcal Pneumonia (Rhodococcus Equi)

This is the most serious cause of pneumonia in foals 1-4 months old. It is not the most common, but it is the most serious. Manure from pneumonic foals is the major source of virulent bacteria. The bacteria live in the dust, and this easily exposes young foals to infection.

Foals should be kept in well-ventilated, dust-free environments, avoiding dirt paddocks and crowded conditions. Manure from infected foals should be removed and composted away from animals. Consult a veterinary health professional to effectively diagnose, prevent serious complications, and avoid contraindications.

Recommendations

Singles: Eucalyptus Blue, Dorado Azul, Eucalyptus Globulus, Oregano, Basil, Copaiba, Ravintsara

Blends: Thieves, Raven, Exodus II, Egyptian Gold, DiGize, ImmuPower

Nutritionals: NingXia Red, MultiGreens, Life 9, Mineral Essence, Inner Defense

Additional: Thieves Household Cleaner, Thieves Waterless Hand Purifier, Thieves Spray, Thieves Laundry Detergent

Application and Usage

Topical: Apply Raven, Copaiba, Thieves, and DiGize to the stomach and chest area multiple times daily. Apply the Raindrop Technique every day to every other day until ailment is resolved.

Ingestion & Oral: Administer orally 20 drops each of Thieves, Exodus II, Ravintsara, Copaiba, and DiGize with 1 oz. NingXia Red and 2 dropperfuls Mineral Essence 4 times daily.

Inhalation: Diffuse Thieves, Exodus II, and/or Ravintsara. Using an equine nebulizer would be the best application, if the foal is quiet enough to wear it. A draped stall for diffusion would be a good alternative. This application can be applied even to newborn foals who have been born into an environment that contains Rhodococcus.

Other: Rhodococcus is extremely contagious. EVERYTHING that the affected animal has come into contact with needs to be washed with a combination of Thieves Household Cleaner with Exodus II. This includes all living spaces, barn area, blankets, tack, etc. Also use Thieves Waterless Hand Purifier, Thieves Laundry Detergent, and Thieves Spray. People who are in the presence of the virus should take all precautions to wash clothing, shoes, etc., as well as hands or any other area that has come into contact with an affected animal.

Ringbone

This is a bone growth in the pastern or coffin joint of a horse. As the disease progresses, the growth encircles the bones. High ringbone is found on the lower part of the large pastern bone or the upper part of the small pastern bone. Low ringbone affects the lower part of the small pastern bone or the upper part of the coffin bone. It usually affects the front legs, but occasionally, it may affect the hind legs. Unless caused by a trauma or injury, the condition is degenerative.

Treatment focuses on pain management and balancing/supporting the horse with proper shoeing. Consult a veterinary health professional for managing the condition in the long term.

Recommendations

Singles: Clove, Wintergreen, Helichrysum, Lavender, Lemongrass, Marjoram, Palo Santo, Peppermint, Pine, Idaho Blue Spruce, Northern Lights Black Spruce, Vetiver, Copaiba, Idaho Balsam Fir, Cypress, Sacred Frankincense, Thyme, Orange

Blends: PanAway, Relieve It, Cool Azul, M-Grain, Deep Relief Roll-On, Believe, R.C., DiGize, Peace & Calming, Stress Away Roll-On

Nutritionals: Sulfurzyme, PowerGize, NingXia Red, MindWise, OmegaGize³, Mineral Essence, Life 9

Additional: Ortho Sport Massage Oil, Ortho Ease Massage Oil, Cool Azul Sports Gel, Cool Azul Pain Relief Cream, Regenolone Moisturizing Cream

Application and Usage

Topical: Apply PanAway many times daily; this is the most effective. Also can apply 3-5 drops Copaiba and at least 3 essential oils to affected area. A combination of R.C. and Wintergreen has been used successfully to dissolve bone spurs; apply 2 times daily. Raindrop Technique helps the spinal area cope with inflammation and imbalanced movement; administer 2 times weekly.

Ingestion & Oral: Combine 1-2 oz. NingXia Red, 4-6 dropperfuls Mineral Essence, 1-2 oz. Sulfurzyme, and 1-2 Life 9. Administer combination orally at least 2 times daily. Add 20 drops Copaiba with 10 drops Wintergreen and 10 drops DiGize to help with pain. Check for imbalanced calcium and magnesium levels.

Inhalation: Diffuse Thyme, Orange, Peace & Calming, Stress Away Roll-On, and Lavender.

Other: Try applying Ortho Sport Massage Oil, Ortho Ease Massage Oil, Cool Azul Sports Gel, Cool Azul Pain Relief Cream, or Regenolone Moisturizing Cream for both the leg with the ringbone and the compensatory leg.

Ringworm

A skin condition that can affect any horse is ringworm, but it is most commonly found in young or debilitated horses. Like lice, this fungus can be spread horse to horse or via shared use of grooming equipment or tack.

Ringworm may start out as only one or two patches but quickly spreads. One-time grooming is not recommended, as brushing may spread the fungus to other parts of the body. Youngsters, senior horses, and horses in poor condition are more likely to be affected.

Recommendations

Singles: Tea Tree, Melaleuca Quinquenervia, Myrrh, Copaiba, Blue Cypress, Roman Chamomile, Palmarosa, Geranium, Idaho Blue Spruce, Northern Lights Black Spruce, Peppermint, Ocotea, Hyssop, Lemongrass, Rosemary, Mountain Savory

Blends: Melrose, Purification, Thieves, Australian Blue, Exodus II, Egyptian Gold, The Gift, Infect Away, ParaGize, PuriClean

Nutritionals: NingXia Red, Rehemogen, K&B, Sulfurzyme, MultiGreens, Mineral Essence, Life 9

Additional: Thieves Household Cleaner, Thieves Waterless Hand Purifier, Animal Scents Shampoo, Animal Scents Ointment, Tender Tush, ClaraDerm, Ortho Sport Massage Oil, Ortho Ease Massage Oil

Application and Usage

Topical: Wash affected area with Thieves Household Cleaner, dry, and apply chosen oils directly to affected area. Ringworm can be transferable, so be sure to wash your hands with Thieves Household Cleaner and Thieves Waterless Hand Purifier.

Ingestion & Oral: Administer the following supplements to lessen the horse's reaction to the fungus. Combine 4 MultiGreens, 1-2 oz. NingXia Red, 4-6 dropperfuls Mineral Essence, 1-2 oz. Sulfurzyme, and 1-2 Life 9. Administer combination orally at least 2 times daily.

Inhalation: Diffuse Melrose, Purification, Thieves, and Tea Tree.

Other: Use Thieves Household Cleaner to clean the affected area as well as the horses' stalls. Wash the affected animal with Animal Scents Shampoo. Layer applied oils with Animal Scents Ointment, Tender Tush, ClaraDerm, Ortho Sport Massage Oil, or Ortho Ease Massage Oil.

Rotavirus Diarrhea

Diarrhea can be a serious condition in horses, due to their size and the volume of their gastrointestinal tract. They dehydrate quickly from the condition, and this may result in serious complications.

The signs of diarrhea may be obvious, but they may also be symptoms of a larger issue. Consequently, they may be mistaken for something other than rotavirus. Rotaviral signs include lethargy, colic, loss of appetite, and profuse, watery, foul-smelling diarrhea. It usually occurs in foals younger than two-months-old.

The virus destroys the cell lining of the small intestine, causing poor absorption of nutrients. It is highly contagious among foals, so strict hygiene and quarantine practices should be observed. There is a vaccine for pregnant mares to protect the newborn foal. Consult a veterinary health professional to diagnose and prevent serious complications.

Once your veterinarian has confirmed it is rotavirus causing the diarrhea, the foal may be given fluids intravenously to prevent further dehydration. Probiotics may help the foal digest its feed. Nutritional supplements may be administered to make up for the malabsorption. Electrolytes may be given to help replace minerals and salts lost through diarrhea. With proper treatment, it's unlikely that the foal will suffer any lasting damage. But left untreated, the dehydration and lack of nutrition can lead to death.

Herbs such as slippery elm and marshmallow, along with the amino acid glutamine, will also speed gut healing. Canned pumpkin is a wonderful food that is high in vitamin C, which helps the gut to recover.

Recommendations

Singles: Eucalyptus Blue, Dorado Azul, Eucalyptus Globulus, Hyssop, Peppermint, Lemongrass, Palmarosa, Lemon, Oregano, Laurus Nobilis, Copaiba, Ocotea, Melissa, Ravintsara, Helichrysum, Myrrh, Cistus, Tea Tree, Melaleuca Quinquenervia

Blends: Thieves, Exodus II, Egyptian Gold, DiGize, AromaEase, ImmuPower, Purification

Nutritionals: Mineral Essence, NingXia Red, MultiGreens, Power Meal, Detoxzyme, Life 9, Allerzyme, MightyZymes, Super C Chewable, Sulfurzyme

Additional: Thieves Household Cleaner, Thieves Waterless Hand Purifier, Thieves Laundry Detergent, Thieves Spray

Application and Usage

Topical: Apply Ravintsara, Copaiba, and DiGize on stomach area and spine. Administer Raindrop Technique daily on spine as needed, adding ImmuPower.

Ingestion & Oral: Administer orally 10 drops each of Copaiba, Cistus, DiGize, Ravintsara, Exodus II, 2 MultiGreens, 2 Detoxzyme, 1-2 oz. NingXia Red, 4-6 dropperfuls Mineral Essence, 1-2 oz. Sulfurzyme, and 1-2 Life 9 2-4 times daily. Syringe directly into horse's mouth if needed.

Inhalation: Diffuse Thieves, ImmuPower, Exodus II, Purification, Eucalyptus Blue, Tea Tree, Melaleuca Quinquenervia, and Egyptian Gold, to assist quarantine measures.

Other: Rotavirus is extremely contagious. EVERYTHING that the affected animal has come into contact with needs to be washed with a combination of Thieves Household Cleaner with Exodus II. This includes all living spaces, barn area, blankets, tack, etc. Also use Thieves Waterless Hand Purifier, Thieves Laundry Detergent, and Thieves Spray. People who are in the presence of the affected animal should take all precautions to wash clothing, shoes, etc., as well as hands or any other area that has come into contact with an affected animal.

Saddle Sore (*see* Girth Galls)

Sarcoids

Sarcoids are skin tumors that primarily affect horses younger than four years old. Sarcoids account for roughly 40 percent of all tumors in horses and are suspected to be caused by both papillomavirus and retrovirus.

Sarcoids are considered only partially malignant. They don't generally spread to other areas, but they may become locally invasive. They frequently occur in horse families and may be found anywhere on the body. General types are warty, fibroblastic, flat, mixed verrucous, and fibroblastic. Consult a veterinary health professional to rule out serious, underlying causes.

Recommendations

Singles: Mountain Savory, Palo Santo, Peppermint, Ravintsara, Thyme, Melissa, Cassia, Tea Tree, Melaleuca Quinquenervia, Eucalyptus Blue, Eucalyptus Globulus, Basil, Grapefruit, Sacred Frankincense, Frankincense, Myrrh, Melissa, Laurus Nobilis, Hyssop, Cistus, Copaiba

Blends: Thieves, Longevity, Exodus II, Egyptian Gold, Australian Blue, ImmuPower, R.C., Melrose, Purification, Trauma Life, Raven, The Gift

Nutritionals: Organic Dried Wolfberries, NingXia Red, MultiGreens, ImmuPro, Sulfurzyme, Inner Defense, PowerGize, Life 9, Mineral Essence

Additional: Animal Scents Ointment, Tender Tush, Thieves Household Cleaner, Animal Scents Shampoo

Application and Usage

Topical: Apply Copaiba with 3 or more suggested oils on location 3 times daily. Administer Raindrop Technique 2 to 3 times weekly, adding ImmuPower, Thieves, and Melrose.

Ingestion & Oral: Administer orally 10-15 drops each Longevity, Copaiba, Mountain Savory, and Ravintsara with 1-2 oz. NingXia Red, 4-6 dropperfuls Mineral Essence, 1-2 oz. Sulfurzyme, and 1-2 Life 9 at least 2 times daily.

Other: Each case responds differently. Sometimes rotating the type of essential oil used every week or so works best. Use Animal Scents Ointment and Tender Tush as carriers for essential oils. Use Thieves Household Cleaner or Animal Scents Shampoo to wash the affected area. If an area becomes raw or irritated, apply Animal Scents Ointment or Tender Tush over top of oils applied directly on location.

Scours (see Diarrhea)

Scratches

Scratches is a common skin condition of horses and is known by a variety of different names, depending on the geographical location. It occurs predominantly during the damp and wet winter months. It is seen in all breeds but often affects those animals with long hair around the fetlock area and those kept in poor or unhygienic conditions.

Areas that are usually affected include the bulbs of the heels, as well as the fetlock and pastern regions of the legs. The back legs are more often affected than the front. The condition is usually started by damage to the skin from local contamination by dirt or grit. This adheres to the skin in the damp and wet conditions, causing irritation and inflammation, particularly to the skin and underlying tissues at the back of the pastern and heel region.

Recommendations

Singles: Tea Tree, Eucalyptus Globulus, Eucalyptus Radiata, Eucalyptus Blue, Mountain Savory, Lemongrass, Patchouli, Rosemary, Helichrysum

Blends: Thieves, Purification, Melrose, Exodus II, Raven, DiGize, Egyptian Gold, ImmuPower, R.C.

> ### 🐎 Veterinarian Tips and Suggestions
>
> ## Screw Worm
>
> There is a round worm called a bore or screw worm that bores into the spine of a horse (especially wild horses). It will cause a huge boil-like abscess on the spine. When lanced, a larva worm will come out of that abscess. Sometimes the abscess will actually break open and ooze.
>
> Pour Thieves into the hole to flush out the larva worm and then fill the hole with a mixture of 12 drops of Melrose and 5 drops of Mountain Savory.

Nutritionals: NingXia Red, Mineral Essence, Sulfurzyme, Life 9

Additional: Thieves Household Cleaner, Thieves Spray

Application and Usage

Topical: Scabby material should be gently eased off the skin by gentle washing with Thieves Household Cleaner. Spray Thieves Spray directly on affected area and let soak. Dry the area and apply any 2 suggested essential oils. Repeat 2 times daily if possible.

Ingestion & Oral: With severe cases, administer orally 20 drops each of Melrose, DiGize, ImmuPower, Thieves, and Exodus II with 1-2 oz. NingXia Red, 4-6 dropperfuls Mineral Essence, 1-2 oz. Sulfurzyme, and 1-2 Life 9 at least 2 times daily.

Inhalation: Diffuse Purification, Thieves, Melrose, ImmuPower, Tea Tree, and Lemongrass.

Other: For stalled horses, always ensure that the bedding is clean and dry. When wet, try to dry your horse's legs. Brushing out any mud and grit and trimming the feathers off pasterns will make this easier and much less of a problem. Avoid clipping the legs completely. Avoid contact with wet and muddy areas and keep susceptible horses out of the rain as much as possible.

Seedy Toe (see White Line Disease)

Sesamoiditis

The ligaments in the fetlock keep the horse's sesamoid bone in place. When a competitive horse strains during racing, the stress on the fetlock may cause the ligaments to tear. This condition may be best managed with a focus on pain, inflammation reduction, and rest. Relaxing the tendons may help to prevent the condition in competition animals. Consult a veterinary health professional to rule out serious, underlying causes, prevent serious complications, and avoid contraindications.

Recommendations

Singles: Peppermint, Copaiba, Clove, Idaho Balsam Fir, Helichrysum, Lavender, Lemongrass, Marjoram, Palo Santo, Pine, Wintergreen, Cypress, Idaho Blue Spruce, Northern Lights Black Spruce, Blue Cypress, Cedarwood, Orange

Blends: PanAway, Deep Relief Roll-On, Cool Azul, Longevity, Aroma Siez, Relieve It, M-Grain, Trauma Life, Stress Away Roll-On, Peace & Calming

Nutritionals: AgilEase, BLM, PowerGize, MegaCal, Mineral Essence, Super C Chewable, NingXia Red, Organic Dried Wolfberries, Sulfurzyme, Life 9

Additional: Ortho Ease Massage Oil, Animal Scents Ointment, Regenolone Moisturizing Cream, Cool Azul Pain Relief Cream

Application and Usage

Topical: Apply by layering 3-4 drops of chosen oils over entire area, followed with Regenolone Moisturizing Cream or Cool Azul Pain Relief Cream over top.

Ingestion & Oral: Administer orally 1 AgilEase or BLM, 1-2 oz. NingXia Red, 4-6 dropperfuls Mineral Essence, 1-2 oz. Sulfurzyme, and 1-2 Life 9 at least 2 times daily. Syringe directly into the horse's mouth if needed. Finely ground gelatin can also provide raw materials for the body to rebuild these tissues.

Inhalation: Diffuse Stress Away Roll-On, Peace & Calming, Idaho Balsam Fir, Cedarwood, and Orange.

Other: When treating horses with sensitive skin, you may need Ortho Ease Massage Oil or Animal Scents Ointment over the top after oils are applied. Check for imbalanced mineral levels, especially copper and zinc.

Splints (see also Sesamoiditis)

In horses, splints are a calcification along the splint bone, causing temporary lameness. This may be the result of injury, strain from aggressive training, faulty conformation, or improper shoeing. The condition is most common in younger horses. Usually, the lameness will subside once the injured area ossifies. In rare situations,

the outgrowth of bone will encroach on the suspensory ligament or carpometacarpal articulation.

Anti-inflammatory treatment and rest are key for recovery. Consult your veterinary health professional about options and to determine the severity of the case. Splints are common and can result in nothing more than a slight blemish on a horse's leg, but they may also cause severe and problematic lameness.

Recommendations

Singles: Copaiba, Idaho Balsam Fir, Idaho Blue Spruce, Cypress, Northern Lights Black Spruce, Wintergreen, Peppermint, Helichrysum, Eucalyptus Radiata, Ocotea

Blends: PanAway, Trauma Life, Valor, Relieve It, R.C., Deep Relief Roll-On, Purification, Stress Away Roll-On, Peace & Calming, Sacred Mountain, Gentle Baby

Nutritionals: NingXia Red, Mineral Essence, Sulfurzyme, Life 9, AgilEase, BLM

Additional: Ortho Sport Massage Oil, Regenolone Moisturizing Cream, Ortho Ease Massage Oil, Cool Azul Sports Gel, Cool Azul Pain Relief Cream

Application and Usage

Topical: Apply 2-4 times daily Copaiba, R.C., Wintergreen, and Cypress with any combination of suggested oil(s) directly over the affected area; then cover lightly with Regenolone Moisturizing Cream or Cool Azul Pain Relief Cream.

Ingestion & Oral: Administer orally 1 AgilEase or BLM, 1-2 oz. NingXia Red, 4-6 dropperfuls Mineral Essence, 1-2 oz. Sulfurzyme, and 1-2 Life 9 at least 2 times daily.

Inhalation: Diffuse R.C., Purification, Stress Away Roll-On, Peace & Calming, Sacred Mountain, Trauma Life, or Gentle Baby.

Other: Apply Ortho Sport Massage Oil, Regenolone Moisturizing Cream, Ortho Ease Massage Oil, Cool Azul Gel, and/or Cool Azul Pain Relief Cream directly to affected area. Apply independently or layer with suggested oils.

Strangles

Strangles is a contagious infection caused by *Streptococcus equi*. The incubation period ranges from 3-14 days, with the first symptom being fever in the 103º-106ºF range. Mucoid nasal discharge, lethargy, and submandibular lymphadenopathy follow the fever. The swollen lymph nodes make it difficult for the horse to swallow. In rare cases, the infection may lead to brain abscess.

Diagnosis is confirmed by bacterial culture from abscesses or nasal swabbing. The suffering animals should be kept in warm, dry, and dust-free environments. Warm compresses help to ease lymphadenopathy. Consult your veterinary health professional to confirm diagnosis, monitor effectiveness of treatment, and prevent complications.

Recommendations

Singles: Ravintsara, Melissa, Cassia, Cinnamon Bark, Laurus Nobilis, Copaiba, Lemongrass, Tea Tree, Melaleuca Quinquenervia, Mountain Savory, Oregano, Helichrysum, Cypress, Peppermint, Ocotea, Basil, Eucalyptus Globulus, Lemon, Orange, Tangerine, Grapefruit

Blends: Thieves, Exodus II, Purification, ImmuPower, Egyptian Gold

Nutritionals: Inner Defense, MultiGreens, NingXia Red, Mineral Essence, Longevity Softgels, Life 9, Sulfurzyme

Additional: Thieves Dentarome Ultra Toothpaste, Thieves Household Cleaner, Thieves Waterless Hand Purifier, Thieves Laundry Detergent, Thieves Spray

---

Veterinarian Tips and Suggestions

Strangles

- Perform the Raindrop Technique with Thieves.
- Apply 4 drops Thieves on the inside of the bottom lip (for a large horse, 8 drops).
- After 2 hours repeat Raindrop Technique with Oregano (or Plectranthus Oregano) and Thyme. Also, put 2 drops Oregano and 2 drops Thyme on the inside of the bottom lip (for a large horse, 4 drops each).
- Repeat the last two steps every 2 hours until the horse begins to improve. As the horse continues to improve, change treatments to every 4 hours, every 6 hours, and then morning and night.

Application and Usage

Topical: Apply Exodus II, Ravintsara, Copaiba, Eucalyptus Globulus directly onto swollen areas 4-6 times daily. Administer Raindrop Technique daily with ImmuPower and Copaiba. Apply 10-20 drops DiGize on stomach area.

Ingestion & Oral: Administer orally 20 drops each of Exodus II, Melissa, Ravintsara, and Copaiba with 1-2 oz. NingXia Red, 4-6 dropperfuls Mineral Essence, 1-2 oz. Sulfurzyme, 1-2 Life 9, 2-4 times daily. Also feed the affected animal hay cubes soaked in any combination of suggested oils. Limit the horse's consumption of inflammatory grains and sugars. Provide the horse a second water bucket flavored with Peppermint or Citrus of choice.

Veterinarian Tips and Suggestions

Swollen Sheath

Geldings and stallions occasionally suffer from swollen sheath with an abscess and infection. It can be caused by:

- Eating hay too rich in protein. Ideal levels of protein should be 12 to 15 percent, and alfalfa hay can have protein as high as 26 percent.
- Not extracting the penis and letting it clean off.

Treatment

- Put on rubber gloves.
- Clean inside the sheath and remove debris with soap and water. Use a half cap of Thieves Household Cleaner diluted in a half gallon of water.

- Clean outside the sheath by applying Myrrh oil and Rosemary with Tea Tree. The ratio is 15 drops of Myrrh, 15 drops of Rosemary, and 10 drops of Tea Tree.
- Clean and disinfect morning and night until infection and swelling subside.
- Maintenance: The sheath should be cleaned out once a month. Make sure the horse is fed adequate water and grass hay and gets sufficient exercise to increase circulation.
- Perform a Raindrop Technique with Oregano (or Plectranthus Oregano), Thyme, and Mountain savory every 3 to 6 months.

Inhalation: Diffuse in a draped stall or use an equine nebulizer; sterilize after each use. Diffuse Thieves, Exodus II, and Ravintsara together.

Other: Use oils of choice; then poultice with Thieves Dentarome Ultra Toothpaste to draw infection out on abscesses and lymphatics or use heat packs to bring abscesses to fruition. Strangles is extremely contagious. EVERYTHING that the affected animal has come into contact with needs to be washed with a combination of Thieves Household Cleaner with Exodus II. This includes all living spaces, barn area, blankets, tack, etc. Also use Thieves Waterless Hand Purifier, Thieves Laundry Detergent, and Thieves Spray. People who are in the presence of the virus should take all precautions to wash clothing, shoes, etc., as well as hands or any other area that has come into contact with an affected animal.

Tendon Conditions

Most tendon injuries are caused by minor repetitive stress, rather than heavy stress all at once. They occur most often in horses that aren't properly exercised. Also at risk are horses without adequately trimmed hooves and horses with poor pastern conformation.

Tendon injuries usually indicate the fiber bundles in the tendon have been overly stretched and/or ruptured. To catch tendon injuries at the onset, examine the tendons before every session of heavy training or intense competition for tenderness or swelling. Consult a veterinary health professional to prevent serious complications.

Recommendations

Singles: Peppermint, Copaiba, Clove, Idaho Balsam Fir, Helichrysum, Lavender, Lemongrass, Marjoram, Palo Santo, Pine, Idaho Blue Spruce, Northern Lights Black Spruce, Wintergreen, Frankincense, Cypress, Blue Cypress, Myrrh, Dorado Azul, Patchouli

Blends: PanAway, Deep Relief Roll-On, Cool Azul, Aroma Siez, Relieve It, M-Grain, Melrose, Evergreen Essence, Christmas Spirit, Sacred Mountain, Transformation

Nutritionals: NingXia Red, Mineral Essence, Sulfurzyme, Life 9, AgilEase, BLM, PowerGize, Super C Chewables, Organic Dried Wolfberries

Additional: Ortho Ease Massage Oil, Ortho Sport Massage Oil, Cool Azul Sports Gel, Cool Azul Pain Relief Cream, Animal Scents Ointment, Dentarome Ultra Toothpaste, Regenolone Moisturizing Cream

Application and Usage

Topical: Select 3-4 suggested oils and layer with Copaiba, one over the other, 3 times daily. Cover oils with Regenolone Moisturizing Cream, Animal Scents Ointment, or Cool Azul Pain Relief Cream.

Ingestion & Oral: Administer orally 20 drops Copaiba with 1-2 oz. NingXia Red, 4-6 dropperfuls Mineral Essence, 1-2 oz. Sulfurzyme, 1-2 Life 9, and 5 AgilEase or BLM at least 2 times daily. Finely ground gelatin can also provide raw materials for the body to rebuild these tissues. Check for imbalanced mineral levels, especially copper and zinc.

Other: Use Lemongrass if a ligament is also involved. If scurf (dry, flaky skin) develops, use with V-6 and administer Raindrop Technique, adding Copaiba. Use Thieves Dentarome Ultra Toothpaste as a poultice, adding Peppermint and Copaiba to draw down heat and inflammation. Use Ortho Ease Massage Oil, Ortho Sport Massage Oil, or Cool Azul Sports Gel for all compensatory legs. If oils or supplies are limited, use Animal Scents Ointment over top on all four legs.

Tetanus (Lockjaw)

Generally, tetanus is preventable through vaccine. If an animal cannot be vaccinated or an owner has reason to believe the animal would be at risk, then the horse must be protected at every turn. Horses actually have *Clostridium tetani* in their digestive tract, and the bacterial spores are omnipresent in soil.

As with other animals, horses contract it through puncture wounds, open lacerations, surgical incisions, or exposed tissues. Consult a veterinary health professional to discuss options and prevent serious complications.

Recommendations

Singles: Copaiba, Helichrysum, Laurus Nobilis, Juniper, Tea Tree, Melaleuca Quinquenervia, Mountain Savory, Cinnamon Bark, Cassia

Blends: Exodus II, Thieves, Egyptian Gold, DiGize, Longevity, Clarity, ImmuPower, Melrose, Purification

Nutritionals: Life 9, NingXia Red, Mineral Essence, Sulfurzyme, AgilEase, PowerGize, Inner Defense

Additional: Thieves Household Cleaner

Application and Usage

Topical: Clean area with undiluted Thieves Household Cleaner prior to applying oils. Apply 10 drops each of DiGize, Copaiba, and Thieves on stomach area 2 times daily. Administer Raindrop with ImmuPower once daily.

Ingestion & Oral: Combine 1-2 oz. NingXia Red, 4-6 dropperfuls Mineral Essence, 1-2 oz. Sulfurzyme, 1-2 Life 9, and 2 Inner Defense. Administer combination orally at least 2 times daily. For additional support, administer 20 drops each of Helichrysum and Exodus II and 10 drops each of Longevity and Copaiba. This can be added to the supplement dosage or can be administered independently.

Inhalation: Diffuse Exodus II, Thieves, Egyptian Gold, Melrose, and Purification.

Other: Use Thieves Household Cleaner directly on affected area or to clean the horse's area.

Thrush

In horses, thrush is deterioration of the frog with secondary infection stemming from the central and collateral sulci. The anaerobic bacterium *Fusobacterium necrophorum* thrives in wet conditions and affects horses with untrimmed frog areas. In the absence of proper hoof hygiene, the infection takes hold and produces tenderness and pain in the foot while releasing a black, foul-smelling exudate.

Prevention is best with thrush. Horses should be kept in stalls with clean, dry shavings and have their feet picked on a regular basis. If a horse contracts thrush, it is best to move it to a clean, dry area. Wash the affected hoof with an antiseptic foot wash, then clean and trim the frog area. Consult a veterinary health professional to prevent serious complications and avoid contraindications.

Recommendations

Singles: Cassia, Cinnamon Bark, Eucalyptus Globulus, Lemongrass, Tea Tree, Melaleuca Quinquenervia, Mountain Savory, Ocotea, Oregano, Black Pepper, Thyme, Copaiba, Clove, Hong Kuai, Patchouli, Ravintsara, Sage, Blue Cypress

Blends: Thieves, Exodus II, Melrose, Purification, R.C., Raven, Egyptian Gold, The Gift, DiGize, Valor, Valor II

Veterinarian Tips and Suggestions

Thrush

Wash the affected hoof with Thieves Household Cleaner and trim away the dead and diseased frog tissue. Work with your veterinarian and/or farrier if more than surface tissue is involved.

Check for mineral imbalances such as copper and zinc, since shortfalls can affect the horse's immune system.

Feed low sugars, low starch (starches in grains break down to sugar) intake, as higher levels feed inflammation in the body.

Soak the foot in Thieves Household Cleaner for 20 minutes. When the foot is dry, add essential oils to the frog and sulcus area and then pack with Thieves Dentarome Ultra Toothpaste to seal the oils and protect and dry out the frog. The area may be sensitive to hotter oils.

Keep the foot out of the mud and spread dry, clean shavings in stall area to help dry out the hoof.

Nutritionals: NingXia Red, Mineral Essence, Sulfurzyme, Life 9

Additional: Thieves Household Cleaner, Thieves Spray

Application and Usage

Topical: Wash area with undiluted Thieves Household Cleaner; let soak for up to 30 minutes. Wash and dry area; then apply copious amounts of chosen oils 3 times daily. Administer Raindrop Technique 2-3 times per week.

Ingestion & Oral: Administer orally 10 drops each Copaiba, DiGize, and Melrose with 1-2 oz. NingXia Red, 4-6 dropperfuls Mineral Essence, 1-2 oz. Sulfurzyme, 1-2 Life 9 at least 2 times daily. Syringe directly into the horse's mouth if needed.

Other: Use Valor or Valor II with the Raindrop Technique to boost the immune system and support any compensation the horse adopts due to pain or tenderness. Remove all of the damaged, necrotic infected tissue after using essential oils. Clean the horse's area and the affected area regularly with Thieves Household Cleaner and Thieves Spray.

Tick Bites

Ticks are blood-sucking parasites that attach themselves to animals and people. As they feed, ticks can transmit many diseases. Skin wounds caused by ticks can lead to secondary bacterial infections and screwworm infestations.

Recommendations

Singles: Peppermint, Citronella, Eucalyptus Globulus, Lemongrass, Melissa, Ocotea, Cassia, Oregano, Thyme, Tea Tree, Melaleuca Quinquenervia, Hyssop, Geranium, Patchouli, Clove, Ravintsara, Copaiba

Blends: Melrose, Purification, Thieves, Egyptian Gold, Longevity, Infect Away, Mendwell, RepelAroma, Raven, ImmuPower, Exodus II, Clarity, DiGize

Nutritionals: Longevity Softgels, Inner Defense, NingXia Red, Mineral Essence, Sulfurzyme, Life 9

Additional: Ortho Ease Massage Oil, Ortho Sport Massage Oil, Cool Azul Sports Gel, Cel-Lite Magic Massage Oil, Thieves Spray, Thieves Waterless Hand Purifier, Animal Scents Ointment, Tender Tush, Rose Ointment

Application and Usage

Topical: Apply chosen oil directly to tick and gently remove to ensure you get the head; then reapply chosen oil. Use Animal Scents Ointment, Tender Tush, or Rose Ointment after applying oils if needed. Use Purification, Thieves, or Melrose directly on the bite many times throughout the next day. Administer Raindrop Technique 1 to 2 times per week.

Ingestion & Oral: Administer orally 10 drops Thieves, 10 drops Longevity, 1-2 oz. NingXia Red, 4-6 dropperfuls Mineral Essence, 1-2 oz. Sulfurzyme, and 1-2 Life 9 1 time daily during tick season.

Inhalation: Diffuse Melrose, Thieves, Purification, and Longevity.

Other: Remove the tick by using tweezers as close to the skin as possible, without squeezing the tick's contents into the bite. Drop into rubbing alcohol or save in a sealed plastic bag to take to authorities to ascertain its disease levels. Look for other ticks that may be embedded close by or in the mane, tail, belly, armpit, or groin areas. Use any of the following to coat the legs to deter ticks' adhesion: Ortho Ease Massage Oil, Ortho Sport Massage Oil, Cool Azul Sports Gel, or Cel-Lite Magic Massage Oil. For further prevention or treatment of affected area, use Thieves Spray and Thieves Waterless Hand Purifier.

Transporting (Shipping Fever)

A specified recovery interval should be part of the preshipment plan for horses making long journeys. For road journeys of 6 to 12 hours, a rest period of 1 day is likely to be sufficient. When horses travel longer than 12 hours by road or are transported by plane, a recovery period of 2 to 3 days should be planned.

Research at the University of California Davis reported that horses transported 24 hours by road in a commercial van in hot summer conditions clearly showed changes in physiological parameters. Higher levels of the stress hormone cortisol caused elevated ratios of two types of white blood cells that did not return to baseline during the 24-hour recovery process. The study by Carolyn Stall (UC-Davis) and Ann Rediek (Cal State-Fresno), both MS, PhD, stated that the least desirable confinement during transport was cross-tying. Horses cross-tied experienced larger increases of selected stress parameters than horses traveling without being tied; i.e., in box stalls.

Horses traveling long distances for performance events should arrive 5 to 6 days prior to the competition date to comply with medication withdrawal rules in the event of travel-associated illness. Horses with shipping fever might need 3 to 4 weeks to resume athletic activity.

Recommendations

Singles: Lavender, Cedarwood, Roman Chamomile, Palo Santo, Frankincense, Sacred Frankincense, Valerian, Vetiver, Ylang Ylang, Copaiba, Peppermint,

---

Veterinarian Tips and Suggestions

Transporting

Use Grounding essential oil to help horses feel connected to the earth while traveling. Acquaint animals ahead of time to the oil you want to use. This will calm stress during shipping in a nonstressful environment. If a horse smells Lavender each time it goes into a trailer and it had a stressful first event with Lavender in the trailer, the horse will remember its first experience and expect a stressful recurrence.

Support the horse's legs with Aroma Siez, Ortho Ease Massage Oil, Ortho Sport Massage Oil, Cool Azul Sports Gel, Cel-Lite Magic Massage Oil, and Relaxation Massage Oil. They use their legs to maintain their balance and can tire during long trailer rides.

Idaho Balsam Fir, Northern Lights Black Spruce, Geranium, Orange, Lemon, Tangerine, Grapefruit, Idaho Blue Spruce, Eucalyptus Globulus, Eucalyptus Radiata, Eucalyptus Blue, Wintergreen

Blends: Tranquil Roll-On, Peace & Calming, Peace & Calming II, Gentle Baby, Inner Child, Grounding, DiGize (to calm gut), Humility, Inspiration, 3 Wise Men, Sacred Mountain, Acceptance, Valor, Harmony, White Angelica, AromaEase, Stress Away Roll-On

Nutritionals: NingXia Red, Mineral Essence, Sulfurzyme, Life 9

Application and Usage

Topical: Use Valor on poll, withers, and sacrum. Rub auricular points on ears with Acceptance and/or Lavender and/or Peace & Calming. Administer Raindrop Technique 1 week prior to shipping and upon arrival at destination to boost the immune system. Apply Grounding to bulbs of feet and to stomach area. Apply Peace & Calming or Lavender to nose. Apply Orange oil to the chest.

Ingestion & Oral: Administer 10-20 drops of Lavender inside lower lip for calming effect. In cases with animals who have high anxiety, substitute Valerian for Lavender. Administer 10 drops each of DiGize and Copaiba to prevent gastric upset each day of travel and during competition.

Inhalation: Diffuse Lavender, Stress Away Roll-On, Cedarwood, any citrus oil, Valerian, Peace & Calming, or Acceptance.

Other: Ideally prepare the horse with the above protocol prior to approaching the vehicle.

Tumors

Cancer can be described as a growth disorder of cells. It begins when an apparently normal cell starts to grow in an uncontrolled and invasive way. The result is a ball of cells known as a tumor, which continues to expand in size. When the tumor involves connective tissue such as muscle, it is called a sarcoma.

Recommendations

Singles: Frankincense, Sacred Frankincense, Tsuga, Orange, Tangerine, Copaiba, Lavender, Ledum, Idaho Blue Spruce, Northern Lights Black Spruce, Sacred Sandalwood, Royal Hawaiian Sandalwood, Idaho Balsam Fir, Clove, Grapefruit

Blends: ImmuPower, Exodus II, 3 Wise Men, GLF, JuvaCleanse, Release, Egyptian Gold, Stress Away Roll-On, The Gift, Sacred Mountain

Nutritionals: NingXia Red, Mineral Essence, Sulfurzyme, Life 9, ImmuPro, Essentialzyme

Application and Usage

Topical: Apply copious amounts of Copaiba, Frankincense, and Sacred Frankincense with any suggested oil on location of tumor 2-4 times daily. Also apply Release over the tumor for additional support. Administer Raindrop Technique 3-4 times per week.

Ingestion & Oral: Administer orally 2 times daily 20 drops each of Frankincense or Sacred Frankincense, Copaiba, Tsuga, Orange or Grapefruit, Idaho Balsam Fir or Idaho Blue Spruce or Northern Lights Black Spruce, 3 oz. NingXia Red, 4-6 dropperfuls Mineral Essence, 1-2 oz. Sulfurzyme, 1-2 Life 9, 3 crushed ImmuPro, and 6 crushed Essentialzyme.

Inhalation: Diffuse Frankincense, Sacred Frankincense, Orange, Tangerine, Grapefruit, Idaho Blue Spruce, Northern Lights Black Spruce, ImmuPower, and Sacred Mountain.

Other: Change feed, improve mineral balance, or control high stress levels that have brought on the immune imbalance and allowed the disease to manifest. Feed no grains, high-sugar grasses, sugar treats, high-sugar fruit, or vegetables such as apples or carrots. Offer celery, cucumbers, hay cubes, romaine lettuce, fennel, pumpkin and its seeds, berries, watermelon rinds, cantaloupe rinds, and sunflower seeds.

Veterinarian Tips and Suggestions

Tumors/Cancer
(For Veterinarians Only)

Shave area near the tumor and have a licensed veterinarian inject Sacred Frankincense or Frankincense with a hypodermic syringe directly into the tumor. Only a licensed veterinarian should inject an animal using a needle.

Alternate with Clove oil every four days. Keep saturated with Sacred Frankincense or Frankincense. If the area is open, put a plug in the opening to hold the oil in the tumor cavity. Continue until the ailment is resolved.

Tying Up

This is the most common muscle condition in horses, caused by extended exercise or a diet change. The muscle groups along the back and rump will contract and not relax. The typical signs include immobility, stiff walking, sweating, and hard muscle contraction. A colloquial term for the condition is "Monday morning sickness," because it often happens to horses that train or work throughout the week and rest on the weekends. Consult your veterinarian about proper nutrition, type and amount of grain feed, as well as supplements, vitamins, or minerals that may need to be included or excluded.

Recommendations

Singles: Copaiba, Marjoram, Basil, Lavender, Peppermint, Wintergreen, Helichrysum, Cedarwood, Cypress, Black Pepper, Idaho Balsam Fir, Idaho Blue Spruce, Northern Lights Black Spruce, Lemongrass, Dorado Azul, Palo Santo, Rosemary, Roman Chamomile, Orange, Tangerine, Lemon

Blends: PanAway, Mendwell, Trauma Life, Aroma Siez, Transformation, En-R-Gee, Clarity, Gentle Baby, Relieve It, R.C., Valor, Valor II, Peace & Calming, Peace & Calming II

Nutritionals: NingXia Red, Mineral Essence, Sulfurzyme, Life 9

Additional: Ortho Sport Massage Oil, Ortho Ease Massage Oil, Regenolone Moisturizing Cream, Cool Azul Pain Relief Cream

Application and Usage

Topical: Apply Copaiba with at least 3-4 other chosen oils on location. Layer with Ortho Sport Massage Oil and Ortho Ease Massage Oil. Administer Raindrop Technique with Cedarwood, Copaiba, and Lavender applied between Marjoram and Wintergreen. Administer every 5-7 days.

Ingestion & Oral: Administer 1-2 oz. NingXia Red, 4-6 dropperfuls Mineral Essence, 1-2 oz. Sulfurzyme, 1-2 Life 9. Give an additional 3 oz. of NingXia Red and 4-6 dropperfuls Mineral Essence immediately after exercising or competing, as needed.

Inhalation: Diffuse Trauma Life, Roman Chamomile, Orange, Tangerine, Lemon, Peace & Calming, Peace & Calming II, and Lavender.

Other: Apply Ortho Sport Massage Oil, Ortho Ease Massage Oil, Regenolone Moisturizing Cream, Cool Azul Pain Relief Cream.

Vaccination Detoxification

After a vaccination, horses are prone to local muscle soreness or swelling, fatigue, fever, loss of appetite, lethargy, and reduced alertness. If the symptoms seem to last more than 36 hours, it is important to contact your veterinarian. It is doubly important to do so if you observe collapse, hives, colic, difficulty breathing, or continued swelling at the injection site several days after the vaccination.

Recommendations

Singles: Helichrysum, Cardamom, Copaiba, Clove, Black Pepper, Cypress, Citronella, Patchouli, Cedarwood, Lemon

Blends: GLF, ImmuPower, M-Grain, PanAway, JuvaCleanse, DiGize, M-Grain, Purification

Nutritionals: NingXia Red, Sulfurzyme, Mineral Essence, Life 9, Rehemogen, MultiGreens, Digest & Cleanse

Application and Usage

Topical: Administer Raindrop Technique the day after the horse has been vaccinated. Apply Copaiba, Cypress, and PanAway if the vaccination site becomes irritated and inflamed.

Ingestion & Oral: Combine 1-2 oz. NingXia Red, 4-6 dropperfuls Mineral Essence, 1-2 oz. Sulfurzyme, 1-2 Life 9, and 3 Digest & Cleanse with 10 drops each of Copaiba, DiGize, and Helichrysum. To this mixture add 10 drops of one of the following: Helichrysum, GLF, or JuvaCleanse. Syringe everything (except Digest & Cleanse) 2 times daily for 5 days after vaccination.

Inhalation: Diffuse ImmuPower, Cedarwood, Lemon, and Purification.

Warts

Equine papillomavirus (EPV) is responsible for equine papillomas. Multiple warts generally affect younger animals, while mature animals generally manifest single warts.

Most warts will manifest as a bump with a hardened surface. Scattered papillomas tend to develop on the nose, lips, eyelids, bottoms of legs, penis, vulva, mammary glands, and inner surfaces of the ears. They often manifest after mild skin abrasions. In foals, they often shrink or disappear in a few months. In older animals, it is common for papillomas to continue for 18 months.

Although they are less than flattering, they are most often benign. However, some warts will infest an area and continue to form or multiply, and these may require treatment and/or removal. If the warts begin to form lesions, the area may be a constant source of pain and inflammation. Consult your veterinary health professional to monitor wart development, observe treatment, and prevent complications.

Recommendations

Singles: Clove, Melissa, Manuka, Tea Tree, Melaleuca Quinquenervia, Ravintsara, Thyme, Blue Cypress, Geranium, Mountain Savory, Eucalyptus Globulus, Cassia, Oregano, Lemongrass, Black Pepper, Copaiba, Ocotea, Ravintsara, Helichrysum

Blends: Thieves, Australian Blue, Melrose, Exodus II, ImmuPower, Longevity, Egyptian Gold, The Gift, Purification

Nutritionals: NingXia Red, MultiGreens, Mineral Essence, Life 9, Inner Defense, Longevity Softgels, Detoxzyme, Sulfurzyme

Additional: Tender Tush, Animal Scents Ointment, Rose Ointment

Application and Usage

Topical: Combine Copaiba and Thyme with any suggested oil; apply 2-4 times daily on location of wart. Layer oils with Tender Tush, Animal Scents Ointment, or Rose Ointment to soothe irritation. Administer Raindrop Technique 1-2 times weekly.

Ingestion & Oral: Administer orally 1-2 oz. NingXia Red, 4-6 dropperfuls Mineral Essence, 1-2 oz. Sulfurzyme, 1-2 Life 9 with 15 drops each of Longevity, Copaiba, and Melrose 2 times daily.

Inhalation: Diffuse Melrose, Purification, Thieves, ImmuPower, and Longevity.

Other: Apply Tender Tush, Animal Scents Ointment, or Rose Ointment.

West Nile Virus

West Nile diagnosis is made by noting the clinical signs and by positive diagnostic tests on blood or cerebrospinal fluid. Treatment is primarily supportive, with anti-inflammatory drugs and fluids. Some horses require hospitalization and assistance with a sling in order to remain standing.

Work with your veterinarian as these horses may become hard to handle very quickly due to the virus's effects on the brain. IV fluid therapy may be required as well.

Recommendations

Singles: Ravintsara, Cypress, Copaiba, Peppermint, Mountain Savory, Laurus Nobilis (all anticon-

vulsants), Melissa, Manuka, Rosemary, Tea Tree, Melaleuca Quinquenervia, Copaiba, Lemongrass, Clove, Cassia, Oregano, Helichrysum, Cedarwood (to oxygenate), Juniper, Geranium, Lemon

Blends: Thieves, Exodus II, ImmuPower, Valor, Grounding, Raven, Purification

Nutritionals: NingXia Red, Sulfurzyme, Mineral Essence, Life 9, Rehemogen, MultiGreens, MindWise, OmegaGize[3], Inner Defense

Additional: Regenolone Moisturizing Cream, Cool Azul Sports Gel

Application and Usage

Topical: Raindrop daily (if horse will tolerate) with Helichrysum, Juniper, Geranium, and Copaiba. Include placing oils on the brain stem. Juniper, Helichrysum,

---

Veterinarian Tips and Suggestions

West Nile Virus

When treating a horse that is affect with the West Nile Virus, administer the following protocols. For best results, give orally every 3 hours 6 times daily.

- Mix all ingredients and administer orally. Syringe into horse's mouth if necessary.
  - 5 drops Helichrysum
  - 20 drops Exodus II
  - 20 drops Ravintsara
  - 20 drops Melrose
  - 20 drops Oregano
  - 20 drops Copaiba
  - 20 drops DiGize
  - 1 oz. NingXia Red
  - 4 dropperfuls Mineral Essence
  - 1 Life 9
  - 1 oz. Sulfurzyme
  - 6 Detoxzyme

- If horse is becoming dehydrated, syringe Lemon and Peppermint directly into its mouth. If condition is especially severe, add an additional 6 dropperfuls Rehemogen.

- Administer Raindrop Technique daily, adding ImmuPower and Copaiba before Wintergreen. Use V-6 Vegetable Oil Complex oil to soothe irritation, if needed.

- Diffuse undiluted Thieves, ImmuPower, Melrose, Mountain Savory, Lemongrass, Cinnamon Bark, Cedarwood, and Purification. Diffuse as closely to affected animal as possible, using an equine nebulizer if needed.

- For horse exposed to but not showing symptoms of West Nile, administer the following orally 2 times daily:
  - 5-10 drops DiGize
  - 5-10 drops Ravintsara
  - 5-10 drops ImmuPower

---

and Regenolone Moisturizing Cream are supportive to nerve tissue. Also place selected suggested oils on poll, sacrum, withers, and coronary bands.

Ingestion & Oral: Administer essential oils on hay cubes if horse is able to eat, soaked preferred. Provide Peppermint and Lemon in a second water bucket to encourage temperature reduction and/or Cool Azul Sports Gel or Copaiba and Peppermint to reduce inflammation.

Inhalation: Use a nebulizer (if horse is still calm) in a large diffuser stall to accommodate potential recumbent horse that may thrash about. Diffuse Thieves, Exodus II, Ravintsara, ImmuPower, Raven, and Purification.

Other: Diffuse and apply your favorite oils such as Purification to avoid mosquito bites, which can carry these viruses to other horses and people.

White Line Disease (Seedy Toe, Hollow Wall)

This is a condition, usually secondary to laminitis, where the outer surface of the hoof wall seems solid, but the inside tissue has lost density. There may even be a hollow cavity where the tissue has degenerated to the point of being absent. The toe may sound hollow when tapped.

If no lameness is present, the condition may be managed through proper shoeing. Consult a veterinary health professional to prevent serious complications.

Recommendations

Singles: Peppermint, Copaiba, Clove, Cinnamon Bark, Cassia, Lemongrass, Tea Tree, Melaleuca Quinquenervia, Mountain Savory, Oregano, Thyme, Wintergreen, Ginger, Manuka, Blue Cypress, Eucalyptus Globulus, Eucalyptus Radiata, Eucalyptus Blue, Basil, Patchouli, Helichrysum, Idaho Blue Spruce, Northern Lights Black Spruce, Sacred Frankincense, Lavender

Blends: Thieves, Purification, Exodus II, Egyptian Gold, Longevity, PanAway, R.C., Melrose, The Gift, DiGize, Tranquil Roll-On, Stress Away Roll-On, Peace & Calming, White Angelica, Gentle Baby, Trauma Life, T-Away

Nutritionals: NingXia Red, Sulfurzyme, Mineral Essence, Life 9, AgilEase, BLM

Additional: Ortho Sport Massage Oil, Ortho Ease Massage Oil

Veterinarian Tips and Suggestions

White Line Disease

Use Thieves Household Cleaner, Thieves Mouthwash, or Thieves Spray to soak the hoof. When soaking a hoof, place your essential oils in the area of separation and let them soak for approximately 10 minutes; then place the hoof in a soaking boot or bucket that has Thieves Household Cleaner (2 capfuls) or Thieves Mouthwash for 20 minutes to drive the oils in even deeper. Do not soak longer, as it may soften the hoof wall, allowing even more hoof wall separation to occur.

Application and Usage

Topical: Apply any combination of 3-4 oils on location 2-3 times daily. Administer Raindrop Technique weekly.

Ingestion & Oral: Administer orally 1-2 oz. NingXia Red, 4-6 dropperfuls Mineral Essence, 1-2 oz. Sulfurzyme, 1-2 Life 9 with 8-10 drops each of DiGize, Thieves, Copaiba, Mountain Savory, and Lemongrass 2 times daily.

Inhalation: Use calming, supportive oils for emotional balance such as Tranquil Roll-On, Stress Away Roll-On, Peace & Calming, Lavender, White Angelica, Gentle Baby, Trauma Life, and T-Away if horse appears stressed.

Other: Check for imbalanced minerals especially copper, zinc, and selenium. Increase biotin to speed hoof regrowth. Use Ortho Sport Massage Oil and Ortho Ease Massage Oil for compensatory legs. Administer Raindrop Technique for both immune and balance support.

Windgalls (Windpuffs)

These are puffy, fluid-filled swellings around the fetlock joints affecting the forelimbs, hindlimbs, or both. Generally, they are the result of aggressive exercise and trauma. Often, they will go away on their own. Obese or overweight animals are more susceptible.

In the majority of cases, windgalls do not result in lameness. Rest, support bandaging, and mild exercise will usually treat them. They do, however, recur in animals that have a history of developing them. Consult a veterinary health professional to confirm diagnosis and prevent any complications.

Recommendations

Singles: Basil, Copaiba, Cypress, Helichrysum, Idaho Balsam Fir, Idaho Blue Spruce, Northern Lights Black Spruce, Palo Santo, Wintergreen, Lemongrass, Pine, Eucalyptus Globulus, Myrtle, Laurus Nobilis, Cedarwood, Dorado Azul, Hyssop, Peppermint, Grapefruit, Orange, Tangerine

Blends: Aroma Life, Cool Azul, Deep Relief Roll-On, PanAway, Believe, R.C., Relieve It, Transformation, Clarity, En-R-Gee, Purification, DiGize, Stress Away Roll-On, Peace & Calming, Peace & Calming II

Nutritionals: NingXia Red, Sulfurzyme, Mineral Essence, Life 9, MindWise, AgilEase, BLM, PowerGize, Organic Dried Wolfberries

Additional: Cool Azul Sports Gel, Cool Azul Pain Relief Cream, Ortho Sport Massage Oil, Cel-Lite Magic Massage Oil, Ortho Ease Massage Oil

Application and Usage

Topical: Apply Copaiba with any combination of suggested oils, ending in Peppermint; apply a cold compress over top. Administer 2 times daily. Administer Raindrop Technique 1 time a week.

Ingestion & Oral: 1-2 oz. NingXia Red, 4-6 dropperfuls Mineral Essence, 1-2 oz. Sulfurzyme, 1-2 Life 9, 1 oz. MindWise combined with 20 drops Copaiba and 10 drops DiGize.

Inhalation: Diffuse Cedarwood, Stress Away Roll-On, Idaho Balsam Fir, Peace & Calming, Peace & Calming II, Orange, Tangerine, Grapefruit

Other: Apply Cool Azul Sports Gel, Cool Azul Pain Relief Cream, Ortho Sport Massage Oil, Cel-Lite Magic Massage Oil, or Ortho Ease Massage Oil.

Wounds (see Cuts)

Veterinarian Tips and Suggestions

Open Wounds

Case History

A large thoroughbred gelding was attacked by a cougar that clawed a chunk of flesh half the size of a soccer ball out of the horse's buttocks. The horse bled terribly, blood squirting from ruptured blood vessels.

The vet said the prognosis was grim because there was too much torn, damaged, and removed tissue. Even if the horse didn't die, the wound would leave a sizeable scar and indentation.

Treatment Protocol

Day 1

To reduce the pain and stop the bleeding, a 5 cc hypodermic syringe was filled with Helichrysum and sprayed into the wound. The horse became less jittery, and the bleeding stopped. Several minutes later a larger 10 cc syringe of Purification was sprayed into the open wound. It took over 15 ml of Purification to spray down and cover the entire wound.

After several hours, the wound was sprayed with Melrose to disinfect it and was packed with Animal Scents Ointment. To keep hair out of the wound and reduce the possibility of infection, the tail was wrapped and tied up.

Because there was no way to cover or close the wound, the horse was kept in the stable to prevent him from moving around. The animal was closely monitored to reduce the possibility of reinfection caused by the animal lying down, rolling around, and scratching the wound.

Days 2-7

The horse's grain was supplemented with crushed up Essentialzyme, the yellow capsule in Essentialzymes-4, and four scoops of Power Meal, which is dense in the nutrients required for healing and tissue rebuilding.

Three times a day, the open wound was irrigated with Purification and Helichrysum. The vet came regularly to monitor the horse's progress. He remarked that he had never seen muscle tissue regenerate to such a degree.

Weeks 2 to 4

Two times a day, the open wound was irrigated with Purification and Helichrysum.

Weeks 4 to 8

Once a week, the wound was irrigated with Purification and Helichrysum until it was closed.

Results

Today, no indentation or concavity is visible, only a small, circular 2-inch scar.

Testimonials

I had a 26-year-old quarter horse gelding who suffered with heaves for 13 years. We were able to manage his condition with the help of a holistic veterinarian, but he still experienced episodes when his breathing would become critical during the allergy season. One such night, I got home from work to find all four of his legs were swollen; and when I tried to take readings of his breathing and heartbeat, which I did every morning and every night, his heartbeat was all over the place. It was so irregular that I couldn't even count it.

I called my vet and she told me some things I could do for him; but in the meantime, I ran to the house to get my Aroma Life. I put 5 drops in the palm of my hand and rubbed it over his heart; and within 10 seconds, his heart had resumed a rhythmic beat again! I kept checking on him all night, and it remained steady, and the swelling in his legs was gone by morning.

-Jan E.

• •

In 2011 Memphis was very sick with EHV1 and was very nearly euthanized. I sent him to Judy Gillum's for rehab. She began giving him full Equine Raindrop Technique once a week. In between, Judy would apply Aroma Life, Juniper, Valor, Cypress, and Helichrysum daily down his spine. Memphis also got 2-4 ounces of NingXia Red daily.

Although Memphis was not able to return to competition, he is very happy, healthy, comfortable, and rideable as a trail horse.

-Michelle

• •

In 2011 I received a horse for rehab that had been at UC Davis for about five days for EHV1. When I got him, he stumbled so much that he looked as though he had been drugged. I gave him treatments similar to what they did with Memphis. The horse got a full Raindrop every three days, and on the in-between-days, he got several oils layered down his spine, including Cypress, Lemongrass, Juniper, and lots and lots of Valor. I had the horse for only two weeks. Shortly after he went home, he was able to return to full working abilities as a cutting horse, and they were able to begin competing on him toward the end of the year.

-Kendra K.

• •

Ed had laminitis and a huge amount of white line disease that was eating away the inside his foot, very nearly into his coffin bone and almost to the top of his foot. I chose not to have his hoof resected but instead used a needle and syringe to apply undiluted Lemon, Eucalyptus Radiata, Clove, Thieves, and Rosemary. My farrier cut out some of the dead hoof wall to allow air inside and to make applying the oils easier.

The hoof grew out astoundingly well and very quickly. The x-rays of Ed's feet showed that his coffin bones were completely unrotated and back in a normal position! I have since worked with other horses who have either foundered or had laminitis flare-ups, all with outstanding results.

-Kendra K.

• •

Last summer, Ed was bitten by a rattlesnake. By the next day, the bite was very swollen; Ed's head was hanging and he would not eat. He was hot and sweaty, with a temperature of 105°F.

The normal course of veterinary action for a snake bite is steroids and anti-inflammatories. But Ed was not a candidate for steroids, so I gave him Raindrop Technique. I also put some Peppermint in a bucket of water and sponged it over him several times throughout the day. He was in bad shape, so I gave him a half-dose of Banamine in the morning and at night. This, combined with the oils, brought his temperature down.

That afternoon, I added Purification and Thieves over the area of the swelling and then put Ortho Sport Massage Oil on top—and Ed perked up again. He progressed from then on, his temperature dropping by a full degree every 12 hours and his appetite continuing to improve. He was left with only a small scar and a thick area on his neck.

-Kendra K.

Gett Bold is a thoroughbred gelding. My client, Patty, competes with him at hunter/jumper shows. In December 2009, he came in one morning with severe tearing of ligaments in his pelvis, including his sacroiliac ligament. This was far beyond a strain or small ligament tear; this was a very bad soft-tissue injury.

I did my massage work, LED light therapy, and lots of oils. I used Valor, Wintergreen, Lemongrass, and Aroma Siez twice a week for several weeks and then started stretching the sessions out as he improved. It took about a year before he was ready to return to work; but not only did he get sound enough to ride, he also became sound enough to compete. Patty continues to compete with him.

-*Kendra K.*

. . . .

I was out of town for a week and came home to find my mare, Ricki, with a very deep wound on her heel. It was caked with dried mud and manure and smelled putrid. I soaked cotton in diluted Thieves Household Cleaner, wrapped it over the wound, and wrapped it with vet wrap until the crust softened. I sent pictures to my veterinarian, and he concluded that the best thing to do was to clean it and wrap it up, as it was much too late for sutures.

I then began a twice-daily program of wrapping it with cotton-soaked in diluted Thieves Household Cleaner and flushing it out with a syringe full of the solution. After removing the wrap and letting the wound dry, I applied Melrose, Frankincense, Lavender, and Helichrysum. The wound healed with minimal scarring, though the scar does go down Ricki's hoof.

-*Kendra K.*

I worked with a young mare whose previous owner had kept her in a 10x10 stall from age 1 because the owner was afraid of her. The mare was about 3 when I met her. I noticed that the mare would do what was asked but always with a crabby attitude and no enthusiasm.

I had her smell Joy for a few days, and she really had some good release, lots of licking and chewing, softening of eyes, lowered head, and more interest in life. I then had the owner use some Orange oil for the horse to smell and apply on her chest daily for about a week or more. The mare came to life and enjoyed being with people instead of just enduring them.

-*Michelle R.*

. . . .

For a horse hoof with a horizontal cut near the coronary band, I used Patchouli, Basil, Cypress, and Ylang Ylang, mixed equally. I applied 2-3 drops into the crack 2 times daily and saw good results after the second day. The horse would limp but after the second day, he walked without a limp; and the crack healed from the inside out. I continued the drops for 10 days until the wound was completely healed. He really seemed more aware of his feet, too.

-Michelle R.

. . . .

Our two-year-old cutting prospect named DR came down with West Nile Virus. He was so sick that he could barely stand. We immediately used NingXia Red and Banamine on him and then applied Lemon, Frankincense, Thyme, Oregano, Peppermint, PanAway, and Valor. We continued to administer these oils daily. I had DiGize and ImmuPower overnighted and added them to the regimen as soon as they arrived.

On the fourth day of DR's illness, we gave him a Raindrop Technique both morning and night.

After a week, DR was doing much better, and we reduced oil application to once daily. A month-and-a-half later, he was well enough to go back into training.

-*Jerry M.*

. . . .

In 2009 my horse Scout had a horrific accident with a sickle bar mower. He had been literally ripped open from his crest to his shoulder, approximately 3 inches wide and 4 inches deep. The vet came out the night of the accident to suture him up and said that the horse could not be saved.

I initially treated the wound with Purification and Lavender several times daily to prevent infection. I cut away Scout's hair and purchased a hood to keep dirt out of the wound. It was a long process and took many weeks for the incision to begin to heal. Once it was no longer draining, I would drip Purification and Lavender on the sutures and add a layer of Animal Scents Ointment. I would also use Valor daily to give him the strength and courage he needed to fight to live. Scout is now healthy and happy again with minimal scarring.

-Nancie B.

• •

My journey with essential oils began when one of my horses came down with a respiratory infection that quickly developed into pneumonia and fluid on his lungs. The vet was treating him with strong oral antibiotics, but there was little to no improvement. The horse pretty much spent his day lying in the paddock and wasn't very interested in eating.

A friend told me about a woman who used essential oils to heal and gave me Pat's name and phone number. Pat instructed me to use Exodus II, R.C., Rosemary, Oregano, and Thyme 2 times daily. A few days later, the vet noticed a slight improvement in the horse's breathing. I told him about the oils, and he asked that I continue to use the antibiotics as well. By the following Monday, the horse was up and very alert, with his appetite returned. Today he is as sound as a dollar. When I visited with the vet sometime after, he admitted he was amazed because he really expected the horse to die.

-Maria J.

• •

A friend came to my place to go riding. As we were saddling up, her horse began coughing a deep, dry, hacking cough. Apparently, her horse had done this before, and my friend didn't think she could ride him much. I put about 6 drops of Raven on the palm of my hands and rubbed the horse all over his chest and lung area. We then proceeded to head to the trails to ride, and her horse didn't cough once, even when running up the hills.

-Chris S.

• •

Pache, a Paint gelding, had an eye that had been draining down the side of his face for months. I had tried nearly everything. I decided to put "Scar BeGone" (a mixture of 10 drops of Helichrysum, 6 drops of Lavender, 8 drops of Lemongrass, 4 drops of Patchouli,

and 5 drops of Myrrh) in a roll-on bottle and rub it down Pache's face and along the tract of the tear ducts. Then I put 2 drops of Lavender in 4 ounces of distilled water and put drops of this mixture into his eye. I put Lavender and Thieves on the palms of my hands and held them over Pache's eyes for about 30 seconds. I did this for three days, and the issue was solved.

-Chris S.

• •

Pache wouldn't let anyone ride him. I thought it might be a back issue, so I called the vet. She came out and examined him and was going to do a Raindrop Technique on him. She balanced him with Valor and applied Frankincense to his coronal bands. She then felt she needed to apply DiGize. She opened the bottle and didn't even get any on him as he just pushed his way to her and inhaled it from the bottle. Pache proceeded to push past the vet and began rolling. He dropped and rolled twice and got up and started eating hay like he was starving.

The next morning we discovered that it wasn't a back issue at all; his intestines had been blocked. It could have been a life-threatening issue, but it was resolved quickly with essential oils.

-Chris S.

• •

A couple was camping at the horse park a mile from my house. Their horse had colic, and every vet they called refused to come help. I went down there with oils in hand. When I got there, the horse was definitely uncomfortable, pawing the ground and not standing still. I made a cup with the horse's lower lip and put 10 drops of Peppermint and 10 drops of DiGize in it. The owner walked her around, and she appeared to calm down.

We sat down and waited and after a little while, the horse began to pull back again, threw herself on the ground, and then got up and paced and pawed.

I repeated the essential oil treatment and added a few drops of each oil directly on her belly. She again calmed down and began eating grass. It was getting fairly late, so I left a couple more treatments and went home. I found out the next day that the horse had one more episode, was treated again, and then was totally normal.

-Chris S.

One summer my normally sweet mare named Abby began attacking other horses and at times even turning that rage on me. The vet started with some tests, which showed high levels of testosterone in Abby's system, caused by a grapefruit-sized tumor on one of her ovaries. The vet scheduled a surgery to remove the tumor and the ovary in one week.

During this week-long wait, my Aunt Sara called and asked me if I would help her make a video about the Raindrop Technique with animals. Aunt Sara said she would use a lot of Peace & Calming and hoped that would help Abby relax. The filming went great, and after applying lots of Peace & Calming to Abby, she only tried to bite, paw, and kick a tiny bit.

When the day of the surgery arrived, the vet did another ultrasound to check on the size of the tumor. To everyone's surprise, the tumor was gone! Abby walked out with a clean bill of health. She is still living a healthy, happy life today.

-Mindy S.

. . . .

Two years ago my daughter got a registered pony who had gotten a thorn stuck in her back flank. The spot was over an inch in diameter and was about an inch deep. We had the vet do a checkup to make sure nothing was still imbedded in it. We ended up having to do a debridement to the area to get rid of all the dead tissue and to get the maggots out. The vet then gave her a shot of antibiotic, due to the systemic infection she developed. We also packed the open wound with Animal Scents Ointment and gauze. We changed dressings 3 times daily, along with applying Purification and Frankincense around area.

When the vet came back the next week, the sore had shrunk to less than an inch in diameter, and the inside had completely healed shut. After 3 weeks, we could barely see the wound, just the bare patch of skin where the hair was just starting to grow back. My 5-year-old daughter would go out every afternoon to wash and brush the pony and then apply a mixture of Myrrh, Lavender, and Melrose to the patch. It took about 10 months before there was really no noticeable scar at all.

-Jaci S.

My horse's muzzle was covered in warts, so I applied Abundance, castor oil, and zinc cream to keep it protected from the sun during the day. At night I applied Abundance. Within three days, the warts were falling off; and he is still wart-free three months later.

-Charlene C.

. . . .

My 20-year-old spotted saddle horse is a worrier, especially when she cannot see our other three horses. To shoe her, we usually have to tie up one of the other horses somewhere close, so she will not be anxious. I decided to try Peace & Calming this time to help. I put 2 drops in my palms, rubbed them together under my horse's nose, and applied my palms to the horse's ears. Within a minute, the horse dropped her head and was completely relaxed. Both my shoer and I were amazed. When we had just one more shoe to go, the oils seemed to wear off; so I reapplied the same way, and within 30 seconds my horse relaxed again.

-Stacy L.

. . . .

My stallion had a sarcoid show up on his inner thigh. I tried most conventional means for three years to get rid of it. After I was introduced to Young Living Essential Oils, I tried many different oils and saw lots of improvements. Laurus Nobilus almost worked, but ultimately it was Grapefruit oil that completely healed the area. I used it three times daily for three months.

-Pam F.

. . . .

A 3-year-old thoroughbred filly named Annie was sent to my rehab facility for injured horses. I was her last hope. She had stepped on a roofing nail that had penetrated her hoof all the way to the coffin bone. She'd spent five weeks in a hospital and had undergone three surgeries. The owner was phoned during the third surgery to give permission to euthanize due to the extensive bone infection. She said no.

The horse arrived here by ambulance, and within four days of using Young Living essential oils and supplements, the infection was eradicated! I then used Young Living products to help the tissue regenerate. To everyone's amazement, the filly made a full recovery.

-Pam F.

Our stallion (Latigo) had founder, which caused laminitis so badly that he could not get up. His legs and feet were swollen, and he was running a high fever. I called the vet and he said Latigo was too far gone; and if he came out of the fever, the vet would just put him to sleep. Not wanting to do that, I called another vet and she said the same thing. So, I called one more vet and the answer was the same.

I called my mom Nancy, and with her guidance, I went to work with the oils. Foundering is sometimes caused by increase of sugars and carbohydrates, which increases the insulin levels, which causes imbalance of the normal bowel flora, leading to production of endotoxins. The endotoxin causes insulin resistance. It has some similarity to type II Diabetes in humans.

Because of this insulin resistance, I concentrated Ocotea, Dill, and Coriander over his pancreas and kidneys as part of the Raindrop Technique. I massaged Ortho Sport Massage Oil all over his whole body to reduce his whole-body inflammation and on his feet, ankles, and legs. I also used Aroma Siez and Cypress for circulation, Peppermint for inflammation and fever, Ortho Sport Massage Oil on his legs, and EndoFlex to support his endocrine system. I got cold water to soak his feet in with Thieves, Cypress, and Peppermint and applied those three oils from the knees down. Then I gave him a Raindrop Technique, repeated it every two hours, and applied the oils every two hours all night long. I kept changing the water I was soaking his feet in, so it was cold all of the time. It was a long siege, but it was worth it.

The next morning, he was able to get up; but he couldn't walk to get his food or water for 3 days. I carried his food and water to him. Then after a week, he was able to walk with just a small limp. The vet said that she has seen only one other person bring a horse out of laminitis that was that bad, but it took him a year of constant caring. Latigo was over it in a month's time. Since then he has been fine and has fathered 3 more colts.

-Jodi R.

I have two horses that I started taking to shows last year. They were very stressed, and their first responses were flight, bucking, and rearing. I had recently signed on as a member of Young Living and had started carrying a bottle of Peace & Calming with me. I rubbed some on the horses' noses, and they were noticeably calmer and more able to think.

I also use Thieves on thrush (a hoof infection), and it works really well.

-Carol P.

. . . .

I have a Tennessee Walker gelding who had a case of thrush in the hoof. My husband and I had used Coppertox several times on the infection without much luck.

My husband soaked the hoof in warm water with Epsom salt and then used extra virgin olive oil mixed with several drops of Thieves. When my husband opened the bottle of oil with the Thieves added to it, the horse immediately cranked his head around to deeply sniff the contents of the bottle for quite a long time. We used the Thieves oil blend for only two days on the hoof, and the thrush was cleared up completely.

-Joyce F.

. . . .

I had a colt that got into a wire fence and cut her hind leg down to the bone and tendon, ripping all the flesh and hide off of the leg from fighting to get out of the fence.

We put Peace & Calming on her, and she just laid there without even a struggle in trying to get up. The wound was bad, but I wanted to give her a chance. We cleaned up the leg with the Thieves Household Cleaner diluted in water and then applied Ortho Sport Massage Oil all over the area, inside and out. After putting Thieves around the outside of the wound and Melrose inside the wound, I put Animal Scents Ointment on top and wrapped the leg.

Miraculously, the colt recovered and all hair grew back except right at the top. It took a long time, but she is now a grown horse, and you can't tell that she had ever been hurt.

-Nancy S.

Several years ago, I had a stallion that had somehow cut his front leg very deeply, just above the hoof. His foot became infected and swollen. All I had at that time was Ortho Sport Massage Oil, so I saturated it and left the horse in the corral for the night. When I got there the next morning, I was shocked to see that he was walking around the corral without a limp. The swelling was gone and so was the infection.

-Nancy S.

••••••••••••••••••••••••••••••••••••••

My husband Blaine and I took a nice horseback ride to a camping site where we were planning on staying. After setting up camp, we checked on the horses again; but my horse Snowball was not acting right. Snowball kept lying down, getting back up, and then lying down again, which is typically a sign of colic. I gave Snowball DiGize inside her lower lip and rubbed her with Ortho Sport Massage Oil and Peppermint to help relax the muscles. Snowball seemed to be improving, but I was out of DiGize. I decided to add some water to the DiGize bottle and give that to Snowball. It did the trick and within four hours, Snowball was much better. By the next morning, she was completely fine.

-Nancy S.

••••••••••••••••••••••••••••••••••••••

My horse Polly, had to have a hysterectomy; afterward, she came home with colic. The vet gave her a shot to relax the muscles and some mineral oil, but it wasn't working; so we decided to try essential oils. I applied 20 drops of DiGize inside Polly's lower lip and rubbed Ortho Sport Massage Oil with Peppermint all around her flank and stomach. Fifteen minutes later she was fine and did not lie down again.

-Nancy S.

••••••••••••••••••••••••••••••••••••••

My new horse Trigger was really sick with colic. I put 20 drops of DiGize under his lip and 6 drops each of Peppermint and DiGize on the front of his front feet. I also put 6 drops of DiGize in some Ortho Sport Massage Oil and massaged from his flank down under his stomach. In less than three minutes, Trigger was improving. I walked him around for an hour and then gave him 40 drops of DiGize inside his lip to help with worms.

I also noticed that he had a cough. The next day, Trigger was better but still acted sick; so I dewormed him with 10 ounces of ParaFree and applied R.C., Melaleuca Ericifolia, Raven, and Oregano. I also did the Raindrop Technique on his spine with Oregano and Thyme, plus he received DiGize again.

The next day you wouldn't believe that he was the same horse! He had a sparkle in his eyes, and his cough was gone. He came up to eat his grain and wouldn't let another horse take it away from him. Days before, he wouldn't eat and didn't care if they took his grain.

-Nancy S.

••••••••••••••••••••••••••••••••••••••

I had a horse that foundered because she had an abscess under the hoof. I used a hot compress to treat it. The horse did not get better, so I decided to apply diluted Lavender, Helichrysum, and Melrose to the foot. After 45 minutes of sleeping, the horse walked without a limp.

-Nancy S.

••••••••••••••••••••••••••••••••••••••

A client of mine called about some bumps that had appeared on a 4-year- old quarter horse. The client had tried a variety of over-the-counter ointments, both for bacterial and fungal infections, with poor results. I diagnosed the horse as having warts and sold him a bottle of Young Living Melrose oil with instructions to apply it sparingly twice daily.

When I visited the client again a few weeks later, the warts were worse. Two weeks later the client called to tell me that the warts were almost all gone. The client admitted that he hadn't tried the Melrose oil until after the follow-up but was too embarrassed to say so at the time.

-John H.

••••••••••••••••••••••••••••••••••••••

I received a call from a barn manager that she had a Buckskin gelding that needed a good home. He was a retired show horse, due to a hind leg injury, and had spent the last year locked in his stall under the premise of rehabbing his injury. He had a past history of abuse, neglect, and being taken for granted.

I spent a lot of time connecting with him, massaging him, doing acupressure, and using essential oils. When I returned a week later to check on him and do another treatment, he had gained 100 pounds, and the trainer had changed nothing.

During another visit, I treated him with essential oils for a recurring bout of laminitis. He could hardly walk and had a lot of heat in his lower forelimbs. I applied the oils daily for three days, along with doing energy work and "Sore No More" clay packs on his legs. He responded really well and was back to walking normally and without any heat present within a few days.

-Dr. Bernadette H.

. . . .

I was called out on emergency to treat a horse's colic with essential oils. The owner didn't have the money to take him in for emergency care, treatment, and possibly surgery. She had been giving him beet pulp prior to my arrival without much success.

When I got there, I treated him orally, topically, and rectally with essential oils in conjunction with a lot of energy work and some body massage. I repeated this over the course of two-and-a-half hours, with gut sounds improving. When I came back to check on him the next day, his eyes were brighter than I had ever seen in him, and he was relaxed and comfortable. To this day, he has not had a colic relapse!

-Dr. Bernadette H.

. . . .

I have worked on a 12-year-old mare numerous times for chiropractic and acupuncture treatments. Each treatment, I would use at least one essential oil on her, which the horse absolutely loved. In the midst of the treatments, the mare was sent to a trainer for 60 days of training. The owner called me when the horse returned to the barn for chiropractic care. When I arrived, the mare was really checked out and not present. I adjusted her and did an essential oil treatment to help her process the training event. Within minutes, I could see her come back into her body; her eyes started to brighten, and she turned her head and nuzzled into my chest.

-Dr. Bernadette H.

A client of mine had a horse that stepped on a nail and penetrated the margin of the coffin bone. A severe, deep infection set in, and the horse was transported to the equine hospital. After a week of expensive and extensive therapy, euthanasia was scheduled for the next day.

They reached out to me, and essential oils were started immediately. Oils were applied directly to the wound in the bottom of the foot and around the coronary band several times daily. In three days, the horse was putting weight on the foot. In another four days, the horse was walking with barely a limp. Three weeks later, the horse was doing amazingly well and everyone, especially the owner, was ecstatic.

-Dr. Barbara F.

. . . .

I was called out to look at an old horse who had gotten down and was unable to arise on his weak, unsteady legs. Despite being well taken care of all of his life, he was now suffering. I instructed the owner to put Frankincense on top of the horse's head and a few drops in his mouth. Frankincense is an oil that I use to help spiritually connect an animal with its person in end-of-life situations. The horse was not even able to get into an upright position, and the strain on his heart and lungs was beginning to show.

After carefully assessing the situation, I gently broke the news to the guardian that the horse was wanting to end his life. She said she instinctively knew this. The end for this aged horse was completely quiet and peaceful.

-Dr. Barbara F.

. . . .

I got a call one night about a 24-year-old mare named Bricky, who was suffering from a severe case of colic. Surgery is often the only hope for survival in cases like this. I instructed the owner to place 3 drops of DiGize inside of Bricky's mouth and to put the same amount of oil on her lower abdomen as often as every hour. One drop of Peppermint was also to be placed on the abdomen as needed.

All throughout the night, the owner applied the oils as directed. Toward early morning, Bricky's vital signs were completely within the normal range and her mucous membranes were moist and pink. I did another oil treatment but this time applied DiGize and

ImmuPower to the horse's jugular vein areas and let her sniff the Peppermint. Bricky continued to improve and made a full recovery in less than 24 hours from her initial bout of colic.

-Dr. Barbara F.

....

I had a horse with a severe rear leg injury with all the tendons and ligaments severed; but because of essential oils (ingested as antibiotics), the horse could walk the day after surgery. Dr. Cliff Honnas, who used to be the head vet at Texas A&M, did the surgery and warned me and the horse's owner, Alana, that there would be ups and downs in the healing process. But, the horse healed wonderfully, and Dr. Honnas would text me when the mare was running out of oils because he didn't want to be without them.

-Candace H.

....

A mare had a thoracic chest abscess that was coming out the nose. There was a poor prognosis, including imminent death. I did Raindrop Technique three days in row, adding Sacred Frankincense and Frankincense. I then left Dr. Honnas with a mix of V-6, Sacred Frankincense, and Frankincense. Dr. Honnas said that they achieved in 4-5 weeks what he would have expected in 4-5 months, and there was no need to remove part of the lung because there was no necrosis.

-Candace H.

....

I created a spray blend of Thieves, Tsuga, Lavender, Palo Santo, Purification, and Egyptian Gold in water. It was applied to a world champion who was injured on a fence panel. After a month-and-a-half, the scar from the injury was barely visible.

-Candace H.

....

A two-year-old half-Arabian filly was presented for examination of multiple head wounds. The veterinarian asked for one week to attempt to achieve improvement before euthanizing. The owner agreed to re-evaluate at the end of one week.

Along with conventional veterinary care and medication, they scrubbed the wound with Thieves Foaming Hand Soap and applied a daily alternative therapy of Lavender, Palo Santo, Tsuga, and Thieves. After viewing the improvement in the animal's condition at the end of the first week, the owner agreed to allow continued treatment.

After a month, the wounds continued to heal very well; however, the filly was unable to open her mouth for oral examination. I provided an herbal formula of comfrey root powder, white oak bark powder, black walnut hull powder, lobelia herb powder, skullcap herb powder, marshmallow root powder, mullein leaf powder, cayenne powder, and gravel root powder, which was applied daily to break down scar tissue. Two months later, the horse could use her mouth normally.

-Candace H.

....

A Paint mare presented for routine artificial insemination developed changes in the iris coloration five days later. I determined to use JuvaCleanse, JuvaPower, Lemongrass, Bergamot, and Tranquil Roll-On internally to address the out-of-range biomarkers. After 10 days of nutritional supplementation, the irises returned to normal, but there was still a uveitis present in the left eye. I then used Raven, Chelex, Black Spruce, Life 5 [now Life 9], and Thyromin to help.

-Candace H.

....

I work with horses and often use oils when teaching or training them in new things. I carry Peace & Calming, Valor, and Grounding and let the horse choose which one it needs. Often they only need a few sniffs, but they all respond to one or more of the blends. I use Lavender on their cuts and scrapes and rarely need a vet.

-Rowena B.

....

A 4-month-old colt had the hide on one side of its body stripped off. The wound was sprayed with Melrose to disinfect and Helichrysum to control the pain. The wound was then sealed with the formula now known as Animal Scents Ointment. Within several months, the hair and skin had completely grown in, and the animal had made a full recovery.

-Gary Y.

Livestock and Wildlife

Bovidae and Cervidae

Bovidae

Bovidae are ruminant animals that have cloven hooves. There 143 species, including African buffalo, water buffalo, bison, antelopes, gazelles, sheep, goats, muskoxen, and domestic cattle.

Essential oils are used similarly to horses for these animals. Regular use of oils in feeds, water, udder washes, and post-milking teat dips are wonderful ways to gain health benefits on a routine basis.

Other Bovidae include:

Aepycerotinae: Impala

Alcelaphinae: Bontebok, Blessbok, Hartebeest, Wildebeest

Antilopinae: Antelopes, Dama and Thompson Gazelles, Dikdik, Purifiedbok

Bovinae: Cattle, Buffalo, Bison, and Antelope species: Lesser Kudu, Nyala, Giant and Common Eland, Greater Kudu, Mountain Nyala, Bongo

Caprinae: Musk Oxen, Markhor, Tahr, American Mountain Goats, Tur, Aoudad, Red Sheep, Dall Sheep, Domestic Sheep, Urials, Mouflon, American Bighorn Sheep, Chamois, Ibex, Serows

Cephalophinae: Duikers

Hippotraginae: Arabian, Beisa, Fringe Eared, Scimitar Horned Oryx, Addax, Roan, and Sable

Reduncinae: Reedbuck, Lechwe, Nile Lechwe, and Kob

Cervidae

Cervidae are ruminant animals and are considered to be in the "Deer Family." There are 23 genres and more than 47 species, with three subfamilies.

Capreolinae: Caribou, Moose, Brocket deer, White-tailed deer, Mule deer, Roe deer, Huemul deer, Taruca deer, Marsh deer, Pampas deer, and Pudu deer.

Other Cervidae include:

Cervinae: Axis, Elk, Elds, Fallow, Muntjacs, Pere David's deer, Red deer, Barasingha, Rusa, Sika, and Tufted deer

Hydropotinea: Chinese Water deer

When working with wild animals, it is best to contact a veterinarian or those who have experience capturing and handling them. When treating these animals, the treatment is limited to the length of time the tranquilization works or the length of time trailered or stalled. The primary concern is getting the animals treated quickly, reversed, and up or standing.

A good place to start is with Thieves Household Cleaner. Make a strong dissolution of the cleaner as a spray. Add extra oils to it, as desired.

Basic Spray:
- 2-4 oz. Thieves Household Cleaner in a glass or Bisphenol-free (BPA) spray bottle
- 20 drops each: Thieves, Purification, Cedarwood, Rosemary, Cistus, Lavender, and Copaiba
- Top with purified or distilled water.

This spray will help eliminate pathogens and external parasites. It may be diffused and used in a misting system.

Use to clean wounds, trailers, and barns.

If concerned with internal parasites, consider adding equal proportions ParaGize and DiGize to the water and feed.

If concerned with keeping the animal calm, diffuse T-Away, Trauma Life, Peace & Calming, Joy, Stress Away Roll-On, Vetiver, or Valerian.

If concerned with infection, consider Infect Away or PuriClean.

If there is an open wound, add 20 drops Melrose and 10 drops Northern Lights Black Spruce to water, agitate, and spray wound if you can. Also, apply 5 drops each of both oils to the wound.

If the animal is extremely ill, consider adding the Raindrop oils. Mist down topline and on area of concern. In cases of punctures, thrush, or deep cuts, flush the area with a needleless syringe. It may also be used as a top dressing on feed when the animals are stalled.

Bovidae and Cervidae Conditions

Abscess

An abscess is characterized as a mass of pus that has accumulated within the tissue of the body. Signs and symptoms of abscesses include redness, pain, warmth, and swelling. The swelling may feel fluid filled when pressed. The area of redness often extends beyond the swelling.

Recommendations
Singles: Thyme, Tea Tree, Elemi, Myrrh, Roman Chamomile, Lavender, Hinoki, Copaiba
Blends: Thieves, Purification, Melrose, Exodus II
Nutritionals: NingXia Red, Ningxia Organic Dried Wolfberries, MultiGreens, Sulfurzyme
Additional: Thieves Household Cleaner, Thieves Spray, Animal Scents Ointment

Applications and Usage
Topical: Apply oils of choice neat to area. If hot oil, dilute with V-6 or other carrier oil. Or add oils to Thieves Household Cleaner spray. Mist on area or flush as needed down topline.
Ingestion & Oral: The animal must be reversed from any tranquilization before drenching or feeding. Add desired oils to NingXia Red or purified water. Draw up in a syringe or drench gun. Drench the animal. Also, try adding as a top dressing to feed.

Inhalation: While the animal is tranquilized, diffuse Clarity. If animals are domestic enough to handle, drop oils of choice in palm of hand and hold over nostrils or use an ambu bag.
Other: Wash affected area with Thieves Household Cleaner and Thieves Spray. Layer oils with Animal Scents Ointment. Administer Raindrop Technique as needed.

Aches and Pains

Aches and pains on animals can be difficult to determine their source. Pain symptoms can remain unknown because of masking factors like assuming it is the animal's natural testy personality showing, or pain could manifest as other ailments that present differently than normal.

To treat chronic or acute pain, the source of the pain must first be located and treated. When administering essential oils to animals that are experiencing pain, be extremely cautious. When treating animals, they should always be stalled or tethered to prevent harmful reflex movement, especially if you inadvertently amplify their pain symptoms while administering treatment.

Veterinarian Tips and Suggestions

Aches and Pains

Try this blend when treating animals for pain. Combine these oils and use a roll-on bottle or dilute with V-6 or other carrier oil and administer in a glass spray bottle. Spray or roll generously over affected area 3 times a day until symptoms subside or root cause of pain is determined.

- 5-10 drops Helichrysum
- 5-10 drops Copaiba
- 5-10 drops Idaho Balsam Fir, Northern Lights Black Spruce, Vetiver, or Evergreen Essence

Recommendations

Singles: Idaho Balsam Fir, Lavender, Eucalyptus Radiata, Clove, Copaiba, Northern Lights Black Spruce, Idaho Blue Spruce, Frankincense, Helichrysum, Elemi, Basil, Rosemary, Tea Tree, Marjoram, Thyme, Cypress, Ginger, Sacred Sandalwood, Royal Hawaiian Sandalwood, Vetiver, Valerian

Blends: Thieves, PanAway, Relieve It, Deep Relief Roll-On, Aroma Siez, AromaEase, Evergreen Essence

Nutritionals: NingXia Red, Sulfurzyme, MultiGreens

Additional: Thieves Household Cleaner, Animal Scents Ointment, Cool Azul Sports Gel, Cool Azul Pain Relief Cream

Applications and Usage

Topical: Apply neat to area. If hot oil, use V-6 or another carrier oil. Or add oils to Thieves Household Cleaner spray. Mist on area or flush as needed down topline. Use Cool Azul Sports Gel or Cool Azul Pain Relief Cream on location.

Ingestion & Oral: The animal must be reversed from any tranquilization before drenching or feeding. Add desired oils to NingXia Red or purified water. Draw up in a syringe or drench gun. Drench the animal. Also try adding as top dressing to feed.

Other: Raindrop Technique

Afterbirth Not Expelling

The placenta and afterbirth tissue not expelling themselves causes a life-threatening infection.

Recommendations

Singles: Copaiba, Myrrh
Blends: DiGize, Thieves, Melrose

Applications and Usage

Topical: Apply 10 drops each suggested oils topically on tummy area, where hair is thinner, every 30 minutes until the tissue expels itself.

Ingestion & Oral: Administer orally 20 drops each DiGize, Copaiba, Thieves, and Melrose 2-3 times daily.

Other: Administer 20 drops each Myrrh, Copaiba, and Melrose inserted into the birthing canal with a no-needle syringe every 30 minutes.

Anesthesia Detoxification or Tranquilization Reversal

Some animals have difficulty waking up fully after a surgery or procedure where a veterinarian used anesthesia (local or general). Naturopaths have long considered anesthesia to promote the formation of toxins in humans and animals. Symptoms range from nausea to inflammation of the throat to trouble standing and walking. Consult your veterinary health professional.

Recommendations

Singles: Wintergreen, Raindrop oils, Lemongrass, Frankincense, Palo Santo, Northern Lights Black Spruce, Cedarwood, Rosemary

Blends: DiGize, Exodus II, Stress Away Roll-On, Joy, Clarity

Nutritionals: NingXia Red, Ningxia Organic Dried Wolfberries, Sulfurzyme, MultiGreens

Additional: Thieves Household Cleaner

Applications and Usage

Topical: Apply Clarity on brainstem, Joy over the heart, and Stress Away Roll-On along topline. Make a dissolution with Thieves Household Cleaner. Add Raindrop oils and other desired oils. Mist along top line.

Ingestion & Oral: The animal must be reversed from any tranquilization before drenching or feeding. Add desired oils to NingXia Red or purified water. Draw up in a syringe or drench gun. Drench the animal. May be added as top dressing to feed.

Inhalation: Drop Clarity in your hands and cup over nostrils. Diffuse if stalled.

Other: Raindrop Technique

Black Quarter

Black Quarter is a disease that causes swelling of the legs, lameness, and death in cattle.

Recommendations
Singles: Copaiba, Peppermint
Blends: DiGize, Thieves

Applications and Usage
Ingestion & Oral: Administer orally 30 drops each DiGize, Copaiba, Peppermint, and Thieves 30 drops each directly into mouth 2 times daily until condition is corrected.

Bloat or Colic (*see also* Equine Colic)

Bloat is characterized by a rapid buildup of gases in the intestines and stomach, caused mostly by plant fermentation. This condition may be life threatening if gas is not expelled rapidly enough, resulting in high internal pressure pushing against vital organs.

Recommendations
Singles: Black Pepper, Tarragon, Lavender, Vetiver, Valerian, Ylang Ylang, Patchouli, Coriander, Copaiba, Ginger, Peppermint
Blends: DiGize, Stress Away Roll-On, Joy, Aroma Siez, Tranquil Roll-On, DiGize

Applications and Usage
Topical: Apply oils in frogs of hooves and around navel. Also try applying 10 drops each suggested oils topically on tummy area, where hair is thinner, 4 times daily.
Ingestion & Oral: Drop suggested oils under tongue or in mouth. Also administer orally 20 drops each DiGize, Copaiba, Ginger, and Peppermint 2-3 times daily.
Inhalation: Apply desired oil in nostrils. Diffuse if stalled.
Other: Raindrop Technique

Bottle Babies in Cervidea and Botinae
(except Cattle, Buffalo & Bison)

Bottle Babies are animals that have been orphaned by their mothers or have been pulled from them to be raised by hand.

It is especially important during the first few days of a new baby's life for it to intake colostrum. Contact a veterinarian or a local goat's milk producer to find some.

If you cannot find fresh goat's milk, buy some from the grocery store.

People often mistakenly try to feed a replacement milk or cow's milk to exotic hoof stock. Cow's milk is harder on the animal's digestive system and can cause severe health issues and in some cases death.

When first feeding a bottle baby, be sure to have a warm, damp cloth available to stimulate the anus, simulating the baby's response to nursing to help prevent impaction. If impaction does occur, use oils that will help move things along.

If the animal scours (diarrhea), drench it with 1 quart castor oil and 25 drops DiGize.

Recommendations
Singles: Coriander, Lemon, Peppermint
Blends: DiGize, T-Away, Joy, Stress Away Roll-On
Nutritionals: NingXia Red

Applications and Usage
Topical: Apply 1 drop chosen oil on hooves and on navel.
Ingestion & Oral: Add 1 drop chosen oil in a single serving of milk.
Inhalation: Place 1 drop chosen oil in hands and cover animal's nostrils.

Botulism

Botulism in cattle can occur for many reasons. These reasons can range from cattle eating near poultry droppings to cattle eating food contaminated with deceased animals. Cattle may also eat animal bones in response to mineral deficiencies. Good and proper nutrition throughout the year, especially during winter, will help prevent botulism from affecting cattle.

Recommendations
Singles: Copaiba, Peppermint, Tea Tree
Blends: DiGize, Thieves
Nutritionals: K&B

Applications and Usage
Ingestion & Oral: Administer orally 30 drops each DiGize, Copaiba, Peppermint, and Thieves, plus 8 dropperfuls K&B directly into mouth 2 times daily until condition is corrected.

Broken Bones

Broken bones may result from a variety of issues, including environmental, nutritional, or inadvertent accidents. Bone diseases may be congenital, hereditary, nutritional, or traumatic. These include spinal ataxia and abnormal bone formation due to parathyroid hypoplasia. Consult your veterinary health professional.

Recommendations

Singles: Helichrysum, Frankincense, Wintergreen, Clove, Peppermint, Lemongrass, Palo Santo, Palmarosa, Copaiba, Lavender, Vetiver, Valerian, Northern Lights Black Spruce, Raindrop oils

Blends: Exodus II, PanAway, Relieve It, Egyptian Gold, Thieves

Nutritionals: NingXia Red, Ningxia Organic Dried Wolfberries, Sulfurzyme

Additional: Thieves Dentarome Ultra Toothpaste, Cool Azul Pain Relief Cream

Applications and Usage

Topical: Carefully apply oils over area in question. If the animal is sensitive to touch, combine oils with carrier oil in spray bottle and mist area thoroughly. Apply oils to help aid recovery; use Thieves Dentarome Ultra Toothpaste or Cool Azul Pain Relief Cream combined with chosen oils as a poultice.

Ingestion & Oral: The animal must be reversed with Wintergreen from any tranquilization before drenching or feeding. Add desired oils to NingXia Red or purified water. Draw up in a syringe or drench gun. Drench the animal. May be added as top dressing to feed.

Inhalation: Use suggested oils to help calm distressed animal. Rub chosen oils between palms and hold over the animal's nose.

Other: Raindrop Technique

Broken Horns

Cervidea: Broken horns may pose significant health challenges for a horned animal. If injured while a cervidea is in velvet or soft horn, the horn may fall partially or completely off. If the animal is in the hard-horn phase of horn growth, horn impact often breaks just the ends of the tines, which can be chipped or broken.

If a deer breaks a horn (antler) off at the pedestal (base closest to the skull), the pedestal may be damaged and mal-formed. This may affect antler growth for years to follow. If the antler breaks extremely close to the pedestal, the break may result in a broken skull plate. Consult your veterinarian.

Bovinae: In rare cases, broken horns can sometimes lead to death. Horns broken near the base or below the base may result in a broken skull plate.

To save an animal's life, a veterinarian may remove both horns if the break is severe. It is not rare to see some breeds that have a broken horn that was broken when the animal was young. These horns can grow crooked or curled and may impair the vision or grow in a manner that is a detriment to the animal.

Most common however are simple chips or cracks near the ends of horns. In those cases, the animal will be fine. Always consult an expert to discuss your options.

Recommendations

Singles: Lemongrass, Helichrysum, Frankincense, Elemi, Geranium, Copaiba, Black Pepper, Raindrop oils, Palmarosa, Coriander, Tea Tree, Northern Lights Black Spruce, Roman Chamomile, Lavender, Cistus, Cedarwood, Rosemary

Blends: Thieves, Purification, Exodus II, Egyptian Gold, The Gift, Believe, Joy, Stress Away Roll-On, Clarity

Nutritionals: NingXia Red, Ningxia Organic Dried Wolfberries, Sulfurzyme

Additional: Thieves Household Cleaner, Animal Scents Ointment

Applications and Usage

Topical: Clean the area thoroughly with Thieves Household Cleaner spray with oils added. Apply Clarity to the brainstem, Joy and Believe to the heart, and Stress Away Roll-On down topline. If bleeding, apply Black Pepper, Helichrysum, and Frankincense to base of skull where it is bleeding. Mist a spray of Thieves Household Cleaner on area or flush as needed down topline.

Ingestion & Oral: The animal must be reversed with Wintergreen from any tranquilization before drenching or feeding. Add desired oils to NingXia Red or purified water. Draw up in a syringe or drench gun. Drench the animal. May be added as top dressing to feed.

Other: Clean affected area with Thieves Household Cleaner. Apply Animal Scents Ointment directly to area, with or without suggested oils. Administer Raindrop Technique as needed.

Cattle Measles

Cattle measles are a result of cattle consuming feed or pasture hay that has been contaminated by human fecal matter. The disease is only manifest after slaughter when meat can be inspected for small cysts that contain immature tapeworms.

Human consumption of meat with cattle measles can result in the transfer of tapeworms to human intestines.

Recommendations

Singles: Oregano, Lemongrass, Ocotea, Copaiba, Peppermint
Blends: DiGize
Nutritionals: ParaFree

Applications and Usage

Ingestion & Oral: Administer directly into the mouth 20 drops each DiGize, Lemongrass, Ocotea, ParaFree (open capsule), Copaiba, and Peppermint for 21 days. Repeat if needed.

Cold or Influenza

Influenza in cattle is manifest similarly as in other cloven hoofed animals. Usually symptoms include extreme thirst, nasal discharge, difficulty eating, and general lethargy. Affected cattle should be separated from the herd and treated separately.

Applications and Usage

Singles: Raindrop oils, Eucalyptus Globulus, Eucalyptus Radiata, Eucalyptus Blue, Myrtle, Lavender, Lemon (or any citrus oil), Frankincense, Elemi, Idaho Balsam Fir, Northern Lights Black Spruce, Idaho Blue Spruce, Peppermint, Ravintsara
Blends: Thieves, Purification, ImmuPower, Egyptian Gold, Exodus II, R.C., Raven, Mountain Savory, Evergreen Essence
Nutritionals: NingXia Red, Ningxia Organic Dried Wolfberries
Additional: V-6 Vegetable Oil Complex

Recommendations

Topical: Rub oils topically on nose or snout; be conscious of hot oils and dilute with V-6 or other carrier oil if needed. Apply chosen oils to neck, flank, and chest.
Ingestion & Oral: Combine desired oils with NingXia Red and syringe or combine with feed and water. Always leave optional second bucket of clean drinking water for your animal.

Veterinarian Tips and Suggestions

Cold or Influenza

Combine all listed ingredients in a 14-oz. container and drench:

- 2 oz. NingXia Red
- 10-15 drops Oregano
- 8-13 drops Mountain Savory
- 8-10 drops Lavender, Lemon, and Peppermint combined
- 5 drops Elemi
- 5 drops Copaiba
- 5 drops Evergreen Essence
- Top with purified water.

Inhalation: Rub chosen oils between your palms and cup hands over the nose of the animal for 30 seconds at a time or as long as the animal allows. Re-apply 2-3 times per session.
Other: Administer Raindrop Technique.

Cuts, Scrapes, and Abrasions

Treating wounds should be done with care and caution. Ensure the animal is restrained and will not thrash about during treatment. This is to protect both the animal and the person administering treatment. Key to treating any open wound is to monitor progress daily to encourage proper healing and to prevent infection.

Recommendations

Singles: Helichrysum, Lavender, Raindrop oils, Hinoki, Elemi, Frankincense, Copaiba, Northern Lights Black Spruce
Blends: Thieves, Relieve It, Mendwell, T-Away, Joy
Supplement: NingXia Red
Additional: Thieves Household Cleaner, Animal Scents Ointment

Applications and Usage

Topical: Apply to location, hooves, or down topline. Clean with Thieves Household Cleaner with desired oils added.
Ingestion & Oral: Top dress
Inhalation: Drop oil in hand; cup over nose.
Other: Apply Animal Scents Ointment on location, with or without suggested oils as needed. Administer Raindrop Technique for additional support.

Foot Rot (Infections of the foot)

Foot rot generally refers to any infection affecting the lower leg and the hoof area. Typical symptoms may include but are not limited to swelling of the foot, odor, limping, and general lameness.

Foot rot can be caused by many external factors, including wet, humid conditions, along with cattle living in areas having high concentrations of urine and feces for long periods of time. This leads to the creation of a mud-like condition that is particularly harmful to cows with foot rot.

Recommendations

Singles: Oregano, Thyme, Basil, Clove, Hyssop, Tea Tree, Melaleuca Ericifolia, Melaleuca Quinquenervia, Ravintsara, Cinnamon Bark, Ginger, Lemon, Lemongrass, Geranium, Ocotea, Black Pepper, Myrrh, Cistus

Blends: Exodus II, Melrose, Thieves, Purification, Raven, Egyptian Gold, DiGize

Additional: Thieves Household Cleaner

Applications and Usage

Topical: Apply equal parts any 1 or combination of suggested oils and Copaiba on location 2-4 times daily until condition is corrected.

Ingestion & Oral: Administer directly into the mouth 10 drops each DiGize and Thieves 1 time daily.

Other: Wash affected area with a solution of 4 capfuls of Thieves Household Cleaner in 1 gallon of water.

Grass Tetany

Grass tetany is a result of magnesium deficiency in the diet of cows. Symptoms can include muscle spasms, faltering, irritability, and general incoordination. Full recovery can be achieved only through restoring magnesium nutrient levels via diet.

Recommendations

Singles: Copaiba

Blends: DiGize

Nutritionals: MegaCal, Mineral Essence, NingXia Red

Applications and Usage

Ingestion & Oral: Administer directly into the mouth 15 drops each DiGize and Copaiba and dissolve 2 scoops MegaCal and 6 dropperfuls Mineral Essence in 6 oz. NingXia Red 2 times daily for 4-6 days. Then supplement with 2-3 oz. NingXia Red, 6 dropperfuls Mineral Essence, and 2 scoops MegaCal 1 time daily.

Hardware Disease

Hardware disease is a condition in which cattle ingest harmful objects, resulting in these objects getting lodged in the intestinal tract or rectum.

This condition can cause major damage and even death. Objects are generally field items and may include wire, glass, metal, bone, or any other indigestible item.

Typical treatment can include surgery or laxatives to help pass objects. Always consult your veterinarian professional when encountering hardware disease.

Recommendations

Singles: Copaiba, Cistus, Peppermint

Blends: DiGize

Applications and Usage

Topical: Apply 30 drops Peppermint on throat down to stomach and belly area.

Ingestion & Oral: Administer ⅓ bottle ICP mixed in 3 gallons of water. Administer orally 10 drops each DiGize, Copaiba, and Cistus directly into mouth.

Lactate or Lactic Acid

In handling wild animals, one of the common things to watch for when capturing them is lactate or lactic-acid buildup. This is a condition in which muscles are being overexerted, generally because the animal is panicking and thrashing about.

This overexertion leads to the buildup of lactate because of the lack of oxygen getting to the exerted muscles. This buildup can cause soreness even days later. The soreness and inflammation can cause a variety of symptoms. In wild animals, this can lead to sickness and even death.

Recommendations

Singles: Wintergreen, Helichrysum, Peppermint, Clove, Lavender, Northern Lights Black Spruce, Frankincense, Elemi, Copaiba, Vetiver, Valerian, Lemon, Myrrh, Raindrop oils, Lemongrass, Palo Santo

Blends: Cool Azul, Joy, DiGize, ParaGize, T-Away, Trauma Life, Stress Away Roll-On, Deep Relief Roll-On, PanAway, Relieve It, Clarity, Aroma Life, Aroma Siez, Evergreen Essence, Thieves

Nutritionals: NingXia Red

Additional: Ortho Ease Massage Oil, Ortho Sport Massage Oil, Thieves Spray, Cool Azul Pain Relief Cream, Cool Azul Sports Gel

Applications and Usage
Inhalation: Administer Wintergreen, Helichrysum, or PanAway in nostrils.

Other: Apply Thieves Spray with pain blends, massage oils, or Cool Azul products added to help with soreness.

Lumpy-Skin Disease
Lumpy-Skin Disease is usually transmitted through direct contact with an affected area or spread through biting insects. Symptoms include lumps forming on the skin of animals. If you suspect your animals have this disease, contact your veterinarian immediately.

Recommendations
Singles: Lavender, Tea Tree, Lemongrass, Geranium, Clove, Basil

Blends: DiGize, Thieves, Purification, Egyptian Gold, Raven

Nutritionals: ParaFree

Additional: Thieves Household Cleaner

Applications and Usage
Topical: Wash affected area with a solution of 4 capfuls Thieves Household Cleaner in 1 gallon of water. Dry area. Apply 1 or more of the suggested oils on location. Repeat as often as needed.

Ingestion & Oral: Apply directly into mouth 20 drops each DiGize, Thieves, and ParaFree 2 times daily.

Other: Administer Raindrop Technique daily.

Mastitis
This inflammation of the mammary gland is reported in almost all domestic mammals worldwide. It is primarily caused by bacterial infection of the mammary gland and will generally reduce milk productivity.

Most infections are mild but severe cases may become systemic and should be treated. Consult a veterinary health professional to rule out serious, underlying causes, prevent serious complications, and avoid contraindications.

Recommendations
Singles: Mountain Savory

Blends: DiGize, Melrose, Thieves

Additional: Thieves Household Cleaner

Applications and Usage
Topical: Wash affected area with a solution of 4 capfuls of Thieves Household Cleaner in 1 gallon of water. Dry area. Apply on location any 1 or more of the following: DiGize, Mountain Savory, Thieves, and Melrose. Follow with Animal Scents Ointment 2 times daily.

Ingestion & Oral: Administer directly into the mouth 10 drops each DiGize and Melrose 2 times daily.

Other: Apply Animal Scents Ointment on teat as needed.

Myopathy
Myopathy is characterized as a muscular affliction. Usually this malady presents as muscle fibers not operating correctly, resulting in muscular weakness. Symptoms of myopathy include painful stiffness, cramps, and uncontrollable muscle twitching.

In wild animals, myopathy is sometimes referred to specifically as capture myopathy. This disease is usually brought about by stress due to being handled or captured. This sudden onset of stress and muscle tetany often results in the death of the animal. This is especially true in small animals such as rodents and birds. It is also referred to as Shock Disease.

Recommendations
Singles: Wintergreen, Helichrysum, Peppermint, Clove, Lavender, Northern Lights Black Spruce, Frankincense, Elemi, Copaiba, Vetiver, Valerian, Lemon, Myrrh, Raindrop oils, Lemongrass, Palo Santo

Blends: Cool Azul, Deep Relief Roll-On, Joy, DiGize, ParaGize, T-Away, Trauma Life, Stress Away Roll-On, PanAway, Relieve It, Clarity, Aroma Life, Evergreen Essence, Thieves

Nutritionals: NingXia Red

Additional: Thieves Household Cleaner, Thieves Spray, Ortho Ease Massage Oil, Ortho Sport Massage Oil, Cool Azul Pain Relief Cream, Cool Azul Sports Gel

Applications and Usage
Topical: Apply Wintergreen, Helichrysum, and PanAway in hooves; Joy on heart; Clarity on brainstem; DiGize or ParaGize dropped into mouth and around navel; Stress Away Roll-On, T-Away, or Trauma Life down topline; and Thieves Household Cleaner spray with desired oils misted down topline and on belly.

Inhalation: Wintergreen, Helichrysum, or PanAway in nostrils.

Other: Thieves Household Cleaner, Thieves Spray with pain blends added. Oils applied topically can be layered with Ortho Ease Massage Oil, Ortho Sport Massage Oil, Cool Azul Pain Relief Cream, and/or Cool Azul Sports Gel.

Parasites

A parasite is an organism that lives on or in a host and gets its food from or at the expense of its host. Parasites can cause disease.

Recommendations

Singles: Oregano, Thyme, Fennel, Tea Tree, Clove, Tarragon, Lemon, Ravintsara, Eucalyptus Radiata, Nutmeg, Laurus Nobilis, Geranium, Rosemary, Cedarwood

Blends: ParaGize, Purification, DiGize

Nutritionals: NingXia Red, MultiGreens, Sulfurzyme

Applications and Usage

Topical: Apply to stomach.

Ingestion & Oral: Mix in feed or water.

Other: Administer Raindrop Technique.

Prussic Acid Poisoning

Prussic acid can build up in plants, mainly sorghum. There are many reasons for this build up, including plants being young, damaged, or wild.

The result of an animal eating plants with high levels of prussic acid can lead to asphyxiation and death. Symptoms include difficulty breathing, foaming at the nose and mouth, and inability to stand. The onset of symptoms is extremely rapid after ingestion. Immediately consult a veterinary professional.

Recommendations

Singles: Copaiba, Peppermint

Blends: DiGize, Purification

Nutritionals: K&B

Applications and Usage

Ingestion & Oral: Administer directly into mouth 30 drops each DiGize, Copaiba, Peppermint, and Purification, plus 8 dropperfuls K&B 2 times daily until condition is corrected.

Puncture Wound

A puncture wound has a small entry hole caused by a pointed object that can vary in width and depth. Treatment of puncture wounds is similar to the treatment of other wounds. Always be sure to have the animal stalled or tethered to prevent thrashing injuries to yourself or the animal.

Recommendations

Singles: Black Pepper, Frankincense, Clove, Elemi, Geranium, Myrrh, Onycha, Wintergreen, Raindrop oils

Blends: Thieves, The Gift, Exodus II, Egyptian Gold, Mendwell, PuriClean, Purification, ParaGize

Nutritionals: NingXia Red

Additional: Thieves Household Cleaner, Animal Scents Ointment

Applications and Usage

Topical: Clean with Thieves Household Cleaner with desired oils added. Drop oils in wound. Top with Animal Scents Ointment if desired. It's good to let a puncture drain. Flush to keep draining.

Ingestion & Oral: NingXia Red

Inhalation: Drop oils in hand and cup over nostrils. If tranquilized, apply Wintergreen in nostrils.

Other: Clean around wound with diluted Thieves Household Cleaner. Topical oils can be layered with Animal Scents Ointment.

Respiratory Care

Treat inflammation of the respiratory system and excessive build up in the nose or throat.

Recommendations

Singles: Eucalyptus Blue, Peppermint, Lemon, Lavender, Myrtle, Rosemary, Eucalyptus Globulus, Eucalyptus Radiata, Northern Lights Black Spruce, Frankincense, Copaiba, Raindrop oils

Blends: Raven, R.C., Breathe Again Roll-On, Thieves, Stress Away Roll-On, Infect Away, ParaGize, DiGize

Nutritionals: NingXia Red, Sulfurzyme

Applications and Usage

Topical: Apply ParaGize or DiGize in hooves and on navel. Also apply Thieves and Stress Away Roll-On with 3-4 suggested oils on topline.

Ingestion & Oral: Feed NingXia Red and Sulfurzyme. Add desired oils as a top dressing.

Inhalation: Eucalyptus Blue or any desired oils in the nostrils.

Veterinarian Tips and Suggestions

Respiratory Care

Use the following custom blend to help with respiratory care. The blend may be administered multiple ways, including misting over the animal's nose, oral drenching, or diffusing in an enclosed stall. Combine the following and store in a large glass container.

- 5-10 drops EACH of the following oils
  - Lavender
  - Copaiba
  - Lemon
  - Northern Lights Black Spruce
  - Peppermint
  - Frankincense

- 2-4 oz. of Thieves Household Cleaner for external application or
- 2-4 oz. of NingXia Red or water for internal application

When administering orally, combine blend in 14-oz. glass bottle with water. Add NingXia Red to oral blend for additional support.

Tetanus

Tetanus in cattle often occurs due to wound infections, particularly during castration and dehorning. The best prevention methods include vaccination and immediate cleaning of wounds.

Recommendations

Singles: Thyme, Mountain Savory, Myrrh
Blends: DiGize, Thieves
Nutritionals: ParaFree

Applications and Usage

Topical: Administer Raindrop Technique daily.
Ingestion & Oral: Administer directly into mouth 20 drops each DiGize, Thyme, Thieves, and ParaFree (open capsule) 2-4 times daily.

Three-Day Stiff Sickness

Three-Day Stiff Sickness is characterized by lameness or sickness in which the afflicted animal will become lethargic or lay down for a period of approximately 3 days. The animal will generally get better on its own, but caretakers should carefully monitor the animal's health and provide food, water, and supplements to aid in recovery. This is usually spread by insects from one cow to another.

Recommendations

Blends: DiGize, Thieves, ImmuPower
Nutritionals: ParaFree

Applications and Usage

Topical: Administer Raindrop Technique daily.
Ingestion & Oral: Administer directly into mouth 20 drops each DiGize, Thieves, ImmuPower, and ParaFree (open capsule) 2 times daily.

Tick Damage

Ticks can often harm cattle in a variety of ways, including spreading disease and causing sores or wounds. The best way to deal with ticks is to take preventive measures. Work toward eradication and quarantine as soon as signs of ticks appear.

Recommendations

Singles: Lavender, Tea Tree, Hinoki, Lemongrass, Geranium
Blends: Thieves, Purification

Applications and Usage

Topical: Wash affected area with a solution of 4 capfuls Thieves Household Cleaner in 1 gallon of water. Dry area. Apply topically on location any 1 or more of the suggested oils.

Worms

Worms can cause challenging issues, particularly in calves. Best preventive measures include deworming regularly.

Recommendations

Singles: Oregano, Peppermint, Cinnamon Bark
Blends: DiGize, ParaGize

Applications and Usage

Ingestion & Oral: Administer orally 20 drops each DiGize, Oregano, Peppermint, and Cinnamon Bark for 14 days. Repeat if needed.

Deer-Specific Conditions

Misting of wild animals may be the most desired application. Single oils and blends may be mixed with Thieves Household Cleaner and water to make a spray of your choice.

Raindrop Technique may be varied to develop individual spray bottles for each of the Raindrop Kit oils. In an 8-ounce glass bottle, combine 1 cap Thieves Household Cleaner and 60 drops of a Raindrop Kit oil; fill with distilled or purified water. Shake well before each use. Mist the animal's top line. Repeat with each of the kit's oils. Be sure to label each bottle for future usage.

Anesthesia Support

A veterinary procedure requiring anesthesia may need to be performed on a deer. Using essential oils may assist the deer to better tolerate anesthesia reversal when it is time to wake up. Some animals become depressed after anesthesia.

Recommendations

Singles: Eucalyptus Blue, Wintergreen, Helichrysum, Lavender, Peppermint

Blends: Joy, JuvaCleanse, JuvaFlex, Stress Away Roll-On, T-Away

Nutritionals: JuvaSpice, JuvaTone

Applications and Usage

Topical: 1. Apply 1 drop Joy to the palm of your nondominant hand. Swirl your fingertip from the opposite hand around in the oil. Gently apply to animal's front feet as close to all coronary bands as possible. 2. Repeat technique on both feet with Stress Away Roll-On. 3. Apply 1 drop of Eucalyptus Blue or oil of your choice to the palm of your nondominant hand. Swirl your fingertip from the opposite hand around in the oil. Gently apply to animal's abdominal area to support its liver.

Ingestion & Oral: Administer 1-5 drops essential oil on a favorite treat or foodstuff daily to support the liver.

Inhalation: After opening a Wintergreen essential oil bottle, just hold it a few inches away from the animal's nose. There is no need to apply it to the animal. Once it begins to arouse, just hold it there for another minute or so.

Bovine Tuberculosis (Deer)

This health challenge is present when an animal is exposed to contagious airborne bacteria of this specific causation. Signs include chronic cough with bloody discharge, fatigue, fever, weakness, and weight loss.

Recommendations

Singles: Cedarwood, Clove, Dorado Azul, Eucalyptus Radiata, Frankincense, Geranium, Idaho Balsam Fir, Lemon, Lemongrass, Tea Tree, Melissa, Myrtle, Myrrh, Mountain Savory, Orange, Oregano, Peppermint, Ravintsara, Rosemary, Sacred Sandalwood, Royal Hawaiian Sandalwood, Thyme

Blends: Breathe Again Roll-On, Citrus Fresh, Exodus II, ImmuPower, Infect Away, Inspiration, Longevity, Melrose, Purification, Raven, R.C., Sacred Mountain, Thieves

Nutritionals: Essentialzyme, ImmuPro, Inner Defense, Life 9, Longevity Softgels, MultiGreens, Rehemogen, Super C Chewable

Additional: Thieves Household Cleaner

Applications and Usage

Topical: Mist multiple times daily with an 8-oz. sprayer containing a blend of 2 oz. Thieves Household Cleaner, water, and 60 drops each Cedarwood, Melrose, Rosemary, and Purification. Fill with purified or distilled water.

Ingestion & Oral: The same single oils and/or blends may be applied to a treat or foodstuff used for topical application or diffusion. Oils should be given at least 2 times daily.

Inhalation: Alternate diffusing R.C. and Raven. Diffuse a blend of equal parts of immune-enhancing and respiratory oils.

Other: Administer Raindrop Technique as needed.

Veterinarian Tips and Suggestions

Bovine Tuberculosis

A variation of Gary Young's human formula for rectal implants may work well. In 2 tablespoons V-6 Vegetable Oil Complex, combine 2 drops Oregano, 4 drops Myrrh, 5 drops Clove, 6 drops Ravintsara, and 15 drops Frankincense. Feed 2 times daily.

Veterinarian Tips and Suggestions

Brain Abscess

In 2 tablespoons V-6 Vegetable Oil Complex, combine 2 drops Rosemary, 4 drops Myrrh, 5 drops Clove, 6 drops Blue Cypress, and 15 drops Frankincense. Feed 2 times daily.

Brain Abscess

This abscess is similar to any other abscess but is contained within the brain itself. This can often result from horns breaking too close to the pedestal (base of the skull), causing the bone of the skull to fracture. Direct application of oils is not possible, so inhalation and diffusing are possible ways to get oils to the proper destination.

Recommendations

Singles: Myrrh, Black Pepper, Blue Cypress, Cedarwood, Eucalyptus Globulus, Frankincense, Helichrysum, Lavender, Lemon, Lemongrass, Melissa, Palo Santo, Peppermint, Rose, Rosemary, Sacred Frankincense

Blends: Brain Power, Clarity, Common Sense, Egyptian Gold, Exodus II, Longevity, ParaGize, Sacred Mountain, Thieves

Nutritionals: Inner Defense, Life 9, Longevity softgels, MindWise, NingXia Red, Ningxia Organic Dried Wolfberries, OmegaGize[3], ParaFree, Rehemogen, Sulfurzyme, Super C Chewable

Applications and Usage

Topical: Mist base of the brain with a single oil or blend of your choice several times daily.

Ingestion & Oral: The same single oils and/or blends may be applied to a treat or foodstuff used for topical application or diffusing. Oils should be given at least 2 times daily.

Inhalation: Diffuse an immune-enhancing essential oil or blend throughout the day.

Other: Administer Raindrop Technique as needed.

Corn Toxicity

Corn toxicity refers to the general condition in which deer overeat a high carbohydrate food, not necessarily just corn. Overeating is not unexpected when a single foodstuff is too plentiful. Overeating can be dangerous, however, when the food includes a high carbohydrate source. This can lead to diarrhea, which will result in dehydration, nutrient deficiencies, and even death.

Recommendations

Singles: Cardamom, Dill, Helichrysum, Juniper, Lemon, Mastrante, Peppermint, Tarragon

Blends: AromaEase, DiGize, GLF, JuvaCleanse, JuvaFlex, Thieves

Nutritionals: Allerzyme, Detoxzyme, Digest & Cleanse, Essentialzyme, Inner Defense, JuvaTone, NingXia Red, Ningxia Organic Dried Wolfberries, Sulfurzyme

Applications and Usage

Topical: Mist lower thoracic spine with a single oil or blend of your choice several times daily.

Ingestion & Oral: The same single oils and/or blends may be applied to a treat or foodstuff used for topical application or diffusing. Oils should be given at least 2 times daily.

Inhalation: Alternate diffusing digestion-enhancing and liver-supporting essential oils or blends throughout the day.

Other: Administer Raindrop Technique as needed.

Hair Loss Syndrome (see also Lice)

Hair loss may be for a variety of reasons: disease, insect infestation, tissue injury caused by fighting, or just rubbing because it feels good.

Recommendations

Singles: Basil, Cedarwood, Clary Sage, Cypress, Geranium, Ginger, Hyssop, Laurus Nobilis, Lavender, Roman Chamomile, Rosemary, Sage, Thyme, Western Red Cedar, Ylang Ylang

Blends: ImmuPower, R.C.

Nutritionals: NingXia Red, Ningxia Organic Dried Wolfberries, Sulfurzyme, Super B

Additional: Thieves Household Cleaner

Applications and Usage

Topical: Mist topline and area of concern with a single oil or blend of your choice extended in Thieves Household Cleaner several times daily.

Ingestion & Oral: The same immune- and growth-stimulating enhancing single oils and/or blends may be applied to a treat or foodstuff used for topical application or diffusing. Oils should be applied at least daily.

Inhalation: Diffuse an immune-enhancing essential oil or blend throughout the day.

Other: Administer Raindrop Technique as needed.

Horn Removal Support (see Anesthesia Support and Wounds)

Lice (see also Flea and Tick Repellant)

The tiny multilegged insects called lice like to move from animal to animal. They burrow into the skin to lay eggs. Lice in deer are usually commonplace and can cause many health challenges.

Recommendations

Singles: Black Pepper, Citronella, Eucalyptus Globulus, Ginger, Lavender, Palmarosa, Peppermint

Blends: ImmuPower, Melrose, Purification, Thieves

Nutritionals: Allerzyme, Essentialzyme, ImmuPro, Life 9, MightyZymes, NingXia Red, Ningxia Organic Dried Wolfberries, OmegaGize[3], Sulfurzyme

Additional: Animal Scents Shampoo, Thieves Household Cleaner, ClaraDerm, LavaDerm Cooling Mist, V-6 Vegetable Oil Complex

Applications and Usage

Topical: Any of the oils may be added to Animal Scents Shampoo if your deer is tame enough to bathe. If not, dilute the oils with Thieves Household Cleaner, V-6, or water to thoroughly mist the hair coat.

Other: Combine 30-60 drops each of Purification and Melrose in a bottle of LavaDerm Cooling Mist to spray on areas. Use Animal Scents Shampoo, ClaraDerm spray, and LavaDerm Cooling Mist to treat and prevent lice infestations.

Lyme Disease

Lyme disease is caused by tick bites, providing quite a health challenge. Symptoms of Lyme disease include joint pain, fever, and in extreme cases, damage to internal organs.

Recommendations

Singles: Helichrysum, Mountain Savory, Ocotea, Oregano, Thyme

Blends: Clarity, Egyptian Gold, Exodus II, Longevity, ParaGize, Sacred Mountain, Thieves

Nutritionals: Essentialzyme, Inner Defense, Life 9, Longevity softgels, MightyVites, NingXia Red, Ningxia Organic Dried Wolfberries, OmegaGize[3], ParaFree, Sulfurzyme, Super C Chewable

Additional: Thieves Household Cleaner

Applications and Usage

Topical: Mist topline with a single oil or blend of your choice extended in Thieves Household Cleaner several times daily during crisis.

Ingestion & Oral: The same immune-enhancing single oils and/or blends may be applied to a treat or foodstuff used for topical application or diffusing. Oils should be given at least 2 times daily.

Inhalation: Diffuse an immune-enhancing essential oil or blend throughout the day.

Other: Administer Raindrop Technique as needed.

Mange (Demodectic)

Mange is characterized by hair loss, open sores from scratching, weight loss, loss of vision, and lethargy. Mange is typically caused by a small, burrowing mite that causes extreme discomfort. This discomfort causes the animal to itch the affected area, causing open sores to form, which can lead to infections.

Be extremely careful when handling animals with mange as the mange-causing mite is very transferable to other animals.

Recommendations

Singles: Black Pepper, Citronella, Eucalyptus Globulus, Ginger, Lavender, Palmarosa, Peppermint

Blends: ImmuPower, Melrose, Purification, Thieves

Nutritionals: Allerzyme, Essentialzyme, ImmuPro, Life 9, MightyZymes, NingXia Red, Ningxia Organic Dried Wolfberries, OmegaGize[3], Sulfurzyme

Additional: Thieves Household Cleaner, Animal Scents Ointment, Animal Scents Shampoo

Applications and Usage

Topical: Mist infected areas with a single oil or blend of your choice extended in Thieves Household Cleaner several times daily.

Ingestion & Oral: The same immune-enhancing and skin-supporting single oils and/or blends used for topical application or diffusing may be applied to a treat or foodstuff. Oils should be given at least 2 times daily.

Inhalation: Diffuse an immune-enhancing essential oil or blend throughout the day.

Other: Administer Raindrop Technique as needed. Use Animal Scents Ointment, Animal Scents Shampoo, and Thieves Household Cleaner to help take care of a mange condition.

Nasal Bots (Squirrel, Rabbit, Deer)

Nasal bots refer to small, hatching fly larvae that burrow in the nasal passages of the host deer. The flies generally do not pose a lethal threat to the host; however, they can lead to discomfort and irritability.

Recommendations

Singles: Eucalyptus Globulus, Melaleuca Quinquenervia

Blends: Purification

Applications and Usage

Topical: Mist the nasal flares with Purification or a single oil.

Inhalation: Diffuse an immune-enhancing essential oil or blend throughout the day.

Parasites (Lung Flukes, Arterial Worms, Stomach Worms)

A parasite is anything that resides inside of you or your pet that is not part of your body. It derives benefits at the expense of its host.

Recommendations

Singles: Basil, Bergamot, Cinnamon Bark, Clove, Fennel, Ginger, Melaleuca Quinquenervia, Nutmeg, Oregano, Tangerine, Thyme

Blends: Citrus Fresh, DiGize, Inner Defense, ParaGize, Thieves

Nutritionals: ParaFree

Additional: Thieves Household Cleaner

Veterinarian Tips and Suggestions

Parasites

In 2 tablespoons V-6 Vegetable Oil Complex, combine 4 drops each Ginger and DiGize. Feed as needed.

Applications and Usage

Topical: Misting of wild animals may be the most desired application. Single oils and blends may be mixed with Thieves Household Cleaner and water to make a spray of your choice. Apply along the animal's topline, while concentrating on lower back area in front of hips.

Ingestion & Oral: The same single oils and/or blends with 1 opened ParaFree capsule may be applied to a treat or foodstuff used for topical application or diffusing.

Inhalation: Diffuse an immune-enhancing essential oil or blend.

Other: Administer Raindrop Technique as needed.

Wounds

When kept in close proximity or territory, animals have a tendency to want to assert their authority. Authority battles may result in skin and tissue injury.

Recommendations

Singles: Blue Tansy, Cistus, Elemi, Eucalyptus Globulus, Frankincense, German Chamomile, Laurus Nobilis, Lavender, Ledum, Lemongrass, Manuka, Tea Tree, Myrrh, Neroli, Ocotea, Onycha, Palmarosa, Palo Santo, Patchouli, Peppermint, Roman Chamomile, Rose, Rosemary, Sacred Frankincense, Thyme, Tsuga

Blends: Common Sense, Egyptian Gold, Exodus II, Infect Away, Lady Sclareol, Longevity, Melrose, Mendwell, Present Time, Purification, Raven, SARA, The Gift, Thieves, White Angelica

---

Veterinarian Tips and Suggestions

Wounds

In a 32-ounce glass misting bottle, combine 4 oz. Thieves Household Cleaner with 30-60 drops each of Lavender, Tsuga, Palo Santo, Egyptian Gold, and Thieves. Fill with purified or distilled water. Mist area of concern at least 1 time daily.

Nutritionals: Inner Defense, Life 9, Longevity Softgels, NingXia Red, Ningxia Organic Dried Wolfberries, Sulfurzyme

Additional: Genesis Hand and Body Lotion, Animal Scents Ointment, ClaraDerm, LavaDerm Cooling Mist, Lavender Hand and Body Lotion, Rose Ointment, Thieves Household Cleaner

Applications and Usage

Topical: Misting of wild animals may be the most desired application. Single oils and blends may be mixed with Genesis Hand and Body Lotion or any of the other lotions to make a skin-supporting lotion of your choice. Apply lotion or spray on area of concern at least 1 time daily until trauma is resolved.

Ingestion & Oral: The same single oils and/or blends may be applied to a treat or foodstuff used for topical application or diffusing.

Inhalation: Diffuse an immune-enhancing essential oil or blend.

Other: Administer Raindrop Technique as needed. Use Animal Scents Ointment, ClaraDerm Cooling Mist, Genesis Lotion, LavaDerm Cooling Mist, Lavender Hand and Body Lotion, Rose Ointment, and Thieves Household Cleaner on location.

Goat and Sheep Conditions

Goats and sheep suffer from many diseases caused by bacteria, viruses, parasites, and other noninfectious agents. The diagnosis of these diseases is difficult because many of them resemble one another.

Many of the common symptoms of these diseases are provided here, helping animal handlers to detect problems at the earliest stage. Handlers may take steps as recommended to prevent further deterioration in the condition of the animal until it is brought under the supervision of a health specialist. Many health conditions for these animals can be prevented or minimized if timely preventive health care has been adopted.

Acetonemia

This condition generally is brought about by feeding sheep and goats a high carbohydrate diet. This is especially prominent during times of pregnancy. Symptoms of acetonemia include lethargy, listlessness, poor reflexes, lack of appetite, and general immobility. This condition can lead to death if corrective action is not taken.

Recommendations

Singles: Ginger, Copaiba, Peppermint
Blends: DiGize
Nutritionals: K&B, Life 9

Applications and Usage

Ingestion & Oral: Administer orally 6 dropperfuls K&B; 10 drops each Copaiba, DiGize, Ginger, and Peppermint; and 1 Life 9, 2 times daily.

Allergic Dermatitis

Allergic dermatitis generally is a result of an animal being bitten by an insect such as a mosquito, gnat, or fly and in turn experiencing an allergic reaction. Treatment of a low-severity response can be achieved with home application; serious reactions should be treated by a veterinarian professional.

Recommendations

Singles: Copaiba
Blends: Melrose, Purification, DiGize, Thieves
Nutritionals: NingXia Red, Life 9
Additional: Thieves Household Cleaner

Applications and Usage

Topical: Apply on location of dermatitis 5-8 drops each Copaiba, Melrose, or Purification 2 times daily.

Ingestion & Oral: Administer orally or in food 5 drops each Copaiba and DiGize and 1 Life 9 dissolved in 1 tablespoon NingXia Red 2 times daily.

Other: Wash affected area with Thieves Household Cleaner daily.

Anemia

Anemia in goats and sheep refers to a low red blood cell count. Symptoms include discoloration of the folds of skin around the eye and the accumulation of fluid on the jawline of the animal, generally referred to as "bottle jaw."

The cause of anemia can be many, including worm infestation, poor diet, or genetic factors. Consult your veterinarian to help with a proper diagnosis.

Recommendations

Singles: Helichrysum, Copaiba
Blends: DiGize
Nutritionals: NingXia Red, Life 9, Mineral Essence, Detoxzyme

Applications and Usage

Ingestion & Oral: Administer orally 5 drops each Copaiba, DiGize, and Helichrysum; 2-4 oz. NingXia Red; ½ Life 9; 4 dropperfuls Mineral Essence; and 3 Detoxzyme 2 times daily.
Other: Supplement with iron.

Anthrax

Anthrax is an infectious disease caused by the bacterium *Bacillus*, a spore-forming bacterium that can remain alive but dormant in the soil for many years.

Keep in mind that this condition can be transferred to humans if anthrax spores are breathed in while treating affected animals. General symptoms include open sores, muscle tetany, flu-like symptoms, including diarrhea and fever, and issues regarding eating and drinking.

Recommendations

Singles: Thyme, Clove, Sacred Frankincense
Blends: DiGize, Purification, Thieves, Raven, Longevity, Melrose
Nutritionals: ParaFree, Inner Defense, Life 9
Additional: Thieves Household Cleaner

Applications and Usage

Topical: Administer Raindrop Technique daily.
Ingestion & Oral: Administer in mouth 20 drops each DiGize, Thyme, Clove, Sacred Frankincense; 1 ParaFree (open capsule); ½ Life 9, 2-4 times daily.
Inhalation: Diffuse Thieves, Raven, Longevity, or Melrose in enclosed barn.
Other: Spray the entire habitat, including the ground in the barn, with ½ cup Thieves Household Cleaner in 1 gallon of water with 30 drops Purification every day for 10 days.

Arthritis

Symptoms of arthritis include joint stiffness and pain, swollen limbs, and inflammation of the foot and leg area. Arthritis can result from many factors, including infection, injury, and age. Be sure to look for other causative ailments when addressing arthritis.

Recommendations

Singles: Copaiba, Myrrh, Wintergreen, Idaho Balsam Fir, Idaho Blue Spruce
Blends: DiGize, Thieves, PanAway
Nutritionals: Life 9, Sulfurzyme, Mineral Essence

Applications and Usage

Topical: Apply Thieves and Myrrh on navel liberally on goat kids.
Ingestion & Oral: Administer 1 Life 9, 1 Sulfurzyme, and 1-2 oz. Mineral Essence 1 time daily.

Bloat

Bloat is most often caused by sheep and goats ingesting feed too fast, causing it to ferment in the animal's digestive tract. This can cause an excess amount of gas, leading to discomfort, bloat, and even death.

Generally, feeds to avoid include lush feed and grain. Try feeding drier feed instead.

Recommendations

Singles: Ginger, Peppermint, Copaiba
Blends: DiGize
Nutritionals: Digest & Cleanse, Life 9

Applications and Usage

Topical: Apply on stomach area, where hair is thinner, 10 drops each DiGize, Ginger, Peppermint, and Copaiba 4 times daily.
Ingestion & Oral: Administer orally 20 drops each DiGize, Ginger, Peppermint, and Copaiba 2-3 times daily and 4 Digest & Cleanse and 1 Life 9, 4 times daily.

Big-Head (see Worms)

Bluetongue

Bluetongue is a viral disease that is usually transmitted by gnats or other biting insects. This disease can also be transmitted from mother to baby, so ensuring that pregnant or birthing animals are kept in areas as bug free as possible is important.

Symptoms of bluetongue include swelling of the face, mouth, and tongue area, with the tongue turning blue, hence the name. Other indications include nasal discharge, ulcers, diarrhea, lameness, and even death.

Recommendations

Singles: Copaiba, Citronella, Lemon

Blends: Purification, RepelAroma, ImmuPower, Melrose, Longevity, DiGize
Nutritionals: Life 9, NingXia Red
Additional: Thieves Household Cleaner

Applications and Usage

Topical: Apply onto affected area using the layering technique Copaiba, Purification, RepelAroma, Citronella, and ImmuPower 2-3 times daily.

Ingestion & Oral: Administer orally 1 oz. NingXia Red; ½ Life 9; 10 drops each Copaiba, DiGize, Longevity, Lemon, and ImmuPower 2-3 times daily.

Inhalation: Diffuse any of the following in an enclosed barn: Longevity, Melrose, ImmuPower, or Purification.

Other: Wash EVERYTHING down with 20 drops Purification, ½ cup Thieves Household Cleaner in 1 gallon of water.

Bronchitis

Bronchitis can be brought on for many reasons. Cause can be environmental, including poor ventilation in housing, exposure to cold or inclement weather, or animals breathing in large amounts of dust or debris.

Other causes include viral transmission of disease, worm infestations, or parasites. Symptoms include swollen and inflamed mouth, nasal passage, and lungs. This can lead to coughing, sneezing, and shortness of breath.

Recommendations

Singles: Copaiba
Blends: DiGize, Thieves, ParaGize, Raven, Purification
Nutritionals: Mineral Essence
Additional: Thieves Household Cleaner

Applications and Usage

Topical: Apply topically on stomach 10 drops Thieves and Raven 2 times daily.

Ingestion & Oral: Administer orally 10 drops each Copaiba, DiGize, Thieves, and ParaGize and 4 dropperfuls Mineral Essence 2 times daily.

Inhalation: Diffuse Thieves or Raven in enclosed barn.

Other: Spray the entire habitat, including the ground in the barn, with ½ cup Thieves Household Cleaner in 1 gallon of water with Purification added every day for 10 days. Apply Raindrop Technique 3 times weekly.

Caseous Lymphadenitis

Caseous Lymphadenitis (CL) is an infection found in goat and sheep species. It is sometimes referred to as abscess, due to boil-like pus pockets that tend to rupture and drain. These pustules are specific to lymph nodes. This is highly contagious for other animals and is transmitted through pus from broken or draining abscesses. When treating, take special care to cleanse all tools or instruments prior to working with other animals.

Recommendations

Singles: Lavender, Tea Tree, Clove, Frankincense, Sacred Frankincense
Blends: Thieves
Additional: Thieves Household Cleaner, Animal Scents Ointment

Applications and Usage

Topical: Drop 3-4 drops Thieves down spine of infected goat 1 time daily. Also, when enlarged lymph node is accessible, inject 5-6 drops Thieves with a syringe into pustule. When pustule ruptures, debride tissue and clean thoroughly with Clove, Lavender, and Tea Tree. Deep flush with highly diluted Thieves Household Cleaner. Then drop on 3-4 drops each Lavender and Tea Tree for an open wound and pack with Animal Scents Ointment. Repeat daily or as needed until abscess disappears.

Other: On other noninfected goats, apply 3-5 drops Thieves daily (for at least 3 weeks) to prevent infection spread. Clean barn with Thieves Household Cleaner when needed to prevent spread.

Chlamydiosis

Chlamydiosis is also commonly known as Chlamydia. It is the most frequent cause of abortion in goats in North America. This virus is usually spread through fluids and waste, including feces, discharge, and afterbirth.

The virus is generally undetectable in nonpregnant animals. However, once the animal becomes pregnant, symptoms will appear, which include birth of weak, underdeveloped lambs or kids or abortion of pregnancy.

Recommendations

Singles: Copaiba, Oregano
Blends: Raven, Thieves, DiGize
Nutritionals: Life 9, NingXia Red
Additional: Thieves Household Cleaner

Applications and Usage

Ingestion & Oral: Apply orally or in food 8-10 drops each Raven, Thieves, Copaiba, and DiGize; 1 drop Oregano; and 1 Life 9 dissolved in 1 tablespoon NingXia Red 1-2 times daily.

Other: Wash goats with diluted Thieves Household Cleaner.

Coccidiosis

Coccidiosis is caused by the protozoan coccidia. This disease generally affects the digestive tract of sheep and goats and is especially common and damaging to younger animals. General symptoms include low development weight, hair loss, diarrhea, and poor appetite.

Prevention is the approach. Maintaining cleanliness and sanitation will help reduce the animal's exposure to coccidia.

Recommendations

Singles: Copaiba, Thyme
Blends: ParaGize, DiGize, Melrose, Thieves, Purification
Nutritionals: Life 9, NingXia Red
Additional: Thieves Household Cleaner

Applications and Usage

Ingestion & Oral: Administer orally or in food 3-4 drops each ParaGize or DiGize, Melrose, Copaiba, and Thyme and 1 Life 9 dissolved in water or NingXia Red 2 times daily.

Inhalation: Diffuse Thieves or Purification in enclosed barn.

Other: Spray the entire habitat, including the ground in the barn, with ½ cup Thieves Household Cleaner in 1 gallon of water with Purification added every day for 10 days.

Colibacillosis

Colibacillosis is an acute disease of lambs and kids, affecting them during the first few days of life. It is generally caused by the *E. Coli* bacteria.

Symptoms will include diarrhea, dehydration, and low appetite. When afflicted with this disease at such a young age, many cases will result in the death of the animal.

Recommendations

Singles: Copaiba
Blends: Melrose, Thieves, DiGize, Purification
Nutritionals: Life 9, NingXia Red

Applications and Usage

Ingestion & Oral: Administer orally or in food 8-10 drops Melrose, Thieves, Copaiba, and DiGize and 1 Life 9 dissolved in 1 tablespoon NingXia Red 1-2 times daily.

Inhalation: Diffuse Thieves, Purification, and Melrose in the barn if kept isolated with doors and windows closed.

Contagious Ecthyma

Commonly known as "orf," this viral disease is characterized by open sores on the mouth and lips of the affected animal. This afflicts mostly younger animals but can be found in adults as well. Contagious ecthyma is transferable through contact to humans, so use precautionary measures when treating.

Recommendations

Singles: Copaiba
Blends: DiGize, Purification, Thieves
Additional: Thieves Household Cleaner

Applications and Usage

Topical: Clean lesions daily with diluted Thieves Household Cleaner, wearing gloves.

Ingestion & Oral: Administer orally 5 drops each Copaiba, DiGize, Purification, and Thieves 2 times daily.

Cystitis

Cystitis is a general urinary tract infection that can affect the kidney, urethra, and bladder. General symptoms include animals acting agitated, bloody urine, inability to urinate, excessive urination, and diminished appetite and fluid intake.

This condition can quickly become life threatening, especially if there is a complete blockage of the urethra, leading to an inability to urinate. Consult your veterinary professional immediately.

Recommendations

Singles: Copaiba, Cedarwood, Clove
Blends: DiGize, Melrose
Nutritionals: K&B

Applications and Usage

Ingestion & Oral: Administer orally or in food 10 drops each Copaiba, DiGize, Melrose, Cedarwood, and Clove and 6 dropperfuls K&B 2 times daily.

Deworming

Use the following deworming protocol every 4-6 weeks or as needed for best results.

Recommendations

Blends: DiGize, ParaGize
Nutritionals: ParaFree

Applications and Usage

Ingestion & Oral: Administer 10-15 drops each DiGize and ParaGize or ParaFree in feed morning and evening for 1 week.

Dysentery

Dysentery in sheep and goats is generally seen only in very young babies; but in some cases, it can be found in adults. Most often dysentery is caused by bacteria, which will lead to severe infection of the intestines.

Symptoms include bloody diarrhea, dehydration, weakness, and eventually death.

Antibacterial treatment is the best course of action, under the recommendation and supervision of a veterinary professional.

Recommendations

Singles: Copaiba, Helichrysum
Blends: ParaGize, DiGize, Purification, Thieves
Nutritionals: Life 9, NingXia Red
Additional: Thieves Household Cleaner

Applications and Usage

Ingestion & Oral: Administer orally or in food 8-10 drops each ParaGize or DiGize, Copaiba, and Helichrysum and 1 Life 9 dissolved in water or NingXia Red 2 times daily.
Inhalation: Diffuse Thieves or Purification in enclosed barn.
Other: Spray the entire habitat, including the ground in the barn, with ½ cup Thieves Household Cleaner in 1 gallon of water, with Purification added every day for 10 days.

Ectoparasitic Infestations (Ticks, Sucking Lice) (see Ticks)

Enterotoxemia

Enterotoxemia is extremely similar to dysentery found in sheep and goats and is caused by the bacteria *Clostridium perfringens.* The presence of this bacteria can cause severe intestinal damage and can be deadly.

Sanitation is extremely important when dealing with any bacterial infection, as well as important in prevention of the spread of the bacteria to other animals.

Recommendations

Singles: Copaiba, Peppermint, Helichrysum
Blends: DiGize, Thieves, Purification, Exodus II, Thieves
Nutritionals: Life 9, NingXia Red
Additional: Thieves Household Cleaner

Applications and Usage

Topical: Administer on stomach 10 drops each DiGize, Copaiba, Thieves, and Peppermint every 1-3 hours.
Ingestion & Oral: Administer orally or in food 20 drops each Exodus II, DiGize, Copaiba, and Helichrysum and 1 Life 9 dissolved in water or NingXia Red 2 times daily.
Inhalation: Diffuse Thieves or Purification in enclosed barn.
Other: Spray the entire habitat, including the ground in the barn, with ½ cup Thieves Household Cleaner in 1 gallon of water with Purification added every day for 10 days.

Eye Conditions

There are a variety of eye conditions that sheep and goats experience. Some of the most common eye conditions include pinkeye and conjunctivitis. Other conditions result from allergies or secondary infections.

Most conditions are treated similarly, and symptoms are usually universal in red, inflamed eyes and skin with liquid discharge, resulting in crusting and blockage around the eye. If symptoms persist after washing with saline solution and treatment, consult your veterinary professional.

Recommendations

Singles: Copaiba, Lavender, Myrrh
Blends: DiGize, Melrose, Purification

Applications and Usage

Topical: Administer 2-5 drops each Copaiba, Melrose, and Purification near location of eye, *but not in the eye,* 2 times daily.

Ingestion & Oral: Administer orally or in food 5 drops each Copaiba and DiGize 2 times daily.

Foot-and-Mouth Diseases Virus (FMD)

Foot-and-mouth disease is common in many cloven-hoofed animals. This disease is viral in nature and is transferable to other cloven-hoofed animals, but not to humans.

Symptoms first appear as lesions, blisters, and sores on both the mouth and lip areas of the affected animal, as well as the foot and lower leg area. The affected animal should be separated from the herd to prevent transmission of the virus to healthy animals.

Recommendations

Singles: Myrrh, Copaiba, Peppermint, Ravintsara
Blends: DiGize, Thieves, Purification, Exodus II
Nutritionals: Life 9, NingXia Red
Additional: Thieves Household Cleaner

Applications and Usage

Topical: Administer on stomach 10 drops each DiGize, Myrrh, Thieves, and Peppermint 3 times daily. Administer Raindrop Technique 2-3 times weekly.

Ingestion & Oral: Administer orally or in food 20 drops each Exodus II, DiGize, Myrrh, and Ravintsara and 1 Life 9 dissolved in water or NingXia Red 2 times daily.

Inhalation: Diffuse Thieves and Purification in enclosed barn.

Other: Spray the entire habitat, including the ground in the barn, with ½ cup Thieves Household Cleaner in 1 gallon of water with Purification added every day for 10 days.

Fungal Infections

The most common fungal infection in goats and sheep is ringworm. Signs of ringworm include a round, hairless patch developing on the affected animal that slowly grows larger. Lesions may accompany the fungal infection. The ringworm fungus is transferable to humans, so use caution when touching animals with ringworm and use proper protection.

After clipping hair, scrub animal with water and Thieves Household Cleaner.

Recommendations

Singles: Rosemary, Hinoki, Lavender, Idaho Balsam Fir, Copaiba
Blends: Thieves, Melrose, Purification, Infect Away, Mendwell, PuriClean, DiGize
Nutritionals: Life 9, NingXia Red
Additional: Thieves Household Cleaner, Animal Scents Ointment

Applications and Usage

Topical: Wash the affected area with a strong solution of Thieves Household Cleaner. Dry and apply your choice of Melrose, Purification, Infect Away, Mendwell, or PuriClean, and Animal Scents Ointment liberally 2 times daily.

Ingestion & Oral: Administer orally or in food 5-8 drops each DiGize, Copaiba, and Thieves and ½ Life 9 dissolved in water or NingXia Red 2 times daily.

Inhalation: Diffuse Thieves, Purification, or Melrose in enclosed barn.

Other: Spray the entire habitat, including the ground in the barn, with ½ cup Thieves Household Cleaner in 1 gallon of water with Purification added every day for 10 days.

Goat Pox and Sheep Pox

This viral disease is highly contagious among goats and sheep. Symptoms include fever, swelling, and scabbing of mouth, nose, and eye area accompanied by fluid discharge and skin lesions.

Isolate the sick quickly and wash the lesions with Thieves Household Cleaner diluted with warm water daily.

Recommendations

Singles: Myrrh, Tea Tree, Copaiba, Peppermint, Ravintsara
Blends: Thieves, Purification, Melrose, DiGize, Exodus II
Nutritionals: Life 9, NingXia Red
Additional: Animal Scents Ointment, Thieves Household Cleaner

Applications and Usage

Topical: After washing and drying, apply Thieves, Purification, Melrose, Myrrh, and Peppermint on lesions; then apply Animal Scents Ointment 1-2 times daily. Administer on stomach 10 drops each

DiGize, Copaiba, Thieves, Myrrh, and Peppermint 3 times daily. Administer Raindrop Technique 2-3 times weekly.

Ingestion & Oral: Administer orally or in food 20 drops each Exodus II, DiGize, Copaiba, and Ravintsara and 1 Life 9 dissolved in water or NingXia Red 2 times daily.

Inhalation: Diffuse Thieves and Purification in enclosed barn.

Other: Spray the entire habitat, including the ground in the barn, with ½ cup Thieves Household Cleaner in 1 gallon of water with Purification added every day for 10 days.

Heat Stress

Heat stress is common in goats and sheep. It can even cause stroke and death. Rapid breathing is the primary form of cooling, as goats are able to cool off eight times more effectively by panting than by sweating.

Recommendations

Singles: Copaiba, Peppermint, Lavender
Blends: DiGize

Applications and Usage

Topical: Apply on stomach, chest, and throat 10 drops each DiGize, Copaiba, and Peppermint 2-3 times daily.

Ingestion & Oral: Administer orally or in food 10 drops each Copaiba, DiGize, and Peppermint 2-3 times daily.

Hemorrhagic Septicemia

Hemorrhagic septicemia is a bacterial disease and is caused by certain strains of *Pasteurella multocida.* As with any bacterial disease, proper sanitation is key to prevention.

Signs of hemorrhagic septicemia include fever, difficulty breathing, and coughing. Some cases may lead to death if untreated and unchecked.

Recommendations

Singles: Copaiba, Peppermint, Cistus, Ravintsara
Blends: DiGize, Thieves, Purification
Nutritionals: Life 9, NingXia Red
Additional: Thieves Household Cleaner

Applications and Usage

Topical: Apply on stomach, chest, and throat 10 drops each DiGize, Copaiba, Thieves, and Peppermint 2-3 times daily. Administer Raindrop Technique 2-3 times weekly.

Ingestion & Oral: Administer orally or in food 10-15 drops each Thieves, Cistus, Copaiba, Ravintsara, and Peppermint and ½ Life 9 in 2 oz. NingXia Red 2 times daily.

Other: Spray the entire habitat, including the ground in the barn, with ½ cup Thieves Household Cleaner in 1 gallon of water with Purification added every day for 10 days.

Hypocalcaemia

Hypocalcaemia is also known as "milk fever." It is caused by low calcium levels in blood. It can occur the day following kidding. Goats are unable to stand and they breathe slowly. Coma and death are possible.

Recommendations

Singles: Copaiba, Peppermint
Blends: DiGize
Nutritionals: Mineral Essence, MegaCal, Life 9, NingXia Red

Applications and Usage

Topical: Apply on stomach 5 drops each DiGize, Copaiba, and Peppermint 2 times daily.

Ingestion & Oral: Administer orally or in food 5 drops each DiGize and Copaiba, 1 Life 9 dissolved in 3 oz. NingXia Red, 6 dropperfuls Mineral Essence, and 1 scoop MegaCal 2 times daily.

Indigestion

The primary cause of indigestion in sheep and goats is the consumption of dangerous or poisonous plants. This can include extremely "green" plants such as young saplings, noxious weeds, or vegetation sprayed with dangerous herbicides.

Whatever the cause, be sure to carefully monitor the animal's health until the afflicted animal is no longer showing signs of discomfort, and try to eradicate the ailment-causing plant in question.

Recommendations

Singles: Copaiba, Peppermint, Tarragon, Rosemary
Blends: DiGize
Nutritionals: NingXia Red, Mineral Essence, Life 9, MegaCal

Applications and Usage

Topical: Apply on stomach 5-10 drops each DiGize, Copaiba, Peppermint, Tarragon, and Rosemary 2 times daily.

Ingestion & Oral: Administer orally or in food 10 drops each DiGize and Copaiba, 2 Life 9 dissolved in 1 oz. NingXia Red, 4 dropperfuls Mineral Essence, and 1 scoop MegaCal 2 times daily.

Johne's Disease

Johne's disease is also known as paratuberculosis. This disease is bacterial borne and can spread to other animals. General symptoms include weight loss, diarrhea, and appetite loss. The disease-causing bacteria can lie dormant for years, and an affected animal may show no signs of sickness. Be sure to have any newly purchased animals tested before introducing the animals into your herd.

Recommendations

Singles: Copaiba, Peppermint, Ravintsara, Lemon, Thyme
Blends: DiGize, Thieves, Raven, R.C., Purification
Nutritionals: Life 9, NingXia Red
Additional: Thieves Household Cleaner

Applications and Usage

Topical: Apply on stomach, chest, and throat 10 drops each DiGize, Copaiba, Thieves, and Peppermint 2-3 times daily. Administer Raindrop Technique daily.

Inhalation: Diffuse any of the following: Thieves, Raven, Ravintsara, R.C., or Purification.

Ingestion & Oral: Administer orally or in food 10 drops each Thieves, Lemon, Copaiba, Ravintsara, Thyme, and DiGize and 1 Life 9 dissolved in 2 oz. NingXia Red 2 times daily.

Other: Spray the entire habitat, including the ground in the barn, with ½ cup Thieves Household Cleaner in 1 gallon of water with Purification added every day for 10 days.

Labial Dermatitis

Labial dermatitis has similar symptoms as contagious ecthyma. The mouth and lip areas become cracked and inflamed. This condition can be brought on by a variety of reasons, including excessive pan feeding, transmission of viral disease, or excessive licking or chewing on foreign objects like metallic barnyard items.

Always monitor the activity of the animals to determine the harmful activity that is the root cause of labial dermatitis.

Recommendations

Singles: Copaiba, Palmarosa, Myrrh
Blends: Purification, Mendwell, PuriClean, Melrose, Raven, Infect Away
Nutritionals: Life 9, NingXia Red
Additional: Thieves Household Cleaner

Applications and Usage

Topical: Apply on location of dermatitis 8-10 each Copaiba and one of the following: Purification, Palmarosa, Myrrh, Infect Away, Mendwell, or PuriClean 2 times daily. Wash affected area with ½ cup Thieves Household Cleaner in 1 gallon of water.

Ingestion & Oral: Administer orally or in food 1 Life 9 dissolved in 1 tablespoon NingXia Red 1-2 times daily.

Inhalation: Diffuse Thieves, Purification, Melrose, or Raven in enclosed barn.

Other: Spray the entire habitat, including the ground in the barn, with ½ cup Thieves Household Cleaner in 1 gallon of water with Purification added every day for 10 days.

Lice

Lice infestations of an animal or a herd can have detrimental to dangerous effects on the afflicted animals. Animals may experience only mild irritation to an infestation. If lice are disease carrying or cause the animal to rub or scratch excessively, it can lead to infections and possibly death.

Be sure to separate out infested animals from other herd members and treat immediately.

Recommendations

Singles: Northern Lights Black Spruce, Copaiba, Peppermint
Blends: RepelAroma, Purification, ParaGize, DiGize, Thieves, Exodus II

Nutritionals: Life 9, NingXia Red

Additional: Thieves Household Cleaner, Animal Scents Ointment

Applications and Usage

Topical: Wash the affected area with a strong solution of Thieves Household Cleaner. Dry and apply Purification or RepelAroma with Animal Scents Ointment liberally 2 times daily.

Ingestion & Oral: Administer orally or in food 8-10 drops each ParaGize or DiGize, Copaiba, Purification, Thieves or Exodus II, and Peppermint and ½ Life 9 dissolved in water or NingXia Red 2 times daily.

Inhalation: Diffuse Thieves or Purification in enclosed barn.

Other: Spray the entire habitat, including the ground in the barn, with ½ cup Thieves Household Cleaner in 1 gallon of water with Purification added every day for 10 days.

Liver Fluke

Liver flukes are parasitic worms that after ingestion lay eggs in the affected animal. The fluke larvae then migrate to the liver, where they can burrow, causing extensive damage.

An animal with a liver fluke infestation will have symptoms that include weakness, anemia, hemorrhaging, and possibly bottle jaw.

Recommendations

Singles: Ledum, Copaiba, Clove, Peppermint

Blends: Thieves, Purification, ParaGize, DiGize

Nutritionals: ParaFree

Additional: Thieves Household Cleaner

Applications and Usage

Topical: Administer Raindrop Technique 2 times or more weekly.

Ingestion & Oral: Administer orally or in food 10 drops each ParaGize or DiGize, Copaiba, Clove, Peppermint, and Ledum and 3 ParaFree 2 times daily.

Inhalation: Diffuse Thieves or Purification in enclosed barn.

Other: Wash the area with a strong solution of Thieves Household Cleaner. Spray the entire habitat, including the ground in the barn, with ½ cup Thieves Household Cleaner in 1 gallon of water with Purification added every day for 10 days.

Mange

Parasitic mites are the culprit of this skin disease. Mange is apparent when there is evidence of flakey, scruffy dandruff on the skin. Plus, severe itching and hair loss develops. The skin can become thick and hardened.

Clip hair and wash animal with warm water and Thieves Household Cleaner.

Recommendations

Singles: Hinoki, Northern Lights Black Spruce, Copaiba

Blends: Thieves, Melrose, Purification, Infect Away, Mendwell, PuriClean, DiGize

Nutritionals: Life 9, NingXia Red

Additional: Thieves Household Cleaner, Animal Scents Ointment

Applications and Usage

Topical: Wash the affected area with a strong solution of Thieves Household Cleaner. Dry and apply your choice of Melrose, Purification, Infect Away, Mendwell or PuriClean and then seal the oils with Animal Scents Ointment 2 times daily.

Ingestion & Oral: Administer orally or in food 5-8 drops each DiGize, Copaiba, and Thieves and ½ Life 9 dissolved in water or NingXia Red 2 times daily.

Inhalation: Diffuse Thieves, Purification, or Melrose in enclosed barn.

Other: Spray the entire habitat, including the ground in the barn, with ½ cup Thieves Household Cleaner in 1 gallon of water with Purification added every day for 10 days.

Mastitis

Mastitis generally affects nursing mothers. It refers to the infection of the teats and udder of a female goat or sheep.

Symptoms include the skin of the udder appearing red, flaky, and tender. The udder or teats may develop lesions or boils that discharge pus. This disease can affect milk production and quality.

Recommendations

Singles: Myrrh, Tea Tree, Copaiba, Ravintsara, Oregano

Blends: Thieves, Melrose, Purification, Raven, DiGize

Nutritionals: Life 9, NingXia Red

Additional: Thieves Household Cleaner

Applications and Usage

Topical: Apply liberally on teats and udder bag Copaiba, Thieves, Melrose, Myrrh, and Tea Tree 2-3 times daily. Administer Raindrop Technique 2-3 times weekly.

Ingestion & Oral: Administer orally or in food 5-8 drops each Thieves, Copaiba, Ravintsara or Raven or Melrose, Myrrh, Tea Tree, and DiGize; 1 drop Oregano; and 2 Life 9 dissolved in 1 oz. NingXia Red 2 times daily.

Inhalation: Diffuse any of the following: Thieves, Melrose, or Purification in enclosed barn.

Other: Spray the entire habitat, including the ground in the barn, with ½ cup Thieves Household Cleaner in 1 gallon of water with Purification added every day for 10 days.

Melioidosis

Melioidosis is from infection by *Burkholderia pseudomallei,* a Gram-negative bacillus in the family Burkholderiaceae. It affects humans and animals.

This disease is characterized as a bacterial infection that can affect the lungs, spleen, liver and lymph nodes, but any organ can be affected. Symptoms include fever, swollen glands, and general weakness that accompanies infection. Depending on which organ system is infected will also determine accompanying symptoms. Clinical manifestations include respiratory distress, coughing, and profuse yellow nasal and ocular discharge.

Recommendations

Singles: Copaiba, Ravintsara, Oregano, Thyme, Lemon

Blends: Thieves, Purification, ImmuPower, Raven, Melrose, DiGize

Nutritionals: NingXia Red

Additional: Thieves Household Cleaner

Applications and Usage

Topical: Administer Raindrop Technique daily.

Ingestion & Oral: Administer orally 10 drops each Thieves, Copaiba, Ravintsara or Raven or Melrose, DiGize, and Thyme and 3 drops Oregano in 1 oz. NingXia Red 4 times daily. Add 20 drops Lemon or Thieves per gallon of drinking water.

Inhalation: Diffuse Thieves, Purification, or ImmuPower in enclosed barn.

Other: Spray the entire habitat, including the ground in the barn, with ½ cup Thieves Household Cleaner in 1 gallon of water with Purification added every day for 10 days.

Metritis

Metritis takes place after kidding or false pregnancy. Symptoms can include an unusual discharge from vagina with loss of appetite.

Recommendations

Singles: Copaiba, Myrrh, Lemon

Blends: Thieves, Purification, Peace & Calming, Trauma Life, Release, Melrose

Additional: V-6 Vegetable Oil Complex

Applications and Usage

Topical: Administer Raindrop Technique daily.

Ingestion & Oral: Administer 10 drops each Melrose, Copaiba, and Myrrh vaginally into birthing canal in ½ oz. V-6 Vegetable Oil Complex. Administer the same mixture orally 3 times daily. Add 20 drops Lemon or Thieves per gallon of drinking water.

Inhalation: Diffuse Thieves, Purification, Peace & Calming, Trauma Life, or Release in enclosed barn.

Mycoplasmosis

Mycoplasmosis is a disease caused by bacteria that can lead to serious respiratory problems in goat and sheep. Typical symptoms include chronic coughing and shortness of breath. This disease can be especially dangerous to young sheep and goats.

Recommendations

Singles: Copaiba, Peppermint, Ravintsara, Oregano

Blends: Raven, R.C., Thieves, Purification, DiGize

Nutritionals: Life 9, NingXia Red

Additional: Thieves Household Cleaner

Applications and Usage

Topical: Apply on stomach, chest, and throat 10 drops each Raven or R.C., Copaiba, Thieves, and Peppermint 2-3 times daily. Administer Raindrop Technique 2 times weekly.

Ingestion & Oral: Administer orally or in food 5-8 drops each Thieves, Copaiba, Ravintsara or Raven, and DiGize; 1 drop Oregano; and 1 Life 9 dissolved in 2 oz. NingXia Red 2 times daily.

Inhalation: Diffuse Thieves, Raven, Ravintsara, R.C., or Purification in enclosed barn.

Other: Spray the entire habitat, including the ground in the barn, with ½ cup Thieves Household Cleaner in 1 gallon of water with Purification added every day for 10 days.

Nitrate poisoning

Nitrate poisoning affects animals that consume certain forages or water containing excessive amounts of nitrate. The animals suffer respiratory difficulty. A staggering gait, falling, and urine positive for nitrate/nitrite are usual clinical manifestations. Blood becomes a chocolate brown color. Sudden death is a possibility.

Recommendations
Singles: Copaiba, Peppermint, Cedarwood, Helichrysum, Lemon
Blends: DiGize, Thieves, Purification
Nutritionals: Rehemogen, Life 9, NingXia Red, Super C Chewable
Additional: Thieves Household Cleaner

Applications and Usage
Topical: Apply on stomach 10 drops each DiGize, Copaiba, and Peppermint 3 times daily.

Ingestion & Oral: Apply orally 4 dropperfuls Rehemogen; 20 drops each DiGize, Copaiba, Helichrysum, and Lemon; ⅓ Life 9 dissolved in 2 oz. NingXia Red; and 4 Super C Chewable 3 times daily.

Inhalation: Diffuse Thieves, Purification, or Cedarwood in enclosed barn.

Other: Spray the entire habitat, including the ground in the barn, with ½ cup Thieves Household Cleaner in 1 gallon of water with Purification added every day for 10 days.

Parasitic Gastroenteritis and Worm Infestation (see Worm Infestation)

Pesticide Poisoning

Whenever treating vegetation with pesticides, always keep in mind what feeding animals may be affected by the presence of dangerous chemicals.

Sheep and goats tend to consume a larger variety of plants than other farm animals. Some symptoms of sheep or goats who have ingested dangerous pesticide chemicals include vomiting, listlessness, general incoordination, and convulsions.

Always consult a veterinarian professional if you suspect your animals have consumed plants laced with pesticides.

Recommendations
Singles: Copaiba, Peppermint, Cedarwood, Helichrysum
Blends: DiGize, Thieves, Purification, JuvaCleanse
Nutritionals: Life 9, NingXia Red
Additional: Thieves Household Cleaner

Applications and Usage
Topical: Apply on stomach 10 drops each DiGize, Copaiba, and Peppermint every 1-2 hours.

Ingestion & Oral: Administer orally 20 drops each DiGize, Copaiba, and Helichrysum or Juva Cleanse and 1 Life 9 dissolved in water or 2 oz. NingXia Red 3 times daily.

Inhalation: Diffuse Thieves, Purification, or Cedarwood in enclosed barn.

Other: Spray the entire habitat, including the ground in the barn, with ½ cup Thieves Household Cleaner in 1 gallon of water with Purification added every day for 10 days.

Pneumonia

Pneumonia in sheep and goats generally results in lesions on the lungs, coughing, fever, difficulty breathing, and thick, whitish nasal discharge. It is generally transmitted through a virus that is spread through contact.

Infected animals should be separated from the herd until symptoms abate.

Recommendations
Singles: Oregano, Copaiba
Blends: Thieves, Raven, R.C., Purification, ImmuPower, DiGize
Nutritionals: Mineral Essence, Life 9, NingXia Red
Additional: Thieves Household Cleaner

Applications and Usage
Topical: Rub on chest, throat, and belly 10 drops each Thieves and Raven and 1 drop Oregano 2-4 times daily. Administer Raindrop Technique 3 times weekly.

Ingestion & Oral: Administer orally 10 drops each Copaiba, DiGize, Thieves, and Raven; 1 drop Oregano; ½ Life 9 in 1 oz. NingXia Red; and 4 dropperfuls Mineral Essence 2 times daily.

Inhalation: Diffuse Thieves, Raven, R.C, Purification, or ImmuPower in enclosed barn.

Other: Spray the entire habitat, including the ground in the barn, with ½ cup Thieves Household Cleaner in 1 gallon of water with Raven added every day for 10 days.

Polioencephalomalacia

Polioencephalomalacia (PEM) is also called goat polio. It is generally a result of a diet deficient in thiamine (vitamin B1), while recently a high sulfur intake has also been implicated.

This disease affects the nervous system, so symptoms usually include loss of motor function, uncontrollable shaking, stumbling, and in some cases, paralysis. Other symptoms include blindness, arching of the back, and "star-gazing," where the animal's head is thrown backward.

Direct injections of vitamin B1 may correct this condition if caught early enough.

Recommendations

Singles: Cardamom, Copaiba, Lemon

Blends: Longevity, Raven, Melrose, ImmuPower, Purification, DiGize

Nutritionals: NingXia Red, Life 9, Super B, Mineral Essence

Additional: Thieves Household Cleaner

Applications and Usage

Topical: Apply topically on spine and belly using layering technique Cardamom, Copaiba, Longevity, Raven, Melrose, and ImmuPower 2-3 times daily.

Ingestion & Oral: Administer orally 10 drops each Copaiba, DiGize, Longevity, Lemon, and ImmuPower; 4 Super B; ½ Life 9 dissolved in 4 oz. NingXia Red; and 2 dropperfuls Mineral Essence 2 times daily.

Inhalation: Diffuse Longevity, ImmuPower, or Purification in an enclosed barn.

Other: Wash EVERYTHING down with 20 drops Purification or Melrose in ½ cup Thieves Household Cleaner in 1 gallon of water.

Post Birth (Mother)

After birth, it is important to replenish nutrients in the mother to prevent infection and support milk production.

Recommendations

Singles: Copaiba

Blends: Peace & Calming, Gentle Baby

Nutritionals: NingXia Red

Applications and Usage

Topical: Pet 1-2 drops of Peace & Calming or Gentle Baby on mother and kid.

Ingestion & Oral: Administer NingXia Red with 2-3 oz. of diluted water.

Other: Use 5-10 drops of Copaiba on the mother's hind end every few hours to promote healing and prevent infection.

Rabies

Rabies develops usually after 20-60 days of a bite, but not less than 10 days. Rabid goats become strange in behavior, followed by frothing and salivation. Goats have the more aggressive behavior, with excessive bleating and salivating. They will not eat or drink and will slowly become paralyzed. Death is possible within 10 days of onset of disease.

The virus causes inflammation of the brain. Rabies in animals takes one of two forms: dumb, where the animal is calmer than normal, or furious, where the animal is vicious and aggressive. **There is no known treatment for rabies in animals; it is always fatal.** Most states in the U.S. require notification of any possible rabies in animals, domestic or wild.

Rabies is a zoonotic disease that can be passed from animals to man, but humans may recover from rabies if treated before symptoms begin.

Rickets (Trace Element Deficiency)

Rickets is a malady that most often affects young and growing animals. It is brought on by deficiencies of vitamin D, calcium, and phosphorus. These deficiencies are either due to the lack of the necessary minerals in the diet or an animal's inability to absorb the needed nutrients.

Symptoms may include deformed, weak, and easily breakable bones. Other symptoms include stunted growth, difficulty walking or moving, and localized swelling.

Usually augmenting the animal's diet with the needed nutrients will alleviate most of the symptoms.

Recommendations
Singles: Idaho Balsam Fir, Idaho Blue Spruce, Pine
Blends: DiGize
Nutritionals: Life 9, Mineral Essence, Super C Chewable, NingXia Red, MegaCal, SuperCal

Applications and Usage
Ingestion & Oral: Administer orally 5 drops each DiGize, Idaho Balsam Fir, Idaho Blue Spruce, and Pine; ½ Life 9 in 2 oz. NingXia Red; 4 dropperfuls Mineral Essence; and 4 Super C Chewable 2 times daily until condition is corrected.

Ringworm (see Fungal Infections)

Salmonella Infection

Salmonella is a bacterium living mainly in the intestine. Salmonella infections elicit symptoms such as diarrhea, early termination of pregnancy, dehydration, weight loss, and high fever. Salmonella bacteria can be spread to others through ingestion, usually through contaminated food and water.

Recommendations
Singles: Myrrh, Tea Tree, Mountain Savory, Lemon
Blends: Thieves, Purification, DiGize
Nutritionals: NingXia Red, Life 9
Additional: Thieves Household Cleaner

Applications and Usage
Topical: Administer Raindrop Technique 2 times a week.
Ingestion & Oral: Administer orally 10 drops each DiGize, Thieves, Myrrh, and Tea Tree; ½ Life 9 dissolved in 1 oz. NingXia Red 2-3 times daily. Once cleared, continue with NingXia Red, DiGize, and Thieves or Lemon in the water until immune system is restored.
Inhalation: Diffuse Thieves, Purification, or DiGize in enclosed barn.
Other: Spray the entire habitat, including the ground in the barn, with ½ cup Thieves Household Cleaner in 1 gallon of water with DiGize added every day for 10 days.

Scabby Mouth

Scabby mouth is a unique form of dermatitis associated with sheep and goats. It is viral in nature and very transferable between animals through physical contact and internal ingestion of flaked off scabs from affected animals. Symptoms are unique in scabby mouth in that not only are the mouth, lips, and throat affected, but also the feet and ankle area of sheep and goats will develop the same pus-filled sores, scabs, and pustules found in the face area of the affected animal.

As this is a viral, transferable ailment, take precautionary measures when treating affected animals.

Recommendations
Singles: Copaiba, Melissa, Ocotea
Blends: Thieves, Purification, PuriClean, Raven, DiGize, Melrose
Nutritionals: Life 9, NingXia Red
Additional: Thieves Household Cleaner

Applications and Usage
Topical: Wash area with a solution of Thieves Household Cleaner. Dry and apply on location of dermatitis 8-10 drops each Copaiba, Purification or PuriClean, and Melrose 2 times daily.
Ingestion & Oral: Administer orally or in food 5 drops each Copaiba, DiGize, Melissa, and Ocotea and 1 Life 9 dissolved in 1 oz. NingXia Red 2-3 times daily.
Inhalation: Diffuse Thieves, Purification, Melrose, or Raven in enclosed barn.
Other: Spray the entire habitat, including the ground in the barn, with ½ cup Thieves Household Cleaner in 1 gallon of water with Purification added every day for 10 days.

Tetanus

Tetanus is caused by the bacteria *Clostridium tetani*, which produces a toxin that can cause illness and death. Open wounds are especially susceptible to the bacteria, and the bacteria can be transferred through bites by infected animals. Symptoms include convulsions, stiff muscles, jerky movement, and respiratory issues. The rapid onset of these symptoms is usually indicative of tetanus.

If you suspect your animal has tetanus, contact your veterinary professional immediately.

Recommendations

Singles: Thyme, Mountain Savory, Myrrh, Lemon
Blends: Thieves, Purification, ImmuPower, DiGize
Nutritionals: ParaFree, Life 9, NingXia Red
Additional: Thieves Household Cleaner

Applications and Usage

Topical: Administer Raindrop Technique daily.
Ingestion & Oral: Administer orally 20 drops each DiGize, Thyme, Thieves, Mountain Savory, and Myrrh; 1 ParaFree; ½ Life 9 dissolved in 1 oz. NingXia Red 2-4 times daily. Once cleared, continue with NingXia Red, DiGize, and Thieves or Lemon in the water until immune system is restored.
Inhalation: Diffuse Thieves, Purification, or ImmuPower in enclosed barn.
Other: Spray the entire habitat, including the ground in the barn, with ½ cup Thieves Household Cleaner in 1 gallon of water with DiGize added every day for 10 days.

Ticks

Tick infestations in goats and sheep can be very detrimental to their health, especially if the tick carries infectious diseases such as Lyme disease. Check animals regularly for any infestations.

Recommendations

Singles: Black Pepper, Copaiba, Peppermint
Blends: Thieves, RepelAroma, Purification, ParaGize, DiGize, Exodus II
Nutritionals: Life 9, NingXia Red
Additional: Thieves Household Cleaner

Applications and Usage

Topical: Wash the affected area with a strong solution of Thieves Household Cleaner. Apply liberally on affected area RepelAroma, Purification, and Black Pepper 2 times or more daily.
Ingestion & Oral: Administer orally or in food 8-10 drops each ParaGize or DiGize, Copaiba, Purification, Thieves or Exodus II, and Peppermint and 1 Life 9 dissolved in water or 2 oz. NingXia Red 2 times daily.
Inhalation: Diffuse Thieves or Purification in enclosed barn.

Other: Spray the entire habitat, including the ground in the barn, with ½ cup Thieves Household Cleaner in 1 gallon of water with Purification added every day for 10 days.

Tuberculosis

Tuberculosis is an infectious disease usually affecting the lungs. It is very transferable from infected animals to healthy animals. Symptoms include fever, cough, weight loss, and trouble breathing.

Recommendations

Singles: Eucalyptus Radiata, Ravintsara, Thyme, Lemon
Blends: ImmuPower, Longevity, Thieves, Raven, Exodus II, Purification, DiGize
Nutritionals: NingXia Red, Life 9
Additional: Thieves Household Cleaner

Applications and Usage

Topical: Apply on throat, chest, and belly using layering technique Eucalyptus Radiata, Ravintsara, Thyme, and ImmuPower 2-3 times daily.
Ingestion & Oral: Administer orally 1 oz. NingXia Red, ½ Life 9, 8 drops each Eucalyptus Radiata, DiGize, Exodus II, Longevity, Lemon, Ravintsara, and ImmuPower 2-3 times daily.
Inhalation: Diffuse any of the following in an enclosed barn: Longevity, Lemon, Eucalyptus Radiata, Thieves, Raven, Ravintsara, Exodus II, ImmuPower, or Purification.
Other: Wash EVERYTHING down with 20 drops Raven and ½ cup Thieves Household Cleaner in 1 gallon of water.

Tympany (see Bloat)

Urea Poisoning

Urea poisoning is the result of carbonic acid found in urine, blood, and lymph. Urea is sometimes added to an animal's diets and used as a filler in certain commercial feeds. Animals who ingest excessive amounts of urea will suffer from severe abdominal pain, tremors, dyspnea (difficulty in breathing), and bloat.

Recommendations

Singles: Juniper, Helichrysum, Copaiba, Ledum
Blends: DiGize
Nutritionals: K&B, NingXia Red, Detoxzyme

Applications and Usage

Topical: Raindrop Technique, 3 times weekly.

Ingestion & Oral: Administer orally or in food 5 drops each Copaiba, DiGize, Juniper, Helichrysum, and Ledum and 4 dropperfuls K&B 3 times daily. Also administer orally or in food 3 Detoxzyme and 1 oz. NingXia Red 2 times daily.

Warts

Warts are papillomas of the skin and/or mucous membranes. They are caused by a virus. Warts mostly affect younger animals. Single warts may be found in older animals.

In goats, warts are seen mostly on teats and udders. If goats have warts on teats during milking, blood may contaminate the milk.

Recommendations

Singles: Oregano, Clove, Hinoki, Thyme, Lemon
Blends: Melrose, DiGize, Longevity, Thieves, Purification
Nutritionals: NingXia Red, Life 9
Additional: Animal Scents Ointment, Thieves Household Cleaner

Applications and Usage

Topical: Apply directly on affected area Oregano, Clove, Melrose, Hinoki, and Animal Scents Ointment 1-2 times daily. Administer Raindrop Technique 1-2 times weekly.

Ingestion & Oral: Administer orally 5 drops each DiGize, Thyme, Hinoki, Longevity, and Clove and ½ Life 9, 2 times daily. Once cleared, continue with NingXia Red, DiGize, and Thieves or Lemon in the water until immune system is restored.

Inhalation: Diffuse Thieves, Purification, or Clove in enclosed barn.

Other: Spray the entire habitat, including the ground in the barn, with ½ cup Thieves Household Cleaner in 1 gallon of water with DiGize added every day for 10 days.

Worm Infestations

Worm infestations can be deadly to sheep and goats if left unchecked and untreated. Early signs include diarrhea, severe weight loss, and localized edema or swelling. Passed worms in feces may also confirm a diagnosis of a worm infestation.

Recommendations

Singles: Black Pepper, Peppermint, Copaiba, Hinoki, Rosemary
Blends: Thieves, RepelAroma, Purification, DiGize, ParaGize
Nutritionals: Life 9, JuvaPower, ParaFree, NingXia Red
Additional: Thieves Household Cleaner

Applications and Usage

Topical: Wash any affected area on goat with a strong solution of Thieves Household Cleaner. Dry. Apply liberally RepelAroma, Purification, and Black Pepper on affected area 2 times or more daily.

Ingestion & Oral: Administer orally or in food 8-10 drops each ParaGize or DiGize, Copaiba, and Peppermint; 3-4 ParaFree; 3 heaping scoops JuvaPower; and ½ Life 9 dissolved in water or NingXia Red 2 times daily.

Inhalation: Diffuse Thieves, Purification, or DiGize with Peppermint in enclosed barn.

Other: Spray the entire habitat, including the ground in the barn, with ½ cup Thieves Household Cleaner in 1 gallon of water with Purification or DiGize added every day for 10 days.

Alpaca and Llama Conditions

Colic (see Equine or Canine Bloat)

Foot and Mouth Disease (FMDV)

Although not a carrier, camelids may become infected by direct contact with the virus *Aphthae epizooticae* on equipment, other animals, human clothing, or feed. Symptoms include high fever for 2-3 days, followed by mouth blisters and foot infections.

Recommendations

Singles: Cedarwood, Myrrh, Lemon, Tea Tree, Peppermint

Blends: Egyptian Gold, Exodus II, ImmuPower, Infect Away, Mendwell, Purification, Thieves

Nutritionals: AlkaLime, Essentialzyme, ImmuPro, Master Formula, MightyVites, NingXia Red, Ningxia Organic Dried Wolfberries, Super C Chewable

Additional: V-6 Vegetable Oil Complex

Applications and Usage

Topical: Put 1-2 drops of immune-supporting oil in each nasal flare. Apply a custom blend or single oil mixed in V-6 or other carrier oil to areas of concern. In a small jar, blend 10-15 drops each of above single oils. Apply to areas of concern

Ingestion & Oral: On a foodstuff your pet really likes, apply 3-4 or up to 15 drops of a mixture of your chosen oil diluted in 15 ml V-6 or other carrier oil. Or, add 1-5 drops essential oil in 1 gallon of drinking water. Mist food stuffs.

Inhalation: Apply 1 drop immune-supporting single or blend in your nondominant hand. Place your hand near animal's nose. You may also diffuse by placing your favorite diffuser near its housing.

Other: Administer Raindrop Technique daily, if needed. After improvement, administer weekly.

Heat Stress

Overheating may occur due to excessive fleece in warm temperatures.

Recommendations

Singles: Spearmint, Lavender, Peppermint
Additional: LavaDerm Cooling Mist

Applications and Usage

Topical: Put 1-2 drops of cooling oil in each nasal flare and along both sides of neck. Mist with LavaDerm Cooling Mist.

Ingestion & Oral: Add 1-5 drops essential oil of choice in 1 gallon of drinking water.

Inhalation: Apply 1 drop cooling single or blend in your nondominant hand. Place your hand near its nose. You may also diffuse by placing your favorite diffuser near its housing.

Other: Administer Raindrop Technique as needed.

Hypocalcemia

Milk Fever is basically a metabolic disorder related to nutrition. Usually, there is a dietary calcium phosphorus imbalance. Symptoms include refusal to eat, lethargy, weakness, inability or refusal to stand after lying down. Hypocalcemia may result in ketosis.

Recommendations

Singles: Peppermint, Dill, Fennel, Ginger, Juniper, Lemon

Blends: DiGize, EndoFlex, Citrus Fresh

Nutritionals: AlkaLime, Balance Complete, Essentialzyme, MegaCal, Mineral Essence, NingXia Red, Ningxia Organic Dried Wolfberries, Power Meal, Super Cal

Additional: V-6 Vegetable Oil Complex

Applications and Usage

Topical: Put 1-2 drops of digestive-supporting oil in each nasal flare, low back, in front of hips, and navel area. Also apply DiGize mixed in V-6 or other carrier oil.

Ingestion & Oral: 1. On a foodstuff your pet really likes, apply 3-4 or up to 15 drops of your chosen oil, diluted in 15 ml V-6 or other carrier oil. 2. Add 1-5 drops essential oil in 1 gallon of drinking water. 3. Mist food stuffs. 4. Crush 1 Essentialzyme per 150 pounds of bodyweight in foodstuff. 5. After adding AlkaLime to water, the mixture may be syringed into the mouth several times daily.

Inhalation: Apply 1 drop digestive-supporting single or blend in your nondominant hand. Place your hand near its nose. You may also diffuse by placing your favorite diffuser near its housing.

Hypothyroidism

Hypothyroidism is a condition in which the thyroid gland does not produce enough thyroid hormone. This lack of thyroid can have ranging effects on the affected animal, including weight loss, extreme tiredness, and lethargy. If left untreated the condition can lead to death.

Consult your veterinary professional to determine if your animal is suffering from hypothyroidism.

Recommendations

Singles: Myrtle, Ledum, Peppermint, Northern Lights Black Spruce

Blends: EndoFlex, Thieves

Nutritionals: EndoGize, Essentialzyme, MultiGreens, NingXia Red, Power Meal, Sulfurzyme, Thyromin, Balance Complete, Power Meal

Additional: V-6 Vegetable Oil Complex

Applications and Usage

Topical: Put 1-2 drops of thyroid-supporting oil in each nasal flare and again at base of neck where shoulder joins. Apply a blend or single oil mixed in V-6 or other carrier oil to areas.

Ingestion & Oral: On a foodstuff your pet really likes, apply 3-4 or up to 15 drops of a mixture of your chosen oil diluted in 15 ml V-6 or other carrier oil. Or, add 1-5 drops essential oil in 1 gallon of drinking water. Mist food stuffs. Pour out contents of 1 capsule Thyromin per 150 pounds of body weight in foodstuff. Also, 1-2 scoops of nutritional supplements such as Balance Complete or Power Meal may be added to regular foodstuffs.

Inhalation: Apply 1-2 drops thyroid-supporting single or blend in your nondominant hand. Place your hand near its nose. You may also diffuse by placing your favorite diffuser near its housing.

Ketosis

Pregnancy toxemia has almost the same symptoms as Hypocalcemia, but the support is not the same. It often happens late in pregnancy when the diet is lacking in carbohydrates. Ketones are produced as the body begins to metabolize fat for its required energy. Body acidity increases to the point of death.

Recommendations

Singles: Peppermint, Dill, Fennel, Ginger, Juniper, Lemon

Blends: DiGize, EndoGize, Citrus Fresh, Aroma Life

Nutritionals: AlkaLime, K&B, Life 9, Master Formula, NingXia Red, Ningxia Organic Dried Wolfberries, Power Meal, Balance Complete, Rehemogen, Super B, Super Cal

Additional: V-6 Vegetable Oil Complex

Applications and Usage

Topical: Put 1-2 drops of digestive supporting oil in each nasal flare, lower back, in front of hips, and navel area. Apply a custom blend or single oil mixed in V-6 or other carrier oil to lower back, in front of hips, and navel area.

Inhalation: Apply 1 drop digestive-supporting single or blend in your nondominant hand. Place your hand near the animal's nose. You may also diffuse by placing your favorite diffuser near its housing.

Ingestion & Oral: On a foodstuff your pet really likes, apply 3-4 or up to 15 drops of a mixture of your chosen oil diluted in 15 ml V-6 or other carrier oil. Or, add 1-5 drops essential oil in 1 gallon of drinking water. Mist food stuffs. Crush 1 Super B per 150 pounds of body weight in foodstuff. After adding AlkaLime to water, a syringe may be used to put substance into animal's mouth several times daily. Also, 1-2 scoops of nutritional supplements such as Balance Complete or Power Meal may be added to regular foodstuffs.

Parasites (Gastrointestinal) (see Equine Chapter for Respiratory Conditions, Obstructive Pulmonary Disorders)

Sunburn (see also Skin Infestations under Equine)

A newly shorn animal may experience skin burning. There is an additional risk of skin infection and fly bites.

Recommendations

Singles: Carrot Seed, Lavender, Manuka, Tea Tree, Myrrh, Roman Chamomile

Blends: Australian Blue, Infect Away, Repel Aroma

Nutritionals: Mineral Essence

Additional: Animal Scents Ointment, ClaraDerm, Genesis Hand & Body Lotion, LavaDerm Cooling Mist, Lavender Hand & Body Lotion

Applications and Usage

Topical: Add 10-15 drops single oil or blend to 4 oz. glass water misting bottle. Apply Mineral Essence directly to burned skin or dilute it in 4 oz. glass misting bottle filled with water. Drop 1-2 drops of skin-supporting oil into the center of Animal Scents Ointment. Swirl fingertip around to combine essential oil and ointment. Apply to areas of concern.

Other: Use the following individually or layer with chosen oils: Animal Scents Ointment, ClaraDerm, Genesis Hand & Body Lotion, LavaDerm Cooling Mist, and Lavender Hand & Body Lotion.

Urolithiasis (Calculi Formation)

Renal stones are calculi that form when urine is saturated with certain salts and minerals. Passing of stones may be painful.

Recommendations

Singles: Eucalyptus Globulus, Geranium, Hyssop, Juniper, Lemon

Blends: R.C.

Nutritionals: EndoGize, Essentialzyme, ICP, K&B, MultiGreens, Super C Chewable

Additional: V-6 Vegetable Oil Complex

Applications and Usage

Topical: Apply warm compress over kidney area and lower back with 10 drops each Geranium and Juniper or 20 drops of a kidney-supporting oil or blend.

Ingestion & Oral: On a foodstuff your pet really likes, apply 3-4 or up to 15 drops of a mixture of your chosen oil diluted in 15 ml V-6 or other carrier oil. Or, add 1-5 drops essential oil in 1 gallon of drinking water. Crush 1 Super C Chewable per 150 pounds of body weight in foodstuff. After adding supplements such as K&B to water, a syringe may be used to put substance into the mouth several times daily. Also, 1-2 scoops of nutritional supplements such as ICP may be added to regular foodstuffs. Be certain your pet is drinking adequate amounts of water.

Inhalation: Apply 1 drop kidney-supporting single or blend in your nondominant hand. Place your hand near animal's nose. You may also diffuse by placing your favorite diffuser near its housing.

Other: Administer Raindrop Technique as needed.

Poultry Conditions

Birds look healthy to most people most of the time. This becomes challenging to recognize an illness until it's too late. The best rule of thumb is to pay close attention to their droppings (changes or inconsistencies), the sounds they make, and their energy levels.

More and more people are keeping free-range chickens as pets and for egg laying. They have a lively personality and are surprisingly smart, but they do require specific care. Sadly, most owners realize there is a problem only when the chickens have taken a dire turn. Generally, this will require professional, immediate care.

The best thing owners can do is familiarize themselves intimately with each chicken—their color, their personality, their movements, their plumes, their combs, and their eyes. Practice noticing everything about them. Take the time to hold your chickens (carefully). Find their crop, be acquainted with how it normally feels, and monitor for any changes. Pay close attention to their visible skin, their feathers, and their feet and watch for any sign of change.

Air Sac Mite

Birds are particularly susceptible to air sac mites, tiny parasites that pass from bird to bird via close air contact. They generally are transmitted through coughing, and they quickly infest the air sacs of the lungs with eggs. Air sac mites spread quickly within bird populations, particularly those that live in tight quarters. Quarantine infected birds and treat immediately.

Recommendations

Singles: Peppermint

Blends: Purification

Applications and Usage

Topical: Spray affected birds with Purification or Peppermint, 10 drops per every ounce of pure water.

Inhalation: Diffuse Purification or Peppermint for at least 5 days in the area.

Aspergillosis

There are several fungi that can cause an aspergillosis infection in bird populations. Incidence occurs mostly in moldy, humid, or wet settings, where the fungi can infest.

The best prevention is keeping birds and their nests away from these areas. Also, be sure to inspect your bird feed regularly for any telltale signs of mold. Sometimes, aspergillosis infection occurs in tandem with another type of infection.

Recommendations

Singles: Lemon, Ocotea, Thyme
Blends: Melrose, Purification, DiGize, Thieves
Additional: Thieves Household Cleaner

Applications and Usage

Topical: Spray affected birds with 5 drops Lemon, Purification, Ocotea, and DiGize per every ounce of pure water.
Ingestion & Oral: Mix 5 drops each Lemon, Purification, DiGize and Thyme per every pound of grain.
Inhalation: Diffuse Thieves, Purification, Lemon, Melrose, or Ocotea where birds and food are kept.
Other: Wash EVERYTHING down with 4 capfuls of Thieves Household Cleaner in 1 gallon of water.

Avian Chlamydiosis

Caused by the bacteria *Chlamydophila psittaci,* avian chlamydiosis is characterized by respiratory distress, diarrhea, and nasal discharge. If you suspect this disease, contact your veterinarian professional immediately.

Since this disease can transfer to humans, take precautionary measures as you handle the bird.

Recommendations

Singles: Lemon, Ocotea, Eucalyptus Blue, Patchouli
Blends: Purification, Raven, DiGize, R.C., Thieves
Additional: Thieves Household Cleaner

Applications and Usage

Topical: Spray affected birds with 5 drops each Lemon, Purification, Ocotea, and DiGize per every ounce of pure water.
Inhalation: Diffuse Thieves, Purification, Lemon, Raven, or Patchouli where the birds and food are kept.
Other: Wash EVERYTHING down with 4 capfuls of Thieves Household Cleaner in 1 gallon of water.

Avian Encephalomyelitis

Avian encephalomyelitis, also known as epidemic tremors, affects many types of young bird populations, including chickens, ducks, turkeys, pheasants, quail, and pigeons. The virus, in the family Picornaviridae, transmits primarily via the fecal-oral route, but it can also transmit to offpurified from hen to egg.

Symptoms include head, neck, and leg tremors. Cupping the bird in your hand will create a "buzzing" feeling from the tremors. If you place the bird on its side, it will stimulate these tremors to confirm diagnosis.

Recommendations

Singles: Eucalyptus Blue, Ocotea, Ravintsara, Lemongrass, Lemon
Blends: Purification, Exodus II, Thieves, Melrose, Raven
Nutritionals: Life 9
Additional: Thieves Household Cleaner

Applications and Usage

Topical: Spray affected birds with 5 drops each Eucalyptus Blue, Purification, and Ocotea per every ounce of pure water.
Ingestion & Oral: Administer orally or in water 3-4 drops each Purification and Lemongrass, plus 1 Life 9 daily.
Inhalation: Diffuse Exodus II with Eucalyptus Blue, Thieves with Ravintsara, Purification with Lemongrass, Lemon with Raven, or Melrose with Ocotea where the birds and food are kept.
Other: Wash EVERYTHING down with 4 capfuls of Thieves Household Cleaner in 1 gallon of water.

Avian Influenza

Avian influenza may be one of many different strains of viruses that have adapted specifically to transmit through birds as well as infect them. Many of these are zoonotic, meaning they can transmit to humans. Of greatest concern are the infamous 5 subtypes (H5N1, H7N3, H7N7, H7N9, & H9N2) that pose great threat to humans.

If you suspect your bird has this virus, notify your veterinarian immediately and quarantine the bird. Look for coughing, sneezing, discharge from the eyes or nose, and respiratory distress. Avoid droppings from the infected birds.

Recommendations
Singles: Lemon, Ravintsara, Mountain Savory, Thyme
Blends: Purification, Thieves, Exodus II, DiGize, Raven
Nutritionals: NingXia Red, Life 9
Additional: Thieves Household Cleaner

Applications and Usage
Ingestion & Oral: Administer orally 2 drops each Ravintsara or Raven, Exodus II, DiGize, Mountain Savory, and Thyme, plus 1 Life 9 dissolved in 1 oz. NingXia Red 2-4 times daily. Once cleared, continue orally NingXia Red, Purification, and Lemon, plus 1 Life 9 daily until immune system is restored.
Inhalation: Diffuse Thieves, Purification, or Lemon in the bird habitat.
Other: Wash EVERYTHING down with 4 capfuls of Thieves Household Cleaner in 1 gallon of water.

Avian Metapneumovirus
Avian metapneumovirus (aMPV) causes turkey rhinotracheitis, a respiratory condition in turkeys. Symptoms can include a fall in egg production, as well as swollen head syndrome.

Recommendations
Singles: Lemon, Cedarwood, Copaiba, Ravintsara
Blends: Raven, DiGize, Exodus II, Thieves, ImmuPower
Nutritionals: Life 9, NingXia Red
Additional: Thieves Household Cleaner

Applications and Usage
Ingestion & Oral: Administer orally 2 drops each Cedarwood, Raven, Lemon, DiGize, and Copaiba, plus 1 Life 9 dissolved in 1 oz. NingXia Red 2-4 times daily. Also, can replace Exodus II and Ravintsara for Raven and Lemon. Once cleared, continue orally with NingXia Red; Raven, ImmuPower, or Lemon; plus Life 9 until immune system is restored.
Inhalation: Diffuse Thieves, Purification, or Lemon in the bird habitat.
Other: Wash EVERYTHING down with 4 capfuls of Thieves Household Cleaner in 1 gallon of water.

Bordetellosis
Bordetella avium is the primary cause of the highly infectious, acute respiratory disease bordetellosis. Turkeys are particularly susceptible and suffer a high rate of infection, but the mortality rate is relatively low. The disease is synonymous with acute respiratory disease, turkey rhinotracheitis, adenovirus-associated respiratory disease, and acute respiratory disease syndrome.

Recommendations
Singles: Eucalyptus Blue, Cedarwood, Copaiba, Lemon, Ravintsara
Blends: Raven, Exodus II, ImmuPower
Nutritionals: Life 9, NingXia Red
Additional: Thieves Household Cleaner

Applications and Usage
Ingestion & Oral: Administer orally or in water 2 drops each Cedarwood, Raven, Lemon, Eucalyptus Blue, and Copaiba, plus 1 Life 9 dissolved in 1 oz. NingXia Red 2-4 times daily. Also, can replace Exodus II and Ravintsara for Raven and Lemon. Once cleared, continue with NingXia Red, plus Life 9 in water and diffusing Raven or ImmuPower and Lemon until immune system is restored.
Inhalation: Diffuse Exodus II, ImmuPower, and Eucalyptus Blue in the bird habitat.
Other: Wash EVERYTHING down with 4 capfuls of Thieves Household Cleaner in 1 gallon of water.

Botulism
Affecting primarily waterfowl, avian botulism is a paralytic disease resulting from *Clostridium botulinum*. There are seven strains—A through G. The bacteria are common in varying regions and climates and can be found on decomposing plants and animals. Birds ingest it with their food and become affected. This results in weakened muscle control affecting their wings and legs. Waterfowl suffer the greatest mortality rate from drowning due to their specific musculature and environments.

Recommendations
Singles: Mountain Savory, Thyme, Peppermint
Blends: Exodus II, ImmuPower, DiGize, Thieves
Nutritionals: NingXia Red, Life 9
Additional: Thieves Household Cleaner

Applications and Usage
Ingestion & Oral: Administer orally or in water 3 drops each DiGize, Mountain Savory, Thyme,

Thieves, and Peppermint and 1 Life 9 dissolved in 1 oz. NingXia Red 2-4 times daily.

Inhalation: Diffuse Exodus II, ImmuPower, and DiGize in the bird habitat.

Other: Wash EVERYTHING down with ½ cup Thieves Household Cleaner in 1 gallon of water. Spray entire habitat, including soil and ground, for 7-10 days.

Candidiasis

Candidiasis is a condition in the digestive tract of chickens and turkeys caused by the over-abundant presence of the yeast *Candida albicans.*

Usually the cause is some form of damage to the digestive tract, but it can also be due to antibiotics or exposure to an unsanitary water source. If left unchecked, the resulting lesions can cause complications in the lungs, intestines, or on the skin.

Recommendations

Singles: Lemon Myrtle, Ocotea, Lemon, Copaiba, Jade Lemon

Blends: Thieves, Purification, DiGize

Nutritionals: Life 9, Mineral Essence, NingXia Red

Applications and Usage

Ingestion & Oral: Administer orally or in water 2-4 drops each Ocotea, DiGize, and Copaiba, plus 1 dropperful Mineral Essence and 1 Life 9 dissolved in 1 oz. NingXia Red daily. Administer 1 drop Jade Lemon, Lemon, Purification, Thieves, DiGize, or Ocotea per 10 oz. water. Keep the bird away from ALL sugar in food and water.

Inhalation: Diffuse Thieves, Purification, or Lemon Myrtle in bird habitat.

Coccidiosis

Coccidiosis is a species-specific protozoan infection targeting the intestine of birds, resulting in bloody droppings, lethargy, and weight loss. Most outbreaks occur in large-scale poultry operations and occur via fecal exposure. Animals moving from farm-to-farm may spread the disease. Proper hygiene and sanitation practices among flocks may prevent the disease.

Recommendations

Singles: Ocotea, Orange, Lemon, Frankincense, Thyme

Blends: Thieves, Purification, ParaGize, DiGize

Nutritionals: Life 9, NingXia Red

Additional: Thieves Household Cleaner

Applications and Usage

Ingestion & Oral: Administer orally or in water 3-4 drops each ParaGize or DiGize, Ocotea, Orange, and Lemon; 2 drops each of Frankincense and Thyme, plus 1 Life 9 dissolved in 1 oz. NingXia Red 2 times daily.

Inhalation: Diffuse Thieves or Purification in area.

Other: Spray the entire habitat, including the ground, with ½ cup Thieves Household Cleaner in 1 gallon of water plus Purification every day for 10 days.

Coronaviral Enteritis

Coronaviral enteritis is almost exclusive to turkeys and is characterized by weight loss, diarrhea, and depression. This is a viral infection, so quarantine and flock thinning is imperative when signs of the virus first appear.

Recommendations

Singles: Eucalyptus Blue, Oregano, Thyme

Blends: Thieves, Raven, Purification, DiGize

Nutritionals: NingXia Red, Life 9

Additional: Thieves Household Cleaner

Applications and Usage

Ingestion & Oral: Administer orally or in water 2 drops each DiGize, Raven, Eucalyptus Blue, Thyme, and Oregano, plus 1 Life 9 dissolved in 1 oz. NingXia Red 2-4 times daily.

Inhalation: Diffuse Thieves, Purification, and DiGize in bird habitat.

Other: Spray the entire habitat, including the ground, with ½ cup Thieves Household Cleaner in 1 gallon of water with Purification every day for 10 days.

Crop Impaction and Stasis

Crop impaction and stasis are fatal conditions if untreated. The crop is an area that stores the food until it moves into the stomach for digestion. If food doesn't move into the stomach, it gets stuck in the crop. That's why the prognosis is better the earlier the diagnosis. As the food gets stuck, it begins to sour, hence the common name of this condition—sour crop. You can actually diagnose it quickly through smelling an affected chicken's breath. It will smell much like sour milk or yogurt.

One of the best prevention tactics is to keep chickens away from long, stringy-style food sources. Long blades of grass begin to knot in the crop and prevent the food from moving quickly and easily into the stomach.

Recommendations
Singles: Oregano, Ginger, Tarragon, Peppermint
Blends: DiGize, Purification, Thieves
Nutritionals: Life 9

Applications and Usage
Topical: Apply Purification and Tarragon directly onto crop, plus apply 1 drop each DiGize, Thieves, and Peppermint on bird's belly and feet 2-4 times daily.
Ingestion & Oral: Administer orally 1 drop Oregano, 2 drops each DiGize and Ginger, and ½ Life 9 dissolved in 1 tablespoon water.
Inhalation: Diffuse Thieves, Purification, and DiGize in bird habitat.

Cryptosporidiosis

Cryptosporidiosis is a parasitic disease that is transferable through feces of infected birds. This can be transferred to other species, so exercise caution when working with animals that may have this disease.

Preventive measures can be taken by maintaining a clean environment and sanitizing feeders and tools as much as possible.

Recommendations
Blends: Thieves, Raven, R.C.
Additional: Thieves Household Cleaner

Applications and Usage
Inhalation: Diffuse Thieves, Raven, or R.C. in bird habitat.
Other: Spray the entire habitat, including the ground, with ½ cup Thieves Household Cleaner in 1 gallon of water with Raven every day for 10 days.

Duck Viral Hepatitis

Duck viral hepatitis is a deadly, fast moving viral disease that can decimate a flock very quickly. Generally, this disease affects younger fowl but can be found in older avians as well. Quarantine and flock thinning is advised.

Recommendations
Singles: Ledum, Geranium, Eucalyptus Blue, Copaiba
Blends: Thieves, Exodus II
Nutritionals: Life 9, NingXia Red
Additional: Thieves Household Cleaner

Applications and Usage
Ingestion & Oral: Administer orally or in water 2 drops each Ledum, Geranium, Eucalyptus Blue, and Copaiba, plus ½ Life 9 dissolved in 1 oz. NingXia Red 2-4 times daily.
Inhalation: Diffuse Geranium and Exodus II in bird habitat.
Other: Spray the entire habitat, including the ground, with ½ cup Thieves Household Cleaner in 1 gallon of water every day for 10 days.

Ectoparasites

Ectoparasites are small, blood-sucking parasites that reside in warmer climates. Generally, they are not present in large poultry or egg operations but can be found in smaller coops where cleaning and hygiene standards are ignored.

These small bugs in low numbers will not be threatening to a bird's life; but in large numbers, they can contribute to infection, anemia, skin lesions, and unexpected weight loss.

Recommendations
Singles: Orange, Copaiba
Blends: Thieves, Purification, ParaGize, DiGize
Additional: Thieves Household Cleaner

Applications and Usage
Ingestion & Oral: Administer orally or in water 3-4 drops each ParaGize or DiGize, Orange, and Copaiba 2 times daily.
Inhalation: Diffuse Orange and Purification in area for an extended length of time.
Other: Spray the birds and the entire habitat, including the ground, with ¼ cup Thieves Household Cleaner in 1 gallon of water with 80 drops each Orange and Purification every day for 10 days.

Fatty Liver Hemorrhagic Syndrome (FLHS)

Fatty Liver Hemorrhagic Syndrome (FLHS) may occur in laying birds. Those birds are usually caged and are given a high-energy diet. The result of this high-energy diet and little or no range opportunities can lead to FLHS. This can cause hemorrhaging of the liver and is usually fatal.

Ensuring a diet that is low in fat and low in carbohydrates, plus allowing birds free range, will help prevent FLHS.

Recommendations

Singles: Lemon Myrtle, Copaiba, Cistus, Ledum
Blends: DiGize
Nutritionals: Life 9, NingXia Red

Applications and Usage

Ingestion & Oral: Administer orally or in water 2 drops each Ledum, DiGize, Lemon Myrtle, Copaiba, and Cistus, plus ½ Life 9 dissolved in 1 oz. NingXia Red 2-4 times daily.
Inhalation: Diffuse DiGize and Lemon Myrtle in habitat.

Feather Pecking and Bullying

As social creatures, birds in a flock will create a pecking order. Feather pecking results from bullying, which is part of the social order. Sadly, one bird will always be at the bottom. The important thing is to provide sufficiently for the flock to keep birds from competing for resources. This will counteract the reasons for bullying.

Ensure that you are providing sufficient nesting area, perches, roaming space, and food.

Recommendations

Singles: Orange
Blends: Harmony, White Angelica, Acceptance, Inner Child, Stress Away Roll-On, T-Away, Peace & Calming

Applications and Usage

Inhalation: Diffuse Harmony, Inner Child, Stress Away Roll-On, White Angelica, Acceptance, T-Away, Orange, or Peace & Calming in the bird habitat.

Fowl Cholera

Fowl cholera is a contagious, bacterial disease that affects domestic and wild birds worldwide.

Recommendations

Singles: Oregano, Ginger
Blends: Thieves, Purification, Melrose
Nutritionals: NingXia Red, Life 9
Additional: Thieves Household Cleaner

Applications and Usage

Ingestion & Oral: Administer orally or in water 2 drops each Melrose, Thieves, Oregano, and Ginger and ½ Life 9 dissolved in 1 teaspoon NingXia Red 1-2 times daily.
Inhalation: Diffuse Thieves, Purification, or Melrose in the bird habitat.
Other: Wash bird habitat with ½ cup Thieves Household Cleaner in 1 gallon of water.

Fowlpox

Fowlpox is a viral infection of chickens and turkeys. Typical symptoms include lesions in the skin that progress to thick scabs and lesions in the upper GI and respiratory tracts.

Recommendations

Singles: Eucalyptus Blue, Myrrh, Lavender
Blends: Exodus II, Raven, Melrose, Purification, Thieves
Nutritionals: Life 9, NingXia Red
Additional: Thieves Household Cleaner

Applications and Usage

Topical: Spray directly on the birds 5 drops each Lavender, Melrose, and Purification in 4 oz. distilled or purified water 1-2 times daily.
Ingestion & Oral: Administer orally or in water 2 drops each Exodus II, Raven, Eucalyptus Blue, and Myrrh and ½ Life 9 dissolved in 1 oz. NingXia Red 2-4 times daily.
Inhalation: Diffuse Thieves, Raven, or Eucalyptus Blue in area.
Other: Spray the entire habitat, including the ground, with ½ cup Thieves Household Cleaner in 1 gallon of water and 20 drops Raven every day for 10 days.

Gangrenous Dermatitis

Gangrenous dermatitis may affect chickens. Initial symptoms resemble red, yellow, and/or blue lesions. Feather loss and weight loss often accompany these symptoms. This dermatitis mainly occurs where it is wet and humid. It is also the result of untreated necrotic underlying tissue.

Recommendations

Singles: Lemon, Lemongrass, Copaiba
Blends: Thieves, Raven, Melrose
Nutritionals: Life 9, NingXia Red
Additional: Thieves Household Cleaner

Applications and Usage

Ingestion & Oral: Administer orally or in water 2 drops each Thieves, Melrose, Lemon, and Copaiba and ½ Life 9 dissolved in 1 oz. NingXia Red 2-4 times daily.

Inhalation: Diffuse Thieves, Raven, and Lemon in bird habitat.

Other: Spray the entire habitat, including the ground, with ½ cup Thieves Household Cleaner in 1 gallon of water and 20 drops each Lemongrass and Melrose every day for 10 days.

Giardia

Giardia is a common protozoal disease that affects caged birds. Noticeable symptoms include diarrhea and dry, itching skin. One sure sign is the scratching and self-plucking as they try to soothe the itch.

While giardia is treatable with pharmaceuticals, it is notoriously difficult to cure.

Recommendations

Singles: Lavender, Hinoki, Rosemary
Blends: Thieves, ParaGize, DiGize, Purification
Additional: Thieves Household Cleaner

Applications and Usage

Ingestion & Oral: Administer orally 3-4 drops each ParaGize or DiGize, Thieves, and Lavender, plus 1 drop Hinoki in 1 teaspoon olive oil or in water 2 times daily.

Inhalation: Diffuse Thieves or Purification in the bird habitat for an extended length of time.

Other: Spray the entire habitat, including the ground, with ¼ cup Thieves Household Cleaner in 1 gallon of water and 80 drops each of Rosemary and Purification every day for 10 days.

Goose Parvovirus Infection

This virus can be extremely deadly, especially to a young goose. It is most often transmitted through the droppings of affected geese. It can be transmitted to offpurified if an affected breeder is the parent.

Cardiac and breathing problems may occur, and lesions on the tongue and in the mouth may also occur.

Recommendations

Singles: Copaiba
Blends: ParaGize, DiGize, Thieves, Melrose, Purification
Nutritionals: ParaFree
Additional: Thieves Household Cleaner

Applications and Usage

Ingestion & Oral: Administer orally or in water 2-3 drops each ParaGize or ParaFree (puncture softgel and squeeze out drops), DiGize, Thieves, Copaiba, and Melrose 2 times daily.

Inhalation: Diffuse Thieves or Purification in the bird habitat for an extended length of time.

Other: Spray the entire habitat, including the ground, with ¼ cup Thieves Household Cleaner in 1 gallon of water plus 80 drops each Thieves and Purification every day for 10 days.

Helminthiasis

Helminthiasis refers to any worm infestation of avians. This could include any parasitic worm such as roundworms and flatworms. Birds suffering from an infestation will have bloody droppings that can easily be tested for worms. They will also suffer inexplicable weight and appetite loss and will appear lethargic.

Recommendations

Singles: Peppermint, Myrrh, Copaiba
Blends: ParaGize, DiGize, Thieves
Nutritional: ParaFree
Additional: Thieves Household Cleaner

Applications and Usage

Ingestion & Oral: Administer orally or in water 2-3 drops each ParaGize or ParaFree (puncture softgel and squeeze out drops), DiGize, and Copaiba 2 times daily.

Inhalation: Diffuse Thieves or DiGize in the bird habitat for an extended length of time.

Other: Spray the entire habitat, including the ground, with ¼ cup Thieves Household Cleaner in 1 gallon of water with 40 drops each of Thieves and DiGize every day for 10 days.

Hemorrhagic Enteritis/Marble Spleen Disease

These two diseases are close in nature and are both caused by similar viruses, but they mostly affect two distinct bird populations: turkeys and pheasants.

Hemorrhagic enteritis (HE) is an acute gastrointestinal disorder primarily afflicting turkeys that are younger than 4 weeks old. Telltale signs are bloody droppings and extreme lethargy.

Marble spleen disease generally affects pheasants. The symptoms are similar to HE for turkeys; however, they suffer more from pulmonary congestion and enlarged spleens.

The symptoms can be difficult to differentiate from other diseases and may even go undetected until secondary bacterial infections call attention to the problem.

Recommendations

Singles: Cistus, Copaiba, Eucalyptus Blue, Lemon
Blends: DiGize, Thieves
Nutritionals: Life 9, NingXia Red
Additional: Thieves Household Cleaner

Applications and Usage

Ingestion & Oral: Administer orally or in water 2 drops each Cistus, DiGize, Thieves, and Copaiba and ½ Life 9 dissolved in 1 oz. NingXia Red 2 times daily. Once cleared, continue with NingXia Red, Life 9 in water, and diffusing Thieves and Lemon until immune system is restored.

Inhalation: Diffuse Thieves and Eucalyptus Blue in the bird habitat.

Other: Wash or spray EVERYTHING down with 4 capfuls of Thieves Household Cleaner in 1 gallon of water.

Hexamitiasis

Hexamitiasis is a parasitic disease in avians. It is transmitted by certain fowls eating or drinking anything contaminated by fecal matter from an infected bird. Signs of hexamitiasis include weight loss, watery diarrhea, and listlessness.

Recommendations

Singles: Myrrh, Frankincense
Blends: Raven, R.C., Thieves
Nutritionals: Life 9, NingXia Red
Additional: Thieves Household Cleaner

Applications and Usage

Ingestion & Oral: Administer orally or in water 2 drops each Raven, R.C., Thieves, Myrrh, and Frankincense and ½ Life 9 dissolved in 1 oz. NingXia Red 2 times daily.

Inhalation: Diffuse Thieves and Raven in the bird habitat.

Other: Wash or spray EVERYTHING down with 4 capfuls Thieves Household Cleaner in 1 gallon of water. Once cleared, continue with NingXia Red, Life 9 in water, and diffusing Thieves and Raven until immune system is restored.

Infectious Bronchitis

Infectious bronchitis is a highly contagious disease in commercial chicken flocks throughout the world. Symptoms include respiratory signs, decreased egg production, and poor egg quality, as well as possible intestinal issues.

Recommendations

Singles: Eucalyptus Radiata, Eucalyptus Globulus
Blends: Raven, R.C., Thieves
Nutritionals: Life 9, NingXia Red
Additional: Thieves Household Cleaner

Applications and Usage

Ingestion & Oral: Administer in water 2 drops each Raven, R.C., Thieves, Eucalyptus Radiata, and Eucalyptus Globulus, plus ½ Life 9 dissolved in 1 oz. NingXia Red 2 times daily.

Inhalation: Diffuse Thieves and Raven in bird habitat. Once cleared, continue diffusing Thieves and Raven until immune system is restored.

Other: Wash or spray EVERYTHING down with 4 capfuls of Thieves Household Cleaner in 1 gallon of water.

Infectious Bursal Disease

Infectious bursal disease (IBD) is seen in domestic chickens worldwide. It can be isolated readily from an organ of the immune system (the bursa of Fabricius).

Symptoms seen in IBD-infected chicks can include a rapid drop in feed/water consumption, slimy diarrhea, and an unsteady gait. IBD immunosuppression allows susceptibility to other diseases. The viral infection is spread through feces.

Recommendations

Singles: Myrrh, Tea Tree, Cistus
Blends: Thieves, Raven, R.C.
Nutritionals: Life 9, NingXia Red
Additional: Thieves Household Cleaner

Applications and Usage

Inhalation: Diffuse Thieves and Raven in bird habitat. Once cleared, continue diffusing Thieves and Raven until immune system is restored.

Ingestion & Oral: Administer in water 2 drops each Raven, R.C., Thieves, Cistus, Myrrh, and Tea Tree and ½ Life 9 dissolved in 1 oz. NingXia Red 2 times daily.

Other: Wash or spray EVERYTHING down with 4 capfuls of Thieves Household Cleaner in 1 gallon of water.

Infectious Coryza

Infectious coryza is a respiratory disease of chickens characterized by nasal discharge, sneezing, and swelling under the eyes. The disease is almost exclusively seen in chickens.

Recommendations

Singles: Cistus, Myrrh, Thyme
Blends: Melrose, Purification, Raven, Thieves
Nutritionals: NingXia Red, Life 9
Additional: Thieves Household Cleaner

Applications and Usage

Ingestion & Oral: Administer orally or in water 2 drops each Melrose, Purification, Cistus, Myrrh, Thyme, and Raven and ½ Life 9 dissolved in 1 teaspoon NingXia Red 1-2 times daily.

Inhalation: Diffuse Thieves, Purification, or Melrose in the bird habitat.

Other: Wash and spray EVERYTHING down with 4 capfuls of Thieves Household Cleaner in 1 gallon of water.

Infectious Laryngotracheitis

Infectious laryngotracheitis (ILT) is a highly contagious, herpesvirus infection of chickens and pheasants.

Respiratory symptoms include shortness of breath, rattled breathing, sneezing, coughing, and wheezing. It may be possible to hear rales with a stethoscope. Secondary symptoms include conjunctivitis, respiratory discharge (nasal/ocular), and tracheitis.

Recommendations

Singles: Lavender, Ravintsara, Eucalyptus Blue, Melissa
Blends: Exodus II, Purification

Applications and Usage

Topical: Apply Lavender, Melissa, and Ravintsara on feet 2-3 times daily.

Ingestion & Oral: Administer orally 5 drops each Lavender, Ravintsara, Exodus II, Eucalyptus Blue, and Melissa in 1 oz. pure water 1-2 times daily.

Inhalation: Diffuse together, Melissa, Purification, Ravintsara, and Eucalyptus Blue in the bird habitat.

Lice

Lice, although not lethal to chickens, can still cause much discomfort with itching. The birds respond by overgrooming, which causes feather loss.

Birds should be checked often so treatment can be administered to prevent further infection. Also, be sure to take the necessary precautions so that the lice are not transferred.

Recommendations

Singles: Cedarwood, Orange, Eucalyptus Blue, Lemongrass, Eucalyptus Radiata
Blends: Purification, Melrose

Applications and Usage

Topical: In a glass spray bottle, combine 4 oz. pure water (not tap), and 20 drops each Cedarwood, Orange, Melrose, Purification, and Eucalyptus Blue. Spray on bird up to 4 times daily.

Inhalation: Combine the following and diffuse in the birds' habitat: Cedarwood, Purification, Melrose, Lemongrass, and Eucalyptus Radiata.

Marek's Disease

Marek's disease is a viral herpes-rooted illness. There is a vaccine available; however, it is only effective for birds younger than five months old. Characteristics of this disease include stiffness, paralysis, and tremors.

This disease is contagious, so vaccination and quarantine are essential in halting contraction and spread.

Recommendations

Singles: Copaiba, Ravintsara, Eucalyptus Blue, Melissa
Blends: Exodus II, Purification

Applications and Usage
Topical: Apply Copaiba, Melissa, and Ravintsara onto feet 2-3 times daily.

Ingestion & Oral: Administer orally Copaiba, Ravintsara, Exodus II, Eucalyptus Blue, and Melissa together in pure water 1-2 times daily.

Inhalation: Diffuse together Melissa, Purification, Ravintsara, and Eucalyptus Blue in bird habitat.

Mycoplasma

Mycoplasma is a microorganism-borne disease that commonly affects chickens and turkeys. Symptoms include nasal discharge, rattling cough, and decreased egg production. This is a highly contagious disease that can last for long periods of time. Clean environments and microbe prevention is the best solution.

Recommendations
Singles: Lavender, Pine, Idaho Balsam Fir

Blends: Thieves, Purification, R.C., Raven

Nutritionals: NingXia Red, Life 9

Additional: Thieves Household Cleaner

Applications and Usage
Ingestion & Oral: Administer orally or in water 2 drops each Thieves, Purification, Lavender, Pine, Idaho Balsam Fir, and Raven and ½ Life 9 dissolved in 1 teaspoon NingXia Red 1-2 times daily.

Inhalation: Diffuse Thieves, Purification, or R.C. in the bird habitat.

Other: Wash and spray EVERYTHING down with 4 capfuls of Thieves Household Cleaner in 1 gallon of water.

Mites

Mites are infestations of barely visible insects that burrow into the upper layer of skin and lay eggs. The infestation causes discomfort and can carry infectious microorganisms.

Mites specifically affecting birds come in many subclasses, different sizes, and afflict various tissues on a bird's body. While they may not pose a direct threat to health, they can make them uncomfortable and expose them to secondary infections.

Recommendations
Singles: Cedarwood, Eucalyptus Blue, Lemongrass, Eucalyptus Radiata

Blends: Purification, Melrose

Applications and Usage
Topical: Make a spray in a glass spray bottle of 4 oz. pure water (not tap), adding in 20 drops each Cedarwood, Melrose, Purification, and Eucalyptus Blue. Spray on birds up to 4 times daily.

Inhalation: Combine and diffuse the following in the bird habitat: Cedarwood, Purification, Lemongrass, and Eucalyptus Radiata.

Molting

Molting is when birds lose their feathers. While most birds molt 1-2 times a year as a natural shedding or feather turnover, anything more than that may indicate a larger issue. Birds may molt due to stress, an autoimmune disease, or serious infections.

During the natural 2 times-yearly variety molt, the process draws on the bird's energy and may leave it susceptible to other infection. The best way to support your birds as they molt is to be sure they have the right vitamins, minerals, food, water, and nesting comfort.

If caused by West Nile Virus, please add that protocol to the following instructions.

Recommendations
Singles: Lavender, Orange, Eucalyptus Blue

Blends: Stress Away Roll-On, Peace & Calming, Gentle Baby, Sacred Mountain

Nutritionals: NingXia Red, Mineral Essence

Applications and Usage
Topical: Make a spray in a glass spray bottle of 4 oz. pure water (not tap), adding in 10 drops each Gentle Baby, Lavender, and Orange and 5 drops Eucalyptus Blue. Spray on birds up to 6 times daily.

Ingestion & Oral: Administer orally or in water 1 oz. NingXia Red and 1 dropperful Mineral Essence daily.

Inhalation: To reduce stress, diffuse Stress Away Roll-On, Peace & Calming, Lavender, Gentle Baby, or Sacred Mountain.

Mycotoxicoses

Mycotoxicoses refers to the effects of fungus and mold affecting avians. The most common source of this malady is when fowl consume feed that has been improperly stored and has developed mold or fungus.

Always be sure to store feed properly in a cool, dry location, checking regularly for signs of fungal growth.

Recommendations

Singles: Tea Tree
Blends: Purification, Melrose, Thieves
Nutritionals: NingXia Red, Life 9
Additional: Thieves Household Cleaner

Applications and Usage

Topical: Make a spray in a glass spray bottle of 4 oz. pure water (not tap), adding in 10 drops each Purification, Tea Tree, and Melrose. Spray on bird up to 6 times daily.
Ingestion & Oral: Administer orally or in water 2 drops each Thieves, Purification, Tea Tree, and Melrose and ½ Life 9 dissolved in 1 teaspoon NingXia Red 1-2 times daily.
Inhalation: Diffuse Thieves, Purification, or Melrose in bird's habitat.
Other: Wash and spray EVERYTHING down with 4 capfuls of Thieves Household Cleaner in 1 gallon of water.

Newcastle Disease (Paramyxovirus Infections)

Newcastle disease is an infection of virulent Newcastle Disease Virus (NDV). Signs of NDV include respiratory issues (coughing, ragged breathing) and erratic behavior (nervousness, irritability).

This viral disease is transferrable to other avians and should be reported immediately to a veterinarian professional.

Recommendations

Singles: Copaiba, Hyssop, Ravintsara, Melissa
Blends: Thieves, Raven, Exodus II, DiGize
Nutritionals: NingXia Red
Additional: Thieves Household Cleaner

Applications and Usage

Topical: Apply Copaiba, Ravintsara, and Hyssop on feet 2-3 times daily.

Ingestion & Oral: Administer orally 2 drops each Copaiba, DiGize, Exodus II, Melissa, and Ravintsara in 1 tablespoon NingXia Red 1-2 times daily.
Inhalation: Diffuse any of the following in the bird habitat: Thieves, Raven, Ravintsara, or Exodus II.
Other: Wash and spray EVERYTHING down with 2 oz. of Thieves Household Cleaner in 1 gallon of water.

Osteomyelitis

Osteomyelitis refers to the swelling of bones in avians. This particular condition can happen due to myriad factors but most often affects avians that are convalescing for a period of time. Since birds are accustomed to being on their feet, these recovery periods mean that the knee and ankle joint will sit against a hard surface. This causes sores, which lead to osteomyelitis. The best course of action is to address the root sickness so that the animal can recover and begin to move about as normal.

Recommendations

Singles: Northern Lights Black Spruce, Idaho Balsam Fir
Blends: Purification

Applications and Usage

Topical: Apply Northern Lights Black Spruce, Idaho Balsam Fir, and Purification directly on inflamed area daily.
Ingestion & Oral: Add Northern Lights Black Spruce to drinking water. Always leave an oil-free second water source.

Quail Bronchitis

Quail bronchitis is a highly contagious respiratory disease, most often found in Bobwhite quail. This disease is of particular interest as it strikes popular game birds and can have devastating consequences on game bird farms. Quail bronchitis is very transferable among other quail and is oftentimes fatal. Symptoms include a rattling cough, nasal discharge, discolored and watery droppings, and ocular weeping.

Recommendations

Singles: Lemon, Ravintsara, Ginger, Copaiba
Blends: Thieves, Raven, ImmuPower
Nutritionals: Life 9, NingXia Red
Additional: Thieves Household Cleaner

Applications and Usage

Ingestion & Oral: Administer orally or in water 2 drops each Ravintsara, Ginger, Thieves, and Copaiba and ½ Life 9 dissolved in 1 oz. NingXia Red 2 times daily. Once cleared, continue with NingXia Red, Thieves or ImmuPower, and Lemon until immune system is restored.

Inhalation: Diffuse Thieves, Raven, or Lemon in the bird habitat.

Other: Wash and spray EVERYTHING down with 2 oz. Thieves Household Cleaner in 1 gallon of water.

Riemerella Anatipestifer Infection

Riemerella anatipestifer is a contagious bacterial infection that strikes small birds. The highest incidence is among ducks that are 1-7 weeks old. It also infects a significant population of turkeys and geese. Other waterfowl, chickens, and pheasants may be occasionally affected.

Symptoms include neck and head tremors, nasal discharge, sneezing, coughing, and birds lying on their backs.

Recommendations

Singles: Copaiba, Ginger, Lemon
Blends: Thieves, Raven, ImmuPower, DiGize
Nutritionals: NingXia Red, Life 9
Additional: Thieves Household Cleaner

Applications and Usage

Ingestion & Oral: Administer orally or in water 2 drops each DiGize, Thieves, and Copaiba, 1 drop Ginger, and ½ Life 9 dissolved in 1 oz. NingXia Red 2 times daily. Once cleared, continue with NingXia Red, Thieves or ImmuPower, and Lemon in the water until immune system is restored.

Inhalation: Diffuse Thieves, Raven, or ImmuPower in the bird habitat.

Other: Wash and spray EVERYTHING down with 3 oz. of Thieves Household Cleaner in 1 gallon of water.

Rotaviral Infections (affecting Chickens, Turkeys, Quail, Pheasants, and Pigeons)

Rotaviral infections are one of the most common causes of diarrhea and enteritis in avians. This particularly affects young birds, but chickens have been tested for presence of the virus in cases that indicate infection without clinical signs. The infection route is oral, and most birds will reach a maximum viral excretion within 2-5 days. Additional symptoms include inflamed vents, dehydration, and weight loss.

Recommendations

Singles: Eucalyptus Blue, Melissa, Copaiba, Lemon
Blends: DiGize, Exodus II, ImmuPower, Raven
Nutritionals: NingXia Red, Life 9
Additional: Thieves Household Cleaner

Applications and Usage

Ingestion & Oral: Administer orally or in water 2 drops each DiGize, Exodus II, Melissa, and Copaiba and ½ Life 9 dissolved in 1 oz. NingXia Red 2 times daily. Once cleared, continue with NingXia Red, DiGize or ImmuPower, and Lemon in the water until immune system is restored.

Inhalation: Diffuse Exodus II, Raven, ImmuPower, or Eucalyptus Blue in the bird habitat.

Other: Wash and spray EVERYTHING down with 4 oz. Thieves Household Cleaner in 1 gallon of water.

Salmonellosis

Most birds carry Salmonella. Unfortunately, chickens are hit much harder than any other bird. The bacteria pose little harm to chickens but cause food poisoning in humans. The transfer usually occurs through exposure to raw meat or eggs.

Making it a priority to treat live poultry helps prevent the spread of Salmonella to eggs or prepared poultry. Thoroughly cooking chicken products and washing hands after handling these products raw will help ensure food safety.

Recommendations

Singles: Lemon, Tea Tree
Blends: Thieves, DiGize
Nutritionals: NingXia Red, Life 9
Additional: Thieves Household Cleaner

Applications and Usage

Ingestion & Oral: Administer orally or in water 2 drops each DiGize, Thieves, Lemon, and Tea Tree and ½ Life 9 dissolved in 1 oz. NingXia Red 2 times daily. Once cleared, continue with NingXia Red, DiGize, and Thieves in the water until immune system is restored.

Inhalation: Diffuse Thieves and DiGize in the bird habitat.

Other: Wash and spray EVERYTHING down with 4 oz. of Thieves Household Cleaner in 1 gallon of water.

Scald

Scald is a form of chemical burn on the skin of chickens, usually on the legs and feet. The skin takes on a reddish hue, becomes noticeably raw, and results in pain for the chickens. Scald happens almost exclusively as a result of ammonia from droppings coming in contact with the birds' skin and chemically burning it.

Provide dry bedding, flooring, and clean the housing continually. Also, be sure to provide enough free range for the flock to move around. Good ventilation is also essential, because ammonia may create vapors that are toxic to the lungs and can cause breathing difficulties.

Recommendations

Singles: Copaiba, Helichrysum, Myrrh
Blends: Purification, Thieves, DiGize
Additional: Thieves Household Cleaner

Applications and Usage

Topical: Apply Copaiba, Helichrysum, and Myrrh directly on inflamed area multiple times daily.

Ingestion & Oral: Put Copaiba and Purification in drinking water.

Inhalation: Diffuse Thieves and DiGize in the bird habitat.

Other: Wash and spray EVERYTHING down with 4 oz. Thieves Household Cleaner in 1 gallon of water.

Trichomoniasis

Trichomoniasis is caused by a protozoan parasite called *Trichomonas gallinae*. In domestic fowl, pigeons, doves, songbirds, and hawks, it is characterized by yellow accumulations in the throat and weight loss. It has been termed "canker," "roup," and in hawks, "frounce."

Recommendations

Singles: Ocotea, Copaiba, Cistus, Jade Lemon, Lemon
Blends: DiGize, Purification, Thieves, Raven, R.C.
Nutritionals: Life 9

Applications and Usage

Ingestion & Oral: Administer orally or in water 2-4 drops each Ocotea, DiGize, Copaiba, and Cistus; 1 drop Jade Lemon, Lemon, Ocotea, or Purification; and ½ Life 9 dissolved in water 2 times daily. Keep the bird away from ALL sugar in food and water.

Inhalation: Diffuse Purification, Thieves, R.C., or Raven.

Viral Infections

Caged birds can potentially suffer from several serious viral illnesses. These include polyma, Pacheco's disease, and Psittacine beak and feather disease. Amounts of oils to use vary according to each unique situation and diagnosis.

Recommendations

Singles: Melissa, Ravintsara, Ocotea, Basil, Eucalyptus Blue, Lemon, Lemongrass, Copaiba
Blends: DiGize, Exodus II, Thieves, Raven, ImmuPower
Nutritionals: Life 9, NingXia Red
Additional: Thieves Household Cleaner

Applications and Usage

Ingestion & Oral: Administer orally or in water 2-4 drops of any combination of DiGize, Exodus II, Melissa, Ravintsara, Ocotea, Basil, Eucalyptus Blue, Raven, ImmuPower, Lemon, Lemongrass, Thieves, and Copaiba and ½ Life 9 dissolved in 1 oz. NingXia Red 2 times daily. Once cleared, continue with NingXia Red, DiGize, and any of the above oils in the water until immune system is restored.

Inhalation: Diffuse any of the above oils in the bird habitat.

Other: Wash and spray EVERYTHING down with 4 oz. Thieves Household Cleaner in 1 gallon of water. Repeat as needed.

Worms

Many roundworms and tapeworms can affect your chickens. The parasitic worms that infest chickens can reside all along the gastrointestinal tract as well as the windpipe. If worms infest the windpipe, the birds will most likely suffer from a form of respiratory disease.

Symptoms include weight loss, strange droppings (usually taking on a foamy consistency), pale skin, and lethargy. The secondary symptom may be anemia if the worm burden is high or the infestation has lasted for a length of time.

Recommendations
Singles: Thyme, Mountain Savory
Blends: ParaGize, Purification, Thieves, DiGize
Nutritionals: Life 9, ParaFree

Applications and Usage
Ingestion & Oral: Administer orally 2-4 drops each ParaGize or ParaFree (puncture softgel and squeeze out drops), DiGize, Thyme, and Mountain Savory and ½ Life 9 dissolved in 1 teaspoon water 1-2 times daily. Keep the bird away from ALL sugar in food and water.
Inhalation: Diffuse Purification or Thieves in the bird habitat.

Swine (Pig) Conditions

These animals can often be exposed to oils in similar ways as dogs. Raindrop Technique is often used. Diffusing for these animals is best with an "air-style" diffuser, as they are in the barns or larger areas. Oral essential oils are commonly used and are easily added to feed.

Abscesses

Abscesses happen to pigs for a variety of reasons, including bites or kicks from others in the herd, scrapes from the pen, trauma from a fall or kick, as a complication from an injection (at the injection site), or from another bacterial infection. Pigs may experience pain, swelling, fever, and tenderness at the site.

Recommendations
Singles: Frankincense, Oregano, Lemongrass, Tea Tree, Lavender, Helichrysum
Blends: PanAway, Melrose, T-Away, Thieves, Infect Away, PuriClean, Mendwell, Purification
Nutritionals: NingXia Red

Applications and Usage
Topical: Essential oils may be applied neat over the affected area or sprayed onto the abscess site; 2 times daily applications are recommended.
Ingestion & Oral: NingXia Red for piglets, syringe 5-10 cc of NingXia Red into mouth 1 time daily; for finishing and market-weight hogs, add 4 oz. NingXia Red to bowl of drinker. If using a nipple-type drinker, add 2-4 oz. of NingXia Red to water container.

Anemia

Anemia (insufficient numbers of red blood cells) is usually caused in young pigs from a deficiency of iron in the first few weeks of life. Other factors such as gastric ulcers, trauma, or warfarin toxicity may cause internal bleeding leading to chronic anemia.

Recommendations
Singles: Cistus, Helichrysum, Frankincense, Copaiba
Blends: DiGize, ParaGize
Nutritionals: Mineral Essence, Rehemogen
Additional: V-6 Vegetable Oil Complex

Applications and Usage
Topical: Essential oils may be applied topically, undiluted or diluted 50:50 with V-6.
Ingestion & Oral: Iron supplementation based on feed analysis; Rehemogen and Mineral Essence (1-2 droppers per day per pig). A beginning recipe may be adding 5-7 drops of suggested essential oil or blend per gallon of water.

Arthritis/Joint infection

When pigs display lameness or arthritis, it's generally the result of infection, not a result of age. Most cases will occur due to injury (lacerations, bites, punctures, kicks, bruises, falls, etc.). Pigs may exhibit lameness ranging from mild limping to immobility.

Recommendations

Singles: Frankincense, Palo Santo, Idaho Balsam Fir, Helichrysum, Copaiba, Peppermint, Ravintsara, Eucalyptus Radiata, Thyme, Basil, Cypress, Marjoram

Blends: PanAway, Deep Relief Roll-On, ImmuPower, Exodus II, Thieves, R.C., Aroma Siez

Nutritionals: NingXia Red, MultiGreens

Additional: V-6 Vegetable Oil Complex

Applications and Usage

Topical: Essential oils can be applied in Raindrop style, mixed together in a bottle with a roller ball, and applied to the spine. This is just one recipe that can be used:

- 15 drops Copaiba
- 15 drops Frankincense
- 6 drops Idaho Balsam Fir
- 6 drops Thyme
- 6 drops Basil
- 8 drops Cypress
- 8 drops Marjoram
- 8 drops Peppermint

Dilute 50:50 with V-6 Vegetable Oil Complex and roll up the spine 1 time daily. This blend can also be applied to affected joints.

Ingestion & Oral: Administer NingXia Red, 5-10 cc syringed into mouth or added to drinking water daily; MultiGreens, contents of 2 capsules added to drinking water daily.

Aujeszky's Disease (Pseudorabies)

Although Aujeszky's disease has been eradicated in commercial hog operations in the United States, this serious viral infection is still prevalent in some parts of Europe, Southeast Asia, Central and South America, and Mexico. Feral pigs may be affected and be carriers as well.

Mortality in young pigs is high. Symptoms start as anorexia and lethargy, quickly progressing to seizures and paralysis. Older pigs may develop respiratory symptoms or reproductive problems, including abortions, mummified piglets, and stillbirths.

Recommendations

Singles: Frankincense, Oregano, Thyme, Ravintsara

Blends: Thieves, Exodus II, ImmuPower

Applications and Usage

Ingestion & Oral: Oils are best administered in drinking water: 1-2 drops per gallon of water for piglets, 5-6 drops per gallon for mid-weight pigs, and 10-12 drops per gallon for sows and market-weight hogs.

Bacterial Infections/Diseases

Pigs suffer from a variety of porcine illnesses as a result of bacterial infection. These include *Bordetella bronchiseptica*, listeria, *E. coli*, leptospirosis, campylobacter, erysipelas, clostridial species, streptococcal species, pasteurella species, etc. Amounts of oils to use vary according to each unique situation and diagnosis.

Recommendations

Singles: Frankincense, Oregano, Thyme

Blends: Thieves, Exodus II, ImmuPower

Applications and Usage

Topical: In an acute outbreak of disease, essential oils can be misted and diffused 2 times daily.

Ingestion & Oral: Oils are best administered in drinking water: 1-2 drops per gallon for piglets; 5-6 drops per gallon for mid-weight pigs; and 10-12 drops per gallon for sows, boars, and market-weight hogs.

Blue Eye Disease

Blue eye disease is a viral affliction that is identified often by loss of appetite and convulsions. Additional symptoms include respiratory distress, pneumonia, and encephalitis. Left untreated, it can cause several complications, including sterility and corneal scarring, where the eye turns blue.

Recommendations

Singles: Copaiba, Ravintsara, Lemongrass

Blends: Exodus II, DiGize, ImmuPower, Raven

Additional: Thieves Household Cleaner

Applications and Usage

Ingestion & Oral: Administer preferably in mouth but at least in food or water 10 drops each Copaiba, Exodus II, DiGize, and ImmuPower 2 times daily.

Inhalation: Diffuse Raven or Ravintsara, DiGize, and Lemongrass in the pig habitat.

Other: Wash and spray EVERTHING AND EVERYWHERE with ¼ cup Thieves Household Cleaner per 1 gallon of pure water.

Diarrhea (Pig Scours)

There are many causes for scours in piglets, but the most common offenders are *E. coli*, clostridial organisms, and coccidia. The most important one is *E. coli*, due to the high mortality rate associated with these bacteria. Adequate intake of colostrum is crucial to the piglet's immune system.

Recommendations

Singles: Copaiba, Cistus
Blends: Thieves, DiGize
Nutritionals: NingXia Red
Additional: Thieves Household Cleaner

Applications and Usage

Ingestion & Oral: Administer preferably in mouth but at least in food or water 10 drops each Copaiba, DiGize, Thieves, and Cistus 2 times daily.

Other: Wash and spray everything with ¼ cup Thieves Household Cleaner per gallon of pure water. Essential oils should be mixed accordingly and given orally 1 time daily:

- 1 drop Thieves
- 2 oz. NingXia Red
- Syringe 5 cc into newborn piglets' mouths for five consecutive days.

Dipped Shoulder ("Humpy Back")

As some pigs approach maturity, their bodies change shape, and they start to take on the appearance of two different pigs joined together at the middle. The back, above and behind the ribs, becomes increasingly dipped, while above the middle and rear abdomen becomes humped.

The condition is abnormal and unsightly but, in the absence of other diseases, the pigs remain healthy and normal in every other way. Although it is thought to be a developmental disease, no known cause has been determined.

Recommendations

Singles: Valor, Valor II, Copaiba, Frankincense
Blends: PanAway, T-Away, Highest Potential
Nutritionals: NingXia Red

Applications and Usage

Topical: Administer Raindrop Technique as needed.
Ingestion & Oral: Administer 1 to 2 tablespoons NingXia Red syringed into mouth 1 time daily.

Foot-and-Mouth Disease

Foot-and-mouth disease is a highly contagious viral illness that spreads quickly through herds. Pigs will demonstrate reduced appetite, over-salivating, chomping, and fever. Most importantly, they will show swollen vesicles on the feet and mouth.

It is important to detect and treat early. Piglets may suffer sudden death from cardiac failure. Early signs in swine include a decrease in appetite, rapid onset fever, and death due to cardiac failure. Quarantine infected animals immediately.

Recommendations

Singles: Myrrh, Mountain Savory, Thyme, Oregano, Lemongrass, Frankincense
Blends: DiGize, ImmuPower, Thieves
Additional: Thieves Household Cleaner

Applications and Usage

Ingestion & Oral: Administer preferably in mouth but at least in food or water 10 drops each Myrrh, Mountain Savory, Thyme, Oregano, Lemongrass, DiGize, ImmuPower, and Frankincense 2 times daily.

Inhalation: Diffuse Thieves, DiGize, and Lemongrass in the pig habitat.

Other: Wash and spray EVERTHING AND EVERYWHERE with ¼ cup Thieves Household Cleaner per 1 gallon of pure water.

Fractures (Broken Bones)

Broken bones can happen for a variety of reasons. Genetically, some pigs are more prone to breaks. In some cases, the propensity for broken bones stems from a mineral deficiency. Whatever the cause, be sure to consult your veterinarian for proper treatment.

Recommendations

Singles: Wintergreen, Copaiba, Blue Cypress, Peppermint, Lemongrass, Rosemary, Marjoram
Blends: T-Away, Valor, Valor II, Thieves, R.C., Egyptian Gold, Aroma Siez

Applications and Usage

Topical: Essential oils should be diluted 50:50 and applied to location at least 2 times daily.

Gastric Ulcers

The stomach of a pig does not have the full covering of a protective mucus as does a human's. The location where the esophagus enters the stomach is especially vulnerable to stomach acid burns. Recent research implicates *Helicobacter suis,* a variant of the bacteria that causes human stomach ulcers, although not with the same frequency as in humans.

Finely ground feed particles are believed to be a cause of ulcers, even when the feed is pelleted. High moisture feed sometimes contributes to ulcers.

Recommendations
Singles: Copaiba, Cistus
Blends: Thieves

Applications and Usage
Ingestion & Oral: Administer preferably in mouth but at least in food or water 10 drops each Copaiba, Thieves, and Cistus 2 times daily.

Glässer's Disease

Glässer's disease is caused by the bacterium *Haemophilus parasuis* (Hps). Symptoms include pain, fever, lameness, and sudden onset death.

Recommendations
Singles: Copaiba, Oregano, Peppermint
Blends: Thieves, Melrose
Additional: Thieves Household Cleaner

Applications and Usage
Ingestion & Oral: Administer preferably in mouth but at least in food or water 10 drops each Copaiba, Oregano, Thieves, Melrose, and Peppermint 2 times daily.
Inhalation: Diffuse Thieves and Melrose in the pig habitat.
Other: Wash and spray EVERTHING AND EVERYWHERE with ¼ cup Thieves Household Cleaner per 1 gallon of pure water.

Hematoma

A hematoma is a kind of bruising where blood pools in the tissue just below the skin surface. It is usually caused by physical trauma. Most commonly, the blood vessels rupture on the ear, shoulders, hind quarters, or flanks.

Recommendations
Singles: Cistus, Helichrysum, Copaiba, Cypress, Hinoki, Lavender
Blends: T-Away, Mendwell, Gentle Baby

Applications and Usage
Topical: Essential oils may be applied neat, directly onto the hematoma; 2 times daily application is advised.

Intestinal Torsion

Intestinal torsion occurs when the bowel twists and forms an obstruction or pseudo-obstruction. The causes are unknown, but most cases occur within swine that are on a high-grain diet. Piglets younger than 6 months have a higher incidence.

Symptoms include strained breathing, bloating, lying down and getting up repeatedly, and a general condition of severe pain or noises suggesting the pig is suffering from extreme pain.

Recommendations
Singles: Cistus, Ginger, Helichrysum
Blends: DiGize

Applications and Usage
Ingestion & Oral: Administer preferably in mouth but at least in food or water 10 drops each Cistus, Helichrysum, DiGize, and Ginger 2 times daily.

Large Roundworm

Pigs have a high incidence of large roundworm that lodges in the small intestine. If the pigs have a high infestation, they may suffer from obstruction of the small intestines or bile duct.

Early symptoms include reduced appetite, weight loss, and slow growth. Advanced symptoms include complete loss of appetite or vomiting. This usually afflicts piglets under the age of 3 months. Mature pigs may show no symptoms.

Recommendations
Singles: Copaiba, Oregano
Blends: ParaGize, DiGize, Purification, Thieves
Nutritionals: ParaFree
Additional: Thieves Household Cleaner

Applications and Usage
Ingestion & Oral: Administer preferably in mouth but at least in food or water 10 drops each Copaiba, Oregano, ParaGize or DiGize 2 times daily. Open 1 capsule ParaFree add to 2 oz. water and syringe into mouth.
Inhalation: Diffuse Thieves and Purification in the pig habitat.
Other: Wash and spray EVERTHING AND EVERYWHERE with ¼ cup Thieves Household Cleaner per 1 gallon of pure water.

Mange (Sarcoptic or Demodectic)

Mange is the result of either *Sarcoptes scabiei* or *Demodex phyllodes*. Sarcoptic mange (sometimes called scabies) is more widespread. It is important to treat quickly, because the discomfort causes the pig to rub against scratchy surfaces to relieve itself. This will damage the skin surface, make the swine more susceptible to secondary illness, and spread the mites among the herd. The presence of mange may affect growth rate.

Once a herd is clear, it is easy to prevent recurrence by properly managing newly introduced animals.

Recommendations

Singles: Lavender, Citronella, Lemongrass, Frankincense, Patchouli, Tea Tree

Blends: Purification, Melrose, Gentle Baby, PuriClean, Mendwell

Additional: Tender Tush, Animal Scents Ointment

Applications and Usage

Topical: Essential oils can be sprayed onto affected pigs 2 times daily. Ulcerated, broken, or irritated skin may benefit from Animal Scents Ointment or Tender Tush applied over the lesions daily.

Mastitis

Mastitis is an infection of the mammary gland (or glands) caused by bacteria or resulting from a secondary infection. It's common among herds and may spread quickly among sows that are feeding their farrow.

It can be acute or chronic, depending on the strain of bacteria. Some strains cause a systemic infection that is toxic to piglets. It starts after farrowing, becoming pronounced within 12 hours.

Recommendations

Singles: Melissa, Lavender, Frankincense, Peppermint, Copaiba, Hyssop, Idaho Balsam Fir, Mountain Savory

Blends: PanAway, Thieves, Infect Away

Nutritionals: NingXia Red, Longevity Softgels

Ingestion & Oral: Administer 2 oz. NingXia Red daily and 2 Longevity Softgels 2 times daily.

Applications and Usage

Topical: Coat affected teat and gland with 3 drops of PanAway and 3 drops of Idaho Balsam Fir. Then apply 3 drops of Peppermint. Affected glands should have oils applied 3 times daily for best results.

Veterinarian Tips and Suggestions

Mastitis

- 3 drops PanAway
- 3 drops Idaho Balsam Fir
- 3 drops Peppermint

Coat affected teat and gland with 3 drops PanAway and 3 drops Idaho Balsam Fir. Then apply 3 drops Peppermint. Affected glands should have oils applied 3 times daily for best results.

Metritis (Uterine Infection)

Metritis is inflammation of the womb caused by a bacterial infection. It is fairly common in the immediate post-farrowing period. Sows act lethargic, have a malodorous vaginal discharge, run a fever, and may not be producing adequate milk.

Recommendations

Singles: Oregano, Thyme, Mountain Savory, Lemongrass, Copaiba, Cypress, Frankincense, Clove, Tea Tree, Eucalyptus Globulus, Myrrh

Blends: Thieves, Melrose, Exodus II, Egyptian Gold, Infect Away, PuriClean, Immune Power

Nutritionals: NingXia Red, MultiGreens

Additional: V-6 Vegetable Oil Complex

Applications and Usage

Topical: Essential oils should be diluted in a 1:4 ratio (1 drop of essential oil to 4 drops of V-6 or other carrier oil) and infused directly into the vaginal vault 2 times daily. Oils may also be applied topically, as in Raindrop Technique style.

Ingestion & Oral: Administer orally 2 oz. NingXia Red and 1-2 MultiGreens daily.

Navel Bleeding ("Pale Pig Syndrome")

Bleeding around the navel or incomplete passage of blood through the umbilical cord at birthing time are causes for "pale pig syndrome."

Recommendations

Singles: Cistus, Helichrysum, Lavender, Myrrh

Blends: T-Away, Mendwell

Topical: After washing affected area, apply oils topically to support healing.

Parasites (Intestinal)

Most porcine parasites are the result of worms infesting the gastrointestinal tract. Common types include whipworm, porcine roundworm, and red stomach worm.

Recommendations

Blends: DiGize, ParaGize
Nutritionals: ParaFree

Applications and Usage

Topical: Essential oils may be applied on the underside of the abdomen 1 time daily.

Ingestion & Oral: Administer orally 2-3 drops DiGize and ParaGize or ParaFree (puncture softgel and squeeze out drops) daily.

Parvovirus

Most herds probably have some incidence of porcine parvovirus. The good news is that herd-developed immunity will generally pass from mother to piglets. Most herds will usually show at least some parvovirus in the young, which is not often fatal or even detectable without testing.

Young sows which are not immune are most often at risk, along with any unborn fetuses that will contract the disease. This will most often lead to stillbirths or aborted fetuses.

Recommendations

Singles: Copaiba, Oregano, Peppermint
Blends: Thieves, Melrose, Purification, DiGize, ParaGize
Additional: Thieves Household Cleaner

Applications and Usage

Ingestion & Oral: Administer preferably in mouth but at least in food or water 10 drops each Copaiba, Oregano, DiGize, ParaGize, and Peppermint 2 times daily.

Inhalation: Diffuse Thieves, Melrose, and Purification in pig habitat.

Other: Wash and spray EVERTHING AND EVERYWHERE with ¼ cup Thieves Household Cleaner per 1 gallon of pure water.

Pneumonia

Pneumonia is rare among swine. When it does occur, it is usually as a complication to swine influenza, *Mycoplasma hyopneumoniae,* PRRS virus, or a virulent strain of *Actinobacillus pleuropneumoniae.* Young animals are more susceptible.

Symptoms will include rapid/labored breathing, cough, fever, dehydration, huddling, and loss of appetite. Mortality rates are generally low, but if the herd is introduced to the virus and trying to recover from another illness, death rates may climb. This is especially true for sows.

Recommendations

Singles: Eucalyptus Blue, Oregano, Ravintsara
Blends: Thieves, Raven
Additional: Thieves Household Cleaner

Applications and Usage

Ingestion & Oral: Administer preferably in mouth but at least in food or water 10 drops each Eucalyptus Blue, Oregano, Thieves, and Raven or Ravintsara 2 times daily.

Inhalation: Diffuse Thieves and Raven in the pig habitat.

Other: Wash and spray EVERTHING AND EVERYWHERE with 1/4 cup Thieves Household Cleaner per 1 gallon of pure water.

Porcine Influenza

Also known as "swine flu," porcine influenza stems from a series of influenza A viruses. The virus may transmit through various means, and incubation is short.

The onset in the herd will be fast, acute, and widespread. It usually travels by contact with newly introduced animals, birds, carrier pigs, people (who are infected or who are handling other infected animals), and other contaminating factors. New strains evolve quickly and illness among the herd can be difficult to manage.

Symptoms include fever, coughing, and loss of appetite. It is surprisingly simple to diagnose because it spreads so dramatically.

Recommendations

Singles: Tarragon, Oregano, Lemongrass, Ginger
Blends: Thieves, Raven, DiGize
Additional: Thieves Household Cleaner

Applications and Usage

Ingestion & Oral: Administer preferably in mouth but at least in food or water 10 drops each Tarragon, Oregano, Ginger, Thieves, and Raven or DiGize 2 times daily.

Inhalation: Diffuse Thieves, Lemongrass, and Raven in the pig habitat.

Other: Wash and spray EVERTHING AND EVERYWHERE with ¼ cup Thieves Household Cleaner per 1 gallon of pure water.

Porcine Reproductive and Respiratory Syndrome

PRRS is a member of the genus *Arterivirus* with two phases: reproductive failure and postweaning respiratory diseases with attacks on the macrophages in the lungs. The macrophages are a crucial part of the swine's immune system.

When the virus takes hold, it may decimate up to 40 percent of the macrophages in the lungs and open the swine to a host of secondary infections.

Recommendations

Singles: Copaiba, Oregano, Lemongrass, Ravintsara, Cedarwood

Blends: Thieves, Raven, DiGize

Additional: Thieves Household Cleaner

Applications and Usage

Ingestion & Oral: Administer preferably in mouth but at least in food or water 10 drops each Copaiba, Oregano, Lemongrass, DiGize, Raven or Ravintsara, Cedarwood, and Thieves 2 times daily.

Inhalation: Diffuse Thieves, Lemongrass, Cedarwood, and Raven in the pig habitat.

Other: Wash and spray EVERTHING AND EVERYWHERE with ¼ cup Thieves Household Cleaner per 1 gallon of pure water.

Respiratory Conditions

Respiratory issues in swine herds can be a result of multiple issues, including bacterial and viral infections. The best way to alleviate these issues is to address the root cause.

Recommendations

Singles: Eucalyptus Radiata, Ravintsara, Peppermint, Copaiba, Dorado Azul, Frankincense, Laurus Nobilis

Blends: Raven, Breathe Again Roll-On, R.C., Thieves, Exodus II, ImmuPower

Nutritionals: NingXia Red, Inner Defense, Longevity Softgels

Applications and Usage

Topical: Several drops of oils diluted 50:50 can be dripped onto the neck or the back. Raindrop oils diluted 50:50 can also be applied.

Ingestion & Oral: Administer orally 1-2 oz. NingXia Red 1 time daily, 1 Inner Defense 2 times daily, and 1 Longevity Softgel 1 time daily. Administer 1-2 drops of suggested oil per liter of water.

Ruptures (Hernias)

Ruptures, whether inguinal or umbilical, are frequently common. Surgery is needed to repair the abdominal muscle wall defect. Essential oils may be used to support soft tissue repair.

Recommendations

Singles: Frankincense, Helichrysum, Lavender, Cypress, Marjoram, Myrrh, Manuka

Blends: PanAway, Aroma Siez, Mendwell, T-Away

Additional: Ortho Sport Massage Oil, Animal Scents Ointment

Applications and Usage

Topical: Essential oils should be diluted at least 50:50 and applied around the surgical site 2 times daily. Apply Animal Scents Ointment following administration of essential oils.

Salmonellosis (see Bacterial Diseases)

Swine Dysentery

Swine dysentery is a bacterial disease caused by *Brachyspira hyodysenteriae* that spreads very quickly through herds. It is important to treat quickly. Symptoms include bloody diarrhea, reduced appetite, and dehydration.

Some pigs will serve as carriers and only exhibit symptoms with a change of feed or under stressful conditions. Herds that recover are generally immune to the strain.

Recommendations
Singles: Peppermint
Blends: Thieves, DiGize
Additional: Thieves Household Cleaner

Applications and Usage
Ingestion & Oral: Administer preferably in mouth but at least in food or water 10 drops each Peppermint, Thieves, and DiGize 2 times daily.
Inhalation: Diffuse Thieves and DiGize in the pig habitat.
Other: Wash and spray EVERTHING AND EVERYWHERE with ¼ cup Thieves Household Cleaner per 1 gallon of pure water.

Udder Edema
Udder edema is when fluid builds up around the udder due to blockage or infection. The swelling can be painful for the sow. Treat quickly and monitor for change. If the swelling remains the same or increases, consult your veterinary professional immediately.

Recommendations
Singles: Cypress, Frankincense, Helichrysum, Fennel, Peppermint, Grapefruit, Juniper, Copaiba
Blends: T-Away, Mendwell, PanAway, Thieves

Applications and Usage
Topical: Apply 3 drops each PanAway, Peppermint, Copaiba, Helichrysum to affected teats 2-3 times daily.

> ### 🐄 Veterinarian Tips and Suggestions
> ## Udder edema
> - 3 drops PanAway
> - 3 drops Peppermint
> - 3 drops Copaiba
> - 3 drops Helichrysum
>
> Mix all together and apply to affected teats 2-3 times daily.

Livestock and Wildlife Breeding

Rut (*see also* Rogue)
As animals approach the breeding seasons, the males can often become tough to handle. They are more aggressive, showing dominance to both genders while warding off other males either by intimidation or injury. The males like their harems. They like to mark their territories by scraping the ground, rubbing shrubs and trees, mounding dung, and secreting a poignant musk.

The discarded bachelor groups, satellite groups comprised of young males wanting more, or old males that want to re-establish their herds, will challenge one another. This can cause injury or death. It is suggested that these males be removed so that the herd may flourish. It is warranted to be mindful of personality traits, confirmation, and desirability of the animals that you remove and/or replace to create a healthy, vibrant herd.

Males that are of breeding age, in rut, are seeking females for breeding that are in estrus. As the males' necks swell, they secrete a powerful musk and are ready to fight.

Recommendations
Singles: Shutran, Northern Lights Black Spruce, Idaho Blue Spruce, Wintergreen
Blends: Joy, Stress Away Roll-On, ParaGize, DiGize
Nutritionals: NingXia Red

Applications and Usage
Topical: Apply chosen suggested oils or blends in hooves, on navel, and down top line.
Inhalation: Administer Wintergreen to reverse; also helps for animals to not smell other males or females.
Ingestion & Oral: Top dress feed or drop in mouth.

Exotic and Wild Animals

It is important to address the need or the why to capture and handle exotic and wild animals. The primary reason is to be a steward for them. It is responsible ownership to tend them when they have been injured, are off feed, need to be moved to another pasture, or sold. Owning and ranching exotic hoof stock is similar to ranching domestics, just a lot more involved.

The mode of capture, the type of tranquilizer used, and the issues that preempted the capture dictate the essential oil protocol used. A good tip to remember is to always use a dewormer or an antiparasitic product while you have your hands on them.

Another reason to handle them is when one becomes unruly or "rogue." Zebra, Blesbok, and other species can become at best a challenge and sometimes belligerent to their owners, handlers, and pasture mates, causing injury and sometimes death. They also will tear up feeders and equipment and walk over or tear down fences.

Certain times of the year, when the females are in estrus and the males are rutted up in pursuit of them, can be dangerous times to handle exotics.

At all times, it is vital to watch for myopathy, lactating issues, and any other forms of stress.

Raccoon Conditions

Racoons are generally considered pests and can certainly be a nuisance. Therefore, before you consider owning one, be sure to check on whether this "exotic" pet is legal in your area and find a veterinarian who is willing to treat it, should the need arise.

Consider obtaining a pet racoon from a breeder who has raised the racoon so that it's familiar with being handled, is more social, and is less prone to biting.

No matter how cute they look, they are not like having pet cats or dogs. They will tear up your house, do whatever they want, and have razor sharp claws and teeth.

If you choose to venture into the "wild," then here are some health concerns to watch for in your pet racoon. And good luck!

Conjunctivitis

Conjunctivitis may occur due to a foreign object getting in an eye, an allergy, or a bacterial or viral infection. Signs include bloodshot sclera (white portion of eye), discharge, burning, itching, or swelling.

Recommendations
Singles: Eucalyptus Radiata, Frankincense, Lavender
Blends: Infect Away, ParaGize, T-Away, Thieves
Nutritionals: ImmuPro, Inner Defense, Life 9, Ningxia Organic Dried Wolfberries, NingXia Red
Additional: V-6 Vegetable Oil Complex

Veterinarian Tips and Suggestions

Conjunctivitis

Variation of Stanley Burrough's Master Eye Cleanse

Combine the following in a dropper bottle:

- 10 parts water
- 2 parts honey
- 1 part apple cider vinegar

Carefully holding your pet's front feet to prevent it from scratching at its eyes, allow 1 drop of the blend to drop into an eye. It does sting at first but is soothing within a few minutes.

Applications and Usage

Topical: Put 1 drop of Lavender in your hand. Rub hands together until no oil is visible. Cup hand over eye area without touching the eye. Try to hold for 10 minutes in this position, if possible.

Ingestion & Oral: On a foodstuff your pet really likes, apply 1 drop of a mixture of your chosen oil diluted in 15 ml V-6 or other carrier oil. Or, add 1-5 drops essential oil in 1 gallon of drinking water. Mist food stuffs.

Inhalation: Diffuse by placing your favorite diffuser near the animal's housing.

Other: Apply a warm compress to the outside of the eye. Be sure it is not too hot as to burn your pet. You may want to dampen its environment's bedding to prevent too much dust getting into an eye. If due to infection, try Raindrop Technique using each diluted oil individually. Raccoons are normally quite hairy per square inch. Hair acts to pull oils into the body. Try using a 4-ml bottle of V-6 or other carrier oil to which you have added just 1-2 drops of an oil. Roll the bottle of diluted oil between your palms until the V-6 and essential oil are well mixed. Use just 1 drop of a well-mixed dilution of each essential oil for a Raindrop Technique session. You may repeat daily if needed until vision improves. After improvement, go to weekly Raindrops.

Distemper

Distemper is a contagious viral infection that attacks several systems: respiratory, gastrointestinal, and nervous.

Recommendations
Singles: Cinnamon Bark, Clove, Cypress, Dorado Azul, Manuka, Eucalyptus Radiata, Eucalyptus Blue, Frankincense, Lemon, Lemongrass, Mastrante, Melissa, Mountain Savory, Myrrh, Neroli, Orange, Oregano, Petitgrain, Pine, Ravintsara, Sage, Tea Tree, Thyme
Blends: Egyptian Gold, ImmuPower, Joy, Longevity, Raven, R.C., The Gift, Thieves
Nutritionals: ImmuPro, Inner Defense, Life 9, Longevity Softgels, MightyVites, Mineral Essence, NingXia Red, OmegaGize[3]
Additional: V-6 Vegetable Oil Complex

Applications and Usage

Topical: Apply 1 drop of a single or blend in 1 tablespoon Manuka and honey or other carrier oil in the palm of your nondominant hand. Swirl your fingertip from the opposite hand around in the oil. Gently apply to animal's chest, throat areas, and front paws. Apply 1-2 drops in palm of hand, rub hands together, and then gently apply to area. In an 8-oz. glass misting spray bottle, add 2-3 drops of an essential oil or blend of your choice. Mist area as needed.

Ingestion & Oral: On a foodstuff your pet really likes, apply 1 drop of a mixture of your chosen oil diluted in 15 ml V-6 or other carrier oil. This may be done several times daily based on severity of symptoms. Or, add 1-5 drops essential oil in 1 gallon of drinking water. Mist food stuffs. Gently apply to the gum areas.

Inhalation: Diffuse by placing your favorite diffuser near its housing.

Other: Administer Raindrop Technique using each Raindrop Kit oil individually after having diluted each oil. Try using a 4-ml bottle of V-6 or other carrier oil and 1-2 drops of an essential oil. Roll the bottle of diluted oil between your palms until the V-6 and essential oil are well mixed. Use just 1 drop of a well-mixed dilution of each essential oil for a Raindrop Technique session. You may repeat daily if needed until condition improves. After improvement, go to weekly Raindrops or as needed.

Giardia

Giardia is a protozoa that infects through feces or contaminated water. Symptoms may include diarrhea, lethargy, and weight loss.

Recommendations

Singles: Northern Lights Black Spruce, Ginger, Lemon, Mountain Savory, Nutmeg, Oregano, Peppermint

Blends: AromaEase, DiGize, Thieves

Nutritionals: Allerzyme, ComforTone, Digest & Cleanse, Essentialzyme, Inner Defense, MightyZyme

Additional: V-6 Vegetable Oil Complex

Applications and Usage

Topical: Apply 1 drop of a single or blend in 1 tablespoon carrier oil of your choice in palm of your nondominant hand. Swirl your fingertip from the opposite hand around in the oil. Gently apply to animal's chest, throat areas, and front paws. Apply

1-2 drops in palm of hand, rub hands together, and then gently apply to area. In an 8-oz. glass misting spray bottle, add 2-3 drops of an essential oil or blend of your choice. Mist area as needed.

Ingestion & Oral: On a foodstuff your pet really likes, apply 1 drop of a mixture of your chosen oil diluted in 15 ml V-6 or other carrier oil. This may be done several times daily based on the severity of symptoms. Or, add 1-5 drops essential oil in 1 gallon of drinking water. Mist food stuffs.

Inhalation: Apply 1 drop each of an immune- and a gastrointestinal-supporting essential oil to your nondominant hand. While holding your pet, gently cup your hand over its nose. You may also diffuse by placing your favorite diffuser near its housing.

Other: Mix 1 drop each Thieves and Peppermint in 1 teaspoon V-6. Apply to stomach 2-3 times daily. Administer Raindrop Technique.

Leptospirosis

Leptospirosis is a gram negative bacterial infection that may be transmitted to other mammals. It is believed to be shared through urine transmission, thus contaminating water sources.

Symptoms include fever, flu-like symptoms, dehydration, refusal to eat, pain in low back area, organ failure, including liver and kidneys, as well as stool containing greenish bile or is blood tinged.

Recommendations

Singles: Cinnamon Bark, Lemongrass, Peppermint, Oregano, Thyme

Blends: DiGize, ImmuPower, Infect Away, JuvaCleanse, JuvaFlex

Nutritionals: ImmuPro, JuvaTone, K&B, NingXia Red, Ningxia Organic Dried Wolfberries, Super C

Additional: V-6 Vegetable Oil Complex

Applications and Usage

Topical: Apply 1 drop of a single or blend in 1 tablespoon V-6 or other carrier oil in palm of your nondominant hand. Swirl your fingertip from the opposite hand around in the oil. Gently apply to animal's chest, throat areas, and front paws. Apply 1-2 drops in palm of hand, rub hands together, and then gently apply to area. In an 8-oz. glass misting spray bottle, add 2-3 drops of an essential oil or blend of your choice. Mist area as needed.

Ingestion & Oral: On a foodstuff your pet really likes, apply 1 drop of a mixture of your chosen oil diluted in 15 ml V-6 or other carrier oil. This may be done several times daily based on the severity of symptoms. Or, add 1-5 drops essential oil in 1 gallon of drinking water. Mist food stuffs.

Inhalation: Diffuse by placing your favorite diffuser near its housing.

Other: Administer Raindrop Technique.

Parasites

When a body's pH is out of balance or immunity is down, it becomes a host for other life forms such as bacterial, fungal, viral, or helminths of various types. These organisms need to live inside another body to survive.

Recommendations

Singles: Cinnamon Bark, Clove, Eucalyptus Globulus, Fennel, Ginger, Hyssop, Lemon, Lemongrass, Tea Tree, Mountain Savory, Oregano, Rosemary, Spearmint, Tangerine, Thyme

Blends: DiGize, Longevity, ParaGize

Nutritionals: Digest & Cleanse, Essentialzyme, ICP, Longevity Softgels, Ningxia Organic Dried Wolfberries, ParaFree

Additional: V-6 Vegetable Oil Complex

Applications and Usage

Topical: Apply 1 drop of a single or blend in 1 tablespoon V-6 or carrier oil of your choice in palm of your nondominant hand. Swirl your fingertip from the opposite hand around in the oil. Gently apply to all paws and abdominal area. Apply 1-2 drops in palm of hand, rub hands together, and then gently apply to abdominal area and down inside and outside of both rear legs to paws and pads. In an 8-oz. glass misting spray bottle, add 2-3 drops of an essential oil or blend of your choice and fill with distilled or purified water. Mist body as needed.

Ingestion & Oral: On a foodstuff your pet really likes, apply 1 drop of a mixture of your chosen oil diluted in 15 ml V-6 or other carrier oil. This may be done several times daily based on the severity of symptoms. Or, add 1-5 drops essential oil in 1 gallon of drinking water. Mist food stuffs.

Inhalation: Diffuse by placing your favorite diffuser near animal's housing.

Other: Administer Raindrop Technique.

> ### 🐄 *Veterinarian Tips and Suggestions*
>
> ## Pneumonia
>
> If pet is not eating well, mix 1 tablespoon Balance Complete thickened to a paste with 50:50 dilution of water and NingXia Red to be fed in small amounts (3-5 ml) 3 times daily. Add 1-2 drops Longevity blend to the mix.

Pneumonia

An upper airway infection such as pneumonia may be the root cause of sneezing or conjunctivitis. Or, its origin could be bacterial or viral. For more information, see Conjunctivitis and Fever.

Recommendations

Singles: Eucalyptus Radiata, Clove, Copaiba, German Chamomile, Hyssop, Lemon, Northern Lights Black Spruce, Tea Tree, Mountain Savory, Oregano, Peppermint, Roman Chamomile, Thyme

Blends: Breathe Again Roll-On, Citrus Fresh, Egyptian Gold, Evergreen Essence, Exodus II, ImmuPower, Infect Away, Melrose, Peace & Calming, Raven, R.C., Stress Away Roll-On, Thieves, Longevity

Nutritionals: Inner Defense, ImmuPro, Life 9, Longevity Softgels, NingXia Red, ParaFree, Sulfurzyme, Super B, Super C Chewable, Balance Complete

Additional: V-6 Vegetable Oil Complex

Applications and Usage

Topical: Apply 1 drop of a single or blend in 1 tablespoon V-6 or other carrier oil in palm of your nondominant hand. Swirl your fingertip from the opposite hand around in the oil. Gently apply to paws, chest, spine, and abdomen. Or, drop 1-2 drops of oil in palm of your hand, rub hands together, and then gently apply to animal's neck, chest, and back. Mist body as needed.

Ingestion & Oral: On a foodstuff your pet really likes, apply 1 drop of a mixture of your chosen oil diluted in 15 ml V-6 or other carrier oil. This may be done several times daily based on the severity of symptoms. Or, add 1-5 drops essential oil in 1 gallon of drinking water. Mist food stuffs.

Gently apply selected oils to the gum areas. Try adding ⅛ teaspoon NingXia Red or up to ¼ Super C Chewable to drinking water supply. It may be best to alternate daily.

Inhalation: Diffuse by placing your favorite diffuser near its housing.

Other: Administer Raindrop Technique daily until respiratory distress improves.

Salmonellosis

There are many strains of Salmonella. Infection may include dehydration due to diarrhea, rough hair coat, abdominal swelling or bloat, loss of pregnancy, and weight loss.

Recommendations

Singles: Cinnamon Bark, Cistus, Clove, Copaiba, Juniper, Lemon, Lemongrass, Lemon Myrtle, Tea Tree, Mountain Savory, Rosemary, Thyme

Blends: DiGize, Egyptian Gold, Evergreen Essence, Exodus II, Infect Away, Purification, Thieves

Nutritionals: Inner Defense, Life 9, Longevity Softgels, NingXia Red, Super C Chewable

Additional: V-6 Vegetable Oil Complex

Applications and Usage

Topical: Put 1 drop each digestion- and immune-supporting essential oil of your choice in your hand. Rub hands together until no oil is visible. Stroke your pet from its head to its tail area. Apply 1 drop of a single or blend in 1 tablespoon V-6 or carrier oil of your choice in palm of your nondominant hand. Swirl your fingertip from the opposite hand around in the oil. Gently apply to animal's tummy area, spine, and pads of all feet. Topical applications may need to be applied 3-5 times daily.

Ingestion & Oral: On a foodstuff your pet really likes, apply 1 drop of a mixture of your chosen oil diluted in 15 ml V-6 or other carrier oil. Or, add 1-5 drops

essential oil in 1 gallon of drinking water. Mist food stuffs.

Inhalation: Diffuse by placing your favorite diffuser near animal's housing.

Other: Administer Raindrop Technique.

Skin Infestations (Fleas, Lice, and Mites)

Insects such as fleas, lice, or mites may find your pet to be a lovely place to visit.

Recommendations

Singles: Cedarwood, Citronella, Eucalyptus Globulus, Lavender, Lemongrass, Tea Tree, Pine, Xiang Mao, Rosemary

Blends: Citrus Fresh, Purification, RepelAroma

Additional: Thieves Household Cleaner, V-6 Vegetable Oil Complex

Applications and Usage

Topical: Apply 1 drop of a single or blend in 1 tablespoon V-6 or other carrier oil in palm of your nondominant hand. Swirl your fingertip from the opposite hand around in the oil. Gently apply to all paws, inside and outside of legs, groin area (avoid sensitive parts), armpits, spine, and abdominal area. In an 8-oz. glass misting spray bottle, add 2-3 drops of an essential oil or blend of your choice and fill with distilled or purified water. Mist affected area as needed several times daily. Apply selected immune-supporting oil or blend directly to affected areas several times daily.

Other: In an 8-oz. glass bottle filled with distilled water, combine 2 capfuls Thieves Household Cleaner and 2 drops each Purification, RepelAroma, Rosemary, and Pine.

Rogue Animals

A rogue animal is one that has become dangerous by attacking pasture mates or humans and/or tears up feeders, equipment, and fences to the detriment of its herd. The animal needs to be removed from its environment. Removal methods vary: netting out of a helicopter, darting with tranquilizers from the helicopter or on the ground, or trapping in a drop net or in a pen with a drop gate.

Recommendations

Singles: Wintergreen (to reverse tranquilization and support the respiratory system), Helichrysum, Lavender, Lemon, Frankincense, Elemi, Northern Lights Black Spruce, Copaiba, Valerian, Ravintsara, Hinoki, Myrrh

Blends: Clarity, Thieves, R.C., Raven, Joy, Aroma Life, Stress Away Roll-On, ParaGize, DiGize, Purification, Animal Scents essential oils, PanAway, Relieve It, Trauma Life

Nutritionals: NingXia Red, Ningxia Organic Dried Wolfberries

Additional: Progessence Plus, Animals Scents Ointment, Thieves Household Cleaner

Applications and Usage

Topical: Drop neat down top line, in hooves if able, on the heart and belly if you can.

Ingestion & Oral: Drop in mouth. NOT Zebras… EVER! They will bite your fingers off. If stalled, use as a top dressing in feed and in water.

Inhalation: Apply oil in nostril.

Other: Make Thieves Household Cleaner spray with the Raindrop oils. Add oils that repel flies, parasites, and anything else you wish to address. Keep it in your vet kit. Mist on animals while contained. Typically, these animals will get up much quieter than without using essential oils. When using Wintergreen, be ready for them to come out of the drug much faster. Be very mindful that these are wild animals; and when drugged, they are still just as dangerous.

Testimonials

I use Young Living oils on my alpacas. Using Thieves soap to wash surrounding eye area, drops of Frankincense around the eye, and Lavender oil diluted with water sprayed into the eye, my alpacas blink and close their eyes, that's when I spray onto eyelids and lashes. I used this successfully to clear a severe eye infection several years ago and recently again this winter. I use Animal Scents Ointment all over on the alpacas for their skin issues. Thank God and Gary Young for Young Living Essential Oils.

– *Karen B.*

. . . .

Recently, when I was back home on my parents' beef cattle farm, we went out to "work" a few bull calves. (For those non-farm folks, this just means we were treating, tagging, and recording information for 1,000-pound male cows).

Dad and Mom had a very young large bull that had a stick driven into its hoof from stepping on it wrong. He'd been limping for a day or two, and his entire lower leg and hoof area were very swollen. We caught this injured bull in the chute, and he was jumping wildly. He was frustrated, uncomfortable, and downright mad. (Ever seen bull riding at a rodeo? Yes, kind of like that.) Not only was he compromising his already injured hoof, but he was dangerous. There was no way my Dad was going to be able to grab his leg, pull out the stick, and inspect and repair his injury.

I had my oil bag with me, knowing that I'd need to rub my kids down with Peppermint and Purification to keep them from getting ticks and chiggers as they romped about the farm. When I saw the bull acting so wildly, I grabbed my Peace & Calming. With the bottle open, I ever so carefully lowered it in front of the bull's face, close to his nose. After about a minute, he wasn't moving at all, so I dropped about 7 drops right on the end of his nose, so he could continue to inhale the oil, thinking it would also penetrate his hide to his bloodstream. I kid you not, that bull stood there perfectly still for another 10 minutes while my Dad lifted his foot, pulled out the rest of the stick, and then rubbed and cleaned his hoof.

We pulled out the "swelling" by squeezing from his knee joint down to his foot as fluid gushed and sprayed out. I also dropped Thieves and Lemon into the wound to fight the infection and PanAway for the pain and swelling. That bull didn't move a muscle. He was a totally different animal than the one who was jumping mad a few minutes prior.

Even when we opened the head chute, he wouldn't walk through to get out; we had to open the side chute. My Dad (a 52-year-old lifetime farmer) was amazed. We all were. None of us had ever seen any of our cattle calm down so quickly and stay calm, even during pain and pressure on a very tender wound! I mean, he DIDN'T MOVE A MUSCLE!

It was a huge testament to the effectiveness of Young Living Essential Oils. These essential oils have a million different uses. Mom and Dad knew that they were using a completely natural, organic, safe, and age-old method. They are SO excited (as am I), and they've decided to get their oils into spray bottles, just to take with them to work cattle from now on!

-*Jordan S.*

. . . .

We use Animal Scents on our show cattle on any open sores they develop, mainly behind the ears from the halters or across the nose. I was always leery to apply any other ointments on the nose, since it is so close to the eyes. Plus, I get a little cautious with what we use on the show cows, since they are normally worth well over $2,000 to $3,000 each! However, I know the oils are safe, no matter what we deal with at the time.

But my most amazing story is that just last week, I convinced my husband to let me try oils on a breech calf. We diagnosed this because my husband inserted an arm into the cow's birth canal because the mom was having troubles delivering.

I applied Peppermint to the left side of the heifer's stomach, repeating every 5 minutes. After 3 applications, we could literally watch her stomach "flip." It looked like she had gotten really big on the right side. Then, it went back to normal.

My husband then reinserted his arm to find out the calf had turned head first! The entire time I also kept applying Lavender and Peace & Calming to the mom's head between the ears. She didn't get agitated or wild like they normally tend to do. When it came to push, the calf was out after the mom pushed only 2 times! Both mom and baby are doing great.

These oils saved my $3,000 heifer and now a $2,500 bull calf. If I could say thank you to every person who developed and now "produces" these awesomely amazing oils, I would probably break down in tears, even though they don't know how they helped save an addition to our cattle herd and what it means to our future breeding.

- Jaci S.

. . . .

Three years ago, Cleo, our milk cow, came down with mastitis and ended up with gangrene, which is called Blue Bag. I called three different vets, and they said there was nothing they could to do to save her bag except to remove it, which would have made her of no use. The other option was to put her to sleep.

Blue Bag is a viral mastitis that cannot be treated with antibiotics. The bag turns black and blue with gangrene, which is why it's called Blue Bag. In all of the research I found, there was nothing to save the cow except to remove the bag.

One of the vets gave some stuff to inject into the infected quarter to kill it, so the gangrene would not spread to the other quarters. But then her entire bag turned black and blue. They said the only thing left to do was remove the bag or kill her. Even if they were able to save her from the Blue Bag, she would never produce milk again.

So, that was when I called my mom and started injecting the oils inside the bag and putting oils on her 2 times a day. I would alternate with Thieves, Melrose, and ImmuPower. Then I massaged her entire bag with Orange, Lavender, Frankincense, and Citrus Fresh 2 times a day. Within two weeks, she started to get better, and I let her dry up. Later she had a baby and was fine. She even had milk in the quarter that she was supposed to have been killed. Last year, she raised her own calf, along with two bum calves, and had milk galore in all quarters.

-Jodi R.

I received a call from a friend who had a heifer that birthed a very large calf that had to be pulled. Both the calf and mama were traumatized by the ordeal; and the calf, after an extended time following the birth, would/could not stand nor would she nurse.

I gave my friend some suggestions for various oils to put on the calf, as well as in its mouth: Oregano (diluted), Valor, Peppermint, and Frankincense. However, my friend had limited oils available at the time, so she drenched the calf with NingXia Red and several drops of DiGize. After some time, the calf arose (with help from its human friends) and drank a tiny bit of milk from its mother. By morning, the little heifer calf was standing and nursing on its own.

-Dr. Barbara F.

. . . .

Millie was attacked by a cougar. It tore all the meat and hide off of Millie's hip. She had disappeared for three days, and I did not know what had happened to her. When she came home, I was so shocked to see how injured she was and full of maggots. I called Game and Fish and they confirmed that she was attacked by a cougar.

My veterinarian wanted to put her down; I said no. I applied PanAway and then washed her wound off with the hose, trying to get rid of all the maggots. They were all over her, inside and out. As they were coming out of legs, stomach, and hip, I sprayed her. I used Thieves mixed with V-6 and sprayed the maggots. They dropped dead! Then I made another spray of Melrose and Purification and sprayed her with that, sealing the wound with Animal Scents Ointment. I did that 2 times a day, and the flesh started to slowly grow back. A month later, it was all grown back.

-Jodi R.

Pocket Pets

Introduction

Pocket pets are quite delightful individuals that depend upon you for everything—their environment, food and water, and companionship. Of top importance in their dependence upon you is their health.

Their environment includes the temperature and humidity inside your home. Some pets become stressed when temperatures get too high or too low. The same stress occurs when the humidity is incorrect. Foodstuff and water need to be as natural and as organic as possible.

One of the biggest issues a pocket pet faces is chlorinated and/or fluoridated water. Lemon oil may assist in removing or diluting some chemicals found in water.

Safety and Guidelines When Using Essential Oils for Pocket Pets

Pocket pets are each unique and vary greatly physically. Some are very hairy and some are not. When using essential oils on a pocket pet, you must consider the number of hairs per square inch. The more hair, the faster essential oils applied to its coat are absorbed. In some situations, more essential oil is not always better. Be sure to closely monitor your pocket pet when applying oils, especially when working with pocket pets with long hair.

An example of a pocket pet with long hair is the chinchilla. The chinchilla coat is very thick. Diluting an essential oil before application would just make a big mess. Instead, apply 1 drop of an essential oil to your hand. Do not let the oil evaporate; and using a petting motion, work the oil through the hair into the skin.

Also, consider body weight. If 1 drop is good for a human, then 1 drop may be too much for a pocket pet. Diffusion may be a great solution to your dilemma about a pocket pet's health challenge. Just diffuse 1-6 drops of a single essential oil or combination of oils in a room where your pet is housed.

Misting or spraying essential oils diluted in water may also be a great solution for those pets that prefer you do not touch them. A 4-oz. spray bottle with 1-4 drops of oil added may be suitable for a light spray bath.

Safety Guidelines When Using Oral Supplementation for Pocket Pets

Most human oral supplementation is permissible for pocket pets. Veggie tablets are wonderful, as you can cut them into four pieces and give 1/4 tablet at a time.

Capsule products are more difficult to determine when measuring what constitutes 1/4. For a capsule application, open a capsule and remove its contents.

Diluted NingXia Red may be offered in a separate container from a pet's water. Add enough NingXia Red to give the separate water container a deep red color. Usually, this is just a teaspoon. If an animal is unwilling or unable to drink, try using an eyedropper to syringe the solution into the corner of its mouth or add it to food.

Herbal tinctures and decoctions, such as Mineral Essence and K&B, should be diluted prior to offering them to a pocket pet. The dilution may be similar to using essential oils in drinking water. It takes only about 2-10 drops in a quart of water. Use a glass eyedropper to syringe product into the corners of a pet's mouth. Be certain to reduce the amount of product and dilute it even further if the pet says "NO" to your original dilution.

Drinking water may be improved by adding 1 drop essential oil per quart of spring water. Just select any oil based on what body system or health challenge you are trying to support.

Administer Raindrop Technique®

Raindrop Technique is wonderful for health challenges. The traditional Raindrop Technique is the preferred method of applying the Raindrop oils to pocket pets. That is, apply 1 Raindrop oil at a time in the typical order of Oregano, Thyme, V-6, Basil, Cypress, Wintergreen, Marjoram, and Peppermint. Each oil is applied separately and feathered up the spine separately (from base of tail to base of neck). You can also put 1 drop of each Raindrop Kit essential oil in the palm of your petting hand. Just stroke the hand up and down the spine. Be certain to wipe the bottom of each paw as well. Start with the rear paws.

If there is concern a pet may wipe its eyes with a paw, just skip the front ones. For small animals like pocket pets, one drop of each oil is enough.

If you are hesitant to apply this amount of oil to your pocket pet or if this is your pet's first time experiencing the Raindrop Technique, another method of application is to dilute Raindrop oils with a carrier oil. Try performing the Raindrop Technique using each diluted Raindrop Kit oil individually. Try using 5 ml of V-6 Vegetable Oil Complex or other carrier oil to which you have added just 1-5 drops of an oil. Mix well. It is this well-mixed dilution that you use just 1 drop of for each essential oil for a Raindrop Technique session.

Keep in mind that for longer-haired pocket pets like chinchillas, hair acts to pull oils into the body, so more oil is not necessarily needed for those types of animals.

Pocket Pet Conditions

This section consists of conditions that are specific to most pocket pets regardless of species. Many pocket pets share the same conditions, and treatment is often the same. For example, ferrets are prone to many of the same conditions as chinchillas.

Some conditions may have a specific animal listed next to the condition, as those conditions more predominantly affect the specified animal. This does not mean that the condition is not relevant to other pocket pets. The same protocols can work for other pocket pets.

Keep in mind the relative size and body weight of the pet you are treating, as protocols should be adjusted accordingly. Larger pocket pets may require larger quantities of oils; smaller pocket pets may require less than stated in the protocols.

Adrenal Disease (Adrenal Gland Tumor) (Ferret)

Studies indicate that almost 70 percent of ferrets develop this health challenge. Artificial lighting and captivity may contribute to unhappy or stressed ferrets. Also, chemicals in food and treats directly contribute to adrenal and digestive issues.

Recommendations
Singles: Clove, Frankincense, Ginger, Idaho Balsam Fir, Ledum, Myrrh, Nutmeg, Rosemary, Copaiba
Blends: EndoFlex, En-R-Gee, Forgiveness, Inner Child, Joy, Longevity, Peace & Calming, Thieves
Nutritionals: EndoGize, Essentialzyme, Allerzyme, Longevity Softgels, NingXia Red, Slique Essence, CortiStop
Additional: V-6 Vegetable Oil Complex, Progessence Plus

Application and Usage
Topical: Place 1 drop of a single or blend in 1 teaspoon oil of your choice in the palm of your hand. Gently apply to all paws and lower back area. Apply 1-2 drops in the palm of your hand, rub hands together, and then gently apply to lower back area and down inside and outside of both rear legs to paws and pads. In a 4-oz. glass misting spray bottle, add 2-5 drops of an essential oil or blend of your choice. Mist body as needed.

Ingestion & Oral: On foodstuff your pet really likes, apply 1-5 drops of a mixture of your chosen oil diluted in 5 ml V-6 or other carrier oil. This may be done several times daily based on the severity of symptoms. Mix 1-5 drops essential oil in ½ gallon drinking water. Mist foodstuffs. Feed pet meaty bones at least 2 times daily.

Inhalation: To hand diffuse, apply 1 drop suggested essential oil to your hand. While holding your pocket pet, gently cup your hand over its nose. You may also diffuse by placing your favorite diffuser near your pet's housing.

Other: Administer Raindrop Technique. You may repeat daily, if needed, until lethargy improves. After improvement, administer weekly Raindrops or as needed.

Anesthesia Support (after a procedure)

There may be a need to perform a veterinary procedure requiring anesthesia on your pet. Using essential oils may assist your pet to better tolerate anesthesia reversal when it is time to wake up. Some animals become depressed after anesthesia.

Recommendations
Singles: Grapefruit, Helichrysum, Lavender, Peppermint, Wintergreen
Blends: DiGize, JuvaCleanse, JuvaFlex, Stress Away Roll-On, T-Away, Joy
Nutritionals: JuvaSpice, JuvaTone

Application and Usage
Topical: Apply 1 drop of Joy to the palm of your hand. Gently apply to animal's front toes on both feet as close to all nail beds as possible. Gently pet the animal with 1-2 drops Stress Away Roll-On on your hands.

Ingestion & Oral: Add 1 drop DiGize or JuvaCleanse to a favorite treat daily to support liver.

Inhalation: Diffuse after opening a Wintergreen essential oil bottle; just hold it a few inches away from your pet's nose. There is no need to apply it to the animal. Once it begins to arouse, just hold it there for another minute or so.

Other: Apply 1 drop of Grapefruit or JuvaFlex to the palm of your hand. Gently apply to animal's abdominal area to support its liver.

Aplastic Anemia (Ferret)

High levels of estrogen due to a failure to reproduce may cause bone marrow suppression of formation of both red and white blood cells. Symptoms include appetite loss, lethargy, hair loss, pale gums, weakness in rear legs, and swollen vulva.

Recommendations

Singles: Carrot Seed, Lavender, Lemon, Clary Sage, Ylang Ylang

Blends: ImmuPower, DiGize, JuvaCleanse, JuvaFlex, SclarEssence

Nutritionals: ImmuPro, JuvaSpice, JuvaTone, NingXia Red, PowerGize, CortiStop, Rehemogen, Digest & Cleanse

Additional: V-6 Vegetable Oil Complex, Progessence Plus

Application and Usage

Topical: Place 1 drop of a single or blend in 1 teaspoon V-6 or other carrier oil of your choice in the palm of your hand. Gently apply to all paws, abdominal area, and down spine. Apply 1-2 drops in the palm of your hand, rub hands together, and then gently apply to spinal area. In a 4-oz. glass misting spray bottle, add 2-5 drops of an essential oil or blend of your choice. Mist area as needed.

Ingestion & Oral: On foodstuff your pet really likes, apply 1 drop of DiGize or JuvaCleanse diluted in 5 ml V-6 or other carrier oil. This may be done several times daily based on severity of symptoms. Mix 1-5 drops essential oil in ½ gallon drinking water. Mist foodstuffs.

Inhalation: To hand diffuse, apply 1 drop ImmuPower to your hand. While holding your pocket pet, gently cup your hand over its nose. You may also diffuse by placing your favorite diffuser near your pet's housing.

Other: Try Raindrop Technique. You may repeat daily if needed until energy levels improve. After improvement, go to weekly Raindrops or as needed.

Appetite Loss (Ketosis Included) (Guinea Pig)

Though appetite loss may be due to illness, dehydration, drafty environment, changes in foodstuffs, or teeth alignment issues, it may also be due to ketosis. Ketosis can be a normal digestive process. Problems may occur when ketones accumulate in tissues or blood. Signs include appetite loss, difficult or labored breathing, hypoglycemia, lethargy, convulsions, and death.

Recommendations

Singles: Celery Seed, Frankincense, Ledum, Ocotea, Orange, Palo Santo, Dill, Coriander

Blends: Abundance, Citrus Fresh, EndoFlex, JuvaCleanse, JuvaFlex

Nutritionals: Allerzyme, Detoxzyme, Essentialzyme, JuvaTone, MightyVites, Mineral Essence, NingXia Red, Organic Dried Wolfberries, Super C Chewable, Life 9

Additional: V-6 Vegetable Oil Complex

Application and Usage

Topical: Apply 1 drop of a suggested single or blend in 1 teaspoon V-6 or other carrier oil in the palm of your hand. Gently apply to all paws, spine, belly, and rear legs (inside and outside). Apply 1-2 drops in the palm of your hand, rub hands together, and then gently apply to area. In a 4-oz. glass misting spray bottle, add 2-5 drops of an essential oil or blend of your choice. Mist area as needed.

Ingestion & Oral: On foodstuff your pet really likes, apply 1 drop of a mixture of your chosen oils diluted in 5 ml V-6 or other carrier oil. This may be done several times daily based on severity of symptoms. Mix 1-5 drops essential oil in ½ gallon drinking water. Mist foodstuffs. Gently apply to the gum areas.

Inhalation: To hand diffuse, apply 1 drop suggested essential oil blend to your hand. While holding your pocket pet, gently cup your hand over its nose. You

---

Veterinarian Tips and Suggestions

Appetite Loss

Swirl a wooden toothpick that has been dipped into an oil bottle around in drinking water. Be sure to monitor the water to determine whether a "picky" pet is drinking the flavored offering. Always be sure to give your pet a non-oil-infused water option as well.

may also diffuse by placing your favorite diffuser near your pet's housing.

Other: Raindrop Technique may support a body while waiting for a body to absorb more vitamin C.

Barbering (Alopecia) (Guinea Pig)

Barbering behavior may be found in pets housed together. It is often the result of stress or dominant behavior. Hair loss has also been seen in later pregnancy stages.

Recommendations

Singles: Idaho Balsam Fir, Lavender, Valerian, Vetiver, German Chamomile, Roman Chamomile

Blends: RutaVaLa, SARA, Stress Away Roll-On, Surrender, T-Away, Trauma Life, Harmony, Release

Nutritionals: Allerzyme, Essentialzyme, NingXia Red, Organic Dried Wolfberries, Super B, Super C Chewable, Super Cal, Mineral Essence, Digest & Cleanse

Additional: V-6 Vegetable Oil Complex

Application and Usage

Topical: Apply 1 drop of a suggested single or blend in 1 teaspoon V-6 or other carrier oil in the palm of your hand. Gently apply to all paws, spine, and abdomen. In a 4-oz. glass misting spray bottle, add 2-5 drops of an essential oil or blend of your choice. Mist area as needed to decrease activity.

Ingestion & Oral: On foodstuff your pet really likes, apply 1 drop of a mixture of your chosen oils diluted in 5 ml V-6 or other carrier oil. This may be done several times daily based on severity of symptoms. Mix 1-5 drops essential oil in ½ gallon drinking water. Mist foodstuffs. Gently apply to the gum areas.

Inhalation: To hand diffuse, apply 1 drop suggested essential oil blend to your hand. While holding your pocket pet, gently cup your hand over its nose. You may also diffuse by placing your favorite diffuser near your pet's housing.

Barbering (Rodents)

Barbering behavior may be found in pets housed together. It is often the result of stress or dominant behavior.

Recommendations

Singles: Idaho Balsam Fir, Lavender, Valerian, Vetiver, German Chamomile, Roman Chamomile

Blends: RutaVaLa, SARA, Stress Away Roll-On, Surrender, T-Away, Trauma Life, Harmony, Release, Peace & Calming

Nutritionals: Allerzyme, Essentialzyme, NingXia Red, Organic Dried Wolfberries, Super B, Super C Chewable, Super Cal, Life 9, Mineral Essence

Additional: V-6 Vegetable Oil Complex

Application and Usage

Topical: Apply 1 drop of a suggested single or blend in 1 teaspoon V-6 or other carrier oil in the palm of your hand. Gently apply to all paws, spine, and abdomen. Apply 1-2 drops in the palm of your hand, rub hands together, and then gently apply to area. In a 4-oz. glass misting spray bottle, add 2-5 drops of an essential oil or blend of your choice. Mist area as needed to decrease activity.

Ingestion & Oral: On foodstuff your pet really likes, apply 1 drop of a mixture of your chosen oils diluted in 5 ml V-6 or other carrier oil. This may be done several times daily based on severity of symptoms. Mix 1-5 drops essential oil in ½ gallon drinking water. Mist foodstuffs. Gently apply to the gum areas.

Inhalation: To hand diffuse, apply 1 drop suggested essential oil blend to your hand. While holding your pocket pet, gently cup your hand over its nose. You may also diffuse by placing your favorite diffuser near your pet's housing.

Bloat (Chinchilla)

Bloat refers to any abnormal distention of the abdominal area. It may be due to improper digestion of foodstuff, dietary imbalances, poor gastrointestinal function, or buildup of fluids or gas.

Recommendations

Singles: Angelica, Cardamom, Copaiba, Coriander, Fennel, Frankincense, Ginger, Lavender, Nutmeg, Ocotea, Orange, Peppermint, Spearmint, Tarragon

Blends: Abundance, AromaEase, Citrus Fresh, DiGize, Gentle Baby, ParaGize, Thieves

Nutritionals: AlkaLime, Digest & Cleanse, Essentialzyme, Essentialzymes-4, MegaCal, ParaFree, Life 9, Mineral Essence

Application and Usage

Topical: Apply 1 drop of essential oil of your choice to palm of your hand. Gently apply to animal's rear leg foot pads or toes. Or, put 1-2 drops essential oil in your hands and rub them together. Then stroke your pet's abdominal area, as well as the pads of its feet. Apply 1-2 drops in the palm of your hand, rub hands together, and then gently apply from base of ears, down sides of neck, down inside and outside of both front legs to front paws and pads. In a 4-oz. glass misting spray bottle, add 2-5 drops of an essential oil or blend of your choice. Mist as needed.

Ingestion & Oral: Add 1 drop diluted essential oil to a favorite treat daily to support liver and digestion. Or, mix 1-5 drops essential oil in ½ gallon drinking water. Mist foodstuffs.

Inhalation: To hand diffuse, apply 1-2 drops to your hand. While holding your pocket pet, gently cup your hand over its nose. You may also diffuse by placing your favorite diffuser near your pet's housing.

Other: Administer Raindrop Technique. You may want to add additional diluted oils before Peppermint.

Bone Fracture (Chinchilla)

Bone fracture is an injury to a bone. There are several different types of fractures. A veterinarian may require an X-ray to determine which type your pet has suffered.

Recommendations

Singles: Cedarwood, Cypress, Helichrysum, Idaho Balsam Fir, Juniper, Northern Lights Black Spruce, Sacred Sandalwood, Royal Hawaiian Sandalwood, Vetiver, Wintergreen, Idaho Blue Spruce, Copaiba, Frankincense, Peppermint

Blends: Infect Away, Mendwell, PanAway, Stress Away Roll-On, Valor, Valor II, Sacred Mountain, Deep Relief Roll-On, Cool Azul

Nutritionals: AgilEase, Balance Complete, Master Formula, MightyVites, Organic Dried Wolfberries,

---

Veterinarian Tips and Suggestions

Bone Fracture

If you are able to access the fracture site, apply several times daily 1-2 drops of diluted mix of 5 ml Ortho Ease or Ortho Sport combined with 1 drop each of Idaho Balsam Fir, Northern Lights Black Spruce, Idaho Blue Spruce, Copaiba, Cypress, Helichrysum, Lemongrass, any of the tree essential oils, and Wintergreen.

NingXia Red, Sulfurzyme, Super B, Super Cal, BLM

Additional: V-6 Vegetable Oil Complex, Ortho Ease Massage Oil, Ortho Sport Massage Oil

Application and Usage

Topical: Apply 1 drop of essential oil of your choice to the palm of your hand. Gently apply to animal's foot pads or toes. Or, put 1-2 drops essential oil in your hands and rub them together. Then stroke your pet and apply to pads of its feet.

Ingestion & Oral: On foodstuff your pet really likes, apply 1 drop of a mixture of your chosen oil diluted in 5 ml V-6 or other carrier oil. Combine 1 teaspoon NingXia Red diluted 50:50 with water with 1 drop each of diluted Copaiba, Frankincense, and Idaho Balsam Fir to be applied to multiple treats throughout a day. Mix 1-5 drops essential oil in ½ gallon drinking water. Mist foodstuffs.

Inhalation: To hand diffuse, apply 1-2 drops to your hand. While holding your pocket pet, gently cup your hand over its nose to support its stress-coping mechanisms. You may also diffuse by placing your favorite diffuser near your pet's housing.

Other: Administer Raindrop Technique. You may want to add additional diluted oils before Peppermint. You may repeat daily if needed until fracture improves. After improvement, but before being healed, administer weekly Raindrops. Try layering oils with Ortho Ease Massage Oil and Ortho Sport Massage Oil.

Breathing Issues (Chinchilla)

Breathing problems may arise due to a variety of issues, from a cold, to asthma, to pneumonia. Many breathing issues are due to overcrowding and poor ventilation. High humidity is also an issue. You may need a veterinarian to confirm whether it is a routine cold or something much more.

Signs of breathing issues may include panting in small breaths, gasping for air, difficult open-mouthed breathing, nasal discharge, etc. If the lymph nodes appear swollen and your pet is lethargic, you probably need to get to a veterinary office. Chinchillas may be prone to going downhill in a hurry.

Recommendations

Singles: Basil, Clary Sage, Cedarwood, Dorado Azul, Eucalyptus Blue, Eucalyptus Globulus, Eucalyptus Radiata, Fennel, Frankincense, Hong Kuai, Hyssop,

Idaho Balsam Fir, Mountain Savory, Myrtle, Northern Lights Black Spruce, Peppermint, Tsuga, Ylang Ylang, Ravintsara, Copaiba, Lemon, Lavender

Blends: Aroma Life, Breathe Again Roll-On, Inspiration, ParaGize, Raven, R.C., Thieves

Nutritionals: Inner Defense, MightyVites, Allerzyme, Organic Dried Wolfberries, NingXia Red, ParaFree, Life 9, Digest & Cleanse

Additional: V-6 Vegetable Oil Complex

Application and Usage

Topical: Apply 1 drop of essential oil of your choice to palm of your hand. Gently apply to animal's throat, chest, rear-leg foot pads, or toes. Put 1-2 drops essential oil in your hands and rub them together. Then stroke your pet's abdominal area and apply to pads of feet.

Ingestion & Oral: On foodstuff your pet really likes, apply 1 drop of a mixture of your chosen oil diluted in 5 ml V-6 or other carrier oil. Or, mix 1-5 drops essential oil in ½ gallon drinking water. Mist foodstuffs.

Inhalation: To hand diffuse, apply 1-2 drops to your hand. While holding your pocket pet, gently cup your hand over its nose to support its stress-coping mechanisms. You may also diffuse by placing your favorite diffuser near your pet's housing.

Other: Administer Raindrop Technique. You may want to add additional diluted oils before Peppermint. You may repeat daily if needed until breathing distress improves. After improvement, go to weekly Raindrops.

Calcium Metabolism (Hypocalcemia) (Chinchilla)

Calcium metabolism deficiency is often due to a parathyroid gland imbalance.

Recommendations

Singles: Dorado Azul, Lemongrass

Blends: EndoFlex, Slique Essence

Nutritionals: Allerzyme, EndoGize, Essentialzyme, Essentialzymes-4, MightyVites, Mineral Essence, MultiGreens, Organic Dried Wolfberries, NingXia Red, Power Meal, Rehemogen, Slique Tea, Thyromin, Life 9

Additional: V-6 Vegetable Oil Complex

Application and Usage

Topical: Apply 1 drop of EndoFlex to the palm of your hand. Gently apply to animal's stomach, all foot pads, or toes. Or, put 1-2 drops essential oil in your hands and rub them together. Then stroke down your pet's throat where it attaches to its body in the chest area and apply to pads of its feet.

Ingestion & Oral: On foodstuff your pet really likes, apply 1 drop of a mixture of your chosen oil diluted in 5 ml V-6 or other carrier oil. Or, combine 1 ounce NingXia Red diluted 50:50 with water to be applied to multiple treats throughout a day. Or Mix 1-5 drops essential oil in ½ gallon drinking water. Mist foodstuffs.

Inhalation: To hand diffuse, apply 1-2 drops to your hand. While holding your pocket pet, gently cup your hand over its nose to support its stress-coping mechanisms. You may also diffuse by placing your favorite diffuser near your pet's housing.

Other: Administer Raindrop Technique weekly.

Calcium: Phosphorus Imbalance
(see Calcium Metabolism)

Colds (Chinchilla)

Colds in pocket pets manifest with symptoms such as runny nose, sneezing, and wheezing. This can lead to upper respiratory tract infections if left unchecked.

Recommendations

Singles: Basil, Lavender, Lemon, Peppermint, Pine, Ravintsara, Rosemary, Thyme, Copaiba, Lemongrass

Blends: Australian Blue, ImmuPower, JuvaCleanse, JuvaFlex, Purification, Raven, R.C., Sacred Mountain, Thieves, GLF, DiGize

Nutritionals: Essentialzyme, Essentialzymes-4, Detoxzyme, ImmuPro, Inner Defense, Digest & Cleanse, Life 9, Allerzyme, MightyVites, MultiGreens, Organic Dried Wolfberries, NingXia Red, Sulfurzyme, Super C, Super C Chewable.

Additional: V-6 Vegetable Oil Complex, Thieves Household Cleaner

Application and Usage

Topical: Mix 1 drop of a single or blend in 1 teaspoon V-6 or other carrier oil in the palm of your hand. Gently apply to animal's front paws and pads, chest, neck, and back. Also try 1-2 drops in the palm of your hand, rub hands together, and then gently stroke from ear base down neck to back.

Ingestion & Oral: On foodstuff your pet really likes, apply 1 drop of a mixture of your chosen oil diluted in 5 ml V-6 or other carrier oil. Mix 1-5 drops essential oil in ½ gallon drinking water. Mist foodstuffs.

Inhalation: To hand diffuse, apply 1-2 drops to your hand. While holding your pocket pet, gently cup your hand over its nose. You may also diffuse by placing your favorite diffuser near your pet's housing.

Other: Administer Raindrop Technique. You may repeat daily if needed until symptoms resolve. Try using Thieves Household Cleaner for cleaning housing and toys.

Constipation (Chinchilla)

Constipation is described as a lack of/or insufficient gastrointestinal movement. Constipation in animals may have a variety of causes: dehydration, depression, improper nutritional balance of too much fiber, carbohydrates, fats or proteins, overeating, eating things not recommended such as toys or bedding, and parasite load.

Recommendations

Singles: Basil, Copaiba, Fennel, Geranium, Ginger, Lemon, Marjoram, Nutmeg, Orange, Patchouli, Peppermint, Roman Chamomile, Rosemary, Sage, Sacred Sandalwood, Royal Hawaiian Sandalwood, Tangerine, Tarragon

Blends: AromaEase, DiGize, JuvaCleanse, JuvaFlex, GLF, ParaGize

Nutritionals: Allerzyme, ComforTone, Essentialzyme, Essentialzymes-4, ICP, JuvaSpice, Life 9, MultiGreens, Organic Dried Wolfberries, NingXia Red, Sulfurzyme, Mineral Essence, ParaFree

Additional: V-6 Vegetable Oil Complex

Application and Usage

Topical: Place 1 drop of a single or blend in 1 teaspoon V-6 or other carrier oil in the palm of your hand. Gently apply to animal's stomach area. Store unused portion in a 2-5 ml bottle for later use. Also try 1-2 drops in the palm of your hand, rub hands together, and then gently stroke stomach.

Ingestion & Oral: On foodstuff your pet really likes, apply 1 drop of a mixture of your chosen oil diluted in 5 ml V-6 or other carrier oil. Mix 1-5 drops essential oil in ½ gallon drinking water. Mist foodstuffs.

Inhalation: To hand diffuse, apply 1-2 drops to your hand. While holding your pocket pet, gently cup your hand over its nose. You may also diffuse by placing your favorite diffuser near your pet's housing.

Other: Administer Raindrop Technique. You may repeat daily if needed until the gastrointestinal tract functions daily.

Conjunctivitis (Chinchilla)

Conjunctivitis may occur due to a foreign object getting in an eye, allergy, or bacterial or viral infection. Signs include bloodshot sclera (white portion of eye), discharge, burning, itching, or swelling.

Recommendations

Singles: Eucalyptus Radiata, Jasmine, Lavender, Helichrysum

Blends: Infect Away, ParaGize, T-Away, Thieves

Nutritionals: ImmuPro, Inner Defense, Life 9, MultiGreens, Organic Dried Wolfberries, NingXia Red, Digest & Cleanse, Longevity Softgels

Additional: V-6 Vegetable Oil Complex

Application and Usage

Topical: Put 1 drop of Lavender in your hand. Rub hands together. Cup hand over eye area without touching the eye. Try to hold for 10 minutes in this position.

Ingestion & Oral: On foodstuff your pet really likes, apply 1 drop of a mixture of your chosen oil diluted in 5 ml V-6 or other carrier oil. Mix 1-5

Conjunctivitis
(Variation of Stanley Burrough's Master Eye Cleanse)

Combine the following in a dropper bottle: 10 parts water, 2 parts honey, and 1 part apple cider vinegar. Carefully holding your pet's front feet to prevent it from scratching at its eyes, allow 1 drop of blend to drop into an eye. It does sting at first but is soothing within a few minutes.

drops essential oil in ½ gallon drinking water. Mist foodstuffs.

Inhalation: To hand diffuse, apply 1 drop to your hand. While holding your pocket pet, gently cup your hand over its nose. You may also diffuse Purification by placing your favorite diffuser near your pet's housing.

Other: Apply a warm compress to the outside of the eye. Be sure it's not too hot as to burn your pet. You may want to dampen its environment's bedding to prevent too much dust getting into an eye. Chinchillas like dust baths! If due to infection, try applying the Raindrop Technique. You may repeat daily if needed until vision improves. After improvement, go to weekly Raindrops.

Coprophagy (Eating Feces) (Rodents)

Coprophagy, or eating of feces, is a common practice of both mice and rats. The behavior is based on dietary needs and increases during pregnancy.

Recommendations
Singles: Fennel, Ginger, Peppermint, Spearmint
Blends: AromaEase, DiGize
Nutritionals: Essentialzyme, ICP, Life 9, Master Formula, MightyVites, MultiGreens, NingXia Red, Organic Dried Wolfberries, Mineral Essence, Super B, Allerzyme
Additional: V-6 Vegetable Oil Complex

Application and Usage
Topical: Rats: Apply 1 drop of diluted suggested single or blend in 1 teaspoon (10 drops) V-6 or other carrier oil in the palm of your hand. Gently apply to rear paws, stomach area, and low back.

Note: Mice may require greater dilution for topical applications. Apply 1 drop in the palm of your hand, rub hands together, and then gently apply to areas. Mice have very thin skin. In a 4-oz. glass misting spray bottle, add 2-5 drops of an essential oil or blend of your choice. Fill with spring or distilled water. Mist as needed.

Ingestion & Oral: On foodstuff your pet really likes, apply 1 drop diluted in 5 ml V-6 or other carrier oil. This may be done several times daily based on severity of symptoms. Add 1 drop essential oil in ½ gallon drinking water. Mist foodstuffs. Gently apply to the gum areas.

Inhalation: To hand diffuse, apply 1 drop suggested essential oil blend to your hand. While holding your pocket pet, gently cup your hand over its nose. You may also diffuse by placing your favorite diffuser near your pet's housing.

Other: Apply Raindrop Technique daily during crisis and then weekly until condition improves.

Dental Disease

Improper diet and nutrition may allow dental disease to occur around the gum areas. Pocket pets tend to chew on almost anything during times of stress or excitement. Use essential oils to help with damages or disease that may accompany periods of chewing. Be sure, however, to address the root cause of chewing to prevent further damage.

Recommendations
Singles: Tea Tree, Myrrh, Orange, Wintergreen
Blends: Citrus Fresh, Melrose, The Gift, Thieves, DiGize
Nutritionals: Allerzyme, Detoxzyme, Inner Defense, NingXia Red, OmegaGize[3], Animal Scents Pet Chews, divided up into small portions suitable for your pet's size.

Dental Disease

Dilute 1 part Thieves Mouthwash with 10 parts distilled water. Gently use a plastic eyedropper to wash the gums around an infected tooth. Plastic eyedroppers may not be reused. Be cautious with glass eyedroppers, because animals may bite down and break them in their mouths.

Additional: V-6 Vegetable Oil Complex, Thieves Mouthwash

Application and Usage

Topical: Place 1 drop of a single or blend in 1 teaspoon V-6 or other carrier oil in the palm of your hand, rub hands together, and then gently apply to area. In a 4-oz. glass misting spray bottle, add 2-5 drops of an essential oil or blend of your choice. Mist area as needed.

Ingestion & Oral: On foodstuff your pet really likes, apply 1 drop of a mixture of your chosen oil diluted in 5 ml V-6 or other carrier oil. This may be done several times daily based on severity of symptoms. Mix 1-5 drops essential oil in ½ gallon drinking water. Mist foodstuffs. Gently apply to the gum areas. Spray Thieves Mouthwash into mouth 2 times daily.

Inhalation: To hand diffuse, apply 1 drop suggested essential oil to your hand. While holding your pocket pet, gently cup your hand over its nose. You may also diffuse by placing your favorite diffuser near your pet's housing.

Other: Administer Raindrop Technique. You may repeat daily if needed until appetite improves. After improvement, go to weekly Raindrops or as needed.

Diarrhea

Diarrhea is the opposite of constipation. With diarrhea, the stool is too loose and watery. Diarrhea has many causes: lack of dietary fiber, dietary intake of high fat and protein, infection, milk replacement for youngsters, nervousness or stress, parasites, and respiratory or stomach ailments. Be certain not to wait too long to seek veterinary assistance. Severe dehydration may be a dangerous complication of diarrhea.

Recommendations

Singles: Copaiba, Cardamom, Cistus, Geranium, Ginger, Lavender, Myrrh, Nutmeg, Ocotea, Peppermint, Roman Chamomile, Sacred Sandalwood, Royal Hawaiian Sandalwood, Spearmint, Tea Tree

Blends: AromaEase, DiGize, Gentle Baby, ParaGize, Peace & Calming, Stress Away Roll-On, Thieves

Nutritionals: AlkaLime, Allerzyme, ICP, JuvaSpice, Life 9, MultiGreens, ParaFree, Detoxzyme, Digest & Cleanse, K&B

Additional: V-6 Vegetable Oil Complex

Application and Usage

Topical: Put 1 drop essential oil of your choice in your hand. Rub hands together until no oil is visible. Stroke your pet from its head to its tail area. Place 1 drop of a single or blend in 1 teaspoon V-6 or other carrier oil in the palm of your hand. Gently apply to animal's stomach area and pads of its feet.

Ingestion & Oral: On foodstuff your pet really likes, apply 1 drop of a mixture of your chosen oil diluted in 5 ml V-6 or other carrier oil. Mix 1-5 drops essential oil in ½ gallon drinking water. Mist foodstuffs.

Inhalation: To hand diffuse, apply 1 drop to your hand. While holding your pocket pet, gently cup your hand over its nose. You may also diffuse by placing your favorite diffuser near your pet's housing.

Other: Administer Raindrop Technique. You may repeat daily if needed until diarrhea improves. After improvement, go to weekly Raindrops.

Diarrhea (Bacterial)

Loose stools may be caused by protozoan infestations, dietary imbalances, or other forms of infection. Dehydration may be a severe complication of diarrhea requiring a veterinarian to administer fluids.

Distemper (see also Environmental Terrain for Housing and Water suggestions)

Distemper is a contagious viral infection that attacks several systems: respiratory, gastrointestinal, and nervous.

Recommendations

Singles: Basil, Cinnamon Bark, Clove, Cypress, Dorado Azul, Eucalyptus Blue, Hong Kuai, Hyssop, Lemon, Lemongrass, Melissa, Mountain Savory, Oregano, Palo Santo, Ravintsara, Tea Tree, Thyme, Copaiba

Blends: Egyptian Gold, ImmuPower, Longevity, Oola Family, Raven, The Gift, Thieves

Nutritionals: ImmuPro, Inner Defense, Life 9, Longevity Softgels, MightyVites, Mineral Essence, NingXia Red, OmegaGize[3], Digest & Cleanse

Additional: V-6 Vegetable Oil Complex

Application and Usage

Topical: Place 1 drop of a single or blend in 1 teaspoon of V-6 or other carrier oil in the palm of your hand. Gently apply to gums, front paws, chest, and throat area. Apply 1-2 drops in the palm of your hand, rub hands together, and then gently apply to area. In a 4-oz. glass misting spray bottle, add 2-5 drops of an essential oil or blend of your choice. Mist area as needed.

Ingestion & Oral: On foodstuff your pet really likes, apply 1 drop of a mixture of your chosen oil diluted in 5 ml V-6 or other carrier oil. This may be done several times daily based on severity of symptoms. Mix 1-5 drops essential oil in ½ gallon drinking water. Mist foodstuffs.

Inhalation: To hand diffuse, apply 1 drop suggested essential oil to your hand. While holding your pocket pet, gently cup your hand over its nose. You may also diffuse by placing your favorite diffuser near your pet's housing.

Other: Administer Raindrop Technique. You may repeat daily if needed until condition improves. After improvement, go to weekly Raindrops or as needed.

Ear Infection (Otitis Media) (Chinchilla)

Recommendations

Singles: Clove, Laurus Nobilis, Ravintsara, Patchouli, Geranium, Juniper, Lavender, Myrrh, Tea Tree, Myrtle, Basil

Blends: Egyptian Gold, ImmuPower, Infect Away, Melrose, Mendwell, ParaGize, Purification, Thieves, Valor II, Longevity

Nutritionals: ImmuPro, JuvaSpice, Life 9, MightyVites, Organic Dried Wolfberries, NingXia Red, Sulfurzyme, MultiGreens, Longevity Softgels

Additional: V-6 Vegetable Oil Complex

Application and Usage

Topical: Place 1 drop of a single or blend in 1 teaspoon V-6 or other carrier oil in the palm of your hand. Gently apply to front paws and around base of both ears. Apply 1-2 drops in the palm of your hand, rub hands together, and then gently apply to base

> ### Veterinarian Tips and Suggestions
> ## Ear Infection
> In 1 teaspoon V-6 or other carrier oil, combine 1 drop each of Lavender, Copaiba, and Melrose or Purification.

inside ears, neck, paws, hocks, and back. Apply 1 drop of oil to a cotton swab. Roll swab inside ear flap or well, but not way down into canal.

Ingestion & Oral: On foodstuff your pet really likes, apply 1 drop of a mixture of your chosen oil diluted in 5 ml V-6 or other carrier oil. This may be done several times daily based on the severity of symptoms. Mix 1-5 drops essential oil in ½ gallon drinking water. Mist foodstuff.

Inhalation: To hand diffuse, apply 1 drop to the palm of your hand. While holding your pocket pet, gently cup your hand over its nose. You may also diffuse by placing your favorite diffuser near your pet's housing.

Other: Administer Raindrop Technique. You may repeat daily if needed until ear condition improves. After improvement, go to weekly Raindrops or as needed.

Ear Masses (Aural Cholesteatomas) (Gerbil)

Gerbils may begin to develop inner ear masses after two years of age. A veterinarian can confirm if your pet's head tilt is due to pressure against an eardrum. This condition may cause permanent damage.

Recommendations

Singles: Copaiba, Elemi, Eucalyptus Radiata, Frankincense, Geranium, Grapefruit, Helichrysum, Juniper, Lavender, Tea Tree, Myrrh, Orange, Palo Santo, Sacred Frankincense, Ravintsara, Rosemary, Idaho Blue Spruce

Blends: Infect Away, ImmuPower, Longevity, Melrose, Mendwell, Purification, Valor, Valor II

Nutritionals: Essentialzyme, Allerzyme, Detoxzyme, Life 9, Digest & Cleanse, ImmuPro, JuvaPower, JuvaSpice, Longevity Softgels, MightyZymes, NingXia Red

Additional: V-6 Vegetable Oil Complex

> ### Veterinarian Tips and Suggestions
> ## Ear Masses
> Combine 1 tablespoon of V-6 Vegetable Oil Complex with 3 drops each of Copaiba, Palo Santo, Longevity, Lavender, and Idaho Balsam Fir. Label bottle for further usage. Wipe a small amount around ear base daily.

Application and Usage

Topical: Put 1 drop suggested essential oil of your choice in your hand. Stroke your pet from its head to its tail area. Place 1 drop of a single or blend in 1 teaspoon V-6 or other carrier oil in the palm of your hand. Gently apply to animal's stomach area, pads of feet, and in and around ear base.

Ingestion & Oral: On foodstuff your pet really likes, apply 1 drop of a mixture of your chosen oil diluted in 5 ml V-6 or other carrier oil. Mix 1-5 drops essential oil in ½ gallon drinking water. Mist foodstuffs.

Inhalation: To hand diffuse, apply 1 drop suggested oil or blend to your hand. While holding your pocket pet, gently cup your hand over its nose. You may also diffuse by placing your favorite diffuser near your pet's housing.

Other: Administer Raindrop Technique as needed.

Enteritis (Bacterial) (Guinea Pig)

Inflammation of the small intestinal tract may be due to bacterial infections such as Salmonella, E. coli, or Clostridium.

Recommendations

Singles: Basil, Citronella, Clove, Copaiba, Eucalyptus, Geranium, Tea Tree, Mountain Savory, Nutmeg, Oregano, Tarragon

Blends: AromaEase, DiGize, ImmuPower, JuvaCleanse, ParaGize, Thieves, Melrose, Exodus II

Nutritionals: Life 9, NingXia Red, Organic Dried Wolfberries, ParaFree, Digest & Cleanse, Longevity Softgels, Detoxzyme, Allerzyme

Additional: V-6 Vegetable Oil Complex, Thieves Household Cleaner

Application and Usage

Topical: Apply 1 drop of a suggested single or blend in 1 teaspoon V-6 or other carrier oil in the palm of your hand. Gently apply to all paws, spine, and abdomen. Apply 1-2 drops in the palm of your hand, rub hands together, and then gently apply to area. In a 4-oz. glass misting spray bottle, add 2-5 drops of an essential oil or blend of your choice. Fill with spring or distilled water. Mist area as needed.

Inhalation: To hand diffuse, apply 1 drop suggested essential oil blend to your hand. While holding your pocket pet, gently cup your hand over its nose. You may also diffuse by placing your favorite diffuser near your pet's housing. Repeat with any digestive-aiding oil (e.g., DiGize) and combine with any suggested oil.

Other: Clean area, toys, and drinking containers with diluted Thieves Household Cleaner. Administer Raindrop Technique as needed.

Environmental Terrain (housing)

The area where your pocket pet resides may have an influence on its general well-being. Misting lightly with diluted Thieves Household Cleaner the area and its toy components weekly, if not daily, will assist in providing a nicer, cleaner, healthier place for your pet to live.

Recommendations

Singles: Cedarwood, Hinoki, Lemon, Lemongrass, Xiang Mao, Rosemary, Idaho Balsam Fir, Idaho Blue Spruce, Northern Lights Black Spruce, Neroli, Geranium, Lavender

Blends: Christmas Spirit, Melrose, Purification, Thieves, Citrus Fresh

Additional: Thieves Household Cleaner

Application and Usage

Environmental: Clean housing regularly with diluted Thieves Household Cleaner combined with any combination of suggested oil.

Environmental Terrain (water sources)

Water to drink or play in must be kept free of extra visitors. Your pocket pet may develop a health crisis by drinking contaminated water.

Recommendations

Singles: Jade Lemon, Lemon, Lemongrass, Xiang Mao

Blends: Purification, Thieves

Veterinarian Tips and Suggestions

Environmental Terrain

In a 32-oz. sprayer, mix 2 caps Thieves Household Cleaner, 10 drops Cedarwood, Hinoki, Melrose, and Purification. Fill with distilled water. Spray area weekly or diffuse as desired.

Application and Usage

Ingestion & Oral: In a gallon container of water, add 1-5 drops of your favorite oil blend. Use this water for drinking and play areas.

Other: Apply essential oils to small areas of water by inserting a wooden toothpick in the oil of your choice and then swirling the toothpick in the water for about a minute.

Epilepsy (seizures) (Gerbil)

Seizures in 20 percent of gerbils may be inherited or a response to sudden stress such as new housing or handling. Seizures may begin about 2-3 months of age and decline after 6 months of age. Many veterinarians suggest you handle babies often from birth through three weeks of age to attempt to get them used to people. Some seizure indications are twitching ears and whiskers and a mild trance. More severe signs are muscle spasms and stiffness.

Recommendations

Singles: Copaiba, Frankincense, Helichrysum, Idaho Balsam Fir, Idaho Blue Spruce, Jasmine, Laurus Nobilis, Lavender, Melissa, Roman Chamomile, Valerian, Vetiver

Blends: Peace & Calming, RutaVaLa, SARA, Surrender, T-Away, Tranquil Roll-On, Trauma Life, Valor, Valor II

Nutritionals: Essentialzyme, Essentialzymes-4, MightyVites, MultiGreens, NingXia Red, OmegaGize[3]

Additional: V-6 Vegetable Oil Complex

Application and Usage

Topical: Put 1 drop essential oil of your choice in your hand. Rub hands together lightly. Stroke your pet from its head to its tail area. Place 1 drop of a single or blend in 1 teaspoon V-6 or other carrier oil in the palm of your hand. Gently apply to animal's stomach area and on all feet.

Ingestion & Oral: On foodstuff your pet really likes, apply 1 drop of a mixture of your chosen oil diluted in 5 ml V-6 or other carrier oil. Mix 1-5 drops essential oil in ½ gallon drinking water. Mist foodstuffs.

Inhalation: To hand diffuse, apply 1 drop of a suggested essential oil to your hand. While holding your pocket pet, gently cup your hand over its nose. You may also diffuse by placing your favorite diffuser near your pet's housing.

Eye Tears (Chromodacryorrhea in Rats) (Rodents)

Don't panic! Your pet is not bleeding from its eyes. Harderian glands, located behind the eyes, secrete proteins that will color the tears red. This usually occurs due to stress from pain or restraint or an underlying chronic disease.

Recommendations

Singles: Cedarwood, Copaiba, Lavender, Lemon, Frankincense, Helichrysum

Blends: Peace & Calming, Purification, Tranquil Roll-On

Nutritionals: Master Formula, MightyVites, MultiGreens, NingXia Red, Organic Dried Wolfberries, Super B, Super C Chewable

Additional: V-6 Vegetable Oil Complex, Animal Scents Ointment, Animal Scents Shampoo, Thieves Household Cleaner

Application and Usage

Topical: Put 1 drop diluted Peace & Calming and suggested essential oil of your choice in your hand. Rub hands together lightly. Stroke your pet from its head to its tail area.

If there is an immune-mediated health challenge, repeat with an immune-stimulating oil or blend. Place 1 drop of a single or blend in 1 teaspoon V-6 or other carrier oil in the palm of your hand. Gently apply to animal's tummy area, spine, and pads of all feet. Make an indentation in center of Animal Scents Ointment. Add 1 drop of oil of your choice. Swirl around with finger. Gently apply on irritated areas being careful not to get into the eyes.

To keep pet clean of contaminants, topically apply Animal Scents Ointment, Animal Scents Shampoo, and Thieves Household Cleaner (diluted) liberally on pet.

Ingestion & Oral: On foodstuff your pet really likes, apply 1 drop of a mixture of your chosen suggested oil diluted in 5 ml V-6 or other carrier oil. Mix 1-5 drops essential oil in ½ gallon drinking water. Mist foodstuffs.

Inhalation: To hand diffuse, apply 1 drop calming oil or blend to your hand. While holding your pocket pet, gently cup your hand over its nose. You may also diffuse by placing your favorite diffuser near your pet's housing.

Other: If your pet has a health challenge, apply Raindrop Technique daily during the crisis and then weekly until condition improves.

Fever

In an 8-oz. misting spray bottle filled with distilled water, combine 2-4 drops Peppermint with equal amounts of Lavender and Copaiba. Gently mist your pet every 20 minutes until fever signs are reduced.

Fever

Recommendations

Singles: Basil, Bergamot, Clove, Cypress, Eucalyptus, Fennel, Ginger, Lavender, Ledum, Lemon, Laurus Nobilis, Tea Tree, Peppermint, Roman Chamomile, Rosemary

Blends: ImmuPower, Thieves

Nutritionals: ImmuPro, Life 9, MightyVites, Mineral Essence, Organic Dried Wolfberries, NingXia Red, Super C Chewable

Additional: Thieves Household Cleaner

Application and Usage

Topical: Cold, wet compresses may be applied to armpits, feet, groin, and neck. Before application, compress material may be dipped in a large bowl of water with 1 drop of Peppermint and 1 capful of Thieves Household Cleaner. Be sure to wring out your compress material before applying.

Ingestion & Oral: In a quart (32-oz.) container of water, add 1-2 drops Peppermint. If your pet doesn't feel like drinking, a small syringe of mix may be held to the mouth.

Inhalation: To hand diffuse, apply 1 drop to your hand. While holding your pocket pet, gently cup your hand over its nose. Diffuse oil(s) of your choice into the air or near housing.

Other: Apply Raindrop Technique as needed.

Fleas and Ear Mites (Rabbits)

Many different species can be infected with fleas or ear mites. Due to the delicate nature of rabbits' gastrointestinal tract and the way their liver detoxifies medication, the traditional treatment of fleas and ticks used in cats and dogs should not be used with rabbits. This can make it a little more challenging, and one must be persistent to win the battle of the pests. Diatomaceous earth should not be used, because it is dangerous if inhaled and can cause impactions if ingested.

Ear mites cannot be seen by the naked eye, but their evidence is seen by the crusty brown debris the tiny mites produce. The ears will be very sensitive and could be raw and even bleeding. Ear mites are highly contagious to other rabbits, so check and treat all animals sharing the same living space.

Evidence of fleas is not as easy to find. Fleas feed on blood and produce blood-tinged stool that looks like it contains tiny brown flecks. A small sample of the "Flea Dirt" can be dusted on a wet white paper towel. If the brown flecks turn red, there is most likely a flea issue. Fleas cannot fly but they can jump. If there are multiple animals in the home, check each one. All will need to be treated to stop the infestation. The life cycle of the flea includes millions of eggs per day.

CAUTION: Never apply essential oils down into the ear canal.

Recommendations

Singles: Lavender, Hong Kuai, Rosemary, Black Pepper, Juniper, Tea Tree, Eucalyptus Radiata, Cedarwood, Palo Santo, Hinoki, Geranium, Basil, Citronella, Orange, Clove

Blends: Purification, DiGize

Nutritionals: MultiGreens

Additional: Animal Scents Ointment, Rose Ointment

Application and Usage

Topical: Purification can be applied to the coat daily. Apply 1-2 drops per every 5 pounds of body weight. Massage well into the coat. Always start out with 1 drop and see how the rabbit does. Make sure it is eating and is active every day. Layer oils with Animal Scents Ointment or Rose Ointment.

Inhalation: Diffuse Orange, Clove, and Purification.

Other: Carefully clean out ear mite debris using moist cotton balls. Do not put any cotton swabs inside the ear canal. If the debris is too heavy, a veterinary appointment may be needed. If there are any raw areas, apply Purification onto fingertip and rub into ear. Then apply a thin layer of Animal Scents Ointment directly onto raw areas. All bedding MUST be changed daily to remove the eggs that are waiting to hatch. Spray all new bedding with 8 drops Purification mixed in 8-10 oz. of water. This should continue at least 1-2 weeks after there is no evidence of pests.

Fungal Infections (see also Ringworm) (Rodents)

Though uncommon, there are various fungal infestations that may affect mice or rats. When present, it is usually caused by *Trichophyton mentagrophytes*. There may be hair loss on your pet's head, neck, or tail. There may or may not be crusting of skin.

Recommendations

Singles: Cinnamon Bark, Clove, Copaiba, Dorado Azul, Eucalyptus Radiata, Geranium, German Chamomile, Lavender, Lemon, Lemon Myrtle, Tea Tree, Mountain Savory, Myrrh, Ocotea, Oregano, Palmarosa, Roman Chamomile, Rosemary, Sage, Thyme

Blends: Abundance, Australian Blue, Egyptian Gold, ImmuPower, Infect Away, Melrose, PuriClean, Raven, R.C., Thieves, Exodus II

Nutritionals: Digest & Cleanse, Essentialzyme, Essentialzymes-4, Life 9, MightyVites, MultiGreens, NingXia Red, Organic Dried Wolfberries, Super C Chewable

Additional: V-6 Vegetable Oil Complex, Animal Scents Ointment

Application and Usage

Topical: Rats: Apply 1 drop of suggested immune single or blend in 1 teaspoon V-6 or other carrier oil in the palm of your hand. Gently apply to rear paws, stomach area, and lower back.

Note: Mice may require greater dilution for topical applications. Apply 1 drop in the palm of your hand, rub hands together, and then gently apply to areas.

Note: If you have mice, you may just want to rub your hands together and hold your hands above your pet without touching it. Mice have very thin skin. In a 4-oz. glass misting spray bottle, add 2-5 drops of an essential oil or blend of your choice. Fill with spring or distilled water. Mist as needed. Also, try layering topically applied oils with Animal Scents Ointment.

> #### Veterinarian Tips and Suggestions
> ## Fungal Infections
> In 2-oz. container, combine Animal Scents Ointment with 2 drops each Australian Blue and Melrose, plus 5 drops Copaiba. Mix well. Apply daily using a cotton swab to the area. Be careful not to transfer the fungi to yourself.

Ingestion & Oral: On foodstuff your pet really likes, apply 1 drop suggested oil or blend diluted in 5 ml V-6 or other carrier oil. This may be done several times daily based on severity of symptoms. Add 1 drop essential oil to ½ gallon drinking water. Mist foodstuffs. Gently apply to the gum areas.

Inhalation: To hand diffuse, apply 1 drop suggested essential oil blend to your hand. While holding your pocket pet, gently cup your hand over its nose. You may also diffuse by placing your favorite diffuser near your pet's housing.

Other: Apply Raindrop Technique daily during crisis and then weekly until condition improves.

Fur Chewing

Fur chewing may be hereditary or due to environmental causes, including stress. Your pet may learn the behavior from watching another pet, and it's possible another pet is doing the fur chewing on its friends.

Recommendations

Singles: Angelica, Bergamot, Cardamom, Cedarwood, Dill, Grapefruit, Lavender, Lemon, Lemongrass, Marjoram, Orange, Nutmeg, Patchouli, Roman Chamomile, Sacred Sandalwood, Royal Hawaiian Sandalwood, Neroli, Geranium, Valerian, Vetiver (stress coping)

Blends: Abundance, Harmony, Peace & Calming, T-Away, Tranquil Roll-On, Valor, Valor II, Stress Away Roll-On, Inner Child

Nutritionals: AgilEase, Balance Complete, Essentialzyme, Essentialzymes-4, ICP, Life 9, MightyVites, Mineral Essence, MultiGreens, Organic Dried Wolfberries, NingXia Red, Super B

Additional: V-6 Vegetable Oil Complex

Application and Usage

Topical: Place 1 drop of a single or blend in 1 teaspoon V-6 or other carrier oil in the palm of your hand. Gently apply to all paws, around base of both ears, and stroke down the entire spine. Apply 1-2 drops

> #### Veterinarian Tips and Suggestions
> ## Fur Chewing
> To help calm your pet, try diffusing 1 drop each of Bergamot, Cardamom, Patchouli, and Valerian or Roman Chamomile in your pet's area.

of your choice of essential oil or blend in the palm of your hand, rub hands together, and then gently apply to base of ears, neck, paws, hocks, and back.

Ingestion & Oral: On foodstuff your pet really likes, apply 1 drop of a mixture of your chosen oil diluted in 5 ml V-6 or other carrier oil. Mix 1-5 drops essential oil in ½ gallon drinking water. Mist foodstuffs.

Inhalation: To hand diffuse, apply 1 drop to your hand. While holding your pocket pet, gently cup your hand over its nose. You may also diffuse by placing your favorite diffuser near your pet's housing.

Gastroenteritis (see Constipation, Diarrhea, and Environmental Terrain)

Gastroenteritis may be due to too much fiber, a diet high in carbohydrates, protein or fat, or drinking water that has chemicals, mold, or bacteria residing in it.

Gastrointestinal Foreign Body (Ferret)

Ferrets often require surgery for eating things they should not. Plastic and rubber items have no nutritional value but are fascinating to ferrets. See Anesthesia Support for more post-surgical support information. Signs include lethargy, appetite loss, constipation, diarrhea, tender abdominal area, or vomiting.

If you have found that your pet has ingested a foreign object, administer 3 drops DiGize orally and apply 1 drop Peppermint on stomach. Continue applying as needed until the object is passed or until surgery can be performed to remove the object. If you suspect your pet has ingested a foreign object, consult your veterinarian immediately.

Gastrointestinal Stasis (GI Stasis) (Rabbits)

Gastrointestinal digestion halting is generally due to stress and can cause bloating and unfavorable bacteria to multiply. This condition commonly turns into a life-threatening situation due to shock. It begins with a form of stress, stopping the digestion of food in the rabbit's body. The key is quick interaction before this becomes advanced. If not treated, the stomach can become distended and full of gas.

Signs include increased respiration, depression, not eating, and the animal's chin may be wet from drinking excessive amounts of water. Any of these signs should be taken very seriously. Quick and early action is the key to a successful recovery. Diet is an enormous component to preventing this condition. See the section on Healthy Rabbit Diet to learn more.

Recommendations

Singles: Frankincense, Patchouli, Copaiba, Ginger, Peppermint, Spearmint, Orange
Blends: DiGize, AromaEase, ParaGize
Nutritionals: MultiGreens, Life 9

Application and Usage

Topical: At first sign of suspected GI stasis, apply 1-3 drops of DiGize or other oil of choice to stomach, spine, and ear tips. If the rabbit does not start eating within 30 minutes, veterinary action will be needed. Many times, subcutaneous fluids are needed from a veterinarian to reverse dehydration, which could hinder the effectiveness of the essential oils.

Ingestion & Oral: Administer Life 9 and 1-2 drops DiGize orally, if possible.

Inhalation: Diffuse Frankincense, Spearmint, and Orange.

Hair Coat

Environmental conditions may contribute to hair loss. If an environment has more than 50 percent humidity, coats tend to become matted and rough. Fighting with companions may result in hair loss from rear ends and tails. Another cause may include animals chewing on their own coat. Patches may disappear due to rubbing on cages or burrowing.

Recommendations

Singles: Cedarwood, Geranium, Lavender, Rosemary, Royal Hawaiian Sandalwood, Sacred Sandalwood, Sage
Nutritionals: Master Formula, MultiGreens, NingXia Red, Sulfurzyme
Additional: V-6 Vegetable Oil Complex, ClaraDerm, LavaDerm Cooling Mist

Application and Usage

Topical: Put 1 drop essential oil of your choice in your hand. Rub hands together lightly. Stroke your pet from its head to its tail area. Place 1 drop of a single or blend in 1 teaspoon V-6 or other carrier oil in the palm of your hand. Gently apply to areas. Mist pet's area with spray of your favorite singles or blends.

Ingestion & Oral: On foodstuff your pet really likes,

apply 1 drop of a mixture of your chosen oil diluted in 5 ml V-6 or other carrier oil. Mix 1-5 drops essential oil in ½ gallon drinking water. Mist foodstuffs.

Inhalation: To hand diffuse, apply 1 drop essential oil to your hand. While holding your pocket pet, gently cup your hand over its nose. You may also diffuse by placing your favorite diffuser near your pet's housing.

Other: Spray ClaraDerm or LavaDerm Cooling Mist on your pet.

Hair Loss (see Barbering and Mites)

Heart Murmur (Chinchilla)

According to a study published in the American Veterinary Medical Association Journal, approximately 23 percent of all chinchillas have heart murmurs. These pets may tire easily and have respiratory distress (coughing, sneezing, and squeaking) symptoms. See other categories for more information.

Recommendations

Singles: Helichrysum, Coriander, Frankincense, Lavender, Marjoram, Ocotea, Orange, Palo Santo, Ylang Ylang

Blends: Aroma Life, Aroma Siez, Build Your Dreams, Clarity, EndoFlex, Harmony, Hope, Into the Future, Motivation, Sacred Mountain, Thieves, White Angelica

Nutritionals: Allerzyme, Essentialzyme, Longevity Softgels, Master Formula, MightyVites, MindWise, Mineral Essence, NingXia Red, Organic Dried Wolfberries, OmegaGize[3], PowerGize, Sulfurzyme, Super B, MultiGreens

Additional: V-6 Vegetable Oil Complex

Application and Usage

Topical: Place 1 drop of a single or blend in 1 teaspoon V-6 or other carrier oil in the palm of your hand. Gently apply to all paws with special concentration on the front ones. Apply 1-2 drops in the palm of your

---

Veterinarian Tips and Suggestions

Heart Murmur

In a 15-ml bottle of V-6 or other edible carrier oil, add 4 drops Helichrysum, plus 2 drops Copaiba. Give 1 drop of mixture orally 2 times daily.

---

hand, rub hands together, and then gently apply from base of ears, down sides of neck, down inside and outside of both front legs to front paws and pads. In a 4-oz. glass misting spray bottle, add 2-5 drops of an essential oil or blend of your choice. Fill bottle with spring or distilled water. Mist as needed.

Ingestion & Oral: On foodstuff your pet really likes, apply 1 drop of a mixture of your chosen oil diluted in 5 ml V-6 or other carrier oil. This may be done several times daily based on the severity of symptoms. Mix 1-5 drops essential oil in ½ gallon drinking water. Mist foodstuffs.

Inhalation: To hand diffuse, apply 1 drop suggested essential oil to your hand. While holding your pocket pet, gently cup your hand over its nose. You may also diffuse by placing your favorite diffuser near your pet's housing.

Other: Administer Raindrop Technique. You may repeat daily if needed until energy levels improve. After improvement, go to weekly Raindrops or as needed.

Heat Stroke (see Fever)

Heat stroke may occur when an animal is housed in an area of more than 80°F or 27°C. Heat and cold tolerance will vary with specific animals. During especially hot or cold seasons, be especially attentive for signs of distress. Signs may be panting, high body temperature, open mouth breathing, and a reluctance to move. Also see Fever.

Hutch Burn (Rabbits)

Hutch burn is characterized by redness and inflammation on the genital area caused by unsanitary conditions. This can also happen in older or overweight rabbits that urinate on themselves. Immediate action must be taken to prevent infection or maggot infestation. This can become serious very quickly.

Recommendations

Singles: Lavender, Blue Cypress, Laurus Nobilis
Blends: Mendwell, PuriClean, Infect Away, Australian Blue, Gentle Baby, Purification, DiGize
Nutritionals: MultiGreens
Additional: Animal Scents Shampoo, Animal Scents Ointment, Rose Ointment

Application and Usage

Topical: Carefully and gently wash area with Animal Scents Shampoo. Rabbits do not like baths, so it is recommended to just wash the soiled area with lukewarm water. Be very careful to support the hind quarters to prevent back injury. Pat dry with towel. Apply selected oils directly on sores. Then apply Animal Scents Ointment or Rose Ointment. Do this daily until area is completely healed.

Inhalation: To hand diffuse, apply Lavender and Purification in nebulizing diffuser.

Other: DiGize can be used 1 drop topically to support the gastrointestinal tract. Try also Animal Scents Shampoo, Animal Scents Ointment, and Rose Ointment.

Insulinomas (Pancreatic Tumors) (Ferret)

Pancreatic tumors may be due to poor diet, treats with chemical preservatives, and nutrition low in protein and fat. Signs include lethargy, rear-leg weakness, and hypoglycemia due to excess insulin production.

Recommendations

Singles: Sacred Frankincense, Frankincense, Copaiba, Tsuga, Northern Lights Black Spruce, Coriander, Grapefruit, Ledum, Nutmeg, Ocotea, Spearmint

Blends: EndoFlex, Joy, Longevity, Peace & Calming, DiGize

Nutritionals: Essentialzyme, JuvaTone, Longevity Softgels, NingXia Red, Power Meal, ImmuPro, MindWise, Mineral Essence, MultiGreens

Additional: V-6 Vegetable Oil Complex

Application and Usage

Topical: Place 1 drop of a single or blend in 1 teaspoon V-6 or other carrier oil in the palm of your hand. Gently apply to rear paws, spine, and up inside of rear legs. Apply 1-2 drops in the palm of your hand, rub hands together, and then gently apply to area. In a 4-oz. glass misting spray bottle, add 2-5 drops of an essential oil or blend of your choice. Fill bottle with spring or distilled water. Mist area as needed.

Ingestion & Oral: On foodstuff your pet really likes, apply 1 drop of a mixture of your chosen oil diluted in 5 ml V-6 or other carrier oil. This may be done several times daily based on severity of symptoms. Mix 1-5 drops essential oil in ½ gallon drinking water. Mist foodstuffs. Gently apply to the

---

Veterinarian Tips and Suggestions

Insulinomas

Combine 1/8-1/4 tablet each of Essentialzyme, ImmuPro, and JuvaTone in 1 teaspoon NingXia Red and 1/8 teaspoon Power Meal. Add 1 drop of your pet's favorite oil to provide a more enticing food.

---

gum areas. Also try increasing meat content of the affected animal's diet.

Inhalation: To hand diffuse, apply 1 drop suggested essential oil to your hand. While holding your pocket pet, gently cup your hand over its nose. You may also diffuse by placing your favorite diffuser near your pet's housing.

Other: Administer Raindrop Technique. You may repeat daily if needed until condition improves. After improvement, go to weekly Raindrops or as needed.

Irritable Bowel Syndrome

There can be many causes for Irritable Bowel Syndrome (IBS) in pocket pets. Everything from diet to viruses and bacteria can cause IBS. Symptoms include loose stools, blood in stools, lethargy, dehydration, and lack of appetite. If you suspect your pet may have IBS, take steps to isolate the root cause to better eliminate the possibility of future flare ups.

Recommendations

Singles: Peppermint, Copaiba, Ginger, Cistus

Blends: AromaEase, DiGize

Nutritionals: Allerzyme, Essentialzyme, MightyZyme, Life 9, JuvaTone, NingXia Red, Power Meal, MindWise, OmegaGize³

Additional: V-6 Vegetable Oil Complex

Application and Usage

Topical: Place 1 drop of a single or blend in 1 teaspoon V-6 or other carrier oil in the palm of your hand. Gently apply to rear paws, spine, and rear legs. Apply 1-2 drops in the palm of your hand, rub hands together, and then gently apply to area.

Ingestion & Oral: On foodstuff your pet really likes, apply 1 drop of a mixture of your chosen oil diluted in 5 ml V-6 or other carrier oil. This may be done several times daily based on severity of symptoms. Mix 1-5 drops essential oil in ½ gallon drinking water.

Mist foodstuffs. Gently apply to the gum areas. Also try increasing meat content in the animal's diet.

Inhalation: To hand diffuse, apply 1 drop suggested essential oil to your hand. While holding your pocket pet, gently cup your hand over its nose. You may also diffuse by placing your favorite diffuser near your pet's housing.

Other: Administer Raindrop Technique. You may repeat daily if needed until condition improves. After improvement, go to weekly Raindrops or as needed.

Joint Issues (Vitamin C Deficiency Induced) (Guinea Pig)

In guinea pigs, joint issues often occur when there is a vitamin C deficiency. Signs may include weight loss due to appetite loss, diarrhea, bleeding under the skin, lameness, and swollen joints

Recommendations

Singles: Carrot Seed, Orange, Idaho Balsam Fir, Palo Santo, Helichrysum

Blends: DiGize, Deep Relief Roll-On, PanAway

Nutritionals: AgilEase, Essentialzyme, Mineral Essence, NingXia Red, Organic Dried Wolfberries, Super C Chewable (10 mg per day vitamin C required), MightyVites, Master Formula

Additional: V-6 Vegetable Oil Complex, Cool Azul Pain Relief Cream, Cool Azul Sports Gel, Ortho Sport Massage Oil, Ortho Ease Massage Oil

Application and Usage

Topical: Apply 1 drop of a suggested single or blend in 1 teaspoon V-6 or other carrier oil in the palm of your hand. Gently apply to all paws, spine, and legs. Repeat with suggested oil. Apply 1-2 drops in the palm of your hand, rub hands together, and then gently apply to area.

Ingestion & Oral: On foodstuff your pet really likes, apply 1 drop of a mixture of your chosen oils diluted in 5 ml V-6 or other carrier oil. This may be done several times daily based on severity of symptoms. Mix 1-5 drops essential oil in ½ gallon drinking water. Mist foodstuffs. Gently apply to the gum areas. Try adding ½ teaspoon NingXia Red or up to ¼ Super C Chewable tablet to ingested water supply. AgilEase may also be added to drinking water in similar amounts as Super C Chewable. It may be best to alternate daily.

Inhalation: To hand diffuse, apply 1 drop suggested essential oil blend to your hand. While holding your pocket pet, gently cup your hand over its nose. You may also diffuse by placing your favorite diffuser near your pet's housing.

Other: Raindrop Technique may support your pet's body while waiting for vitamin C levels to rise. Also try layering topically applied oils with Cool Azul Pain Relief Cream, Cool Azul Sports Gel, Ortho Ease Massage Oil, and Ortho Sport Massage Oil.

Kidney Disease (Glomerulonephritis) (Gerbil)

It is not uncommon for a one-year-old or older gerbil to develop kidney blood-vessel inflammation. Signs include dehydration, excessive thirst, excessive urination, and weight loss. A veterinarian may decide to run tests to determine if tumor(s) are also present, as this is also a risk with this health challenge.

Recommendations

Singles: Copaiba, Cypress, Fennel, Frankincense, Helichrysum, Hyssop, Juniper, Ledum, Lemon, Lemongrass, Palo Santo

Blends: Aroma Life, Aroma Siez, Exodus II, JuvaCleanse, Thieves, PuriClean

Nutritionals: Essentialzyme, Detoxzyme, K&B, Longevity Softgels, MightyVites, MultiGreens, NingXia Red, Organic Dried Wolfberries, Rehemogen, Super C Chewable

Additional: V-6 Vegetable Oil Complex

Application and Usage

Topical: Put 1 drop essential oil or blend of your choice in your hand. Stroke your pet from its head to its tail area. Place 1 drop of a single or blend in 1 teaspoon oil of your choice in the palm of your hand. Gently apply to animal's lower back and rear feet, including between pads.

Ingestion & Oral: On foodstuff your pet really

> ### Veterinarian Tips and Suggestions
>
> ## Kidney Disease
>
> Combine 1 drop each of Copaiba, Cypress, Helichrysum, Juniper, and Lemongrass in 1 teaspoon V-6 Vegetable Oil Complex. Gently stroke blend along spine, middle back, and legs 2-4 times daily or as needed.

likes, apply 1 drop of a mixture of your chosen oil diluted in 5 ml V-6 or other carrier oil. Mix 1-5 drops essential oil in ½ gallon drinking water. Mist foodstuffs.

Inhalation: To hand diffuse, apply 1 drop over kidney area or suggested oil or blend to your hand. While holding your pocket pet, gently cup your hand over its nose. You may also diffuse by placing your favorite diffuser near your pet's housing.

Other: Administer Raindrop Technique as needed.

Kidney Disorders (Nephrosis) (Rodents)

This health challenge is described as chronic and progressive. It occurs more often on castrated males. It is often due to being fed a high protein diet. Signs include a gradually less active pet with a rough hair coat. Veterinary tests may reveal increased albumin levels in urine.

Recommendations

Singles: Copaiba, Cypress, Fennel, Frankincense, Helichrysum, Hyssop, Juniper, Ledum, Lemon, Lemongrass, Palo Santo

Blends: Aroma Life, Aroma Siez, Exodus II, JuvaCleanse, JuvaFlex, Thieves, PuriClean

Nutritionals: Allerzyme, Detoxzyme, Essentialzyme, K&B, Longevity Softgels, MightyVites, MightyZyme, MultiGreens, NingXia Red, Organic Dried Wolfberries, Rehemogen, Super C Chewable

Additional: V-6 Vegetable Oil Complex

Application and Usage

Topical: Put 1 drop essential oil or blend of your choice in your hand. Stroke your pet from its head to its tail area. Place 1 drop of a single or blend in 1 teaspoon V-6 or other carrier oil in the palm of your hand. Swirl your fingertip from the opposite hand around in the oil. Gently apply to animal's lower back and rear feet, including between pads.

Veterinarian Tips and Suggestions

Kidney Disorders

Combine 1 drop each of Cypress, Juniper, Copaiba, Helichrysum, and Lemongrass in 1 teaspoon V-6 Vegetable Oil Complex. Gently stroke blend along spine, back, and legs 2-4 times daily or as needed.

Ingestion & Oral: On foodstuff your pet really likes, apply 1 drop of a mixture of your chosen oil diluted in 5 ml V-6 or other carrier oil. Mix 1-5 drops essential oil in ½ gallon drinking water. Mist foodstuffs.

Inhalation: To hand diffuse, apply 1 drop on kidneys or suggested oil or blend to your hand. While holding your pocket pet, gently cup your hand over its nose. You may also diffuse by placing your favorite diffuser near your pet's housing.

Other: Administer Raindrop Technique as needed. Also try reducing dietary protein ingestion.

Lead Poisoning (Gerbil)

Gerbils like to chew on things. Things like old metal pipes or lead-based painted wood may be a source of lead.

Recommendations

Singles: Clove, Coriander, Helichrysum, Juniper, Copaiba

Blends: JuvaCleanse, DiGize, Longevity, GLF

Nutritionals: Longevity Softgels, NingXia Red, Organic Dried Wolfberries, Detoxzyme, K&B, MindWise, MultiGreens

Additional: V-6 Vegetable Oil Complex

Application and Usage

Topical: Put 1 drop suggested essential oil of your choice in your hand. Rub hands together until no oil is visible. Stroke your pet from its head to its tail area. Place 1 drop of a single or blend in 1 teaspoon V-6 or other carrier oil in the palm of your hand. Gently apply to animal's tummy area, all feet, and entire spine.

Ingestion & Oral: On foodstuff your pet really likes, apply 1 drop of a mixture of your chosen oil diluted in 5 ml V-6 or other carrier oil. Mix 1-5 drops essential oil in ½ gallon drinking water. Mist foodstuffs.

Inhalation: To hand diffuse, apply 1 drop of suggested oil or blend to your hand. While holding your pocket pet, gently cup your hand over its nose. You may also diffuse by placing your favorite diffuser near your pet's housing.

Other: Administer Raindrop Technique as needed.

Lumps (Cervical Lymphadenitis) (Guinea Pig)

Swelling of lymph nodes in the neck may be due to a variety of causes, including but not limited to, a Strep infection resulting from a fighting wound, mouth abrasions caused by overgrown teeth, or coarse foodstuffs scraping the mouth cavity.

Recommendations

Singles: Lavender, Palo Santo, Tsuga, Copaiba, Frankincense, Sacred Frankincense, Lemon, Myrrh, Ginger, Geranium, Ocotea, Lemongrass

Blends: Egyptian Gold, ImmuPower, Thieves, Exodus II

Nutritionals: ImmuPro, MightyVites, MultiGreens, NingXia Red, Organic Dried Wolfberries, Super C Chewable

Additional: V-6 Vegetable Oil Complex, Thieves Household Cleaner, Animal Scents Ointment, Rose Ointment

Application and Usage

Topical: Apply 1 drop of a suggested single or blend in 1 teaspoon V-6 or other carrier oil in the palm of your hand. Gently apply to all paws, cervical spine, and legs. Also apply around the outside of the lumps. Repeat with suggested oils. Apply 1-2 drops in the palm of your hand, rub hands together, and then gently apply to area. In a 4-oz. glass misting spray bottle, add 10 drops of an essential oil or blend of your choice. Mist area as needed.

Ingestion & Oral: On foodstuff your pet really likes, apply 1 drop of a mixture of your chosen oils diluted in 5 ml V-6 or other carrier oil. This may be done several times daily based on severity of symptoms. Mix 1-5 drops essential oil in ½ gallon drinking water. Mist foodstuffs. Gently apply to the gum areas. Try adding ½ teaspoon NingXia Red or up to ¼ Super C Chewable tablet and ¼ tablet ImmuPro to ingested water supply. It may be best to alternate daily.

Inhalation: To hand diffuse, apply 1 drop suggested essential oil blend to your hand. While holding your pocket pet, gently cup your hand over its nose. You may also diffuse by placing your favorite diffuser near your pet's housing.

Other: Cleanse any open neck wound area with diluted Thieves Household Cleaner; dry area before applying immune enhancing or suggested oils. Layer applied oils with Animal Scents Ointment or Rose Ointment. Also administer Raindrop Technique as needed.

Lymphoma (Cancer of White Blood Cells)

Lymphoma is an immune health challenge involving the lymphatic system. Symptoms can include external signs such as enlarged lymph nodes.

Recommendations

Singles: Frankincense, Sacred Frankincense, Laurus Nobilis, Lavender, Sacred Sandalwood, Royal Hawaiian Sandalwood, Cypress, Ravintsara, Idaho Blue Spruce, Idaho Balsam Fir, Northern Lights Black Spruce, Copaiba, Tsuga, Ledum, Myrrh, Spearmint, Orange, Pine

Blends: ImmuPower, Longevity, 3 Wise Men

Nutritionals: Allerzyme, Detoxzyme, Essentialzyme, Life 9, Longevity Softgels, ImmuPro, MightyVites, NingXia Red, Power Meal, Super C Chewable, MultiGreens, Mineral Essence

Additional: V-6 Vegetable Oil Complex

Application and Usage

Topical: Place 1 drop of a single or blend in 1 teaspoon V-6 or other carrier oil in the palm of your hand. Gently apply to all paws, spine, and rear legs. Apply 1-2 drops in the palm of your hand and then gently apply to area. In a 4-oz. glass misting spray bottle, add 5 drops of an essential oil or blend of

Veterinarian Tips and Suggestions

Lumps

Combine the following in an 8-oz. glass spray bottle: 1 capful Thieves Household Cleaner, 2 drops each of Lavender, Egyptian Gold, Lemongrass, and Thieves. Fill with distilled water. Spray area several times daily.

Veterinarian Tips and Suggestions

Lymphoma

Combine 1 drop each of ImmuPower, Laurus Nobilis, Idaho Blue Spruce, Sacred Frankincense, Orange, Tsuga, Pine, and 8 drops Copaiba in a 5-ml bottle filled with V-6 carrier oil. Apply on stomach and inside of legs 2-4 times daily.

your choice. Fill with spring or distilled water. Mist area as needed.

Ingestion & Oral: On foodstuff your pet really likes, apply 1 drop of a mixture of your chosen oils diluted in 5 ml V-6 or other carrier oil. This may be done several times daily based on severity of symptoms. Mix 1-5 drops essential oil in ½ gallon drinking water. Mist foodstuffs. Gently apply to the gum areas.

Inhalation: To hand diffuse, apply 1 drop suggested essential oil blend to your hand. While holding your pocket pet, gently cup your hand over its nose. You may also diffuse by placing your favorite diffuser near your pet's housing.

Other: Administer Raindrop Technique. You may repeat daily if needed until condition improves. After improvement, go to weekly Raindrops or as needed.

Mammary Glands (Tumors) (Rodents)

Fibroadenoma is a common tumor of mammary glands in rats. They may occur from the neck to the belly area in both males and females. Most of these benign tumors in rats are removed surgically. In mice, most are malignant. The most common tumors are mammary adenocarcinomas or fibrosarcomas.

Recommendations

Singles: Copaiba, Clove, Frankincense, Sacred Frankincense, Ginger, Idaho Balsam Fir, Lavender, Myrrh, Nutmeg, Rosemary, Orange, Grapefruit

Blends: Citrus Fresh, EndoFlex, Inner Child, Joy, Longevity, Peace & Calming, ImmuPower

Nutritionals: Detoxzyme, Essentialzyme, Longevity Softgels, ImmuPro, MultiGreens, Mineral Essence, Power Meal, NingXia Red, Organic Dried Wolfberries

Additional: V-6 Vegetable Oil Complex, Progessence Plus, Thieves Household Cleaner

Application and Usage

Topical: Apply 6 drops of any combination of singles or blends in 1 teaspoon V-6 or other carrier oil in the palm of your hand. Gently apply to all paws, spine, and abdominal area. Apply 1-2 drops in the palm of your hand, rub hands together, and then gently apply to lower back area, abdominal area, and down inside and outside of both rear legs to paws and pads. Complete application by applying from bottom of neck and down abdominal area 2-4 times daily.

Ingestion & Oral: On foodstuff your pet really likes, apply 6 drops of a mixture of your chosen oil diluted in 5 ml V-6 or other carrier oil. This may be done several times daily based on the severity of symptoms. Mix 1-5 drops essential oil in ½ gallon drinking water. Mist foodstuffs.

Inhalation: To hand diffuse, apply 1 drop immune enhancing oil or blend to your hand. While holding your pocket pet, gently cup your hand over its nose. You may also diffuse by placing your favorite diffuser near your pet's housing.

Other: Apply Raindrop Technique using each Raindrop Kit oil individually after having diluted each oil. Try using a 5-ml bottle of V-6 or other carrier oil to which you have added just 1-2 drops of an oil. Mix well. Use just 1 drop of each diluted essential oil for a Raindrop Technique session. You may repeat daily if needed until health challenge improves. Then use weekly until situation is resolved. Also try applying Progessence Plus skin serum and cleaning affected area of animal with diluted Thieves Household Cleaner.

Mange, Fleas and Mites (see also Skin Infections in Chinchilla section)

Mites often present health challenges on and in the skin tissue. Secondary ulcerative infections may occur in damaged tissue.

Recommendations

Singles: Citronella, Geranium, Basil, Copaiba, Tea Tree, Black Pepper, Rosemary, Palmarosa, Lemongrass, Palo Santo, Pine, Xiang Mao

Blends: Infect Away, ParaGize, Purification, Thieves, PuriClean

Nutritionals: MultiGreens, Rehemogen, ImmuPro, NingXia Red, Organic Dried Wolfberries, OmegaGize[3], ParaFree

Additional: V-6 Vegetable Oil Complex, Animal Scents Ointment, ClaraDerm, Thieves Household Cleaner, Thieves Waterless Hand Purifier

Application and Usage

Topical: Apply 4 drops of suggested single or blend in 1 teaspoon V-6 or other carrier oil in the palm of your hand. Gently apply to all paws, affected areas, and spine. Repeat with suggested oil. In a 4-oz. glass misting spray bottle, add 2-5 drops of an essential oil or blend of your choice. Mist the affected areas as needed.

Veterinarian Tips and Suggestions

Mange

Combine 3 drops each of Copaiba, Purification, Basil, Lemongrass, Geranium, and Thieves into ClaraDerm or LavaDerm spray. Mist the affected areas daily or as needed until at least 2 weeks after last sign of infestation.

Ingestion & Oral: On foodstuff your pet really likes, apply 5 drops suggested oil or blend diluted in 5 ml V-6 or other carrier oil. This may be done several times daily based on severity of symptoms. Mix 1-5 drops essential oil in ½ gallon drinking water. Mist foodstuffs. Gently apply to the gum areas.

Inhalation: To hand diffuse, apply 1 drop suggested essential oil blend to your hand. While holding your pocket pet, gently cup your hand over its nose. You may also diffuse by placing your favorite diffuser near your pet's housing.

Other: Apply Raindrop Technique daily during crisis and then weekly until condition improves. For additional support, layer Animal Scents Ointment and ClaraDerm spray with topically applied oils. Be careful not to contact exposed areas, as you don't want to transfer a health challenge to yourself. Use Thieves Household Cleaner and Thieves Waterless Hand Purifier to help clean any exposed areas that may become contaminated. See Environmental Terrain to support housing from providing continued exposure.

Neurological Disease (LCMV) (see also Viral Infections)

Lymphocytic choriomeningitis due to a possible viral infection may result in neurological symptoms or merely a slight fever.

Recommendations

Singles: Clove, Ravintsara, Melissa, Basil, Helichrysum, Juniper, Lemongrass, Tea Tree, Palmarosa, Copaiba, Geranium

Blends: Brain Power, Longevity, Thieves, Exodus II, Raven, EndoFlex, Melrose

Nutritionals: Detoxzyme, Longevity Softgels, OmegaGize[3], MultiGreens, NingXia Red, Organic Dried Wolfberries, Sulfurzyme

Additional: V-6 Vegetable Oil Complex

Veterinarian Tips and Suggestions

Neurological Disease

Combine 4 drops each of Helichrysum, EndoFlex, Copaiba, and Lemongrass, Melissa, Ravintsara, Exodus II, Melrose, or Geranium in a 5-ml glass bottle. Fill with a fatty based oil or V-6 Vegetable Oil Complex. Be certain to label accordingly. Apply to spine.

Application and Usage

Topical: Rats: Apply 1 drop of diluted (1 drop oil to 10 drops V-6 or carrier oil of choice) suggested single or blend in the palm of your hand. Gently apply to all paws, stomach area, and spine.

Note: Mice may require greater dilution for topical applications. Apply 1 drop in the palm of your hand, rub hands together, and then gently apply to areas. Mice have very thin skin. In a 4-oz. glass misting spray bottle, add 3-6 drops of an essential oil or blend of your choice. Fill with spring or distilled water. Mist spine as needed.

Ingestion & Oral: On foodstuff your pet really likes, apply 1-4 drops suggested oil or blend diluted in 5 ml V-6 or other carrier oil. This may be done several times daily based on severity of symptoms. Mix 1 drop essential oil in ½ gallon drinking water. Mist foodstuffs. Gently apply to the gum areas.

Inhalation: To hand diffuse, apply 1 drop suggested essential oil blend to your hand. While holding your pocket pet, gently cup your hand over its nose. You may also diffuse by placing your favorite diffuser near your pet's housing.

Other: Apply Raindrop Technique daily during crisis and then weekly until condition improves.

Parasites (Internal)

When a body's pH is out of balance or immunity is down, it becomes a host for other life forms such as bacterial, fungal, viral, or helminths of various types. These organisms must live inside another body to survive.

Recommendations

Singles: Cinnamon Bark, Clove, Fennel, Lemongrass, Manuka, Tea Tree, Mountain Savory, Oregano, Peppermint, Rosemary, Tarragon

Blends: DiGize, Longevity, ParaGize

Nutritionals: Digest & Cleanse, Detoxzyme, ICP, Longevity Softgels, Organic Dried Wolfberries, ParaFree

Additional: V-6 Vegetable Oil Complex

Application and Usage

Topical: Apply 4 drops of a single or blend in 1 teaspoon oil of your choice in the palm of your hand. Gently apply to all paws and abdominal area. Apply 1-2 drops in the palm of your hand, rub hands together, and then gently apply to abdominal area and down inside and outside of both rear legs to paws and pads. In a 4-oz. glass misting spray bottle, add 4-6 drops of an essential oil or blend of your choice. Mist body as needed.

Ingestion & Oral: On foodstuff your pet really likes, apply 1-4 drops of a mixture of your chosen oil diluted in 5 ml V-6 or other carrier oil. This may be done several times daily based on the severity of symptoms. Mix 1-5 drops essential oil in ½ gallon drinking water. Mist foodstuffs.

Inhalation: To hand diffuse, apply 1 drop suggested essential oil to your hand. While holding your pocket pet, gently cup your hand over its nose. You may also diffuse by placing your favorite diffuser near your pet's housing.

Other: Administer Raindrop Technique. You may repeat daily if needed until energy levels improve. After improvement, go to weekly Raindrops or as needed.

Pneumonia

An upper airway infection such as pneumonia may be the root cause of sneezing or conjunctivitis. For more information, see Conjunctivitis and Fever.

Recommendations

Singles: Goldenrod, Clove, Copaiba, Eucalyptus Blue, Eucalyptus Radiata, Oregano, Eucalyptus Globulus, Cedarwood, Ocotea, Lavender, Dorado

> ### Veterinarian Tips and Suggestions
>
> ## Pneumonia
>
> If pet is not eating well, mix 1 tablespoon Balance Complete thinned to a paste with 50:50 dilution of water and NingXia Red to be fed in small amounts (3-5 ml) 3 times daily. Also try adding 1-2 drops Lemon and 1 drop Longevity blend to the mix.

Azul, Hyssop, Lemon, Blue Spruce, Northern Lights Black Spruce, Lemongrass, Myrtle, Tea Tree, Thyme, Ravintsara

Blends: Egyptian Gold, Infect Away, Melrose, Thieves, Exodus II, R.C., Breathe Again Roll-on, Raven, Longevity, ImmuPower

Nutritionals: Essentialzyme, Detoxzyme, Inner Defense, JuvaSpice, Life 9, Longevity Softgels, Master Formula, MightyVites, MindWise, Mineral Essence, NingXia Red, Organic Dried Wolfberries, OmegaGize[3], PowerGize, Sulfurzyme

Additional: V-6 Vegetable Oil Complex

Application and Usage

Topical: Place 1 drop of a single or blend in 1 teaspoon V-6 or other carrier oil in the palm of your hand. Gently apply to front paws, chest, and stomach. Also try applying 1-2 drops in the palm of your hand, rub hands together, and then gently apply to neck, chest, and back. Mist body as needed.

Ingestion & Oral: On foodstuff your pet really likes, apply 1-6 drops of a mixture of your chosen oil diluted in 5 ml V-6 or other carrier oil. This may be done several times daily based on the severity of symptoms. Mix 1-5 drops essential oil in ½ gallon drinking water. Mist foodstuffs.

Inhalation: To hand diffuse, apply 1-2 drops to your hand. While holding your pocket pet, gently cup your hand over its nose. You may also diffuse by placing your favorite diffuser near your pet's housing.

Other: Administer Raindrop Technique. You may repeat daily if needed until breathing distress improves. After improvement, go to weekly Raindrop Techniques.

Pneumonia (Bacterial)

Bacterial pneumonia is a respiratory infection caused by a bacterial infection.

Recommendations

Singles: Cedarwood, Wintergreen, Black Pepper, Lemon, Lemongrass, Myrtle, Tea Tree, Ginger, Ravintsara, Basil, Clove, Copaiba, Eucalyptus Globulus, Geranium, Mountain Savory, Oregano, Thyme, Cinnamon Bark, Ocotea

Blends: ImmuPower, ParaGize, Raven, R.C., Thieves, Exodus II, Melrose

Nutritionals: Detoxzyme, Balance Complete, Life 9, Longevity Softgels, Digest & Cleanse, NingXia Red, Organic Dried Wolfberries, ParaFree, Super C Chewable

Additional: V-6 Vegetable Oil Complex, Thieves Household Cleaner

Application and Usage

Topical: Apply 1 drop of a suggested single or blend in 1 teaspoon V-6 or other carrier oil in the palm of your hand. Gently apply to all paws, cervical spine, chest, and all legs. Repeat with suggested oils as needed. Apply 1-2 drops in the palm of your hand, rub hands together, and then gently apply to area. In a 4-oz. glass misting spray bottle, add 4-6 drops of an essential oil or blend of your choice. Fill bottle with spring or distilled water. Mist area as needed.

Ingestion & Oral: On foodstuff your pet really likes, apply 1-4 drops of a mixture of your chosen oils diluted in 5 ml V-6 or other carrier oil. This may be done several times daily based on severity of symptoms. Mix 1-5 drops essential oil in ½ gallon drinking water. Mist foodstuffs. Gently apply to the gum areas. Try adding ¼ teaspoon NingXia Red or up to ¼ Super C Chewable tablet to ingested water supply. It may be best to alternate daily.

Inhalation: To hand diffuse, apply 1 drop suggested essential oil blend to your hand. While holding your pocket pet, gently cup your hand over its nose. You may also diffuse by placing your favorite diffuser near your pet's housing. Repeat with suggested oils.

Other: Apply the Raindrop Technique. Clean housing area, including drinking water and toys, with diluted Thieves Household Cleaner daily until crisis is over. Refer to Environmental Terrain (housing) for weekly suggestions to maintain a healthier lifestyle.

Protein Digestion (Amyloid Deposits) (Gerbil)

After approximately 10 months of age, gerbils may tend to develop deposits in the endocrine and lymph systems and various organs, including the gastrointestinal tract, heart, liver, pancreas, spleen, and reproductive glands. Indications of deposits may include appetite loss, dehydration, and weight loss. The condition may result in death.

Recommendations

Singles: Black Pepper, Coriander, Dill, Mastrante, Ginger, Peppermint

Blends: AromaEase, DiGize, EndoFlex, GLF, ParaGize, JuvaFlex

Nutritionals: Essentialzyme, Essentialzymes-4, JuvaTone, NingXia Red, Organic Dried Wolfberries, JuvaCleanse

Additional: V-6 Vegetable Oil Complex

Application and Usage

Topical: Put 1 drop suggested essential oil of your choice in your hand. Stroke your pet from its head to its tail area. Place 1 drop of a single or blend in 1 teaspoon V-6 or other carrier oil in the palm of your hand. Gently apply to animal's stomach area, spine, and pads of all feet.

Ingestion & Oral: On foodstuff your pet really likes, apply 1 drop of a mixture of your chosen oil diluted in 5 ml V-6 or other carrier oil. Mix 1-5 drops essential oil in ½ gallon drinking water. Mist foodstuffs.

Inhalation: To hand diffuse, apply 1-2 drops suggested oil or blend to your hand. While holding your pocket pet, gently cup your hand over its nose. You may also diffuse by placing your favorite diffuser near your pet's housing.

Other: Administer Raindrop Technique as needed.

Pododermatitis (Guinea Pig)

Swollen feet may need proper nail trimming or may become infected by Staph bacteria. Signs include a refusal to move, crying out, and ulcerated feet.

Recommendations

Singles: Frankincense, Eucalyptus Radiata, Laurus Nobilis, Geranium, Copaiba, Juniper, Ginger, Cypress, Helichrysum, Hyssop, Lavender, Lemongrass, Lemon Myrtle, Tea Tree, Mountain Savory, Myrrh, Palo Santo, Patchouli, Thyme, Xiang Mao

Blends: Abundance, Gentle Baby, Infect Away, Melrose, Purification, Thieves, Egyptian Gold,

---

Veterinarian Tips and Suggestions

Pododermatitis

Dilute 1 drop each Lavender, Copaiba, and Purification or Melrose in 1 pint of water and 1 capful Thieves Household Cleaner. Soaking affected feet in this solution may be done daily until there is resolution of the issue.

Exodus II, M-Grain, Relieve It, En-R-Gee

Nutritionals: Essentialzyme, JuvaTone, Life 9, MightyVites, MultiGreens, NingXia Red, Organic Dried Wolfberries, Super C Chewable

Additional: V-6 Vegetable Oil Complex, Thieves Household Cleaner

Application and Usage

Topical: Apply 1 drop of a suggested single or blend in 1 teaspoon V-6 or other carrier oil in the palm of your hand. Gently apply to all paws, spine, belly, and all legs. Apply 1-6 drops in the palm of your hand, rub hands together, and then gently apply to area. In a 4-oz. glass misting spray bottle, add 2-8 drops of an essential oil or blend of your choice. Mist area as needed.

Ingestion & Oral: On foodstuff your pet really likes, apply 1 drop of a mixture of your chosen oils diluted in 5 ml V-6 or other carrier oil. This may be done several times daily based on severity of symptoms. Mix 1-5 drops essential oil in ½ gallon drinking water. Mist foodstuffs. Gently apply to the gum areas. Try adding ¼ teaspoon NingXia Red or more to ¼ Super C Chewable tablet to ingested water supply. It may be best to alternate daily.

Inhalation: To hand diffuse, apply 1 drop suggested essential oil blend to your hand. While holding your pocket pet, gently cup your hand over its nose. You may also diffuse by placing your favorite diffuser near your pet's housing. Repeat with suggested oils.

Other: Refer to Environmental Terrain (housing) for daily cleaning during crisis and then perform weekly at a minimum to attempt prevention. Best practices include cleaning entire area thoroughly with Thieves Household Cleaner

Pyometra

Pyometra is an infection of the uterus. Hormonal changes are a known cause. Vaginal discharge is often an early warning symptom. If the cervix is closed, the uterus could rupture. A veterinary diagnosis may be a lifesaver. Vaginal discharge is often an early warning sign.

Recommendations

Singles: Clary Sage, Geranium, Lemon, Myrrh, Tea Tree, Myrtle, Melissa

Blends: ImmuPower, Infect Away, Thieves, Melrose, Purification, Mendwell, PuriClean

Nutritionals: ImmuPro, NingXia Red, MindWise, Life 9, Longevity Softgels, MultiGreens

Additional: V-6 Vegetable Oil Complex

Application and Usage

Topical: Apply 1-2 drops of a single oil or blend in 1 teaspoon oil of your choice in the palm of your hand. Gently apply to all paws and abdominal area. Apply 1-2 drops in the palm of your hand, rub hands together, and then gently apply to abdominal area and down inside and outside of both rear legs to paws and pads. Pay special attention to the inside of the hocks. In a 4-oz. glass misting spray bottle, add 2-5 drops of an essential oil or blend of your choice. Mist body as needed.

Ingestion & Oral: On foodstuff your pet really likes, apply 1 drop of a mixture of your chosen oil diluted in 5 ml V-6 or other carrier oil. This may be done several times daily based on the severity of symptoms. Mix 1-5 drops essential oil in ½ gallon drinking water. Mist foodstuffs.

Inhalation: To hand diffuse, apply 1 drop essential oil to your hand. While holding your pocket pet, gently cup your hand over its nose. You may also diffuse by placing your favorite diffuser near your pet's housing.

Other: Administer Raindrop Technique. You may repeat daily if needed until conditions improve. After improvement, go to weekly Raindrop Techniques or as needed.

Respiratory Infection and Pasteurellosis
(Rabbits)

This type of bacterial infection in rabbits can take the form of abscesses and/or respiratory congestion with nasal and/or eye discharge. The secretion is very thick and off-white. Abscesses can form anywhere on the body, including inside the mouth. Veterinary care will be needed to lance and drain the abscesses. The material is usually very thick and challenging to evacuate. Anesthesia is often needed for this. Special care is needed for rabbit anesthesia. Going to an exotic veterinarian would be best.

Recommendations

Singles: Copaiba, Lavender, Tea Tree, Eucalyptus Radiata, Myrtle, Ravintsara, Laurus Nobilis

Blends: Melrose, DiGize, Purification, Infect Away, PuriClean, Mendwell, Raven

Nutritionals: MultiGreens, Life 9, Longevity Softgels

Application and Usage

Topical: Apply Lavender and Purification or any other oil directly on abscess

Inhalation: Diffuse Lavender in a nebulizing diffuser starting 3-4 times a day. Slowly work up to diffusing constantly. Tea Tree can also be added with the Lavender.

Other: Pasteurellosis can live in the rabbit body for life and come out during times of stress in the form of respiratory infection or abscess. Persistent diffusing of essential oils like Lavender will help. While treating, closely monitor eating and behavior. Syringe feeding may be necessary during recovery time.

Respiratory Issues (see also Pneumonia-Bacterial and Environmental Terrain/Housing) (Rodents)

Dyspnea is shortness of breath, usually due to inflammation in the airways. High ammonia levels in cages present an environmental factor. There may be additional health challenges presented by ear infection.

Chronic Respiratory Disease (CRD) in mice is often due to *Streptobacillus moniliformis*. It may cause cervical lymphadenitis and polyarthritis progressing to pneumonia and fatal septicemia. As natural hosts of these bacteria, rats co-exist without complications. CAR (cilia-associated respiratory bacillus) and *Mycoplasma pulmonic* have been found in 95 percent of pet rats and mice.

Causation is often due to high ammonia levels in housing, inherited tendency, and vitamins A or E deficiency.

Ringtail (see also Environmental Terrain/Housing in Chinchilla section and Tail Slip in Gerbil section) (Rodents)

This condition occurs more in newborn and young nursing rats than mice. The tail develops a circular ring or sore at the base. The tail may fall off by itself or require amputation. Conditions predisposing young animals are low humidity, too absorbent litter or bedding, and diet deficient in essential fatty acids.

Recommendations

Singles: Basil, Bergamot, Lavender, Lemongrass, Lemon, Blue Cypress, Hong Kuai, Idaho Balsam Fir, Ledum, Myrrh, Palo Santo, Rosemary, Sage, Hyssop, Juniper, Tsuga, Geranium, Palmarosa, Patchouli, Roman Chamomile

Blends: Egyptian Gold, Melrose, EndoFlex, Exodus II, Infect Away, Longevity, Mendwell, Peace & Calming, PuriClean, Purification, Thieves, DiGize, ImmuPower, R.C., Raven

Nutritionals: Essentialzyme, Longevity Softgels, Life 9, NingXia Red, Organic Dried Wolfberries, OmegaGize[3], Digest & Cleanse

Application and Usage

Topical: In a 4-oz. glass misting spray bottle, add 1-2 drops of an essential oil or blend of your choice. Fill with spring or distilled water. Mist body area as needed.

Inhalation: To hand diffuse, apply 1 drop immune-enhancing oil or blend to your hand. While holding your pocket pet, gently cup your hand over its nose. You may also diffuse by placing your favorite diffuser near your pet's housing.

Ringworm (Dermatophytosis)

Ringworm is a fungal infection of the skin. It appears as a ring-type rash.

Recommendations

Singles: Clove, Copaiba, Dorado Azul, Blue Cypress, Eucalyptus Blue, Geranium, German Chamomile, Lavender, Lemon, Lemon Myrtle, Tea Tree, Mountain Savory, Myrrh, Ocotea, Oregano, Palmarosa, Roman Chamomile, Rosemary, Thyme, Lemongrass

Blends: Abundance, Australian Blue, Egyptian Gold, ImmuPower, Infect Away, Melrose, PuriClean, Raven, R.C., Thieves

---

Veterinarian Tips and Suggestions

Ringworm

Combine 5 drops each of Australian Blue and Melrose. Add the mixture to 10 drops Copaiba. Mix well. Apply directly on affected area 2 times daily. Be careful not to transfer the fungi to yourself. You may also add 7 drops of an oil or blend to the center of 1 oz. Animal Scents Ointment, swirl around with cotton swab to mix in the oil, and then apply to the affected area.

Nutritionals: Digest & Cleanse, Essentialzyme, Essentialzymes-4, Life 9, MightyVites, MultiGreens, NingXia Red, Organic Dried Wolfberries, Super C Chewable

Additional: V-6 Vegetable Oil Complex, Thieves Household Cleaner, Animal Scents Ointment

Application and Usage

Topical: Apply 1 drop of a suggested single or blend in 1 teaspoon of V-6 or other carrier oil in the palm of your hand. Gently apply to all paws and abdominal area. Apply 1-2 drops in the palm of your hand, rub hands together, and then gently apply to abdominal area and down inside and outside of both rear legs to paws and pads. In a 4-oz. glass misting spray bottle, add 2-5 drops of an essential oil or blend of your choice. Mist affected area as needed several times daily. Apply selected suggested oil or blend directly to affected areas several times daily.

Ingestion & Oral: On foodstuff your pet really likes, apply 1 drop of a mixture of your chosen suggested oil diluted in 5 ml V-6 or other carrier oil. This may be done several times daily based on the severity of symptoms. Mix 1-5 drops essential oil in ½ gallon drinking water. Mist foodstuffs.

Inhalation: To hand diffuse, apply 1 drop suggested essential oil to your hand. While holding your pocket pet, gently cup your hand over its nose. You may also diffuse by placing your favorite diffuser near your pet's housing.

Other: Clean the area with diluted Thieves Household Cleaner before applying suggested essential oils. This may need to be done daily for up to 4 weeks. Also try administering the Raindrop Technique. You may repeat daily if needed until skin improves. After improvement, go to weekly Raindrops or as needed for immune support. Also layer Animal Scents Ointment with suggested oils topically.

Salmonellosis (Gerbil)

There are many strains of Salmonella. Infection may include dehydration due to diarrhea, rough hair coat, abdominal swelling or bloating, loss of pregnancy, and weight loss.

Recommendations

Singles: Clove, Copaiba, Eucalyptus Radiata, Geranium, Ginger, Hinoki, Hong Kuai, Juniper, Lavender, Patchouli, Lemon, Lemongrass, Lemon Myrtle, Tea Tree, Mountain Savory, Ocotea, Oregano, Rosemary, Tarragon, Thyme, Xiang Mao

Blends: AromaEase, Christmas Spirit, Melrose, DiGize, Egyptian Gold, Exodus II, Infect Away, Light Your Fire, Purification, Thieves

Nutritionals: Allerzyme, Detoxzyme, Essentialzyme, JuvaTone, Longevity Softgels, MightyVites, NingXia Red, Organic Dried Wolfberries, Super C Chewable, ImmuPro, MultiGreens

Additional: V-6 Vegetable Oil Complex, Thieves Household Cleaner

Application and Usage

Topical: Put 1 drop each of digestion-aiding oil and suggested essential oil of your choice in your hand. Stroke your pet from its head to its tail area. Place 1 drop of a single or blend in 1 teaspoon V-6 or other carrier oil in the palm of your hand. Gently apply to animal's stomach area, spine, and pads of all feet.

Ingestion & Oral: On foodstuff your pet really likes, apply 1 drop of a mixture of your chosen oil diluted in 5 ml V-6 or other carrier oil. Mix 1-5 drops essential oil in ½ gallon drinking water. Mist foodstuffs.

Inhalation: To hand diffuse, apply 1 drop each of digestion-aiding oil and any suggested oil or blend to your hand. While holding your pocket pet, gently cup your hand over its nose. You may also diffuse by placing your favorite diffuser near your pet's housing.

Other: Administer Raindrop Technique as needed. See Environmental Terrain to support both housing and water supplies. Best practices include cleaning pet's area with Thieves Household Cleaner regularly.

Scurvy (Citamin C Deficiency) (Guinea Pig)

Guinea Pigs require approximately 10 mg of vitamin C daily as they don't readily make it within their own bodies. Deficiency signs include diarrhea, poor hair coat, joint swelling, lameness, lethargy, loose teeth, and vocalizing. Vitamin C deficiency may also greatly contribute to other smaller health challenges becoming larger issues.

Recommendations

Singles: Orange, Peppermint, Tarragon

Blends: Citrus Fresh, DiGize, AromaEase

Nutritionals: MightyVites, MultiGreens, NingXia Red, Organic Dried Wolfberries, Super C Chewable

Additional: V-6 Vegetable Oil Complex

Application and Usage

Topical: Apply 1 drop of a suggested single or blend in 1 teaspoon V-6 or other carrier oil in the palm of your hand. Gently apply to all paws, spine, belly, and all leg joints. Repeat with suggested oil. Apply 1-2 drops in the palm of your hand, rub hands together, and then gently apply to area. In a 4-oz. glass misting spray bottle, add 2-5 drops of an essential oil or blend of your choice. Mist as needed.

Ingestion & Oral: On foodstuff your pet really likes, apply 1 drop of a mixture of your chosen oils diluted in 5 ml V-6 or other carrier oil. This may be done several times daily based on severity of symptoms. Mix 1-5 drops essential oil in ½ gallon drinking water. Mist foodstuffs. Gently apply to the gum areas. Try adding ⅛ teaspoon NingXia Red or up to ¼ Super C Chewable tablet to ingested water supply. It may be best to alternate daily.

Skin, Dry

Recommendations

Singles: Geranium, Jasmine, Lavender, Ylang Ylang, Blue Cypress, Mastrante, Myrrh, Neroli, Patchouli, Roman Chamomile, German Chamomile, Sacred Sandalwood, Royal Hawaiian Sandalwood, Vetiver, Palmarosa

Blends: Gentle Baby, Mendwell

Nutritionals: NingXia Red, OmegaGize[3], MindWise, Allerzyme, Sulfurzyme, Super B

Additional: V-6 Vegetable Oil Complex, Animal Scents Ointment, ART Renewal Serum, Genesis Hand & Body Lotion, Lavender Hand & Body Lotion, Rose Ointment, ART Sheerlumé Brightening Cream, Sensation Hand & Body Lotion, Sensation Massage Oil

Application and Usage

Topical: Place 1 drop of a single or blend in 1 teaspoon Manuka, V-6, or other carrier oil in the palm of your hand. Gently apply to area of concern. Apply 1-2 drops in the palm of your hand, rub hands together, and then gently apply to area. In a 4-oz. glass misting spray bottle, add 2-5 drops of an essential oil or blend of your choice. Mist area as needed.

Other: Also layer with oils or apply separately if needed: Animal Scents Ointment, ART Renewal Serum, Genesis Hand & Body Lotion, Lavender Hand & Body Lotion, Rose Ointment, ART Sheerlumé Brightening Cream, Sensation Hand & Body Lotion, Sensation Massage Oil.

Skin Infections (see also Pododermatitis and Skin Infestations)

Most skin infections are due to mite infestation causing your pet to scratch. Tears in the skin may become infected by Staph bacteria. Clipping rear toe nails shorter is needed.

Skin Infestations (Fleas and Mites)

Recommendations

Singles: Cedarwood, Citronella, Eucalyptus Radiata, Lavender, Lemongrass, Tea Tree, Pine, Xiang Mao

Blends: Citrus Fresh, Purification, RepelAroma

Additional: V-6 Vegetable Oil Complex, Thieves Household Cleaner

Application and Usage

Topical: Place 1 drop of a single or blend in 1 teaspoon V-6 or other carrier oil in the palm of your hand. Gently apply to all paws, inside and outside of legs, groin area (avoid sensitive parts), armpits, spine, and abdominal area. Apply 1-2 drops in the palm of your hand, rub hands together, and then gently apply to abdominal area, spine, and down inside and outside of all legs to paws and pads. In a 4-oz. glass misting spray bottle, add 2-5 drops of an essential oil or blend of your choice. Fill with spring or distilled water. Mist affected area as needed several times daily. Apply selected suggested oil or blend directly to affected areas several times daily.

Veterinarian Tips and Suggestions

Skin Infestations

In an 8-oz. glass bottle filled with distilled water, combine 2 capfuls of Thieves Household Cleaner, 2-4 drops each of Purification, RepelAroma, Rosemary, Hinoki, and Pine. Shake well and spray affected areas 2-3 times per day until symptoms disappear.

Slobbers (Teeth, Overgrown or Malocclusion) (Guinea Pig)

Guinea Pigs may have a tooth that has overgrown. There may be a concern of nutritional imbalances, injury, or genetics. Signs to see a veterinarian for dental assistance include slobbering (called slobbers) and a lack of appetite. See Anesthesia Support for additional information after returning home.

Sore Hocks (Rabbits)

In almost all cases, sore hocks are caused from not having enough soft bedding in living quarters, so the fur on ventral hocks becomes worn away. Sores develop in this area and can break open and become infected. Serious cases involve the sores to be open down to the bone. Certain rabbit breeds like the Rex have very short, fine fur and are more susceptible to this. To prevent this, it is recommended to not have wire flooring.

Recommendations
Singles: Lavender, Palmarosa, Tea Tree, Helichrysum, Myrrh, Blue Cypress, Copaiba
Blends: Infect Away, Mendwell, PuriClean
Additional: Animal Scents Ointment, Rose Ointment

Application and Usage
Topical: Apply selected oils directly on the clean wound and then apply Animal Scents Ointment or Rose Ointment 2 times daily until the sores are completely healed.
Other: Twice daily, spritz bedding with 8 oz. of water with 10 drops of your rabbit's favorite calming oil (e.g., Lavender) to prevent further complications. Proper bedding would include shredded paper, fine Aspen wood shavings, or a soft towel, as long as the rabbit will NOT chew or eat the towel.

Stomach Ulcers (Gastric Ulcers)

Stomach ulcers are a sore in the stomach lining. Signs may include teeth grinding, excess salivation, and weight loss. Conventional pain relievers and anti-inflammatories may be a cause.

Recommendations
Singles: Copaiba, Cistus, Cypress, Manuka, Tea Tree, Dill, Fennel, Ginger, Lemon, Peppermint, Lavender, Sacred Frankincense

Veterinarian Tips and Suggestions

Stomach Ulcers
Combine 5 ml Manuka with 10 drops Copaiba. To apply, stroke gently around abdominal area and on the back feet.

Blends: Citrus Fresh, DiGize, ParaGize, AromaEase, PuriClean
Nutritionals: Essentialzyme, Essentialzymes-4, NingXia Red, Organic Dried Wolfberries, Power Meal, Allerzyme, MindWise, Life 9
Additional: V-6 Vegetable Oil Complex

Application and Usage
Topical: Apply 1-6 drops of a single or blend in 1 teaspoon V-6 or other carrier oil in the palm of your hand. Gently apply to all paws and abdominal area. Apply 1-2 drops in the palm of your hand, rub hands together, and then gently apply to abdominal area and down inside and outside of both rear legs to paws and pads. In a 4-oz. glass misting spray bottle, add 2-5 drops of an essential oil or blend of your choice. Fill with spring or distilled water. Mist body as needed.
Ingestion & Oral: On foodstuff your pet really likes, apply 1 drop of a mixture of your chosen oil diluted in 5 ml V-6 or other carrier oil. This may be done several times daily based on the severity of symptoms. Mix 1-5 drops essential oil in ½ gallon drinking water. Mist foodstuffs.
Inhalation: To hand diffuse, apply 1 drop calming oil and 1 drop suggested essential oil to your hand. While holding your pocket pet, gently cup your hand over its nose. You may also diffuse by placing your favorite diffuser near your pet's housing.
Other: Administer Raindrop Technique. You may repeat every other day if needed until eating improves. After improvement, go to weekly Raindrop Techniques or as needed.

Tail Slip

Picking up by the tail may be dangerous to your pet. Loss of tail hair or skin is called tail slip. Areas exposed by tail slip may rot. Amputation may be required.

Tail Slip

In a 4-oz. sprayer, combine 1 teaspoon Thieves Household Cleaner and 4 drops of suggested oil or blend. Fill with distilled or spring water. Spray living area lightly several times daily or as needed.

Recommendations

Singles: Blue Cypress, Copaiba, Patchouli, Tea Tree, Manuka, Cypress, Helichrysum, Myrrh, Lavender, Tsuga, Roman Chamomile, Geranium, Palmarosa

Blends: Australian Blue, Thieves, Sensation, Gentle Baby, Aroma Siez, Melrose, Infect Away, Mendwell, PuriClean, Purification

Nutritionals: Master Formula, MightyVites, MultiGreens, NingXia Red, Organic Dried Wolfberries, Super C Chewable

Additional: V-6 Vegetable Oil Complex, Animal Scents Ointment, Thieves Household Cleaner

Application and Usage

Topical: Put 1 drop suggested essential oil of your choice in your hand. Stroke your pet from its head to its tail area. Place 1 drop of a single or blend in 1 teaspoon V-6 or other carrier oil in the palm of your hand. Gently apply to animal's stomach area, spine, and pads of all feet. Make an indentation in center of 1 oz. Animal Scents Ointment. Add 1 drop of oil of your choice and swirl around with finger. On exposed tail area, gently apply this mixture daily or as needed.

Ingestion & Oral: On foodstuff your pet really likes, apply 1 drop of a mixture of your chosen suggested oil diluted in 5 ml V-6 or other carrier oil. Mix 1-5 drops essential oil in ½ gallon drinking water. Mist foodstuffs.

Inhalation: To hand diffuse, apply 1 drop suggested oil or blend to your hand. While holding your pocket pet, gently cup your hand over its nose. You may also diffuse by placing your favorite diffuser near your pet's housing.

Other: To prevent infection, clean pet's area well with Thieves Household Cleaner. Also layer Animal Scents Ointment with suggested oils on location or apply singly. See Environmental Terrain for suggestions to maintain as clean an environment as possible.

Tear Glands (Excess Porphyrin Secretion) (Gerbil)

A reddish-brown protein may accumulate around your pet's eyes and nostrils. It is excreted by tear glands. It may cause skin irritations, which may lead to bleeding in the area, hair loss, itching, redness, and scabby sores, which may become infected. The secretions may occur due to high humidity (more than 50 percent), room temperature too high or too low, overcrowding, or just because it doesn't like its roommates.

Recommendations

Singles: Cedarwood, Copaiba, Lavender

Blends: Peace & Calming, Purification, Tranquil Roll-On, Gentle Baby

Nutritionals: Master Formula, MightyVites, MultiGreens, NingXia Red, Organic Dried Wolfberries, Super C Chewable

Additional: V-6 Vegetable Oil Complex, Animal Scents Ointment, Animal Scents Shampoo

Application and Usage

Topical: Put 1 drop calming essential oil of your choice in your hand. Rub hands together lightly. Stroke your pet from its head to its tail area. Apply 1-3 drops of a single or blend in 1 teaspoon V-6 or other carrier oil in the palm of your hand. Gently apply to animal's head, nose, and pads of all feet. Make an indentation in the center of 1 oz. Animal Scents Ointment. Add 1-3 drops oil of your choice and swirl around with finger. Gently apply on irritated areas, being careful not to get into the eyes.

Ingestion & Oral: On foodstuff your pet really likes, apply 1 drop of a mixture of your chosen suggested oil diluted in 5 ml V-6 or other carrier oil. Mix 1-5 drops essential oil in ½ gallon drinking water. Mist foodstuffs.

Inhalation: To hand diffuse, apply 1 drop calming oil or blend to your hand. While holding your pocket pet, gently cup your hand over its nose. You may also diffuse by placing your favorite diffuser near your pet's housing.

Other: Also try washing affected area with Animal Scents Shampoo. After drying thoroughly, apply Animal Scent Ointment with chosen suggested oils.

Teeth, Overgrown (Chinchilla)

Chinchillas may have a tooth that has overgrown. Signs suggesting need to see a veterinarian for dental assistance include slobbering and a lack of appetite. See Anesthesia Support for additional information after returning home. Apply Copaiba, Myrrh, or Helichrysum on gums 2 times daily before and after visiting the veterinarian.

Thiamine Deficiency (Chinchilla)

Chinchillas may also have a B vitamin or Thiamine deficiency.

Recommendations

Singles: Frankincense, Lavender, Vetiver, Ginger, Copaiba

Blends: Stress Away Roll-On, Tranquil Roll-On, T-Away, Trauma Life, Citrus Fresh

Nutritionals: Essentialzyme, Essentialzymes-4, JuvaSpice, MightyVites, NingXia Red, Organic Dried Wolfberries, Super B, Balance Complete, Power Meal

Additional: V-6 Vegetable Oil Complex

Application and Usage

Topical: Apply 1 drop of a single calming essential oil or blend in 1 teaspoon V-6 or other carrier oil in the palm of your hand. Gently apply to all paws and abdominal area. Apply 1-2 drops in the palm of your hand, rub hands together and then gently apply to abdominal area, spine, and around base of ears. In a 4-oz. glass misting spray bottle, add 2-5 drops of an essential oil or blend of your choice. Fill with spring or distilled water. Mist body as needed.

Ingestion & Oral: Mix ¼ capsule Super B in 1 teaspoon Balance Complete or Power Meal with ⅛ teaspoon JuvaSpice. Combine with 1 tablespoon NingXia Red diluted 50:50 with water. Lastly, add 1 drop of your pet's favorite tasting oil or Citrus Fresh. Present as a foodstuff several times weekly.

Inhalation: To hand diffuse, apply 1 drop calming essential oil to your hand. While holding your pocket pet, gently cup your hand over its nose. You may also diffuse by placing your favorite diffuser near your pet's housing.

Tumors, Benign

A tumor is a walled-off area of cells the body may build as it attempts to isolate affected tissue. It is a type of health challenge defense. Tumors of concern should be diagnosed by a veterinarian and biopsies taken to determine the exact nature of the tumor. After a diagnosis has been reached, treatment and recovery with oils may begin.

Recommendations

Singles: Clove, Copaiba, Frankincense, Sacred Frankincense, Grapefruit, Lavender, Ledum, Myrrh, Ocotea, Orange, Palo Santo, Tangerine, Xiang Mao, Tsuga, Idaho Balsam Fir, Idaho Blue Spruce

Blends: Australian Blue, Egyptian Gold, Exodus II, GLF, Longevity, Sacred Mountain, ImmuPower

Nutritionals: Allerzyme, Essentialzyme, JuvaTone, Longevity Softgels, Master Formula, MightyVites, ImmuPro, MightyZymes, MultiGreens, NingXia Red, Organic Dried Wolfberries, OmegaGize³, Sulfurzyme, Super C Chewable

Additional: V-6 Vegetable Oil Complex

Application and Usage

Topical: Apply 1 drop of a suggested single or blend in 1 teaspoon V-6 or other carrier oil in the palm of your hand. Gently apply to all paws, spine, and abdominal area. Apply 1-2 drops in the palm of your hand, rub hands together, and then gently apply to lower back area and down inside and outside of both rear legs to paws and pads. In a 4-oz. glass misting spray bottle, add 2-5 drops of an essential oil or blend of your choice. Mist body as needed.

Ingestion & Oral: On foodstuff your pet really likes, apply 1 drop of a mixture of your chosen oil diluted in 5 ml V-6 or other carrier oil. This may be done several times daily based on the severity of symptoms. Mix 1-5 drops essential oil in ½ gallon drinking water. Mist foodstuffs.

Inhalation: To hand diffuse, apply 1 drop suggested uplifting essential oil to your hand. While holding

---

Veterinarian Tips and Suggestions

Tumors, Benign

Combine ⅛ -¼ capsule of Allerzyme and ImmuPro in 1 teaspoon NingXia Red and ⅛ teaspoon Power Meal. Add 1 drop of Copaiba and Sacred Frankincense to the mixture and present as foodstuff.

your pocket pet, gently cup your hand over its nose. You may also diffuse by placing your favorite diffuser near your pet's housing.

Other: Administer Raindrop Technique. You may repeat daily if needed until health challenge begins to improve and then weekly until situation is resolved.

Tumors, Reproductive (Hedgehog)

These common types of tumors are found within the reproductive system of an older Hedgehog. The basis of support is the same as for other forms of tumor formation. Additional oils may be chosen to support the reproductive system.

Recommendations

Singles: Cedarwood, Clary Sage, Clove, Lavender, Frankincense, Geranium, Idaho Balsam Fir, Myrrh, Orange, Palo Santo, Tsuga, Sacred Frankincense, Copaiba, Peppermint

Blends: ImmuPower, JuvaCleanse, Longevity, Mister

Nutritionals: Allerzyme, Essentialzyme, Longevity Softgels, MightyVites, MightyZyme, NingXia Red, Organic Dried Wolfberries, Super C, ImmuPro

Additional: V-6 Vegetable Oil Complex, Progessence Plus, Thieves Household Cleaner

Application and Usage

Topical: Apply 1 drop of a suggested single or blend in 1 teaspoon V-6 or other carrier oil in the palm of your hand. Gently apply to rear paws and pads, spine, and abdominal area. Apply 1-2 drops in the palm of your hand, rub hands together, and then gently apply to lower back area and down inside and outside of both rear legs to paws and pads. In a 4-oz. glass misting spray bottle, add 2-5 drops of an essential oil or blend of your choice. Fill with spring or distilled water. Mist body as needed.

Ingestion & Oral: On foodstuff your pet really likes, apply 1 drop of a mixture of your chosen oil diluted in 5 ml V-6 or other carrier oil. This may be done several times daily based on the severity of symptoms. Mix 1-5 drops essential oil in ½ gallon drinking water. Mist foodstuffs.

Inhalation: To hand diffuse, apply 1 drop suggested uplifting essential oil to your hand. While holding your pocket pet, gently cup your hand over its nose. You may also diffuse by placing your favorite diffuser near your pet's housing.

> ### 🐀 Veterinarian Tips and Suggestions
>
> ## Tumors, Reproductive
>
> Combine in a 4-oz. sprayer containing 1 teaspoon Thieves Household Cleaner the following essential oils: 5 drops each of Frankincense, Sacred Frankincense, Copaiba, Lavender, Palo Santo, and 1 drop Peppermint. Fill sprayer with water. Mist along lower back and belly several times daily.

Other: Administer Raindrop Technique. You may repeat daily if needed until health challenge begins to improve. Then weekly until situation is resolved. Also try applying Progessence Plus skin serum to affected area.

Tumors, Skin and Belly Areas (see also Ear Masses) (Gerbil)

On the belly of an older gerbil, there is a marking gland. It may develop a mass that may become an open, infected sore. Be sure to clean pet's area regularly with Thieves Cleaner, as the open sores are repeatedly in contact with the pet's housing. Ask your veterinarian for guidance on changes in diet that can help alleviate tumor growth.

Recommendations

Singles: Copaiba, Clove, Frankincense, Idaho Blue Spruce, Northern Lights Black Spruce, Ginger, Idaho Balsam Fir, Ledum, Myrrh, Nutmeg, Rosemary, Tea Tree, Lavender

Blends: Citrus Fresh, Egyptian Gold, EndoFlex, Exodus II, Longevity, Thieves, Melrose

Nutritionals: EndoGize, Essentialzyme, Longevity Softgels, NingXia Red, Organic Dried Wolfberries, ImmuPro

Additional: V-6 Vegetable Oil Complex, Progessence Plus

Application and Usage

Topical: Place 1 drop of a single or blend in 1 teaspoon V-6 or other carrier oil in the palm of your hand. Gently apply to all paws, spine, and abdominal area. Apply 1-2 drops in the palm of your hand, rub hands together, and then gently apply to lower back area and down inside and outside of both rear legs to paws and pads. In a 4-oz. glass misting spray bottle, add 2-5 drops of an essential oil or blend of your choice. Fill with spring or distilled water. Mist body as needed.

Ingestion & Oral: On foodstuff your pet really likes, apply 1 drop of a mixture of your chosen oil diluted in 5 ml V-6 or other carrier oil. This may be done several times daily based on the severity of symptoms. Mix 1-5 drops essential oil in ½ gallon drinking water. Mist foodstuffs.

Inhalation: To hand diffuse, apply 1 drop of a calming and uplifting essential oil to your hand. While holding your pocket pet, gently cup your hand over its nose. You may also diffuse by placing your favorite diffuser near your pet's housing.

Other: Administer Raindrop Technique. You may repeat daily if needed until health challenge improves and then weekly until situation resolves. Also try applying Progessence Plus skin serum to tumors or sores to aid in recovery.

Tumors, Skin Swellings (Rodents)

Most skin swellings in rats or mice are due to tumor formation or abscess.

Tumors, Surface Skin Areas (Hedgehog)

As a hedgehog ages, it may develop fast-growing tumors along the back of the neck or jaw line. A veterinarian may require a biopsy of the mass.

Tyzzer's Disease (Gerbil)

A common bacterial infection that infects stressed young gerbils may result in Tyzzer's disease. It is transmitted through contaminated feces. Signs include appetite loss, back hunched up, depression, diarrhea, and hair coat roughness.

Recommendations

Singles: Cistus, Clove, Ginger, Hong Kuai, Lemongrass, Lemon Myrtle, Mountain Savory, Myrrh, Nutmeg, Rosemary, Tangerine, Thyme, Xiang Mao, Tea Tree

Blends: AromaEase, DiGize, Exodus II, En-R-Gee, Melrose, Egyptian Gold, Infect Away, Longevity, Thieves, Mendwell, PuriClean

Nutritionals: Essentialzyme, Longevity Softgels, Life 9, ImmuPro, NingXia Red, Organic Dried Wolfberries, Super C Chewable

Additional: V-6 Vegetable Oil Complex

Application and Usage

Topical: Place 1 drop of a single or blend in 1 teaspoon V-6 or other carrier oil in the palm of your hand. Gently apply to all paws and lower back area. Apply 1-2 drops in the palm of your hand, rub hands together, and then gently apply to lower back area and down inside and outside of both rear legs to paws and pads. In a 4-oz. glass misting spray bottle, add 2-5 drops of an essential oil or blend of your choice. Fill with spring or distilled water. Mist body as needed.

Ingestion & Oral: On foodstuff your pet really likes, apply 1 drop of a mixture of your chosen oil diluted in 5 ml V-6 or other carrier oil. This may be done several times daily based on the severity of symptoms. Mix 1-5 drops essential oil in ½ gallon drinking water. Mist foodstuffs.

Inhalation: To hand diffuse, apply 1 drop calming and uplifting essential oil to your hand. While holding your pocket pet, gently cup your hand over its nose. You may also diffuse by placing your favorite diffuser near your pet's housing.

Other: Administer Raindrop Technique. You may repeat daily if needed until lethargy improves. After improvement, go to weekly Raindrops or as needed. See Environmental Terrain to support housing and water sources.

Urinary Calculi (Guinea Pig)

Stone formation may cause difficulty urinating, bloody urine, and a hunched back position.

Recommendations

Singles: Cypress, Fennel, Juniper, Copaiba, Helichrysum

Blends: PanAway, R.C., DiGize

Nutritionals: K&B, Mineral Essence, Detoxzyme

Additional: V-6 Vegetable Oil Complex

Application and Usage

Topical: Apply 1 drop of a suggested single or blend in 1 teaspoon other carrier oil in the palm of your hand. Gently apply to rear paws and low back. Repeat with suggested oil. Apply 1-2 drops in the palm of your hand, rub hands together, and then gently apply to area. In a 4-oz. glass misting spray bottle, add 2-5 drops of an essential oil or blend of your choice. Mist as needed.

Ingestion & Oral: On foodstuff your pet really likes, apply 4 drops Copaiba, diluted in 5 ml V-6 or other carrier oil. This may be done several times daily based on severity of symptoms. Mix 1-5 drops essential oil in ½ gallon drinking water. Mist foodstuffs. Gently apply to the gum areas.

Inhalation: To hand diffuse, apply 1 drop suggested essential oil blend to your hand. While holding your pocket pet, gently cup your hand over its nose. You may also diffuse by placing your favorite diffuser near your pet's housing.

Other: Apply Raindrop Technique daily during crisis and then weekly until condition improves.

Viral Infections (Rodents)

This is a common health challenge for these pets. Your pet does not have the mumps. Its salivary glands and lymph nodes on the neck are swollen.

Recommendations

Singles: Basil, Blue Cypress, Cinnamon Bark, Clove, Eucalyptus Globulus, Geranium, Helichrysum, Hinoki, Hyssop, Lemon, Lemon Myrtle, Laurus Nobilis, Lemongrass, Tea Tree, Melissa, Mountain Savory, Myrrh, Oregano, Palmarosa, Ravintsara, Eucalyptus Blue, Rosemary, Thyme, Ocotea

Blends: Australian Blue, Egyptian Gold, ImmuPower, Infect Away, Longevity, Melrose, ParaGize, PuriClean, Raven, R.C., Thieves, Exodus II

Nutritionals: Digest & Cleanse, Essentialzyme, Essentialzymes-4, ImmuPro, Life 9, Longevity Softgels, MightyVites, MultiGreens, NingXia Red, Organic Dried Wolfberries, Super C Chewable

Additional: V-6 Vegetable Oil Complex

Application and Usage

Topical: Rats: Apply 1 drop of diluted (1 drop oil to 10 drops V-6) suggested immune single or blend in the palm of your hand. Rub hands together. Gently apply to all paws, stomach area, and spine.

Note: Mice may require greater dilution for topical applications. Apply 1 drop in the palm of your hand, rub hands together, and then gently apply to areas.

Note: If you have mice, you may just want to rub your hands together and hold your hands above your pet without touching it. Mice have very thin skin. In a 4-oz. glass misting spray bottle, add 2-5 drops of an

essential oil or blend of your choice. Fill with spring or distilled water. Mist as needed.

Ingestion & Oral: On foodstuff your pet really likes, apply 1 drop suggested oil or blend diluted in 5 ml V-6 or other carrier oil. This may be done several times daily based on severity of symptoms. Add 1 drop essential oil in ½ gallon drinking water. Mist foodstuffs. Gently apply to the gum areas.

Inhalation: To hand diffuse, apply 1 drop suggested essential oil blend to your hand. While holding your pocket pet, gently cup your hand over its nose. You may also diffuse by placing your favorite diffuser near your pet's housing.

Other: Apply Raindrop Technique daily during crisis and then weekly until condition improves. See Environmental Terrain (Housing) and (Water) for additional areas of concern.

Wobbly Hedgehog Syndrome (Hedgehog)

This neurological challenge may progress to paralysis before a pet is 2 years of age. As a body reawakens, there may be pain.

Recommendations

Singles: Basil, Cedarwood, Copaiba, Cypress, Frankincense, Geranium, Ginger, Helichrysum, Northern Lights Black Spruce, Idaho Blue Spruce, Juniper, Lemongrass, Nutmeg, Peppermint, Petitgrain, Pine, Ravintsara, Valerian

Blends: Deep Relief Roll-On, Exodus II, Egyptian Gold, PanAway, The Gift, Valor, Valor II

Nutritionals: Master Formula, MightyVites, Mineral Essence, MultiGreens, Life 9, NingXia Red, Organic Dried Wolfberries, OmegaGize[3], Sulfurzyme, Super B

Additional: V-6 Vegetable Oil Complex

Application and Usage

Topical: Apply 1 drop of a suggested single or blend in 1 teaspoon V-6 or other carrier oil in the palm of your hand. Gently apply to all paws, pads, and entire spine. Apply 1-2 drops in the palm of your hand, rub hands together, and then gently apply to entire spine and down inside and outside of both rear legs to paws and pads. In a 4-oz. glass misting spray bottle, add 2-5 drops of an essential oil or blend of your choice. Mist body as needed.

Ingestion & Oral: On foodstuff your pet really likes, apply 1 drop of a mixture of your chosen oil diluted in 5 ml V-6 or other carrier oil. This may be done several times daily based on the severity of symptoms. Mix 1-5 drops essential oil in ½ gallon drinking water. Mist foodstuffs.

Inhalation: To hand diffuse, apply 1 drop suggested essential oil single or blend to your hand. While holding your pocket pet, gently cup your hand over its nose. You may also diffuse by placing your favorite diffuser near your pet's housing.

Other: Also try Neuro Auricular Technique or Administer Raindrop Technique.

Wounds

This may occur during overcrowding. Bite wounds may contain *Pasteurella*, gram-negative bacteria. There is the possibility of an abscess occurring. If severe, you may choose to visit a veterinarian.

Recommendations

Singles: Basil, Cistus, Copaiba, Cypress, Frankincense, Helichrysum, Juniper, Lavender, Myrrh, Onycha, Palo Santo, Palmarosa, Roman Chamomile, Rose, Sacred Sandalwood, Royal Hawaiian Sandalwood, Tea Tree, Tsuga, Vetiver (stress coping)

> **Veterinarian Tips and Suggestions**
>
> ## Wounds
>
> Add 5 ml Lavender, PuriClean, or Infect Away to 1 bottle of ClaraDerm. Blend well. Apply to area as often as needed.

Blends: Australian Blue, Egyptian Gold, Infect Away, Melrose, Mendwell, PuriClean, Purification, Thieves, T-Away, The Gift

Nutritionals: NingXia Red, Life 9, ImmuPro, Mineral Essence

Additional: V-6 Vegetable Oil Complex, Animal Scents Ointment, ClaraDerm, LavaDerm Cooling Mist, Rose Ointment

Application and Usage

Topical: Place 1 drop of a single or blend in 1 teaspoon V-6 or other carrier oil in the palm of your hand. Gently apply to all paws and abdominal area. Apply 1-2 drops in the palm of your hand, rub hands together, and then gently apply to area around wound. In a 4-oz. glass misting spray bottle, add 2-5 drops of an essential oil or blend of your choice. Fill with spring or distilled water. Mist area as needed.

Ingestion & Oral: On foodstuff your pet really likes, apply 1 drop of a mixture of your chosen oil diluted in 5 ml V-6 or other carrier oil. This may be done several times daily based on severity of symptoms. Mix 1-5 drops essential oil in ½ gallon drinking water. Mist foodstuffs.

Inhalation: To hand diffuse, apply 1 drop immune and 1 drop suggested essential oil to your hand. While holding your pocket pet, gently cup your hand over its nose. You may also diffuse by placing your favorite diffuser near your pet's housing.

Other: Administer Raindrop Technique. You may repeat daily if needed until skin improves. After improvement, go to weekly Raindrops or as needed. Also try the following carrier products individually or layered with oils when applying to wounds: Animal Scents Ointment, ClaraDerm, LavaDerm Cooling Mist, Rose Ointment

Wry Neck (Loss of Equilibrium) (Rabbits)

Total loss of equilibrium may follow signs of wry neck after an injury, upper respiratory infection, or ear infection. The equilibrium can be lost and the rabbit may circle and even roll. This can become very serious quickly and life threatening. The cause should be identified to enhance treatment options.

Recommendations

Singles: Clove, Lavender, Idaho Blue Spruce, Northern Lights Black Spruce, Tea Tree, Melissa, Mountain Savory, Laurus Nobilis, Lemongrass, Petitgrain, Ravintsara, Sacred Frankincense, Orange, Idaho Balsam Fir, Mastrante, Ocotea

Blends: Valor, Valor ll, DiGize, Melrose, Thieves, Purification, Mendwell, Infect Away, PuriClean, Exodus II, Peace & Calming, Inner Child, Trauma Life

Nutritionals: MultiGreens

Application and Usage

Topical: Apply Valor on back of neck, DiGize on spine, and Exodus II on stomach. Also apply 1-2 suggested oils on the spine 3 times daily.

Inhalation: Diffuse Lavender, Tea Tree, Purification, Peace & Calming, Sacred Frankincense, Inner Child, Trauma Life

Other: Make sure the rabbit is able to eat enough during the illness and recovery. Syringe feeding may be needed, as well as other nursing care.

Tips for Healthy Rabbits

Bedding

Bedding can either help prevent respiratory infections or be the cause of them. There are many types of bedding for a rabbit's cage or litter box to choose from, but only a couple would be considered safe. Cedar shavings can be very irritating to the respiratory mucus membranes of the sinus and lungs. Pine has been shown to elevate blood liver enzymes. Cat litter is too dusty and irritating to the respiratory tract. Corncob bedding may be ingested by a rabbit and cause gastrointestinal impactions. The best choice would be Aspen wood shavings. The second-best choice would be shredded paper.

Diffusing and misting bedding with certain essential oils like Lavender, Purification, Orange, Idaho Balsam Fir, Tea Tree, Mastrante, and Ocotea can be beneficial to keeping a respiratory tract healthy.

Tips for Healthy Rabbits

Diet

Many diseases and health issues can be prevented with a healthy diet.

A truly healthy diet for rabbits consists of 80 percent hay. For rabbits older than one year, it should be Timothy hay. Rabbits that are under a year and still growing or a mother doe that is either pregnant or nursing should get alfalfa hay. It has much more calcium that is needed for growing babies. Too much calcium for the adult rabbit over time will cause bladder and /or kidney stones.

The remaining 20 percent of the diet should be a variety of fresh organic greens. These would consist of all kinds of lettuce (except for iceberg, which has no nutritional value) parsley, kale, spinach, carrot tops, etc. Certain veggies should be avoided if the rabbit has a history of frequent GI stasis because these are gas producer foods and could aggravate a flare up. These consist of broccoli, cabbage, cauliflower, and Brussels sprouts. Other food that is high in sugar like bananas, apples, and carrots should also be avoided for GI stasis-prone bunnies.

Grains are not at all appropriate for bunnies, even though rabbits are particularly fond of them. Oatmeal, crackers, and breads are like candy to bunnies and very addictive. These foods can quickly damage a healthy rabbit's gastrointestinal flora. These foods can make them more prone to GI stasis.

Rabbits are "hind gut fermenters." This means they have flora, or healthy bacteria, that live in their cecum and are imperative for proper digestion and absorption of vitamins and minerals. In fact, rabbits need to "eat" their stool to get all they need for being healthy. These special softer stools that they eat right as they are exiting the anus are called cecotropes. They are also known as "night feces." Bunnies that are overweight from too many carbs are unable to reach their hind end and eat these. The result is a poor immune system and much higher chances of GI stasis.

For some rabbits, hay and greens are not enough. Commercial pellets are available. However, many of the commercial brands are filled with toxins like soybean oil and food coloring. Many also contain cereal-like treats, which are not healthy for gut flora and cause obesity. Care needs to be taken when choosing an appropriate pellet. The reason for pellets in the first place was for the food rabbit industry where longevity is not a goal. It was a convenient feeding for large breeding facilities for meat and show but was not designed for a pet house rabbit to live a full life capacity of 10-14 years.

When a healthy pellet has been chosen, feed only about 2 tablespoons per 5 pounds of body weight per day. This small amount will be eaten within 20 minutes to an hour. Always feed pellets with plenty of greens.

Testimonials

I had a breeding female rabbit that got into a fight with another female. The result was a severe tear in the skin around her neck. I immediately used Lavender oil (about 20 drops). I repeated this every 4 hours until I could get her to a vet 3 days later. The vet was amazed that there was no infection and congratulated me when I told him the treatment. The tear could not be stitched, so we continued for 5 days with the oil. She healed perfectly.

-Rowena B.

Calvin and Hobbes were Mini Rex brothers, and both lived to be 12 years and 8 months old! This is way past the life expectancy for rabbits, which is normally 5-10 years. Ten years can usually happen, if they are fed an organic green diet with 80-90 percent hay. No pellets. I have not found any pellets without toxic ingredients. During a molt, which usually happens twice a year for bunnies, it is common for them to have some intestinal stress from ingesting the extra hair. It can turn into GI stasis, which is a life-threatening emergency (like colic in horses). All I would do is rub 1-2 drops of DiGize oil on by fingers and massage into their ears. Within 4-10 minutes, they would be eating and acting completely normal! This happened whenever they had any digestive discomfort, and it worked every time, except once when Hobbes was dehydrated. I had a bag of Lactated Ringers Solution at home and gave him about 35cc. It took him only an hour to start eating.

-Cindy W.

Simon thought he was a person. He was a Blue Dutch that had so much love to give. He suffered with chronic respiratory infections. He HATED to be restrained and given oral antibiotics. After trying lots of oils, the one that worked overnight was Young Living Lavender! I needed to apply it only once, just 1 drop on my finger, and then massaged on his ears. It would last months before respiratory infection came back. As he got older, I started to diffuse Lavender 24/7 right next to his cage to keep his lungs and nose clear. I used the Young Living glass nebulizing diffuser, which is full strength. Sometimes I would add Melaleuca Alternifolia [Tea Tree] to the diffuser with the Lavender. He lived almost 13 years.

-Cindy W.

Reptiles

The reptile family is one of the most diverse in the animal kingdom. This diversity may lead to challenges when trying to care for the health of your reptile. Each species has its own unique health challenges and preferred environment. Independent studying about your reptile's specific needs is crucial to taking care of your pet properly. Knowing and identifying common health issues with your reptile will help you properly care for its individual needs.

Unique challenges to reptiles include managing their exposure to parasites and bacteria; ensuring their diet is adequate and specific to their needs; and keeping their environment not only clean but also making sure the temperature, humidity, and surroundings are also specific to their needs.

Always monitor the overall appearance of your reptile to immediately address signs of sickness or poor health. Signs of poor health may include changes in behavior, changes in eating patterns, and varying appearance (specifically in skin tone, color, and texture). If you are suspicious that your reptile is becoming ill, consult your veterinarian professional immediately.

Reptile Conditions

Burns

Improper heating elements such as hot rocks or caves can cause burns on reptiles, especially snakes.

Recommendations
Singles: Lavender, Copaiba, Myrrh, Lemon, Orange
Blends: Purification, Thieves
Nutritionals: NingXia Red
Additional: Animal Scents Ointment, Thieves Household Cleaner

Application and Usage
Topical: Depending on the severity of the burn, soak your reptile with cool water and 6 drops Lavender infused in ¼ cup Epsom salt. Then remove from water. Apply Helichrysum, Copaiba, and Myrrh on location of burn; cover with a thin layer of Animal Scents Ointment 1-2 times daily. Apply Animal Scents Ointment to reptile as needed.

Continued on page 427

Safety Guidelines When Using Essential Oils with Reptiles

Like most animals, reptiles have a much larger capacity to smell and taste as compared to humans. This is due to an organ called the Jacobson's organ, or vomeronasal organ (VNO). This organ is typically located in the roof of the reptile's mouth and is thought to act as a bridge between a reptile's smell and taste senses, almost making it one combined "hypersense" and not two distinct senses. A common way reptiles will use this sense involves tongue flipping. For example, snakes and salamanders will flip their tongues to gather scents from their surroundings and then press their tongues to the roof of their mouths where the VNO is located. In a sense, they are simultaneously smelling and tasting their surroundings. In this example, you can see how hypersensitive reptiles are to "new" smells and tastes. Keep this in mind when introducing new oils to your reptile.

Even handling reptiles with essential oil residue on your hands may trigger an unforeseen behavior with your reptile. A good way to test an oil is to place a small drop somewhere in your animal's environment and see how your reptile reacts to it. If it is drawn to that area, that oil may work. Also, monitor the reactions when you have certain oils on your person or your hands. Watch for different behaviors or actions.

A reptile's skin is also extremely sensitive. When administering oils, keep in mind to introduce them slowly and keep them diluted from the start until the animal is comfortable with neat application.

Also, be sure to be conscious of hot oils and oils that can have adverse effects on the skin if exposed to sunlight, like some citrus oils. Always have a carrier oil on hand to dilute oils if needed when applying topically. Some reptiles absorb chemicals through their skin. Essential oils can be a great soother to these types of reptiles; and simply holding your reptile with essential oils on your hands will work wonders.

When it comes to introducing oils to your reptile orally, usually citrus oils are preferred. Some methods include spraying diluted oil on food or putting a small amount in your pet's water. Remember to always have a fresh water option available for your reptile.

Ingestion & Oral: Combine NingXia Red with equal parts water and a few drops of Lemon or Orange. Allow for direct ingestion or spray on food before serving.

Inhalation: From at least 6 feet away, diffuse Purification, Thieves, or Lemon to keep down risk of infection.

Other: Dilute 1 capful Thieves Household Cleaner in 28 oz. water. Regularly clean all feeding and watering dishes, living environment, and anything your reptile touches

External Parasites

Ticks are very common on wild-caught stock, especially the Ball Python. Snake mites can quickly spread but are species specific, so they won't harm other reptiles. They are usually concentrated around the eyes, nostrils, and mouth and are very tiny. Also, they may be red or black in color, and their feces can show up as white flakes.

Recommendations
Singles: Lemon, Orange
Blends: Purification, Thieves
Nutritionals: NingXia Red
Additional: Thieves Household Cleaner

Application and Usage
Topical: Add 8 drops Purification to 4 oz. pure water. Mist directly on location of the mites 2-4 times daily. Also spray the same mixture inside the cage 1-2 times weekly.

Ingestion & Oral: Combine NingXia Red with equal parts water and a few drops of Lemon or Orange. Allow for direct ingestion or spray on food before serving.

Inhalation: From at least 6 feet away, diffuse Purification, Thieves, or Lemon to keep down risk of infection.

Other: Dilute 1 capful Thieves Household Cleaner in 28 oz. water. Regularly clean all feeding and watering dishes, living environment, and anything your reptile touches.

Injuries/Wounds

Loss of a tail and various scrapes are very common injuries. If you startle some reptiles, their tail will fall off; and some are just very excitable and nibble on clutch mates' tails. They can also injure themselves in their cages.

Recommendations
Singles: Lemon, Orange, Copaiba, Lavender, Helichrysum
Blends: Thieves, Purification
Nutritionals: NingXia Red
Additional: V-6 Vegetable Oil Complex, Animal Scents Ointment

Application and Usage
Topical: Combine 1 cup Epsom salt with 10 drops each Lavender and Thieves. Put 2 tablespoons of the infused salt into a warm water soak and let the animal soak for 15-30 minutes. Then apply a thin layer of Animal Scents Ointment to the injury 2 times daily. Mix 50/50 Animal Scents and coconut or V-6 oil to use with newer thin-skinned animals. Work up to using Animal Scents full strength, especially on the thinner-skinned lizards. Apply 1-2 drops Helichrysum and Copaiba neat or mixed with Animal Scents Ointment directly on injury location.

Ingestion & Oral: Combine NingXia Red with equal parts water and a few drops of Lemon or Orange. Allow for direct ingestion or spray on food before serving.

Inhalation: From at least 6 feet away, diffuse Purification, Thieves, or Lemon to keep down risk of infection.

Other: Dilute 1 capful Thieves Household Cleaner in 28 oz. water. Regularly clean all feeding and watering dishes, living environment, and anything your reptile touches.

Internal Parasites

Endo-parasitic diseases that infect reptiles can be single-celled protozoa and amoeba, which can cause regurgitation and diarrhea. The parasite coccidia can have an extremely severe form that is difficult to diagnose and treat. These are highly contagious parasites and are a result of dirty caging and drinking water. Improper temperature and humidity can also lead to these issues.

Larger parasitic organisms include various types of worms. Roundworms, hookworms, pinworms, and tapeworms are internal parasites that occur most frequently with wild-caught specimen. However, infected feeders can be a route of infection for reptiles as well. Signs include bloody mucous stools and lack of appetite.

Recommendations
Singles: Lemon, Orange
Blends: Purification, Thieves, DiGize
Nutritionals: NingXia Red
Additional: Thieves Household Cleaner

Application and Usage
Ingestion & Oral: Combine NingXia Red with equal parts water and a few drops of Lemon or Orange. Allow for direct ingestion or spray on food before serving. Also add 1-5 drops DiGize to food or water to support healthy digestion.

Inhalation: From at least 6 feet away, diffuse Purification, Thieves, or Lemon to keep down risk of infection.

Other: For prevention and to remove all parasites, dilute 1 capful Thieves Household Cleaner in 28 oz. water. Regularly clean all feeding and watering dishes, living environment, and anything your reptile touches.

Metabolic Bone Disease

This is a general "catch all" name for vitamin D3 and calcium deficiency. It causes soft bones or shells, swollen joints, tremors, weakness, and more. It is generally caused by poor husbandry, including incorrect temperatures, incorrect humidity, poor diet (not enough calcium and too much phosphorous), and lack of sunlight (vitamin D3 production).

Recommendations
Singles: Copaiba, Orange, Lemon, Tangerine, Grapefruit
Blends: Citrus Fresh
Nutritionals: NingXia Red, MegaCal, OmegaGize[3]

Application and Usage
Topical: Apply Copaiba on all swollen joints as needed throughout the day.

Ingestion & Oral: Combine 1 oz. NingXia Red, a pinch of MegaCal, and 1 dissolved OmegaGize[3]. Administer 1 time daily in food or syringe if needed.

Inhalation: Diffuse Orange, Lemon, Tangerine, or Grapefruit in the room.

Shedding Problems

It seems every reptile will have a shed that is not "complete" from time to time. But lizards that do not shed completely can lose toes or tail tips when the leftover shed is not removed right away.

Recommendations
Singles: Lavender, Lemon, Orange
Blends: Thieves, Purification
Nutritionals: NingXia Red
Additional: Thieves Household Cleaner

Application and Usage
Topical: Add 2 tablespoons Lavender and Thieves infused with Epsom salt or 1 capful Thieves Household Cleaner to a soaking bath and let the animal soak for 15-30 minutes. Then examine all the toes to check for shed that may be stuck. It is always a good idea to check for the spectacle scales on a snake's shed to make sure they are not retained.

Ingestion & Oral: Combine NingXia Red with equal parts water and a few drops of Lemon or Orange. Allow for direct ingestion or spray on food before serving.

Shedding and Skin Conditions

To infuse, use a pint jar of Epsom salt with 15 drops Lavender. Use this for soaking a variety of issues: stuck sheds, minor injuries, scrapes, and minor burns. Add 1 tablespoon per quart of warm water. When an injury is more serious, or for a bearded dragon that is missing half its tail, soak in warm water with ¼ cup Lavender and Epsom salt infusion of 1 capful Thieves Cleaner to 2 gallons of water. This really helps with a more extensive shed issue, and it is great for cleaning and helping heal injuries.

Inhalation: From at least 6 feet away, diffuse Purification, Thieves, or Lemon to keep down risk of infection.

Other: Dilute 1 capful Thieves Household Cleaner in 28 oz. water. Regularly clean all feeding and watering dishes, living environment, and anything your reptile touches.

Stomatitis (Mouth Rot)

Stomatitis is noted by a "cottage-cheese" appearance in the lining of the mouth, oral inflammation, and necrotic tissue. It is usually caused by stress related to poor husbandry, including dirty cage, wrong temperature, wrong humidity, and poor nutrition.

Recommendations

Singles: Copaiba, Helichrysum, Orange, Lemon, Tangerine, Grapefruit
Blends: Citrus Fresh
Nutritionals: NingXia Red
Additional: Thieves Household Cleaner

Application and Usage

Ingestion & Oral: Administer 1 drop each of Copaiba and Helichrysum in mouth or on food 2 times daily. Combine NingXia Red with equal parts water and a few drops of Lemon or Orange. Allow for direct ingestion or spray on food before serving.

Inhalation: Diffuse Orange, Lemon, Tangerine, or Grapefruit.

Other: Dilute 1 capful Thieves Household Cleaner in 28 oz. water. Regularly clean all feeding and watering dishes, living environment, and anything your reptile touches.

Upper Respiratory Infection/Pneumonia

Upper Respiratory Infection is characterized by discharge from mouth or nose, difficulty breathing, holding mouth open, loss of appetite, weight loss, and wheezing or crackling when breathing.

Recommendations

Singles: Copaiba, Lemon, Ginger, Eucalyptus Blue, Ravintsara, Orange
Blends: Raven, R.C., Thieves
Nutritionals: NingXia Red
Additional: Thieves Household Cleaner

Application and Usage

Topical: Apply diluted Eucalyptus Blue, Raven, or R.C. to belly and front legs of affected reptile.

Ingestion & Oral: Combine 1 drop each of Copaiba, Lemon, Ginger, and Eucalyptus Blue. Administer in mouth or in food 2 times daily. Combine NingXia Red with equal parts water and a few drops of Lemon or Orange. Allow for direct ingestion or spray on food before serving.

Inhalation: Diffuse Thieves, Lemon, Raven, R.C., or Ravintsara.

Other: Dilute 1 capful Thieves Household Cleaner in 28 oz. water. Regularly clean all feeding and watering dishes, living environment, and anything your reptile touches.

Testimonial

My Chinese Water Dragon, named Boga, wouldn't eat food on its own; and it didn't swallow food by itself, even if I thrust food into its throat. I was doing everything I could to keep him alive; but after a few months, Boga became thin and couldn't open his eyes or move by himself. I spread Purification around, dripped a drop of it in the wash basin, and let Boga bathe in it. After that, Boga was immediately fine. His skin color came back and became emerald green on the third day of bathing. After a week, Boga was healthier than before.

-Nanako K.

Index

3 Wise Men: 88, 131, 133, 158, 169, 173, 211, 219, 225, 229, 262, 274, 282, 293, 299, 312, 405

Abrasions: 103, 129, 162, 175, 313, 330, 405

Abscess: 154, 168, 179, 192, 234, 253, 256, 261, 266, 270, 284, 285, 306, 308, 322, 324, 326, 336, 341, 369, 411, 418, 420

Absolutes: 12

Abundance: 28, 52, 53, 58, 96, 131, 133, 175, 184, 185, 229, 261, 285, 320, 388, 389, 399, 409, 411

Abuse: 78, 99, 101, 192, 193, 226, 322

Acceptance: 88, 131, 133, 135, 151, 155, 156, 176, 181, 192, 193, 196, 203, 219, 226, 227, 241, 254, 262, 264, 265, 267, 312, 361

Acetonemia: 339

Aches and Pains: 78, 326, 327

Acne: 43, 45, 46, 50, 55, 60, 62-65, 68, 71, 72, 74-76, 78, 80, 82, 154, 224, 298

Adrenal Disease: 211, 387

Afterbirth Not Expelling: 327

Aggression: 100, 156, 193, 194, 197, 264

AgilEase: 107, 128, 155, 157, 168, 170, 196-198, 203, 214, 218-221, 226, 261, 262, 265, 267, 268, 271, 294, 296-299, 307, 309, 315, 316, 390, 399, 403

Air Sac Mite: 356

Alcohols: 5, 12

Aldehydes: 5

AlkaLime: 107, 354, 355, 389, 394

Alkanes: 5, 121

Allergic Dermatitis: 339

Allergies: 3, 6, 15, 51, 66, 108, 154, 155, 159, 162, 163, 171, 172, 194, 200, 206, 216, 224, 226, 239, 272, 275, 277, 283, 288, 343

Allerzyme: 108, 154-157, 159-161, 164, 185, 194, 195, 200, 226, 236, 284, 305, 336, 337, 379, 387-389, 391-396, 401, 402, 404, 405, 412-414, 416, 417

Alpaca: 354

Amazonian Ylang Ylang: 38

Amoebic Gill Disease: 245

Anaplasmosis: 277

Anemia: 143, 157, 194, 195, 225, 277, 281, 288, 339, 347, 360, 369, 388

Anesthesia Detoxification: 261, 327

Anesthesia Support: 335, 337, 387, 400, 414, 416

Angelica: 15, 28, 38, 90-96, 100, 101, 105, 121, 130-133, 148-150, 155, 166, 171, 172, 176, 184, 189, 192-194, 196, 197, 203, 219, 227, 260, 300, 312, 315, 338, 361, 389, 399, 401

Animal Scents Dental Pet Chews: 103, 204, 211, 215, 219

Animal Scents Ointment: 103, 104, 106, 129, 154, 159, 163, 168, 172, 173, 175, 177, 178, 190, 192, 194, 199, 206, 208, 209, 212, 216-218, 221, 223-225, 230, 231, 237, 252-255, 261, 266, 267, 271, 274-276, 282, 285, 288, 291-293, 298-302, 304, 306, 307, 309, 311, 314, 316, 319-321, 324, 326, 327, 329, 330, 332, 333, 337-339, 341, 344, 347, 353, 355, 356, 373, 375, 383, 384, 397-399, 401, 402, 405-407, 411-415, 420, 421, 425, 427

Animal Scents Shampoo: 23, 104, 128, 159, 163, 173, 177, 194, 199, 206, 208, 213, 216, 223-225, 238, 261, 274, 292, 297-300, 302, 304, 306, 337, 338, 397, 401, 402, 415

Anise: 28, 38, 90, 97, 102-104, 108-111, 114, 116, 130, 132, 249

Anorexia: 140, 165, 195, 279, 370

Anthrax: 340

Anxiety: 25, 39, 45, 47, 56, 60, 63-65, 67, 69, 70, 73-75, 78, 79, 81, 82, 85, 89, 97, 101, 124, 129, 153, 156, 158, 174, 176, 192, 194-197, 199, 200, 205, 232, 237, 312

Aplastic Anemia: 388

Apoplexy: 136

Appetite Loss: 346, 362, 388, 400, 403, 409, 418

Appetite, Poor: 155, 170, 173, 175, 297, 342

Application Codes: 130-133

Aroma Ease: 88, 281

Aroma Life: 88, 131, 133, 156-160, 162, 164-167, 174, 175, 185, 194, 198, 205, 211, 212, 215, 219, 232, 266, 277, 280, 290, 293-296, 299, 313, 316, 317, 331, 332, 355, 382, 391, 401, 403, 404

Aroma Siez: 88, 131, 133, 148, 155, 168, 170, 183, 184, 194, 197, 199, 202, 205, 215, 218, 219, 221, 222, 230, 232, 258, 259, 261, 265, 266, 268, 272, 273, 282, 283, 287, 290, 294, 296, 298, 300, 307,

309, 311, 313, 318, 321, 327, 328, 331, 370, 371, 375, 401, 403, 404, 415

Aroma Sleep: 192, 193

ART Renewal Serum: 121, 413

ART Sheerlumé Brightening Cream: 121, 413

Arthritis: 38, 41, 44, 46, 47, 52-55, 58, 59, 61, 65, 69, 71-73, 77, 78, 82, 83, 97, 108, 117, 122, 128, 155, 168, 196, 203, 242, 261, 340, 369

Aspergillosis: 136, 357

Asthma: 50, 78, 85, 155, 171, 253, 271, 273, 390

Atomizing: 21, 283, 284

Aujeszky's Disease: 370

Aural: 21, 395

Australian Blue: 131, 133, 154, 159, 184, 185, 203, 216, 222, 226, 229, 266, 281, 282, 293, 294, 299, 300, 304, 305, 314, 355, 392, 399, 401, 411, 415, 416, 419, 420

Autoimmune Disorders: 262, 277

Avian Chlamydiosis: 138, 357

Avian Encephalomyelitis: 357

Avian Influenza: 137, 357

Avian Metapneumovirus: 358

Awaken: 88, 95, 102, 131, 133, 197, 219

Bacterial Diseases: 245, 375

Bacterial Infections: 155, 161-163, 168, 172, 200, 247, 267, 272, 311, 363, 370, 396

Balsam Canada: 58, 89, 90, 92, 95-97, 99, 100

Barbering: 389, 401

Barking Excessively: 197

Basil: 15, 25, 28, 39, 88, 89, 95, 96, 114, 130, 132, 138, 152-154, 158, 161, 163, 168, 169, 175, 179, 183-185, 194, 197, 198, 201, 204, 206, 213, 215, 218, 221-224, 227-229, 259, 261, 262, 266, 268, 269, 271, 276, 277, 280, 282-284, 288, 290-295, 298, 300, 301, 303, 305, 308, 313, 315, 316, 318, 327, 331, 332, 336, 338, 368, 370, 386, 390-392, 394-396, 398, 406-408, 411, 419, 420

Basil Vitality: 39

Bay Laurel: 48, 61, 89, 116

Bedding: 24, 129, 164, 194, 200, 203, 208, 228, 235, 266, 269, 271, 272, 297, 306, 368, 378, 392, 393, 398, 411, 414, 421

Behavior Modification: 156, 193, 195

Believe: 1, 6, 7, 27, 28, 65, 89, 91, 143, 148-150, 157, 158, 167, 172, 184, 185, 187, 190, 196, 197, 199, 200, 203, 219, 222, 231, 236, 237, 258, 262, 265, 266, 274, 282, 287, 289, 290, 294, 296, 298-300, 304, 309, 316, 322, 329

Bergamot: 15, 28, 39, 52, 88-102, 104, 105, 121-126, 130, 132, 148-150, 154, 156, 167, 174, 184, 185, 196, 197, 203, 222, 223, 229, 285, 291, 300, 324, 338, 398, 399, 411

Bergamot Vitality: 39

Biblical Sweet Myrrh: 40

Bird: 16, 22, 31, 135-150, 356-369

Birthing & Delivery: 171, 222, 263, 264

Birthing and Delivery: 263, 264

Bite Buster: 89

Bitter Orange: 69, 88, 93, 94, 96, 97

Black Pepper: 40, 90, 94, 96, 98, 107, 109, 115, 130, 132, 163, 164, 184, 185, 192, 201-203, 208, 213, 215, 216, 218, 227, 229, 263, 264, 267, 285, 291, 292, 294, 296, 299-303, 310, 313, 314, 328, 329, 331, 333, 336, 337, 352, 353, 398, 406, 408, 409

Black Pepper Vitality: 40

Black Quarter: 328

Black Spruce: 41, 69, 88-102, 104, 105, 107, 123, 148-150, 155-158, 169, 170, 173, 174, 176, 184, 192, 193, 196-199, 203, 206, 218, 219, 221, 222, 226, 254, 261, 262, 265, 266, 268, 271, 273, 277, 281-283, 286, 290, 293, 294, 296, 298, 303, 304, 307, 309, 312, 313, 315, 316, 324, 326, 327, 329-334, 346, 347, 355, 366, 376, 379, 380, 382, 390, 391, 396, 402, 405, 408, 417, 419, 421

Blackhead: 137

BLM: 108, 155, 157, 168, 170, 196-198, 203, 218-221, 226, 232, 236, 241, 261, 262, 265, 267, 268, 271, 294, 297-299, 307, 309, 315, 316, 390

Bloat: 328, 340, 352, 354, 381, 389

Blockage: 137, 155, 167, 174, 268, 271, 342, 343, 376

Blood Clots: 56, 156, 158, 274

Blood Disorders: 156, 157

Blue Cypress: 41, 88-90, 92, 96, 98, 99, 101, 105, 122, 160, 163, 164, 170-172, 176, 184, 185, 198, 200, 201, 203, 215, 216, 222, 223, 226-229, 266, 269, 274, 276, 282, 285, 289, 292-295, 299-301, 304, 307, 309, 310, 314, 315, 336, 371, 401, 411, 413-415, 419

Blue Eye Disease: 370

Blue Tansy: 41, 88, 90, 92, 94, 97-102, 105, 112, 122, 184, 185, 274, 338

Bluetongue: 340

Body and Environment: 121

Body Care Products: 121

Bone Conditions: 265

Bone Fracture: 390

Bordetellosis: 358

Boredom: 152, 182, 197, 200, 216

Bottle Babies: 328

Botulism: 328, 358

Bovidae: 325, 326

Bovine Tuberculosis: 335

Brain Abscess: 308, 336

Brain Power: 89, 131, 133, 158, 170, 172, 197, 200, 211, 219, 225, 229, 278, 291, 295, 336, 407

Breathe Again Roll-On: 156, 171, 184, 185, 194, 199, 200, 202, 215, 222, 229, 269, 272, 273, 283, 285, 333, 335, 375, 380, 391, 408

Breathing Issues: 390, 391

Broken Bones: 157, 197, 329, 371

Broken Horns: 329

Bronchitis: 46, 50, 66, 98, 302, 341, 363, 366

Brucella Canis: 198

Bruised Soles: 266

Build Your Dream: 89

Bumblefoot: 137, 138, 142

Burns: 52, 61, 62, 72, 95, 124, 147, 371, 425, 429

Calamus: 41, 91

Calcium Metabolism: 391

Calluses: 198, 213, 222

Canadian Fleabane: 42, 94, 108, 109

Cancer: 38, 46-48, 50, 53, 57, 68, 70, 73, 74, 76, 77, 110, 111, 129, 136, 157, 158, 168, 169, 172, 173, 199, 206, 213, 228, 230, 235-237, 241, 253, 266, 295, 312, 405

Candidiasis: 138, 141, 359

Canine: 23, 124, 125, 130-133, 181, 184-186, 188, 192, 196, 202, 205, 214, 215, 220, 223, 224, 229, 236, 241, 354

Canker: 266, 267, 368

Capillaria: 138, 141

Carboxylic Acids: 5

Cardamom: 28, 42, 88, 89, 96, 101, 102, 114, 116, 184, 200, 291, 313, 336, 350, 389, 394, 399

Cardamom Vitality: 42

Cardiomyopathy: 156, 158, 165, 167

Carrot Seed: 28, 43, 104, 124, 168, 184, 195, 198, 217, 234, 252, 291, 355, 388, 403

Carrot Seed Vitality: 43

Caseous Lymphadenitis: 341

Cassia: 28, 43, 91, 94, 97, 98, 102, 109, 116, 130, 132, 261, 266, 277, 278, 280, 285, 291, 298, 299, 301, 305, 308-311, 314, 315

Castration: 267, 282, 334

Cats: 9-11, 16, 17, 20, 22, 24, 30, 31, 107, 108, 117, 130-133, 151-170, 172-175, 178, 236, 278, 378, 398

Cattle: 10, 17, 32, 325, 328, 330, 331, 334, 383, 384

Cattle Measles: 330

Cedarwood: 28, 43, 45, 88-90, 92-96, 98-101, 122, 123, 130, 132, 136, 143-146, 148-150, 156, 158, 159, 161, 164-167, 170, 172, 174, 176, 184, 185, 192, 193, 195-197, 200-203, 211, 212, 215, 219, 222, 225-229, 236, 241, 269, 272, 274, 278, 283, 284, 287, 292, 294, 295, 299, 303, 307, 311-314, 316, 326, 327, 329, 333, 335, 336, 342, 349, 354, 358, 364, 365, 375, 381, 390, 396-400, 408, 413, 415, 417, 419

Cel-Lite Magic Massage Oil: 122, 217, 270, 277, 294, 295, 298-300, 311, 316

Celery Seed: 28, 44, 92, 94, 130, 132, 168, 184, 195, 207, 209, 217, 291, 388

Celery Seed Vitality: 44

Cellulitis: 276

Cervidae: 325, 326

Chapter: 19, 25, 87, 94, 141, 152, 158, 185, 274, 355

Chemistry: 13, 37, 49, 51, 87, 91, 152, 182, 209

Chewing: 83, 103, 129, 200, 216, 231, 242, 318, 346, 393, 399, 400

Chickens: 31, 137, 138, 142, 356, 357, 359-365, 367-369

chinchilla: 385, 389-392, 395, 401, 406, 411, 416

Chinese water dragon: 429

Chlamydiosis: 138, 341, 357

Choking: 103, 110, 251, 268

Christmas Spirit: 28, 89, 131, 133, 147, 184, 185, 197, 204, 222, 229, 285, 291, 292, 298, 309, 396, 412

Cinnamon Bark: 9, 28, 44, 88-92, 95, 96, 101, 105, 111, 114, 116, 124-126, 129, 130, 132, 152, 184, 185, 208, 220, 223, 227, 229, 261, 266, 267, 274, 284-286, 289, 291, 298, 299, 301, 308-310, 314, 315, 331, 334, 338, 378-381, 394, 399, 407, 408, 419

Cinnamon Bark Vitality: 44

Cistus: 28, 44, 75, 93, 95-97, 100, 102, 104, 128, 130, 132, 157, 168, 173-175, 184, 185, 195, 201, 205, 208-212, 214-216, 219, 221, 222, 227, 229, 242, 248, 262, 263, 267, 274, 281, 282, 293, 299, 300, 305, 326, 329, 331, 338, 345, 361, 363, 364, 368, 369, 371-373, 381, 394, 402, 414, 418, 420

Citronella: 28, 45, 60, 89, 96-98, 104, 105, 130, 132, 163, 184, 185, 206, 208, 229, 278, 288, 291, 292, 301, 311, 313, 337, 340, 341, 373, 381, 396, 398, 406, 413

Citrus Fresh: 16, 28, 32, 89, 131, 133, 155,

158, 160, 162, 163, 167, 174, 184, 197, 199, 200, 203-205, 207, 209-213, 217, 219, 225, 263, 264, 277, 300, 335, 338, 354, 355, 380, 381, 384, 388, 389, 393, 396, 406, 412-414, 416, 417, 428, 429

Citrus Fresh Vitality: 89

Citrus Hystrix: 45, 90, 92, 96, 99-101, 105

ClaraDerm: 122, 154, 159, 163, 168, 172, 173, 175, 218, 223, 224, 252, 263, 264, 267, 274-276, 282, 284, 293, 299, 300, 302, 304, 337, 339, 355, 356, 400, 401, 406, 407, 420, 421

Clarity: 63, 75, 89, 91, 96, 156, 170, 184, 185, 197, 200, 214, 218, 219, 222, 229, 295, 300, 309, 311, 313, 316, 326, 327, 329, 331, 332, 336, 337, 382, 401

Clary Sage: 11, 28, 45, 90, 93, 94, 96, 99, 101, 108-110, 122, 130, 132, 185, 207, 250, 263, 286, 336, 388, 390, 410, 417

Clove: 9, 28, 31, 46, 81, 88, 90, 93-95, 97, 101, 105, 107-109, 111-114, 116, 122-126, 129, 130, 132, 152, 156, 157, 160, 169, 184, 185, 192, 199, 203, 204, 207, 208, 210, 211, 218, 220, 221, 223-230, 234, 241, 253, 261, 262, 266, 267, 269, 272, 274-280, 283, 285, 289-294, 296-302, 304, 307, 309-315, 317, 327, 329, 331-333, 335, 336, 338, 340-342, 347, 353, 373, 378, 380, 381, 387, 394-396, 398, 399, 404, 406-408, 411, 412, 416-419, 421

Clove Vitality: 46

Clubfoot: 268

Coccidiosis: 139, 342, 359

Coffin Bone Infection: 267

Cognitive Dysfunction: 200

Cold and Influenza: 268

Cold Compress: 19, 316

Cold or Influenza: 330

Colds: 50, 58, 62, 66, 74, 78, 98, 128, 268, 391

Colibacillosis: 342

Colic: 52, 106, 128, 250, 253, 269-271, 275, 281, 285, 287, 289, 291, 297, 299, 305, 313, 319, 322-324, 328, 354, 423

Columnaris: 246

Combava: 45

ComforTone: 108, 201, 208, 210, 379, 392

Common Sense: 14, 15, 31, 89, 131, 133, 183, 219, 336, 338

Conjunctivitis: 159, 200, 279, 343, 364, 378, 380, 392, 393, 408

Constipation: 159, 201, 269, 392, 394, 400

Contagious Ecthyma: 342, 346

Contracted Tendons: 271

Cool Azul: 90, 122, 129, 196-198, 203, 219-221, 252, 253, 261-263, 265-268, 271, 274, 276-278, 281, 284, 287, 288, 290, 294-301, 304, 307, 309, 311, 313-316, 327, 329, 331-333, 390, 403

Cool Azul Pain Relief Cream: 122, 129,

196-198, 203, 219-221, 252, 253, 261-263, 265, 266, 268, 271, 278, 281, 287, 290, 294-301, 304, 307, 309, 313, 316, 327, 329, 331-333, 403

Cool Azul Sports Gel: 122, 129, 196, 203, 219-221, 252, 253, 261-263, 265, 266, 268, 271, 276-278, 281, 287, 290, 294-298, 301, 304, 307, 309, 311, 314-316, 327, 331-333, 403

Copaiba: 28, 31, 32, 46, 47, 89-91, 96, 100, 105-107, 122, 123, 128, 130, 132, 136-150, 152, 154-175, 179, 184, 185, 189, 192, 194-230, 232, 233, 236-239, 241, 245-248, 252, 261-316, 326-334, 339-353, 358-376, 380-382, 387, 389-392, 394-412, 414-420, 425, 427-429

Copaiba Vitality Balsam Copaiba: 46

COPD: 271

Coprophagia: 201

Coprophagy: 393

Coriander: 28, 47, 88, 89, 91-96, 99-102, 104, 105, 121-125, 130, 132, 160, 185, 205, 220, 229, 274, 286, 289, 321, 328, 329, 388, 389, 401, 402, 404, 409

Coriander Vitality: 47

Corn Toxicity: 336

Cornea: 138, 165, 201

Corns: 272

Coronaviral Enteritis: 359

Coronavirus: 163, 202, 229

CortiStop: 108, 387, 388

Coryza: 139, 364

Cough: 58, 154, 165, 170, 202, 215, 234, 253, 268, 269, 271-273, 282, 302, 319, 322, 335, 352, 365, 366, 374

Coumarins: 5

Courage: 46, 55, 69, 96, 101, 102, 203, 236, 319

Cramp: 110, 139

Crop Impaction and Stasis: 359

Cruciate Ligament Injury: 203

Cryptosporidiosis: 360

Cumin: 28, 47, 48, 93, 97, 103, 104, 109, 116

Cushing's Disease: 108-110, 273, 274

Cuts: 58, 78, 82, 95, 97, 103, 106, 175, 251, 274, 280, 287, 289, 299, 301, 316, 324, 326, 330

Cypress: 12, 25, 41, 48, 88-90, 92, 96, 98-101, 105, 122, 130, 132, 141, 142, 148, 150, 153, 155-160, 162-165, 168, 170-172, 175, 176, 179, 183-185, 192, 193, 196, 198, 200, 201, 203, 207, 209, 211, 213-216, 218-220, 222, 223, 225-230, 248, 255, 259, 261-263, 265-272, 274, 276-282, 285, 287, 289, 290, 292-296, 298-301, 304, 307-310, 313-318, 321, 327, 336, 370-373, 375, 376, 378, 386, 390, 394, 398, 401, 403-405, 409, 411, 413-415, 418-420

Cystitis: 46, 81, 203, 228, 269, 342

Dalmatia Bay Laurel: 48

Dalmatia Juniper: 48

Dalmatia Sage: 49

Dandruff: 65, 78, 159, 347

Davana: 49, 88, 90, 92, 97-102, 105, 122, 123

Deep Relief Roll-On: 129, 155, 157, 168, 170, 184, 196, 199, 203, 216, 219, 221, 222, 226, 253, 261, 262, 265, 266, 268, 271, 274, 281, 285, 287, 288, 292, 294-296, 298, 304, 307, 309, 316, 327, 331, 332, 370, 390, 403, 419

Deer: 277, 288, 291, 325, 329, 335-338

Dehydration: 138, 140, 147, 161, 201, 286, 289, 299, 305, 336, 342, 343, 351, 367, 374, 375, 379, 381, 388, 392, 394, 400, 402, 403, 409, 412

Dental Disease: 203, 274, 393

Dental Disorders: 159, 164, 173

Detoxification: 8, 9, 19, 21, 55, 94, 108, 117, 183, 204, 261, 313, 327

Detoxzyme: 108, 160, 161, 164, 168-170, 173-175, 192, 194, 195, 199-202, 204, 205, 207-213, 217-221, 223-230, 238, 253, 270, 271, 276, 278, 287-291, 301, 302, 305, 314, 336, 340, 353, 388, 392-396, 403-409, 412, 418

Deworming: 160, 173, 204, 275, 297, 334, 343

Diabetes: 43, 46-50, 53, 68, 73, 106, 160, 166, 172, 174, 205, 206, 214, 273, 321

Diabetes Mellitus: 174, 273

Diarrhea: 54, 81, 139, 140, 143, 148, 154, 161, 164, 170, 179, 188, 205, 210, 220, 221, 256, 269, 275, 276, 286, 297, 299, 304-306, 328, 336, 340, 342, 343, 346, 351, 353, 357, 359, 362, 363, 367, 370, 375, 379, 381, 394, 400, 403, 412, 418, 428

Diet: 13, 103, 107, 109, 111, 113, 147, 148, 151, 154, 155, 157-161, 164, 165, 167, 172-174, 178, 181, 190, 192, 194-196, 200, 204, 206, 210, 211, 214, 216, 224, 228, 238, 247, 251, 269, 283, 288, 290, 299, 313, 331, 339, 350, 355, 361, 372, 393, 400, 402-404, 411, 417, 422, 423, 425, 428

Diffusing: 8, 9, 17, 20, 21, 135, 136, 153, 157, 163, 164, 171, 182, 190, 196, 198, 211, 225, 284, 334-339, 358, 363, 364, 369, 399, 411, 421

Digest & Cleanse: 109, 185, 192, 195, 199-202, 205-208, 210, 213, 220, 222, 225, 230, 276, 281, 283, 284, 290, 291, 299, 313, 336, 340, 379, 380, 388, 389, 391, 392, 394-396, 399, 408, 409, 411, 412, 419

DiGize: 28, 90, 128, 129, 131, 133, 136-150, 154-157, 159-162, 164, 165, 167-175, 179, 184, 185, 192, 194, 195, 200-202, 204-210, 213, 215, 217-221,

223, 227-230, 232, 236, 238, 241, 247, 248, 252, 253, 255, 256, 261, 264, 266-268, 270, 271, 274-279, 281, 284-293, 296-306, 308-316, 318, 319, 322, 323, 326-328, 330-334, 336, 338-355, 357-363, 366-372, 374-376, 379-382, 384, 387-389, 391-394, 396, 398, 400-404, 407, 409-412, 414, 418, 421, 423, 428

DiGize Vitality: 128, 253, 255, 256, 275

Dill: 28, 49, 103, 111, 130, 132, 160, 166, 167, 184, 205, 220, 263, 264, 274, 287, 289, 300, 321, 336, 354, 355, 388, 399, 409, 414

Dill Vitality: 49

Dilution: 7-10, 19-22, 27, 30, 37, 93, 95, 97, 98, 100, 104, 105, 126, 130-133, 144, 152-155, 157, 160-173, 175, 176, 182, 249, 265, 279, 293, 378-380, 386, 393, 399, 407, 408, 419

Dipped Shoulder: 371

Disease: 2, 44, 46, 48, 66, 69, 72, 75, 80, 81, 94, 97, 98, 107-110, 114, 136, 137, 139-142, 144-146, 148, 149, 151, 156, 157, 159-161, 163-171, 175, 179, 182, 196, 202-204, 206, 209, 211, 213-215, 217, 223, 225, 227, 228, 234, 245, 246, 248, 262, 268, 269, 271-275, 277-279, 283, 286, 288, 289, 291, 294-296, 300, 301, 303, 306, 311, 312, 315, 317, 328, 330-334, 336, 337, 340-342, 344-348, 350, 352, 354, 357-366, 368-372, 374, 375, 387, 393, 397, 403, 407, 411, 418, 428

Distemper: 161, 172, 175, 179, 229, 253, 273, 298, 378, 394

Divine Release: 90, 192, 193

Dogs: 7-10, 17, 29-32, 107-111, 113, 117, 130-133, 165, 175, 178, 181-183, 185-192, 194-206, 208-211, 213-222, 224-231, 234-237, 239-243, 273, 369, 378, 398

Dorado Azul: 50, 51, 89, 90, 93, 100, 104, 105, 116, 122, 130, 132, 143, 154, 156, 162, 163, 171, 172, 184, 185, 195, 196, 200, 207, 214-216, 219, 222, 223, 226, 229, 269, 272, 276, 278-280, 282-284, 291, 292, 294-296, 298, 300, 302, 303, 305, 309, 313, 316, 335, 375, 378, 390, 391, 394, 399, 408, 411

Douglas Fir: 50, 124

Dragon Time: 122, 131, 133, 207, 222, 286

Dragon Time Massage Oil: 122

Dream Catcher: 88, 89, 131, 133, 219, 299

Duck Viral Hepatitis: 360

Dysentery: 343, 375

Ear Fungus: 276, 297

Ear Infection: 161, 228, 233, 395, 411, 421

Ear Masses: 395, 417

Ear Mites: 129, 177, 206, 398

Ear Plaque: 276

Ectoparasites: 360

Edema: 150, 175, 276, 277, 279, 284, 353, 376

Egyptian Gold: 131, 133, 137, 149, 150, 154, 163, 165, 166, 169, 171, 172, 184, 185, 198, 199, 202-204, 206, 210, 213, 214, 216, 218, 222, 223, 225, 227, 229, 237, 261, 267, 269, 273, 276, 278, 280, 282, 283, 285, 291-293, 298-300, 302-306, 308-312, 314, 315, 324, 329-333, 336-338, 354, 371, 373, 378, 380, 381, 394, 395, 399, 405, 408, 409, 411, 412, 416-420

Ehrlichia: 277

Elemi: 11, 28, 50, 90, 97, 105, 122, 123, 130, 132, 212, 219, 220, 294-296, 300, 326, 327, 329-333, 338, 382, 395

Elimination: 108, 109, 111, 167, 174

En-R-Gee: 131, 133, 156, 184, 189, 197, 199, 214, 222, 263, 264, 272, 285, 287, 289, 294, 296, 298-300, 313, 316, 387, 410, 418

Encephalitis: 200, 277, 278, 288, 370

EndoFlex: 28, 90, 131, 133, 159, 160, 166, 167, 184, 207, 214, 218, 274, 286, 287, 289, 293, 299, 321, 354, 355, 387, 388, 391, 401, 402, 406, 407, 409, 411, 417

EndoFlex Vitality: 90

EndoGize: 109, 207, 214, 274, 286, 287, 289, 355, 356, 387, 391, 417

Enteritis: 359, 363, 367, 396

Enterotoxemia: 343

Environmental Care: 126

Environmental Terrain: 394, 396, 400, 407, 409-412, 415, 418, 419

Envision: 131, 133

Epilepsy: 78, 225, 397

EPM: 262, 278

Epulis: 206

Equine: 105, 130-133, 249, 250, 252-256, 261, 262, 267-269, 272-274, 276-284, 286, 288, 289, 293, 296, 303, 309, 313, 314, 317, 323, 328, 354, 355

Equine Herpes Virus: 278, 279

Equine Viral Arteritis: 279

Escherichia Coli: 140

Essentialzyme: 109, 158-163, 165, 166, 168, 169, 171, 174, 185, 193, 199-202, 204, 205, 208-211, 215-220, 225, 227, 229, 230, 232, 238, 255, 276, 290, 293, 312, 316, 335-337, 354-356, 379, 380, 387-389, 391-393, 395, 397, 399, 401-406, 408-412, 414, 416-419

Essentialzymes-4: 109, 158, 185, 193, 195, 196, 203, 205, 207, 210, 219, 220, 236, 255, 289, 290, 316, 389, 391, 392, 397, 399, 409, 412, 414, 416, 419

Esters: 5

Estro: 110, 214, 222, 286

Ethers: 5

Eucalyptus Blue: 51, 89, 100, 130, 132, 141-144, 147, 150, 156, 161, 163, 165, 171, 172, 184, 185, 198, 200-202, 213, 215, 222, 229, 230, 269, 272, 278-283, 285, 299, 300, 303, 305, 306, 312, 315, 330, 333, 335, 357-361, 363-365, 367, 368, 374, 378, 390, 394, 408, 411, 419, 429

Eucalyptus Citriodora: 51, 98, 100

Eucalyptus Globulus: 28, 51, 52, 73, 89, 98, 100, 123, 129, 130, 132, 143, 144, 147, 154, 156, 159, 160, 162-164, 169, 171, 174, 184, 185, 198, 200-202, 206, 222, 224, 226, 229, 241, 245, 269, 272, 276, 278-285, 288, 291, 292, 294, 297, 299-301, 303, 305, 306, 308, 310-312, 314-316, 330, 333, 336-338, 356, 363, 373, 380, 381, 390, 408, 419

Eucalyptus Radiata: 52, 89, 98, 100, 101, 111, 123-126, 129, 130, 132, 143, 144, 147, 156, 163, 171, 184, 185, 198, 200-202, 215, 222, 229, 272, 278, 285, 300, 303, 306, 307, 312, 315, 317, 327, 330, 333, 335, 352, 363-365, 370, 375, 378, 380, 390, 392, 395, 398, 399, 408-410, 412, 413

Eucalyptus Staigeriana: 52, 89

Euthanasia: 176, 178, 236, 323

Evergreen Essence: 91, 131, 133, 155, 156, 167, 184, 222, 266, 296, 298, 300, 309, 327, 330-332, 380, 381

Exodus II: 106, 128, 129, 131, 133, 136-138, 142-147, 149, 150, 154, 157, 158, 161, 163, 165, 171, 184, 185, 192, 198-207, 210, 213, 215, 216, 218, 221-223, 227-230, 256, 261, 264, 266-269, 272-285, 287, 289, 291-293, 298-306, 308-312, 314, 315, 319, 326, 327, 329-331, 333, 335-338, 343-347, 352, 354, 357-361, 364-368, 370, 373, 375, 380, 381, 396, 399, 403-405, 407, 408, 410-412, 416-419, 421

Exotic: 9, 16, 32, 100, 114, 121, 328, 377, 378, 410

External Parasites: 128, 145, 146, 154, 159, 172, 205, 208, 212, 326, 427

Eye Conditions: 162, 201, 280, 293, 343

Eye Tears: 397

False Pregnancy: 109, 110, 171, 207, 348

Fatty Liver: 55, 56, 62, 83, 162, 168, 206, 361

Fatty Liver Hemorrhagic Syndrome: 361

Fatty Liver Syndrome: 162, 168

Feather Pecking and Bullying: 361

Feelings Kit: 192, 196, 260

Feline: 11, 17, 124, 125, 130-133, 151-155, 157-159, 161-165, 167, 170, 172, 177-179

Feline Immunodeficiency Virus: 157, 162, 178

Feline Infectious Peritonitis: 163
Feline Leukemia: 157, 162, 164, 172, 177, 178
FemiGen: 110, 214, 286
Fennel: 28, 52, 88, 90, 94, 95, 97, 99, 102-104, 108-112, 114, 116, 122, 130, 132, 160, 161, 165, 170, 171, 173, 184, 185, 195, 201, 203-205, 207, 210, 220, 229, 242, 249, 250, 263, 264, 268, 275, 281, 286, 287, 289, 297, 312, 333, 338, 354, 355, 376, 380, 389, 390, 392, 393, 398, 403, 404, 407, 414, 418
Fennel Vitality: 52
Ferret: 32, 387, 388, 400, 402
Fever: 49, 138, 140, 149, 154, 165, 175, 179, 207-209, 217, 227, 235, 262, 268, 269, 277-282, 298, 299, 302, 308, 311, 313, 321, 335, 337, 340, 344, 345, 348, 349, 351, 352, 354, 369, 371-374, 379, 380, 398, 401, 407, 408
First Aid: 27, 106, 197, 204, 212, 252, 265
Fish: 16, 111, 115, 116, 148, 245-248, 384
Flea Infestations: 163
Fleas: 73, 128, 157, 163, 172, 208, 216, 232, 237, 381, 398, 406, 413
Fleas and Ear Mites: 398
Fluke or Flat Worms: 140
Foot and Mouth Disease: 354
Foot Rot: 331
Foreign Object: 208, 378, 392, 400
Forgiveness: 88, 90, 93, 131, 133, 156, 158, 176, 184, 192-194, 196, 199, 223, 260, 262, 267, 387
Fowl Cholera: 140, 361
Fowlpox: 361
Fractures: 93, 157, 231, 254, 265, 371, 390
Frankincense: 11, 28, 31, 32, 40, 50, 53, 54, 64, 71, 77, 88-96, 98-102, 104, 105, 107, 108, 113, 117, 122, 123, 125, 129, 130, 132, 137, 139, 141, 148-150, 152, 154-160, 162-164, 166-176, 178, 179, 184, 185, 189, 191-201, 203, 206, 208-214, 216, 217, 219-222, 225-229, 231-233, 236-239, 241-243, 246, 248, 253, 261-263, 265, 271, 274, 277, 280, 282, 286, 287, 293, 295-297, 299, 300, 304, 305, 309, 311, 312, 315, 318-320, 323, 324, 327, 329-336, 338, 340, 341, 359, 363, 369-371, 373, 375, 376, 378, 382-384, 387-391, 395, 397, 400-406, 409, 414, 416, 417, 419-421
Frankincense Vitality: 53
Freedom: 91, 100, 105, 192, 193
French Moult: 141
Frereana Frankincense: 53, 54
Frostbite: 141, 190
Frounce: 138, 141, 368
Fungal Diseases: 246, 247
Fungal Infections: 41, 43, 51, 55, 57, 65, 68, 69, 71, 72, 76, 80, 187, 246, 322, 344, 351, 399

Fur Chewing: 399
Furanoids: 5
Furunculosis in Farmed Salmon: 246
Galbanum: 54
Gallbladder: 55, 64, 72, 78, 79, 92, 108, 168, 208, 209
Gangrenous Dermatitis: 362
Gapeworms: 142
Gastric Dilatation Volvulus: 209
Gastric Ulcers: 209, 281, 369, 371, 414
Gastroenteritis: 349, 400
Gastrointestinal Foreign Body: 400
Gastrointestinal Stasis: 400
Gathering: 23, 91, 131, 133, 184, 185, 193, 219, 226, 229, 234, 300
Genesis Hand & Body Lotion: 122, 339, 355, 356, 413
GeneYus: 92, 170, 219, 229
Gentle Baby: 92, 128, 129, 131, 133, 137, 141, 142, 148-150, 155, 156, 159, 162, 166, 168, 171-176, 184, 185, 197, 222, 225, 263, 264, 282, 287, 293, 296, 297, 299, 300, 307, 312, 313, 315, 350, 365, 372, 373, 389, 394, 401, 409, 413, 415
Geranium: 11, 28, 54, 88-96, 98-102, 104, 105, 112, 121-125, 128-130, 132, 154, 162, 168-174, 178, 184, 185, 188, 189, 192, 195, 196, 198, 203, 205-207, 210, 213, 215, 216, 220, 222-224, 228, 229, 232, 242, 261, 263, 264, 266, 267, 274, 276, 277, 282, 284, 285, 288, 289, 291, 295, 299, 304, 311, 312, 314, 329, 331-336, 356, 360, 392, 394-396, 398-400, 405-413, 415, 417, 419
Gerbil: 395, 397, 403, 404, 409, 411, 412, 415, 417, 418
German Chamomile: 28, 55, 88, 90, 92, 97-102, 105, 108, 112, 116, 122, 155, 156, 159, 162, 168, 172, 173, 184, 185, 192, 193, 196, 198, 216, 219, 222, 226, 234, 252, 262, 266, 269, 274, 276-278, 280, 284-286, 289, 291, 293, 295, 299-301, 338, 380, 389, 399, 411, 413
German Chamomile Vitality: 55
GI Conditions: 210
Giardia: 164, 210, 275, 362, 379
The Gift: 100, 131, 133, 172, 173, 175, 176, 184, 185, 194, 198-201, 223, 229, 266, 272, 276, 278, 282, 283, 285, 291-293, 298-300, 304, 305, 310, 312, 314, 315, 329, 333, 338, 378, 393, 394, 419, 420
Ginger: 28, 55, 88, 90, 94-97, 102-104, 108-111, 114, 116, 130, 132, 136, 138, 139, 143, 147, 149, 154, 155, 159, 161, 162, 164, 167, 169, 171, 172, 184, 192, 195, 198, 201, 205, 208-210, 213, 214, 220, 221, 228-230, 232, 246, 261, 262, 267, 268, 274, 276, 279, 281, 282, 285-287, 299, 315, 327, 328, 331, 336-340, 354, 355, 360, 361, 366, 367, 372, 374, 375, 379, 380, 387, 389,

392-394, 398, 400, 402, 405, 406, 408, 409, 412, 414, 416-419, 429
Ginger Vitality: 55
Gingivitis: 61, 159, 164, 203, 210
Girth Galls: 282, 305
Glässer's Disease: 372
Glaucoma: 162, 164, 211
GLF: 92, 131, 133, 154, 157, 162, 168, 184, 195, 204, 207, 209, 217, 220, 228, 232, 235, 261, 274, 277, 286, 289, 291, 312, 313, 336, 392, 404, 409, 416
GLF Vitality: 92
Goat: 117, 328, 339-341, 344, 347, 348, 350, 353
Goat Pox and Sheep Pox: 344
Goldenrod: 28, 56, 89, 116, 130, 132, 184, 237, 272, 286, 291, 292, 303, 408
Goose Parvovirus Infection: 362
Gout: 72, 142
Grapefruit: 12, 15, 28, 56, 88-90, 92, 96, 98, 99, 101, 113, 116, 118, 122, 130, 132, 148-150, 158, 162, 168, 169, 173, 175, 184, 197-199, 204, 207, 212, 215-217, 225, 241, 251, 261, 277, 289, 291, 294, 305, 308, 312, 316, 320, 376, 387, 388, 395, 399, 402, 406, 416, 428, 429
Grapefruit Vitality: 56
GRAS: 15, 27, 28, 31, 47
Grass Tetany: 331
Gratitude: 28, 176, 184, 192, 223, 264, 299, 300
Greasy Heel: 282
Grooming: 15, 19, 22, 23, 104, 151, 152, 215, 237, 304
Grounding: 41, 48, 50, 58, 66, 69, 73, 76, 81, 82, 92, 93, 99, 131, 133, 156, 157, 171, 192-194, 196, 216, 217, 219, 225-227, 263, 274, 278, 280, 281, 287, 300, 311, 312, 314, 324
Guinea Pig: 388, 389, 396, 403, 405, 409, 412, 414, 418
Gums: 27, 30, 46, 83, 157, 177, 182, 195, 200, 204, 206, 210, 211, 231, 238, 243, 388, 393, 394, 416
Haemoproteus: 142
Hair Coat: 9, 151, 159, 170, 273, 337, 381, 400, 404, 412, 418
Hair Loss Syndrome: 336
Hairballs: 164
Hardware Disease: 331
Harmony: 75, 84, 88, 92, 93, 102, 121, 131, 133, 152, 154, 156, 158, 166, 167, 171, 174, 185, 192-197, 219, 225, 226, 232, 260, 262-265, 296, 297, 300, 312, 361, 389, 399, 401
Heart Conditions: 165, 211
Heart Murmur: 401
Heartworm: 165, 171, 211, 235, 237, 243
Heat Stress: 345, 354
Heat Stroke: 148, 213, 229, 289, 401
Heaves: 271, 282, 283, 317

Hedgehog: 417-419

Helichrysum: 11, 28, 56, 88-92, 94, 95, 97, 100, 101, 105, 106, 122, 123, 128-130, 132, 141-150, 152, 154-160, 162-165, 167-170, 172-175, 179, 184, 185, 194-201, 203-222, 225-229, 231-233, 236, 239, 242, 252, 254, 255, 261, 262, 265-268, 270-272, 274, 276-278, 280-286, 289-296, 298-310, 313-319, 322, 324, 327, 329-332, 335-337, 340, 343, 349, 353, 368-370, 372, 373, 375, 376, 382, 387, 390, 392, 395, 397, 401, 403, 404, 407, 409, 414-416, 418-420, 425, 427, 429

Helminthiasis: 362

Hematoma: 242, 272, 372

Hemorrhagic Enteritis Marble Spleen Disease: 363

Hemorrhagic Septicemia: 248, 345

Hendra Virus: 283

Herpes: 39, 41, 44, 51, 52, 55, 56, 64, 66, 67, 72, 74, 76, 142, 247, 277-279

Herpesvirus: 165, 171, 229, 364

Hexamitiasis: 363

Highest Potential: 88, 92, 131, 133, 158, 185, 193, 195, 197, 219, 254, 260, 264, 300, 371

Hinoki: 57, 90, 94, 95, 97, 99, 104, 105, 143, 154-156, 159, 162, 171, 184, 185, 192-194, 196, 200, 222, 227, 229, 265, 272, 273, 283, 284, 288, 292, 300, 301, 326, 330, 334, 344, 347, 353, 362, 372, 382, 396, 398, 412, 413, 419

Histiocytoma: 212

Hit by Car: 174, 212

Hives: 29, 284, 288, 313

Hong Kuai: 57, 89, 158, 169, 172, 173, 184, 185, 197, 199, 200, 206, 213, 219, 222, 224, 225, 227, 229, 272, 276, 291, 292, 300, 310, 390, 394, 398, 411, 412, 418

Hoof Abscess: 261, 284

Hoof Infections: 254, 285

Hope: 2, 55, 89, 93, 101, 131, 133, 158, 163, 173, 174, 176, 179, 184, 192, 196, 219, 223, 231, 238, 274, 284, 287, 320, 323, 401

Hormonal Disorders: 286

Horner's Syndrome: 213

Horses: 9, 10, 13, 17, 29, 32, 109, 110, 125, 183, 231, 249-253, 256-261, 266-275, 277-284, 286, 288-294, 296, 297, 299-302, 304-307, 309-311, 313-315, 317, 319-322, 324, 325, 423

Hospice Care: 176

Hot Spots: 213, 216

housing: 205, 212, 341, 354-356, 368, 378-381, 387-412, 414-421

Humility: 93, 95, 131, 133, 184, 193, 223, 226, 282, 312

Hypertension: 42, 56, 59, 63, 66, 69, 70, 72, 74, 75, 80, 83, 85, 100, 166, 215, 289

Hyperthermia: 213

Hyperthyroidism: 165-167, 173, 206

Hypertrophic: 156, 158, 165, 167

Hypoadrenocorticism: 286

Hypocalcaemia: 345

Hypocalcemia: 354, 355, 391

Hypothyroidism: 109, 110, 214, 224, 228, 242, 355

Hyssop: 28, 57, 90-93, 95, 96, 98, 100-102, 104, 105, 130, 132, 143-146, 154, 156, 162, 163, 169, 171-173, 184, 185, 198-200, 202, 204, 213, 222, 227, 229, 250, 267, 269, 272, 275, 282, 288, 291-293, 297, 299-305, 311, 316, 331, 336, 356, 366, 373, 380, 390, 394, 403, 404, 408, 409, 411, 419

Ichthyophthirius multifiliis: 246

ICP: 110, 201, 210, 256, 275, 284, 297, 331, 356, 380, 392-394, 399, 408

Idaho Balsam Fir: 28, 58, 89, 90, 92, 95-97, 99, 100, 104, 106, 108, 148-150, 155-158, 167-170, 172-174, 176, 184, 185, 192, 193, 196-200, 203, 206, 216-222, 225, 226, 233, 239, 241, 254, 261, 262, 265-269, 271, 274, 277, 281, 282, 286, 287, 289, 290, 293, 294, 296-298, 300, 304, 307, 309, 312, 313, 316, 327, 330, 335, 340, 344, 351, 365, 366, 370, 373, 387, 389-391, 395-397, 403, 405, 406, 411, 416, 417, 421

Idaho Blue Spruce: 58, 88, 89, 91-96, 98, 99, 101, 102, 116, 148-150, 155-158, 168-174, 176, 184, 185, 192, 193, 196, 198, 199, 203, 206, 218, 219, 221, 222, 226, 261, 263, 265-269, 271-273, 277, 281, 283, 286, 290, 293, 294, 296, 298, 303, 304, 307, 309, 312, 313, 315, 316, 327, 330, 340, 351, 376, 390, 395-397, 405, 416, 417, 419, 421

Idaho Ponderosa Pine: 58

Idaho Tansy: 59, 89, 98, 105, 106, 129, 175, 212, 216, 239, 252, 258, 274, 288, 292, 297, 301

Iditarod: 2, 186, 188-191

ImmuPower: 128, 131, 133, 137, 145-147, 149, 154, 157, 160, 161, 163, 165, 166, 171, 173, 175, 184, 185, 194, 198-203, 207-210, 213-216, 218, 221-224, 227-230, 237, 241, 262, 274, 278-283, 285, 287, 291-293, 297-300, 303, 305, 306, 308-315, 318, 324, 330, 334-337, 341, 348-350, 352, 354, 358, 359, 366-368, 370, 371, 375, 378-380, 384, 388, 392, 394-396, 398, 399, 405, 406, 408, 410, 411, 416, 417, 419

ImmuPro: 110, 111, 129, 158, 169, 173, 192, 194, 198-200, 202, 206, 229, 269, 278, 280, 281, 292, 293, 305, 312, 335, 337, 354, 378-380, 388, 392, 394, 395, 398, 402, 405, 406, 410, 412, 416-420

Impaction: 143, 269, 270, 287, 328, 359

Impaction Colic: 269, 270, 287

Inappropriate Urination: 167, 174

Incontinence: 109, 110, 214, 228

Indigestion: 38, 42, 61, 67, 90, 345

Infect Away: 93, 95, 97, 104, 129, 154, 159-162, 168, 169, 171-173, 175, 184, 185, 200, 201, 204, 206, 207, 212, 213, 216, 218, 222-224, 227, 229, 255, 267, 274, 276, 282, 288, 291-293, 299-302, 304, 311, 326, 333, 335, 338, 344, 346, 347, 354, 355, 369, 373, 378-381, 390, 392, 395, 399, 401, 406, 408-412, 414, 415, 418-421

Infections: 38, 39, 41-46, 49-53, 55, 57, 58, 60-63, 65-69, 71-77, 80-82, 98, 112, 147, 155-157, 159, 161-164, 167-169, 172, 174, 178, 187, 198-200, 202, 206, 207, 216, 217, 222, 225, 228, 246, 247, 254, 256, 264, 267, 272, 274, 278, 280, 285, 291, 302, 311, 322, 331, 332, 334, 337, 343, 344, 346, 351, 354, 363, 365-368, 370, 375, 391, 396, 399, 406, 407, 413, 419, 421, 423

Infectious Bronchitis: 363

Infectious Bursal Disease: 363

Infectious Coryza: 139, 364

Infectious Laryngotracheitis: 364

Inflammation: 25, 45, 53, 58, 63, 72, 85, 90, 95, 97, 106-108, 115, 128, 138, 147, 155, 162, 164, 168, 169, 174, 187-189, 191, 200, 203, 205, 209, 210, 214, 215, 217, 220, 226, 228, 231, 232, 235, 239, 247, 253, 261, 262, 266, 268, 270, 275-278, 282, 287, 288, 290-293, 295, 297, 298, 301, 302, 304, 306, 309, 310, 314, 315, 321, 327, 331-333, 340, 350, 373, 396, 401, 403, 411, 429

Inflammatory Bowel Disease: 72, 159, 206, 214

Injuries: 100, 169, 170, 172, 190, 197, 201, 212, 240, 252, 254, 280, 282, 295, 309, 333, 427, 429

Inner Child: 93, 131, 133, 155, 156, 158, 167, 176, 192-198, 203, 216, 217, 219, 226, 260, 264, 281, 312, 361, 387, 399, 406, 421

Inner Defense: 111, 185, 192, 195, 200, 202-205, 207, 210-213, 215-218, 221-225, 227-230, 237, 269, 275-278, 280, 281, 283, 289, 291, 296, 298, 300, 301, 303, 305, 308-311, 314, 335-340, 375, 378-381, 391-394, 408

Inner Harmony: 93, 193, 361

Insect Bite: 288, 291

Inspiration: 96, 131, 133, 197, 203, 219, 312, 335, 391

Insulin Resistance: 251, 273, 289, 321

Insulinomas: 402

Internal Parasites: 29, 128, 170, 171, 297, 326, 407, 428

Intestinal Torsion: 372

Into the Future: 131, 133, 192, 196, 218, 260, 267, 401

InTouch: 94

Introduction: 1-3, 135, 151, 181, 249, 385

Irritable Bowel Syndrome: 108, 187, 188, 402

Ishpingo: 59, 70

Jade Lemon: 59, 126, 130, 132, 138, 140-142, 359, 368, 396

Jade Lemon Vitality: 59

Jasmine: 12, 28, 60, 64, 88-96, 98-101, 105, 121-124, 130, 132, 148-150, 172, 174, 176, 185, 200, 225, 277, 392, 397, 413

Johne's Disease: 346

Joint Issues: 403

Joy: 28, 65, 69, 88, 89, 94, 101, 131, 133, 151, 156, 158, 165, 167, 191-193, 196, 197, 203, 205, 211, 217, 219, 254, 260, 264, 277, 318, 326-332, 335, 376, 378, 382, 387, 402, 406

Juniper: 28, 48, 60, 88, 90, 92, 93, 95-97, 103, 104, 108, 112, 116, 122, 123, 130, 132, 142, 164, 166-168, 170, 172, 174, 175, 184, 185, 198-201, 203, 205, 213-218, 228, 229, 234, 255, 261, 262, 266, 276-278, 282, 286, 289, 291, 293-295, 300, 309, 314, 317, 336, 353-356, 376, 381, 390, 395, 398, 403, 404, 407, 409, 411, 412, 418-420

JuvaCleanse: 28, 94, 131, 133, 154, 157-159, 162, 164, 167-169, 184, 195, 199, 204, 205, 207, 209, 217, 220, 228, 235, 261, 262, 270, 274, 277, 283, 286, 289, 291, 295-297, 312, 313, 324, 335, 336, 349, 379, 387, 388, 392, 396, 403, 404, 409, 417

JuvaCleanse Vitality: 94

JuvaFlex: 28, 94, 131, 133, 154, 157, 159, 162, 168, 175, 184, 195, 204, 207, 216, 217, 228, 235, 277, 291, 299, 335, 336, 379, 387, 388, 392, 404, 409

JuvaFlex Vitality: 94

JuvaPower: 111, 163, 291, 301, 302, 324, 353, 395

JuvaSpice: 111, 291, 335, 387, 388, 392, 394, 395, 408, 416

JuvaTone: 111, 201, 204, 207, 217, 228, 230, 289, 291, 335, 336, 379, 387, 388, 402, 409, 410, 412, 416

K&B: 112, 142, 143, 162-164, 168, 169, 175, 199, 200, 203, 204, 209, 214, 215, 220, 227, 228, 232, 242, 255, 277, 284, 289, 291, 304, 328, 333, 339, 342, 353, 355, 356, 379, 386, 394, 403, 404, 418

Kennel Cough: 202, 215

Ketones: 5, 49, 355, 388

Ketosis: 354, 355, 388

Kidney Disease: 165, 166, 206, 211, 214, 215, 225, 289, 403

Kidney Disorders: 46, 214, 404

Kidney Failure: 157, 166, 167, 178, 255, 295

KidScents MightyVites: 112, 114

KidScents MightyZyme: 112, 114

Kitty Litter: 153, 156

Kitty Raindrop: 153, 155, 156, 158, 171, 175

Koi Herpes: 247

Labial Dermatitis: 346

Lacerations: 147, 168, 201, 216, 274, 289, 309, 369

Lactate or Lactic Acid: 331

Lactones: 5

Lady Sclareol: 131, 133, 172, 286, 338

Lameness: 168, 219, 254, 262, 265, 266, 284, 294, 307, 315, 328, 331, 334, 340, 369, 372, 403, 412

Laminitis: 267, 274, 281, 289, 290, 299, 315, 317, 321, 323

Large Roundworm: 372

Laurus Nobilis: 28, 48, 61, 89, 130, 132, 152, 154, 162, 165, 169, 184, 185, 198-204, 215, 218, 223, 224, 227, 229, 261, 262, 267, 269, 272, 276, 277, 283, 291, 298-300, 305, 308, 309, 314, 316, 333, 336, 338, 375, 395, 397, 398, 401, 405, 409, 410, 419, 421

Laurus Nobilis Vitality: 61

LavaDerm Cooling Mist: 123, 154, 159, 168, 172, 173, 216, 217, 252, 274, 275, 282, 284, 337, 339, 354-356, 400, 401, 420, 421

Lavandin: 20, 21, 28, 61, 62, 97, 98, 104, 105

Lavender: 11, 20, 21, 28, 61, 62, 64, 78, 88-93, 95-101, 104-106, 110, 117, 122-125, 128-130, 132, 136, 138, 139, 141-143, 146, 149, 150, 152, 154-156, 158, 159, 162, 165-179, 183-185, 192-194, 196-201, 205-207, 209, 211-214, 216, 218-222, 224-228, 230-232, 234, 236-239, 241, 252, 261, 263-269, 271, 272, 274, 277, 280-282, 284-290, 293-302, 304, 307, 309, 311-313, 315, 318-320, 322, 324, 326-339, 341, 343-345, 354-356, 361, 362, 364, 365, 369, 372, 373, 375, 378, 381-384, 387-389, 391, 392, 394-402, 405, 406, 408-417, 420, 421, 423, 425, 427-429

Lavender Hand & Body Lotion: 123, 339, 355, 356, 413

Lavender Vitality: 61

Lead Poisoning: 143, 404

Ledum: 62, 90, 92, 94, 129, 130, 132, 154, 158, 162, 168, 175, 179, 184, 207, 217, 228, 232, 262, 274, 286, 289, 291, 312, 338, 347, 353, 355, 360, 361, 387, 388, 398, 402-405, 411, 416, 417

Lemon: 7, 12, 15, 28, 32, 52, 59, 62-64, 66, 67, 88-92, 94-96, 98-101, 104, 105, 108, 109, 111-116, 118, 122-126, 130, 132, 136-138, 140-143, 145, 147-150, 154-161, 163, 167-169, 173-175, 184, 185, 192, 194, 195, 197, 199-202, 204, 209-211, 214, 217, 219, 222, 225, 228-230, 234, 235, 246, 247, 261, 262, 267, 269, 273-277, 280, 282, 285, 289, 291-294, 300, 305, 308, 312-315, 317, 318, 328, 330-336, 340, 341, 346, 348-359, 361-363, 366-368, 378-383, 385, 388, 391, 392, 394, 396-399, 403-405, 408-412, 414, 418, 419, 425, 427-429

Lemon Myrtle: 63, 64, 96, 137, 138, 141, 142, 147, 148, 150, 156, 160, 184, 185, 199, 217, 222, 229, 276, 293, 359, 361, 381, 399, 409, 411, 412, 418, 419

Lemon Vitality: 59, 62

Lemongrass: 28, 63, 71, 84, 90, 93, 96, 97, 103, 104, 108, 110, 111, 115, 116, 118, 123, 128-130, 132, 143, 144, 146, 150, 156, 157, 160, 163, 165, 167, 168, 170, 172, 174, 184, 185, 189, 192, 196-199, 202-204, 206, 208, 212-218, 220-230, 232, 235, 238, 239, 261-263, 265-269, 271-273, 275-280, 282, 283, 285-294, 296-311, 313-319, 324, 327, 329-332, 334-336, 338, 357, 362, 364, 365, 368-371, 373-375, 378-381, 390, 391, 394, 396, 399, 403-409, 411-413, 418, 419, 421

Lemongrass Vitality: 63

Leptospirosis: 293, 370, 379

Leucocytozoonosis: 143

Lice: 22, 46, 73, 104, 143, 145, 290, 304, 336, 337, 343, 346, 364, 381

Lick Granuloma: 216

Life: 0-2, 5, 6, 10, 11, 16, 19, 22, 26, 35, 37, 48, 67, 88, 90, 92-94, 96, 101, 107, 113, 115, 125, 128, 129, 131, 133, 136-145, 147-152, 154-177, 184, 185, 192-196, 198-233, 235-239, 247, 254, 260, 263-267, 269, 271-278, 280-283, 287, 290, 291, 293-318, 320, 323, 324, 326, 328, 329, 331, 332, 335-337, 339-353, 355, 357-369, 378, 380-382, 388, 389, 391-405, 407-412, 414, 416, 418-423

Light the Fire: 94, 299

Lime: 12, 28, 45, 64, 88, 89, 94, 96, 98, 100, 108, 113, 114, 118, 126, 294

Lime Vitality: 64

Lipoma: 217, 271

Live Your Passion: 94, 219

Liver Disease: 75, 168, 170, 206, 217, 225, 277, 291, 295

Liver Fluke: 347

Livestock: 17, 29, 32, 130-133, 198, 301, 325, 376

Llama: 354

Longevity: 28, 32, 65, 78, 94, 113, 131, 133,

149, 154, 157, 158, 163, 168, 169, 173, 184, 185, 192, 196-203, 205, 206, 208, 210-214, 216, 217, 222-227, 229, 230, 238, 241, 253, 261, 262, 266, 267, 269, 270, 273, 275, 276, 281, 283-285, 287, 288, 290-294, 296, 298-302, 305-311, 314, 315, 335-341, 350, 352, 353, 373, 375, 378, 380, 381, 387, 392, 394-396, 401-412, 416-419, 422

Longevity Softgels: 94, 113, 185, 192, 196, 197, 200-202, 205, 206, 208, 211-214, 217, 222-227, 229, 230, 253, 267, 273, 283, 284, 298, 308, 311, 314, 335-337, 339, 373, 375, 378, 380, 381, 387, 392, 394-396, 401-412, 416-419

Longevity Vitality: 94

Lumps: 199, 225, 298, 332, 405

Lumpy-Skin Disease: 332

Lyme Disease: 227, 277, 291, 337, 352

Lymphoma: 169, 405

M-Grain: 28, 131, 133, 164, 184, 185, 199-201, 219, 223, 229, 261, 267, 282, 283, 285, 290, 291, 293, 294, 296, 298-300, 304, 307, 309, 313, 410

Maggots: 144, 320, 384

Magnify Your Purpose: 131, 133, 197, 219

Malaria: 40, 51, 144

Mammary Glands: 169, 207, 298, 313, 406

Mandarin: 12, 28, 64, 85, 89, 96, 98, 117

Mange: 169, 177, 223, 292, 337, 338, 347, 373, 406, 407

Manuka: 65, 154, 159, 162, 206, 210, 216-218, 224, 228, 276, 277, 300, 301, 314, 315, 338, 355, 375, 378, 379, 407, 413-415

Marek's Disease: 142, 364

Marjoram: 25, 28, 65, 88, 90, 95, 96, 98, 100, 118, 122, 123, 130, 132, 153, 158, 165, 168, 170, 175, 183, 185, 199, 211, 214, 216, 218, 219, 221, 232, 239, 242, 258, 259, 261-263, 266, 268, 271, 273, 282, 290, 294, 296, 300, 304, 307, 309, 313, 327, 370, 371, 375, 386, 392, 399, 401

Marjoram Vitality: 65

Massage: 9, 17, 22, 25, 26, 37, 48, 73, 87, 104, 105, 122-125, 128, 172, 183, 189, 190, 196-198, 201, 203, 217-221, 226, 253, 254, 258, 259, 261-264, 266, 268-271, 273, 276, 277, 280, 281, 285-288, 290-301, 304, 307, 309, 311, 313, 315-318, 321-323, 331-333, 375, 390, 398, 403, 413, 423

Massage Oil: 9, 105, 122-124, 128, 183, 189, 196-198, 203, 217-221, 226, 253, 259, 261-263, 266, 268-271, 277, 280, 285-288, 290-301, 304, 307, 309, 311, 313, 315-317, 321, 322, 331-333, 375, 390, 403, 413

Mast Cell Tumor: 169, 242

Master Formula: 113, 114, 201, 203, 205, 207, 209, 354, 355, 390, 393, 397, 400, 401, 403, 408, 415, 416, 419

Mastitis: 169, 217, 264, 332, 347, 373, 384

Mastrante: 66, 94, 205, 273, 289, 291, 336, 378, 409, 413, 421

Megaesophagus: 218

Melaleuca Ericifolia: 66, 184, 185, 192, 222, 229, 322, 331

Melaleuca Quinquenervia: 66, 90, 95, 105, 122, 130, 132, 152, 184, 185, 222, 229, 267, 273, 277, 278, 280, 281, 285, 291, 297-299, 302, 304, 305, 308-311, 314, 315, 331, 338

Melanoma: 232, 241, 292

Melioidosis: 348

Melissa: 28, 31, 32, 67, 89-94, 96, 98, 115, 122, 129, 142-146, 150, 154, 160, 161, 163, 165, 169, 171, 177, 184, 185, 194, 202, 207, 213, 216, 218, 221, 222, 228-230, 247, 262, 269, 273, 276-281, 283, 284, 288, 291, 293, 300, 301, 305, 308, 311, 314, 335, 336, 351, 364-368, 373, 378, 394, 397, 407, 410, 419, 421

Melrose: 106, 129, 131, 133, 139, 140, 143, 144, 149, 154, 159, 169, 171-173, 175, 178, 179, 184, 185, 192, 198-204, 210, 212, 213, 215, 216, 218, 221-224, 227-230, 241, 252-256, 258, 261, 264, 266, 267, 269, 272-274, 276-278, 280-283, 285, 288, 291-293, 297-306, 309-311, 314-316, 318, 320-322, 324, 326, 327, 331, 332, 335, 337-344, 346-348, 350, 351, 353, 357, 361, 362, 364-366, 369, 372-374, 380, 384, 393, 395, 396, 399, 407-412, 415, 417-421

Mendwell: 93, 95, 97, 104, 129, 154, 159, 160, 162, 168, 169, 173-175, 184, 185, 200, 201, 206, 212, 216, 218, 223, 229, 255, 265, 267, 271, 274, 282, 292-294, 298-300, 302, 311, 313, 330, 333, 338, 344, 346, 347, 354, 369, 372, 373, 375, 376, 390, 395, 401, 410, 411, 413-415, 418, 420, 421

Metabolic Bone Disease: 144, 428

Metritis: 348, 373

Micromeria: 67

MindWise: 114, 165, 166, 172, 173, 185, 193, 195, 200, 211, 212, 214, 215, 218, 219, 225, 226, 229, 262, 278, 282, 289, 292-296, 298, 299, 301, 302, 304, 314, 316, 336, 401, 402, 404, 408, 410, 413, 414

Mineral Essence: 114, 128, 129, 138, 140-142, 144, 148-150, 157, 159, 160, 162, 164-168, 185, 192, 193, 195-199, 201, 203-205, 209, 211, 213, 214, 216-229, 232, 238, 252, 262-264, 267, 272, 274-278, 280-289, 291-316, 331, 340, 341, 345, 346, 349-351, 354-356,

359, 365, 369, 378, 386, 388, 389, 391-394, 398, 399, 401-403, 405, 406, 408, 418-420

Mismothering: 264

Mister: 131, 133, 189, 222, 250, 286, 417

Mites: 106, 126, 129, 161, 169, 177, 206, 216, 292, 347, 356, 365, 373, 381, 398, 401, 406, 413, 427

Molting: 365

Monoterpenes: 5

Moon Blindness: 293

Motivation: 74, 91, 94, 95, 101, 131, 133, 197, 212, 219, 401

Mountain Savory: 9, 28, 67, 93, 97, 100, 104, 106, 130, 132, 138, 152-154, 163, 175, 184, 185, 192, 195, 198, 202-204, 213, 215, 216, 218, 220-223, 227-229, 249, 253, 256, 258, 261, 263, 264, 266-269, 273, 275-278, 280, 281, 283, 285, 291-294, 297-301, 303-306, 308-310, 314, 315, 330, 332, 334, 335, 337, 351, 352, 358, 369, 371, 373, 378-381, 391, 394, 396, 399, 407-409, 411, 412, 418, 419, 421

Mountain Savory Vitality: 67

MultiGreens: 114, 115, 144, 157-160, 162, 163, 165, 166, 168-171, 173-176, 185, 192, 195-202, 204-207, 213, 214, 219-221, 225, 227-229, 232, 265, 267, 274, 276-278, 280-283, 288-294, 298, 299, 301-305, 308, 313, 314, 326, 327, 333, 335, 355, 356, 370, 373, 391-395, 397-407, 410, 412, 415, 416, 419, 421

Muscle Wasting: 218

Muscular Conditions: 61, 294

Mycoplasma: 184, 365, 374, 411

Mycoplasmosis: 348

Mycotoxicoses: 275, 366

Myopathy: 332, 377

Myrrh: 28, 40, 50, 68, 88, 90-93, 95, 96, 98, 100, 102-104, 106, 109, 119, 122-124, 129, 130, 132, 138, 141, 144, 149, 154, 158, 160, 162, 166-169, 171-173, 175, 176, 179, 184, 185, 191, 192, 198, 199, 204, 206, 208-210, 212, 214-219, 222, 223, 227, 229, 230, 237, 238, 252, 256, 261-264, 266, 267, 274, 276, 277, 280, 282, 284, 286, 292, 296, 298-300, 304, 305, 308, 309, 319, 320, 326, 327, 331-336, 338, 340, 343-348, 351, 352, 354, 355, 361-364, 368, 371, 373, 375, 378, 382, 387, 393-395, 399, 405, 406, 409-411, 413-420, 425

Myrtle: 28, 63, 64, 68, 89, 90, 93, 95-98, 100, 104, 112, 118, 119, 129, 130, 132, 137, 138, 141, 142, 147, 148, 150, 156, 160, 169, 171, 172, 184, 185, 199, 214, 215, 217, 222, 223, 229, 262, 269, 272, 273, 276, 283, 286, 293, 300, 301, 316, 330, 333, 335, 355, 359, 361, 381, 391,

395, 399, 408-412, 418, 419
Nasal Bots: 338
Navel Bleeding: 373
Navicular Syndrome: 294
Nebulizing: 21, 402, 411, 423
Neroli: 12, 28, 69, 88, 93, 94, 96, 97, 130, 132, 155, 156, 174, 185, 192, 193, 195-197, 203, 219, 226, 229, 338, 378, 396, 399, 413
Nervous System Disorders: 295
Neurologic Conditions: 106, 172, 218
Neurological Conditions: 169
Neurological Disease: 278, 407
Newcastle Disease: 144, 366
Niaouli: 66, 90, 95, 105, 122
NingXia Nitro: 115, 200, 295
NingXia Red: 29, 30, 32, 98, 115, 136, 137, 139-141, 143-150, 152-176, 178, 179, 185, 192-230, 232, 234-236, 238, 240, 261-269, 271-275, 277-318, 326-334, 336, 337, 339-355, 358-371, 373, 375, 376, 378-382, 384, 386-420, 425, 427-429
Ningxia Wolfberry: 112, 113, 115-119
Nitrate Poisoning: 349
Northern Lights Black Spruce: 69, 90-102, 104, 105, 107, 123, 148-150, 155-158, 169, 170, 173, 174, 176, 184, 192, 193, 196, 198, 199, 203, 206, 218, 219, 221, 222, 226, 254, 261, 262, 265, 266, 268, 271, 273, 277, 281-283, 286, 290, 293, 294, 296, 298, 303, 304, 307, 309, 312, 313, 315, 316, 326, 327, 329-334, 346, 347, 355, 366, 376, 379, 380, 382, 390, 391, 396, 402, 405, 408, 417, 419, 421
Nutmeg: 28, 69, 90, 94-96, 115-118, 130, 132, 184, 197, 216, 262, 274, 277, 278, 281, 286, 287, 289, 295, 333, 338, 379, 387, 389, 392, 394, 396, 399, 402, 406, 417-419
Nutmeg Vitality: 69
Nutrition: 1, 112, 136, 141, 144, 159, 232, 245, 251, 305, 313, 328, 354, 393, 402, 429
Nutritional Supplements: 107, 305, 355, 356
Nutritional Support: 94, 107, 110, 119, 268
Obedience Training: 197, 219, 227
Ocotea: 59, 70, 88, 89, 92-96, 98-101, 104, 106, 108, 116, 117, 130, 132, 136, 138-142, 149, 154, 155, 160-165, 169, 170, 172, 173, 184, 185, 192, 194, 195, 197, 200-205, 210, 213, 216, 218-224, 227, 229, 248, 253, 266, 269, 272-278, 280, 282, 283, 286-293, 296, 297, 299-301, 304, 305, 307, 308, 310, 311, 314, 321, 330, 331, 337, 338, 351, 357, 359, 368, 388, 389, 394, 399, 401, 402, 405, 408, 411, 412, 416, 419, 421
OmegaGize3: 115, 116, 160, 164-166, 170, 172-175, 185, 192-200, 203, 205, 207, 209, 211-221, 224-227, 229, 230, 232,

235, 236, 238, 278, 293-296, 298, 299, 301, 302, 304, 314, 336, 337, 378, 393, 394, 397, 401, 402, 406-408, 411, 413, 416, 419, 428
Onchocerciasis: 296
Oola Balance: 95
Oola Faith: 196, 203
Oola Family: 394
Oola Field: 219
Oola Finance: 96
Oola Fitness: 96
Oola Friends: 96
Oola Fun: 197, 219
Oola Grow: 96, 203
Open Wounds: 106, 129, 255, 309, 316, 351
Oral Drops: 30
Orange: 12, 15, 28, 32, 56, 69, 70, 88, 89, 91-97, 99-101, 105, 111-113, 115-118, 126, 130, 132, 136, 141-144, 148-150, 155, 156, 158, 161, 166-168, 170, 176, 192, 193, 195-199, 203, 204, 209, 212, 216, 217, 219, 241, 263, 264, 291-294, 296, 297, 301, 304, 307, 308, 312, 313, 316, 318, 335, 359-361, 364, 365, 378, 384, 388, 389, 392, 393, 395, 398-401, 403, 405, 406, 412, 416, 417, 421, 425, 427-429
Orange Vitality: 70
Oregano: 9, 25, 26, 28, 37, 71, 73, 90, 93, 104, 105, 111, 114, 122-124, 130, 132, 138, 152, 153, 161, 163, 164, 179, 183-185, 192, 198, 201-205, 208, 210, 213, 215, 216, 218, 220-223, 225, 227-230, 234, 237, 249, 250, 254, 256, 258, 259, 261, 264-267, 269, 272, 273, 275-278, 280, 281, 283-285, 287, 291-293, 296, 298, 299, 301, 303, 305, 308, 310, 311, 314, 315, 318, 319, 322, 330, 331, 333-335, 337, 338, 341, 342, 347-350, 353, 359-361, 369-375, 378-380, 384, 386, 394, 396, 399, 407, 408, 411, 412, 419
Oregano Vitality: 71, 256
Ortho Ease Massage Oil: 123, 183, 196-198, 203, 218-221, 226, 261-263, 269, 271, 280, 285-288, 293-301, 304, 307, 309, 311, 313, 315, 316, 331-333, 390, 403
Ortho Sport Massage Oil: 123, 128, 189, 196-198, 203, 218-221, 226, 253, 259, 261-263, 266, 268, 269, 271, 280, 285, 287, 288, 290-301, 304, 307, 309, 311, 313, 315-317, 321, 322, 331-333, 375, 390, 403
Osteomyelitis: 366
Owie: 97
Oxides: 5
Pain: 6, 20, 22, 23, 25, 29, 30, 45-47, 50, 57-59, 65, 67, 69, 72, 82, 83, 87, 95, 97, 98, 106, 108, 111, 112, 122, 128, 129, 154-156, 159, 168, 170, 173, 176, 178, 190, 193, 196-199, 203, 218-221, 225,

226, 228, 230-233, 236, 239, 243, 252-255, 261-263, 265, 266, 268-271, 274, 278, 280-282, 285, 287, 290-292, 294-301, 303, 304, 306, 307, 309, 310, 313, 314, 316, 324, 326, 327, 329, 331-333, 337, 340, 352, 368, 369, 372, 379, 383, 397, 403, 414, 419
Palmarosa: 28, 71, 89, 91, 92, 94-96, 100, 101, 104, 105, 122-124, 130, 132, 154, 162, 169, 171-173, 175, 184, 185, 199, 204, 216, 219, 222, 223, 252, 261-263, 267, 274, 277, 280, 282, 285, 291, 297, 299-302, 304, 305, 329, 337, 338, 346, 399, 406, 407, 411, 413-415, 419, 420
Palo Santo: 71, 89, 91-93, 95-98, 100, 101, 104-106, 129, 130, 132, 155, 157, 163, 168, 170, 173, 175, 176, 184, 185, 196-199, 203, 212, 214, 216, 219, 221, 222, 226, 227, 236, 258, 261-263, 265, 266, 268, 272, 281, 282, 288, 290-294, 296, 298, 300, 304, 305, 307, 309, 311, 313, 316, 324, 327, 329, 331, 332, 336, 338, 370, 388, 394, 395, 398, 401, 403-406, 409, 411, 416, 417, 420
PanAway: 97, 106, 128, 129, 131, 133, 155-157, 168, 170, 174, 175, 184, 196, 198, 199, 203, 213, 216, 218-221, 223, 226, 232, 233, 238, 242, 253, 261-263, 265-268, 271, 272, 274, 281, 285, 287, 288, 290-292, 294-298, 304, 307, 309, 313, 315, 316, 318, 327, 329, 331, 332, 340, 369-371, 373, 375, 376, 382-384, 390, 403, 418, 419
Pancreatitis: 170, 206, 220, 229, 238
ParaFree: 116, 129, 142, 145, 154, 155, 161, 163, 170, 173, 174, 185, 192, 195, 205-208, 210, 212, 219-221, 223, 224, 227, 230, 235, 236, 274-276, 278, 284, 291, 296, 297, 301, 302, 322, 330, 332, 334, 336-338, 340, 343, 347, 352, 353, 362, 369, 372, 374, 380, 389, 391, 392, 394, 396, 406, 408, 409
ParaGize: 97, 104, 128, 129, 138-140, 145, 154, 157, 159-162, 164, 165, 168, 170, 173, 174, 179, 184, 185, 194, 195, 201, 203, 204, 208, 210, 212, 216, 220, 221, 223, 224, 227, 229, 241, 247, 248, 256, 271, 275, 291, 292, 296, 300, 301, 304, 326, 331-334, 336-338, 341-343, 346, 347, 352, 353, 359, 360, 362, 369, 372, 374, 376, 378, 380, 382, 389, 391, 392, 394-396, 400, 406-409, 414, 419
Parasite Diseases: 247
Parasites: 29, 39, 45, 46, 49, 53, 57, 63, 66, 73, 79, 84, 97, 104, 128, 129, 143, 145, 146, 148, 154, 155, 157, 159, 161, 168-173, 204, 205, 208, 211, 212, 220, 224, 229, 245, 247, 248, 253, 262, 270, 274, 275, 288, 293, 297, 302, 311, 326, 333, 338, 339, 341, 355, 356, 360, 374, 380, 382, 394, 407, 425, 427, 428

Parvo: 175, 221

Parvovirus: 161, 202, 229, 362, 374

Patchouli: 28, 72, 79, 88, 90, 93-95, 97, 100, 101, 103-105, 108, 116, 124, 130, 132, 140, 145, 154, 155, 159-166, 169, 170, 172, 173, 175, 179, 184, 185, 196, 199-201, 204, 206, 210, 213, 216, 218, 220-224, 226, 252, 261, 262, 266, 267, 274-276, 281, 282, 285-288, 291, 292, 296, 297, 299-301, 306, 309-311, 313, 315, 318, 319, 328, 338, 357, 373, 392, 395, 399, 400, 409, 411-413, 415

Patella: 22, 221

PD 80/20: 116, 207, 214, 219, 286, 287, 295

Peace & Calming: 38, 61, 91, 92, 97, 128, 129, 131, 133, 136, 147-150, 155-158, 161, 162, 165-172, 174-176, 183, 192, 193, 195-198, 203, 209, 212, 215-217, 219-222, 225, 226, 232, 233, 236-239, 242, 252, 254, 255, 263-265, 268, 270, 274, 276, 280, 281, 285-287, 289, 290, 293-295, 297, 304, 307, 312, 313, 315, 316, 320, 321, 324, 326, 348, 350, 361, 365, 380, 383, 387, 389, 394, 397, 399, 402, 406, 411, 415, 421

Peace & Calming II: 97, 136, 174, 192, 193, 196, 212, 219, 222, 254, 255, 263, 268, 270, 280, 295, 312, 313, 316

Pelodera: 297

Peppermint: 15, 25, 28, 31, 32, 72, 79, 88-91, 94-105, 108, 109, 111, 112, 114-116, 119, 122-125, 128-130, 132, 143, 153, 155, 157, 159-164, 167, 168, 170, 171, 173, 175, 179, 183-185, 189, 194-197, 200, 201, 204, 205, 207-210, 213-215, 218-222, 228-230, 232, 234, 242, 246-253, 259, 261-264, 268-271, 273-288, 290-292, 294, 296-299, 301, 303-305, 307-309, 311, 313-319, 321-324, 328-340, 343-349, 352-356, 358-360, 362, 370-376, 379, 380, 383, 384, 386, 387, 389-394, 398, 400, 402, 407, 409, 412, 414, 417, 419

Peppermint Vitality: 72, 128

Periostitis: 298

Pesticide Poisoning: 349

Petitgrain: 28, 73, 130, 132, 170, 184, 200, 201, 213, 219, 225, 378, 419, 421

Petting: 17, 22, 23, 153, 163, 196, 385, 386

Phenols: 5, 9, 71, 152

Pig: 369-376, 388, 389, 396, 403, 405, 409, 412, 414, 418

Pigeon Fever: 298

Pine: 28, 58, 73, 88, 91, 92, 96, 98, 100, 102, 128-130, 132, 148-150, 156, 167, 219, 261, 263, 265, 269, 273, 283, 290, 296, 298, 304, 307, 309, 316, 351, 365, 378, 381, 391, 405, 406, 413, 419, 421

Plectranthus Oregano: 73, 90, 93, 104, 105, 122, 254, 256, 258, 265, 308

Pneumonia: 72, 74, 98, 145, 173, 239, 269, 302, 303, 319, 349, 370, 374, 380, 390, 408, 411, 429

Pocket Pet: 385-412, 414-421

Pododermatitis: 409, 413

Poisoning: 8, 143, 145, 204, 209, 215, 236, 247, 275, 295, 333, 349, 352, 367, 404

Polioencephalomalacia: 350

Porcine Influenza: 374

Porcine Reproductive and Respiratory Syndrome: 375

Post Birth: 350

Potomac Fever: 299

Poultry: 31, 103, 137, 146, 328, 356, 359, 360, 367

Poultry Ticks: 146

Power Meal: 116, 128, 253, 255, 262, 270, 276, 278, 287, 294, 305, 316, 354, 355, 391, 402, 405, 406, 414, 416

PowerGize: 116, 192, 199, 200, 214, 218, 294, 296, 304, 305, 307, 309, 316, 388, 401, 408

Pox: 146, 149, 344

Pregnancy & Delivery: 171, 221, 222

Pregnancy and Birthing: 171

Present Time: 88, 97, 131, 133, 184, 192, 193, 196, 203, 219, 223, 260, 262, 338

Progessence Plus: 123, 207, 214, 286, 295, 382, 387, 388, 406, 417, 418

Protein Digestion: 409

Proud Flesh: 106, 274, 299, 300

Prussic Acid Poisoning: 333

Puncture Wound: 261, 284, 285, 300, 333

Pure Protein Complete Vanilla Spice: 117

PuriClean: 93, 95, 97, 104, 129, 154, 159, 160, 162, 167-169, 171-175, 184, 185, 200, 201, 203, 204, 206, 212, 213, 216, 220-224, 227, 229, 255, 267, 274, 276, 282, 288, 291-293, 297, 299-302, 304, 326, 333, 344, 346, 347, 351, 369, 373, 399, 401, 403, 404, 406, 410, 411, 414, 415, 418-421

Purification: 20, 28, 31, 32, 52, 58, 63, 97, 106, 129, 131, 133, 136-147, 149, 150, 154-156, 159-167, 169, 171-175, 179, 184, 185, 192, 194, 195, 197, 199-213, 215-218, 220-224, 227-230, 232, 234, 237-239, 245-247, 250, 252, 255, 261, 266, 267, 269, 272, 274, 276-279, 281, 282, 284, 285, 288, 289, 291-294, 296-311, 313-320, 324, 326, 329-335, 337-354, 356-362, 364-366, 368, 369, 372-374, 381-384, 392, 393, 395-398, 401, 402, 406, 407, 409-413, 415, 420, 421, 425, 427-429

Purity: 6, 7, 11, 27, 35, 80, 187

Pyometra: 109, 110, 171, 222, 410

Pythiosis: 300

Quail Bronchitis: 366

Queensland Itch: 301

R.C.: 89, 98, 128, 129, 131, 133, 143, 144, 147, 156, 159, 171, 184, 185, 194, 196, 199-202, 215, 223, 224, 226, 227, 229, 241, 245, 250, 253, 265, 266, 268, 269, 272, 273, 278, 281, 283, 290, 298-300, 303-307, 310, 313, 315, 316, 319, 322, 330, 333, 335, 336, 346, 348-350, 356, 357, 360, 363-365, 368, 370, 371, 375, 378, 380, 382, 391, 392, 399, 408, 411, 418, 419, 429

Rabbit: 338, 398, 400, 410, 411, 414, 421-423

Rabies: 175, 301, 350

Raccoon: 378

Rain Rot: 302

Raindrop Technique: 15, 17, 22, 25, 26, 128, 153, 158, 162, 168, 169, 183, 194, 196, 198, 199, 202-206, 208, 210-215, 217, 220-224, 226-229, 233-238, 240, 253, 256-259, 262, 263, 267, 269, 272-274, 276, 277, 279-285, 287-300, 302-306, 308-322, 324, 326-330, 332-341, 344-349, 351-354, 356, 369, 371, 373, 378-381, 386-399, 401-410, 412, 414, 417-421

Rats: 393, 397, 399, 406, 407, 411, 418, 419

Raven: 129, 131, 133, 137, 140-147, 149, 150, 154, 156, 163, 165, 166, 171, 184, 185, 192, 198-202, 204, 207, 213, 215, 223, 224, 227-230, 250, 253, 267-269, 272, 273, 277-280, 282-285, 292, 293, 298-300, 302, 303, 305, 306, 310, 311, 314, 315, 319, 322, 324, 330-333, 335, 338, 340-342, 346-352, 357-368, 370, 374, 375, 378, 380, 382, 391, 392, 394, 399, 407, 408, 410, 411, 419, 429

Ravintsara: 74, 93, 98, 100, 130, 132, 136, 137, 142-147, 149, 150, 156, 160-163, 165, 171, 184, 185, 192, 198, 200-202, 204, 207, 210, 213, 215, 221, 222, 224, 227-230, 241, 261, 262, 269, 272, 273, 276-280, 282-285, 291, 293, 300, 302, 303, 305, 306, 308-311, 314, 315, 330, 331, 333, 335, 344-349, 352, 357, 358, 364-368, 370, 374, 375, 378, 382, 391, 394, 395, 405, 407, 408, 410, 419, 421, 429

Reconnect: 93, 98

Rectal Instillation: 30

Red Shot: 98

Regenolone Moisturizing Cream: 123, 196-198, 203, 218, 221, 263, 265, 266, 268, 278, 287, 290, 294-300, 304, 307, 309, 313-315

Rehemogen: 117, 142, 143, 145, 146, 156, 157, 185, 195, 204, 217, 227, 228, 261, 264, 270, 278, 284, 289, 292, 301, 303, 304, 313, 314, 335, 336, 349, 355, 369, 388, 391, 403, 404, 406

Relaxation Massage Oil: 124, 263, 268, 271, 294, 296-298, 311

Release: 26, 38, 55, 74, 77, 89-91, 96, 98, 99, 101, 109, 129, 131, 133, 158, 159, 162, 167-169, 174, 176, 184, 185, 192-196, 198, 199, 203, 207, 212, 217, 219, 221, 236, 250, 260, 261, 263, 264, 268, 271, 287, 291, 294, 296, 298, 299, 312, 318, 348, 389

Relieve It: 28, 129, 131, 133, 155, 159, 168, 170, 171, 184, 185, 196, 198, 199, 203, 213, 216, 219-221, 223, 226, 229, 261, 263, 265, 266, 268, 271, 272, 281, 285, 287, 290-292, 294-296, 298, 304, 307, 309, 313, 316, 327, 329-332, 382, 410

RepelAroma: 98, 105, 128, 129, 163, 185, 206, 208, 212, 223, 227, 228, 282, 288, 291, 292, 300, 301, 311, 341, 346, 347, 352, 353, 381, 413

Reptile: 425-429

Reptiles: 32, 130-133, 425-428

Respiratory Care: 333, 334

Respiratory Conditions: 45, 51, 52, 58, 81, 155, 171, 174, 302, 355, 375

Respiratory Infection and Pasteurellosis: 410

Respiratory Infections: 41, 45, 51, 53, 55, 57, 61, 62, 65, 66, 69, 72, 74, 82, 159, 163, 222, 274, 302, 421, 423

Respiratory Issues: 165, 171, 351, 366, 375, 411

Rhodococcal Pneumonia: 303

Rickets: 350

Riemerella Anatipestifer Infection: 367

Ringbone: 303, 304

Ringtail: 411

Ringworm: 43, 51, 55, 57, 65, 68, 80, 106, 172, 223, 304, 344, 351, 399, 411

Rodents: 32, 332, 389, 393, 397, 399, 404, 406, 411, 418, 419

Rogue Animals: 382

Roman Chamomile: 11, 28, 37, 49, 74, 88-96, 99-101, 105, 106, 112, 117, 122-125, 129, 154-156, 159, 171, 173, 184, 185, 192-196, 198, 203, 209, 212, 222, 225, 226, 234, 261-263, 266, 274, 276, 282, 284, 286, 287, 293, 295, 301, 304, 311, 313, 326, 329, 336, 338, 355, 380, 389, 392, 394, 397-399, 411, 413, 415, 420

Rose: 13, 28, 44, 74, 75, 88-96, 98-102, 104, 105, 118, 122-124, 130, 132, 141, 156, 159, 165, 168, 171, 173-176, 199, 216, 236, 263-265, 274, 275, 282, 288, 293, 298-300, 302, 311, 314, 336, 338, 339, 398, 401, 402, 405, 413, 414, 420, 421

Rose Ointment: 92, 124, 141, 168, 173, 175, 199, 216, 274, 275, 282, 288, 293, 298-300, 302, 311, 314, 339, 398, 401, 402, 405, 413, 414, 420, 421

Rosemary: 11, 15, 28, 60, 75, 78, 89, 90, 94-97, 101, 103-105, 108, 110-112, 115, 117, 123-126, 129, 130, 132, 156, 159, 160, 171, 184, 185, 192, 198, 202, 204, 206-208, 210, 213, 215, 217, 219, 223, 224, 227, 229, 234, 250, 256, 261, 267, 269, 272-274, 276, 277, 283, 285, 288, 291, 294, 295, 298-301, 304, 306, 308, 313, 314, 317, 319, 326, 327, 329, 333, 335, 336, 338, 344, 346, 353, 362, 371, 380, 381, 387, 391, 392, 395, 396, 398-400, 406, 407, 411-413, 417-419

Rosemary Vitality: 75

Rosewood: 76

Rotaviral Infections: 367

Rotavirus Diarrhea: 304

Royal Hawaiian Sandalwood: 76, 77, 88-96, 98, 100-102, 105, 122, 148, 149, 158, 169, 172, 173, 176, 185, 196, 199, 200, 203, 216, 225, 226, 262, 282, 292, 293, 299, 312, 327, 335, 390, 392, 394, 399, 400, 405, 413, 420

Ruptures: 341, 375

Ruta: 76, 88, 89, 91, 98-101, 105, 117

RutaVaLa: 98, 99, 131, 133, 146, 158, 165, 172, 183, 185, 192, 196, 213, 219, 226, 268, 270, 280, 286, 287, 294, 389, 397

RutaVaLa Roll-On: 99, 131, 133, 158, 165, 183, 192, 196, 213, 219, 226, 268, 270, 287

Sacred Frankincense: 77, 88, 89, 91-93, 95, 98-101, 117, 122, 123, 130, 132, 141, 148-150, 154, 157-159, 163, 164, 166, 167, 169, 171-176, 184, 185, 192, 193, 195, 196, 198-201, 203, 209-212, 214, 216, 217, 219, 222, 225-229, 231, 237, 238, 241, 253, 262, 263, 265, 271, 274, 277, 280, 282, 286, 287, 293, 295-297, 299, 300, 304, 305, 311, 312, 315, 324, 336, 338, 340, 341, 395, 402, 405, 406, 414, 416, 417, 421

Sacred Mountain: 28, 141, 143, 148-150, 155, 156, 158, 159, 168, 172, 174, 176, 184, 192, 203, 219, 222, 238, 254, 264, 266, 293-297, 307, 309, 312, 335-337, 365, 390, 392, 401, 416

Sacred Sandalwood: 77, 148, 149, 158, 169, 172, 173, 176, 185, 196, 200, 203, 216, 225, 226, 262, 282, 292, 293, 299, 312, 327, 335, 390, 392, 394, 399, 400, 405, 413, 420

Safety: 47, 135, 152, 182, 249, 367, 385, 386, 426

Sage: 11, 15, 28, 45, 49, 77, 78, 90-96, 99-101, 105, 108-110, 112, 122, 130, 132, 176, 184, 185, 207, 214, 222, 224, 242, 250, 263, 286, 310, 336, 378, 388, 390, 392, 399, 400, 410, 411, 417

Sage Vitality: 77

Salmonella Infection: 351, 381, 412

Salmonellosis: 367, 375, 381, 412

SARA: 99, 156, 192, 193, 196, 320, 338, 389, 397

Sarcoids: 297, 305

Sarcoptic Mange: 223, 292, 373

Scabby Mouth: 351

Scald: 302, 368

SclarEssence: 99, 207, 214, 250, 286, 388

SclarEssence Vitality: 99

Scrapes,: 95, 97, 175, 324, 330, 369, 427, 429

Scratches: 201, 282, 306

Screw Worm: 256, 306

Scurvy: 58, 62, 412

Seavey, Mitch: 2, 186, 191

Sebaceous Cysts: 224

Seborrhea Oleosa: 224

Seed to Seal: 14, 152, 182, 250

Seizures: 142, 146, 149, 166, 169, 172, 173, 175, 225, 231, 243, 370, 397

Sensation: 23, 72, 90, 99, 121, 123, 124, 150, 158, 165, 173, 185, 211, 286, 413, 415

Sensation Hand & Body Lotion: 124, 413

Sensation Massage Oil: 124, 413

Sensitivity: 5, 9, 37-39, 48, 56, 58, 63, 64, 70, 77, 79, 80, 85, 87-102, 154, 161, 182, 223

Sesamoiditis: 306, 307

Sesquiterpenes: 5, 9, 40, 68, 76, 81, 101

Shampoo: 19, 23, 104, 105, 128, 129, 159, 163, 173, 177, 194, 199, 206, 208, 213, 216, 223-225, 232, 235, 238, 239, 261, 274, 292, 297-300, 302, 304, 306, 337, 338, 397, 401, 402, 415

Shedding Problems: 428

Sheep: 325, 339-345, 347-349, 351-353

Shutran: 99, 100, 189, 196, 203, 227, 250, 286, 376

Sinusitis: 46, 98, 147

Skin Conditions: 39, 43, 47, 54-56, 59, 60, 62, 64, 68, 69, 72-74, 76, 77, 80, 81, 111, 169, 172, 175, 216, 302, 429

Skin Infections: 45, 49, 65, 68, 81, 216, 406, 413

Skin Infestations: 355, 381, 413

Skin Tags: 225

Skin, Dry: 124, 125, 190, 237, 413

SleepEssence: 117

SleepyIze: 99

Slique Essence: 99, 220, 387, 391

Slique Tea: 99, 117, 391

Slobbers: 414

Snakes: 32, 425, 426

SniffleEase: 100

Sore Hocks: 414

Sour Crop: 147, 359

Spanish Sage: 78, 92, 94-96, 99-101, 105

Spearmint: 28, 79, 88-90, 92, 94, 96-99, 101-104, 115, 116, 119, 122, 124, 125, 130, 132, 155, 159, 163, 168, 184, 185, 197, 200, 201, 205, 207-210, 214, 220, 229, 252, 268, 269, 276, 278, 280, 281, 291, 354, 380, 389, 393, 394, 400, 402, 405

Spearmint Vitality: 79
Spikenard: 79
Splints: 307
Spondylosis Deformans: 225
Spritzing: 21
Squamous Cell Carcinoma, Oral: 173
Stallion and Mare Reproduction: 286
Stargazing: 147, 148
Steroid Alternative: 226
Stomach Ulcers: 46, 371, 414
Stomatitis: 429
Storage: 0, 14, 37, 160, 272
Strangles: 256, 298, 308, 309
Stress Away: 136, 137, 141, 145-150, 155-158, 164-172, 175, 176, 183, 184, 192, 193, 195-198, 200, 203, 209, 211, 216, 217, 219-223, 225, 226, 263, 264, 268, 270, 274, 281, 285-287, 289, 290, 293-298, 304, 307, 312, 315, 316, 326-329, 331-333, 335, 361, 365, 376, 380, 382, 387, 389, 390, 394, 399, 416
Stress Away Roll-On: 136, 137, 141, 145-150, 155-158, 164-172, 176, 219, 263, 264, 268, 270, 274, 281, 285-287, 289, 290, 293-298, 304, 307, 312, 315, 316, 326-329, 331-333, 335, 361, 365, 376, 380, 382, 387, 389, 390, 394, 399, 416
Sublingual Application: 30
Submissive Urination: 203, 226, 228
Sulfurzyme: 117, 128, 129, 144, 154, 155, 157, 160, 163, 165, 166, 168-170, 175, 176, 185, 192, 194-200, 203-207, 209, 212-221, 224-227, 235-238, 254, 261-263, 265-268, 270-274, 276-278, 280, 282-316, 326, 327, 329, 333, 336, 337, 339, 340, 355, 380, 390, 392, 395, 400, 401, 407, 408, 413, 416, 419
Sunburn: 65, 83, 355
Super B: 118, 156, 158, 162, 163, 165, 166, 168-170, 172, 175, 185, 195, 203, 214, 216, 219, 290, 293, 295, 336, 350, 355, 380, 389, 390, 393, 397, 399, 401, 413, 416, 419
Super C: 118, 129, 157, 158, 165, 166, 174, 175, 203, 218, 226, 278, 280-283, 293, 294, 296, 298, 299, 301, 305, 307, 309, 335-337, 349, 351, 354, 356, 379-381, 388, 389, 392, 397-399, 403-405, 409, 410, 412, 413, 415-419
Super C Chewable: 118, 158, 165, 166, 174, 175, 203, 218, 226, 278, 280-283, 294, 296, 298, 299, 301, 305, 307, 335-337, 349, 351, 354, 356, 380, 381, 388, 389, 392, 397-399, 403-405, 409, 410, 412, 413, 415, 416, 418, 419
Super Cal: 118, 226, 354, 355, 389, 390
Surrender: 100, 131, 133, 176, 203, 219, 254, 264, 389, 397
Swine: 369, 371-375

Swine Dysentery: 375
Swollen Sheath: 256, 308
T-Away: 100, 105, 128, 129, 148-150, 154-159, 164, 168-171, 174, 175, 184, 185, 193, 194, 198, 200, 208, 209, 212, 216, 219, 223, 227, 254, 260, 267, 300, 315, 326, 328, 330-332, 335, 361, 369, 371-373, 375, 376, 378, 387, 389, 392, 397, 399, 416, 420
T.R. Care: 193
Tail & Mane Sheen: 105, 129
Tail Slip: 411, 414, 415
Tangerine: 12, 15, 28, 32, 79, 88-90, 92-94, 96-102, 105, 108, 112, 113, 115, 118, 122, 124, 130, 132, 148-150, 156, 159, 168, 197, 212, 217, 219, 270, 277, 291, 294, 298, 308, 312, 313, 316, 338, 380, 392, 416, 418, 428, 429
Tangerine Vitality: 79
Tapeworms: 148, 173, 204, 275, 297, 330, 369, 428
Tarragon: 28, 80, 90, 97, 103, 104, 108-110, 116, 130, 132, 159-161, 164, 170, 173, 184, 185, 204, 210, 214, 220, 221, 241, 268, 271, 275, 276, 292, 296, 297, 328, 333, 336, 346, 360, 374, 375, 389, 392, 396, 407, 412
Tarragon Vitality: 80
Tea Tree: 28, 65, 66, 80, 95, 97, 98, 103-105, 116, 117, 122, 124, 128, 130, 132, 152, 163, 169, 172, 174, 175, 177, 184, 185, 187-190, 192, 198-204, 206-208, 210, 213, 215, 216, 218, 220-224, 227-229, 241, 246, 247, 252, 256, 258, 261, 262, 267, 269, 272-274, 276-278, 280-283, 285, 288, 291, 292, 296-306, 308-311, 314, 315, 326-329, 331-335, 338, 341, 344, 347, 348, 351, 354, 355, 364, 366-369, 373, 378, 380, 381, 393-396, 398, 399, 406-415, 417-421, 423
Tear Glands: 415
Teeth, Overgrown: 405, 414, 416
Tendon Conditions: 117, 309
Terpenes: 5, 58
Tetanus: 46, 309, 334, 351
Thiamine Deficiency: 416
Thieves: 20, 22, 23, 28, 31, 32, 46, 75, 101, 106, 111, 124-126, 129, 131, 133, 136-140, 143-147, 149, 150, 154, 156, 158, 160, 161, 163, 164, 167, 169, 171-175, 177, 179, 184, 185, 192, 194, 198-208, 210-213, 215-225, 227-230, 235-237, 239, 242, 248, 250, 252, 254-256, 261-269, 272-294, 296-306, 308-311, 314, 315, 317-319, 321, 324, 326-355, 357-376, 378-384, 387, 389, 391-399, 401, 403-413, 415, 417-421, 425, 427-429
Thieves Dentarome Plus Toothpaste: 124, 204, 211

Thieves Dentarome Ultra Toothpaste: 125, 250, 266, 267, 274, 282, 284-286, 293, 297-302, 308-310, 329
Thieves Foaming Hand Soap: 126, 223, 224, 324
Thieves Fresh Essence Plus Mouthwash: 125, 204, 211
Thieves Fruit & Veggie Spray: 126, 138
Thieves Household Cleaner: 22, 23, 126, 136-140, 144-146, 149, 150, 158, 161, 164, 167, 173, 192, 194, 198, 199, 202, 203, 205, 206, 208, 210, 212, 213, 216, 219-225, 227-229, 248, 250, 252, 256, 261, 264-267, 273-276, 279-286, 291, 292, 297-306, 308-310, 315, 318, 321, 326, 327, 329-353, 357-368, 370-372, 374-376, 381, 382, 392, 396-398, 405-407, 409, 410, 412, 413, 415, 417, 425, 427-429
Thieves Laundry Soap: 126, 158, 164, 194
Thieves Spray: 126, 208, 216, 217, 252, 267, 274, 275, 279, 280, 282, 291, 297, 298, 301, 303, 305, 306, 308-311, 315, 326, 331-333, 394
Thieves Vitality: 101, 256
Thieves Waterless Hand Purifier: 125, 223, 224, 252, 280, 303-305, 308, 309, 311, 406, 407
Three-Day Stiff Sickness: 334
Thrombocytopenia: 227
Thrush: 310, 321, 326
Thyme: 9, 25, 26, 28, 80, 81, 94, 109, 111, 113, 116, 117, 123, 130, 132, 138, 139, 149, 152, 153, 161, 163, 175, 179, 183-185, 192, 198, 199, 204, 207, 213, 217, 220, 221, 225, 227, 229, 230, 234, 256, 258, 259, 261, 262, 266, 267, 269, 275-278, 280, 281, 283, 285, 288, 291, 292, 296-302, 304, 305, 308, 310, 311, 314, 315, 318, 319, 322, 326, 327, 331, 333-338, 340, 342, 346, 348, 352, 353, 357-359, 364, 369-371, 373, 378-381, 386, 391, 394, 399, 408, 409, 411, 412, 418, 419
Thyme Vitality: 80, 256
Thyromin: 119, 207, 214, 224, 225, 262, 286, 287, 324, 355, 391
Tick Bites: 227, 288, 292, 311, 337
Tick Damage: 334
Ticks: 104, 106, 129, 146, 228, 237, 277, 288, 292, 302, 311, 334, 343, 352, 383, 398, 427
Tipping: 22
Torticollis: 140, 148
Toxoplasmosis: 164, 173
Tranquil Roll-On: 156, 158, 165, 170, 172, 192, 193, 196, 219, 263, 268, 270, 274, 281, 282, 284, 285, 287, 295, 296, 312, 315, 324, 328, 397, 399, 415, 416
Transformation: 101, 131, 133, 157, 159,

164, 170, 173, 174, 176, 178, 184, 192, 193, 197, 199, 200, 207, 208, 213, 219, 223, 229, 240, 264, 266, 272, 294-296, 298, 309, 313, 316

Transporting: 156, 157, 212, 311

Trauma: 38, 45, 48, 82, 98, 99, 101, 128, 129, 131, 133, 141, 148-150, 156, 157, 164, 166-168, 170, 171, 174-176, 184, 192-196, 198-201, 203, 208, 209, 212, 213, 216, 217, 219, 223, 227, 228, 233, 254, 260, 262-267, 271, 272, 277, 280, 281, 287, 293, 294, 296-298, 300, 303, 305, 307, 313, 315, 326, 331, 332, 339, 348, 369, 372, 382, 389, 397, 416, 421

Trauma Life: 128, 129, 131, 133, 141, 148-150, 156, 157, 164, 166-168, 170, 171, 174-176, 184, 192-196, 198, 200, 203, 208, 209, 212, 216, 217, 219, 223, 227, 233, 254, 260, 263-267, 271, 272, 277, 280, 281, 287, 294, 296-298, 300, 305, 307, 313, 315, 326, 331, 332, 348, 382, 389, 397, 416, 421

Trichomoniasis: 141, 368

Tsuga: 28, 81, 130, 132, 158, 169, 173, 199, 214, 293, 294, 312, 324, 338, 391, 402, 405, 411, 415-417, 420

Tuberculosis: 46, 71, 72, 83, 98, 149, 335, 352

TummyGize: 102, 159-162, 164, 167, 168, 201, 204

Tumors: 129, 159, 169, 172, 207, 211, 217, 228, 230, 266, 273, 276, 305, 312, 402, 406, 416-418

Tumors, Benign: 230, 406, 416

Tumors, Reproductive: 417

Tumors, Skin and Belly Areas: 417

Tumors, Skin Swellings: 418

Tumors, Surface Skin Areas: 418

Tying Up: 313

Tyzzer's Disease: 418

Udder Edema: 376

Upper Respiratory Infection: 421, 429

Urea Poisoning: 352

Urinary Calculi: 418

Urinary Conditions: 56, 174, 203, 228

Urinary Tract Conditions: 56, 156, 159, 164, 174

Urolithiasis: 356

Uropygial Gland Infection: 149

V-6 Vegetable Oil Complex: 9, 14, 15, 20, 22, 23, 30, 37, 87, 125, 129-133, 154, 155, 160, 161, 165, 168, 169, 172, 179, 182, 183, 196, 227, 249, 253, 259, 261-263, 265, 269, 270, 273, 280, 288, 300, 314, 330, 335-338, 348, 354-356, 369, 370, 373, 378-381, 386-397, 399-410, 412-420, 427

Vaccination: 175, 228, 268, 313, 334, 364

Vaccination Detoxification: 313

Vaccinosis: 175, 228

Valerian: 11, 28, 81, 88, 91, 98-101, 105,

106, 117, 129, 130, 132, 155, 156, 166, 172, 174, 192, 193, 196, 198, 216, 219, 225, 255, 262, 274, 276, 295, 311, 312, 326-329, 331, 332, 382, 389, 397, 399, 419

Valor: 25, 102, 129, 153, 155-158, 166-168, 170-172, 174, 176, 185, 189, 192-198, 203, 212, 219, 221, 222, 225-227, 229, 233, 235-239, 242, 243, 254, 257, 259, 260, 263-265, 268, 278-281, 284, 289, 294, 295, 299, 300, 307, 310, 312-314, 317-319, 324, 371, 384, 390, 395, 397, 399, 419, 421

Valor II: 153, 155-158, 166, 168, 170, 172, 174, 192, 193, 196, 198, 203, 212, 219, 222, 225-227, 260, 263, 278, 289, 294, 295, 299, 300, 310, 313, 371, 390, 395, 397, 399, 419

Vanilla: 81, 82, 88, 100, 115, 117, 121

Vestibular Disease: 228

Vetiver: 28, 82, 88, 90-98, 100-102, 104-106, 116, 117, 122, 123, 125, 130, 132, 155, 166, 172, 174, 185, 192, 193, 196, 199, 200, 216, 219, 243, 261, 263, 268, 274, 287, 294, 304, 311, 326-329, 331, 332, 389, 390, 397, 399, 413, 416, 420

VHS: 248

Viral Conditions: 171, 229, 278, 283

Viral Infections: 39, 41, 44, 51, 52, 55, 57, 61, 67, 72, 74, 76, 157, 161, 164, 167, 169, 178, 368, 375, 407, 419

Vita Flex: 23, 183, 258, 259

Vomiting: 83, 138, 144, 154, 161, 166, 182, 207, 210, 217, 220, 221, 228, 229, 232, 286, 349, 372, 400

Warts: 41, 44, 230, 242, 276, 297, 313, 314, 320, 322, 353

Water: 1, 2, 5, 8, 9, 13, 15-17, 19-24, 27, 29, 31, 32, 43, 46, 62, 67, 74, 80, 87, 103-105, 108-117, 121-126, 129, 136-147, 149-151, 153, 158, 159, 161, 164, 165, 167, 172-174, 178, 179, 181, 182, 186, 197, 201, 202, 204, 205, 207, 211, 213, 214, 217, 220, 223-225, 232, 238, 239, 245-250, 253, 256, 261, 263, 266, 268, 270, 271, 274, 275, 277-281, 284, 285, 287, 288, 290-293, 297-300, 302, 308, 315, 317, 319, 321, 322, 324-327, 329-335, 337, 338, 340-372, 374-376, 378-383, 385-421, 425-429

West Nile Virus: 141, 148, 149, 314, 318, 365

Western Red Cedar: 82, 91, 336

Whirling Disease: 248

White Angelica: 28, 131, 133, 148-150, 155, 171, 172, 176, 189, 192-194, 196, 197, 203, 219, 227, 260, 300, 312, 315, 338, 361, 401

White Fir: 82, 88, 91-93, 96, 101, 102, 196-198

White Light: 102

White Line Disease: 306, 315, 317

White Lotus: 83, 93, 96, 99

Wild Animals: 326, 331, 332, 335, 338, 339, 377, 382

Wildlife: 160, 325, 376

Windgalls: 315

Wingtip Edema: 150

Wintergreen: 25, 28, 83, 90, 97, 98, 105, 107, 108, 118, 122-125, 128, 130, 132, 138, 152, 153, 155, 168, 170, 183, 184, 187, 189-191, 196-198, 203, 210, 215, 216, 218-222, 224, 226, 227, 232, 234, 250, 254, 259, 261, 262, 265-268, 271, 272, 281, 285, 288, 290, 294-298, 300, 303, 304, 307, 309, 312-316, 318, 327, 329, 331-333, 335, 340, 371, 376, 382, 386, 387, 390, 393, 408

Wobbly Hedgehog Syndrome: 419

Wolfberry Eye Cream: 125, 274, 275

Worm Infestations: 49, 341, 353

Worms: 42, 44-46, 53, 57, 72, 97, 104, 129, 140, 142, 148, 165, 170, 185, 247, 275, 296, 297, 322, 334, 338, 340, 347, 353, 362, 369, 374, 428

Wounds: 24, 50-52, 58, 72, 81, 84, 103, 106, 125, 126, 129, 154, 162, 175, 194, 199, 212, 216, 231, 237, 247, 255, 267, 274, 285, 296, 300, 301, 309, 311, 316, 324, 326, 330, 333, 334, 337, 338, 351, 420, 421, 427

Wry Neck: 148, 421

Xiang Mao: 84, 96, 130, 132, 159, 184, 185, 222, 229, 266, 273, 285, 291, 292, 300, 381, 396, 406, 409, 412, 413, 416, 418

Yacon Syrup: 119

Yarrow: 28, 84, 90, 95

Ylang Ylang: 28, 38, 85, 88-102, 104, 105, 110, 121-125, 130, 132, 150, 155, 156, 158, 165-167, 171, 172, 174, 176, 185, 192, 196, 211, 216, 264, 286, 311, 318, 328, 336, 388, 391, 401, 413

Young, Gary: 38, 50, 54, 77, 89, 100, 105, 187, 190, 191, 233, 335, 383

Young Living: 6-8, 14, 38, 40, 51, 77, 81, 88, 89, 104, 117, 122, 152, 177, 182, 186, 187, 189-191, 204, 211, 232-239, 242, 243, 252, 279, 320-322, 383, 423

Yuzu: 85, 115